D0161867

survey research and analysis:
applications in parks, recreation, and human dimensions

survey research and analysis:
applications in parks, recreation, and human dimensions

Jerry J. Vaske

Human Dimensions of Natural Resources
Colorado State University
Fort Collins, Colorado

Venture Publishing, Inc.
State College, Pennsylvania

Production Manager: Richard Yocum
Manuscript Editing: Michele L. Barbin

Cover by StepUp Communications, Inc.

Library of Congress Catalogue Card Number: 2008930451
ISBN-10: 1-892132-79-6
ISBN-13: 978-1-892132-79-6

To:

*Nicky, Alexis, TJ, Harley, Sonny
and my wife "Mo"*

table of contents

1   the science of survey research 1

2   linking theory and concepts to survey research. 17

3   the evolution of theory 35

4   conceptualization and measurement 59

5   levels of measurement: once over again 79

6   hypothesis testing and effect size 97

7   writing and constructing surveys 121

8 survey implementation, sampling, and weighting data....173

9   an introduction to SPSS for Windows 223

10   constructing SPSS data files 241

11   frequencies and descriptive statistics 259

12   data manipulation techniques 285

13   crosstabulations 315

14 means and *t*-tests 343

15 analysis of variance 375

16 bivariate correlation and regression 409

17 logistic regression and discriminant function analysis . . 453

18   psychological scales and reliability analysis............501

19   missing data, response patterns, and outliers........533

20   mediator and moderator variables in path analysis ..575

preface

There are numerous excellent books available on survey research (e.g., Dillman, 1978, 2007; Fowler, 1993; Salant & Dillman, 1994; Schuman & Presser, 1996; Sudman & Bradburn, 1974, 1983; Tourangeau, Ripps, & Rasinski, 2000). General research methodology texts often cover survey research topics (e.g., Babbie, 2003; Gliner & Morgan, 2000; Huck & Cormier, 1996; Morgan, Gliner, & Harmon, 2006). Thousands of journal articles have explored specific survey design and implementation issues including: (a) overview articles (e.g., Krosnick, 1999; Tourangeau, 2004), (b) survey mode effects (e.g., Cole, 2005; Gaede & Vaske, 1999), (c) writing questions (e.g., Conrad & Schober, 2005; Schaeffer & Presser, 2003), (d) response scale effects (e.g., Browne-Nuñez & Vaske, 2006; Greenleaf, 1992a, 1992b; Schwarz, Hippler, Deutsch, & Strack, 1985), (e) survey length (e.g., Dillman, Sinclair, & Clark, 1993; Moore, Halle, Vandivere, & Mariner, 2002), (f) response rates (e.g., Church, 1993; Connelly, Brown, & Decker, 2003; Fox, Crask, & Kim, 1988; Heberlein & Baumgartner, 1978), (g) response patterns (e.g., Bishop & Smith, 2001; Vaske & Beaman, 2006), and (g) response bias (e.g., Tarrant & Manfredo, 1993; van der Vaart, 2004).

Similarly, there is no scarcity of available statistics books (e.g., Coolidge, 2006; Jaeger, 1990; Keller, 2006; Salkind, 2007; Sirkin, 2005) or useful and readable "how to" use the Statistical Package for Social Science (SPSS) software manuals (e.g., Argyrous, 2005; Cronk, 2006; Field, 2005; Holcomb, 2006; Leech, Barrett, & Morgan, 2005; Mertler & Vannatta, 2005; Morgan & Griego, 1998; Morgan, Griego, & Gloeckner, 2001).

Collectively, this *partial* listing of methods and statistics books, articles, and manuals raise a fundamental question: Why does the world need another book called *Survey Research and Analysis: Applications in Parks, Recreation, and Human Dimensions*? There are several reasons why this book can make a contribution to the literature. First, the content of methodology and statistics books is often generic. The examples described in these methods texts intentionally cover a wide range of topics to address the needs of multiple audiences. Although there are exceptions to this general rule, no book currently focuses specifically on statistical and methodological applications in parks, recreation, and human dimensions. This book attempts to overcome this shortcoming by concentrating on data from actual research projects. My personal experiences in teaching methods/statistics, as well as working with natural resource managers on research projects, suggest that students and professionals find methodology and statistics more difficult to grasp when the examples and illustrations are foreign to them.

Second, methods and statistics books generally do not contain direct ties back to the theories used by the researcher. In part, this can be attributed to the wide range of audiences that many books are intended to reach. Theories from a variety of disciplines (e.g., social psychology, sociology, economics) are used by parks, recreation, and human dimensions researchers. Theory is important because it extends the generalizability of the findings; improves the rigor and confidence in the research; provides a structure for integrating and building upon previous findings; and moves beyond the endless, repetitive cycle of purely descriptive research. In short, theory-based research improves the integrity and credibility of an empirical study. Writing surveys that have a theoretical foundation, however, necessitates an understanding of the concepts and their relationships that have been reported in the literature.

Natural resource managers face real and specific problems that often require societal acceptance of their actions. Survey research can inform natural resource management decisions and policy issues by attempting to describe and predict human thought and action toward natural environments. The utility, credibility, and acceptance of this advice, however, is greatly enhanced when the research is theoretically grounded, methodologically sound, and appropriately analyzed and reported.

Pedagogical Approach

This book is predicated on the assumption that the best way to learn research methodology and statistics is to become directly involved in the conduct of scientific inquiry. Consequently, a considerable amount of time is devoted to analyzing data from actual research projects. Data sets for this book can be downloaded at: http://www.venturepublish.com. The data examine both general public surveys and population specific surveys in the field.

General public surveys regard:

- wolf reintroduction in Colorado
- a trapping ban initiative in Colorado
- wildfire management in Colorado, Washington, and California

Population specific surveys include:

- New Hampshire State Park visitors
- Colorado State Park visitors
- Lake Mead National Recreation Area visitors
- Columbia Icefield visitors
- Colorado skiers and snowboarders
- Wisconsin hunters
- Students' knowledge of the endangered fish of the Upper Colorado River Basin

For each of the studies examined, this book: (a) discusses why the project was initiated; (b) evaluates the theoretical/research design, sampling procedures, and survey instrument;

(c) analyzes the data using SPSS; and (d) interprets the findings from both a managerial and a theoretical perspective. Emphasis is placed on understanding data manipulation techniques and what statistics are appropriate for addressing specific methodological problems. In blending theoretical, methodological, and statistical considerations in an applied approach, the goal is to achieve the following objectives:

1. Explain the relationship between theory and research.

2. Distinguish between conceptualization and measurement.

3. Describe the processes associated with: (a) writing survey questions, and (b) constructing and implementing different types of surveys (e.g., on-site, mail, telephone, electronic).

4. Differentiate the various sampling strategies used by researchers (e.g., simple random, systematic, stratified, cluster) and the procedures that can be used to weight data to approximate populations of interest.

5. Provide guidelines for understanding what types of statistical techniques are appropriate for analyzing a variety of research questions and hypotheses.

6. Describe the steps in conducting data analysis using SPSS (e.g., frequencies, crosstabs, *t*-tests, analysis of variance, correlation, regression, logistic regression, discriminant analysis). When this book went to press, SPSS 15 was the latest version of the software.
   SPSS 16 is now available. For purposes of the topics covered here, the menu structure, dialog boxes, and menu selections in version 16 are virtually identical to those in version 15. For each analytical technique presented, the menu choices and statistics in the SPSS dialog boxes are described in call-out boxes for each specific analysis option.

7. Provide examples of interpreting SPSS computer printouts and constructing data tables, figures for journal articles, and technical reports. Output from the SPSS analyses are also described using call-out boxes that detail the meaning and interpretation of the findings. Sample journal style tables are used to illustrate the conversion of output data to usable information.

Chapter Overview

This book is based on the assumption that survey research should employ the standards of science when addressing both theoretical and applied questions. Chapter 1 overviews the characteristics of science as they apply to survey research. The goal is to introduce the topics covered in this book, as well as highlight those not addressed. Chapter 2 provides an overview of some of the concepts used by parks, recreation, and human dimensions researchers. The goals of this chapter are to: (a) illustrate how social science theory can be used to define and shape the content of surveys, and (b) clarify conceptual distinctions. Without an initial understanding of the different concepts (e.g., values, attitudes, norms) used by researchers, it is difficult, if not impossible, to write survey items that measure those concepts. Chapter 3 extends this discussion by focusing on the theories that have evolved in the literature. Emphasis is placed on the processes researchers go through when thinking about how concepts are theoretically related to each other and what variables should be measured on the survey to test the predicted conceptual relationships.

Chapter 4 examines the processes researchers go through when conceptualizing and measuring variables in a survey. Six common properties of measurement are discussed: (a) precision, (b) accuracy, (c) reliability, (d) validity, (e) representativeness, and (f) generalizability. Measurement has been broadly defined as the assignment of numbers to the different characteristics (i.e., values) of variables according to rules. Since the 1950s, four levels of measurement (i.e., nominal, ordinal, interval, ratio) have been discussed in most statistics and methods books and have led to considerable debate and confusion. At the heart of this controversy is the nature of the relationship between ordinal and interval scales, and the appropriate statistics for such measures. Chapter 5 addresses these issues by: (a) outlining the different positions in the measurement-statistics relationship debate, (b) offering an alternative measurement hierarchy (i.e., dichotomous, categorical, continuous), and (c) providing some practical guidelines for determining which statistics are appropriate given different measurement levels.

Social scientists are interested in answering three basic questions when examining the relationships between variables. First, is an observed effect real or should it be attributed to chance? (i.e., statistical significance). Second, if the effect is real, how large is it (i.e., effect size)? Third, is the effect large enough to be useful (i.e., practical significance or importance)? Chapter 6: (a) reviews the basic steps in hypothesis testing (i.e., statistical significance), (b) highlights the major problems with the approach, and (c) discusses the strengths and weaknesses of three procedures commonly used to supplement hypothesis tests (i.e., effect sizes, confidence intervals, odds ratios) for communicating the practical significance or importance of empirical data.

Thirty years ago my graduate advisor at the University of Wisconsin, Dr. Thomas A. Heberlein, told me that any human dimensions professional with a stack of paper, a typewriter, and a Xerox machine can, and probably will, conduct a survey at some point in his or her career. This statement holds true today with the exceptions that the typewriter has been replaced with a personal computer and the Xerox machine is now a color laser printer. Unfortunately, many novice researchers often mistakenly believe that designing and implementing a survey simply involves quickly writing a few questions and asking a few people to respond. Writing and constructing questionnaires are complex tasks that *always* require multiple drafts of the instrument. Chapter 7 outlines a series of general guidelines and recommendations that should be followed to ensure that a survey is conducted in a scientifically rigorous manner and results are representative of and generalizable to the population of interest. This chapter also discusses the general advantages and disadvantages of survey research and offers recommendations for constructing specific types of surveys (e.g., on-site, mail, telephone, electronic).

Once a first draft of a questionnaire has been constructed, steps that follow in the survey research process include asking experts to review the questionnaire, pretesting the instrument, finalizing sampling procedures, administering the final questionnaire, and conducting a nonresponse bias check if necessary. Chapter 8 discusses these steps and examines various approaches for selecting samples of potential respondents, and administering questionnaires to these individuals. Response rates, nonresponse checks, and approaches for weighting data are also examined in chapter 8.

The data collected in parks, recreation, and human dimensions surveys can result in hundreds of variables and thousands of respondents. For the researcher, this implies that a considerable amount of time and energy must be devoted to: (a) carefully entering the data into a computerized database, (b) running preliminary analyses to identify any problems (e.g., missing data, potential outliers in the data) that could influence the results, (c) checking the reliability and validity of the data, and (d) transforming the data to create composite indices of the underlying dimensions. Some analysts have suggested that as much as 80% of a researcher's time is devoted to these preliminary data manipulation steps. Consequently, this book devotes several chapters to these topics. Chapter 9 introduces the SPSS statistical software package that is used throughout the book. Chapter 10 walks the reader through the steps required for creating an SPSS data file. Chapter 11 describes the basic descriptive statistics necessary for understanding a variable's distribution. Specific data manipulation strategies for transforming the data are examined in chapter 12. Procedures for testing the reliability of a set of indicators for a concept are covered in chapter 18. Chapter 19 deals with handling missing data and outliers.

Statistics provide a systematic way of summarizing what has been learned and facilitate conclusions about the data. The appropriate statistics depend on the types of research questions or hypotheses asked: (a) difference questions, (b) associational questions, and (c) descriptive questions. Difference questions address how far apart two or more groups are on a variable of interest. Association questions focus on how closely two or more variables are related. Understanding these three basic kinds of questions (i.e., difference, association, descriptive) facilitates selecting the appropriate test statistic. For example, difference questions involve statistics such as chi-square (chapter 13), *t*-tests (chapter 14) and analysis of variance (chapter 15). Association questions are examined using tests such as correlation and regression (chapter 16). Regression models attempt to predict survey respondents' beliefs, attitudes, and behaviors. The model used in the analysis, however, depends on how the variables are measured. If all of the independent and dependent variables are continuous variables, ordinary least squares regression techniques can be used (chapter 16). If the dependent variable is dichotomous, logistic regression or discriminant analysis is the appropriate analysis strategy (chapter 17). Finally, given the complexities of the concepts and their relationships (chapters 2 and 3), researchers are frequently interested in the causal relationships between variables. Chapter 20 provides a brief introduction to path analysis, an analytical technique for estimating the magnitude of the linkages between variables, and using these estimates to provide information about the underlying causal process.

acknowledgements

No book, including this one, is ever solely the effort of one individual. The basic content of this book is a product of lecture notes developed for my undergraduate and graduate courses at the University of Maryland and Colorado State University. These courses have been taught every semester for approximately 25 years. Following each semester, the notes were revised based on personal observation and student feedback about what aspects were clear and what topics needed more explanation. I would like to acknowledge the assistance of these students who used earlier versions of this book and provided helpful feedback for improvement.

Two colleagues were particularly instrumental in this book. Dr. Mark D. Needham, Oregon State University, is a coauthor on chapter 7 (Writing and Constructing Surveys) and chapter 8 (Survey Implementation, Sampling, and Weighting Data). Dr. Lori B. Shelby, George Mason University, is a coauthor on chapter 15 (Analysis of Variance) and chapter 19 (Missing Data, Response Patterns, and Outliers). I greatly appreciate their insights on these topics and their contributions to the book. Dr. Shelby also provided invaluable support in editing the entire manuscript. Laura Sample helped with proofreading.

I would also like to thank my friends and colleagues who allowed me to use their data sets as illustrations of the statistical topics: Dr. Alan D. Bright (Colorado State University), Dr. Alan R. Graefe (The Pennsylvania State University), and Dr. Michael J. Manfredo (Colorado State University). Drs. George A. Morgan (Colorado State University) and Jeffrey A. Gliner (Colorado State University) provided reviews and suggestions for improving the text.

This book is dedicated to "Nicky, Alexis, TJ, Harley, and Sonny" (the five miniature schnauzers who are a big part of my life) and to my wife Maureen "Mo" Donnelly. Each of the schnauzers is a champion in his or her own right: Nicky for obedience and agility; Alexis and TJ for conformation; Harley because he is Harley; and Sonny because he is cute. Their companionship made the many long hours sitting in front of the computer bearable. Finally, I would like to thank "Mo" who put up with me while writing this book. Without her support, this book would not have been completed.

J. J. V.
Fort Collins, Colorado

1

the science of survey research

Human dimensions of natural resources refers to an area of investigation that attempts to describe, predict, understand, and affect human thought and action toward natural environments (Manfredo, Vaske, & Sikorowski, 1996). Attempts to understand what people "do and say" are certainly not new to human dimensions or parks and recreation in general. In fact, human dimensions pervade recreation management. Natural resource managers and agency personnel at all levels (local, state, federal), for example, encounter people on a daily basis, form impressions about the public(s) they serve, and consider those impressions when making decisions. Public involvement activities (e.g., public meetings, open houses) are often conducted to obtain people's reaction to management and planning alternatives. Pamphlets and brochures are routinely produced and distributed with the intent of influencing the thoughts and behavior of the public. In the arena of wildlife management, inventories of hunting participation and harvest are conducted annually to facilitate the formulation of regulations. Similarly, park agencies regularly collect data on the customers they serve. All of these activities fall under the heading of human dimensions.

Although the emphasis on human dimensions is not new, the focus on the *science* of human dimensions is relatively new. This chapter overviews the characteristics of science as they apply to survey research. The goal is to introduce the topics covered in this book, as well as highlight those not addressed. As will be argued throughout this text, survey research should employ the standards of science when addressing both theoretical and applied questions.

The Characteristics of Scientific Inquiry

The most prominent characteristics of scientific inquiry concern reliability, validity, representativeness, and generalizability. Future chapters explain in detail these defining characteristics of science. The following provides a brief introduction.

Overall **study reliability** addresses the repeatability of findings; the degree to which study results fluctuate over time. For example, if one used a thermometer on a healthy person five times in one hour, only minor variations in readings would be expected (i.e., the thermometer would be reliable). Similarly, the reliability of a survey of individuals' attitudes deals with whether the results would be similar if administered repeatedly.

Measurement reliability refers to the consistency of responses to a set of questions designed to measure a given concept. For example, a survey might be interested in individuals' attitudes toward wildland fires and measure this concept by asking respondents to evaluate the extent to which wildfires are: (a) good or bad, (b) beneficial or harmful, and (c) positive or negative. Each of these three variables could be coded on a seven-point scale (extremely good, beneficial, or positive [+3]; extremely bad, harmful, or negative [–3]). Individuals who feel that a wildfire is "extremely bad" are also likely to feel that wildfires are "extremely harmful" and be "extremely negative" toward wildfires. This consistency in the pattern of respondents' answers reflects measurement reliability.

Validity can be described in terms of the: (a) overall validity of a study (or the research in general), and (b) validity of the measurement. Campbell and Stanley (1966) define two broad types of overall study (i.e., research) validity — internal and external. ***Internal validity*** refers to the extent to which a researcher can infer that one variable caused another variable to change and depends on the strength of the research design (Morgan, Gliner, & Harmon, 2000). Experimental designs are often high on internal validity because subjects are randomly assigned to treatment conditions and the influence of extraneous variables is controlled or eliminated. ***External validity*** asks the question of generalizability: to what populations, settings, and variables can this effect be generalized (Campbell & Stanley, 1966).

Measurement validity deals with the accuracy of generalizations and is concerned with whether the variables in the survey measure the concepts that they were intended to measure. An investigator, for example, may develop a set of survey items to measure wildlife value orientations (i.e., patterns of basic beliefs about wildlife, chapter 2). Validity concerns include: are all of the basic beliefs (e.g., animal rights, animal welfare) associated with the value orientation represented by the items on the survey? (***content validity***); can we predict behavioral or attitudinal differences among the public(s) based on the value orientation measures? (***predictive validity***); and do the item groupings measure what they are purported to measure (e.g., do items addressing animal rights values actually measure that construct)? (***construct validity***).

Representativeness is largely a sampling issue and is concerned with how well results of the inquiry mirror the population of interest (e.g., all residents living in a given state or province). Two types of sampling methods — probability and nonprobabilty — are discussed in the scientific literature. Probability sampling designs are typically employed in survey research to allow inferences about representativeness with acceptable levels of confidence.

Generalizability addresses the breadth of inferences that can be drawn. Questions of generalizability might ask: "If a study's target population is wildlife viewers interested in watching elk, can the results be generalized to all wildlife viewers?" or "Can studies conducted in Colorado be generalized to those conducted in other states?" Generalizability focuses on a study's link to theory development and testing.

None of these defining characteristics should be considered absolutes. Statements regarding these qualities are matters of degree accompanied with varying degrees of certainty. Different forms of human dimensions inquiry (e.g., public meetings, surveys) vary in how well they attend to concerns of reliability, validity, representativeness, and generalizability.

Goals of Survey Research

Survey researchers typically have more than one goal for conducting a study (e.g., exploration, description, explanation). These varying goals influence the extent to which the characteristics of science come into play. Some studies, for example, are exploratory, whereas other studies emphasize describing a population or explaining the relationships among variables.

Two types of exploratory surveys that are used to collect preliminary information are elicitation surveys or focus groups. ***Exploratory surveys*** are useful when the researcher: (a) does not have a basic understanding of what kinds of topic-related concerns are important to individuals in a given population, (b) is interested in exploring the feasibility of a larger study, or (c) wants to develop a methodology that is broader in scope. Sometimes, elicitation surveys or focus groups are used to collect this preliminary information. An elicitation survey usually involves a series of fill-in-the-blank questions that are administered to a small sample of individuals from the population of interest. The questions ask individuals to describe their thoughts and feelings on a given issue (e.g., the development of a new recreation facility, a proposed reintroduction of a wildlife species, a presidential candidate). A ***focus group*** typically involves a moderator bringing 6 to 12 individuals from a population of interest together for directed questioning. This approach provides a flexible format for the moderator to explore the participants' attitudes and perceptions about the topic.

Elicitation surveys and focus groups allow the researcher to get a feel for the type and range of issues important to people in the population of interest. This information can then be used to develop questions that will be included on a survey administered to a larger sample of individuals. It is important to recognize, however, that the small sample sizes and open-ended nature of the questioning often limit the representativeness and generalizability of the findings from elicitation surveys and focus groups.

As the name suggests, ***descriptive surveys*** describe the characteristics and reported behaviors of a sample or population of individuals. The U.S. Census, for example, attempts to profile the American population in terms of where they live, how long they have lived in a given location, and other sociodemographic information (e.g., age, sex, occupation, education, income). Similarly, understanding national trends in wildlife recreation has been facilitated by surveys of American households conducted approximately every five years by the U.S. Fish and Wildlife Service (USFWS). Questions on types and frequency of hunting and hunters' expenditures have been included in the national survey since 1955. Information on nonconsumptive activities (e.g., wildlife observation, photography) has been collected since 1980.

Explanatory studies address the question of why things happen, and are undertaken to identify possible causal variables of a given situation or event, thereby contributing to understanding. For example, researchers might be interested in why people support or oppose the development of a new recreation facility, or why they agree or disagree with the reintroduction of a given wildlife species in a certain location.

Although it is useful to distinguish among these three goals—exploration, description, explanation—of survey research, many research projects include all three. An elicitation study, for example, might be conducted initially to identify the range of beliefs and feelings that people hold toward a topic. The results obtained from the elicitation study could then be used to inform the questions for a larger survey that describes who holds specific opinions and who is likely to behave in a particular way (e.g., vote for or against an event). These same data could also be used to explain the relationship between respondents' attitudes and behaviors (i.e., why they behave the way they do). The theoretical and practical utility of descriptive and explanatory analyses depends on how well the researcher has addressed concerns regarding reliability, validity, representativeness, and generalizability.

Designing a Survey Research Project

In general, survey research involves three major sequential tasks. First, the researcher specifies questions or hypotheses that will be examined in the study. These questions/hypotheses should be framed within a theoretical context to help guide decisions regarding the kinds of questions that should be included in the survey. Second, the methodology for the survey is delineated. This task involves: (a) specifying the meaning of the concepts and variables included in the investigation (i.e., *conceptualization*); (b) specifying how the variables will be measured (i.e., *operationalization*); (c) selecting a survey method (e.g., mail, telephone, web), constructing, and implementing the survey; and (d) deciding who will be included in the study (i.e., sampling design, chapter 8). Finally, once the surveys have been collected, the information must be analyzed. Statistics provide a systematic way of summarizing what has been learned and facilitate drawing conclusions about the data. Figure 1.1 provides a schematic of these tasks. The following introduces some basics about each step in the process.

A thorough literature review of previous theories and research informs each of these steps, especially the development of hypotheses and methodology. Theory (a collection of hypotheses) allows scientific studies to build upon one another to form a greater whole that leads to broader knowledge. As will be argued throughout this text, theory is more than an academic exercise; it is the cornerstone against which explanation, prediction and, ultimately, control of phenomena are judged.

Hypotheses and Research Questions

All survey projects begin with hypotheses and/or research questions. A *hypothesis* is a predictive statement about the relationship between two or more variables. Hypotheses may be driven by past research. For example, empirical studies have demonstrated that conflict occurs more often among participants engaged in different recreation activities (i.e., out-group conflict) compared to those engaged in the same activity (i.e., in-group conflict). Researchers might be interested in whether this pattern persists as a recreationist's skill level increases. One study (Vaske, Dyar, & Timmons, 2004), for example, hypothesized that as skill level increases, out-group and in-group conflict will increase for both skiers and snowboarders. The analyses supported the hypothesis.

Research questions are similar to hypotheses, but are stated in question format. For an applied discipline like parks, recreation and human dimensions, research questions may originate from an agency interested in solving a problem. For example, the Colorado Division of Wildlife

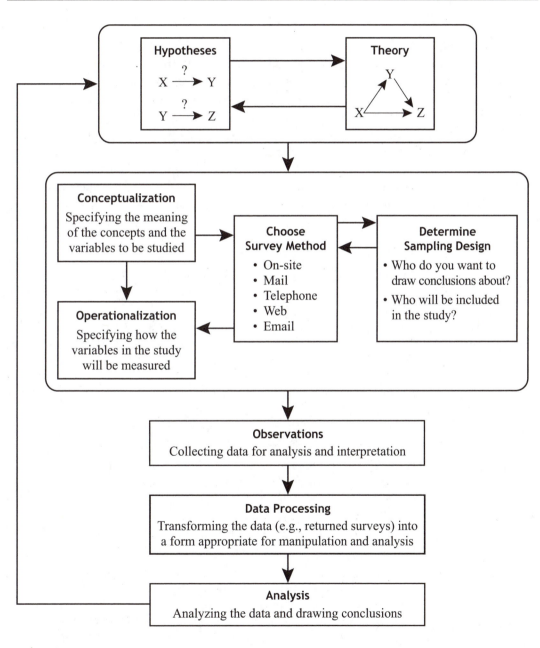

Source: Babbie (2003)

Figure 1.1   The Survey Research Process

was interested in the extent to which conflict existed between hunters and wildlife viewers on Mt. Evans, 70 miles west of Denver. To address this applied question, the researchers (Vaske, Donnelly, Wittmann, & Laidlaw, 1995) used past research to develop and test research questions based on a theoretical distinction between interpersonal versus social values conflict. Interpersonal conflict can occur when the physical presence or behavior of an individual or group interferes with the goals of another individual or group. Social values conflicts can arise when different groups do not share the same norms and/or values, independent of the physical presence or actual contact between the groups. Theory provided the medium for understanding the specific situation on Mt. Evans.

It is useful to think of three types of research questions: (a) difference questions, (b) associational questions, and (c) descriptive questions (Morgan & Harmon, 2000). Difference and association questions imply at least two variables, whereas ***descriptive questions*** focus on a single variable (Table 1.1). ***Difference questions*** examine how far apart two or more groups are with respect to some dependent variable (e.g., conflict, satisfaction, crowding). In the Vaske et al. (1995) study on Mt. Evans, for example, the independent variable was whether the recreationist was a hunter or wildlife viewer. The dependent variable was the type of conflict (i.e., interpersonal vs. social values). Chapter 2 describes this distinction between independent and dependent variables. For the moment, simply recognize that the researchers were interested in the question of whether hunters and wildlife viewers differed in their evaluations of conflict.

Table 1.1   Examples of Three Kinds of Basic Research Hypotheses / Questions

Basic Question	Definition / Example	
Difference (Group Comparison)	For this type of hypothesis or research question, respondents are divided into groups (i.e., the independent variable, such as hunters and wildlife viewers) and the groups are compared in terms of their answers to one or more dependent variables (e.g., experienced interpersonal or social values conflict).	
	Example hypothesis:	Wildlife viewers will experience more social values conflict than hunters.
	Example question:	Do wildlife viewers experience more social values conflict than hunters?
Association (Relational)	For this type of hypothesis or research question, the responses to the independent variable (e.g., How many other recreationists did you see today? [variable = reported encounters]) are related to the responses on the dependent variable (e.g., Did you feel crowded today?).	
	Example hypothesis:	As reported encounters increases, crowding increases.
	Example question:	Do increases in the number of other recreationists a person remembers seeing increase perceptions of crowding?
Descriptive	For this type of research question, responses to a single variable are described in terms of (a) the percent of respondents in each category of a variable, or (b) the variable's central tendency (e.g., mean, μ), and variability (e.g., standard deviation, σ).	
	Example 1:	What percent of respondents experienced social values conflict?
	Example 2:	On average, how many people did the respondents see during their visit?

Adapted from Morgan & Harmon (2000)

Association questions focus on how strongly two or more variables are related (Table 1.1). Chapter 3, for example, examines the strength of the relationship between variables such as the number of people in a recreation area (i.e., user density) and perceived crowding (i.e., an evaluation of the experience).

Understanding these three basic kinds of questions (i.e., difference, association, descriptive) facilitates selecting the appropriate test statistic (Figure 1.2). For example, difference questions involve inferential statistics such as *t*-tests (chapter 14) and analysis of variance (chapter 15). Association questions are examined using inferential tests such as correlation and regression (chapter 16). Descriptive questions are usually not answered with inferential statistics; they are explored by describing or summarizing the data (e.g., frequency counts, means) one variable at a time.

Conceptualization

As we go through life, we observe certain patterns in human behavior. For example, some students: (a) never study, (b) do not attend class, (c) fail to turn in their assignments on time, and (d) do not actively participate in assigned group projects. We might describe these people as lazy. Laziness is shorthand for describing this collection of behaviors. Note, however, that laziness does not really exist; it is merely a term that we agree upon and use for describing these behaviors when we communicate with others. Stated otherwise, laziness is a concept.

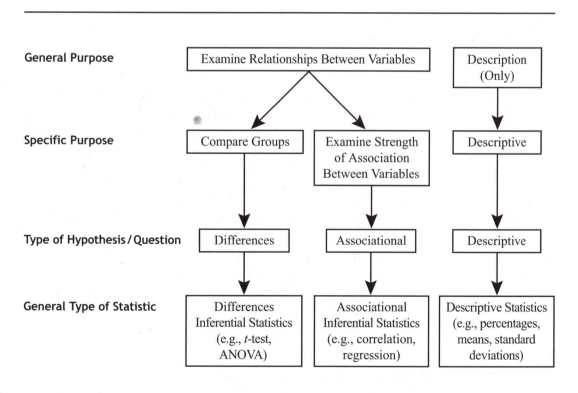

ANOVA = Analysis of Variance; Adapted from Morgan, Gliner, & Harmon (1999, 2006)

Figure 1.2   Relationship between Purpose of Research and Appropriate Statistics

Concepts are constructed from our beliefs about reality and reflect generally shared meanings. Human dimensions researchers, for example, use the concept of motivation when discussing an individual's goals or reasons for participating in a recreation activity. Sometimes, this broad concept is subdivided into the constructs of *intrinsic* and *extrinsic* motivation. Intrinsic motivations refer to things that you do for yourself (e.g., to get exercise, to be outdoors). Extrinsic motivations are things that you do for others (e.g., to be with friends, to prove to others that you can do an activity). Similar to laziness, intrinsic and extrinsic motivations cannot be seen; they are merely ways to describe people.

Conceptualization is the process of specifying precisely what we mean by the use of particular terms (e.g., motivation, satisfaction, crowding, conflict). The Recreation Experience Preference (REP) scales, for example, were developed for measuring the different motivations that people have for participating in recreation activities (Driver & Tocher, 1970). This research suggested that recreation experiences were defined from a psychological perspective as *packages* or *bundles* of psychological outcomes desired from participation in activities (Manfredo, Driver, & Tarrant, 1996). These bundles included concepts such as: (a) achievement / stimulation, (b) family togetherness, (c) introspection, and (d) escape. These concepts were often further subdivided into more specific concepts. The escape dimension, for example, can be conceptualized as escape from personal, social, or physical pressure. These REP scales are useful because they help clarify the concepts of interest when differentiating trip-specific motivations for leisure (e.g., why people took a particular trip), activity-specific motivations (e.g., why people engage in a particular activity), and the satisfaction obtained from participation (e.g., the degree to which goals were attained).

Operationalization

Concepts are mental images of how the researcher and / or the respondent view the world. The conversion of these abstract mental images into something that is measurable is called *operationalization*. This measurement process links abstract theoretical concepts to empirical indicators that give credence to the presence or absence of a concept. In survey research, the indicators typically are the variables in the survey.

As the name implies, a *variable* contains a logical collection of responses (attributes) to a question. Sex is a variable with two possible responses: male or female. If the sample of respondents contains only males, sex is not variable; it is a constant. Days of recreation participation per year is a variable with responses that can range from 0 to 365. Both sex and days of participation can be thought of as *single-item indicators* of their respective concepts. Many of the psychological concepts employed by human dimensions researchers are too complex to be represented by a single question on a survey. For example, an REP concept such as "escape from personal and social pressures" could be measured with three variables: (a) to release built up tensions, (b) to get away from the usual demands of life, and (c) to reduce the feeling of having too many things to do. Each of these questions might be measured on a seven-point response scale (e.g., strongly agree [+3], moderately agree [+2], slightly agree [+1], neither agree nor disagree [0], slightly disagree [–1], moderately disagree [–2], strongly disagree [–3]). As will be discussed in chapter 18, a researcher can test the extent to which the three variables reflect the underlying concept of "escape from personal and social pressure." The test, Cronbach's alpha (α), provides a measure of reliability. If measurement reliability can be demonstrated, the responses to the three questions are typically combined into a ***multi-item composite index*** that represents the underlying concept.

Reliability is one of the basic properties of measurement. Other measurement properties of variables include: (a) level of measurement, (b) mutually exclusive and exhaustive, (c) precision, (d) accuracy, (e) validity, and (f) predictive potential. Although the details about these properties will be discussed in chapter 4, the notion of levels of measurement deserves a few comments here. In general, four levels of measurement (i.e., nominal, ordinal, interval, and ratio) have been commonly discussed in the literature (e.g., Stevens, 1946, 1951) and used in statistical software packages (e.g., Statistical Package for the Social Sciences [SPSS]). Sex is a *nominal variable* because: (a) the responses merely name or label the attributes of the variable (i.e., male or female), and (b) the attributes cannot be logically rank ordered. For example, one cannot say that males are superior to females or that females are better than males (unless, of course, you want to pick a fight or are extremely foolish).

Days of participation per year as measured in the above example is a *ratio level variable* (i.e., 0, 1, 2 … 365) because the attributes can be: (a) named (e.g., the number 2 implies that the individual hunted twice during the year), (b) logically rank ordered (e.g., 2 is greater 1), (c) the distance between the attributes is equal and meaningful (e.g., the distance between 5 and 10 is equal to the distance between 10 and 15), and (d) there is a true zero point (i.e., 0 implies that the individual did not engage in the activity).

The three variables described for the REP scale example above pose a different type of measurement issue. The attributes (or responses) to these variables ranged from –3 (strongly disagree) to +3 (strongly agree). Stevens (1946, 1951) would argue that these types of variables constitute ordinal level measures because the attributes can be named and rank ordered, but the distance between the responses is not necessarily equal. In other words, the difference between "strongly agree" (+3) and "moderately agree" (+2) may not be conceptually equal to the difference between "slightly agree" (+1) and "neutral" (0). For those who are new to statistical analysis, the first reaction might be "ok, these variables are ordinal measures, so what?" The problem here is not what you call a variable, but rather what you can do with the variable from an analysis perspective.

Stevens contends that associated with each level of measurement (i.e., nominal, ordinal, interval, ratio) is a unique set of permissible mathematical operations that constrain the statistical manipulations that can be performed. From this perspective, computing means and standard deviations are only appropriate for interval or ratio level measures;[1] such calculations are not appropriate (according to Stevens) for ordinal level measures. Consider the following example. Student grades are typically awarded on a scale of "A, B, C, D, or F" and are assigned numerical values of 4, 3, 2, 1, and 0, respectively. Such grades, however, are ordinal (not numerical data). Undergraduate students who receive an A (4), B (3), or C (2) in a course, often pass the course. Students who receive a D (1) or F (0) often fail the course. Pragmatically then, the difference

---

[1] The attributes of an interval variable can be named or labeled, can be rank ordered, and have an equal and meaningful distance between the two attributes. There is, however, no absolute 0 point. Examples include Fahrenheit or Celsius temperature.

between a 3 (B) and a 2 (C) is not the same as the difference between a 2 (C) and a 1 (D). In the former situations (i.e., A, B, C), the student passed the course; in the latter, the person failed the course. If grades are considered as ordinal measures, as Stevens would recommend, then colleges and universities should not compute a student's "grade point average" (GPA).

Given that means and standard deviations form the foundation for more advanced statistics (e.g., correlation, regression, analysis of variance), following Stevens's position poses a major problem for university administrators who calculate students' GPAs and, for researchers who use survey response scales similar to the REP example.

Although more than half a century has passed since Stevens's (1946, 1951) influential work on the relationship between measurement levels and appropriate statistics, the debate continues today (Baker, Hardyck, & Petrinovich, 1966; Binder, 1984; Labovitz, 1967, 1970; Velleman & Wilkinson, 1993; Zumbo & Zimmerman, 1993). At the heart of this controversy is the nature of the relationship between ordinal and interval scales, and the appropriate statistics for such measures. Chapter 5 presents alternative theoretical and empirical views on this debate. For the moment, however, simply note that most social scientists recognize that the psychological concepts of greatest interest to human dimensions (e.g., value orientations, attitudes, beliefs, norms) are continuous (i.e., ratio) at the unobserved level (i.e., in the population), even though they are usually observed (i.e., measured) as variables with a limited number of responses (e.g., 7-point scale) in a sample.

Choice of Method

Human dimensions researchers employ a variety of data collection techniques such as observational studies, content analyses, experiments, and surveys. The choice of one methodology or the combination of methodologies depends in part on how much is known about the research question(s) to be addressed. *Observational studies*, for example, are useful when the researcher is interested in the actual behaviors of individuals. Chase and associates (Chase & Godbey, 1983; Chase & Harada, 1984) linked the attendance records (i.e., observational data) of members maintained by a health club with attendance reported on a member survey. The self-reported participation was substantially higher than the actual attendance.

Content analysis might prove useful for researchers interested in better understanding where a given discipline stands on a particular issue. This analytical technique involves the manual or automated coding of documents (e.g., newspapers, transcripts, journal articles) to obtain counts of words or phrases for purposes of statistical analysis (Krippendorff, 2004). The American Psychological Association (Wilkinson & The Task Force on Statistical Inference, 1999), for example, now argues that researchers should report "effect sizes" (i.e., measures of the strength of association between variables) for all primary results, although relatively few researchers did so before 1999. An interesting empirical question is: "To what extent have researchers and journal editors followed this advice?" The question could be answered by a content analysis that counts the number of articles in a given journal that have reported effect size measures in relation to those articles that did not report such statistics (see Vaske, Shelby, & Manfredo, 2006, as an example).

With *experimental* designs, the researcher randomly assigns subjects to one or more treatment conditions (i.e., the independent variables) and measures the effect of a manipulation on dependent variables of interest. This method is appropriate when the concepts are well-defined and the goal is to explain variable relationships rather than descriptions of a sample or population. Experiments can be conducted in laboratories or in natural environments. The advantage of laboratory experiments lies in the researcher's ability to eliminate or control extraneous variables such that the relationship between the independent and dependent variables can be clarified (i.e., internal validity). Explanation of the relationships is the focus; less attention is placed on the representativeness of the sample (e.g., students in Psychology 101) or the generalizability of the results (i.e., external validity).

For applied fields like parks, recreation, and human dimensions, experiments conducted in the natural environments are often more interesting. Natural settings, however, introduce a host of logistical and ethical challenges that must be addressed. Heberlein and Kuentzel (2002), for example, conducted a series of experiments from 1979 to 1989 at the Sandhill Wildlife Demonstration Area in Wisconsin to examine how hunter numbers influence the quality of the experience under alternative hunting season frameworks. The strength of these studies lies in the researchers' ability to randomly assign hunters to high- and low-density hunting conditions independent of the hunters' own preferences. This design allowed the researchers to clarify the relationships among several variables (i.e., hunter numbers, success, satisfaction, season structure), but it is debatable whether today's university human subjects review committee would allow the experimental manipulation of randomly assigning individuals to areas where a large density of people are carrying guns.

In contrast to the experiments by Heberlein and Kuentzel (2002) where the researchers manipulated the independent variables (e.g., hunter density) and measured the hunters' responses using a survey, most surveys do not involve this type of manipulation. Rather, surveys are sent to a sample of individuals from a population, and the data are used to describe and/or to explain the relationships among variables of theoretical or applied interest. Similar to each of the other methodologies (i.e., observational, content analysis, experiments), surveys have advantages and disadvantages. For example, because relatively large samples are feasible, the representativeness of the data is potentially enhanced. Given that numerous questions can be asked, the measurement reliability and measurement validity of the data can be examined empirically. The use of standardized questions facilitates the comparisons of groups (e.g., hunters vs. wildlife viewers) within the sample as well as between studies, thereby increasing the ability to generalize the findings.

Standardized questions, however, do have some disadvantages. First, on-site self-administered and mailed surveys are not flexible. Once the instrument is written and printed, changes to the survey become costly. Telephone surveys and personal interviews allow more flexibility in this regard, but changing the instrument compromises the ability to compare respondents' answers between different versions of the survey. Second, independent of the survey mode (e.g., mail, telephone, personal interview, Internet), the questions must be understandable by all respondents. This task is far more difficult than most novice survey researchers realize.

As the title implies, this book focuses on survey research. Its chapters detail issues related to: (a) writing questions, (b) constructing the survey, and (c) implementing the instrument (chapters

7 and 8). Space considerations do not allow for detailed examination of other data collection methodologies such as observational studies, content analysis, and experiments.

Sampling Design

Survey researchers are interested in making inferences about the population of people that they study. With rare exceptions (e.g., U.S. Census, employee studies), it is not possible to contact all of the individuals in a population. A bridge is needed to connect the goals of the study with the practical considerations (e.g., time, cost) of conducting the research. Sampling designs, or the methods by which members of a population are selected for the study, provide this bridge.

There are two basic approaches to sampling—probability and nonprobability samples. *Probability sampling* techniques involve random samples of individuals. Potential survey respondents are selected such that every member of a population (e.g., all students enrolled in a university) has a known chance (i.e., probability) of being included in the sample. *Nonprobablity samples* do not allow the researcher to generalize to a population of interest, but are sometimes chosen for convenience (e.g., students exiting the university's library) or based on some other criteria. Given that nonprobablity samples can lead to erroneous conclusions (e.g., the attitudes of students who use the library may be different from those who do not use the library), probability samples are generally preferred because they allow researchers to collect relatively few surveys and still generalize to the population.

A sample is representative of the population from which it was selected if the aggregate characteristics of the sample closely approximate the same aggregate characteristics in the population. For example, if the goal of a study is to compare male and female health club members in terms of their frequency of using the club, and the member population is known to be 60% male and 40% female, the ratio of males to females in the sample should closely reflect this population distribution.

For some survey projects where the population can be readily described (e.g., percent male vs. percent female) and identified (e.g., membership in a club, hunting/fishing license sales), selecting a simple random sample (SRS, chapter 8) of respondents is relatively straightforward. In other situations, the identification of whom to include in the study is less obvious. For example, researchers might be interested in generalizing to a population of visitors to a national park, but the National Park Service does not generally gather contact information on their clients. The sampling design for these types of studies becomes more complex. Chapter 8 discusses the tradeoffs that researchers must make in selecting among different sampling methods (e.g., SRS, systematic, stratified, cluster).

Data Processing

The data processing requirements for a survey project are enhanced greatly if: (a) the research questions and hypotheses are theoretically grounded, (b) the concepts have been delineated and operationalized properly, (c) the survey is understandable to the respondents and an adequate response rate has been obtained, and (d) the sampling design allows the researcher to state a known probability of an individual being included in the study. Unfortunately, the social (e.g., cultural factors) and psychological concepts (e.g., values, attitudes, norms) that drive human behavior are complex. Researchers are typically more interested in describing and explaining these underlying (and unobserved) conceptual influences and their relationships, rather than merely summarizing specific variables from the survey.

For the researcher, this implies that a considerable amount of time and energy must be devoted to: (a) carefully entering the data into a computerized database, (b) running preliminary analyses to identify any problems (e.g., missing data, potential outliers in the data) that could influence the results, (c) checking the reliability and validity of the data, and (d) transforming the data to create composite indices of the underlying dimensions. Analysts at SPSS have suggested that as much as 80% of a researcher's time is devoted to these preliminary data manipulation steps. Consequently, this book devotes several chapters to these topics.

Survey Analysis

Stevens's (1951) discussion of levels of measurement stimulated the classification of statistical procedures into two categories. ***Parametric statistics*** (e.g., t, F) require the estimation of at least one parameter (e.g., a population mean, μ, or a population standard deviation, σ). These statistics assume that the samples being compared are drawn from a population that is normally distributed. The frequency distributions of the samples are assumed to be meaningful and the measures are, from Stevens's perspective, assumed to be interval or ratio. ***Nonparametric statistics*** (e.g., analysis of variance by ranks, better known as the Kruskal-Wallis H test) do not require the estimation of population parameters and no assumptions are made about the equivalence of units along the scale or about the shape of the distribution of scores in the population.

The association of parametric statistics with interval and ratio scales, and nonparametric statistics with nominal and ordinal scales has provided the foundation for several statistical books (e.g., Blalock, 1979; Senders, 1958; Siegel, 1956). If one buys the arguments advanced in these texts, parametric statistics (e.g., correlation, regression, t-tests, analysis of variance) should not be used by any researcher who has less than interval level data. In effect, this prevents most social science researchers from using parametric statistics for much of their data.

As discussed by Borgatta and Bohrnstedt (1980), however, the assertion that parametric statistics require interval or ratio level data seems to be based on confusion between measurement theory and statistical theory. Measurement theory and statistical theory lie in distinct domains. In the development of surveys, measurement issues (e.g., reliability, validity) are a primary concern. The validity aspect brings into focus the meaning of responses (i.e., the numbers) to a variable.

In statistical analyses and especially in the tests of null hypotheses (chapter 6), differences and relatedness of numbers are of concern. The meaning of the numbers does not enter the picture. In other words, "the numbers do not know where they come from" (Lord, 1953, p. 751). The only requirements for any parametric statistical procedure are that the mathematical assumptions underlying the procedure must be met or approximated (Savage, 1957). For example, with analysis of variance (ANOVA) problems, the mathematical model assumes normality, independence, and homogeneity of variance (chapter 15). As long as these three assumptions are met, the calculation of the ANOVA F statistic is appropriate. Similar ideas apply for other inferential statistical procedures (e.g., correlation, regression). Thus, the question of whether a given set of data is ordinal or interval is important if we wish to attach meaning to the numbers (i.e., ***measurement theory***). It is not important if we wish to estimate the probability that the two sets of numbers have been drawn from a single population (i.e., ***statistical theory***).

As an alternative to the Stevens's (1951) classification scheme (i.e., nominal, ordinal, interval, ratio), a variable's level of measurement is described in this book as ***dichotomous*** (a variable with only two response categories), ***categorical*** (a nominal variable with three or more response categories that are either ordered or not ordered) and ***continuous*** (an ordered variable with a distribution that is normally distributed [bell-shaped] in the population sampled, chapters 6 and 11).[2]

Differentiating between dichotomous and categorical variables for statistical analysis is impor-tant for two reasons. First, computing the average of a three (or more) level categorical variable that is unordered does not make sense. For example, if the survey question asks for respondents' political party affiliation and the response categories are democrat (coded as a 1), republican (2), and independent (3), a mean of 1.52 implies that respondents are, on average, somewhere between democrat and republican. Likewise, calculating a mean for an ordered categorical variable (e.g., elementary school, high school, undergraduate university, graduate university) does not make sense. Computing an average for a dichotomous variable, however, does have meaning. For example, if individuals are asked to report their sex (females = 0, males = 1), a mean of .55 implies that 55% of the respondents were male. Second, a dichotomous variable can be used as an independent variable (called a *dummy variable*) in a regression analysis (see chapter 16 for additional discussion of this statistical approach).

Continuous variables combine Stevens's (1951) measurement levels of ordinal, interval, and ratio. If one accepts this approach, the example survey questions presented earlier in this chapter, the composite multiple-item indices (e.g., REP computed scales), as well as students' grade point averages can be analyzed using inferential (i.e., parametric) statistics. In other words, it is appropriate for a researcher to compute an average score for a set of attitudinal items or for a university to compute a student's mean GPA (apologies to all of the students who are reading this book). It is important that the variables (or their errors) are at least approximately normally distributed (chapters 6 and 11) in the population. Moreover, the choice of inferential statistic depends on research questions/hypotheses and level of measurement (see Figure 1.2, p. 7).

---

[2] See Morgan, Gliner, and Harmon (1999) for a slight variation on this proposed labeling scheme.

Chapter Summary

This chapter introduced the basic topics examined (and not examined) in this book. Emphasis was placed on applying the standards of science (i.e., reliability, validity, representativeness, generalizability) when conducting survey research. Regardless of a study's goals (e.g., exploration, explanation, prediction), all survey research projects involve three major sequential tasks. First, the researchers specify the hypotheses or questions to be examined. A hypothesis is a predictive statement about the relationship between two or more variables. Research questions are similar to hypotheses, but are stated in a question format. These questions/hypotheses should be framed within a theoretical context to help guide decisions regarding the kinds of questions that should be included in the survey.

The second major task involves: (a) specifying the meaning of the concepts and variables to be included in the investigation (i.e., conceptualization), (b) specifying how the variables will be measured (i.e., operationalization), (c) selecting a survey method (e.g., mail, telephone, web), and (4) deciding who will be included in the study (i.e., sampling design).

Finally, the collected information is analyzed. Statistics provide a systematic way of summarizing what has been learned and facilitate conclusions about the data. The appropriate statistics depend on the types of research questions/hypotheses asked: (a) difference questions, (b) associational questions, and (c) descriptive questions. Difference questions address how far apart two or more groups (the independent variable) are on a dependent variable of interest (e.g., satisfaction, crowding, conflict). Association questions focus on how closely two or more variables are related. Difference and associational research questions (hypotheses) involve two or more variables and are analyzed using inferential statistics. Descriptive questions usually summarize a single variable.

Review Questions

1. Describe four major characteristics of scientific inquiry.

2. Define and differentiate *study reliability* from *measurement reliability*.

3. Define and differentiate *study validity* from *measurement validity*.

4. Define three major goals of survey research.

5. Depict the survey research process in a diagram.

6. Give a definition of a hypothesis.

7. What is the difference between a hypothesis and a research question?

8. Define three types of research questions. Why is it useful to differentiate among these different types of research questions?

9. What do researchers mean by the term *concept*?

10. What is the difference between *conceptualization* and *operationalization*?

11. List five basic properties of measurement.

12. Describe Stevens' four levels of measurement.

13. Define four different types of data collection used by researchers.

14. What differentiates *experiments* from *surveys*?

15. What are the two advantages and two disadvantages of surveys?

16. When is a sample representative of a population?

17. What is the difference between *parametric* and *nonparametric* statistics?

18. Describe the difference between *dichotomous*, *categorical*, and *continuous* variables?

19. Why is it important to differentiate *dichotomous* and *categorical* variables?

2

linking theory and concepts to survey research

Social scientists explore people's thoughts and actions toward a wide variety of issues. Contemporary examples include topics such as reducing conflict among recreationists; understanding the relationships among value orientations, attitudes, norms, and behavior; educating individuals about management practices; or predicting support for policy changes. To understand, explain and predict why people think and act the way they do in different situations often requires asking numerous survey questions. A mail survey, for example, might include hundreds of survey questions (variables). While long surveys are sometimes necessary, the selection of specific items should be guided by social science theory.

Theory is important because it extends the generalizability of the findings; improves the rigor and confidence in the research; provides a structure for integrating and building upon previous findings; and moves beyond the endless, repetitive cycle of purely descriptive research. In short, theory-based research improves the integrity and credibility of an empirical study (Manfredo, 1989). Empirical verification of theory is more than an academic exercise; it is the cornerstone against which explanation and prediction are judged. Theory provides the medium for studies to build upon one another into a greater whole that leads to broader knowledge.

This chapter defines and differentiates what researchers mean by a *theory*, a *concept*, and a *variable*. Emphasis is placed on how concepts are theoretically related to each other and what variables on a survey should be measured to test the predicted relationships. The chapter concludes with an overview of some of the concepts used by social science researchers. In adopting this approach, the goals are to: (a) illustrate how theory can be used to define and shape the content of social science surveys, and (b) clarify conceptual distinctions. Without an initial understanding of the different concepts (e.g., values, attitudes, norms) used by social science researchers, it is difficult, if not impossible, to write survey items that measure those concepts. Similarly, knowledge of how different researchers use the same word (e.g., norm, attitude) is essential for students (and professionals) when attempting to apply the concept to natural resources and recreation issues.

Theories — Concepts — Variables

All research in both the physical and social sciences begins with a problem or an unanswered question. As applied to human dimensions and recreation issues, physical scientists might be interested in whether different types of footwear (e.g., lugged vs. smooth soles) have more or less impact on a trail's surface. Wildlife biologists are often interested in how the presence of recreationists influences the reproductive success of animals. Social scientists examine issues that contribute to or detract from the quality of a recreational experience. Regardless of one's disciplinary perspective, theory offers a systematic explanation of observed events.

Theories state suspected relationships among concepts. *Concepts*, the basic building blocks of theory, are abstract elements representing our mental images of reality. They reflect the different properties that an object (e.g., people, wildlife) may possess. Sometimes these mental images are obvious because we are familiar with the abstraction. The physical scientist studying trail erosion problems, for example, employs concepts like the "depth" of the trail as a gauge for thinking about the relative impact of lugged- versus smooth-soled shoes. Trails that show more erosion are deeper and are more impacted than those that are level with the adjacent terrain. A wildlife biologist might use the concept of "weight" as an indicator of whether an animal will be able to successfully produce offspring. We use concepts like "depth" and "weight" in everyday life to describe the properties of physical things or people. A river, for example, might be described as shallow or deep. A person might be characterized as thin or weight-challenged.

The concepts used by human dimensions and recreation researchers are typically more complex and sometimes less obvious than depth or weight. Because everyone may not share our mental images of these abstractions, it is important to clarify what we mean by a concept. "Conflict," for example, has been studied extensively in the recreation literature. Despite the volume of conflict-related research, there has never been agreement on how the concept of recreation conflict should be measured (Graefe & Thapa, 2004). In part, differences in conceptual definitions can be attributed to the theoretical foundation of the study. Most researchers, for example, have examined interpersonal conflict (a.k.a. goal interference) using the model proposed by Jacob and Schreyer (1980). For interpersonal conflict to occur, the physical presence or behavior of an individual or a group of recreationists must interfere with the goals of another recreationist or group. A person attempting to photograph wildlife, for example, may experience interpersonal conflict if the animal is scared away by the arrival of other visitors. Using the goal interference model of conflict, some studies have measured conflict as the extent to which visitors find encounters with others to be desirable or undesirable (Thapa & Graefe, 2003; Watson, Niccolucci, & Williams, 1994), or more directly, asked survey respondents to indicate the extent to which encounters with others interfered with their enjoyment (Graefe & Thapa, 2004; Watson, Williams, & Daigle, 1991). This approach to conflict predicts that for those recreationists for whom the interaction with others has negative consequences (e.g., disrupts the experience, or inhibits one's ability to watch wildlife, hunt game or catch fish), conflict increases.

Another theoretical approach to the study of recreation conflict has emphasized differences in norms (Ruddell & Gramann, 1994) and / or values (Saremba & Gill, 1991), as opposed to differences in motivations (i.e., goals). Conflict is predicted to occur between groups who do not share the same norms or values independent of the physical presence or actual contact between the groups (Carothers, Vaske, & Donnelly, 2001; Morgan, Newman, & Wallace, 2007; Vaske, Donnelly, Wittmann, & Laidlaw, 1995). For example, although encounters with llama packing trips may be rare, individuals may philosophically disagree about the appropriateness of using these animals in the backcountry (Blahna, Smith, & Anderson, 1995). Vaske et al. (1995) provided support for this social values versus interpersonal conflict distinction in a comparison of hunters and nonhunters on Mt. Evans. Even though nearly all of the nonhunters did not physically observe any hunting-associated events (e.g., seeing hunters, seeing an animal being shot), many expressed a conflict in social values. Simply knowing that hunting occurred on the mountain was sufficient to activate perceptions of conflict. Using this model of recreation conflict implies that survey items need to identify respondents' beliefs about the occurrence of different events or situations (e.g., response options of "never," "occasionally," "frequently," "always") and the extent to which these situations are deemed unacceptable (e.g., "not at all" to "totally unacceptable"). The combination of these beliefs and evaluations yields an indicator of the conflict concept.

A researcher's choice of theoretical framework thus influences what concepts and associated measured variables are important for an investigation. Complex concepts like conflict are sometimes referred to as **constructs**. The term *construct* reinforces the idea that the building blocks of theory (i.e., concepts) are not real, but mental constructions. While concepts are the domain of theory, a variable is a concept's empirical counterpart. **Variables** are the questions that are actually included on the survey. A variable must be able to vary or have different values. If it doesn't vary, it is a constant. Sex, for example, is a variable because it has two values— male or female. Age is a variable because it has numerous values; on a survey, age typically ranges between 18 to less than 100. The lower bound of 18 is often dictated by the desire to only include adults in a survey. The upper bound occurs because there are relatively few individuals in any population who are a century old. These ranges, however, are not fixed. Sometimes researchers are interested in studying children; other investigators are concerned with the aged. When we measure a construct in a way that gives varying values, we label the measure a variable.

For purposes of this book, the word *variable* implies an indicator or empirical measure such as grades in school. Theoretical variables are used here to refer to unmeasured or abstract latent constructs like academic achievement. This distinction is important to understand. *Concepts*, *constructs*, and *theoretical variables* all represent abstract and unmeasured properties of people, places, and things. They reflect our abstractions of the world. *Variables* (or more precisely, *measured variables*) refer to concrete, measured expressions of these properties. Measured variables can be counted, categorized, and assigned numerical values.

Diagramming Theories

Understanding the complexities of the world and the theoretical relationships that might exist among the concepts of interest can be a daunting task. Visualizing these relationships is often easier if the theorist draws a picture. Figure 2.1 (p. 20), for example, shows a diagram of the theoretical concepts and measured variables predicted by Bratt (1999) to influence environmentally responsible behavior (i.e., recycling behavior).

In Figure 2.1, the words inside the ovals are concepts and the words in the rectangles are measured variables. The arrows connecting the ovals illustrate the hypothesized relationships

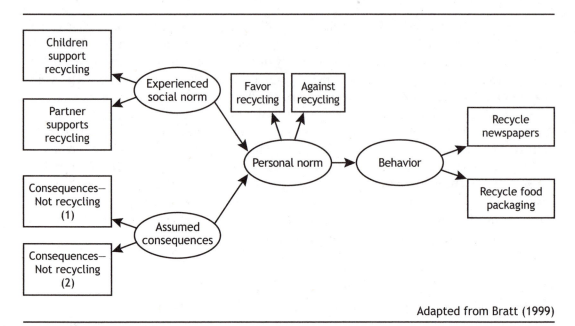

Adapted from Bratt (1999)

Figure 2.1   The Influence of Norms on Recycling Behavior

between the concepts. For example, people who recognize or "assume the consequences of their actions" are more likely to hold a personal norm in favor of recycling. The arrows connecting the rectangles to each oval depict what variables were used to measure each construct. The theoretical concept of behavior (the oval), for example, was represented by two measured variables (the rectangles)—recycling newspapers and recycling food packaging.

The study reported by Bratt (1999) is interesting because it represents a blending of the concepts discussed in Fishbein and Ajzen's (1975) theory of reasoned action and Schwartz's (1977) norm activation theory. Both theories, for example, address the concept of norms, but the theorists have different mental images of what the construct means. For Fishbein and Ajzen (1975), social norms refer to what a person thinks other people think is appropriate. Bratt (1999) used two measured variables as indicators of this subjective social norm. Respondents were asked whether they believed their spouse and children thought they should recycle paper products. Possible answers were: "yes, strong opinions," "yes, but not very strong opinions," "no," and "don't know."

Schwartz's (1977) activation theory defines a norm as an internalized sense of obligation to behave in given manner in a particular situation (i.e., a personal norm). As originally conceived, two conditions were necessary to "activate" the norm. Individuals must possess an *awareness of the consequences* (AC) their behavior has on others and they must accept some responsibility for their actions (i.e., *ascription of responsibility* [AR]). Bratt's (1999) study addressed a slightly modified version of the AC concept and did not include the AR construct.

From a larger perspective, it is common for any given study to contain only a subset of the concepts originally proposed by the theory or to operationalize (i.e., measure) the concepts in a slightly different way. Schwartz's initial model focused on moral norms as they influenced individuals' willingness to engage in altruistic behavior to help other humans. Research has documented the utility of the AC and AR constructs in predicting environmental behaviors.

Specific issues have included: (a) recycling (Bratt, 1999; Hopper & Nielsen, 1991); (b) littering, the purchase of lead-free gasoline, and other energy conserving behaviors (Heberlein, 1971); (c) environmental conservation behavior (Black, 1978); (d) support for environmental laws and regulations with links to moral judgments about government and industry responsibilities (Stern, Dietz, & Black, 1986); (e) yard burning (Van Liere & Dunlap, 1978); (f) water pollution related to human waste dumped by boaters (Cottrell & Graefe, 1997); and (g) efforts to recover the desert tortoise (Vaske & Donnelly, 2007).

Bratt's concept of AC was measured with two variables (Figure 2.1). Respondents indicated their beliefs about the collective and individual consequences of not recycling on the environment. One of the specific questions asked "What damage is caused to the environment if people in general do not recycle?" The second survey item asked "If you disregard how others behave, what damage do you think is caused to the environment if you as an individual do not recycle?" Similarly, two measured variables were used to represent the individual's personal norm about recycling. One of these survey items was stated in the positive, "I should deliver paper for recycling in order to contribute to environmental protection." The second question was couched in the negative, "I should throw paper in the ordinary garbage. It is too inconvenient to separate paper and deliver it to containers meant for paper waste." Finally, the behavior concept was measured with two self-reported behaviors (Figure 2.1). "When you throw away household waste, how much of the following materials do you sort out from other waste and place in or deliver to separate containers for recycling?" Separate questions were asked for newspapers and paper used in food packaging.

According to the theory in Figure 2.1, individuals who "experienced the social norm" (i.e., believe that their children and spouse think they should recycle) and who have "assumed the consequences" of their actions are more likely to hold a personal norm in favor of recycling. These theoretical considerations result in a ***hypothesis***, or an expectation about the way things ought to be in the world if the theoretical expectations are correct. The direction of arrows implies that the "social norm" and the "assumed consequences" cause the activation of the "personal norm." In reality, it is usually impossible to prove causation (see Box 2.1), especially in survey research where the researcher has not experimentally manipulated the variables in question.

Box 2.1 Criteria for Determining Causation

1. The predictor or independent variable (i.e., cause) and criterion or dependent (i.e., effect) variables must be empirically related to one another.

2. The predictor variable must occur earlier in time than the criterion variable.

3. The observed relationship cannot be explained away as an artificial product of the effect of another earlier variable.

Consistent with Schwartz's (1977) original theory, Bratt's (1999) empirical example postulates that the AC construct causes the personal norm to be activated. Other concepts (e.g., age, education, sex) might be hypothesized to affect a person's AC, but a theory must start somewhere. Theories vary in their range, some including more causal links than others. However extensive, any theory has to choose some concepts as starting points (i.e., causes where starting points are unknown or at least not stated).

Exogenous versus Endogenous Constructs

In Figure 2.1, the starting concepts are the social norm and assumed consequences. Such starter concepts are referred to as ***exogenous constructs*** because their causes originate from outside the theory. Exogenous concepts have causal arrows pointing away from them, but not to them. In their measured form, such variables are often referred to as ***independent variables***, because they are independent of (not caused by) other variables in the model.

Endogenous constructs are caused by other concepts in the model. When presented in a diagram (or path model like Figure 2.1), endogenous concepts have arrows pointing to them. Personal norm, for example, is an endogenous concept because the model predicts that the construct is caused by the social norm and the assumed consequences concepts. The measured forms of these endogenous constructs are referred to as ***dependent variables***. If we ignore for the moment the behavior construct in Figure 2.1, this exogenous–endogenous construct (or independent–dependent measured variable) distinction works. When the entire path model is considered, however, a slightly expanded labeling strategy might be easier to understand and help clarify the relationships among the constructs / variables of interest.

Mediating Constructs

The personal norm construct sits in between the behavior concept and the two starter concepts (i.e., social norm and assumed consequences). The concept "mediates" the relationship between social norm / assumed consequences and recycling behavior. In contrast to the social norm and assumed consequences constructs, where the arrows always point away from the constructs (i.e., they are always exogenous constructs), or the behavior construct, where the arrow only points to the concept (i.e., it is always a endogenous construct), the personal norm concept sometimes has arrows pointing to it and sometimes the arrow points away from it. The personal norm concept might be more appropriately labeled a ***mediator*** in this model (see chapter 20 for more information on mediation).

Bratt's (1999) analysis supported the linkages shown in Figure 2.1. Social norms and assumed consequences influenced recycling behavior, but the causal linkage was *fully mediated* by the personal norm construct. Fishbein and Ajzen's (1975) theory of reasoned action would have predicted a direct link (arrow) between the social norm and behavior constructs. Had this causal relationship been observed in the Bratt study (in addition to the arrows shown in Figure 2.1), the personal norm construct would be described as a *partial mediator*. In other words, the social norm would have had a direct influence as well as indirect influence (i.e., mediated by the personal norm) on behavior.

Whether or not a construct serves as a mediator or is exogenous to another construct depends on what the theory predicts and what concepts are included in the theory. All theories are tentative or preliminary explanations of how the world works and all are subject to empirical verification. Not finding a causal linkage between social norms and behavior does not invalidate the theory of reasoned action. Fishbein and Ajzen's (1975) attitude-behavior model does not address the idea of a personal norm (only the subjective social norm). The inclusion (or exclusion) of additional concepts can change the observed relationships.

Bratt's (1999) analyses adopted structural equation modeling to examine which measured (i.e., observed) variables were related to specific latent (unobserved) concepts and how the concepts were related to each other. Although structural equation models (SEM) are beyond the scope of this book (see Byrne, 1994; Kline, 1998; Maruyama, 1998, for a detailed discussion of SEM), thinking causally about a problem and constructing an arrow diagram that reflects causal processes often facilitates a clearer statement of the hypotheses and the generation of additional insights into the topic at hand.

Social Science Theories and Concepts

Many of the concepts discussed by researchers can be categorized into two broad theoretical traditions—cognitive and motivational/satisfaction. *Cognitive theories* examine the concepts underlying the process of human thought to action, such as values, attitudes, and norms, and examine the relationships among them, especially to predict behavior. *Motivational theories* are explanatory approaches for understanding human behavior and address why we do what we do. *Satisfaction theories* attempt to explain why people evaluate their experiences in a given way. This section defines and provides examples of the major theoretical orientations and the associated concepts used in literature. What is important to note is that different researchers measure the same concepts differently. Without an understanding of what a concept means, it is impossible to write survey questions that measure the concept.

A Cognitive Approach

The *cognitive approach* emphasizes attitude and value theories (Bem, 1970; Fishbein & Ajzen, 1975; Fulton, Manfredo, & Lipscomb, 1996; Vaske & Donnelly, 1999; Vaske, Donnelly, Williams, & Jonker, 2001; Whittaker, Vaske, & Manfredo, 2006). These theories propose that human thought is arranged into a hierarchy of cognitions. Cognitions refer to the collection of mental processes and activities used in perceiving, remembering, thinking, and understanding, as well as the act of using these processes (Ashcroft, 1994). This approach explores values, value orientations (patterns of basic beliefs), attitudes, and norms in an effort to understand how these concepts influence behavior. Each of these elements build upon one another in what has been described as an inverted pyramid (Figure 2.2, p. 24).

Values

Rokeach (1973) defines *values* as desirable end states of existence (e.g., a comfortable life, freedom, self-respect) or appropriate modes of conduct (e.g., honesty, fairness, forgiving). From this perspective, values are basic evaluative beliefs that are shaped by family, friends, and significant others early in life (Manfredo, Teel, & Bright, 2004). These enduring characteristics of a person guide life decisions and give direction to one's attitudes, norms and behaviors. Because values are stable beliefs that are central to one's identity, they are difficult to change (Bem, 1970).

The study of values has become common in the human dimensions and recreation literature. Human dimensions of wildlife researchers (Bright, Manfredo, & Fulton, 2000), for example, have used values to segment stakeholder groups and predict their attitudes toward controversial

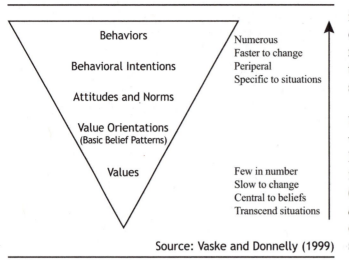

Behaviors

Behavioral Intentions

Attitudes and Norms

Value Orientations
(Basic Belief Patterns)

Values

Numerous
Faster to change
Periperal
Specific to situations

Few in number
Slow to change
Central to beliefs
Transcend situations

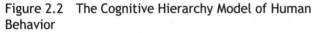

Source: Vaske and Donnelly (1999)

Figure 2.2   The Cognitive Hierarchy Model of Human Behavior

issues (e.g., trapping, relocation of nuisance animals). Other researchers have used the concept to identify consumer lifestyle segments (Homer & Kahle, 1988).

Unfortunately, the concept of values has multiple definitions. Brown (1984), for example, differentiated between ***held values*** (i.e., ideals or life goals) and ***assigned values*** (i.e., the process of evaluating). Held values are similar to the Rokeach's (1973) definition of the concept. Assigned values are similar to the construct of attitudes (Manfredo, Teel et al., 2004). How a researcher thinks about a concept and the associated theory influences what questions need to be included in the survey to test the variable relationships.

Because much of the early, applied work on values was not explained in the context of theory, students and even professionals sometimes confuse the concepts of values and attitudes. Kellert (1980), for example, developed a typology that suggested human evaluations could be expressed by 10 dimensions (e.g., utilitarian, naturalistic, aesthetic, negativistic). Kellert's (1985, 1987) review of changing trends in American's relationship with wildlife indicated a shift from utilitarian to more appreciative evaluations. Whether this shift reflects a change in wildlife values or a change in wildlife attitudes has been debated in the literature (Manfredo, Teel et al., 2004). Similarly, the New Environmental Paradigm (Dunlap & Van Liere, 1978) is sometimes described as a measure of environment attitudes, and other times portrayed as a worldview (i.e., a value). Although these types of descriptive approaches to the study of values illustrate how the public views wildlife and natural resources, their lack of theoretical structure limits their application for prediction of specific attitudes, norms or behavior.

Values differ from attitudes in at least four ways. First, values represent single, stable beliefs that individuals use as standards for evaluating attitudes and behavior. Attitudes, on the other hand, reflect an organization of several beliefs and evaluations. Second, values transcend situations, issues and objects. In the social psychological literature, an ***object*** can be any entity that is being evaluated (e.g., a person, situation, wildlife, forests, the environment). Thus, if a person holds "honesty" as a value, the individual is expected to be honest when completing IRS tax forms, conducting business deals, or interacting with friends. Attitudes are specific to situations, issues, and objects. From this perspective, research articles that discuss wildlife values (Kellert, 1980, 1987; Steinoff, 1980), forest values (Steel, List, & Schindler 1994), and environmental values (Dunlap & Van Liere, 1978; Weigel & Weigel, 1978), implicitly confuse the concepts of values and attitudes. Values are not specific to particular objects like wildlife, forests and the environment. Third, values are the most central component of a person's belief system, whereas attitudes vary with respect to how strongly they are held. Fourth, values tend to be limited in number (dozens), while attitudes can be numerous (thousands). Rokeach (1973), for example, identifies 18 instrumental values (e.g., ambitious, logical, obedient) and 18 terminal values (e.g., a comfortable life, happiness, freedom). Similarly, Schwartz (1992) discusses 10 fundamental value domains (e.g., universalism, achievement, power). Both Rokeach and Schwartz purport to offer a comprehensive listing of values, yet neither identifies a specific value for environmentalism or natural resources (Manfredo, Teel et al., 2004).

Value Orientations (and Basic Beliefs)

Because values tend to be widely shared by all members of a culture, values are unlikely to account for much of the variability in specific attitudes, norms and behaviors (Manfredo, Teel et al., 2004; Stern, 2000; Vaske & Donnelly, 2007). *Basic beliefs*, on the other hand, reflect our thoughts about specific objects or issues, and give meaning to the more global cognitions represented in values. *Value orientations* are the patterns of direction and intensity among these basic beliefs (Fulton et al., 1996; Vaske & Donnelly, 1999, 2007). Basic beliefs and value orientations help explain how positions toward specific issues evolve from broad values.

A person has a number of basic beliefs about the environment (e.g., wildlife or nature) in which they live, and these beliefs can be grouped to indicate a specific orientation. One wildlife value orientation focuses on a single "rights-use" continuum that is measured by the degree of agreement with a series of statements about "wildlife use" and "wildlife rights" (Fulton et al., 1996). Example statements include "Recreational use of desert environments is more important than protecting the endangered species that live there" (i.e., use) and "The rights of endangered species to live is more important than the negative effects that their recovery may have on humans" (i.e., rights).

The wildlife "rights-use" orientation is similar to the biocentric-anthropocentric value orientation continuum (Shindler, List, & Steel, 1993; Steel et al., 1994; Thompson & Barton, 1994; Vaske & Donnelly, 1999, 2007; Vaske et al., 2001). An anthropocentric value orientation represents a human-centered view of the nonhuman world (Eckersley, 1992; Pinchot, 1910). The approach assumes that providing for human uses and benefits is the primary aim of natural resource allocation and management, whether those uses are for commodity benefits (e.g., timber) or for aesthetic, spiritual, or physical benefits (e.g., recreation). The environment is seen as "material to be used by humans as they see fit" (Scherer & Attig, 1983). There is no notion that the nonhuman parts of nature are valuable in their own right or for their own sake. In short, an anthropocentric value orientation emphasizes the instrumental value of natural resources for human society, rather than their inherent worth (Steel et al., 1994).

In contrast, a biocentric value orientation is a nature-centered or eco-centered approach. The value of all ecosystems, species, and natural organisms is elevated to center stage. Human desires and human values are still important, but are viewed from a larger perspective. This approach assumes that environmental objects have inherent as well as instrumental worth and that human economic uses and benefits are not necessarily the most important uses of natural resources. In matters of natural resource management, these inherent values are to be equally respected and preserved, even if they conflict with human-centered values (Thompson & Barton, 1994).

Biocentric and anthropocentric value orientations are not mutually exclusive. Rather, these value orientations can be arranged along a continuum with biocentric viewpoints on one end and anthropocentric orientations on the other. The mid-point of this scale represents a mixture of the two extremes. Research conducted in Colorado (Vaske & Donnelly, 1999; Vaske et al., 2001) and Oregon (Shindler et al., 1993; Steel et al., 1994) supports this conceptual continuum. Figure 2.3 illustrates these relationships relative to the cognitive hierarchy. The numbers connecting the ovals indicate that individuals on the biocentric end of the value orientation continuum were more likely to have a positive attitude toward wildland preservation. In turn, people with a positive attitude were more likely to vote for wildland preservation (Vaske & Donnelly, 1999).

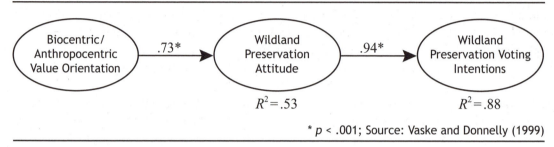

* $p < .001$; Source: Vaske and Donnelly (1999)

Figure 2.3   A Value-Attitude-Behavior Model Predicting Wildland Preservation Voting Intentions

Depending on the author, these latent constructs (i.e., rights-use, biocentric-anthropocentric) have been labeled general environmental values, value orientations, general attitudes, and even "world views" (Whittaker et al., 2006). Regardless of the label, each concept fundamentally measures an underlying general "environmental values" dimension.

To effectively use these concepts in a parks, recreation and human dimensions survey, it is important to recognize what is and what is not being measured. Natural resource applications of the cognitive hierarchy have generally not measured "values" (e.g., Bright, Manfredo, & Fulton, 2000; Fulton et al., 1996; Vaske & Donnelly, 1999, 2007; Whittaker et al., 2006). The "starter concepts" in these investigations were "value orientations." As noted earlier, "values" are not likely to show much variation in a given population. If the concept and its associated measured variables does not vary, it cannot predict another concept that varies depending on the situation. For example, two individuals may share the same value, say universalism, which emphasizes equality. One individual might believe that humans and animals (or nature) should have similar rights (i.e., a rights value orientation). The other individual, however, only applies this value to humans, not animals (i.e., a use value orientation). Thus, the "universalism value" for both individuals is the same (a constant), but the value orientation varies (rights or use) depending on what is being evaluated (humans or animals/nature). Based on the differences in the two individuals' value orientations, their attitudes and voting behavior for management policies would likely be quite different, even though they share the same underlying value. Values can guide value orientations, but their influence on other concepts in the cognitive hierarchy (e.g., attitudes, norms, behavior) is "indirect" (i.e., value orientations mediate the relationship between values and attitudes, norms and behavior). Value orientations, on the other hand, are predicted to "directly" influence higher order concepts such as attitudes and norms.

Attitudes

Attitudes are one of the most frequently studied concepts in the social sciences (Eagly & Chaiken, 1993; Manfredo, Teel et al., 2004). ***Attitudes*** are defined as the evaluation, either favorable or unfavorable, of an entity (e.g., person, object, or action). The concept is important because attitudes can predict and influence behavior. While value orientations are believed to direct attitudes, attitudes are believed to directly influence behavior. Short-term behavior change typically will not become permanent unless one changes the accompanying constructs causing the behavior, such as underlying attitudes. Knowing what influences behavior helps us predict it more accurately.

Attitude questions on surveys are typically framed in terms of like-dislike, good-bad, positive-negative. Much of the research in parks, recreation, and human dimensions of natural resources dealing with opinions, preferences, and perceptions is actually an examination of attitudes. Perceived crowding, for example, is typically defined as a negative evaluation of a certain number of people in a given situation (e.g., at a campsite). Defined in this manner, crowding is an attitude about how people feel about seeing others while engaged in an activity like camping (Shelby, Vaske, & Heberlein, 1989; Vaske & Shelby, 2008). Similarly, a person's overall evaluation (i.e., satisfaction) of a particular recreation experience as either positive or negative is an attitude.

Attitudes have both an evaluative and a cognitive dimension. The evaluative component refers to whether the individual views the attitude object as positive or negative. The cognitive aspect refers to the beliefs associated with the attitude object. Beliefs are what we think are true, but are not necessarily objective facts. It is important to understand both the cognitive and evaluative characteristics of attitudes, because an understanding of only one aspect is inadequate for accurately predicting behavior. For example, one person may have a cognitive belief that wolves are dangerous to humans and evaluate wolves negatively because of fear. Another person may also believe wolves are dangerous, but feel positively toward them because they are excited by the potential danger. Both individuals share the belief that wolves are dangerous, but their evaluations of this belief are different.

Beliefs, attitudes, and behaviors are most strongly related when measured at "corresponding levels of specificity" (Ajzen & Fishbein, 1980; Fishbein & Manfredo, 2002). For example, to determine whether a person will vote to support wolf reintroduction, we should determine their attitudes toward *wolf reintroduction*, not just their beliefs about or attitudes toward wolves (Bright & Manfredo, 1996). When there is a direct correspondence between the attitude and behavior measures (e.g., specific to specific), a relatively strong correlation will be observed. When there is no correspondence (e.g., general to specific), the magnitude of the relationship declines (Whittaker et al., 2006).

Ajzen and Fishbein (1980) identify four specificity variables across which measurements of attitude and behavior should correspond: target (e.g., deer); context (e.g., deer are causing Lyme disease); action (e.g., conduct a special hunt); and time (e.g., next month). Specific survey questions should more closely approximate public sentiment than broadly worded questions.

Norms

Norms can refer to what most people are doing (a ***descriptive norm***) or what people "should" or "ought to" do (an ***injunctive norm***) in a given situation (Cialdini, Kallgren, & Reno, 1991).

Social norms are standards shared by the members of a social group (Vaske, Shelby, Graefe, & Heberlein, 1986), whereas ***personal norms*** are an "individual's own expectations, learned from shared expectations and modified through interaction" (Schwartz, 1977). In many definitions, norms are also intimately tied to the concept of sanctions — punishment for people who break norms (Grasmick, Blackwell, Bursik, & Mitchell, 1993; Heywood, 2002). Norms that are widely shared by most members of society (e.g., littering, dumping human waste) often become legal mandates complete with formal sanctions (e.g., fines) for noncompliance.

Norms can help explain why people (either individually or collectively) often act in regular ways, as well as aid our understanding of *irregular* human behavior (Heywood, 1996a). Anti-litter evaluations illustrate a norm that is strong and widely held (Heywood & Murdock, 2002); yet litter is often present, even in wilderness. Norms are interesting precisely because they vary by the proportion of people who hold them, their strength in an individual or group, the level of agreement about them, their influence on behavior, and their wider enforcement of social regularities. If norms were unbreakable rules for behavior, they would be indistinguishable from descriptions of behavior itself. Norms, like attitudes, however, are not static within or across people, or across situations. In a given social context, some people may have a well-formed norm that dominates their behavior or evaluation, while others may have only an emerging norm that barely influences what individuals do or think (Heywood, 1996b). Still others may be unaware of a norm, becoming bewildered when sanctions are brought against them for breaking it. Even well-formed norms may fail to influence behavior because of competing norms, attitudes, or motivations.

Different social psychologists define and use the concept of norms differently (see Vaske & Whittaker, 2004, for a review). Some concentrate on the variables that serve to focus (Cialdini, Kallgren, & Reno, 1991; Cialdini, Reno, & Kallgren, 1990) or activate a norm (e.g., Bratt, 1999; Schwartz, 1977), while others address how social pressure can influence behavior or aid in the diffusion of ideas (Ajzen & Fishbein, 1980; Fishbein & Ajzen, 1975). Still others emphasize the structural characteristics of norms (Shelby, Vaske, & Donnelly, 1996; Vaske, Shelby et al., 1986) to help evaluate appropriate behavior or conditions. Knowing how different researchers use the same basic concept (e.g., norms), clarifies what theoretical approach is most appropriate for examining a given situation or problem. For example, if the issue involves promoting responsible environmental behavior (e.g., not littering, recycling newspapers), norm focus/activation models may be more appropriate. If the issue involves determining standards for acceptable recreation use impacts, structural approaches may be a better choice.

The theories also differ in how they measure and think about the concept of norms. Norm focus/ activation theories and the structural norm approach measure norms at the individual level (i.e., personal norms) and then aggregate the data to derive social norms. The theory of reasoned action, in contrast, focuses primarily on perceived social norms (i.e., subjective norms) and does not directly address the concept of a personal norm (which is subsumed within a person's attitude).

Norms can be linked to attitudes and are often construed as a parallel construct. Like attitudes, norms have both cognitive and affective components (the strength of obligation can be tied to emotions such as guilt), as well as the ability to influence behavior (Heywood, 2002). Some attitudes and norms are more global than others, and the specificity of each is critical for determining whether the attitude or norm will accurately predict behavior.

Norms are different from attitudes, however, because of the added dimension of obligation. With an attitude, the evaluative scale focuses on whether the behavior is judged positively or negatively. With a norm, the scale examines whether the behavior is acceptable or unacceptable, or how much or how little of the behavior is acceptable. Beliefs about internal or external sanctions are the additional components that do not find parallels in attitude models. An attitude is favorable or disfavorable of a behavior; a norm carries with it the expectation of sanctions if some behavior is not performed. An illustration of the attitude-norm distinction can be applied to littering. "I disfavor littering" may be the attitude, but the norm is proscriptive: "Littering is unacceptable." The norm rises from the attitude, but with additional elements implicit, including: "People should not litter," "I will sanction people who litter," "I expect people to sanction me if I littered," and "I will feel guilty if I litter."

Norms, like attitudes, are not tangible things, but latent constructs researchers use to describe how cognitions and affective responses are represented in an individual. As with attitude research, norm research measures dimensions of these latent constructs, with implicit understanding that they will be related to each other and the behavior we are trying to understand, predict, and possibly control. The multiplicity of dimensions provides more alternatives for understanding when a norm is activated, salient, and relevant. As with attitude work, no theory of norms is likely to effectively encompass all of the ways the concept may be used to understand how people think or act in social situations.

A fundamental issue in understanding norms is the idea of norm strength. The ability of a norm to predict individual or group behavior is influenced by how strongly a norm is held in that individual or group. A norm does not just exist or not exist; there is a matter of degree. As a construct represented in a person's mind, a norm may be weakly held, difficult to access, without much sense of obligation, with no connection to moral values, and may be associated with low expectations of trivial external sanctions. As such, one would not expect the norm to affect behavior. However, if the norm is strong, has a sense of obligation attached, and brings expectations of serious sanctions or a high probability of sanctions, it may affect behavior. The research challenge is to measure this variety of information that can be collected about normative concepts in people or across groups, and then relate that to behavior.

Summary: Organizing Social Concepts via the Cognitive Approach

Social science concepts, such as values, attitudes, and norms, have been applied in various ways in parks, recreation, and human dimensions contexts. The cognitive approach has been proposed as one way for examining how values → value orientations → attitudes → norms influence behavior. The previous section provides a description of the concepts studied within the cognitive approach, and indicates the proposed relationships among them. The cognitive approach suggests that a person's value orientations determine the higher order concepts (attitudes and norms), and that these, in turn, affect behaviors.

There are several benefits to the cognitive approach. First, by understanding how the whole cognitive structure is formed, from values to behavior, we can look at the influence of each individual concept and predict the influence on individual's actions. This approach helps us understand, for example, how a person's value orientation for wildlife use can predict their likelihood of supporting legal hunting. A second benefit of this approach is the potential to understand how these concepts work beyond one specific study. In other words, attitudes and norms are proposed to influence behavior in a specific way, regardless of the particular issue we examine. Third, the approach facilitates an understanding of regional differences in values, attitudes, norms, and behaviors. Within a culture, we can assume these concepts operate in the same manner, although to different degrees, across individuals. This allows us to focus on the actual differences in attitudes / norms using consistent methodology across study samples. The approach may also discern why conflict among individuals is occurring and whether common ground can be obtained. For example, although two individuals may have drastically different behaviors while fishing, they may share similar values and norms regarding wildlife recreation and this shared interest can be used to ensure management emphasizes this agreement. Finally, this approach can facilitate the understanding of how these concepts work across cultures. This can help us to understand whether values, attitudes and norms influence behavior similarly across cultures or how specific attitudes and norms may differ.

While cognitive approaches can help us understand how behavior may be derived, there are other approaches. Motivation theory has been proposed as another way to answer questions such as "Why do people recreate with friends, hike alone, or go wildlife viewing with family?"

Motivational and Satisfaction Approaches

Substantial research has been directed toward understanding recreationists' motivations for and satisfactions associated with participation in an activity. Motivations drive the recreationists' interest in activities prior to participation. Satisfaction refers to individuals' evaluations after the experience.

Motivation

A *motivational approach* suggests that people are driven (i.e., motivated) to take actions to achieve particular goals (i.e., they seek certain outcomes from their experiences). Two enduring approaches to investigating motivations have emerged in the literature. One, introduced by Hendee (1974), emphasized a multiple satisfaction approach. This approach suggested that recreationists seek a variety of benefits and outcomes. Although Hendee applied his arguments to demonstrate that hunters define satisfaction beyond merely harvest, this multiple satisfaction idea is appropriate for all types of experiences. Recreationists, for example, may seek outcomes such as solitude, being outdoors, or socializing with friends and family.

Second, Driver and his associates (see Driver, Brown, & Peterson, 1991, for a review) empha-sized the importance of understanding the bundle of "desired psychological outcomes" derived from recreation participation. Recreation was proposed as a way for achieving certain outcomes (e.g., achievement, stress release, family togetherness). The Recreation Experience Preference (REP) scales (i.e., concepts) and the survey items (i.e., variables) used to measure these out-comes were selected based upon a review of the personality trait and motivation literature. In more than 30 studies, these concepts and variables have demonstrated their usefulness in helping to understand the nature of outdoor recreation experiences and recreationists themselves (Manfredo, Driver, & Tarrant, 1996).

Recognizing the diversity of experiences desired by participants in recreation activities, researchers have noted the importance of differentiating users into homogeneous and meaningful subgroups. Bryan (1977), for example, proposed the concept of recreation specialization, which he defined as a "continuum of behavior from the general to the specific, reflected by equipment and skills used in the sport" (p. 29). Within the continuum, individuals may range from the novice to the specialist. Variations between user classes reflect differences in motivations, the extent of prior experience with and commitment to an activity. As people become more specialized, they become more particular in their setting preferences and equipment. More specialized users are also more likely to have specific managerial requirements and are more likely to communicate with managers. Research has applied the concept of specialization to angling (Bryan, 1977; Graefe, 1980), hunting (Miller & Graefe, 2000), wildlife viewing (McFarlane, 1996), boating (Donnelly, Vaske, & Graefe, 1986), canoeing (Kauffman & Graefe, 1984), and skiing (Thapa & Graefe, 2003; Vaske, Dyar, & Timmons, 2004).

Satisfaction

Motivation research focuses on what initiates behavior, while satisfaction studies focus on the outcomes received from recreation experiences (Manfredo, Vaske, & Decker, 1995). A number of different types of satisfactions may be associated with a recreation experience (e.g., time with family, enjoyment of the outdoors, exercise). Satisfaction is similar to Driver's notion of experience benefits (Driver et al., 1991). Satisfaction, however, can also refer to a feeling of pleasure or enjoyment derived from experiences. Using this latter definition, the concept of satisfaction becomes an attitude, or the evaluation of something. In recreation-related contexts, we often are interested in satisfaction with a particular event or action.

Satisfaction is one of the most common social inquiries in recreation management because it appears simple to ask. The use of overall measures of satisfaction, however, is questionable because they tend to only measure major changes in the quality of service delivery (Manfredo et al., 1995). An individual's satisfaction is complex and dependent upon a variety of aspects related to the experience, including one's expectations.

This recognition of the complex nature of satisfaction is part of the multifaceted discrepancy model for satisfaction. This model proposes that overall satisfaction is a function of more specific satisfaction with individual components of an experience. For example, overall satisfaction with a bird-watching trip may be a function of how satisfied one was with the weather, numbers and species of birds seen, encounters with other people, accessibility to the site, and the facilities there. Satisfaction with one of these particular components of a recreation experience is a function of the discrepancy between one's expectation for that component and what actually occurred. Therefore, if a birdwatcher expected to see a certain species of bird and did not, his or her satisfaction level may be low for that facet.

Despite its widespread application, there is still a need to further understand what influences satisfaction (the motivations and expectations that determine a person's evaluation of an experience). Managers are interested in the relationship between satisfaction and participation, which is not as direct as one might expect. A person can have a dissatisfying experience but continue to participate in an activity and vice versa. Certain satisfactions may be more important and outweigh others. It becomes important to not just measure individual or overall satisfaction, but to determine the relative importance of different facets of satisfaction and the other factors that motivate behavior.

Overall, motivation approaches have made contributions in several areas. The first is in identifying the benefits of leisure, such as determining the worth of a particular recreation program. Knowing the worth of recreation can help in prioritizing budgeting and policy planning among agencies. The second contribution of understanding motivations is in leisure counseling. There has been increasing interest in the therapeutic benefits derived from recreation participation, based on the assumption that need satisfaction is a critical component of physical and mental health. By understanding the relationship between recreation and the motivations met during engagements, it is possible to guide people to activities that will enhance their well-being. Third, identifying the types of motivations provided in different recreational environments and activities can help improve service delivery. This is particularly the case in market segmentation research and research that has advocated an experience-based approach to recreation management. Fourth, understanding motivations of an increasingly diverse agency workforce can improve organizational performance and the satisfaction of employees. Fifth, motivations can help identify the causes for conflict among publics. Goal interference models (see Graefe & Thapa, 2004, for a review), for example, suggest that conflict occurs when the behaviors of one group are perceived to inhibit motivation satiation by another group. Sixth, an understanding of user motivations can help managers identify activity substitutes, important when assessing the impact of allocation decisions (Manfredo & Anderson, 1987). For example, if managers eliminate an opportunity (e.g., close a facility or a hunting/fishing season) for which there are abundant substitutes, the potential impact is likely to be smaller than if the opportunity had no or few substitutes (Hunt, Haider, & Armstrong, 2002; Sutton & Ditton, 2005). A basic definition of substitutability holds that activities are substitutable only when they satiate the same motivations (Vaske, Donnelly, & Shelby, 1990). Finally, motivations can help in understanding crowding because perceptions of crowding are believed to stem in part from the types of motivations associated with an experience.

Chapter Summary

Theories assemble claims about causally related concepts. Concepts and constructs represent abstract and unmeasured properties of our mental images of reality. Variables refer to concrete, measured expressions of these properties. Theory guides research by highlighting what constructs are appropriate and what variables should be measured.

Exogenous constructs (or independent variables in their measured form) are predicted by theory to cause endogenous constructs (or measured dependent variables). A mediating construct links exogenous and endogenous constructs. Causality is often difficult to demonstrate in surveys because the researcher does not experimentally manipulate the variables in the study. Suggestive evidence for causal linkages among the constructs can be enhanced, however, by the logic used to develop the theory.

Two general theoretical approaches have proven useful for understanding recreation behavior. The *cognitive hierarchy* examines the process from thoughts to actions. Concepts such as values, value orientations (i.e., patterns of basic beliefs), attitudes, and norms have proven useful in explaining and predicting human behavior. *Motivation theory* considers what drives our actions.

This chapter has tried to clarify the different concepts used by recreation and natural resource researchers. Understanding the similarities and differences among the concepts is essential when attempting to develop surveys intended to help resolve applied problems. While lengthy surveys with multiple questions are sometimes necessary, the selection of specific questionnaire items should be guided by social science theory. Theory-based approaches to survey design greatly enhance our ability to understand, explain, and predict issues of concern to natural resource managers. Information about other parks, recreation, and human dimensions concepts can be found in Manning (1999).

Review Questions

1. Give a definition for *theory*.

2. Give five reasons why theory is important in parks, recreation, and human dimensions research.

3. Define *concept* and give two examples.

4. Explain the distinction between a *concept* and a *variable*.

5. Define *hypothesis* and give three examples.

6. Explain the difference between an *exogenous* and an *endogenous* construct.

7. What is the relationship between *exogenous–endogenous constructs* and *independent–dependent variables*?

8. Give an example of a mediator variable.

9. Differentiate the cognitive approach from the motivation approach to research.

10. Give three benefits of using the cognitive approach to studying natural resource issues.

11. Identify four contributions of motivation research.

12. Define the concept of *values*.

13. Explain why values do not directly influence behavior.

14. How do *values* differ from *value orientations*?

15. Define the concept of *attitude*.

16. How do *values* differ from *attitudes*?

17. How do *norms* differ from *attitudes*?

18. How does *motivation* differ from *satisfaction*?

3

the evolution of theory

Chapter 2 differentiated what researchers mean by theory, concept, and variable. This chapter is concerned with theories that have evolved in the natural resource and recreation literature. Emphasis is placed on the processes researchers go through when thinking about how concepts are theoretically related to each other and what variables should be measured on the survey to test the predicted conceptual relationships. While the theories discussed here are most frequently associated with the human dimensions/recreation research, the concepts and their characteristics can be linked directly to the ideas presented in chapter 2. For example, crowding is commonly investigated in the recreation literature. Most researchers define crowding as a negative evaluation of a certain number of people in a given situation (e.g., at a campsite). Defined in this manner, crowding is an attitude about how people feel about seeing others while engaged in an activity like camping. Similarly, the concepts can be measured at different levels of specificity, which influences how strongly the measured variables will be correlated with each other. Recreation satisfaction, for example, can be measured as an overall evaluation (a general attitude) or the concept can be measured relative to how the number of people camping near them negatively affected their satisfaction with their camping experience (a specific attitude). Social psychology theory would hypothesize that the specific crowding measure would have a stronger relationship to the specific satisfaction variable than would the general satisfaction survey item.

Two general logical systems—deductive and inductive—are described in this chapter and illustrated with examples. The deductive examples focus on a traditional recreation model that has been used to address social carrying capacity concerns. By tracing the evolution of this capacity model and its associated concepts (e.g., crowding, satisfaction), the intent is to demonstrate how theories evolve as researchers continually test and refine their thinking. Three guidelines—internally logical, parsimonious, and generalizable—are discussed for evaluating deductive theories. The chapter concludes with examples that show the process of moving from inductive explanations of the findings reported in the satisfaction literature to deductive hypotheses generated by this theorizing.

Deductive and Inductive Theories

Theory-based survey research employs both deductive and inductive logic when attempting to understand and explain the relationships among the concepts of interest. Deductive approaches begin with general theories and associated hypotheses. The predicted conceptual relationships are tested in specific studies. If the results of these studies continually support the hypothesized relationships and lead to the same conclusion, the theorist and researcher has evidence for arguing in favor of the original model. Conversely, if after repeated trials, the results consistently fail to support the predicted conceptual relationship, the original hypothesis is rejected and the theorist must search for an alternative explanation. Unfortunately, empirical findings seldom yield such consistency (either positive or negative). Some studies might support the predicted relationships while others fail to support the hypotheses.

Using inductive logic, the theorist starts with these contradictory findings and searches for a "pattern" in the data that might explain the specific observations. For example, the original hypotheses may only apply to certain types of recreationists (e.g., hunters) and not others (e.g., wildlife viewers). Alternatively, the hypotheses may be appropriate for visitors to backcountry or wilderness resources, but not when used in frontcountry locations. Because researchers may have collected the information at different points in time (e.g., on-site vs. off-site), used different types of surveys (e.g., mail vs. phone), or measured different variables to reflect the same concepts, the discrepancies in the findings might be attributable to methodological differences. Whatever the suspected reason for the contradictory findings, this process of moving from particular study findings to general principles creates new theories.

The two systems of logic—deduction and induction—work together in what has been described as the wheel of science (Wallace, 1971). Both approaches facilitate scientific advances; they simply differ in their starting points. Deduction begins with specific hypotheses suggested by prior theory and tests the relationships using observations from specific studies. Induction starts with patterns of observations in an effort to produce empirical generalizations that lead to new theories (Figure 3.1).

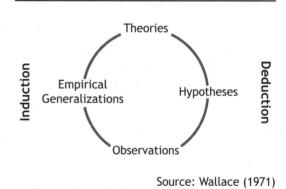

Source: Wallace (1971)

Figure 3.1   The Wheel of Science

Deductive Logic to Inductive Explanations

Much of the early research on social carrying capacity was concerned with the relationship between visitor numbers (or actual density) and visitor satisfaction. *Actual density* is a descriptive concept that refers to the number of people per unit area. It is measured by counting the number of people and the space they occupy. It can be determined objectively by participant observers (e.g., research assistants) who simply count the number of visitors in a given setting or by automated recording devices such as motion detectors and time-lapse cameras. Actual density cannot be measured on the survey because respondent-provided answers will always be based on their subjective beliefs and or evaluations of the situation. Understanding a concept like actual density is important, however, because visitor numbers can often be directly manipulated by a managing agency. Whenever use limits or restrictions on certain kinds of recreation are imposed, the actual density of visitors in an area is affected.

As described in chapter 2, ***visitor satisfaction*** is a complex psychological concept. When measured on a survey, the concept can reflect the visitors' overall evaluation of an experience (i.e., a general attitude) or the construct can be subdivided into specific motivations for visiting a recreation resource (e.g., opportunities for solitude, relaxation, social interactions with friends). The measured variables reflecting the satisfaction concept have ranged from a single evaluative question to multiple items assessing the extent to which the person's different motivations were realized. In the simplest measured form, researchers ask a question like "Overall, how would you rate your trip today?" In numerous studies, the potential answers were: "poor," "fair," "good," "very good," "excellent," or "perfect."

Theorizing about the Capacity Model: Phase 1

Wagar (1964) hypothesized that this relationship between actual density and visitor satisfaction would not be constant, but would vary according to the outdoor recreation activity and the kinds of needs or desires that the activity participants sought. In spite of this early recognition that satisfaction depends on the motives underlying participation, many subsequent studies simply measured the extent to which satisfaction is influenced by the actual density of visitors.

The earliest of these studies proposed theoretical models that assumed enjoyment from a recreation experience is inversely correlated with the number of people present (Alldredge, 1972). Accordingly, intrusions into an individual's solitude were hypothesized to reduce visitor satisfaction (Figure 3.2).

Figure 3.2 Initial Proposed Relationship between Actual Density and Visitor Satisfaction

From an historical perspective, the hypothesized negative relationship can be defended using deductive logic. Agencies that sponsored much of the earlier carrying capacity research are responsible for managing wilderness areas. The Wilderness Act of 1964 (16 U.S.C. § 1131 et seq.) defines wilderness as an area that "…has outstanding opportunities for solitude." Given this definition, it is logical to predict an inverse relationship between numbers of people and visitor satisfaction. As visitor numbers increase, satisfaction should decrease.

In Figure 2.1 (p. 20), the theoretical concepts were displayed using ovals and the measured variables were represented by rectangles. Because Figure 3.2 only shows the measured variables, only the rectangles are necessary to depict the hypothesized relationship. Actual density is the independent variable and visitor satisfaction is the dependent measure.

Table 3.1 (pp. 39–41) summarizes studies that have examined the relationship between actual density and visitor satisfaction (The other variable relationships in the table follow this discussion).

Cell entries in columns 5 through 7 give the citation for the study, the resource where the study was conducted, and the activity that was included in the investigation. The cell entries in columns 2 through 4 are correlations. Details associated with calculating these coefficients are presented in chapter 16. For the moment, simply note that the Pearson's correlation (symbolized as *r*) represents the strength of association between a pair of variables. Because a Pearson's correlation is a standardized effect size statistic, the values can range from –1 (a perfect negative correlation) to +1 (a perfect positive correlation), with a 0 indicating no relationship. The word *perfect* simply means that every time one variable increases or decreases by one value, the second variable increases or decreases by the same amount. Larger values of the coefficient imply that the relationship between the two variables is stronger regardless of whether the direction is positive or negative. Thus, if one pair of variables has a correlation of +.60 and another pair of variables has a correlation of –.60, the effect size is the same, only the direction is different.

Similar to other effect size statistics (chapter 6), Pearson correlations can be interpreted relative to statistical significance or practical significance. **Statistical significance** in Table 3.1 is indicated if there is a * next to the correlation coefficient. The * says that the probability of finding a correlation this extreme for the relationship is less than 5 in 100 (i.e., $p < .05$). In other words, the relationship is not likely to have occurred by chance. When there is no * following a correlation, the relationship between the two variables is not statistically significant. **Practical significance** is concerned with whether the correlation is large enough to be useful. As a general rule of thumb, a Pearson's correlation of .1 (positive or negative) can be thought of as a "minimal relationship." Correlations of .3 (positive or negative) reflect what is "typically" found in human dimensions research, while correlations of .5 or greater can be considered "substantial relationships" (Vaske, Gliner, & Morgan, 2002). Substantial relationships are more likely to have practical significance.

Of the 14 studies examining the relationship between actual density and satisfaction in Table 3.1, only two showed a statistically significant correlation (average $r = .03$). Of the two investigations reporting a statistically significant relationship (Heberlein & Laybourne, 1978; Heberlein, Trent, & Baumgartner, 1982), a positive rather than the predicted negative association was observed. In other words, as actual density increased, satisfaction increased; the opposite of the hypothesized negative relationship. The activity under examination in both of these studies was deer hunting. As noted by the authors, "the presence of hunters outside of one's party is often considered an asset because they move deer and increase the chances of bagging for everyone" (Heberlein & Laybourne, 1978, p. 41). Such an explanation illustrates inductive reasoning for explaining the findings.

Theorizing about the Capacity Model: Phase 2

Given that the empirical evidence consistently failed to support the model in Figure 3.2, researchers theorized that other variables may attenuate (lower) the correlation between actual density and visitor satisfaction (deductive logic). For example, even though there may be many visitors in an area, the geographic characteristics of the resource (e.g., a winding river, a heavily forested area) may limit the amount of contact individuals have with one another. Studies examining this possibility focused on the relationship between visitor encounters with each other, and satisfaction.

Table 3.1 Effects of Density and Encounter Measures on Perceived Crowding and Satisfaction

Independent Variable	Dependent Variable			Citation	Resource	Activity
	Reported Encounters	Perceived Crowding	Visitor Satisfaction			
Actual Density	.39*			Heberlein & Vaske (1977)	Brule River	Canoers
	.52*					Tubers
	.15*					Anglers
	.75*			Hammitt, McDonald, & Noe (1984)	Hiwassee River	Tubers
	.68*			Shelby (1980)	Colorado River	Rafters
	.42*			Shelby & Colvin (1979)	Rogue River	Rafters
Actual Density		.18*	NR	Lee (1975)	Yosemite	Backcountry users
		.05	.00	Shelby (1976, 1980)	Grand Canyon	Rafters
		.32*	-.06	Heberlein & Vaske (1977)	Brule River	Canoers
		.23*	.00			Tubers
		.06*	.11			Anglers
		NR	.00	McConnell (1977)	Beaches	Singles beach
		NR	—			Natural beach
		.29*	.09	Randall (1977)	Sleeping Bear Dunes	Day visitors
		.01	.17*	Heberlein & Laybourne (1978)	Wisconsin	Deer hunters
		.44*	.01	Kuentzel & Heberlein (1998)	Grand River Marsh	Goose hunters: Firing line
		.07	.02			Goose hunters: Managed hunt
		.26*	NR	Absher (1979)	Yosemite	Backcountry users
		.20*	.00	Shelby & Colvin (1979)	Rogue River	Rafters
		.06	NR	Gramann & Burdge (1981)	Lake Shelbyville	Reservoir users
		.26*	NR	Absher & Lee (1981)	Yosemite	Backcountry users
		NR	0	Becker (1981)	Upper Mississippi	River users
		NR	0	Becker (1981)	Lower St. Croix	River users
		NR	NR	Bultena, Field, Womble, & Albrecht (1981)	Mt. McKinley	Hikers
		.09*	.02	Ditton, Fedler, & Graefe (1983)	Buffalo River	Floaters
		.61*	NR	Hammitt et al. (1984)	Hiwassee River	Tubers
		.28*	.10*	Heberlein, Trent, & Baumgartner (1982)	Sandhill Mgt Area	Deer hunters

Table 3.1 continued >>

Table 3.1   Effects of Density and Encounter Measures on Perceived Crowding and Satisfaction (continued)

| Independent Variable | Dependent Variable | | | Citation | Resource | Activity |
	Reported Encounters	Perceived Crowding	Visitor Satisfaction			
Reported Encounters	+		0	Blackwood (1977)	Wolf River	Rafter
		.51*	-.11*	Heberlein & Vaske (1977)	Brule River	Canoers
		.36*	-.15			Tubers
		.18*	.08			Anglers
		NR	0	Becker (1981)	Lower St. Croix	River users
		.46*	-.10	Heberlein & Laybourne (1978)	Wisconsin	Deer hunters
		.48*	.06	Kuentzel & Heberlein (1998)	Grand River Marsh	Goose hunters: Firing line
		.18	.05			Goose hunters: Managed hunt
		+	NR	Schreyer & Nielsen (1978)	West Water Canyon	Floaters
		+	NR		Desolation Canyon	Floaters
		NR	-.02	McDonald & Hammitt (1981)	Hiwassee River	Tubers
		.20*	.07		Deep Creek	Tubers
		.69*	.23*		Chattahoochee River	Rafters
		.30*	.02	Shelby & Colvin (1979)	Rogue River	Rafters
		.50*	.10	Donnelly (1980)	Great Gulf Wilderness	Hikers
		NR	.09	Manning & Ciali (1980)	Vermont Rivers	Anglers
		NR	.06			Floaters
		NR	.08			Swimmers
		.34*	.01	Bultena, Womble, & Albrecht (1981)	Mt. McKinley	Hikers
		.31*	-.02	Vaske, Graefe, & Dempster (1982)	Dolly Sods Wilderness	Hikers
		.63*	NR	Hammitt et al. (1984)	Hiwassee River	Tubers
		.23*	NR	Schreyer (1976)	Dinosaur Ntl Monument	Floaters
		.40*	.00	Graefe, Donnelly, & Vaske (1986)	White Mtn Ntl Forest	Hikers
		.21*	.18*	Vaske, Donnelly, & Tweed (1983)	Fishing Bay WMA	Goose hunters
		-.13	.18	Vaske, Fedler, & Graefe (1986)	Tuchahoe State Park	Goose hunters

Table 3.1 continued >>

Table 3.1 Effects of Density and Encounter Measures on Perceived Crowding and Satisfaction (continued)

| Independent Variable | Dependent Variable | | | Citation | Resource | Activity |
	Reported Encounters	Perceived Crowding	Visitor Satisfaction			
Perceived Crowding			-.14*	Shelby (1976, 1980)	Grand Canyon	Rafters
			-.01	Blackwood (1977)	Wolf River	Rafters
			-.14*	Heberlein & Vaske (1977)	Brule River	Canoers
			-.20*	Randall (1977)	Sleeping Bear Dunes	Day visitors
			-.15*	Shelby & Colvin (1979)	Rogue River	Rafters
			-.01	Donnelly (1980)	Great Gulf Wilderness	Hikers
			-.05	Bultena, Field, Womble, & Albrecht (1981)	Mt. McKinley	Hikers
			-.12*	Ditton, Fedler, & Graefe (1983)	Buffalo River	Floaters
			-.18*	Vaske, Graefe, & Dempster (1982)	Dolly Sods Wilderness	Hikers
			.01	Graefe, Donnelly, & Vaske (1986)	White Mtn Ntl Forest	Hikers
			-.18*	Vaske, Donnelly, & Tweed (1983)	Fishing Bay WMA	Goose hunters
			-.20*	Vaske, Fedler et al. (1986)	Tuckahoe State Park	Goose hunters

(−) minus sign equals negative correlation; (0) zero equals no association; (+) plus sign equals positive relationship; NR - Not Reported; Entries with decimal point refer to zero order correlations. * $p < .05$

Two types of encounter measures have been discussed in the literature. The first involves the effects of ***actual encounters*** on visitor satisfaction. Shelby (1976) and Shelby and Colvin (1979) measured actual encounters (i.e., an objective count) between visitors by putting an observer on float trips in the Grand Canyon and on the Rogue River, respectively. Neither of these studies found a statistical relationship between actual encounters and satisfaction.

Other investigators have examined the relationship between visitors' reported encounters and satisfaction. ***Reported encounters*** refer to the number of other people in a recreation setting that visitors' recall seeing. Actual encounters can be considered an ***objective*** measure, because the researcher systematically made the count. Reported encounters are ***subjective***, reflecting the visitors' beliefs about what they experienced. Although estimates of reported encounters may not be as accurate as those provided by trained observers (Shelby & Colvin, 1981), numerous studies suggest visitors' beliefs about the trip are the important determinants of quality recreation experiences (Kuss, Graefe, & Vaske, 1990). Using the terminology from chapter 2, reported encounters mediates the relationship between actual density and visitor satisfaction (Figure 3.3).

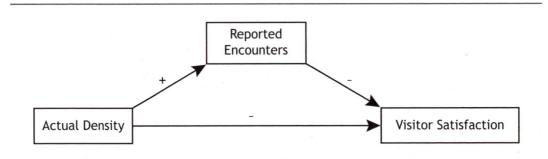

Figure 3.3 Actual Density, Reported Encounters, and Visitor Satisfaction

In Figure 3.3, both actual density and reported encounters are hypothesized to be negatively related to visitor satisfaction. The relationship between actual density and reported encounters is predicted to be positive. As the actual number of people in an area increases, visitors are likely to encounter more individuals. Although there should be a positive relationship between actual density and reported encounters, the strength of the association is expected to be less than perfect (i.e., $r < 1.0$). Rather, the association will be attenuated by: (a) the characteristics of the resource (e.g., winding river systems that limit the amount of time a person is in sight of others), (b) the characteristics of the activity (e.g., trout anglers who fish a particular section of a river cannot avoid encounters with individuals floating the river), (c) the characteristics of the visit (e.g., the time of day a person visits the resource), and (d) the characteristics of the visitors themselves (e.g., people seeking a solitary experience are more likely to notice the presence of others than those for whom solitude is not a primary motivation).

In the six studies (Table 3.1) that examined the relationship between actual density and reported encounters, the Pearson correlations ranged from .15 to .75 (Hammitt et al., 1984; Heberlein & Vaske, 1977; Shelby, 1980; Shelby & Colvin, 1981). This range of values suggests that the relationship may work differently depending on the resource or the activity. The lowest correlation ($r = .15$) was observed for trout anglers on the Brule River (Heberlein & Vaske, 1977); an activity where participants are likely to be on the river either early in the morning or late in the day when the number of other visitors may be lower. At the other end of the range ($r = .75$), the social experience of tubing on the Hiwassee River (Hammitt et al., 1984) revealed a large effect size between the two variables. The average correlation of these six studies ($r = .49$) also indicates that the association between actual density and reported encounters has a "substantial relationship" (Vaske et al., 2002).

Of the 21 studies in Table 3.1 examining the relationship between reported encounters and visitor satisfaction, 18 were not statistically significant, and two were statistically significant but not in the predicted direction (i.e., the relationship was positive). In the one study (Heberlein & Vaske, 1977) showing the predicted negative relationship, the correlation was –.11. Although this association was statistically significant, the size of the coefficient suggests only a "minimal relationship;" one that does not have much practical significance (Vaske et al., 2002).

From a theory development perspective then, including the reported encounter measure as a mediating variable did not improve our understanding of visitor satisfaction. Reported encounters, however, is a specific belief about the number of people present in a given situation. As measured in the studies summarized here, visitor satisfaction is a general attitude reflecting the visitor's overall evaluation of the experience. Consistent with social psychology theory and the specificity hypothesis, reported encounters are not likely to have a strong relationship. Recognition of this limitation stimulated the inclusion of another concept in the model—perceived crowding.

Theorizing about the Capacity Model: Phase 3

While encounters are beliefs about the conditions that were experienced, *crowding* is a negative evaluation of the number of people the individual remembers seeing (i.e., a specific attitude). Crowding involves a value judgment that the number of people encountered is too many (Shelby, Vaske, & Heberlein, 1989; Vaske & Shelby, 2008). The term *perceived crowding* is often used to emphasize the subjective or evaluative nature of the concept. It is commonly measured using a single question that asks people how crowded they felt in a given situation. Answers are given on a nine-point scale ranging from "not at all crowded" to "extremely crowded."

Figure 3.4 (p. 44) shows the path model with the crowding measure included. The model predicts that actual density influences the number of reported encounters between visitors and that encounters influence perceived crowding. Crowding is hypothesized to be negatively related to visitor satisfaction. Given that crowding is a specific attitude and visitor satisfaction, as measured here, is a general attitude, the strength of the relationship is not likely to be large or substantial.

A total of 16 studies (Table 3.1) present data on the relationship between actual density and perceived crowding. Twelve of these investigations reported a positive, statistically significant effect. As use levels increased, recreationists were more likely to evaluate the experience as crowded. The magnitude of the observed correlations ranged from .01 to .61, with an average of .21. As in the case of the satisfaction concept, this suggests that the relationship between actual density and perceived crowding may be mediated by geographic factors or by individuals' beliefs about the experience (e.g., reported encounters). Research related to the effects of

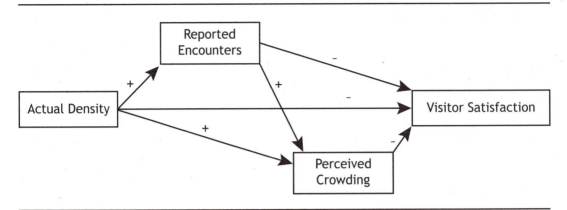

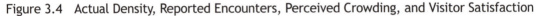

Figure 3.4   Actual Density, Reported Encounters, Perceived Crowding, and Visitor Satisfaction

reported encounters on perceptions of crowding reveals stronger and more consistent levels of association. Of the 20 studies, all but two (Grand River Marsh goose hunters participating in the managed hunt, Heberlein & Kuentzel, 2002; and Tuckahoe State Park goose hunters, Vaske, Fedler et al., 1986) that examined these two variables showed significant positive relationships, with an average correlation of .34. Finally, perceived crowding negatively influenced overall satisfaction as predicted. Of the 12 studies shown in Table 3.1, eight were significant and in the predicted direction. The strength of this relationship, however, was minimal (average $r = -.11$).

Overall, the correlations presented in Table 3.1 fail to support the capacity model's primary hypothesis. On average, recreationists tend to be just as satisfied in high-use settings as they are in low-use settings. Satisfaction may be related to actual density, but the relationship is mediated by the other variables in the model (not summarized here—e.g., norms, expectations, preferences). The observed empirical relationships in Table 3.1 may also have been limited by inadequacies in the way satisfaction is typically measured (i.e., single survey item vs. multiple indicators of the construct; see chapter 4)

As a final note, most explanatory recreation and human dimensions theories and research use a ***probabilistic model*** (as opposed to a deterministic model) of causation. In other words, as the actual number of visitors in an area increases, the probability of seeing more people increases. As the correlations demonstrated, a positive and statistically significant relationship was consistently observed between these two variables. None of these correlations, however, were +1.0. Such a correlation would imply that every time another person entered the resource, visitors' recollection of the number people seen would increase by one (i.e., a ***deterministic model***). Rather, the relationship was attenuated by the characteristics of the resource, the activity, the visitor and the time of day the person visited.

Guidelines for Evaluating Deductive Theories

All deductive theories should have at least three properties: (a) internally logical, (b) parsimonious, and (c) generalizable. This section examines these properties relative to the capacity model and an encounter-norm-crowding model.

Internally Logical

The model presented in Figure 3.4 was derived using deductive logic. As the number of people (i.e., **actual density**) in a recreation area increases, **reported encounters** (e.g., a belief) between these individuals are likely to increase. Since crowding is the negative evaluation (a specific attitude) of a certain number of people seen, when reported encounters increase, crowding should increase. Finally, since most of the early research was conducted in backcountry/wilderness areas where solitude is a desirable attribute of the experience, when perceived crowding increases, visitor satisfaction should decrease.

The causal flow of these variables is clearly defensible from a deductive reasoning perspective. For example, one criterion for determining causation is that the independent variable must occur earlier in time than the dependent variable (chapter 2). Before a visitor can recall seeing other visitors (the dependent measure), people have to be present in the area (the independent variable; in this case, actual density). Before visitors can evaluate a situation as crowded (the dependent variable), they must remember seeing others (the independent variable). Finally, to the extent that satisfaction from a wilderness experience is dependent on solitude, the other variables in the model—density, encounters, and crowding—must occur earlier in time than the satisfaction variable.

Providing evidence for causation, however, requires at least two additional criteria beyond the temporal ordering of the variables (Babbie, 2003). For example, the observed relationship cannot be explained away as a product of the effect of another, earlier variable. In the capacity model (Figure 3.4), actual density occurs earlier in the causal sequence than reported encounters. Actual density was correlated with perceived crowding in 12 of 16 studies, but the magnitude of the observed correlations ranged from .01 to .61, with an average of .21. The effects of reported encounters on perceived crowding revealed stronger and more consistent levels of association (average $r = .34$). In terms of a causal sequencing then, the effect of reported encounters on perceived crowding cannot be explained away as an effect of the earlier actual density measure.

The final criterion for causation noted by Babbie (2003) is that the independent (cause) and dependent (effect) variables must be empirically related to one another. As suggested by the correlations in Table 3.1, this condition was not observed for the relationship between actual density and visitor satisfaction (average $r = .03$). Taken together, these findings suggest that while the capacity model in Figure 3.4 is logical, the path model might be simplified.

Parsimony

A property that guides researchers in revising and evaluating any theory is *parsimony*. A theory with parsimony employs the fewest constructs and linkages necessary to explain the events of interest. If two theories fit the data equally well, the one with more parsimony is generally preferred. Although we may not be interested in eliminating any of the concepts from the capacity model, not all of the linkages (arrows) may be necessary.

The Simon-Blalock method of model testing (see Asher, 1983) is used here to determine the "best-fitting" model for the data by eliminating arrows one by one from Figure 3.4. The results of the technique indicate whether or not a linkage between variables should be included in the model. In statistical terms, this is accomplished by setting the partial correlations equal to 0 (see definition below). If the actual values of the partial correlations approximate 0 (i.e., less than .10), the correlation is judged to be spurious and the given causal arrow is eliminated from the model. A correlation is spurious if the effect is merely an artifact of a particular data set (or in this example, the multiple data sets in Table 3.1), and not a characteristic of the underlying theoretical process.

More simply, the computation procedure begins with a correlation matrix. Table 3.2 shows the average correlations among the variables in the capacity model; Figure 3.5 gives the same findings graphically.

Table 3.2   Average Correlations among the Variables in the Capacity Model

	Actual Density	Reported Encounters	Perceived Crowding	Visitor Satisfaction
Actual Density	1.00			
Reported Encounters	.49	1.00		
Perceived Crowding	.21	.34	1.00	
Visitor Satisfaction	.03	.04	−.11	1.00

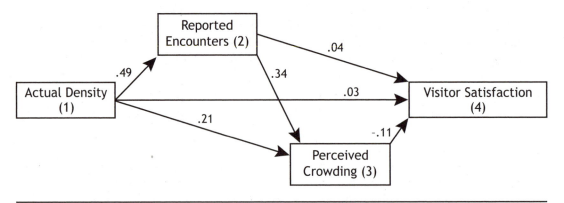

Figure 3.5   Average Correlations among Variables in Capacity Model

The partial correlation between two variables can be expressed as a product of the r's between variables along alternative paths. For example, the predicted partial correlation (r_{23}) between reported encounters and perceived crowding is the product of the correlation on the path between actual density and reported encounters ($r_{12} = .49$) and the path between actual density and perceived crowding ($r_{13} = .21$).

As shown in Table 3.3, this predicted partial correlation for the reported encounters → perceived crowding link is .10. The actual correlation for this linkage based on the data in Table 3.1 is .34. The difference between the actual and predicted correlation is .24. According to the rules for applying the Simon-Blalock technique, if the difference between the actual and predicted values is less than .10, the arrow is eliminated. If the difference is greater than .10, the linkage (i.e., the arrow) is retained in the model. For the path just calculated, the linkage between encounters and crowding is real and should not be eliminated from the model.

Table 3.3 Detecting Real and Spurious Correlations in the Capacity Model

		Predicted	Actual	Difference	Spurious
$r_{12} * r_{13} = r_{23}$	.49 * .21	.10	.34	.24	No
$r_{13} * r_{32} = r_{12}$	.21 * .34	.07	.49	.42	No
$r_{12} * r_{23} = r_{13}$	.49 * .34	.17	.21	.04	Yes
$r_{23} * r_{24} = r_{34}$	.34 * .04	.01	−.11	.12	No
$r_{23} * r_{34} = r_{24}$	.34 * -.11	−.04	.04	.08	Yes
$r_{12} * r_{23} * r_{34} = r_{14}$	.49 * .34 * −.11	−.02	.03	.05	Yes

Calculation of the other partial correlations in the model and computation of the difference between the partial and actual associations suggests that three of the relationships are real and the other three are not necessary to describe the underlying theory. The result of this analysis produces the model shown in Figure 3.6.

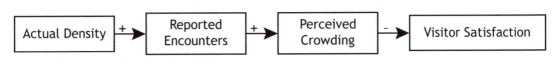

Figure 3.6 Revised Capacity Model Based on the Simon-Blalock Analysis

Although the number of concepts in Figure 3.6 is the same as Figure 3.5, the number of hypothesized linkages has been reduced from six to three. The model based on the Simon-Blalock analysis is more parsimonious.

• • • • •

This section has traced the development of one recreation theory as it has evolved over several decades. The initial model included only two concepts — actual density and visitor satisfaction. When the empirical evidence failed to support the predicted negative relationship, researchers sought to identify variables that mediate the two original concepts and help explain variations in visitor satisfaction. As variables, such as reported encounters and perceived crowding were added, the complexity of the model and the associated hypotheses increased. Use of the Simon-Blalock technique helped to simplify these relationships. From the perspective of creating theories, these analyses highlight the observations at the beginning of this chapter. All theories are tentative or preliminary explanations of how the world works. Given the strength of the relationship between perceived crowding and visitor satisfaction, the final model (Figure 3.6) here does not offer a full explanation of what accounts for a quality recreation experience.

Generalizability

A final property for evaluating human dimensions theories is generalizability. *Generalizability* refers to the extent to which conclusions can be drawn about a population based on information from a sample (Vogt, 1999), or the extent to which information from multiple samples yields the same conclusions. The capacity model just reviewed has been applied to wide range of activities, resources, and situations (i.e., it generalizes). As a second example, consider the relationships between reported encounters, norms, and crowding. In the context here, norms refer to standards for judging the acceptability of behaviors or conditions (Shelby, Vaske, & Donnelly, 1996). Theory predicts that when encounters exceed a visitor's norm for seeing others, crowding will increase (Vaske, Donnelly, & Petruzzi, 1996; Vaske, Shelby, Graefe, & Heberlein, 1986). A paper by Vaske and Donnelly (2002) examined this hypothesis using data from a wide range of studies conducted in the United States and Canada. The activities included canoeing, rafting, kayaking, tubing, motor boating, mountain climbing, day hiking, mountain biking, wildlife viewing, angling, and hunting. The areas studied reflected considerable diversity, with some showing extremely high-density and use impact problems, and others showing low densities and no problems.

Table 3.4 shows the reported encounters-norm-crowding relationship for 24 of the 78 evaluations contexts in Vaske and Donnelly (2002). On average, across all evaluation contexts, 65% of the respondents reported fewer encounters than their norm, while 35% reported more encounters than their norm. As predicted, mean differences in perceived crowding were statistically greater for individuals indicating more encounters than their norm ($t = 12.70$, $p < .001$). Across the 78 evaluation contexts, when the number of encounters was less than the norm, crowding scores averaged 2.07 (i.e., not at all crowded). When encounters exceeded the norm, respondents felt "slightly" to "moderately" crowded with an average score of 4.07 across all evaluation contexts.

Examination of the specific evaluation contexts indicates that the mean differences in perceived crowding between those who had more or fewer contacts than their norm were statistically significant ($p < .05$) in 72 of the 77 evaluation contexts where the comparison could be calculated. Among the 72 tests where a statistical relationship was observed, when encounters exceeded normative tolerance limits, crowding increased significantly. These findings generalize across a wide range of specific evaluation contexts, methodologies, visitor characteristics and management practices. For example, the hypothesized pattern was evident across different:

1. Methodologies
   - Types of surveys (i.e., on-site, phone, mailed)
   - Question formats (repeated item [Brule River] vs. single item [other studies])
2. Years of data collection at the same resource
   - Brule River: 1975 and 1985
   - Columbia Icefield: 1993, 1996, and 2000

Table 3.4   Reported Encounters, Norm Tolerances, and Perceived Crowding (selected studies from Vaske & Donnelly, 2002)

Study site	Evaluation Context		Reported Encounters Compared to Norm		Mean Crowding Scores		t-value	p-value	Effect Size	
	Evaluation by:	Evaluation of:	% Fewer Encounters	% More Encounters	Fewer Encounters	More Encounters			r	p-value
Across all evaluation contexts			65	35	2.07	4.07	12.70	<.001	.470	<.001
RMNP – Bear Lake										
Shuttle parking lot	Visitors	Other visitors	71	29	2.56	3.96	3.53	<.001	.365	<.001
Bear Lake trail	Visitors	Other visitors	52	48	2.76	5.14	9.04	<.001	.562	<.001
RMNP – Longs Peak										
At the trailhead	Hikers	Other hikers	81	19	2.03	5.10	6.55	<.001	.539	<.001
On the trail	Hikers	Other hikers	42	58	3.03	5.20	7.33	<.001	.467	<.001
At the summit	Hikers	Other hikers	41	59	3.14	5.23	5.32	<.001	.469	<.001
Brule River, WI (1975)	Canoers	Other canoers	24	76	2.00	3.70	8.83	<.001	.476	<.001
		Tubers	63	37	2.70	4.30	9.49	<.001	.525	<.001
		Anglers	95	5	4.40	5.70	2.57	.010	.397	<.001
	Tubers	Canoers	41	59	1.70	3.00	5.63	<.001	.487	<.001
		Other tubers	79	21	2.10	3.70	5.70	<.001	.495	<.001
		Anglers	100	0	2.50	--	--	--	--	--
	Anglers	Canoers	35	65	1.60	4.40	7.15	<.001	.562	<.001
		Tubers	65	35	2.60	4.90	5.74	<.001	.499	<.001
		Other anglers	92	8	3.20	5.30	2.71	.010	.486	<.001
Brule River, WI (1985)	Canoers	Other canoers	74	26	2.11	3.44	9.81	<.001	.359	<.001
	Anglers	Other anglers	86	14	2.47	4.00	2.59	.011	.268	.011
Poudre River, CO	Kayakers	Other kayakers at put-in	88	12	1.33	2.50	2.28	.040	.364	<.001
		Other kayakers on river	69	31	1.52	2.59	3.90	<.001	.338	<.001
		Rafters at put-in	73	27	2.13	4.93	6.55	<.001	.525	<.001
		Rafters on the river	40	60	2.14	3.53	4.56	<.001	.312	<.001
	Rafters	Kayakers at put-in	92	8	1.27	2.17	3.24	.005	.334	<.001
		Kayakers on river	80	20	1.24	2.38	5.14	<.001	.454	<.001
		Other rafters at put-in	72	28	1.57	3.22	6.92	<.001	.453	<.001
		Other rafters on river	67	33	1.50	2.26	5.26	<.001	.288	<.001

3. Specific locations where encounters occurred within the same resource
   - Rocky Mountain National Park: trailhead, trail, and summit
   - Poudre River: access area versus on the river
   - Sunwapta/Athabasca Rivers: access area versus on the river
   - Mount Shasta climbers: while climbing, at the summit versus while camping

4. Visitor characteristics
   - Amount of prior experience with the resource (Mt. Evans: 1st time vs. repeat visitors)
   - Country of origin (1993, 1996, and 2000 Columbia Icefield: Canada, USA, Japan, Britain, Germany)

5. Management regulations (i.e., Colorado bow elk hunters)

Although 72 of the 77 tests were statistically significant ($p < .05$), the p-value does not indicate the strength of the relationship (chapter 6). The last two columns of Table 3.4 show the Pearson correlations (i.e., effect size) between those who had more or fewer encounters than their norm and perceived crowding. In the original article (Vaske & Donnelly, 2002), 31 of the 77 relationships had correlations greater than .5 (a substantial relationship). An additional 38 relationships were larger than .3 but less than .5 (a typical relationship), and only 8 had a correlation of less than .3 (a minimal relationship). Across all 77 evaluation contexts, the average correlation was .470. Taken together, these findings suggest that the strength of the encounter-norm-crowding relationship can be characterized as "typical" to "substantial."

Researchers may not always be able to achieve both generalizability and parsimony. To gain greater generality we may have to accept greater complexity and thus, reduce parsimony. Nevertheless, striving for both generalizability and parsimony is a worthwhile goal.

Inductive Explanations to Deductive Logic

The discussion thus far has emphasized deductive theories and suggested that examination of patterns in the data can facilitate an understanding of any discrepancies in the findings. Deductive logic begins with a theory and an associated set of hypotheses. The predicted relationships are examined in one or more studies to determine if the hypotheses are supported. Induction starts with patterns of observations in an effort to produce empirical generalizations that lead to new theories. This section illustrates this process of moving from inductive explanations to deductive logic.

Inductive Theorizing: Empirical Example

Vaske, Donnelly, Heberlein, and Shelby (1982) examined the data collected in 12 separate studies conducted across the United States. Respondents in each study were asked the same question: "Overall, how would you rate your day/trip?" Responses were coded on a six-point scale ranging from poor to perfect. The studies involved different *consumptive* (i.e., hunting and angling) and *nonconsumptive* (e.g., hiking, canoeing, camping) activities.

Tables 3.5a and 3.5b summarize the reported satisfaction ratings by the participants in each of the 17 activities. Savage River anglers and Maryland turkey hunters reported the lowest scores; a majority of the respondents in these surveys rated their day as "poor" or "fair." A little over one third of the 1976 Wisconsin deer hunters and goose hunters, and one-quarter of the 1977 Wisconsin deer hunters checked the lowest response categories. Anglers on the Brule River were more satisfied than any of the other consumptive groups considered, but 22% described their day as poor or fair.

Table 3.5a   Reported Satisfaction Ratings by Percent across Different Recreation Settings and Activities for Consumptive Activities

Overall how would you rate your experience?	Maryland Turkey Hunters	Horicon Goose Hunters	Wisconsin Deer Hunters		Savage River Anglers	Brule River Anglers
			1976	1977		
Poor or fair	57	39	36	25	70	22
Good or very good	32	34	41	30	18	43
Excellent or perfect	11	27	23	25	12	35

Source: Vaske, Donnelly et al. (1982)

Table 3.5b   Reported Satisfaction Ratings by Percent across Different Recreation Settings and Activities for Nonconsumptive Activities

Overall how would you rate your experience?	Great Gulf Hikers	Sleeping Bear Dunes	Apostle Islands			Wolf River Rafters
			Campers	Day Visitors	Boaters	
Poor or fair	5	6	3	0	1	14
Good or very good	20	30	17	28	19	66
Excellent or perfect	75	64	80	72	80	20

Overall how would you rate your experience?	Brule River		Grand Canyon	Rogue River	
	Canoers	Tubers		Floaters	Jet Boaters
Poor or fair	4	5	0	0	0
Good or very good	30	30	18	13	9
Excellent or perfect	67	65	82	87	91

Source: Vaske, Donnelly et al. (1982)

For the nonconsumptive activities, the floaters and jet boat passengers on the Rogue River, the whitewater rafters through the Grand Canyon, and the boaters and campers at the Apostle Islands reported the highest levels of satisfaction. Between 80 and 90% of the visitors to these areas rated their experience as "excellent" or "perfect." Similar evaluations were reported by three-quarters of the hikers in the Great Gulf Wilderness in New Hampshire. About two-thirds of the canoers and tubers on the Brule River (Wisconsin), the day visitors at the Apostle Islands (Wisconsin) and Sleeping Bear Dunes (Indiana) rated their experience as highly.

Overall, these data show that across a wide variety of geographic areas and recreation populations, those who engage in a nonconsumptive activity report higher levels of overall satisfaction than those who engage in a consumptive activity (i.e., hunting and fishing). In 10 of the 11 surveys of nonconsumptive recreation populations, better than 60% indicated their experience was excellent or perfect; whereas in all surveys of consumptive activities, no more than 35% reported this level of satisfaction. These findings, based on over 7,000 responses and using two different methodologies in six different states establish an empirical generalization: Nonconsumptive recreationists are more satisfied than consumptive users.

Based on this pattern of differences, Vaske, Donnelly et al. (1982) theorized that consumptive activities differ from nonconsumptive activities in at least two distinct ways. First, *consumptive activities are dominated by one clear and specific goal, the acquisition of the commodity to be consumed.* For the hunter this is harvesting game; for the angler it is catching fish. As noted in chapter 2, other motivations such as enjoying nature and social companionship are important (Hendee, 1974; Manfredo, Fix, Teel, Smeltzer, & Kahn, 2004), but bagging game and catching fish are still the most central evaluative criteria for the recreationist (Miller & Graefe, 2001; Vaske, Shelby et al., 1986).

The individual's reference group reinforces the importance of the consumable commodity. Other hunters and anglers, friends, and family members inquire about the success of a trip in terms of the number of animals bagged (or fish caught). Even if the consumptive recreationist uses other elements to evaluate his or her experience, the tale is related to others in terms of the bag. The simplicity and clarity of the success criterion makes it difficult to ignore.

By comparison, the goals of nonconsumptive activities are often more diffuse and less central to the definition of the activity. Backcountry hiking involves more than just walking in a roadless area. Seeing nature, being away from home and routine activities, being with friends and family, and perfecting skills, all contribute to the overall evaluation of the experience. These goals are also more general. There are many ways to be close to nature and have fun with friends. River running, for example, is composed of a complex series of events, such as navigating rapids, camping along beaches, strenuous exercise, and leisurely floating. Other than making the trip there is no single criterion on which evaluation hinges. Friends and family are likely to ask nonconsumptive recreationists if they had a good trip, picnic or bicycle ride, while consumptive recreationists are asked, "Did you get anything?"

A second important difference between consumptive and nonconsumptive recreationists involves the amount of control the person has in achieving their goals. Nonconsumptive recreationists have more control in selecting environments that provide the outcomes central to their recreation goals. For this group, the basic goal is to complete the activity (e.g., finishing the hike, running a river, driving a scenic road). Although unforeseen circumstances such as a sprained ankle, low water, or a flat tire can disrupt the experience, individuals can generally choose a setting that allows them to achieve the experience they desire. In contrast, while hunters and anglers may select areas that provide greater opportunities for seeing game and getting shots or strikes, there is no assurance that game will be bagged or fish will be caught. Data from several studies indicate that most hunters are unsuccessful on any given trip (Miller & Graefe, 2001; Vaske, Fedler et al, 1986). For example, less than 1 in 5 Wisconsin deer hunters bags a deer during the nine-day season (Heberlein & Laybourne, 1978) and 50% of the goose hunters at Horicon Marsh in Wisconsin get only one goose per season (Vaske, Donnelly et al., 1982), and fewer than 20% of the turkey hunters in Maryland get a turkey (Donnelly & Vaske, 1981). This means that hunters are less likely to achieve the specific goal that is central to their activity. The presence of a more specific and clear goal less subject to the control of a consumptive recreationist has implications for the participant's overall evaluation of the experience.

The one anomalous nonconsumptive case provides additional support for this inductive theorizing. The rafters on the Wolf River in Wisconsin who had to drag their boats through boulder-strewn rapids because of low water levels said their trip was less than excellent or perfect (Table 3.5b). For this group, the water levels may have kept many of the would-be floaters from achieving the defining objective of river rafting.

Although the Wolf River visitors were less likely to rate their trip as excellent or perfect when compared to 4 of the 6 consumptive samples, it is interesting to note that they were also less likely to rate it as poor or fair. Only 14% of the floaters on the Wolf checked the lowest response categories, while 22 to 70% of the consumptive groups gave this evaluation. This suggests that the Wolf River rafters' subjective goals, such as getting outdoors, having a good time with friends and viewing the scenery of the river, may have been relatively more important for this group than for the consumptive recreationists. For the nonconsumptive users then, it appears that when the defining objective of the activity cannot be achieved, it is easier for them to emphasize these secondary goals. The floaters may have rationalized that the trip was still fun even though the river was low.

In contrast, it is more difficult for the unsuccessful hunter or angler to make this psychological shift. It is clear to the hunter/angler and others, such as hunting/fishing partners, spouse, and children, that he or she came home empty-handed. The pleasures of companionship and being close to nature can only go so far as a substitute. When the bag is empty, the trip is called poor or fair.

From Inductive to Deductive Logic

The inductive theorizing by Vaske, Donnelly et al. (1982) leads to the deductive hypothesis that hunters and anglers who achieve the defining goal (i.e., bag game, catch fish) will report higher satisfaction ratings than those consumptive users who did not bag game or catch fish. Support for this prediction is shown in Table 3.6 (p. 54). Only 12% of the unsuccessful hunters and anglers rated their experience as excellent or perfect, while 40% of the successful consumptive recreationists gave this evaluation. At the same time, the satisfaction ratings by the successful hunters/anglers were substantially lower than those reported by the nonconsumptive recreationists (40% vs. 69% for the excellent-perfect category, respectively).

The findings in Table 3.6 suggest that success is an important indicator of a satisfactory experience but, by itself, is not sufficient to explain the differences between consumptive and

Table 3.6 Satisfaction Ratings by Unsuccessful and Successful Consumptive Recreationists and Nonconsumptive Recreationists

Overall, how would you rate your day / trip?	Consumptive Activities		Nonconsumptive Activities
	Unsuccessful	Successful	
Poor or Fair	52%	27%	4%
Good or Very Good	36%	33%	27%
Excellent or Perfect	12%	40%	69%
Total %	100%	100%	100%
Total *n*	984	352	5,871
M	2.60	3.56	4.74

All means differ significantly at $p < .001$

nonconsumptive recreationists. Among the successful hunters and anglers, satisfaction is much higher, but below the levels reported by nonconsumptive recreationists. It may be that consumptive users are less likely to describe their experience as excellent or perfect unless they bag a trophy or catch limit of fish, both of which are rare events. As consumptive activities, hunting and fishing may place the individual in a striving mode where one is searching for the optimum rather than satisficing or compromising.

The data reported by Vaske, Donnelly et al. (1982) measured success for the consumptive individuals as a simple "yes" or "no" variable, rather than the number or the size of the animals / fish taken. Although this represents a limitation of the study, the yes / no success categorization was the only measure that was available in the studies that were included in their comparative analysis. The influence of number and size of animals / fish taken remains a topic for future study. Remember, all theories are tentative.

Generalizing the Findings

Vaske, Donnelly et al. (1982) theorized that participants in consumptive (i.e., hunting, angling) and nonconsumptive activities differ in terms of the specificity and clarity of their goals and their control in achieving these goals. At issue is whether these findings can be generalized to other types of activities.

The 1982 article argued that nonconsumptive and consumptive uses fall along a continuum of recreation activities. There are some nonconsumptive activities, for example, which like hunting and angling, have more specific goals. The goal of mountain climbing is to reach the summit. The goal of bird watching and other wildlife viewing is to observe particular species of wildlife. For these activities, however, the recreationists may have more control in goal achievement by choosing climbing routes that match their skills and abilities, or by selecting habitats known to have populations of the desired wildlife species.

Puttkammer (1994) explored the generalizability of the specificity / clarity of goals hypothesis using a sample of mountain climbers at Mt. Shasta Wilderness in California. For mountain climbers whose specific goal was to reach the summit, she hypothesized that the satisfaction scores of those who achieved the goal would be higher than for those who did not reach the summit.

The findings supported the predicted relationship. Individuals who were motivated to reach the summit and achieved their goal were more satisfied (91% in the excellent-perfect category) than those who were unsuccessful at reaching the summit (57%). Table 3.7 also suggests two ways these data might be analyzed. When the satisfaction scale is collapsed into the three categories, a chi-square analysis (chapter 13) or simply looking at the percentages are appropriate Alternatively, if the original coding is used (i.e., poor [1] through perfect [6]), a t-test for independent samples can be used to compare the two groups (chapter 14). The t-test indicates that the two groups are statistically different in terms of their satisfaction ratings ($t = 7.70, p < .001$). The average score for the successful group (i.e., reached the summit) was 4.29 on the six-point scale. This implies that their mean rating was in between "very good" and "excellent." For the unsuccessful group, the average satisfaction rating ($M = 3.60$) was "good" and "very good." As will be discussed in chapter 5, not all statisticians would agree with the use of a t-test for these data. In this specific example, the need for a statistical test is less important given the magnitude of differences in the cell percentages (e.g., 57% vs. 91%).

Table 3.7   Satisfaction Ratings by Unsuccessful and Successful Climbers at Mt. Shasta Wilderness

Rating of today's climbing experience	Unsuccessful summit attempt	Successful summit attempt
Poor or fair	9%	0%
Good or very good	35%	9%
Excellent or perfect	57%	91%
Total n	118	189
M^1	3.60	4.29

1. $t = 7.70, p < .001$

Extending the Generalization

Although wildlife viewing is typically considered a nonconsumptive activity, it is similar to consumptive activities in the sense that it has a specific and clear goal (i.e., see wildlife). Vaske, Donnelly, Wittmann, and Laidlaw (1995) examined the specificity/clarity of goal hypothesis among a sample of wildlife viewers on Mt. Evans in Colorado. Two alternative (as opposed to null, chapter 6) hypotheses were advanced:

H_1:   For wildlife viewers whose specific goal is to observe *mountain goats*, the mean satisfaction scores of individuals who observe this species will be higher than for those who do not observe this species.

H_2:   For wildlife viewers whose specific goal is to observe *bighorn sheep*, the mean satisfaction scores of individuals who observe this species will be higher than for those who do not observe this species.

In contrast to the Puttkammer (1994) mountain climber study where the percent differences in excellent/perfect cells were pronounced (57% vs. 91% for the unsuccessful and successful groups, respectively), the percent differences in these cells for both species (i.e., mountain goats and bighorn sheep) were considerably closer (Table 3.8). For example, 59% of the wildlife viewers who wanted to see and actually observed mountain goats rated their experience as excellent or perfect, while 49% of the unsuccessful viewers gave this rating. The difference in percents for the successful and unsuccessful bighorn sheep viewers was only 3% in the excellent/ perfect cells. Differences were thus apparent, but are the differences statistically significant? For the mountain goat viewers the answer is yes ($t = 2.52$, $p = .012$). For the bighorn sheep viewers, the answer is no ($t = 0.95$, $p = .343$).

Table 3.8   Satisfaction ratings by unsuccessful and successful wildlife viewers

Rating of today's visit to Mt. Evans	Observed Mountain Goats		Observed Bighorn Sheep	
	No	Yes	No	Yes
Poor or fair	5%	5%	5%	4%
Good or very good	46%	36%	41%	39%
Excellent or perfect	49%	59%	54%	57%
Total *n*	263	348	193	418
Total *M*	4.27	4.45	4.35	4.42
t	2.52		.95	
p	.012		.343	

Based on these findings, we would accept hypothesis 1 and reject hypothesis 2. The difference in findings for the two wildlife-viewing activities can be partially attributed to the challenge associated with the activity. Even though the Mt. Evans area has the most accessible herd of mountain goats in Colorado, and the road offers excellent wildlife viewing opportunities, mountain goats are seen less often than bighorn sheep. In this sample, 57% saw mountain goats compared to 68% who observed bighorn sheep. Because bighorn sheep are prevalent in the area, they are accustomed to humans, and are seen regularly. Viewing this species may have less impact on visitor satisfaction than observing mountain goats.

Chapter Summary

Theory-based research employs both deductive and inductive logic when attempting to understand and explain the relationships among the concepts of interest. Deductive logic begins with a theory and an associated set of hypotheses. The predicted relationships are examined in one or more studies to determine if the hypotheses are supported. Induction starts with patterns of observations in an effort to produce empirical generalizations that lead to new theories. Both approaches facilitate scientific advances. They simply differ in their starting points on the wheel of science.

All deductive theories strive to be internally logical, parsimonious, and generalizable. A theory with parsimony uses the fewest constructs and linkages (hypotheses) necessary to explain the events of interest. Generalizability means that the results from one study can be used to explain events in another setting or situation. All theories should be considered tentative explanations of the relationships among the concepts, subject to continual testing and refinement.

Review Questions

1. Differentiate *deductive logic* from *inductive logic* by definition and example. Show how each of these approaches contributes to theory construction, both together and separately.

2. Discuss the difference between *objective* and *subjective* measures.

3. Explain the conceptual distinction between *actual density* and *reported encounters*.

4. Explain the conceptual distinction between *reported encounters* and *perceived crowding*.

5. List and explain three properties of deductive theories.

6. Based on the Vaske, Donnelly et al. (1982) article, discuss two distinct ways consumptive activities differ from nonconsumptive activities? Are these conclusions based on inductive or deductive logic? Explain your reasoning.

7. Was the hypothesis that "hunters and anglers who achieve the defining goal (i.e., bagging game) will report higher satisfaction ratings than those consumptive users who did not bag game" supported by the findings from the Vaske, Donnelly et al. (1982) article? What is the basis for your decision?

conceptualization and measurement

As discussed in chapter 2, **theories** state suspected relationships among concepts. **Concepts** are people's mental images of themselves, other people, places, or things. Concepts refer to un-measured (i.e., latent) constructs like academic achievement. For purposes of this book, the word **variable** (or **measured variable**) implies an indicator or empirical measure (e.g., grade in school) of a concept. Variables are the questions that are included in a survey. Responses to survey questions can be counted, categorized and assigned numerical values.

This chapter examines the processes researchers go through when conceptualizing and measuring variables in a survey. **Conceptualization** is the process of specifying precisely what is meant by the use of particular concepts. Six common measurement properties are considered: precision, accuracy, reliability, validity, representativeness, and generalizability. The predictive potential of variables in explaining the relationships among concepts is introduced. The chapter begins by clarifying the distinction between single-item and multiple-item indicators of a concept.

Single-Item versus Multiple-Item Indicators of a Concept

An **indicator** is a variable that specifies how a concept is measured (Vogt, 1999). A concept may be represented by either a **single-item indicator** (i.e., one survey question or variable) or **multiple-item indicators** (i.e., multiple questions or variables).

Single-Item Indicators

Perceived crowding is a psychological concept that exists in the minds of individuals and has frequently been measured with a single-item (Shelby, Vaske, & Heberlein, 1989; Vaske & Shelby, 2008). Heberlein and Vaske (1977), for example, developed a question that asks people to indicate how crowded the area was at the time of their visit. Responses were given on the following scale:

Did you feel crowded on the river today?

1	2	3	4	5	6	7	8	9
Not At All Crowded		Slightly Crowded			Moderately Crowded			Extremely Crowded

In this item, two of the nine scale points label the situation as uncrowded (1 and 2), while the remaining seven points label it as crowded to some degree (3 through 9). The rationale is that people may be reluctant to say an area was crowded because crowding is an undesirable characteristic in a recreation setting. An item that asked, "Did you feel crowded?" with response categories of "No" and "Yes" might lead most people to say "No." The scale needs to be sensitive enough to pick up even slight degrees of perceived crowding just as measures of undesirable chemicals, such as pollutants or carcinogens, need to be sensitive to even low levels of those substances.

Single-item indicators of a concept are sometimes advantageous because they can be: (a) intuitively meaningful, (b) analyzed from different perspectives, (c) compared across recreation activities and settings, and (d) place less burden on survey respondents than multi-item indicators of the concept. The single-item indicator of crowding, for example has proven to be *intuitively meaningful for both researchers and managers* (Shelby & Vaske, 2007; Vaske & Shelby, 2008). When describing a wilderness experience, where the goal is to provide an opportunity for low-density recreation, researchers have traditionally collapsed the scale into a dichotomous variable (i.e., two categories — not crowded vs. some degree of crowding). This provides a conceptually meaningful breakpoint between those who label the situation as not at all crowded (scale points 1 and 2, a positive evaluation), and those who label the situation as slightly, moderately, or extremely crowded (scale points 3 through 9, a negative evaluation). For managers who may not be accustomed to complex statistical procedures, the single-item crowding scale is easy to interpret.

The crowding scale *can be analyzed from different perspectives*. When describing a frontcountry experience, for example, individuals often accept and can tolerate higher densities of people. Collapsing the scale into not at all crowded versus some degree of crowding may be too strict a definition for what constitutes crowding in these situations. For frontcountry settings, the crowding scale might be collapsed into "not at all and slightly crowded" (scale points 1 through 4) versus "moderately and extremely crowded" (scale points 5 through 9; Vaske, Donnelly, & Petruzzi, 1996). Alternatively, a researcher may elect to not collapse the scale at all and simply calculate the average (i.e., the mean) of the scale, or the midpoint of the scale (i.e., the median).

The crowding scale *allows for comparisons between recreation activities and settings*. Since 1975, the single-item crowding measure has been used in 181 studies in the United States, Canada, New Zealand, Ecuador, Sweden, and Taiwan resulting in crowding ratings for 615 different settings and activities (Vaske & Shelby, 2008). These activities included hunting, fishing, rafting, kayaking, canoeing, floating, boating, rock climbing, mountain climbing, backpacking, day hiking, biking, sailing, photography, and driving for pleasure. The areas studied show considerable diversity, with some showing extremely high density and use impact problems, others showing low densities and no problems, and still others actively utilizing management strategies to control densities and use impacts. In total, 85,451 individuals have been asked the crowding question to date.

Analyses of this scale have illustrated the utility of comparing crowding evaluations from different activities and settings (Shelby & Vaske, 2007; Vaske & Shelby, 2008). By contrasting identical indicators of the same concept across a number of activities, resources, and visitor characteristics, aggregated data sets can reveal patterns in the findings and identify causal factors that typically cannot be manipulated in a single study (e.g., the relationship of multiple activities and settings on crowding).

Multiple-Item Indicators

Despite the advantages of single-item indicators, defining a concept with only one question does not necessarily reflect the full meaning and richness of most concepts. Consequently, researchers develop *multiple-item indicators*. Multiple indicators contribute to a more sophisticated understanding of concepts. For example, the single overall indicator of crowding does not incorporate other research findings that show individuals may feel more crowded by certain types of encounters (e.g., rafts vs. kayaks) or at different locations along the river (e.g., at the put-in, on the river, at the take-out). Rather than asking the single question, six questions might be included in the survey (3 for rafts and 3 for kayaks).

Did you feel crowded by the number of **rafts** at each of the following locations?

Did you feel crowded by the number of rafts:	Not at all crowded		Slightly crowded			Moderately crowded		Extremely crowded	
...at the put-in location?	1	2	3	4	5	6	7	8	9
...while on the river?	1	2	3	4	5	6	7	8	9
...at the take-out location?	1	2	3	4	5	6	7	8	9

Did you feel crowded by the number of **kayaks** at each of the following locations?

Did you feel crowded by the number of kayaks:	Not at all crowded		Slightly crowded			Moderately crowded		Extremely crowded	
...at the put-in location?	1	2	3	4	5	6	7	8	9
...while on the river?	1	2	3	4	5	6	7	8	9
...at the take-out location?	1	2	3	4	5	6	7	8	9

As a second example, visitor satisfaction is one of the most common indicators of recreation quality (chapter 3). Similar to the crowding scale, many early recreation satisfaction studies were based on a six-point single-item scale (Heberlein & Vaske, 1977; Shelby, 1976; Vaske, Donnelly, Heberlein, & Shelby, 1982).

Overall, how would you rate your experience on the river today?

_____ Poor	_____ Good	_____ Excellent
_____ Fair	_____ Very good	_____ Perfect

This satisfaction variable provides four response options reflecting a satisfying experience (i.e., good, very good, excellent, and perfect) and two categories representing a nonsatisfying experience (i.e., poor and fair). Similar to the crowding indicator, the rationale for including several positive response options is that people may be reluctant to say that the experience was not satisfying. An item that asked, "Were you satisfied with the experience" (response options "yes" or "no") might lead most people to say "Yes." With no variance (i.e., if everyone says yes), the indicator is not very useful for either researchers or managers.

Although this single-item indicator of satisfaction is sometimes useful for comparing participants engaged in different kinds of consumptive and nonconsumptive activities (chapter 3), researchers have recognized the multiple satisfactions associated with a recreation experience (Hendee, 1974; Manfredo, Fix, Teel, Smeltzer, & Kahn, 2004). Consequently, multiple-item indicators of satisfaction are now routinely incorporated into surveys. For example, the survey questions might be asked as follows:

There are a number of things that could have contributed to your overall evaluation of the experience today. Some of these are listed below. Please indicate how much *each statement* affected your experience.

	Added to my enjoyment today		No effect on my enjoyment today		Detracted from my enjoyment today	
The grade of the rapids we ran	1	2	3	4	5	6
The weather	1	2	3	4	5	6
The natural beauty of the area	1	2	3	4	5	6
The things I learned about the river features	1	2	3	4	5	6
My river guide	1	2	3	4	5	6
The people I met on the river	1	2	3	4	5	6
Other: _____	1	2	3	4	5	6

Interchangeability of Indicators

If several different indicators all represent the same concept, there should be a relatively strong correlation (chapter 16) among the indicators. To the extent that multiple, interchangeable indicators produce similar findings, researchers can reach the same conclusions about the concepts even if they disagree about definitions. The consequences of this observation, however, vary depending on whether the research goal is description or explanation (chapter 1).

With ***descriptive studies***, the indicators used to define the concepts have a greater impact on the study's conclusions than the indicators in explanatory studies. For example, "travel barometers" are sometimes developed to measure and describe the economic impact of tourism in a state. At issue, is what things (i.e., variables) should be included in the definition of economic impact? Among the possibilities are the taxes generated by hotels/motels, restaurants, ski resorts, sporting events (e.g., attendance at baseball, football, or hockey games). Local residents, however, can stay at hotels/motels, eat at restaurants, ski locally, and attend sporting events. The questions become:

(a) How many of the above categories of variables (i.e., hotels/motels, restaurants, ski resorts, sporting events) should be included in the definition of economic impact; and

(b) Because local residents of a state may also participate, what proportion of the taxes generated should be attributed to residents versus tourists?

Answers to these questions influence how much economic impact is associated with tourism. For example, if one study includes taxes generated by (a) hotels/motels, (b) restaurants, (c) ski resorts, but not sporting events, and a second study includes the tax revenues produced from all four variables, the bottom-line additive total from the two studies will not be equal. Similarly, if one researcher excludes the expenditures of residents and focuses on the money spent by nonresidents while a second investigator does not make this differentiation, the total economic impact of tourism on the state from these two descriptive studies will vary substantially.

With ***explanatory studies***, the goal is to examine the relationships among variables. Building on the previous example, a researcher might be interested in the magnitude of the relationship between the number of tourists and the economic impact of tourism (i.e., an association question, chapter 1). Study 1 measured economic impact with 3 of the 4 indicators (i.e., taxes from hotels/motels, restaurants, ski resorts); study 2 included all four indicators. With either study 1 or study 2, a logical hypothesis is that as the number of tourists in the area increases, the economic impact of tourism will increase. Regardless of how the researcher operationally defined the concepts (i.e., number of tourists and economic impact); the predicted positive relationship (a positive correlation) could be observed because the Pearson's correlation is a standardized statistic ranging from -1 to $+1$.

Measurement

Human dimensions researchers often use concepts that are formulated at rather high levels of abstraction (chapter 2). Such abstractions can be quite different from the variables that are empirically measured. *Measurement* is the process of linking abstract concepts to empirical indicators. In other words, measurement and theory are inextricably linked.

Measurement focuses on the observable response (e.g., a checkmark on a survey). Theory is concerned with the ***underlying unobservable concept*** (and directly unmeasureable concept) that is represented by the response. For example, a researcher may be theoretically interested in respondents' wildlife value orientations (chapter 2) and measure the concepts using a series of questions addressing the rights of wildlife (e.g., similar to human rights) or acceptable uses of wildlife (e.g., hunting, wildlife viewing). If there is a strong relationship between empirically grounded indicators (i.e., the observable response) and the underlying unobservable concept, analysis of the empirical indicators can produce useful inferences about the relationships among the underlying concepts. On the other hand, if the theoretical concepts have no empirical indicators, the empirical tenability of the theory remains unknown. At issue is how can researchers determine the extent to which a particular empirical indicator (or set of empirical indicators) represents a given theoretical concept. At the most general level, there are five basic properties of empirical measurement: (a) precision and accuracy, (b) reliability, (c) validity, (d) level of measurement, and (e) predictive potential.

Precision and Accuracy

Precision represents the fineness of distinctions made between the attributes (e.g., responses to a survey question) composing a variable. A person's age, for example, could be measured precisely (e.g., 43 years old) or less precisely (e.g., mid-forties). The length of a hot dog could be measured precisely (11.5 inches) or characterized as "about a foot long." Although precise measurements are generally superior to imprecise measures, the level of precision used in specific questions depends on the respondents' willingness to answer the questions, the researcher's theoretical objectives (chapter 2), and the study's context. Consider the following two income questions:

1. What is your approximate annual household income before taxes?

   $ _____ annual household income to the nearest dollar

2. What is your approximate annual household income before taxes? (Please check (√) one)

   ___ Less than $25,000   ___ $50,000 to $74,999   ___ $100,000 to $124,999

   ___ $25,000 to $49,999   ___ $75,000 to $99,999   ___ $125,000 or more

Question 1 is clearly more precise than question 2. Whether most respondents would answer question 1, however, is debatable. If a majority of respondents do not answer the question, the question has little analytical value. Based on the author's survey research experience, the refusal rate for income questions similar to question 2 is typically less than 10%. Thus, the less precise question 2 may have an advantage over the precise question 1 in this example because the respondents are more willing to offer an answer.

If the researcher's goal is to examine the influence of income on participation in fee-based recreation activities, the response categories given in question 2 may not provide a sufficient number of options at the low end of the scale. For example, to test a hypothesis that "poor individuals are less likely to visit National Parks that charge an entrance fee," additional response options should be added to the question (e.g., less than 7,500; $7,500 to $14,999; $15,000 to $24,999). Theory enters into the choice of measurement precision because of the need to clearly define what is meant by "poor" (e.g., the U.S. government's definition of poverty or some other definition). Context is important because even the revised scale that includes a response option of "less than $7,500" may constitute a substantial amount of income in a developing country.

Similar issues arise for the upper end of the measurement scale. If the study focuses on describing the recreation lifestyles of the rich and famous, the highest response options in question 2 (i.e., $125,000 or more) are likely to be insufficient for the research objectives. People who can afford expensive recreational toys (e.g., yachts, sport cars) typically make more than $125,000. When all respondents check one of the extreme responses (either lower or upper end of the scale), the question needs more variation in response options.

Variations in response precision between the extremes are an equally important measurement consideration. Age, for example, can be measured precisely or less precisely:

3. What is your age? _____ years old

4. What is your age? (Please check (√) one)

___ less than 21 years old	___ 41 to 50	___ 71 to 80
___ 21 to 30	___ 51 to 60	___ 81 to 90
___ 31 to 40	___ 61 to 70	___ over 90

The choice of question 3 versus question 4 depends on the research objectives. If the goal is to examine people who are of retirement age relative to the leisure pursuits that they enjoy, a response of "61 to 70" does not allow the researcher to differentiate those who may have opted to retire at the age of 62 as opposed to 65. If the research question concerns voting age and who will vote for a given presidential candidate, the low end of the response scale for question 4 (less than 21 years old) is inadequate because there is no way to differentiate those who are 18, 19 or 20 years old (i.e., voting age) from those who are less than 18. Similar problems could arise if the research question involved people's views on the legal drinking age relative to how old they are because the legal drinking age varies by state.

Given that survey research projects have multiple objectives (chapter 1) and that respondents tend to answer age questions, the more precise question 3 is superior to the less precise question 4. The researcher can always combine the precise responses into more general categories during analysis depending on the research question to be addressed. It is not possible, however, to separate out responses that have been lumped together (e.g., 61 to 70 years old) on the survey.

It is important to note that measurement precision does not necessarily equal measurement accuracy. ***Measurement accuracy*** refers to how closely the measured variable represents the concept. Assume, for example, that a researcher is interested in measuring a person's place of birth. Saying someone was born in Fort Collins, Colorado (precise) as opposed to the West (imprecise), but, if the person was actually born in Denver, Colorado as opposed to Fort Collins, the more imprecise measure is more accurate.

Reliability

The term *reliability* can refer to either the overall reliability of the study or to the consistency of responses to a set of measured variables (measurement reliability) (Table 4.1). ***Overall study reliability*** addresses the repeatability of findings; the degree to which study results fluctuate over time. For example, is the number of people participating in a recreation program increasing, staying the same, or decreasing? ***Measurement reliability*** refers to the consistency of responses to a set of questions designed to measure a given concept. For example, a survey might be concerned with individuals' attitudes toward wildland fires and measure this concept by asking respondents to evaluate the extent to which wildfires are: (a) good or bad, (b) beneficial or harmful, and (c) positive or negative. Each of these three variables could be coded on a seven-point scale (extremely good/beneficial/positive [+3] to extremely bad/harmful/negative [−3]). Individuals who feel that a wildfire is "extremely bad" are also likely to feel that wildfires are "extremely harmful" and be "extremely negative" toward wildfires. This consistency in the pattern in respondents' answers reflects measurement reliability.

Table 4.1   Research and Measurement Reliability and Validity

Reliability (Stability or Consistency)	Validity (Accuracy and Representativeness)

Research (or Study) Reliability
• If replicated, different studies produce similar results
	Research (or Study) Validity
	• Results of study are accurate and generalizable
	• Dimensions of research (or study) validity
	
	1. Measurement Reliability
	
	2. Internal Validity
	   a. Equivalence of groups on respondent characteristics
	   b. Control of experience/environment variables
	
	3. External Validity
	   a. Population validity (sample respondents represent theoretical population)
	   b. Ecological validity (results are generalizable to real-life outcomes)
	
	4. Measurement Validity and Generalizability of Concepts

Measurement (or Survey Item) Reliability Respondents report the same or very similar answers on the survey Types of Measurement Reliability 1. Test-Retest Reliability 2. Equivalent Form Reliability 3. Internal Consistency Reliability 4. Interrater Reliability	Measurement (or Survey Item) Validity Variables accurately measure concepts they were intended to measure Evidence for Measurement Validity 1. Criterion (Predictive) Validity 2. Content Validity 3. Construct Validity

Adapted from Morgan, Gliner, and Harmon (2006)

Reliability concerns the extent to which a survey yields the same results on repeated trials. Reliability, however, does not ensure accuracy. For example, if you set a scale to shade off five pounds, you will repeatedly get the same measurement, but it will not be accurate (i.e., the measurement is *biased*). The word bias, however, is sometimes used inappropriately by survey researchers (see chapter 19).

The measurement of any phenomenon always contains a certain amount of chance error. The goal of error-free measurement is never attainable in any area of scientific investigation. Two sets of measurements of the same attitudes (or beliefs or norms or value orientations; chapter 2) of the same individuals will never exactly duplicate each other. In other words, unreliability is always present at least to some degree. At the same time, however, while repeated measurements of the same phenomenon never precisely duplicate each other, they do tend to be consistent from measurement to measurement. Respondents with the highest scores on "anti-trapping of wildlife" items (those who are opposed to wildlife trapping) in a survey administered prior to a November ballot are likely to have the highest scores against wildlife trapping in a survey after the November vote. Their responses may not exactly be the same from one measurement to the next, but they will tend to be consistent. This tendency toward consistency found in repeated measurements of the same phenomenon is referred to as reliability. The more consistent the results given by repeated measurement, the higher the reliability of the measuring procedure. Conversely, the less consistent the results, the lower the reliability.

There are four basic methods for estimating the reliability of empirical measurement: (a) test-retest method, (b) alternative-form method, (c) split-halves method, and (d) internal consistency method.

Test-Retest Method

The **test-retest method** simply involves giving the same survey to the same people after a given period of time (Morgan, Gliner, & Harmon, 2006). One then obtains the correlation between scores on the two administrations of the same survey. It is assumed that responses to the survey will correlate across time because they reflect the same true variable. If one obtains exactly the same results on the two administrations of the test, the retest reliability coefficient will be 1.00. Invariably, however, the correlation of measurements across time will be less than perfect for a number of reasons (e.g., the person may be temporarily distracted, may misunderstand the question wording, or may change attitude).

Unfortunately, there are several problems with the test-retest method. First, survey researchers are often only able to measure a phenomenon at a single point in time. Second, a low test-retest correlation does not necessarily indicate that the reliability of the test is low. Rather, it may signify that the underlying theoretical concept itself has changed. For example, an individual's attitude toward trapping wildlife may be very different before and after seeing a video on trapping. True change is mistakenly interpreted as measurement instability in the assessment of retest reliability.

Third, the very process of measuring a phenomenon can induce change in the phenomenon itself (i.e., **reactivity**). In measuring the person's attitude at time 1, the person can be sensitized to the subject under investigation and demonstrate a change at time 2, which is solely due to the earlier measurement. Such reactivity reduces reliability estimates. Alternatively, the test-retest correlations can be overestimated due to memory. For example, if the time interval is short, respondents will remember their previous responses and will appear to be more consistent than they actually are. Memory effects lead to inflated reliability estimates.

Alternative-Form Method

The ***alternative-form method*** is similar to the test-retest method in that it also requires two testing situations. It differs from the retest method in that the same test is not given on the second testing. Rather, an alternative form of the same test is administered. Both forms are intended to measure the same thing. The alternative-form method has the advantage over the test-retest method primarily because it reduces the extent to which individual's memory can inflate the reliability estimate. There are, however, at least two problems with the alternative-form method: (a) the method does not distinguish true change from unreliability of the measure and (b) it is difficult to construct alternative forms that are parallel. Two measures are defined as parallel if they have identical true scores and equal variances.

Split-Halves Method

Both the retest and the alternative-form methods for assessing reliability require two separate administrations with the same group of people. In contrast, the ***split-halves method*** can be conducted on one occasion. Specifically, the total set of items is divided into halves and the scores on the halves are correlated to obtain an estimate of reliability. The halves can be considered approximations to alternative forms.

Unfortunately, there is certain indeterminacy in using the split-halves technique to estimate reliability due to the different ways that the survey items can be grouped into halves. The most typical way to divide the items is to place the even-numbered items in one group and the odd-numbered items in the other group. Other ways of partitioning the total number of items include randomly assigning the items into two groups. For 10-items, there are 125 different possible splits. Each split will probably result in a slightly different Pearson correlation between the two halves which, in turn, will lead to a different reliability estimate. Since the number of different splits is a function of the number of total items, obtaining a consistent estimate of the reliability increases as the number of items increases. Thus, using the split-halves method, it is quite possible that different reliability estimates will be obtained; even though the same items are administered to the same individuals at the same time. Chapter 18 provides an empirical example of the split-halves method for assessing reliability.

Internal Consistency Method

The split-halves method of assessing reliability has limitations because the reliability coefficients obtained from different ways of subdividing the total set of items are not same. There are methods for estimating reliability, however, that do not require either the splitting or repeating of items. These techniques require only a single survey administration and provide a unique estimate of reliability for a given test administration. In general, these coefficients are referred to as measures of ***internal consistency***. The most popular of these reliability estimates is *Cronbach's alpha* (Cronbach, 1951; Cronbach, 2004). Chapter 18 examines the Cronbach alpha in greater detail.

Validity

Validity can also be described in terms of the (a) ***overall validity of a study*** (or the research in general) and (b) the ***validity of the measurement*** (Morgan, Gliner, & Harmon, 2006). Campbell and Stanley (1966) define two broad types of overall study (or research) validity—internal and external. *Internal validity* depends on the strength of the research design. Experimental designs are often high on internal validity because subjects are randomly assigned to treatment conditions and the influence of extraneous variables controlled or eliminated. "*External validity* asks the question of generalizability: to what populations, settings, treatment variables, and measurement variables can this effect be generalized" (Campbell & Stanley, 1966, p. 5).

Measurement validity deals with the accuracy of generalizations and is concerned with whether the variables in the survey measure the concepts they were intended to measure (Table 4.2). An investigator, for example, may develop a set of survey items to measure wildlife value orientations (chapter 2). Validity concerns include: "Are all the basic beliefs associated with the value orientations represented by the items on the survey?" (*content validity*), "Can we predict behavioral or attitudinal differences among the public(s) based on the value-orientation measures?" (*criterion validity*), and "Do the item groupings measure what they are purported to measure?" (e.g., Do items addressing animal-rights values actually measure that construct; *construct validity*).

Table 4.2   Evidence for Measurement Validity

Type of Validity	Evidence for Validity	Usual Statistic	Support for Validity Depends On:
Content	All aspects of the concept are represented in appropriate proportions	None	Agreement by external panel of experts
Criterion			
Concurrent	Test and criterion are measured at the same time	Correlation [1]	Effect size [2]
Predictive	Test predicts some criterion in the future	Correlation [1]	Effect size [2]
Construct			
Convergent	Based on theory, variables predicted to be related are related	Correlation [1]	Effect size [2]
Discriminant	Variables predicted not to be related are not related	*t*-test ANOVA Correlation [1]	Statistically significant Statistically significant Effect size [2]
Factorial	Factor analysis yields theoretically meaningful solution	Factor analysis	Meaningful factor structure consistent with content evidence

[1.] Depending on the data, the type of correlation (e.g., r, r_{pb}, ϕ) will vary.

[2.] Effect size guidelines proposed by Cohen (1988; i.e., weak, medium, strong) or Vaske, Gliner, and Morgan (2002; i.e., minimal, typical, substantial).

Adapted from Morgan, Gliner, and Harmon (2000)

Criterion Validity

Criterion validity comes closest to what is meant by the everyday usage of the term. Criterion validity is at issue when the purpose is to use a survey to estimate behavior that is external to the measuring instrument itself. For example, the validity of the college board is shown in its ability to predict college success; college success is the criterion (a.k.a. predictive validity). Concurrent validity, another form of criterion validity, is similar to predictive validity except that the test and the criterion are measured at the same time (Table 4.2).

Figure 4.1 illustrates predictive validity using Schwartz's (1977) norm activation theory (chapter 2). The concept "awareness of consequences" is measured using three survey items. Survey respondents who agree with the statement "Human behavior upsets the balance in nature" should also agree with the statements "Recycling greatly reduces litter" and "Conservation is important for future generations." In other words one would expect some internal consistency in the responses to these items (i.e., reliability). The concept of "ascription of responsibility" is measured by a single-item indicator (i.e., I feel a personal obligation to protect the environment). Environmentally responsible rehavior (ERB) is the criterion and might be measured by observing a person's behavior. As diagrammed, there are four indicators of ERB (i.e., recycles, does not litter, conserves water, and conserves electricity). As will be demonstrated in the chapter on regression analysis (chapter 16), the multiple correlation between the two survey-based concepts (i.e., awareness of consequences and ascription of responsibility) and the criterion (i.e., environmentally responsible behavior) provides an estimate of criterion validity.

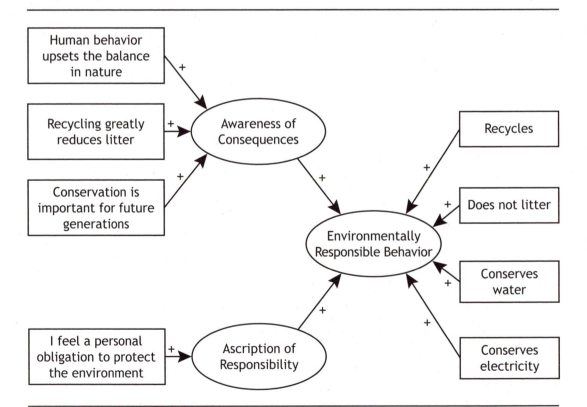

Figure 4.1   Predicting Environmentally Responsible Behavior from Awareness of Consequences and Ascription of Responsibility Concepts

Content Validity

Content validity refers to the degree to which the measure covers the range of meanings included in the concept. For example, a test of mathematical ability (a concept) would not have content validity if it focused on only addition. To be valid the test would also have to include subtraction, division, and multiplication. This example seems obvious because we agree that all four components (i.e., addition, subtraction, division, and multiplication) are important and necessary for defining the concept of mathematical ability. Unfortunately, there is less agreement about what should be included in many of the concepts of interest to parks, recreation, and human dimensions researchers. For example, while we might all believe that ascription of responsibility should be measured with more than just the single-item indicator (Figure 4.1), the question becomes one of asking what else is necessary to reflect this concept.

Construct Validity

Construct validity refers to the way indicators and concepts relate to one another within a system of theoretical relationships (Babbie, 2003). For example, human dimensions researchers have proposed that a person's value orientation toward wildlife can be positioned along a continuum ranging from "rights" to "use" (Fulton, Manfredo, & Lipscomb, 1996; Whittaker, Vaske, & Manfredo, 2006). This continuum is represented by several sets of basic beliefs (e.g., wildlife rights, wildlife welfare, wildlife use). Each of these basic beliefs is based on multiple indicators. For example, three survey items (i.e., The rights of wildlife are more important than human use of wildlife; Animals should have rights similar to the rights of humans; I object to hunting because it violates the rights of an individual animal to exist) might reflect the basic belief of wildlife rights. Multiple items would also be developed for wildlife welfare (a basic belief concept) and wildlife use (another basic belief concept). When we combine these three basic beliefs, the result is a value orientation toward wildlife. More generally, we have a system of theoretical relationships that reflect the idea of a value orientation. To demonstrate construct validity, we would need to show that this pattern of relationships exists in studies conducted in different locations (e.g., Colorado, Alaska).

The example just presented focused on one type of construct validity (i.e., convergent). Evidence for *convergent validity* occurs when relatively large correlations among the concepts are observed. *Discriminant validity*, another type of construct validity, exists when variables predicted not to be related to each other are not correlated. Discriminant evidence can also be demonstrated by showing that groups that should differ on the scale actually do vary statistically. A third type of construct validity, *factorial*, occurs when a factor analysis yields meaningful groupings of items.

Trade-offs among the Measurement Criteria

As suggested throughout this section, there can be tension among these four general measurement quality criteria. While precise measures are generally preferable, precise measures are not always more accurate. Reliable measures are not always accurate (e.g., calibrating a weight scale inaccurately). As will be demonstrated in chapter 18, trade-offs between reliability and validity must also be considered. For example, eliminating some variables from a multiple-item indicator of a concept may yield a more reliable estimate of the concept. There can be, however, instances when keeping these indicators in a concept is justified for validity reasons (even if it reduces the reliability).

Babbie (2003) provides a useful diagram for illustrating this relationship between validity and reliability. Figure 4.2 depicts a series of three targets. The dots represent the extent to which a marksman was successful at hitting each of the targets. The target on the far left of the figure depicts a scenario where the individual consistently hit the same area (i.e., high reliability), but not all of the shots hit the target (i.e., low validity). For the target in the middle of Figure 4.2, the marksman always hit the target (i.e., validity), but his or her shots did not consistently hit the same location (i.e., low reliability). For the last target (far right of Figure 4.2), the marks-man consistently hit (i.e., high reliability) the bulls eye (i.e., high validity). Survey researchers strive to achieve both reliability and validity in the concepts they measure.

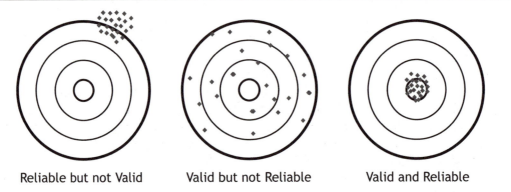

| Reliable but not Valid | Valid but not Reliable | Valid and Reliable |

Source: Babbie (2003)

Figure 4.2   An Analogy of Validity and Reliability

Predictive Potential

Many variables that are commonly believed to influence behavior, often have little predictive potential. For example, popular media commonly assert that values influence environmental attitudes and/or behaviors, but empirical evidence showing direct predictive validity is sparse (chapter 2). Stern (2000), for example, suggests that basic environmental value orientations often have limited effects on specific forms of environmental activism such as signing environ-mental petitions and recycling. Similarly, pro-environmental "values" may not predict support for wildlife management actions such as efforts to protect endangered species in a given loca-tion (Vaske & Donnelly, 2007).

Social-psychological theories offer explanations for these disparities, suggesting that attitudes, beliefs, and norms mediate the relationships between values and behavior (chapter 3). These theories distinguish stable but abstract values from more specific cognitions (e.g., attitudes and norms) that evaluate objects or situations encountered in daily life. These cognitions are best understood as part of a "hierarchy" from general to specific (see chapter 2). Specific belief, attitudinal, or normative variables are more likely to predict behaviors than more general measures like values or value orientations (Fishbein & Ajzen, 1975; Fiske & Taylor, 1991). General "wildlife value orientations," for example, predicted the general acceptability of hunting better than acceptability responses to specific conflict situations (e.g., destroying a moose in a suburban neighborhood during the fall of 2005; Whittaker et al., 2006).

The logical progression of general to specific concepts within the cognitive hierarchy is based on the specificity of the object. For example, attitudes represent a positive or negative evaluation of an object (Table 4.3). If the object is "coyotes," the evaluation reflects cognitions that form a general attitude. If the object is "lethal management of coyotes in Colorado during 2006," the evaluation reflects a narrower context and time frame, and thus a more specific attitude.

Table 4.3   Specificity of Evaluation Objects in the Cognitive Hierarchy

Concept	Specificity of Evaluation Object
Wildlife value orientation	All wildlife
General attitude	Coyotes
Specific attitude	Lethal trapping of coyotes in South Suburban area, Colorado
Behavioral intention	Likelihood of supporting lethal trapping of coyotes in South Suburban area, Colorado

Adapted from Vaske and Needham (2007)

The notion of predictive potential also applies to variables not typically included in the cognitive hierarchy (e.g., demographics). Issues related to general versus specific variables apply here as well. Are survey questions about age, sex, education, and income general or specific variables? A survey response to a question asking about a person's age can be a specific number (e.g., 22, 43, 56) and an individual's sex is specific (i.e., male or female). In the context presented here, however, these demographic variables would be considered general variables. "General" in the sense that a person who is 43 years old is 43 years old regardless of other questions on the survey. The following empirical example by Donnelly and Vaske (1995) illustrates the limited predictive power of demographic variables and other general concepts.

Predictive Potential: Empirical Example

New Hampshire had not had a moose hunt since the early 1900s, but legislation passed in 1985 mandated the Fish and Game Department to study the state's growing moose population, and if deemed biologically feasible, to reintroduce a limited moose hunt. Following two years of study, the agency proposed a three-day season with 75 permits to be issued by a lottery drawing. Two widely advertised public hearings suggested widespread support for the hunt among sportsmen and conservation groups. Two bills introduced into the state legislature, however, indicated opposition to the hunt. The first was designed to eliminate Fish and Game's authority to conduct a hunt, while the other placed a three-year moratorium on the hunt, pending further study of moose diseases and population dynamics.

Opponents of the hunt argued that the biological moose studies were incomplete, that the moose were not in danger of overpopulating their habitat, and that the public hearings were not representative of the majority of residents. Proponents took an opposing stance suggesting that they believed Fish and Game had studied the moose herd sufficiently and that a limited hunt would not endanger the moose population.

To address this issue, a questionnaire was mailed to a simple random sample of New Hampshire residents (n = 1,250) during 1987 (Donnelly & Vaske, 1995). The sample included people living in urban and rural areas as well as those in the northern and southern sections of New Hampshire. After a reminder postcard and one follow-up mailing, a total of 906 usable surveys (72%) were returned.

The predictor variables were respondents' personal characteristics, beliefs about the state's Fish and Game Department, general beliefs about hunting, and specific beliefs about the moose hunt. Determination of the relative importance of these independent variables in explaining the variance in respondents' feelings about the hunt was examined through five regression analyses (chapter 16). Four separate equations were fitted for each set of respondents' characteristics, beliefs about Fish and Game, general beliefs and specific beliefs. A final model included all of the independent variables simultaneously. In all cases, the level of approval of the hunt was the dependent variable.

Current hunting participation, sex and income were significant in the respondent characteristics model, but only 16% of the variation was explained (Table 4.4). Three of the four variables in the Fish and Game model were also statistically significant. This model, however, explained only 26% of the variation. For both the general and specific beliefs reduced models, all of the variables had a significant effect on whether or not individuals approved of the hunt. The general beliefs model explained 52% of the variation in individuals' feelings, whereas the specific beliefs model accounted for 77% of the variance. As hypothesized, the sociodemographics and beliefs about the agency explained less of the variation in the dependent variable than either the general or specific beliefs models. In addition, the specific beliefs about the moose hunt accounted for 25% more of the variance than did the general beliefs model.

As a final step in the analysis, a model was fitted which included all of the predictor variables. Four of the personal characteristics, one of the general belief statements, and all four of the specific beliefs were significant. None of the beliefs about the Fish and Game Department entered the equation. Taken together, this set of independent variables explained 79% of the variance in the dependent measure; only a 2% increase in explanatory power over the specific beliefs reduced model (77%).

Consistent with the social psychological literature, results indicated that specific beliefs were better predictors of residents' reactions to the moose hunt than either general beliefs or personal characteristics. Conversely, the traditional sociodemographic variables were among the poorest predictors of respondents' attitude. These findings suggest that efforts to understand public sentiment towards wildlife management policies need to focus directly on the issues and cannot be generalized from demographic indicators that have less predictive potential.

Table 4.4 Predicting a Specific Dependent Variable Using General and Specific Independent Variables

	Dependent Variable Approve/Disapprove of Moose Hunt			
	Reduced Model		Entire Model	
	β	p	β	p
Sociodemographic characteristics				
Age	−.08	.070	−.01	.633
Sex	−.31	.001	−.04	.010
Education	−.15	.001	−.02	.159
Income	−.15	.001	−.05	.004
Current residence	−.01	.795	−.00	.785
R^2 for Reduced Model	.16			
Wildlife Recreation Activities				
Hunting	.56	.001	.09	.001
Wildlife viewing	−.09	.003	−.03	.063
Wildlife photography	−.04	.250	.00	.795
R^2 for Reduced Model	.31			
Beliefs about the Fish & Game Dept.				
Fish & Game knows enough about the number of moose.	.37	.001	.01	.566
Fish & Game is doing enough to research moose herds' needs.	.13	.001	.00	.877
There should be more money spent on nongame species.	−.17	.001	−.02	.281
Fish & Game has increased the number of moose in NH.	.06	.065	.03	.093
R^2 for Reduced Model	.26			
General beliefs about hunting				
Hunting is a good management practice.	.25	.001	.04	.100
Hunting is necessary to prevent overpopulation.	.37	.001	.07	.002
I don't like hunting.	−.24	.001	−.02	.485
R^2 for Reduced Model	.53			
Specific beliefs about the moose hunt				
There are enough moose to support a controlled hunt	.59	.001	.50	.001
A hunt will kill off too many moose	−.26	.001	−.21	.001
A controlled hunt will leave enough moose for viewing	.11	.001	.07	.001
R^2 for Reduced Model	.77			
R^2 for Entire Model			.79	

Adapted from Donnelly and Vaske (1995)

Chapter Summary

This chapter examined the issues related to conceptualization and measurement of variables in a survey. The indicators of a concept may be represented by either a *single-item* variable (i.e., one survey question) or *multiple-item variables* (i.e., multiple questions). Single-item indicators of a concept can be: (a) intuitively meaningful, (b) analyzed from different perspectives, (c) compared across recreation activities and settings, and (d) placed less burden on survey respondents than multi-item indicators of the concept. Despite these advantages, single-item indicators may not necessarily reflect the full meaning and richness of many parks, recreation, and human dimensions concepts. Multiple-item indicators of a concept contribute to a more sophisticated understanding of concepts.

Measurement is the process of linking abstract concepts to empirical indicators. Six common properties of measurement were discussed: (a) precision, (b) accuracy, (c) reliability, (d) validity, (e) representativeness, and (f) generalizability. Precision represents the fineness of distinctions made between attributes (e.g., responses to a survey question) composing a variable. Survey questions for variables such as age can ask for a precise number (e.g., 43 years old) or can reflect grouped categories of responses (e.g., 40–50 years old). Although precise measurements are generally superior to imprecise measures, the level of precision used in specific questions depends on the respondents' willingness to answer the questions, the researcher's theoretical objectives, and the study's context. Measurement precision, however, does not necessarily equal measurement accuracy. Measurement accuracy refers to how closely the measured variable represents the concept.

Reliability can refer to either the overall study reliability or to the consistency of responses to a set of measured variables (i.e., measurement reliability). *Overall study reliability* addresses the repeatability of findings; the degree to which study results fluctuate over time. *Measurement reliability* refers to the consistency of responses to a set of questions designed to measure a given concept. There are four basic methods for estimating the reliability of empirical measurement: (a) test-retest method, (b) alternative-form method, (c) split-halves method, and (d) internal consistency method. Test-retest reliability involves giving the same test (survey) to the same people after a given period of time. The alternative-form method also requires two testing situations, but uses slightly different questions during the second administration of the survey. The split-halves method can be conducted on one occasion. Reliability is estimated by correlating the responses from the two halves. Internal consistency methods for examining reliability (e.g., Cronbach's alpha) can also be achieved through a single survey administration and can be thought of as all possible split-halves. Cronbach's alpha is one of the most commonly reported measures of reliability in survey research.

Validity can be described in terms of the: (a) overall validity of a study (or the research in general) and (b) the validity of the measurement. *Overall study validity* is typically discussed in terms of internal and external validity. *Measurement validity* deals with the accuracy of generalizations and is concerned with whether the variables in the survey measure the concepts they were intended to measure. Measurement validity involves issues related to content, construct, and prediction. Content validity refers to the degree to which the measure covers the range of meanings included in the concept. Construct validity refers to the way indicators and concepts relate to one another within a system of theoretical relationships. Criterion validity is at issue when the purpose is to use a survey to estimate behavior that is external to the measuring instrument itself.

There are trade-offs among these general measurement criteria. Precise measures are generally preferable, but precise measures are not always more accurate. Reliable measures are not always accurate. For example, shading five pounds off of a scale will give you a reliable weight number, but the number will be inaccurate.

Predictive potential refers to the likelihood that one survey question can explain variation in a second variable. When the two questions are measured at the same level of specificity the predictive potential increases. Specific belief, attitudinal, or normative variables, for example, are more likely to predict specific behaviors than more general measures like values or value orientations. When there is less measurement correspondence between the variables, the predictive potential decreases. For example, a general attitude toward moose is likely to explain less of the variability in respondents' specific behavioral intentions to support a proposed moose hunt than an individual's specific attitude toward the hunt. Understanding such differences in measurement correspondence can facilitate a researcher's choice of what questions to include on a survey and how those questions should be asked.

Review Questions

1. Explain the logic of conceptualization and its relationship to measurement.

2. Explain the difference between a *concept* and an *indicator* of that concept.

3. Discuss the distinction between *single-item* and *multiple-item* indicators of a concept.

4. Discuss the advantages and disadvantages of a *single-item* indicator.

5. What does it mean to say that indicators are interchangeable?

6. Explain the statement: Definitions are more problematic for descriptive research than for explanatory research.

7. Discuss the concepts of *precision* and *measurement accuracy* as they relate to measurement quality.

8. Define reliability and list four strategies for improving the reliability of measures.

9. Discuss three problems with the test-retest method of assessing reliability.

10. Discuss two problems with the alternative-form method of assessing reliability.

11. Define validity and compare the four types of validity.

12. Explain why there may be a trade-off between reliability and validity.

13. Discuss what is meant by predictive potential.

5

levels of measurement: once over again[1]

Measurement has been broadly defined as the assignment of numbers to the different character-istics (i.e., values) of variables according to rules (Stevens, 1951). Stevens went on to describe a hierarchy of four levels of measurement (i.e., *nominal, ordinal, interval, ratio*) and suggested that these scales were necessary for the selection of appropriate statistics. Since the 1950s these four levels of measurement have been discussed in most statistics and methods books and have led to considerable debate and confusion (Baker, Hardyck, & Petrinovich, 1966; Binder, 1984; Labovitz, 1967, 1970; Velleman & Wilkinson, 1993; Zumbo & Zimmerman, 1993). At the heart of this controversy is the nature of the relationship between ordinal and interval scales, and the appropriate statistics for such measures (Borgatta & Bohrnstedt, 1980).

This chapter has three objectives: (a) outline different positions in the measurement-statistics relationship debate, (b) offer an alternative measurement hierarchy (i.e., *dichotomous, categori-cal, continuous*) that is more useful than Stevens's for selecting and interpreting statistics, and (c) provide some practical guidelines for determining which statistics are appropriate given different measurement levels.

Levels of Measurement: Stevens's View

The attributes to a variable (e.g., response options on a survey question) should be exhaustive and mutually exclusive. For the variable, sex, the attributes of males and females exhaust all possible answers and are mutually exclusive. If a survey included a question on party affiliation and only included "Republicans" and "Democrats" as response options, the answers would miss individuals who might belong to other parties or who are Independents. *Mutually exclusive* implies that you must be able to classify every observation in terms of one and only one attribute (i.e., response). For example, if the survey asked about occupation and had the response options of professional, doctor, Ph.D., and white-collar worker, a given individual could be in more than one category—probably all four in this example.

---

[1] This chapter was inspired by an article by Borgatta and Bohrnstedt (1980) with the same title published in *Sociological Methods & Research, 9*(2), 147–160.

All of Stevens's levels of measurement share these characteristics of mutually exclusive and exhaustive. *Nominal* measures, for example, offer names or labels for the variable's characteristics. Examples of nominal variables include sex (male vs. female), religious affiliation (e.g., Catholic, Protestant, Jew), college major (e.g., Psychology, Recreation, Sociology), hair color (e.g., blonde, brunette, red, black), and hair (Yes or No). There is no implied ranking of the variable's attributes. Blondes, for example, are not necessarily more intellectually challenged than individuals with another hair color.

The attributes of an *ordinal* variable can be named or labeled (similar to nominal variables) *and* the responses can be logically rank ordered. In Stevens's view, an example of an ordinal level variable would be the grade (i.e., A, B, C, D, or F) that a student receives in a given course. Other examples might include the overall satisfaction measure discussed in chapter 3 where the response options were poor, fair, good, very good, excellent, and perfect; or the crowding variable with response categories of "not at all," "slightly," "moderately," and "extremely" crowded. Different attributes (e.g., survey response categories) in an ordinal measure represent relatively more or less of the variable.

For *interval* level variables the attributes can be named, rank ordered, *and* the distance between the attributes is equal and meaningful. For example, the distance between 90° and 80° is the same as the distance between 50° and 40° on the Fahrenheit scale, and the different temperatures have clear implications for the clothes a person should wear on a given day. The same logic applies to Celsius temperatures. With interval levels of measurement, however, there is no absolute zero point (e.g., Fahrenheit or Celsius temperatures).

With *ratio* measures, the attributes composing the variable have all of the characteristics mentioned previously (i.e., exhaustive, mutually exclusive, named categories, rank ordered responses, equal distances between categories), *and* there is a true zero point (e.g., Kelvin temperature scale). Most social science variables that meet the requirements for interval measures, also meet the requirements for ratio measures (e.g., length of stay in a campground, number people in a recreation program, length of residence). A person's age, however, represents an interesting exception. Most researchers would treat age as a ratio level variable, but can a person truly be zero years old. If yes, when did the clock start ticking, at the time of conception or the time of birth? Proponents of abortion rights would argue that the time of birth marks the starting point. Individuals who do not support abortion would argue for the time of conception.

According to Stevens (1951), associated with each level of measurement is a unique set of permissible mathematical transformations that leaves the scale invariant. The nature of this invariance sets limits on the kinds of statistical manipulations that can legitimately be applied to scaled data. For example, transformations that are appropriate for interval level data (e.g., computing means, standard deviations, chapter 11) are not, in Stevens's view, appropriate for ordinal level data. Stevens asserts:

> As a matter of fact, most scales used widely and effectively by psychologists are ordinal scales. In the strictest propriety, the ordinary statistics involving means and standard deviations ought not to be used with those scales, for many of these statistics imply a knowledge of something more than the relative rank order of data. (1966, p. 26)

More than five decades have passed since Stevens's (1951) influential paper on the relationship between scales of measurement and appropriate statistics. His taxonomy has been widely accepted (often without criticism) and has served as the foundation for statistical programs designed to assist in the selection of data analysis methods. The Statistical Package for the Social Sciences (SPSS), for example, uses three terms (i.e., nominal, ordinal, and scale) when discussing levels of measurement. Not all statisticians, however, agree about the utility of using Stevens's traditional levels (or SPSS measurement terms) when selecting appropriate statistics (Morgan et al., 2006). Velleman and Wilkinson, for example, concluded:

> Unfortunately, the use of Stevens's categories in selecting or recommending statistical analysis methods is inappropriate and can often be wrong. They do not describe the attributes of real data that are essential to good statistical analysis. Nor do they provide a classification scheme appropriate for modern data analysis methods. (1993, p. 65)

At the heart of this debate is the nature of the relationship between ordinal and interval scales, and parametric and nonparametric statistics. The distinction between ordinal and interval scales is not a black-and-white distinction; many kinds of summated scales (chapter 18) occupy a gray region somewhere in between.

Implications of Stevens's Measurement Levels for Statistics

Stevens's argument has led directly to a classification of statistical procedures into two categories. ***Parametric statistics*** (e.g., t, F) require the estimation of at least one parameter (i.e., population mean, μ, or a population standard deviation, σ). The derivation of these statistics assumes that the samples being compared are drawn from a population that is normally distributed (chapter 6). The frequency distributions of the samples are assumed to be meaningful, and the measures are assumed to be interval or ratio. ***Nonparametric statistics*** (e.g., analysis of variance by ranks) do not require the estimation of population values. No assumptions are made about the equivalence of units along the scale or about the shape of the distribution of scores in the population.

The association of parametric statistics with interval and ratio scales, and nonparametric statistics with nominal and ordinal scales has provided the foundation for several statistical books (e.g., Blalock, 1979; Senders, 1958; Siegel, 1956). Accepting the arguments advanced in these texts, parametric statistics (e.g., t-tests, analysis of variance, Pearson correlations, regressions, factor analysis) should not be used by any researcher who has less than interval level data. The formulas for each of these analysis techniques are based on the computation of means and standard deviations. In effect, Stevens's view prevents most social science researchers from using parametric statistics.

Levels of Measurement: Alternative Viewpoints

Borgatta and Bohrnstedt (1980) argue that most of the scales used widely and effectively in the social sciences are not ordinal scales (e.g., strongly disagree to strongly agree, highly unacceptable to highly acceptable). The survey questions used by social scientists usually fit badly into an interval scale (e.g., a disagree to agree scale is likely to be limited to only 5 or 7 response options), but they are not ordinal scales. Most of the constructs of interest to human dimensions researchers (e.g., value orientations, attitudes toward some object, chapter 2) are conceptualized to be continuous at the latent (i.e., unobserved) level, even though they are usually measured (i.e., observed) as discrete variables (e.g., variables with a limited number of response options such as a 7-point agree-disagree scale).

At the observed level (i.e., the responses on a survey), the variables used by parks, recreation, and human dimensions researchers are likely to be imperfect interval level scales. Unlike physicists who measure variables precisely with the aid of computer technology, social scientists generate measures that are: (a) unquestionably discrete, rather than continuous, and (b) likely to have intervals that are not truly equal. Researchers who have carefully developed the survey instrument, however, can assume that there is a monotonic (i.e., a function or sequence of numbers that steadily increases or decreases) relationship between the observed scale and the underlying latent construct (i.e., a positive difference between two points on the observed scale reflects a positive difference on the latent scale). This is another way of saying that parks, recreation, and human dimensions surveys contain measurement error. Measurement error does affect population parameter estimates (e.g., μ, σ), but the fact that the observations do not correspond perfectly to the underlying latent model in no way implies that the analyses should be confined to nonparametric statistics (Lord, 1953; Savage, 1957).

Level of measurement is not a requirement for the use of parametric statistics as suggested by Stevens (1951, 1966). Baker, Hardyck, and Petrinovich (1966), for example, tested Stevens's permissible transformations notion by constructing three types of distributions (i.e., normal, rectangular, exponential) that were of interval scale nature. They then performed a number of nonpermissible transformations that produced subinterval-type data. Pairs of random samples were selected from the original and transformed distributions, and *t*-values were obtained for each pair. The resulting sampling *t* distributions were similar to the theoretical *t* distributions. They concluded, "Probabilities estimated from the *t* distribution are little affected by the kind of measurement scale used" (p. 308). Similar conclusions have been noted for analysis of variance (e.g., Gaito, 1980; Kempthrone, 1955).

Havlicek and Peterson (1977) empirically examined the effects of the violation of assumptions of normality and of measurement scales on the Pearson correlation coefficient (chapter 16). The effects of such violations were studied separately, and in combination, for samples varying in size from 5 to 60. Simulation procedures were used to generate populations of scores for basic distributions (e.g., normal, positively skewed, negatively skewed; chapter 11). Samples of varying sizes were then randomly selected from specific populations. The results of their study were based on distributions of *r*, which were calculated on 5,000 sets of samples of $n = 5$ or $n = 15$, and 3,000 sets of samples of $n = 30$ or $n = 60$. Results indicated that the Pearson *r* is insensitive to extreme violations of the basic assumptions of normality and of the type of measurement scale. Failure to meet the basic assumptions separately or in combination had little effect upon the results.

An Alternative Levels of Measurement Hierarchy

Stevens (1951) discussed four levels of measurement: *nominal, ordinal, interval*, and *ratio*. SPSS uses three terms: *nominal, ordinal*, and *scale*. Morgan et al. (2006) suggested four terms: *nominal, dichotomous, ordinal*, and *approximately normal* (for normally distributed). In this book, three levels of measurement are described: *dichotomous, categorical*, and *continuous*. These descriptors are from the author's perspective more useful than the traditional, SPSS, or Morgan et al. (2006) measurement terms for the selection and interpretation of statistics. The relationships between these different terms are outlined in Table 5.1 (p. 84).

A *dichotomous* variable has only two response categories (e.g., males vs. females, support vs. oppose a policy). This descriptor is used by Morgan et al. (2006), but not by Stevens (1951) or SPSS. Dichotomous variables are commonly used in a variety of analyses. For example, if a frequency analysis (chapter 11) reveals that 30% of the respondents support a given policy (coded as a "1") and 70% oppose the policy (coded as a "0"), the researcher automatically knows that the mean of the variable is .30. The mean of a dichotomous variable coded as 0 or 1 is always the percent of respondents with a value of 1. This interpretation only applies, however, if the variable is coded as 0 or 1 (not for other codes such as oppose [1] and support [2]). Later chapters will demonstrate how dichotomous variables can be used in *t*-tests (chapter 14), analysis of variance (chapter 15), correlation (chapter 16), and dummy variable regression (chapter 16) as independent variables. If the dependent variable is dichotomous, logistic regression or disciminant analysis is the appropriate analysis strategy (chapter 17).

A *categorical* variable has three or more *unordered* response categories. Examples include religious affiliation (e.g., Catholic, Protestant, Jewish), party affiliation (e.g., Democrat, Republican, Independent), or college major (e.g., Recreation, Sociology, Psychology). Stevens (1951), SPSS, and Morgan et al. (2006) would call "categorical" variables "nominal." Unlike dichotomous variables where the mean can be interpreted, the mean of a categorical variable does not make any sense. For example, if the variable is location of residence where 1 equals North America, 2 equals Asia, and 3 equals Europe, a mean of 1.5 implies that the person lives somewhere in the middle of the Pacific Ocean. Although calculating a mean (or other summary statistics such as median and standard deviation) is illogical, it is important to remember that statistical programs like SPSS will compute the statistic. In addition, categorical variables cannot be used in correlation, regression, or analysis of variance as the dependent variable.

A *continuous* variable has an *ordered* set of response categories (typically 5 or more levels) with a distribution that is approximately normally distributed in the population sampled. In a normal distribution (chapter 11), most responses fall somewhere in the middle of the scale; fewer responses occur at the ends of the scale. In Stevens's (1951) terminology, continuous variables would be labeled "interval" or "ratio." SPSS calls continuous variables "scales" and Morgan et al. (2006) label these measures "approximately normal." Some recreation variables such as age, days of participation, and amount of money spent on an activity are obviously continuous variables although the range of possible responses is not infinite. Few individuals in most samples, for example, are over 100 years old. The maximum number of times a person can engage in a recreation activity per year is 365. The upper limit for expenditures on recreation equipment is only constrained by an individual's income (or willingness to go into debt), but even here there is some maximum for most people. For variables measured on scales such as "strongly disagree"

Table 5.1   Differences in Measurement Terms

| | Stevens (1951) | | Morgan et al. (2006) | | Vaske | | |
	Traditional Term	Traditional Definition	Term	Definitions	Term	Definition	SPSS Term
	NA	NA	Dichotomous	Two categories, either ordered or unordered.	Dichotomous	Two categories, either ordered or unordered.	NA
	Nominal	Two or more *unordered* categories	Nominal	Three or more *unordered* categories.	Categorical	Three or more *unordered* categories.	Nominal
	Ordinal	*Ordered* levels, in which the difference in magnitude between levels is not equal	Ordinal	Three or more *ordered* levels, but the frequency distribution of the scores is *not* normally distributed.			Ordinal
	Interval	Interval: *ordered* levels, in which the difference between levels is equal, but no true zero.	Approximately Normal	Many (at least 5) *ordered* levels or scores, with the frequency distribution of the scores being approximately normal.	Continuous	An *ordered* variable with at least 5 levels and a distribution that is approximately normally distributed in the population sampled.	Scale
	Ratio	Ratio: *ordered* levels; the difference between levels is equal, and a true zero.					

Adapted from Morgan et al. (2006)

to "strongly agree" the range of possible responses is typically constrained to 5 or 7 values. The response values are therefore limited discrete numbers, but, in theory, could fall anywhere between 1 to 5 (or 1 to 7). For purposes of this book, variables with response categories of strongly disagree to strongly agree or highly unacceptable to highly acceptable are considered continuous variables.

The proposed level of measurement hierarchy does not include ordinal variables (Table 5.1). The traditional definition of ordinal focused on whether the interval differences in ordered response categories were equal (Stevens, 1951). Morgan et al. (2006), however, take a different stance when differentiating ordinal from "approximately normal" variables. In their view, ordinal measures: (a) have fewer ordered response categories (i.e., 3 or 4) as compared to approximately normal variables (i.e., 5 or more), and (b) more importantly, the frequency distribution for an ordinal variable is not normally distributed (e.g., G. Morgan, personal communication). The position taken in this book is that the scales used in human dimensions surveys typically have five or more response categories (e.g., strongly disagree [1], moderately disagree [2], slightly disagree [3], neither [4], slightly agree [5], moderately agree [6], strongly agree [7]). In addition, the empirical demonstrations noted earlier (e.g., Baker, Hardyck, & Petrinovich, 1966; Gaito, 1980; Havlicek & Peterson, 1977; Kempthrone, 1955) suggest that parametric procedures are robust and yield valid conclusions even when the data are distorted (i.e., not normally distributed). When the distortions are severe, transformations can be applied to the data (chapter 12). Taken together, the combination of these considerations reduces the need for an ordinal level in the proposed measurement hierarchy.

Distinguishing among Measurement Levels and Variables

To facilitate an understanding of the three levels of measurement (i.e., dichotomous, categorical, continuous) advanced in this book, Tables 5.2a (p. 86) and 5.2b (p. 88) provide a series of examples. Sex is an obvious dichotomous variable, ethnicity is a clear categorical variable, and age is typically described as a continuous measure (Table 5.2a). Education, however, can be characterized as continuous, categorical or dichotomous depending on how the researcher operationalizes the variable. If the respondent is asked to circle a specific number of formal grade levels completed (e.g., 0 through 22), the variable represents a continuous variable. Education can also be measured as a categorical variable (e.g., elementary school, high school, some college, four-year college degree, graduate school). If the responses to this categorical variable are collapsed into "no college degree" versus "college degree," the variable becomes a dichotomous variable. A researcher's choice of operationalizing the variable influences the kinds of statistics that can be computed. For example, for the continuous version of the education variable, computing a mean or average number of grades completed is a logical option. When education is operationalized as a categorical variable, the analysis is constrained to the percentage of individuals who checked each response option; calculating a mean in this situation would not be appropriate.

The income variable poses a different analytical challenge. As measured in Table 5.2a, the variable does have eight ordered response categories, which might imply that the variable could be treated as a continuous measure. The response options, however, are clearly not equal intervals. The low end of the scale is "less than $15,000;" the next response category is "$15,000 to $24,999" (range = $10,000), while the third category spans $25,000 (i.e., $25,000 to $49,999). If

Table 5.2a   Characteristics and Examples of the Three Levels of Measurement

Concept	Survey Question (Variable)	Response Categories	Level of Measurement
Sex	What is your sex?	Male or Female	Dichotomous
Ethnicity	What is your ethnic origin? (check one response)	African American or Black Asian or Pacific Islander Caucasian or White Hispanic or Spanish Origin Native American	Categorical
Age	What is your age?	Fill-in-the-blank response	Continuous
Education	What is the highest year of formal education that you have completed? (circle one number)	0, 1, 2, 3, 4, 5, 6, 7, 8, 9, 10, 11, 12, 13, 14, 15, 16, 17, 18, 19, 20, 21, 22	Continuous
Education	What is the highest year of formal education that you have completed? (check one response)	Elementary school High school Some college 4-year college degree Graduate school	Categorical
Education	What is the highest year of formal education that you have completed? (check one response)	No college degree College degree	Dichotomous
Income	What is your total household income before taxes? (check one response)	Less than $15,000 $15,000 to $24,999 $25,000 to $49,999 $50,000 to $74,999 $75,000 to $99,999 $100,000 to $124,999 $125,000 to $149,999 $150,000 or more	Categorical[1]
Participation	Did you hunt deer in Colorado last year?	No or Yes	Categorical
Participation	About how many years have you hunted deer in Colorado?	Fill-in-the-blank response	Continuous
Substitutability	If you could never go deer hunting again, what one wildlife-oriented activity would you do?	Fill-in-the-blank response	Categorical
Substitutability	Considering all of your other wildlife-oriented activities, how many substitutes do you have for deer hunting? (check on response)	I have no substitutes I have only a few substitutes I have some substitutes I have many substitutes	Categorical[2]

[1.] A judgment call is necessary on the part of the researcher. The variable does have at least five ordered categories (see Table 5.1), but the intervals are clearly not equal. If the researcher is willing to ignore the inequalities between intervals, the variable could be treated as a continuous variable. Otherwise, the variable would be considered a categorical variable. The author's personal preference is for the latter.

[2.] This variable has fewer than 5 response options and thus, would be considered categorical.

the researcher is willing to ignore these differences, the respondents' mean income level could be calculated. Many analysts, however, are likely to treat this income variable as categorical.

One of the participation measures in Table 5.2a, Did you hunt deer in Colorado last year? (coded no or yes), is a dichotomous variable. The other participation variable, About how many years have you hunted deer in Colorado? (a fill-in-the-blank response), is a continuous variable. Not all fill-in-the blank variables, however, are continuous measures. The substitutability question that asks "If you could never go deer hunting again, what one wildlife-oriented activity would you do?" would result in categorical answers (e.g., elk hunting, goose hunting, trout fishing).

The final example in Table 5.2a asks "Considering all of your other wildlife-oriented activities, how many substitutes do you have for deer hunting?" (check one response). The response options are ordered levels ranging from "I have no substitutes" to "I have many substitutes." Given the guidelines presented in Table 5.1 (5 or more categories for a continuous variable), this variable would be treated as categorical. Stevens (1951) and SPSS and Morgan et al. (2006) would call this variable ordinal.

All of the variables in Table 5.2b (p. 88) would be considered continuous measures in the measurement hierarchy described in this book. Each of these variables has at least five or more categories. This collection of measures also reflects the conceptual differences discussed in chapter 2. For example, the object evaluated by the basic beliefs measure refers to all endangered species and the scale is a cognitive evaluation (i.e., strongly disagree to strongly agree). The general attitude measure is also framed relative to all endangered species, but the scale is a negative to positive affective response (as opposed to a cognitive evaluation). The specific belief measure narrows the evaluation object to desert tortoises instead of all endangered species and the measurement scale is a cognitive evaluation (i.e., disagree to agree). The behavioral measure uses a likelihood scale (i.e., extremely unlikely to extremely likely) to measure respondents' voting intentions to increase spending on efforts to recover the desert tortoise.

Table 5.2b   Characteristics and Examples of the Three Levels of Measurement[1]

Concept [2]	Survey Question (Variable)	Response Categories	Level of Measurement
Reported Encounters (a belief)	About how many other visitors did you see while on the trail today?	Fill-in-the-blank response	Continuous
Crowding (an attitude)	Did you feel crowded by other visitors today?	1 = Not at all crowded 2 = Not at all crowded 3 = Slightly crowded 4 = Slightly crowded 5 = Moderately crowded 6 = Moderately crowded 7 = Moderately crowded 8 = Extremely crowded 9 = Extremely crowded	Continuous
Basic belief	The needs of people are always more important than any rights endangered species have. (Check one response)	−3 = Strongly disagree −2 = Moderately disagree −1 = Slightly disagree 0 = Neither 1 = Slightly agree 2 = Moderately agree 3 = Strongly agree	Continuous
General Attitude	My attitude towards all endangered species is:	−3 = Extremely negative −2 = Moderately negative −1 = Slightly negative 0 = Neither 1 = Slightly positive 2 = Moderately positive 3 = Extremely positive	Continuous
Specific Belief	I feel strong personal obligation to protect the desert tortoise in the Mojave Desert	−3 = Strongly disagree −2 = Moderately disagree −1 = Slightly disagree 0 = Neither 1 = Slightly agree 2 = Moderately agree 3 = Strongly agree	Continuous
Behavioral Intention	If you had to vote today, how likely is it that you would vote to increase spending on efforts to recover the desert tortoise? (Check one response)	−3 = Extremely unlikely −2 = Moderately unlikely −1 = Slightly unlikely 0 = Neither 1 = Slightly likely 2 = Moderately likely 3 = Extremely likely	Continuous

[1.] All variables in this table would be considered continuous variables because each has more than five response categories. The difference between general and specific variables is based on the specificity of the "object" evaluated. For example, the object for the general attitude is all endangered species. The object for the specific belief is "desert tortoises in the Mojave Desert."

[2.] The distinction between beliefs, attitudes and behavioral intention is reflected in response categories. For example, the responses for the attitude questions are affective (e.g., positive vs. negative). The responses for the belief statements are cognitive.

Guidelines for Selecting an Appropriate Analysis Strategy

Table 5.3 provides guidelines for selecting an appropriate analysis strategy. Some readers may not be familiar with the specifics of calculating a chi-square, *t*-test, or any of the other statistics mentioned in the table. The details of each of these statistical tests are presented in later chapters. Learning any statistical analysis routine is similar to learning a foreign language. If a person worries too much about where every accent mark should be placed on different words, the details can inhibit the learning process. In statistical analysis, if the researcher becomes overly concerned about what options to check on SPSS menus, the details become mind boggling. Table 5.3 should be treated as a "big picture" roadmap that helps to sort out what tests should be conducted to address specific analysis problems. For the moment, what is important to recognize is that how variables are measured drives what statistical tests are appropriate.

Table 5.3 Guidelines for Selecting an Appropriate Analysis Strategy

Type of Variable		Number of Variables			
Independent Variable	Dependent Variable	Independent Variable	Dependent Variable	Analysis Strategy	Test Statistic
Dichotomous Categorical	Dichotomous Categorical	1	1	Chi-square	χ^2
Dichotomous	Continuous	1	1	*t*-test (groups)	*t*
	Continuous	Cases	2	*t*-test (paired)	*t*
Dichotomous Categorical	Continuous	1	1	1-way ANOVA	*F*
Dichotomous Categorical	Continuous	2 +	1	*n*-way ANOVA	*F*
Dichotomous Categorical	Continuous	2 +	2 +	MANOVA	*F*
	Continuous	Cases	2 +	Repeated measures ANOVA	*F*
Continuous	Continuous	1	1	Correlation	*F*
Continuous	Continuous	1 +	1	Regression	*F*
Dichotomous Continuous	Continuous	1 +	1	Dummy variable regression	*F*
Dichotomous Continuous	Dichotomous	1 +	1	Logistic regression	χ^2
Dichotomous Continuous	Dichotomous Categorical	1 +	1	Discriminant	*F*
Dichotomous Categorical	Dichotomous Categorical	1 +	1 +	Log linear	χ^2

Note: The word "Cases" in the above table refers to the sample of respondents.

The following steps ask a series of questions that hopefully help a researcher identify an appropriate analysis strategy for testing a given hypothesis.

Steps in Selecting an Appropriate Analysis Strategy

1. *What is the independent variable and what is the dependent variable?*

   For example, if you want to examine the relationship between survey respondents' sex (male or female) and how they voted on a trapping ban ballot initiative (for or against), it is reasonable to hypothesize that a person's sex might influence whether the individual voted "for" or "against" the trapping ban. Whether the person voted "for" or "against" the ballot cannot influence the individual's sex. In this example then, sex is the independent variable and voting behavior is the dependent variable. Voting behavior thus depends on the individual's sex.

2. *How is the independent variable coded?*

   In the current example, sex is a dichotomous variable with response options of "male" and "female."

3. *How is the dependent variable coded?*

   In this example, voting behavior is a dichotomous variable with response categories of "voted for" and "voted against."

4. *How many variables included in the analysis?*

   There are two variables (sex and voting behavior) in this example. Therefore, with two dichotomous variables the appropriate analysis strategy is a chi-square (Table 5.3).

A chi-square analysis can be based on (a) two dichotomous variables, (b) a dichotomous independent variable and a categorical dependent variable, (c) a categorical independent variable and a dichotomous dependent variable, or (d) two categorical variables (chapter 13).

Additional Examples

Independent Samples (Groups) t-test. Assume the researcher wants to explore the relationship between "sex" (a dichotomous variable) and "income" (coded as the actual number of dollars a person earned—a continuous variable). The hypothesis is that males make more money than females. Sex is thus the independent variable and income is the dependent variable. An individual's sex might influence how much money he or she earns in a given year. A person's income, on the other hand, cannot influence the individual's sex. With one dichotomous independent variable and one continuous variable, an appropriate analysis strategy is an independent samples *t*-test (chapter 14). The samples are independent because if a respondent is a male, the person cannot be a female (i.e., mutually exclusive).

Paired Samples t-tests. Sometimes the researcher is interested in comparing the responses of the same individuals at two or more points in time. For example, a professor might be interested in testing his or her students on the material presented in this chapter. The test is given prior to a student having had a chance to read the chapter and the person receives a score of 3 out of a possible 100 points (i.e., a continuous level variable). At the end of the course the professor gives the same person the same test and individual's score is 100. To test whether there has been a statistically significant improvement in knowledge of statistics the professor would *pair* the individual's initial test score against that person's final score. When a researcher makes this comparison across all members of the class (cases in SPSS terminology), the appropriate statistical approach becomes a paired samples *t*-test (chapter 14).

One-Way Analysis of Variance (ANOVA). In the independent samples *t*-test example (independent variable = sex [dichotomous]; dependent variable = income [continuous]), the researcher could have conducted a one-way analysis of variance (i.e., one independent and one dependent variable) and produced identical results. The *F*-value from the ANOVA is equal to the square of the *t*-value from the *t*-test (chapter 14). The analysis of variance can be thought of as an extension of the independent samples *t*-test in that the independent variable in an ANOVA can be either dichotomous (identical to the independent samples *t*-test) or categorical. For example, consider the relationship between "party affiliation" (i.e., Democrat, Republican, Libertarian, or Independent—a categorical variable) and "recreation participation" (coded as a continuous level variable—e.g., camping participation). Party affiliation is the independent variable, recreation participation is the dependent variable, and the appropriate analysis strategy is a one-way ANOVA.

n-way ANOVA. The *n*-way ANOVA (2 or more independent variables and 1 dependent variable) represents an extension of the one-way ANOVA. Because *n*-way ANOVA includes more than one dichotomous or categorical independent variable, the researcher can examine not only "main" effects of the predictor variables on the dependent variable, but also the "interaction" effects (chapter 15) of the two independent variables. Cottrell, Vaske, Shen, and Ritter (2007), for example, predicted both main effects (distance of residence from village entrance and tourism employment) and interaction effects on Chinese villager beliefs about the economics of sustainable tourism. Respondents who lived further away from the village entrance *and* who were not employed in tourism perceived less economic potential from tourism than those who lived closer to the entrance *and* were employed in the tourism industry. The combined influence (i.e., the interaction effect) of the two independent variables helped explain respondents' beliefs about sustainable tourism beyond what was learned by examining the predictors separately (i.e., main effects).

Repeated Measures ANOVA. Just as *n*-way ANOVA is an extension of one-way ANOVA, repeated measures ANOVA can be viewed as an extension of a paired samples *t*-test. In the previous example, the professor tested the same students at two points in time (the beginning and end of the semester). Each student's test grade from time 1 was paired with his or her test grade from time 2. If the professor was to administer the same test to the same students, six months after the course was completed, the analytical problem becomes a repeated measures ANOVA. This analysis strategy compares the same individual's responses to the same survey at multiple (3 or more) points in time. Although most professors do not typically track down students after a course has been completed, we do know where you live and, in the interest of science, this additional testing may be necessary.

Correlation and Regression. Based on logic presented in chapter 3, a researcher might hypothesize that as reported encounters with other individuals in a recreation setting increases, perceived crowding will increase. Using the rationale in Table 5.2b, both of these variables are continuous measures and the appropriate analysis strategy is either a correlation or a regression (chapter 16). The independent variable in these analyses would be reported encounters and the dependent variable is perceived crowding. The causal sequence of events has to occur in this order because a recreationist has to recall seeing other individuals (a belief) before the encounters can be evaluated as positive or negative (an attitude). Chapter 3 explains this relationship in greater detail. As will be demonstrated in future chapters, a correlation analysis and a regression will yield identical answers in this situation. In other words, the correlation coefficient will equal the standardized regression coefficient when there is only one independent and one dependent variable.

Other Examples. The other analysis techniques outlined in Table 5.3 are further variations on the examples already presented. For example, a regression analysis can include more than one continuous independent variable (see Donnelly & Vaske, 1995, chapter 4). In dummy variable regression, the dependent variable is continuous (similar to regression), and the independent variable is dichotomous. In logistic regression and discriminant analysis (chapter 17), the dependent measure is typically dichotomous and the independent variables are dichotomous or continuous. With log linear analysis, the variables are dichotomous or categorical, similar to a chi-square analysis.

In Sum: Guidelines for Selecting an Appropriate Analysis Strategy

Table 5.3 provides the basic foundation for the analyses throughout this book. Many of the remaining chapters simply detail the specifics of each analysis. A few summary points, however, should be noted. First, level of measurement influences a researcher's choice of analysis. Second, although statistics books discuss the analysis techniques in separate chapters, the techniques are related to each other (e.g., one-way ANOVA is an extension of an independent sample *t*-test; *n*-way ANOVA is an extension of one-way ANOVA; repeated measures ANOVA is an extension of paired sample *t*-tests; regression is an extension of correlations). Third, thirteen analysis strategies are highlighted in Table 5.3, but there are only three test statistics (i.e., χ^2, t, F) associated with these statistical procedures.

Chapter Summary

Stevens's (1951) influential paper on the relationship between scales of measurement (i.e., nominal, ordinal, interval, ratio) and appropriate statistics has been widely accepted and has served as the foundation for statistical programs designed to assist in the selection of data analysis methods. The Statistical Package for the Social Sciences (SPSS), for example, uses three terms (i.e., nominal, ordinal, and scale) when discussing levels of measurement. Not all statisticians, however, agree about the utility of using Stevens's traditional levels (or SPSS measurement terms) when selecting appropriate statistics.

As argued by others (Borgotta & Bohrnstedt, 1980), Stevens's idea of a relationship between measurement scales and statistical procedures seems to be based on confusion between measurement theory and statistical theory. Questions about the "interpretation of measurements" and questions about the "appropriateness of statistical procedures" lie in distinct domains. Whether a given set of data is ordinal or interval is important if researchers wish to attach meaning to the numbers; it is not important if researchers wish to estimate the probability that two sets of numbers have been drawn from a single population.

In the development of surveys, the researcher is concerned with reliability and validity. The validity aspect brings into focus the meaning underlying the numbers. For example, an average score of −2.98 on a seven-point agree-disagree scale (coded strongly agree [+3] to strongly disagree [−3]) indicates that respondents strongly disagreed with the statement. In statistical procedures and especially null hypothesis significance tests (chapter 6), differences and relatedness of numbers are of concern. The meaning of numbers does not enter the picture. In other words, "The numbers do not know where they come from" (Lord, 1953, p. 751).

In the mathematical statistics literature there are no scale requirements for the use of various statistical procedures. Savage, a mathematical statistician, notes: "I know of no reason to limit statistical procedures to those involving authentic operations consistent with the scale of observed quantities" (1957, p. 340). The only requirements for any parametric statistical procedure are that the mathematical assumptions underlying the procedure must be met or approximated. For example, with ANOVA problems, the mathematical model assumes normality, independence, and homogeneity of variance (chapter 15). As long as these three assumptions are met, the use of the F distribution is appropriate. Similar ideas apply for other procedures (e.g., correlations, regression). The empirical demonstrations noted here (e.g., Baker, Hardyck, & Petrinovich, 1966; Gaito, 1980; Havlicek & Peterson, 1977; Kempthrone, 1955) cast doubt on the assertion that parametric statistics require interval level data. Parametric procedures are, in any case, robust and yield valid conclusions even when the data are distorted (i.e., not normally distributed). If the distortions are severe, various transformations can be applied to the data (chapter 12).

In the parks, recreation, and human dimensions literature, the distinction between ordinal and interval scales is not sharp. Many summated scales (chapter 18) yield scores that, although not strictly interval, are often only mildly distorted versions of the latent underlying construct. Thus, although Stevens did a service for measurement theory in developing scale ideas, his notion has led to a misconception that has been difficult to eliminate.

This chapter introduced an alternative level of measurement hierarchy (i.e., dichotomous, categorical, continuous) that is, from the author's perspective, more useful than Stevens's or SPSS measurement terms for the selection and interpretation of statistics. A *dichotomous* variable has only two response categories (e.g., males vs. females, support vs. oppose a policy). Dichotomous variables are useful when describing a variable's frequency distribution and can be used as independent variables in *t*-tests, analysis of variance, correlation, dummy variable regression, and logistic regression. If the dependent variable is dichotomous, logistic regression or discriminant analysis is an appropriate analysis strategy.

A *categorical* variable has three or more *unordered* response categories. Religious affiliation (e.g., Catholic, Protestant, Jewish), political party affiliation (e.g., Democrat, Republican, Independent), or college major (e.g., Recreation, Sociology, Psychology) are examples of categorical variables. With this level of measurement, there are more constraints on the types of analyses that can be conducted. For example, computing an average religious affiliation does not make sense. In addition, categorical variables cannot be used as dependent variables in correlation, regression, or analysis of variance.

A *continuous* variable has an *ordered* set of response categories (typically 5 or more levels) with a distribution that is approximately normally distributed in the population sampled. Normal distributions are bell-shaped (i.e., most responses are in the middle of the scale; fewer responses occur at ends of the scale, chapters 6 and 11). Continuous variables would be labeled *interval* or *ratio* by Stevens (1951). SPSS calls continuous variables *scales*. Age, days of participation, and amount of money spent on recreation activities are examples of continuous variables. Psychological variables such as beliefs, attitudes, and norms that are measured on five-point or seven-point scales (e.g., strongly disagree to strongly agree, extremely negative to extremely positive) have more discrete response options at the observed level (i.e., the number circled on a survey), but, in theory, the respondent's answer could fall anywhere between 1 and 5 or 1 and 7. This simply means that surveys are relatively crude measurement instruments that contain measurement error. For example, the respondent's true belief about some event, situation, or action might be 1.2478, but what was recorded on the survey was the number 1. The difference between 1.2478 and 1 reflects the amount of measurement error (i.e., .2478). What's key to understand, however, is that measurement error does not imply that researchers cannot use parametric statistics.

A series of examples were presented to facilitate an understanding of what variables should be treated as dichotomous, categorical, or continuous. Guidelines were offered for selecting appropriate analysis strategies based on this measurement hierarchy. Many readers are likely to be unfamiliar with the specifics of the statistical tests (e.g., χ^2, t, F) associated with these analyses (e.g., analysis of variance, correlation, regression). Recognition of the fact that level of measurement influences the appropriate statistical procedure (Table 5.3) is a key take-home message from this chapter. Remaining chapters will fill in the details on how the different analyses are conducted.

Review Questions

1. Differentiate Stevens's four levels of measurement (i.e., nominal, ordinal, interval, ratio) and give an example of each.

2. Differentiate the three levels of measurement (i.e., dichotomous, categorical, continuous) proposed in this book. Give an example of each.

3. Explain why it is important to know the level of measurement for variables in a study.

4. Explain the concepts of *mutually exclusive* and *exhaustive* as they apply to a variable's attributes. Give examples of each.

5. Give an example of one dichotomous variable and one continuous variable. What would be the appropriate statistical test for variables measured at this level?

6. If both your dependent and independent variables are measured at the continuous level, what is an appropriate analysis strategy?

7. Give an example of a categorical level independent variable. Assume your dependent variable is number of people visiting a recreation resource. What is an appropriate analysis strategy for these two variables?

8. If students completed an exam on day one of a course (answers coded 0 through 100) and then the same students took the same exam on the last day of the class, what analysis strategy would you use to compare their answers?

9. If these same students repeated the same exam six months later, how would you analyze the data?

10. Under what circumstances could you use either a *t*-test (groups) or a one-way analysis of variance to analyze data? Give an example.

6

hypothesis testing and effect size

Social scientists are interested in answering three basic questions when examining the relationships between variables (Kirk, 2001). First, is an observed effect real or should it be attributed to chance (i.e., statistical significance)? Second, if the effect is real, how large is it (i.e., effect size)? Third, is the effect large enough to be useful (i.e., practical significance or importance)? This chapter: (a) reviews the basic steps in hypothesis testing (statistical significance), (b) highlights the major problems with the approach, and (c) discusses the strengths and weaknesses of three procedures commonly used to supplement hypothesis tests — effect sizes, confidence intervals, and odds ratios — for communicating the practical significance or importance of empirical data.

Introduction to
Inferential Statistics and Significance Testing

Researchers rarely have data on an entire population of individuals. Rather, data are collected on a sample of individuals and inferences are made about the population. Inferential statistics involve making inferences from sample statistics (e.g., the sample mean [M] and sample standard deviation [SD]) to population parameters (e.g., the population mean [μ] and population standard deviation [σ]). One method for making inferences about a population involves hypothesis testing (a.k.a. null hypothesis significance testing [NHST]).

The logic underlying hypothesis testing is at best confusing and has often been criticized (e.g., Fidler, 2002; Gliner, Morgan, Leech, & Harmon, 2001; Schmidt & Hunter, 2002). Despite these criticisms, NHST continues to be both wildly employed and misunderstood (Morgan, 2003). For example, 97% of the articles published between 1940 and 1999 in the *Journal of Applied Psychology* used NHST (Finch, Cumming, & Thompson, 2001). Before discussing the problems with NHST, it is important to understand the basic approach. Huck and Cormier (1996) outline a seven-step procedure for hypothesis testing:

1. State the null hypothesis (H_0).

2. State the alternative hypothesis (H_1).

3. Select a level of significance (*p*-value).

4. Collect and analyze the sample data (calculate the test statistic).

5. Compare the calculated test statistic value to the critical value from the theoretical distribution for a given statistic.

6. Make a decision (Reject or Fail-to-Reject H_0).

7. Estimate the strength of association (***effect size***).

The first six steps are required in *all* statistical tests (i.e., χ^2, *t*, *F*) and should be conducted in the order listed. Step seven begins to address problems associated with NHST. Huck and Cormier (1996) provide an excellent detailed discussion of all seven steps. The following highlights the major points.

The Hypotheses

Substantive hypotheses are statements involving concepts (e.g., attitudes, norms, behavior) that either predict or explain the phenomena in question (Henkel, 1976; Krueger, 2001). Examples of such *substantive hypotheses* include:

1. Individuals who are aware of the consequences of their actions (i.e., a normative concept, chapter 2) will be more likely to engage in environmentally responsible behavior.

2. Individuals who receive Firewise[1] information will be more like to perform defensible space activities around their home (e.g., clean roof gutters, prune trees, plant fire resistant plants) than individuals who do not receive Firewise information.

The first **hypothesis** makes a *prediction* about the relationship (or association) between two variables. If the two variables (i.e., awareness of consequences [AC], environmentally responsible behavior [ERB]) are measured as continuous variables, either a correlation or a regression could be used to test the hypothesis. As suggested in chapter 5 and demonstrated in chapter 16, either of these analyses would yield identical results because the there is only one independent and one dependent variable. Based on Schwarz's (1977) norm activation model, the independent variable in the regression model would be AC and the dependent variable would be ERB.

The second hypothesis attempts to *explain* why people differ in their defensible space activities. The independent variable in this example is whether the person received Firewise information (a dichotomous yes/no variable). The dependent variable might refer to a summated index of the number of defensible space activities the person does (e.g., cleaning, pruning, planting; see chapters 12 and 18 for details on computing an index). This index would be a continuous variable. In this situation, because there are only two levels to the independent variable, the researcher could use either an independent samples *t*-test or an analysis of variance to test the hypothesis. The *F*-value from the ANOVA is simply the square of the *t*-value.

---

[1] Firewise (sometimes referred to as *defensible space*) refers to activities homeowners can do to protect their homes from forest fire. Defensible space activities include behaviors such as: (a) cleaning roof surfaces and gutters, (b) reducing the density of trees within 100 feet of a home, (c) removing overhanging braches within ten feet of the roof, and (d) ensuring that trees and shrubs are at least 15 feet apart.

The appropriate analysis strategy for these *substantive* hypotheses was driven by the variables' level of measurement. In significance testing, however, what is tested is a *statistical hypothesis*. A *statistical hypothesis* is a statement about population parameters (e.g., μ [population mean], σ [population standard deviation], ρ [population correlation]). Two statements or hypotheses—the *null hypothesis* and the *alternative hypothesis* — are necessary in significance testing. The *null hypothesis* states that there is no relationship between the variables in the population. The *alternative hypothesis* states that there is a relationship in the population.

If the researcher elected to analyze the first hypothesis with a correlation, the null hypothesis would be $\rho = 0$ and the alternative hypothesis might be $\rho > 0$ (Table 6.1). The symbol ρ (rho) refers to the population correlation between the two variables. If regression analysis was used the corresponding hypotheses would be $\beta = 0$ and $\beta > 0$. Beta (β) is the symbol used in regression analyses. For either the correlation or regression analysis, the null hypothesis says that awareness of consequences does not influence a person's behavior. The alternative hypothesis implies that there is positive relationship between the variables as indicated by the "greater than" (i.e., >) symbol.

Table 6.1 Null and Alternative Hypotheses Apply to All Statistical Tests

	Possible H_0	Possible Corresponding H_1
Correlation	$\rho = 0$	$\rho > 0$
Regression	$\beta = 0$	$\beta > 0$
t-tests	$\mu_1 - \mu_2 = 0$	$\mu_1 - \mu_2 \neq 0$
Analysis of Variance	$\mu_1 = \mu_2 = \mu_3$	$\mu_1 \neq \mu_2 \neq \mu_3$

As currently formulated, the alternative hypothesis states a **directional** relationship. As one variable increases (AC), the second variable increases (ERB). The predicted positive relationship is based on norm activation theory (chapter 2). If the theory had hypothesized a negative relationship, the corresponding alternative hypotheses would be $\rho < 0$ and $\beta < 0$. Sometimes there is no theory to guide the statistical hypotheses or prior research does not exist to allow the researcher to speculate on the direction of the relationship. In these situations, a **nondirectional** alternative hypothesis should be used. The alternative hypotheses would be $\rho \neq 0$ and $\beta \neq 0$. Thus theory and prior research help determine whether the hypothesis should be directional or nondirectional.

The Firewise example null hypothesis states that the mean number of defensible activities in the population for those who received the information is equal to the mean number of defensible space activities for those who did not receive the information. Symbolically, this can be represented as $\mu_1 - \mu_2 = 0$ (or the equivalent, $\mu_1 = \mu_2$). The alternative hypothesis shown in Table 6.1 is $\mu_1 - \mu_2 \neq 0$ (i.e., a nondirectional hypothesis). If the researcher believed that receiving information has a positive influence on an individual's behavior, the alternative hypothesis would $\mu_1 > \mu_2$.

An independent samples *t*-test is appropriate in this example because there are only two levels to the independent variable (received Firewise information—yes/no). If the independent variable had three levels— (a) received and carefully read Firewise information, (b) received but did not read the information, and (c) did not receive the information — a one-way analysis of variance would be used. The null hypothesis is $\mu_1 = \mu_2 = \mu_3$ and the alternative hypothesis might be $\mu_1 \neq \mu_2 \neq \mu_3$ (Table 6.1). The researcher, however, does not necessarily have to predict that all three means will differ. One might hypothesize that merely receiving and glancing through the information (but not carefully reading the material) is enough of a stimulus to motivate people to engage in defensible space activities. The alternative hypothesis in this situation would be $\mu_1 = \mu_2 \neq \mu_3$.

The null and alternative hypotheses in these examples were based on a value of 0 (e.g., $\rho = 0$ vs. $\rho > 0$, $\mu_1 - \mu_2 = 0$ vs. $\mu_1 - \mu_2 \neq 0$). A value of 0 is common practice because researchers often do not have sufficient knowledge of the expected relationships to advance another value. In principle, however, any value could be hypothesized. For example, theory predicts that when encounters exceed a visitor's norm for seeing others, crowding will increase. A comparative analysis examining this relationship using data from 13 different studies (72 evaluation contexts) that included both high-density and low-density sites and 12 different activities, supported this hypothesis (chapter 3). Across all 72 evaluation contexts, the average correlation was .469. Future meta-analyses might use this correlation as a starting point for advancing the hypotheses (e.g., $\rho = .469$ vs. $\rho \neq .469$).[2]

Selecting a Level of Significance

NHST involves making a decision about the null hypothesis (H_0). There are two possible choices: *reject the H_0* or *fail-to-reject the H_0*. Rejecting the null hypothesis implies that a statistically significant relationship between the variables was observed. In the Firewise example, this would imply that the mean number of defensible space activities performed by individuals who received the information was greater than the mean number of defensible space activities done by individuals who did not receive the information. This decision is based on the probability value (*p-value*) that is associated with the test statistic (*t*-test in the Firewise example). An outcome that is highly unlikely under the null hypothesis (i.e., one that results in a low *p*-value) leads the researcher to reject the null hypothesis. An outcome that is more likely or probable will result in failure-to-reject the null hypothesis. In these situations, the results of the statistical test were not significant (e.g., $p > .05$).

The *p*-value is often based on the ***normal curve*** (Figure 6.1). This curve is derived from a frequency distribution that is theoretically formed by counting an "infinite" number of occurrences of a variable. The *x* axis (horizontal) is the probability level. The *y* axis is the frequency distribution. To illustrate how this distribution is formed, flip a coin ten times and count the number of "heads" that result from this first trial. Then flip the coin another ten times and record the number of heads. If this process was repeated multiple times, a frequency distribution for the number of times that the coin turned up heads out of each trial of ten could be plotted. The largest number of trials would probably show 5 heads out of 10. Very few trials would result in 0, 1, 9, or 10 heads, and the probability of these outcomes is quite low. If this experiment was repeated an infinite number of times, the frequency distribution would be a normal curve.

---

[2]   Meta-analysis is a quantitative technique that uses specific measures (e.g., an effect size) to indicate the strength of variable relationships for the studies included in the analysis. The technique emphasizes results across multiple studies as opposed to results from a single investigation (see Shelby & Vaske, 2008, for a discussion of the technique, and Shelby & Vaske, 2007, for an example).

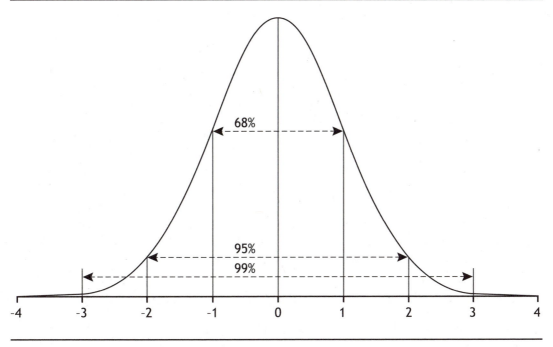

Figure 6.1   The Normal Curve

The area under the normal curve is a probability distribution equal to 1.0. Portions of this curve can be expressed as fractions of 1.0. For example, if the average weight of men living in the United States is 190 pounds, then the probability of a man in the U.S. weighing 190 pounds *or more* is .5. The probability of a male weighing over 260 or less than 120 is considerably smaller. It is important to conceptualize the normal curve as a probability distribution because researchers typically set acceptable probability levels for rejecting the null hypothesis at .05, although there is nothing sacred about this value (see Cohen, 1994; Skipper, Guenther, & Nass, 1967). Other probability values such as $p < .01$ or $p < .001$ could have been selected. One's choice of a significance level is partially determined by the sample size. For very large samples (e.g., $n > 1,000$), a researcher may elect to use $p < .001$. For samples of roughly 400 respondents, $p < .05$ or $p < .01$ are commonly reported in the literature. For smaller samples ($n < 100$), a $p < .1$ is sometimes used. As demonstrated later in this chapter, sample size influences statistical significance. Cross-tabulation analyses (i.e., chi-square, chapter 13) are especially sensitive to sample size; larger samples are more likely to result in statistically significant outcomes than smaller samples.

A normal curve can be divided into areas or units called *standard deviations* (see chapter 11 for a formal definition). Approximately 34% of the area under the normal curve is between the mean and one standard deviation above or below the mean (Figure 6.1). Including both the area to the right *and* to the left of the mean, 68% of the area under the normal curve is within one standard deviation from the mean. Two standard deviations to the left and right of the mean accounts for approximately 95% of a normal curve. Subtracting 95% from 100% equals 5% or the p-value of .05. Probabilities outside two standard deviations of the mean are considered relatively rare events.

Collection and Analysis of Data

Assume that data were collected to test each of the two hypotheses advanced earlier: (a) AC positively influences ERB, and (b) people who receive Firewire information will be more likely perform defensible space activities than those who do not receive the information. The data for each study were obtained from a survey. Chapters 7 and 8 detail the procedures for writing questions, constructing, and implementing a survey. The responses were entered into SPSS and analyzed. The first hypothesis was tested with a Pearson correlation (r) and an r of .478 was observed. The calculated F-value (test statistic) for this relationship was 15.98. As predicted, individuals who were aware of the consequences of their actions were more likely to engage in environmentally responsible behavior (i.e., a positive relationship). The second hypothesis was examined using an independent samples t-test. The resulting means were M (sample mean) = 6.34 for those who received the information and M = 1.12 for those who did not receive the information. This implies that those who received the information did, on average, six defensible space behaviors around their home. Those who did not receive the information only did, on average, one defensible space activity. The calculated t-value (test statistic) for this difference was 12.78.

Compare Calculated Test Statistic Value to Critical Value

Having computed the test statistic (***calculated value***), the next step in the hypothesis testing procedure is to compare the calculated value against the critical value. The ***critical value*** is the value of the theoretical distribution (e.g., F and t in these examples) that is found in tables at the end of statistics books or stored in the memory of statistics programs like the Statistical Package for the Social Sciences (SPSS, chapter 9). The researcher compares the calculated value against the critical value for a desired level of significance and makes a decision. In general, if the calculated value of the statistic (F or t) is relatively large, the probability or p is small (e.g., .05, .01, .001) and the null hypothesis of no difference or relationship is rejected. In other words, if the probability is *less than* the predetermined p-value (e.g., $p < .05$), the results are *statistically significant*. In the two examples here ($F = 15.98$, $t = 12.78$), the researcher would reject the null at a probability level of $p < .001$.

As demonstrated in later chapters, determining statistical significance in SPSS is easy. The output files print the actual significance or probability level (p) so the critical value does not have to be looked up in a table and compared to the calculated value; SPSS does the comparison for the researcher. Regardless of what specific test statistic is used (i.e., χ^2, t, F), if the p is small (typically less than .05), the finding is *statistically* significant, and the null hypothesis is rejected. Table 6.2 illustrates how to interpret *any* inferential test once the probability level (p-value) is known.

Inferential statistics provide a logic for making a decision (e.g., reject or fail-to-reject the null hypothesis), but the decision could still be incorrect. This occurs because the decision is based on the probability of an outcome. There are four possible decisions that can be made in NHST (Table 6.3). Two of these decisions are correct and two are incorrect (errors). The correct decisions involve: (a) not rejecting the null hypothesis when it is true (i.e., there is no difference between the samples), and (b) rejecting the null hypothesis when it is false (i.e., there is a difference). The errors occur when the researcher rejects the null hypothesis when it is true (i.e., ***Type I error***). In the Firewise example, a Type I error is saying there is a *difference* between those who received the information and those who did not, when in fact there is *no difference*. ***Type II errors*** occur when the researcher concludes that there is *no difference* between the

Table 6.2   General Guidelines for Determining Statistical Significance

Probability	Meaning	Null Hypothesis	Interpretation
1.00	$p = 1.00$	Fail-to-Reject	Not Statistically Significant (could be due to chance)
.50	$p = .50$		
.06	$p = .06$	↓	↓
.05	$p < .05$	Reject	Statistically Significant (not likely due to chance)
.01	$p = .01$		
.000	$p < .001$	↓	↓

Adapted from Morgan, Gliner, and Harmon (2006)

samples, when there really was a *difference*. For example, concluding that Firewise information made no difference in the number of defensible space activities performed, when in fact the information made a difference.

Table 6.3   Type I and Type II Errors

	Null is True (No real difference)	Null is False (Difference is real)
Reject Null	Type I error	Correct Decision
Do Not Reject Null	Correct Decision	Type II error

A key consideration in making this decision concerns the alternative hypothesis (i.e., directional vs. nondirectional). For example, the alternative hypothesis for the Firewise example predicted that individuals who received the information would be *more* likely to perform defensible space activities. If the results show the reverse of what was predicted (i.e., those receiving the information were *less* likely to perform Firewise behaviors), the researcher would fail-to-reject the null hypothesis because the findings are opposite of the prediction direction. More importantly, the agency distributing the Firewise information would need to seriously rethink its information campaign.

The directionality of the alternative hypothesis influences relational (or association) questions as well as difference questions (chapter 1). For example, the alternative hypothesis for the relationship between awareness of consequences and environmentally responsible behavior predicted a positive relationship. If a statistically significant (e.g., $p < .05$) negative relationship was observed, the researcher would fail-to-reject the null hypothesis because the findings were in the wrong direction.

Three final points about inferential statistics and hypothesis testing need to be considered. First, because any decision is based on sample data, the researcher is never totally sure that the decision reflects what is actually true in the population. Second, when the null hypothesis is not rejected, it is not actually accepted. The correct conclusion is that the null is not rejected. The word *accept* is problematic because there could be a variety of reasons (e.g., small sample size, poor conceptualization, inadequate measurement, chapter 4) why the study did not result in a rejection of the null hypothesis. Third, the logic and steps of hypothesis testing apply to all statistical tests: chi-square (χ^2), *t*-tests and *F*-tests (e.g., analysis of variance, correlation, regression).

Problems with Null Hypothesis Significance Testing

There are philosophical and practical problems associated with null hypothesis significance testing. From a philosophical perspective, NHST relies on an inappropriate combination of syllogistic reasoning and probabilistic testing (Cohen, 1994). The logic of hypothesis testing is based on a form of syllogistic reasoning called a *modus tollens* (Hofmann, 2002; Krueger, 2001). A proof using a modus tollens is obtained through denial of a consequence (Brody, 1972). Such arguments take the form: if A, then not B; B, therefore not A. For example, "If John has a statistics assignment due tomorrow, he will not go to the basketball game tonight. He went to the game, therefore, he did not have an assignment due." If John is reading this book, he knows he had an assignment due.

Although the modus tollens is used in NHST, the test is based on a probability model. The argument structure of NHST is "If A, then B is highly unlikely. B has occurred, therefore A is highly unlikely." For example, "If it were true that no systematic differences exist between the means of the populations from which the samples were obtained, then the probability that observed means would be as different as they are is less than 5 in 100." NHST does not evaluate the logical nature of an event, but rather evaluates the rareness of an event (Carver, 1978). NHST thus dilutes the logical rigor and value of the syllogism with probabilistic wording, making it impossible to prove or disapprove the null hypothesis (Cohen, 1994; Hofmann, 2002).

From a practical perspective, a major problem with NHST concerns the interpretation of statistical significance. Misinterpretation of statistical significance occurs when one assumes that a statistically significant outcome provides information about the strength of the outcome. A statistically significant outcome only indicates that it is likely that there is *some relationship between the variables*. Statistical significance, however, does not provide information about the strength of the relationship (effect size) or whether the relationship is meaningful (practical significance). Unfortunately, outcomes with lower p-values are sometimes interpreted as having stronger effects than those with higher p-values (Morgan, Gliner, & Harmon, 2006; Vaske et al., 2002). For example, an outcome of $p < .01$ is interpreted as having a stronger effect than an outcome of $p < .05$. In part, this misconception stems from the fact that smaller p-values, *given a constant sample size*, are correlated with larger effect sizes.

Recognizing the limitations of NHST, researchers working in a variety of disciplines (e.g., human dimensions, wildlife biology, education, psychology) have argued that effect sizes should always be reported following tests of significance (e.g., Anderson, Burnham, & Thompson, 2000; Gliner, Vaske, & Morgan, 2001; Johnson, 1999; Kirk, 1996; Snyder & Lawson, 1993; Thompson, 1996, 1997, 2002; Wilkinson & the Task Force on Statistical Inference, 1999). Other investigators have advocated the use of confidence intervals in place of NHST on grounds that confidence intervals provide more information than a significance test, and still include information to determine statistical significance (Borenstein, 1994; Cohen, 1994; Harlow, Mulaik, & Steiger, 1997; Kirk, 1996). Finally, some have suggested using odds ratios for reporting data because they clarify the likelihood of the relationship between the variables (Fleiss, 1981; Rosenthal, 2000).

The increasing use of effect sizes, confidence intervals, and odds ratios as methods used to replace or supplement NHST represents good statistical practice (Robinson & Levin, 1997; Thompson, 2002; Vacha-Haase, 2001). Each of these statistics, however, has strengths and weaknesses and none are necessarily synonymous with "practical significance" (Grissom & Kim, 2005). Practical significance involves a value judgment made by both the researcher and the consumer of research about the theoretical and applied implications of a study's findings. This section briefly reviews the strengths and weaknesses of effect sizes, confidence intervals, and odds ratios for addressing practical significance and offers some guidelines for their use and interpretation.

Assessing Practical Significance

The first step in assessing practical significance involves understanding the dependent measure. Continuous level dependent variables and those that have intuitive meaning typically provide information about practical significance because they are easily interpreted. Estimates of days spent hunting or fishing fall into this category because the potential scale (e.g., 0 to 365 days per year) has an intuitive meaning to both natural resource managers and researchers.

A similar intuitive understanding may hold for a survey question that asks respondents to rate their hunting/fishing experience on a scale that ranges from 0 (i.e., a letter grade of F) to 4 (for a grade of A). Such scales are commonly used in North America to assess a student's performance across all education levels (e.g., grade school, high school, colleges and universities). Thus, if hunters rate their overall experience with an average score of 2.0 (i.e., C) and anglers evaluate their experience with a mean of 3.5 (i.e., B+), the difference is interpretable to wildlife managers, researchers and the public. When measuring scales have intuitive common meanings, Kirk suggests that "confidence intervals can be used to decide whether results are trivial, useful, or important" (1996, p. 755).

Other dependent measures used in the social sciences, however, sometimes lack this intuitive appeal (depending on how the data are presented). Attitude surveys, for example, typically ask respondents to answer belief statements on a particular topic. Response scales for *each* variable may include five to seven points with each point reflecting varying degrees of intensity (e.g., strongly agree to strongly disagree). If the data are reported as percentages (e.g., 80% agree and 20% disagree with a belief statement), interpretation of the findings is likely to be straightforward. If the same variable is summarized as an average score on that item, the results may not be as obvious to all readers. For example, on a five-point scale (strongly agree [1], somewhat agree [2], neutral [3], somewhat disagree [4], strongly disagree [5]), an arithmetic mean of 3.5 may not be easily understood, but it implies that respondents are somewhere between neutral and disagreeing with the statement.

The variables of greatest interest to natural resource managers and social scientists typically involve the latent constructs underlying actual survey items (e.g., an attitude toward a given wildlife issue or a general value orientation toward wildlife, chapter 2). For example, computing a new variable that is an average of an individual's responses to a series of belief statements is a frequently used tool for representing these latent concepts (see chapters 12 and 18). When properly developed, these averaged variables have good psychometric properties (e.g., evidence for reliability and validity) and facilitate understanding the relationships among theoretical constructs (Nunnally & Bernstein, 1994). Despite these advantages, communicating the practical significance of relationships among computed variables can be confusing because the resulting scale is even further removed from the original coding (i.e., the average of multiple items each measured on 7-point agree-to-disagree scales).

Overall, decisions regarding practical usefulness are less straightforward when the analysis strategy of a measuring scale involves unfamiliar units. In such cases, it is necessary to: (a) compute an effect magnitude and a confidence interval for that magnitude[3] and (b) develop guidelines for deciding whether the effect magnitude is useful (Kirk, 1996).

Standardized Effect Size Indices

An *effect size (ES)* is defined as the strength of the relationship between the independent variable and the dependent variable. *ES* computations have been divided into two major types often referred to as the *d* family of indices and the *r* family of indices (Rosenthal, 1994). The *d* effect size indices are expressed in standard deviation units and computed by finding the difference between the means of two groups (e.g., those who voted for a particular wildlife initiative and those who voted against the issue) and then dividing by the appropriate standard deviation. Although Hedge's *g* is used as the *d* effect size indicator for the examples in this chapter, the formulas for both follow:

$$\text{Glass's } \Delta = \frac{\overline{X}_E - \overline{X}_C}{S_{control\ group}}$$

Equation 6.1

$$\text{Hedge's } g = \frac{\overline{X}_1 - \overline{X}_2}{S_{pooled}}$$

Equation 6.2

A second general family of indices is the effect size expressed as a correlation coefficient, *r* (Rosenthal, 1994; Rosenthal, Rosnow, & Rubin, 2000). Using this method, effect sizes are always less than 1.0, varying between −1.0 and +1.0. There is disagreement among researchers about whether it is best to express effect size as *r* or r^2 (eta or eta^2, see Chapter 15). It has been common to use the squared versions because they indicate the percentage of variance in the dependent variable that can be predicted from the independent variable(s). Rosenthal (1994), however, argues that these usually small percentages give you an underestimated impression of the strength or importance of the effect. Cohen (1988) and most meta-analyses also use *r* rather than r^2. Rosenthal and others (Gliner, Vaske et al., 2001; Vaske et al., 2002) argue that it is better to use *r*, eta or *R* (multiple correlation) when presenting the findings as effect sizes and to use the squared versions when discussing explained variance.

If the original means and standard deviations are not available (e.g., as might occur in a meta-analysis based on published literature), both *d* and *r* indices can be computed *indirectly* following, for example, an independent samples *t*-test.

---

[3] Computing a confidence interval around effect sizes involves the use of a noncentral *t* or *F* distribution that can be addressed with proper statistical software (see Cumming & Finch, 2001).

Hedge's $g = \dfrac{2t}{\sqrt{N}}$ for equal sample sizes

Equation 6.3

Hedge's $g = \dfrac{t\sqrt{n_1 + n_2}}{\sqrt{n_1 n_2}}$ for unequal sample sizes

Equation 6.4

$r = \sqrt{\dfrac{t^2}{t^2 + df}}$

Equation 6.5

All ES indices have advantages and disadvantages. One advantage is that effect sizes can be averaged across studies as in a meta-analysis (e.g., see Shelby & Vaske, 2007, for an example). Assuming that the magnitude of the relationship is a key factor in practical importance, effect size indices can be good indicators of practical significance (Grissom & Kim, 2005).

There are, however, at least three disadvantages of ES indices. First, an ES is an abstract statistic calculated from means and standard deviations or presented as a correlation coefficient. Whether such abstractions are comprehensible or meaningful to recreation managers and the public is open to debate. Second, an overall ES statistic may not be sufficient for describing specific group differences. As public servants, recreation managers are responsible for providing opportunities and services to all of their constituents. Information on which groups are satisfied with their experiences and which are not could have practical significance. Finally, not all similar effect sizes are equally important. A "small" effect size may have more practical significance than a "large" effect size in one instance, but not in another. Rosnow and Rosenthal (1996), for example, examined aspirin's effect on heart attacks and demonstrated that those who took aspirin had a statistically significant lower probability of having a heart attack than those in the placebo condition. Although the effect size for this relationship was small (phi = .034, see chapter 13), the practical importance was high, due to both the low cost of taking aspirin and the importance of reducing myocardial infarction. If this same effect size were found for a very expensive prescription heart medication, the practical significance might be lower.

Table 6.4 provides rough guidelines for selecting and interpreting eight effect size measures (Cohen, 1988). The first, *d*, was discussed above. The ***point biserial correlation*** (r_{pb}) is the result of an effect size, *r*, computed indirectly from a *t*-test. This r_{pb} (e.g., a dichotomous independent variable and a continuous dependent variable) is similar to the Pearson correlation, *r* (See Cohen, 1988, p. 82, for details on converting between the two measures). As applied to a 2 x 2 contingency table (i.e., two dichotomous level variables), the effect size index determined from a chi-square is ***phi (ϕ)***:

$\phi = \sqrt{\dfrac{\chi^2}{N}}$

Equation 6.6

Phi is a product moment correlation; so as an effect size, its interpretation is the same as *r* (Cohen, 1988). However, if two dichotomous distributions differ dramatically, the range of phi is restricted.

Table 6.4   Interpretation of Effect Size Indices

Test	Effect Size Index	Effect Size [1]		
		Minimal Relationship	Typical Relationship	Substantial Relationship
Cohen's *d* Measures the difference between two means (e.g., independent samples *t*-test)	*d*	.20	.50	.80
Hedge's *g* Measures the difference between two means (e.g., independent samples *t*-test)	*g*	.20	.50	.80
Glass's Δ Measures the difference between two means (e.g., independent samples *t*-test)	Δ	.20	.50	.80
Point biserial correlation r_{pb} (i.e., dichotomous independent variable and a continuous dependent variable)	r_{pb}	.100	.243	.371
Eta (*η*) Measures the association of a continuous level dependent variable and a dichotomous or categorical independent variable (e.g., analysis of variance)	*η*	.10	.243	.371
Pearson correlation Measures the relationship between two continuous variables	*r*	.10	.30	.50
Multiple correlation coefficient Measures the combined influenced of two or more continuous independent variables and a continuous dependent variable (e.g., regression analysis)	*R*	.14	.36	.51
Phi (*ϕ*) Measures the association between two dichotomous variables (e.g., a 2 x 2 crosstabulation table and a χ^2)	*ϕ*	.10	.30	.50

[1] Cohen (1988) labels these effect sizes as "small," "medium," and "large."

Cohen (1988) provides research examples of small, medium, and large effects to support the suggested *d* and *r* values in Table 6.4. Although researchers may not consider a correlation (*r*) of .5 to be very strong, Cohen argues that a *d* of .8 and an *r* of .5 (which he shows are mathematically similar) indicate "…grossly perceptible and therefore large differences" as is the "IQ difference between college graduates and persons with only a 50-50 chance of passing in an academic high school curriculum" (p. 27). Similarly, a correlation of .5 is according to Cohen (1988, p. 81) "about as high as they come" in predictive effectiveness in applied psychology.

Cohen's (1988) labels (i.e., small, medium, large), however, are relative to each other and to the behavioral sciences in general. The values shown in Table 6.4 could vary between social science disciplines (or subdisciplines), depending on the specific context of the research and the research method used (e.g., surveys, experiments). As applied to issues of practical significance, the labeling is confounded because "small" effect sizes can have, in some examples, more practical importance than "large" effect sizes in other instances (Rosnow & Rosenthal, 1996). Cohen, however, argues that there is more to be gained than lost by offering a common frame of reference for evaluating ES indices (especially when no better alternative exists for making a judgment). Vaske et al. (2002), agreed with Cohen's argument, but suggested a modification in the labels attached to his proposed categories. For example, a "small effect" might be more appropriately labeled ***minimal relationship***. A "medium effect" really reflects what is usually "typical" for behavioral science studies and methods (i.e., a ***typical relationship***). Similarly, a "large effect" might be categorized as a ***substantial relationship***. Substantial indicates that researchers and educated consumers of research would agree that there really is a difference or an association.

There are at least two advantages to the proposed labels. First, the terminology clarifies that the guidelines refer to a relationship, but not necessarily a practical relationship. Second, the labels reinforce the relative nature of the relationships. A word like "typical," for example, highlights that the relationship is common in behavioral science disciplines and methods. The values of the effect size indices (e.g., .10, .30 and .50 for r) suggested by Cohen (1988) were specific to applied psychology and may or may not be appropriate for another discipline. For example, experimental psychology, medicine, or biology could use the same labels, but have different values. Vaske et al. (2002) suggest that when applied to parks, recreation, and human dimensions research, Cohen's proposed values for these ES indices represent a reasonable frame of reference.

Statistical Significance and Effect Size

While most agree that some index of the strength of relationship should accompany reporting of statistical tests, there is some disagreement about reporting effect sizes following analyses that are not statistically significant. Robinson and Levin (1997) introduced a two-step procedure for the evaluation and reporting of empirical results: "First convince us that a finding *is not due to chance* and only then, assess how *impressive* it is (i.e., estimate its magnitude)" (1997, p. 23). In other words, only report effect sizes after a statistically significant finding. The rationale for this approach is that effect sizes reported for outcomes that are not statistically significant represent *chance deviations*, assuming adequate power of the study.[4] The role of power, however, is especially important for the reporting of effect size.

Consider a study that had a relatively small sample size and hence inadequate power to reject the null hypothesis. Some might suggest that these studies need to be replicated with larger sample sizes before reporting effect size. Even though these small sample studies may not find a statistically significant outcome, a case can be made for reporting the results and including an effect size. For example, if a meta-analysis was conducted on the topic, combining these small sample studies with other similar studies would help address overall sample size and power issues. What is persuasive about this argument is that if only statistically significant studies

---

[4] Power refers to the ability to reject a false hypothesis and is, in part, based on the study's sample size.

are reported in the literature, a meta-analysis performed on these topics will tend to overestimate the effect sizes. If all studies are reported in the literature (those with and those without statistically significant outcomes), the resulting effect sizes will more accurately reflect the true state of affairs. In survey research, the problem may not be sufficient power, but rather too much power (Cook & Campbell, 1979; Morgan, Gliner, & Harmon, 2006). Surveys with large sample sizes (e.g., $n > 1,000$) may yield statistically significant results that have little practically utility. The trend toward reporting effect sizes helps to address this issue.

Vaske et al. (2002) recommend a three-step approach for interpreting inferential statistics. First, decide whether to reject the null hypothesis. Second, if the outcome is statistically significant, determine the direction of the effect. If testing a difference between groups, state which group performed better. If testing a correlation, indicate whether the relationship is positive or negative. Finally, estimate the size of the effect. The effect size should be included in the description of results.

Gliner, Vaske et al. (2001) illustrated the relationship between statistical significance and effect size. Data for that paper were obtained from a survey designed to explore Anchorage Alaska residents' attitudes toward a potential moose hunt in Chugach State Park (Whittaker & Manfredo, 1997). The grouping variable was the respondents' reported intention to vote for or against the hunt *if* a referendum were held.[5] Results indicated that 481 would vote for the hunt, while 315 would vote against it, and 137 were unsure. The analyses focused on those who stated an intention to vote either for (60%) or against (40%) the hunt ($n = 796$).

A total of nine dependent variables were examined. Five of these variables were measured at the continuous level. Following techniques developed by Fishbein and Ajzen (1975), attitude toward the proposed hunt was measured by combining respondents' answers to a series of questions about the possible outcomes from the hunt (see Whittaker, Manfredo, Fix, Sinnott, Miller, & Vaske, 2001, for details on how this measure was computed). Two wildlife value orientation indices (i.e., rights-use, appreciative) were computed based on the procedures outlined in Fulton, Manfredo, and Lipscomb (1996). The remaining two continuous level measures included a summated index (chapter 18) of the reported number of negative experiences with moose (e.g., been in a vehicle that has hit a moose, been charged by a moose, had a pet injured or killed by a moose), and a single-item question that asked respondents how many years they had lived in Anchorage. Four dichotomous level variables were also included in the analyses: current hunting participation (yes/no), membership in hunting/fishing organizations (yes/no), membership in animal rights/welfare organizations (yes/no), and the sex of the respondent.

To illustrate the relationship between statistical significance and effect size, different sample sizes of approximately 400, 200, and 100 were selected at random from the original sample of 796 (Gliner, Vaske et al., 2001). For each of these random samples, the 60% (for) versus 40% (against) ratio was maintained. Statistical significance tests and effect size measures for the relationship between the respondents' behavioral intention to vote for or against the proposed moose hunt and the nine dependent variables are shown in Tables 6.5 and 6.6 (p. 112). Table

---

[5] The public does not vote on hunts in Alaska; a governor-appointed Board of Game, which factors public opinion into its decisions, decides these. Using a hypothetical vote to measure intentions was designed to make support or opposition to the hunt as concrete and action-oriented as possible.

6.5 presents t statistics (chapter 14), the Hedge's g and r_{pb} effect size indices, for the five continuous dependent measures and for each of the four different sample sizes (i.e., $n = 796, 398, 200, 100$). Both g and r_{pb} were computed indirectly from the t statistic. Table 6.6 presents the χ^2 (chapter 13), and the effect size ϕ for each of the four dichotomous dependent variables and the four sample sizes.

Four out of five t-tests with the original sample size ($n = 796$) yielded p-values of less than .001 (Table 6.5). These p-values imply that the probability of this outcome, assuming a true null hypothesis, is quite remote (less than five in 10,000) and unlikely to be true. According to the logic of null hypothesis significance testing (HNST), the null hypothesis should be rejected in favor of the alternative hypothesis. In this example, the effect sizes (r_{pb}) for "attitude toward the hunt" ($r_{pb} = .76$) and the "rights-use value orientation" ($r_{pb} = .62$) were substantial (Table 6.6, p. 112). Although the "appreciative value orientation" and "number of negative moose experiences" had the same small p-values ($< .001$) for the original sample size ($n = 798$), the effect sizes for these measures were minimal to typical, and "years in Anchorage" had a minimal effect.

Table 6.5   *t*-values and Effect Size Indices for Four Sample Sizes

Variable	Sample Size	*t*-value	*df*	*p-value*	Mean Difference	Hedge's *g* [1]	r_{pb} [1]
Attitude toward the hunt[2]	796	−29.39	792	< .001	−4.36	−2.13	.76
	398	−19.33	260.5	< .001	−4.29	−2.39	.77
	200	−14.64	132	< .001	−4.51	−2.55	.78
	100	−11.27	98	< .001	−4.63	−2.30	.75
Rights-use value orientation scale[3]	796	−22.36	792	< .001	−1.74	−1.62	.62
	398	−15.54	395	< .001	−1.73	−1.59	.61
	200	−10.64	198	< .001	−1.66	−1.54	.60
	100	−7.62	98	< .001	−1.67	−1.56	.61
Appreciative value orientation scale[3]	796	4.39	792	< .001	.23	.33	.16
	398	4.24	390	< .001	.30	.43	.21
	200	1.55	198	.122	.15	.22	.10
	100	1.74	98	.086	.21	.35	.17
Number of negative experiences with moose	796	−3.45	794	< .001	−.26	.23	.13
	398	−3.54	381	< .001	−.37	−.36	.18
	200	−1.44	198	.152	−.21	−.21	.10
	100	−1.59	98	.116	−.35	−.32	.16
Years in Anchorage	796	−2.41	755	.016	−2.20	−.13	.09
	398	−0.67	381	.500	−0.92	−.07	.03
	200	−1.50	184	.135	−2.59	−.22	.11
	100	−0.91	90	.365	−2.29	−.19	.10

[1.] Effect sizes *g* and *r* computed indirectly from the *t*-test when Levene's test for homogeneity of variance was significant.

[2.] See Whittaker et al. (2001) for details on how this variable was computed.

[3.] See Fulton, Manfredo, and Lipscomb (1996) for details on how these variables were computed.

Table 6.5 also shows that the t-values decreased in size as the sample size was systematically reduced. The first two variables (i.e., "attitude toward the hunt" and the "rights-use value orientation" indices) maintained statistical significance ($p < .001$) regardless of the reduction in sample size. The "appreciative value orientation" and "number of negative experiences with moose," however, were not statistically significant ($p > .05$) for sample sizes less than 400. The "years living in Anchorage" variable was statistically significant only for the largest ($n = 796$) sample size. The larger sample sizes were thus more likely to produce statistically significant results.

On the other hand, across all four sample sizes examined here, the effect sizes were statistically equivalent for each of the five variables analyzed in Table 6.5. A series of pairwise Fisher z transformation comparisons indicated that there were no statistical differences (at $p < .05$) between the effect size (r_{pb}) indices regardless of sample size.[6] Thus, *even though the t-value decreased and p-value increased as the sample size decreased, the effect size remained statistically stable.*

Table 6.6 shows the χ^2 values, p-values, and effect size indices (ϕ), for the four dichotomous dependent variables. For three of these variables (i.e., current hunting participation, membership in hunting or fishing organization, and respondents' sex), as the sample size decreased, the χ^2 values decreased, and the p-value increased.[7] At the same time, there was no statistical change in the effect sizes, which remained stable based on the Fisher z comparisons. Sample size, which directly influences p-values, was independent of effect size.

Table 6.6   Chi-square Statistics and Effect Size Indices for Four Sample Sizes

Variable [1]	Sample Size	x^2	df	p-value	Effect Size (ϕ)
Do you hunt?	796	120.39	1	<.001	.44
	398	49.93	1	<.001	.40
	200	43.64	1	<.001	.54
	100	26.79	1	<.001	.61
Member of hunting or fishing organization	796	27.63	1	<.001	.19
	398	16.24	1	<.001	.20
	200	8.23	1	<.004	.22
	100	4.31	1	<.038	.25
Member of animal rights or welfare organization	796	4.52	1	<.033	−.08
	398	0.21	1	.651	−.04
	200	4.05	1	.044	−.17
	100	3.69	1	.055	−.25
Respondents' sex	796	36.94	1	<.001	−.22
	398	24.13	1	<.001	−.25
	200	12.24	1	<.001	−.26
	100	7.03	1	.008	−.29

[1.]   All variables were dichotomous variables (Yes/No, Male/Female).

[6]   Fisher (1921) developed a transformation now called "Fisher's z transformation" that converts Pearson's r to the normally distributed variable z. Fisher's z has two important characteristics: (a) it is normally distributed and (b) it has a known standard error. The transformation is used for computing confidence intervals on Pearson's correlation and for confidence intervals on the difference between correlations.

[7]   The one exception to this general pattern was the finding for the "member of animal rights or welfare organization" ($n = 398$). This result can be attributed to the random selection process because in the sample of 398, an extremely small number of respondents ($n = 2$) belonged to these organizations.

Taken together, these findings reinforce the importance of reporting both probability levels and effect sizes. Reducing the sample size resulted in smaller *t*-values and larger *p*-values, yet the effect sizes were basically not effected. The findings from the Fisher *z* transformation showing no statistically significant differences among all pairs of effect sizes provides further evidence that sample size and effect size are independent from each other. Communicating the practical significance of this relationship to nonstatisticians, however, might be problematic because the interpretation of a result computed from the continuous-level attitude variable may not necessarily be obvious. For example, this scale ranged from –9 "strong negative attitude" to +9 "strong positive attitude," the interpretation of a mean of 1.23 may not be clear.

Confidence Intervals

Confidence intervals provide a method for estimating population values from sample statistics. A difference between the means of two comparison groups (such as for a hunt vs. against a hunt), for example, represents a difference between two *sample* means. A practical concern is how close the difference is between the two sample means to the difference between the population means. A **confidence interval** is a range of scores on the dependent variable that should contain the true population difference between means. Because a researcher cannot be totally certain that the range of values includes the population parameter, calculation of the confidence interval begins by deciding on the level of risk one is willing to take of stating that the parameter is somewhere in the interval when in fact it is not. If a researcher is willing to accept being wrong 5% of the time, the confidence interval is 95%.

Confidence intervals often provide more practical information than NHST. To illustrate, consider the Anchorage data (Whittaker & Manfredo, 1997; Gliner, Vaske et al., 2001). In the traditional NHST model, a null hypothesis of no difference would be established (i.e., attitude toward the hunt will *not* influence a decision to vote for or against the hunt). It should be noted that one of the criticisms of NHST is that a null hypothesis of no difference is always false and that its rejection is merely dependent upon a large enough sample. Assuming a *p*-value of .05 with 794 degrees of freedom in this example, the critical value of a two-tailed *t* is approximately 1.96 (chapter 14). If the *t*-value exceeds the critical value, the null hypothesis of no difference is rejected in favor of an alternative hypothesis.

The average score on the attitude measure for those who said they would vote "for" the hunt was 2.34 (a positive attitude), while the mean score for those who intended to vote "against" the hunt was –2.02 (a negative attitude), producing a difference between the means of 4.36. The computed *t*-value for this relationship was 29.26 (*p* < .001). Confidence intervals are based on the same information used to obtain a *t*-value, but are expressed differently. In this example:

$$t = \frac{\text{difference between means} - \text{null}}{\text{estimated standard error}} \qquad \text{Equation 6.7}$$

$$t = \frac{4.36 - 0}{.149} = 29.26$$

CI = differences between means – null $\pm$ Critical value * Estimated standard error
CI = (4.36 – 0) $\pm$ 1.96 (.149)
CI = 4.07 to 4.65

This statistically significant finding is consistent with what attitude-behavior theory would predict (chapter 2), but does the confidence interval improve our understanding of practical significance? The answer is a "qualified yes." The lower bound (4.07) indicates that it is likely that there is at least a 4-point difference between the means. The difference between the upper and lower bounds of this confidence interval is .58; approximately half a point on a scale that ranges from –9 to +9. When the lower bound is not close to zero and when the interval (4.07 to 4.65) is small, researchers and practitioners can feel more confident that the result is useful for decision making. Conversely, if the interval is large, researchers and practitioners must be more cautious in their interpretation of the data.

The practical significance of the findings is further enhanced because confidence intervals explicitly require researchers and managers to critically examine the measurement scale. Although those who intended to vote against the hunt had a negative attitude and those voting for the hunt had a positive attitude, neither of the means (i.e., –2.02 vs. 2.34, respectively) was on the far end of the scale (i.e., –9 to +9). This suggests that it might be possible to persuade (e.g., through media campaigns or education programs) Anchorage residents with a negative attitude to shift their feelings about the hunt. Whether such persuasion techniques are appropriate for wildlife agencies is open to debate (see, for example, the Special Issue on Advocacy in *Human Dimensions of Wildlife,* 6(1), 2001); the reason for the "qualified yes" mentioned above. Practical significance includes a judgment about the political consequences of any decision. From a statistical perspective, however, confidence intervals provide information about the precision of a given numerical value from a sample and thus are likely to be important to practitioners.

If confidence intervals provide more information than tests of significance, why aren't they used more frequently? The answer lies in the disadvantages of the approach. First, when the dependent measure is not in easily interpretable units (e.g., a computed variable ranging from –9 to +9), reporting a confidence interval does not facilitate interpretation. When the dependent variable is continuous (e.g., days of participation in an activity), confidence intervals are more intuitive. Second, confidence intervals in the social sciences have been embarrassingly large (Cohen, 1994). Large confidence intervals make conclusions more tentative and weaken the practical significance of the findings. Third, because the same information is used to compute a confidence interval and a *t*-test, both suffer from the same weakness. Setting a significance level of .05 for a *t*-test is no different than an arbitrarily established 95% confidence interval. "The major scientific disadvantage of both methods is that their significance is merely an inference derived from principles of mathematical probability, not an evaluation of substantive importance for the 'big' or 'small' magnitude of the observed distinction" (Feinstein, 1998, p. 355).

Odds Ratios

When both the independent and dependent variables are dichotomous (as opposed to continuous), ***odds ratios*** offer a useful approach for evaluating practical importance. To illustrate, consider three examples from the Anchorage data (Whittaker & Manfredo, 1997; Gliner, Vaske et al., 2001) that demonstrate the relationship between statistical significance, effect size, and odds ratios.

Table 6.7 shows three 2 x 2 contingency tables. The upper part of this table examines the relationship between "voting intention" (for or against the hunt) and "hunting participation" (hunter or nonhunter). For this sample (*n* = 796), 85% of the hunters and 41% of the nonhunters would vote for the hunt. The calculated χ^2 of 120.39 was statistically significant ($p < .001$) and the effect size ϕ was .44 (Gliner, Vaske et al., 2001), suggesting a "typical" to "substantial" relationship between hunting and voting for the hunt. Computing an odds ratio for this relationship provides a practical measure of how much of the vote for the hunt was influenced by whether or not the respondent was a hunter.

Table 6.7   Voting Intentions by Hunting Participation, Respondents' Sex, and Attitude toward the Hunt

	Voting Intention[1]		Estimated odds per level of independent variable	Overall Odds Ratio	Effect Size ϕ	*p*-value
	For hunt	Against hunt				
Hunting participation				8.35	.44	<.001
Hunter	85%	15%	5.67			
	(210)	(37)				
Nonhunter	41%	59%	.68			
	(157)	(230)				
Respondents' sex				2.86	−.22	<.001
Males	72%	28%	2.57			
	(367)	(143)				
Females	47%	53%	.90			
	(151)	(167)				
Attitude toward hunt[2]				48.22	.74	<.001
Positive	90%	10%	8.68			
	(50)	(434)				
Negative	15%	85%	.18			
	(263)	(47)				

[1].   Numbers in parentheses are frequency counts.
[2].   For these analyses, the attitude variable was recoded as a dichotomous variable (−9 thru −.01 = −1 [negative attitude], .00 thru +9 = 1 [positive attitude]).

The odds ratio is defined as the ratio of hunters voting for the hunt (cell A) to hunters voting against the hunt (cell B) divided by the ratio of nonhunters voting for the hunt (cell C) to nonhunters voting against the hunt (cell D):

	Voting Intention	
Hunting participation	For hunt	Against hunt
Hunter	A	B
Nonhunter	C	D

More formally, the equation for an odds ratio is:

$$\text{odds ratio} = \frac{A/B}{C/D}$$

Equation 6.8

A computational shortcut is to divide the cross products:

$$\text{odds ratio} = \frac{AD}{BC}$$

Equation 6.9

For those who hunt, the ratio is 5.67 (Table 6.7). In other words, for those who hunt, for every person who voted against the hunt, 5.67 persons voted for the hunt. For those who do not hunt, only .68 persons voted for the hunt. Dividing the ratio of those who hunt by the ratio of those who do not hunt yields an overall odds ratio of 8.35. The interpretation is that hunters are over 8 times more likely to vote for the hunt than nonhunters. The advantage of this approach is that the findings are expressed in terms that managers and the public can understand (i.e., practical significance).

The middle of Table 6.6 considers the relationship between sex and voting intentions. The chi-square was statistically significant ($\chi^2 = 36.94$, $p < .001$), and the effect size ϕ was .22 (Gliner, Vaske et al., 2001), suggesting a "minimal" to "typical" relationship between sex and voting for the hunt. The overall odds ratio was 2.86, indicating that males were almost three times as likely to vote for the hunt when compared to females. Odds ratios of three or greater have been suggested by some to be worthy of attention, at least within the context of epidemiology (Kraemer, 1992), and thus, may have practical significance.

Taken together, these findings illustrate that odds ratios represent an easy way to index practical significance. There are, however, two disadvantages to odds ratios. First, the approach only applies to comparisons of dichotomous variables. A continuous level measure (e.g., the attitude scale in this chapter) could be collapsed into a dummy variable (i.e., positive vs. negative attitude toward the hunt). The odds ratio results for this dichotomized attitude measure are shown in the lower portion of Table 6.6. For those with a positive attitude toward the hunt, the ratio is 8.68. In other words, for those with a positive attitude, for every person who voted against the hunt, 8.68 persons voted for the hunt. For those with a negative attitude, only .18 persons voted for the hunt. Dividing the ratio of those with a positive attitude by the ratio of those with a negative attitude yields an overall odds ratio of 48.22. This means that people with a positive attitude were 48 times more like to vote for the hunt than those with a negative attitude. These findings reinforce the effect size ($r = .76$) and confidence interval (4.07 to 4.65) approaches by demonstrating the substantial influence attitudes can have on behavior.

There is, however, a cautionary note to this procedure. Dichotomization of one of two continuous variables results in a reduction in explained or predicted variance (r^2; one-fifth to two-thirds) and an associated loss of sample power (one-third to two-thirds; Cohen, 1983, p. 253). Such a price is not trivial and dichotomization should not be adopted blindly.

A second disadvantage of odds ratios is that there is no upper limit and ratios increase more rapidly than corresponding effect sizes (see, for example, the three examples in Table 6.7). When there are only a few cases in one cell relative to the other three cells in the matrix, the odds ratio may become quite large (infinity if there is an empty cell). In these cases, one should be cautious when making an interpretation.

Chapter Summary

This chapter outlined the logic of null hypothesis significance testing (NHST). Following Huck and Cormier (1996), a seven-step process was described. These steps include:

1. State the null hypothesis (H_0).

2. State the alternative hypothesis (H_1).

3. Select a level of significance (p-value).

4. Collect and analyze the sample data (calculate the test statistic).

5. Compare the calculated test statistic value to the critical value from the theoretical distribution for a given statistic.

6. Make a decision (Reject or Fail-to-Reject H_0).

7. Estimate the strength of association (*effect size*).

The first six steps are required in *all* statistical tests (i.e., χ^2, t, F) and should be conducted in the order listed. Step seven begins to address problems associated with NHST.

The major problem with NHST is that the procedure does not tell researchers and practitioners what they want to know (Kirk, 1996). "In scientific inference, what we want to know is the probability that the null hypothesis (H_0) is true given that we have obtained a set of data (D); that is, $p(H_0|D)$. What null hypothesis significance testing tells us is the probability of obtaining these data or more extreme data if the null hypothesis is true, $p(D|H_0)$" (Kirk, 1996, p. 747). Controversy over the continued use of NHST has generated considerable debate (Harlow, Mulaik, & Steiger, 1997). Effect sizes, confidence intervals and odds ratios have all been suggested as methods to replace or supplement tests of significance.

This chapter reiterates the value of using at least one of these methods when presenting scientific data. None of the approaches, however, is a direct index of practical significance. For example, effect sizes offer a standardized estimate of the magnitude of variable relationships, and therefore, comparisons on different variables in the same study or across different studies are meaningful. Effect sizes, however, (a) are abstract statistics, (b) may not be sufficient for describing variations between different groups of interest to practitioners, and (c) do not differentiate when relationships of similar magnitude have "more" or "less" practical significance due to the cost of implementation or political constraints.

Confidence intervals can provide more practical information than NHST by highlighting the lower and upper bounds of what the true value of a parameter might be. There are, however, disadvantages to confidence intervals. First, unless the measuring scale values are familiar, confidence limits may not facilitate interpretation of the findings. Kirk (1996) suggests reporting confidence intervals about a point estimate for familiar measures and reporting effect sizes for unfamiliar measures. Second, confidence limits in the social sciences are often embarrassingly large; thus, weakening the practical significance of the findings (Cohen, 1994). Third, the arbitrary selection of a 95% confidence interval is no different than the arbitrary selection of a significance level in NHST (Feinstein, 1998).

Odds ratios provide a practical indication of the likelihood of the relationship between the variables by expressing the finding in terminology that is easily understandable to researchers and managers. They are, however, limited to dichotomous variables and converting continuous measures to dichotomous (i.e., dummy) variables results in a substantial loss of predicted variance and sample power (Cohen, 1983). Furthermore, odds ratios do not have an upper limit and grow rapidly when there are relatively few cases in one cell. Thus, the pubic and managers could be overly impressed with big ratios.

By highlighting the advantages and disadvantages of effect sizes, confidence intervals and odds ratios, the goal is not to discourage their use. Rather, the intent is to emphasize that no one single statistic will be appropriate for describing the strength of variable relationships or evaluating the practical significance of empirical findings. Moreover, researchers could present two or all three methods (i.e., effect sizes, confidence intervals, odds ratios) when attempting to communicate the practical significance of the data.

The same logic applies to Cohen's (1988) guidelines (i.e., small, medium, large) for interpreting effect sizes. The labels (i.e., minimal, typical, and substantial relationships) for Cohen's (1988) conventions represent an attempt to (a) more clearly differentiate statistical significance from practical significance, and (b) highlight that the relationships are relative to a discipline, study context and/or method. What constitutes a large effect (i.e., narrow confidence interval or large odds ratio) in one context or study may not apply to another discipline or study. Furthermore, practical significance must always involve a value judgment made by both the researcher and the consumer of research about the theoretical and applied implications of a study's findings.

Although this chapter focused on statistical implications, it is equally important to consider the theoretical and practical importance of the examples presented. The data reported here are consistent with the predictions from attitude theory and the value-attitude-behavior cognitive hierarchy (chapter 2). The relationship between attitude toward the hunt and the respondent's voting intention was stronger than the association for either of the two value orientations (rights-use or appreciative). Of these two value orientations, the effect size for rights-use was approximately four times larger than that observed for appreciative; a finding that would not have been apparent if only *p*-values had been considered for the largest two sample sizes. In addition, the psychological variables (i.e., attitude and rights-use) consistently had a stronger relationship to the behavioral intention than any of the demographic indicators (i.e., years living in Anchorage, hunting participation, organizational memberships, or sex); findings that are consistent with prior theorizing and research (i.e., predictive potential, chapter 4).

Review Questions

1. Discuss three basic questions when examining the relationships among variables.

2. List the seven steps involved in hypothesis testing.

3. Define *hypothesis* and give an example.

4. Explain the distinction between a *substantive* and a *statistical* hypothesis.

5. What is the difference between a *null hypothesis* and an *alternative hypothesis*? Give an example of each type of hypothesis.

6. Why are null and alternative hypotheses commonly based on a value of 0? Give an example of when another value might by specified.

7. What is the difference between a *directional* and *nondirectional* alternative hypothesis? Give an example of a directional and an example of a nondirectional alternative hypothesis.

8. What is the difference between the *calculated value* (i.e., test statistic) and the *critical value*?

9. If you found a correlation of $-.60$, $p < .049$ between reported contacts and crowding, would you reject or fail-to-reject the null hypothesis?

10. If the calculated value of a chi-square is 15.34 and the critical value of the chi-square is 10.83, do you reject or fail-to-reject the null hypothesis?

11. What two choices does a researcher have in making a decision about the null hypothesis? What is this decision based on?

12. Why is the direction of the alternative hypothesis (i.e., directional vs. nondirectional) key to making a decision about the null hypothesis?

13. How does a researcher decide what probability value to use in significance testing?

14. Explain the difference between a Type I and a Type II error. Give an example of each.

15. Explain the statement: "When the null hypothesis is not rejected, it is actually not accepted."

16. What does a *p*-value tell you?

17. Describe two major problems with null hypothesis significance tests.

18. List three statistics that are commonly used to supplement hypothesis tests.

19. Define *effect size*. What are the advantages and disadvantages of effect sizes?

20. What are the advantages of using the labels—minimal, typical, and substantial—for describing effect sizes?

21. Would a correlation of .55 be considered a *minimal*, *typical*, or *substantial* effect size?

22. Define *confidence interval*. What are the advantages and disadvantages of confidence intervals?

23. Define *odds ratio*. What are the of advantages and disadvantages odds ratios?

24. What is the recommended three-step approach for interpreting inferential statistics?

7

writing and constructing surveys[1]

It is common to open a newspaper or turn on the television and see results of public opinion surveys asking people about such things as who they would vote for in the next election, how important they consider the environment, or whether they approve of current political decisions. Private companies, governments, universities, and other organizations depend on surveys to gather information about the public and other interest groups. Simply defined, survey research involves administrating questionnaires to a sample of respondents selected from a particular population. The term *survey* implies that data have been gathered using some form of question-naire administered to a sample of individuals (Mitra & Lankford, 1999). A sample should be selected in such a way that it represents the entire population of interest and that observations from the sample can be generalized to the population. This chapter discusses: (a) advantages, disadvantages, and guidelines for conducting different types of surveys; and (b) guidelines for writing survey questions and constructing questionnaires. Chapter 8 provides details regarding sampling procedures and implementing surveys.

Advantages of Survey Research

A fundamental principle of survey research is to use surveys in a scientific way at a reasonable cost to realize benefits of interviewing a representative sample instead of the entire population. There are advantages of this methodology. First, survey research is *useful for describing characteristics of a larger population*. If selected appropriately, a sample of approximately 400 individuals can provide relatively accurate information about a population of one billion people (Salant & Dillman, 1994). Procedures for selecting a sample of people and making accurate population estimates based on sample data are discussed in chapter 8.

Second, surveys *use consistent or standardized questions, so comparisons among groups can be facilitated*. Recent research at Colorado State University, for example, has compared public value orientations toward wildlife in 19 western states (Teel, Dayer, Manfredo, & Bright, 2005), and hunters' responses to chronic wasting disease (CWD) in eight states

---

[1] This chapter was coauthored with Dr. Mark D. Needham, Oregon State University.

(Needham, Vaske, & Manfredo, 2006). These large-scale survey research projects allow for statistical comparisons among residents of different states and other geographical areas.

Third, survey research allows for *large sample sizes that can be obtained in a relatively short period of time*. The sample for the wildlife value orientations study, for example, included over 12,000 mail survey respondents and had a telephone nonresponse survey of 7,600 people to test for differences between mail survey respondents and nonrespondents (Teel et al., 2005). The regional mail survey of hunters' responses to CWD generated almost 10,000 completed questionnaires in just over one month (Needham et al., 2006).

Fourth, *numerous questions can be asked in a single survey*. Given the complexities of many human dimensions topics, multiple questions are often necessary to understand concepts under investigation and can improve the reliability and validity of the measuring instrument. Reliability and validity are discussed in chapters 4 and 18.

Disadvantages of Survey Research

There are, however, some disadvantages of survey research. Survey research, for example, requires that *all questions in a questionnaire must be understandable to all potential respondents*. Researchers should never assume that all respondents will have a high level of reading capability and comprehension or a full understanding of topics being investigated. To illustrate, it would be imprudent to ask the general public a specific question such as "Do you support the Division of Aquatic Resources' policy regarding angling for pelagic fish?" First, not all people will know who the Division of Aquatic Resources is or what their mandate involves. Second, few people other than perhaps some anglers and interested nonanglers will understand specific details and guidelines stipulated in the policy to allow for an informed response. Third, people without a scientific background may not know what "pelagic" means. It is important to ensure that all questions are easy to understand and targeted to the appropriate audience.

Another disadvantage of survey methodology is that *questionnaires are often not flexible*. Mail surveys, for example, cannot be changed once they have been written, printed, and administered. This disadvantage forces researchers to consider several important questions before proceeding with survey implementation, including:

- Do the questions address project objectives and/or hypotheses?

- Are there enough questions to test validity and reliability of concepts examined?

- Has the appropriate literature been examined to inform questions and response scales?

- Are the questions easy to understand for all potential respondents so that people in the sample are able to respond willingly and accurately?

- Is the questionnaire too long?

- Is the layout of the questionnaire attractive, professional, and easy to follow?

- Are the questions grouped into logical sections?

A third disadvantage of survey research is that it can *sometimes seem artificial to respondents*. Some surveys focusing on public willingness to pay or behavior in response to hypothetical conditions may fit into this category. Such hypothetical scenarios may seem artificial to some respondents who have little or no past experience with the topic.

Survey research also *may not always provide data that is within the context of social life*. A few belief statements measured on seven-point scales, for example, may not be adequate to capture the complexity of specific emotions felt after a spouse or child passes away. In these situations, other methodologies may be more useful for addressing project objectives. Alternative data collection techniques include:

- *Document analysis* includes historical or archival analysis, literature reviews, diary methods, and analysis of existing or secondary data such as content or meta-analyses.

- *In-depth interviewing* includes unstructured and semi-structured interviews often followed by qualitative techniques such as ethnographic or content analyses.

- *Participant observation* includes systematic observations and recordings of phenomena such as when a researcher becomes a participant-observer.

- *Experiments* include true or quasi design experiments where participants are assigned to treatment or control groups and assessed via observation or standardized scales.

- *Group techniques* include focus groups, Delphi methodologies, Q-methodologies, and nominal group techniques.

Some of these methodologies are briefly discussed in chapter 1. Given that the focus here is on survey methodology and analysis, however, detailed discussion of these other quantitative and qualitative methodologies are beyond the focus of this book. There are many excellent texts and journal articles examining these alternative methodological techniques.

Things to Consider Before Administering a Survey

Some people believe that designing and implementing a survey is a simple task of quickly writing a few questions and then immediately asking a few people to respond. These people are mistaken. There are several broad steps that should be followed to ensure that a survey is conducted in a scientifically rigorous manner and results are representative of and generalizable to the population of interest. At a minimum, the following steps should be followed in order when designing and implementing a survey:

1. Identify the problem, objectives, and/or hypotheses that the project is trying to solve and information needs for addressing these issues.

2. Review the relevant literature and identify knowledge gaps (see chapters 2 and 3).

3. Decide what should be included in the questionnaire.

4. Select the most appropriate type of survey method for the project.

5. Develop a first draft of the questionnaire.

6. Ask experts to review the questionnaire and revise accordingly based on input.

7. Pretest the questionnaire and revise accordingly based on pretest results.

8. Establish procedures for coding responses, entering data, and analyzing data.

9. Administer the final questionnaire.

10. Conduct a nonresponse bias check if the response rate is lower than desired.

11. Enter and analyze responses; report findings.

This chapter provides an overview of the first five steps. The remaining steps are discussed in chapter 8 and in subsequent chapters of this book.

What Information Should Be Included?

Before deciding on the type of survey to administer and the mechanics of constructing and implementing a survey, it is important to ask a couple of seemingly simple questions: (a) *What problem is this project trying to solve?* and (b) *What new information is needed to solve this problem* (Salant & Dillman, 1994)? If questions are irrelevant for most respondents, do not provide useful information, and/or fail to address project objectives or hypotheses, the survey is likely to be a waste of financial resources, time, and personnel.

Human dimensions research projects typically try to address specific questions or hypotheses to improve understanding about a particular natural resource concept, theory, or problem. It is important to be specific about what the concept, theory, or problem is, why it is important, and what research has already attempted to address the same or a similar issue. Deciding what information the survey should cover seems like a trivial task, but many researchers struggle with this early stage because the focus of a project may be vague, biased, and/or not critical (Salant & Dillman, 1994). A research question such as "How do recreationists' feel about Carter Lake?" for example, is *vague*. More specific questions such as "To what extent are boaters satisfied with boat access at Carter Lake?" "How crowded do hikers feel on the trail around Carter Lake?" and "Do anglers support or oppose the new catch-and-release policy at Carter Lake?" are more specific and provide clearer direction for developing questions and response scales in a questionnaire.

Bias can be introduced even before a single questionnaire has been administered. Writing leading or loaded questions (discussed later in this chapter) and selecting nonrandom samples of participants because their responses align with current policy decisions (see chapter 8) are examples of bias in survey research. Researchers must continually strive to design, implement, and report survey findings objectively if results are to be meaningful and scientifically valid.

Many surveys contain *questions that are peripheral or irrelevant* to project objectives or hypotheses. Although there are many interesting questions about a topic that could be asked, it is important to ensure that every question has a purpose and addresses a specific research objective or hypothesis. It is critical to separate "nice to know" from "need to know" when designing questionnaires (Salant & Dillman, 1994). Long questionnaires containing interesting but nonessential items increase respondent burden, reduce overall response rates, increase question nonresponse, and yield data that are unrelated to project goals.

As discussed in chapter 1, there are approaches that allow researchers to obtain a feel for the type and range of issues that are related to project objectives and important to the population of interest. ***Elicitation surveys***, for example, include a series of open-ended questions that are administered to a small sample of people (Manfredo, 1992). ***Focus groups*** involve a moderator bringing together 6 to 12 individuals from a population of interest for direct questioning (Knap & Propst, 2001; Krueger, 1988; Merton, 1987). Both of these approaches stimulate thinking and elicit ideas on a particular subject. Small sample sizes and the open-ended nature of questioning often limit the representativeness and generalizability of findings from elicitation surveys and focus groups. Information gained from these techniques, however, can be used to develop questions that will be included in a questionnaire to be administered later to a larger sample of individuals. Table 7.1 compares and contrasts focus groups and survey research.

Table 7.1   Focus Groups Cannot Substitute for Surveys

	Focus groups	Surveys
Purpose	Stimulate thinking and elicit ideas on a subject	Determine what proportion of a predefined population has a particular attribute or opinion
Structure	Discussion of a small group led by a moderator	Mail, telephone, in-person, or electronic questionnaire completed by individuals
Capacity to generalize to larger population	No	Yes
Capacity to generate ideas or hypotheses for later testing	Yes	To some extent
Capacity to test ideas or hypotheses	To some extent	Yes
Must questions and answers be formulated ahead of time?	No, but moderator must be ready to guide discussion	Yes, except for open-ended questions

Source: Salant and Dillman (1994)

Once researchers are clear on the problem to be addressed and understand specific information needs, they need to select a particular type of survey for collecting data. When choosing between types of surveys (e.g., telephone, on-site, mail, electronic), researchers should carefully consider issues such as budget, ethics, availability of contact information for potential respondents, design and layout, completion time, and response rates. Each of these issues influences decisions about the type of survey that is most appropriate and feasible for addressing project objectives or hypotheses.

Types of Surveys and Criteria for Choosing Survey Type

There are multiple types of survey methods including mail, telephone, on-site (i.e., in-person, face-to-face), electronic (i.e., Internet, email), drop-off, and mixed mode surveys. None of these methods is inherently superior to the others; each has strengths and weaknesses that should be evaluated in the context of the specific project. Selecting a survey method requires consideration of issues such as survey length, completion time, accuracy of answers, complexity, necessary facilities (e.g., telephone lines), personnel qualifications, and availability of sample contact information (e.g., addresses, telephone numbers). Table 7.2 compares mail, telephone, on-site, and Internet surveys in terms of criteria for human dimensions research.

Table 7.2   Some Broad Criteria for Choosing a Survey Type for Parks, Recreation, and Human Dimensions of Natural Resources Research

	On-site	Mail	Telephone	Internet
Questionnaire construction and design				
Allowable length of survey (minutes to complete)	5–15	30–45	10–20	15–30
Type of questions				
Allowable complexity	Medium	High	Low	High
Success with open-ended (fill-in-the-blank) questions	Low	Medium	High	Medium
Success with screening questions	Medium	Low	High	High
Success with controlling sequence of question completion	Medium	Low	High	High
Success with avoiding item nonresponse	Medium	Low	High	High
Sensitivity to design layout	High	High	Low	Medium
Accuracy of answers				
Likelihood of interviewer distortion/bias	Medium	Low	Medium	Low
Likelihood of social desirability bias	Medium	Low	Medium	Low
Administration considerations				
Cost per completed survey [1]	High	Low	Medium	Low
Anticipated response rates				
General population	Medium	Medium	Low	Medium
Specific user group or stakeholder/interest group	High	Medium	Medium	Medium
Data collection completion time after survey is developed [2]	Medium	Slow	Fast	Fast
Control of survey once developed and administered	High	Low	High	Medium
Need for sample contact list from population	Low	High	High	Medium

[1] Cost is variable depending on circumstances. On-site surveys, for example, can be expensive if they require substantial out-of-state or international travel (e.g., air, vehicle) and accommodation, but can be conducted for a lower cost if these costs are not incurred. Costs for mail surveys can be variable depending on type of postage selected (e.g., bulk, business reply, first class, international).

[2] Completion time is variable depending on number of personnel working on survey administration.

Mail surveys require an address list of a sample from a population. Addresses may be obtained from government agencies, private firms, or another source such as an earlier on-site survey (discussed in mixed-mode surveys). If a project requires information from hunters or anglers, for example, names and addresses of potential respondents might be obtained from a wildlife agency's license sales records. Samples can also be purchased from private firms such as Survey Sampling International (SSI). Mail surveys typically involve multiple ordered mailings such as: (a) initial letter providing advance notification, (b) questionnaire packet (e.g., cover letter, questionnaire, return envelope), (c) postcard reminder to nonrespondents, and (d) additional mailings of the questionnaire packet to remaining nonrespondents (see chapter 8).

There are several strengths of mail surveys (see Dillman, 2007; Salant & Dillman, 1994). Mail surveys generally require fewer resources because personnel are not needed for talking with respondents as they are with on-site (i.e., face-to-face) and telephone surveys. Personnel also do not need as much expertise or training in communicating with people; skills mostly involve clerical tasks such as typing, sorting, stuffing envelopes, and processing incoming and outgoing mail. Compared to other survey methods, mail surveys give personnel and respondents the flexibility of making fewer immediate and high-pressure decisions. Given the lower personnel requirements, additional costs of administering and processing more mail questionnaires are lower than in-person or telephone contacts. Mail surveys are also more likely to ensure respondent anonymity and confidentiality. Respondents have more time to think about questions, which is useful particularly if the instrument contains complex questions. Finally, mail surveys are less sensitive to interviewer bias or distortion, and there is greater probability of avoiding *social desirability bias*, which occurs when respondents provide answers that are consistent with societal norms or perceived viewpoints of the interviewer (e.g., a person did not vote in the last election, but said that they did because it is the politically correct thing to do; DeMaio, 1984).

There are, however, weaknesses of mail surveys. Mail surveys are susceptible to lower response rates than on-site surveys. Fewer individuals may respond to mail surveys because people may have less incentive and a chance to examine questionnaires before deciding whether or not to answer questions. Obtaining high response rates with mail surveys requires an attractive and properly formatted questionnaire that is easy to read and free of complications (Mitra & Lankford, 1999).

Another weakness of mail surveys is that individuals without a high level of reading capability and comprehension may choose to disregard the questionnaire because they struggle reading questions, following instructions, and providing written responses. In mail surveys, researchers also have little control over what happens to the questionnaire after it is mailed, including: (a) who actually completes the questionnaire; (b) if the respondent received advice from others, which could bias answers; (c) if questions were answered in the order in which they appeared, which is important if questions build on each other; and (d) if questionnaires were completed in full or respondents overlooked sections or avoided answering boring or challenging questions (Salant & Dillman, 1994). Finally, mail surveys often require more than one mailing to achieve an appropriate response rate. Multiple mailings necessitate more money and time.

Despite these shortcomings, mail surveys continue to be popular among researchers seeking to gather information from numerous interest groups about their perceptions of various natural resource issues. Mail surveys are particularly useful for large projects in which financial and personnel resources are limited and rapid project completion is not necessary. It is important to remember, however, that mail surveys require a reasonably accurate address list of a sample from a particular population.

Telephone surveys involve selecting a sample from the telephone directory, another list, or using random number techniques. Survey questions are asked by an interviewer who records responses into a computer or onto a form. Telephone surveys can also be automated where questions are asked by a recording and responses are recorded when interviewees press numbers corresponding to their answer (i.e., Interactive Voice Response [IVR], Touch-Tone Data Entry [TDE]; see Dillman, 2007 for a discussion).

Telephone surveys are advantageous because they can rapidly generate data and results. Polling companies (e.g., Gallup, Ipsos-Reid), for example, have enough personnel to conduct public opinion polls in one or two days and report results quickly thereafter. Telephone surveys are one of the quickest methods because time is not spent waiting for the postal service to deliver questionnaires to respondents and then back to researchers, and telephone surveys do not have travel time required for completing on-site/in-person surveys (Frey, 1989; Gad, 2000).

Telephone surveys allow researchers a high degree of control over the sequence in which questions are asked, avoiding influence of others in the household, and ensuring that all questions are answered (i.e., avoid item nonresponse). These surveys also give respondents the flexibility of asking researchers for clarification if questions are confusing. Finally, telephone surveys are not as sensitive to design layout because respondents seldom see the instrument.

There are, however, weaknesses of telephone surveys. Refusals occur because people can simply hang up the telephone. Other people may use answering machines and call display technologies to screen calls; government and private "do not call" telephone lists have also been established (e.g., Crabb, 1999; Tuckel & Feinberg, 1991). If the topic being investigated is of particular interest to the sample group, however, nonresponse may be less of a problem (Dillman, 2007).

Not all people have telephones and among those who do, telephone directories used for drawing samples are often incomplete because they are out of date, do not include unlisted numbers, and often do not include cellular telephone numbers. These issues are problematic for selecting a sample where all members of a population should have an equal or known chance of selection (Salant & Dillman, 1994). Selecting random telephone numbers (i.e., *random digit dialing*) or adding a randomly chosen number to the last digit of each number in the sample (i.e., *add-a-digit dialing*) can be used to partially overcome some of these issues (see chapter 8).

Complex questions such as those involving hypothetical scenarios, visuals (e.g., maps, photographs), or ranking a long series of items are difficult to complete using telephone surveys. As a result, telephone surveys must be relatively short and simplistic for interviewers to communicate questions and for respondents to comprehend and answer in a timely manner. Telephone surveys are also susceptible to interviewer distortion and social desirability bias through leading questions, the interviewer's tone, and by what the respondent thinks the interviewer wants to hear (e.g., Gad, 2000; Mitra & Lankford, 1999; Salant & Dillman, 1994). Training of all interviewers is required before survey administration.

In the last decade, telephone surveys have received less attention in parks, recreation, and human dimensions research. This is partially attributable to the increasing complexity of methodologies used by researchers. Stated choice modeling and conjoint analysis, for example, are becoming popular for examining tradeoffs among social, environmental, and managerial attributes preferred by recreationists (e.g., Kneeshaw, Vaske, Bright, & Absher, 2004; Lawson, Roggenbuck, Hall, & Moldovanyi, 2006). Although data collected from these approaches assists managers with prioritization when faced with challenging decisions, the number and complexity of scenarios and questions required for these methodologies are arguably too complex to convey using telephone surveys.

Researchers often conduct research in diverse geographical areas (e.g., other states, countries), which necessitates long-distance costs when administering telephone surveys. If a large sample size is desired, these rates can be prohibitively costly compared to approaches such as mail and electronic surveys. Telephone surveys also require reasonably accurate lists of telephone numbers for specific samples. These lists are becoming more difficult to obtain due to cellular telephone numbers and unlisted numbers. Regardless, telephone surveys are advantageous especially when rapid turnaround is important, experienced help is available, and questions are relatively straightforward (e.g., Frey, 1989; Khurshid & Sahai, 1995).

On-site (i.e., in-person, face-to-face) surveys are useful when address or telephone lists required for mail or telephone surveys are unavailable, and for surveying people who may be unwilling or unable to respond by mail, telephone, or electronic methods. Interviewers intercept individuals in person and either: (a) read survey questions to respondents and record answers on the questionnaire form (i.e., interviewer-completed), or (b) ask respondents to immediately read and respond to questions themselves (i.e., respondent-completed). On-site surveys are common in tourism and recreation settings where lists of visitor contact information are often unavailable. Trailhead surveys, for example, are common for intercepting backcountry recreationists and obtaining completed questionnaires about issues in remote areas.

On-site surveys typically yield exceptionally high response rates because researchers can explain the rationale and importance of the survey, and ensure that responses remain anonymous and confidential. Researchers retain a high degree of control over who completes the survey and can encourage people to complete all questions (i.e., avoid item nonresponse). On-site surveys also give respondents the ability of asking researchers for clarification if questions are confusing (Groves & McGonagle, 2001).

Like telephone surveys, a major weakness of site intercept survey instruments, especially in human dimensions and recreation research, is that they cannot be too long because few people want to be disrupted for an extended period of time. By comparison, mail and some electronic surveys can be longer and more complex because respondents have the choice of completing questionnaires on their own time at one or more sittings. Most on-site surveys ask people to stop what they are doing to answer questions.

On-site surveys can be costly in terms of time and money. Although these surveys can be completed relatively quickly, they can be more expensive and less efficient than telephone and mail surveys. Time and cost to travel to the study site as well as accommodation costs at the site can increase quickly with on-site studies. This is especially true when the study site is large and potential respondents are widely scattered across the site. It makes little sense conducting an on-site survey when the target sample population is the general public in a large area (e.g., state).

Another weakness of on-site surveys is that interviewers must be trained in interpersonal communication, why the research project is being conducted, format of the questionnaire, and how to respond professionally to anticipated and unanticipated questions (Salant & Dillman, 1994). Supervisors should be present to monitor interviewers and ensure that questionnaires are being filled out completely during survey administration. Extensive training and supervisor presence can increase costs of on-site surveys. Despite these shortcomings, on-site surveys are popular because of their high response rates and ability to reach populations for which no contact list (e.g., addresses, telephone numbers) currently exists.

Electronic surveys are conducted using electronic mail (i.e., email) or websites operated by researchers or private companies (e.g., www.surveymonkey.com). *Email surveys* are relatively simplistic and are often little more than text messages (Dillman, 2007). *Internet surveys* are becoming more common because of their efficiency and dynamic construction and interaction capabilities such as pop-up instructional boxes, drop-down menus with lists of answers, seamless and invisible skip patterns, audio capabilities, animation, and video clips (Couper, Traugott, & Lamias, 2001; Dillman, 2007). Both of these electronic survey methods generally require access to a sample list of email addresses or notification of potential respondents to visit a website.

Electronic surveys can be more efficient than mail, telephone, and on-site surveys because almost no paper, postage, travel, envelope stuffing, or telephone calls are required. Electronic surveys can eliminate the need for data-entry costs because answers can be automatically transferred to an electronic database spreadsheet. Time required for survey implementation and administration can be reduced from several weeks to just a few days or hours (Dillman, 2007). Once the data collection system has been designed, costs of administering additional surveys are less than most other survey methods (Couper, 2000; Dillman, 2007; Gaede & Vaske, 1999).

There are weaknesses associated with electronic surveys. It cannot be assumed, for example, that everyone has past experience with electronic surveys. These surveys need to explain how to respond and proceed through the instrument. Issues of anonymity, security, and confidentiality of electronic responses should be addressed and communicated to respondents (Sills & Song, 2002). For example, if employees are asked by their supervisor to complete an electronic survey about a sensitive topic such as workplace discrimination, fears associated with answers being traced to email or Internet protocol (IP) addresses may inhibit responses rates.

Researchers often cannot control responses to electronic surveys. Some respondents, for example, could complete the questionnaire more than once and bias findings. It is difficult to control whether the person to whom the survey was addressed actually completed the questionnaire. This makes it challenging to generalize results to a known population. A personal identification number (PIN) or other code should be provided to limit questionnaire access to only individuals who were sampled (Couper, 2000).

Computer system issues such as screen configuration and resolution, connection speed (e.g., dial-up vs. high-speed cable), and software availability also complicate administration of electronic surveys. Surveys with large graphics and many drop-down menus and pop-up instructional boxes, for example, may take several minutes instead of a few seconds to download using older machines or Internet service providers with less capacity and capability.

A major weakness with electronic surveys is that many individuals and households do not have computers or email addresses, especially in poorer areas and developing countries. This is problematic when generalizing from surveys of the general public because there is no possibility for drawing a sample in which every individual has an equal chance of being selected (Dillman, 2007; Gaede & Vaske, 1999). This may be less of an issue for specific populations such as university personnel or government employees who generally have access to computers with Internet service. Although more people are obtaining computers every day, "email and web surveying of the general public is currently inadequate as a means of accessing random samples of defined populations of households and/or individuals" (Dillman, 2007, p. 356).

In addition to mail, telephone, on-site, and electronic surveys, there are other types of surveys that have received some attention in parks, recreation, and human dimensions research. ***Drop-off surveys***, for example, combine on-site (i.e., in-person, face-to-face) and mail surveys. Questionnaires are personally delivered to respondents who then complete the questionnaire on their own time and return it by mail or keep it until a later time when the researcher returns to collect the completed questionnaire. These surveys are useful when contact lists required for mail or telephone surveys are unavailable and the instrument is too long to complete on-site in a short period of time.

Mixed-mode surveys involve using two or more types of surveys to compensate for weaknesses of each method (e.g., Groves & Lepkowski, 1985). The most common mixed-mode approach is to use one method to obtain responses from some members of a sample, and use a second or third method to obtain responses from other members (e.g., Dillman, 2007; Schonlau, Asch, & Du, 2003). Email surveys, for example, may be followed by paper questionnaires sent to nonrespondents simply because not everyone has access to email. Another type of mixed-mode survey is to use a different method to collect panel data from the same respondents at a later time period. An initial on-site trailhead survey, for example, may ask for contact information (e.g., address, telephone number) that would allow for other methods in a follow-up mail, telephone, or electronic survey. Mixed-mode surveys may also be used to collect different types of information from the same respondents during the same data collection period.

Different Methods, Different Results

When selecting among survey methods, researchers should be aware that for some questions, certain types of surveys provide different results than other types (de Leeuw, Mellenbergh, & Hox, 1996). To illustrate, a study of visitors to Colorado State Parks used both telephone and mail surveys (Whittaker, Vaske, Donnelly, & DeRuiter, 1998). The purpose of the study was to estimate visitors' willingness to pay a fee increase to visit the parks. The primary research question was: Do income levels, past visitation experience, and willingness to pay differ between mail and telephone survey respondents? Telephone surveys were completed by 618 visitors (79% response rate); mail surveys were completed by 311 other visitors (78% response).

Results showed that past experience with Colorado State Parks (e.g., number of years visiting, number of visits per year) did not differ by survey mode, whereas reported income was slightly higher for mail survey respondents (Table 7.3, p. 132). Telephone survey participants, however, reported significantly higher willingness to pay fee increases (e.g., $4 to $6 per day, $40 to $60 per year) than mail survey respondents (Table 7.4, p. 132). Answers from mail survey participants suggested that strategic bias may have influenced their responses. ***Strategic bias*** occurs when respondents deliberately provide a lower willingness to pay response compared with their true feelings so that they do not pay a high fee once implemented (Loomis, 2004). Conversely, answers from telephone survey participants suggested that social desirability bias may have influenced responses. Given that these respondents were completing the survey by talking with interviewers on the telephone, they may have felt obliged as park visitors to pay more for their experiences and not leave interviewers with an impression that respondents were tightfisted and cheap. It is important for researchers to choose among survey methods by thinking about their strengths and weaknesses, and the potential for survey type to influence project outcomes.

Table 7.3   Differences between Mail Survey and Telephone Survey Respondents' Past Experience and Income Levels

	Survey mode [1]		*t*-value	*p*-value
	Telephone	Mail		
Years living in Colorado	26.1	26.4	0.26	.792
Years visiting Colorado State Parks	20.6	20.1	0.57	.569
Number of State Parks visited per year	9.9	9.1	1.10	.272
Income in dollars	$39,129	$44,779	3.34	.001

[1] Cell entries are means (averages).

Table 7.4   Differences between Mail Survey and Telephone Survey Respondents' Willingness to Pay to Visit Colorado State Parks

Willingness to pay	Survey mode [1]		χ^2-value	*p*-value	Effect size (ϕ)
	Telephone	Mail			
$4 per day	85	73	5.89	.015	.15
$5 per day	77	56	14.55	<.001	.22
$6 per day	67	43	15.37	<.001	.23
$40 per year	70	55	5.39	.020	.14
$50 per year	56	47	2.30	.129	.09
$60 per year	43	32	3.69	.056	.11
More on weekends	49	39	9.54	.002	.10
More for some parks	69	56	14.98	<.001	.13
More for water sites	57	52	2.33	.127	.05

[1] Cell entries are percent that said "yes" they would be willing to pay amount.

The First Draft: Writing Good Survey Questions

General Guidelines for Writing Questions

Writing good questions and constructing an attractive and professional questionnaire that is easy to follow and complete in a timely manner are not trivial tasks. The key to producing useful data is taking time to translate ideas that motivated the survey into good questions (Salant & Dillman, 1994). The following guidelines are offered for writing survey questions. These guidelines are based on various sources (e.g., Dillman, 2000, 2007; Mitra & Lankford, 1999; Salant & Dillman, 1994; Tourangeau, Rips, & Rasinski, 2000) and the authors' own research in parks, recreation, and human dimensions of natural resources.

Guideline 1:
Identify exactly what kind of information you want respondents to provide.
This should be the first step to writing survey questions. It is important to clarify what type of information is needed to meet project objectives and/or hypotheses because it is easy to ask for one type of information when a researcher really wants another. Willingness to pay for park access, for example, is one area of research in recreation management. If the goal is to find out *whether or not* people would be willing to pay, the following question may be appropriate:

> Would you be willing to pay a daily fee to visit Smith Lakes State Park? (please check one)
> ☐ No
> ☐ Yes

Alternatively, if the objective is to estimate *how much* people would be willing to pay for park access, a question such as the following may be more suitable:

> What is the maximum amount that you would be willing to pay per day to visit Smith Lakes State Park? (please write response)
>
> I would be willing to pay $ _____ per day to visit Smith Lakes State Park

Parks, recreation, and human dimensions research is often interested in measuring individuals' behavior and attitudes toward that behavior. A recent study, for example, examined residents' behavioral intentions and attitudes regarding lethal control of coyotes in the South Suburban open space area in Colorado (Vaske & Needham, 2007). To measure behavioral intentions, the following question was asked on a seven-point response scale from "extremely unlikely" to "extremely likely:"

> If you had to decide today how to solve a problem with a nuisance coyote, how likely is it that you would support lethal trapping of coyotes in South Suburban open spaces? (Please circle one number that matches your response)

This study also wanted to examine attitudes about lethal coyote control so an additional question was asked on a seven-point response scale from "extremely negative" to "extremely positive:"

> Overall, how do you feel about lethal trapping of coyotes in South Suburban open spaces? (Please circle one number that matches your response)

Information from the first question describes behavioral intentions toward lethal control of coyotes, whereas information from the second question describes how people feel about lethal control of coyotes. These are two different pieces of information measuring distinctly different concepts described in the literature and outlined in theories such as the theory of reasoned action (Ajzen & Fishbein, 1980; Fishbein & Ajzen, 1975; chapter 2).

Guideline 2:
Use fixed-scale or close-ended questions rather than open-ended questions wherever possible.

Open-ended questions do not provide choices from which to select a particular answer. Open-ended questions are easier to construct, but have several weaknesses (see Salant & Dillman, 1994 for a review). These questions, for example, require tremendous personnel time to enter into a database (e.g., as a "string" variable in SPSS), sort through responses, and code answers into categories or groups. This process takes substantially more time than if answers were specified and coded in advance. Open-ended questions can produce hundreds or even thousands of different responses depending on sample size. An open-ended question such as "Where do you live?" for example, may yield responses from different individuals such as Colorado, Larimer County, Fort Collins, and Red Feather Lakes. All of these areas could be categorized into one category labeled Colorado because Larimer County, Fort Collins, and Red Feather Lakes are all in Colorado. Categorization, however, is challenging and time-consuming, but can be made more efficient using the SPSS `Auto recode` command (Chapter 12).

Respondent burden also increases with open-ended questions, which can increase survey completion time and decrease response rates. If people are asked to write sentences about topics that they may not be interested in or familiar with, there is greater likelihood that questionnaires will be returned incomplete or answers may not provide substantive or useful information. If the general public was mailed a questionnaire asking a specific open-ended question such as "What should be done to improve habitat for the Great Grey Slug?" for example, it is likely that most people will either provide uninformed answers or not answer the question.

Open-ended questions limit the ability to measure reliability and validity of concepts examined in a questionnaire, and rarely provide information that can be compared among groups across an entire sample. Finally, some respondents may write long, detailed, and multi-part answers to a particular question, whereas others may write a brief one- or two-word reply. This presents a challenge for researchers when comparing answers.

Open-ended questions, however, are useful for elicitation surveys. Answers from an elicitation survey can be used to develop fixed-scale questions to include in a questionnaire that will be administered later to a larger sample of individuals. This is important when researchers have little prior knowledge about a topic and are unable to specify response choices. In a recent study of hunters' responses to chronic wasting disease (CWD), for example, there was limited literature and past research to help investigators understand what aspects of the disease would influence hunters to stop hunting (Needham, Vaske, & Manfredo, 2004). An elicitation survey was administered to a sample of hunters who were asked "What circumstances related to CWD would cause you to give up deer hunting?" Responses to this open-ended question showed that the most dominant responses were related to CWD prevalence and potential human health risks associated with the disease. In subsequent larger mail surveys, scenarios portrayed increasing CWD human health risks and prevalence levels among deer and elk, and hunters were asked to select from a set of fixed response options (e.g., hunt, give up).

There are other advantages of open-ended questions. These questions, for example, can be useful at the end of questionnaires to allow respondents to provide additional comments or let researchers know if anything was missing. An appropriate open-ended question at the end of a questionnaire would be "Do you have any other comments about issues discussed in this survey? If so, please write your comments below." Open-ended questions are also useful following a close-ended or fixed scale response question to ask respondents to explain, elaborate, or clarify their answer. This can provide researchers with more insight regarding answers to a particular question (Dillman, 2007; Geer, 1991). Finally, open-ended questions are useful when asking people to provide an estimate of a personal characteristic, routine behavior, or situation in which precise information is needed and can be recalled without a list or scale of answer choices (Geer, 1991). Examples where open-ended questions are useful include:

What is your age? (Please write response) _____ years old

In total, about how many years have you fished in your life? (Please write response)

Number of years _____

In what state or province do you currently live? (Please write response) _____

Taken together, open-ended questions should be used sparingly and only in certain circumstances. Close-ended questions are preferred. Different types of close-ended or fixed-scale questions include: (a) close-ended with ordered response choices, (b) close-ended with unordered response choices, and (c) partially close-ended response choices (Salant & Dillman, 1994). Questions that are ***close-ended with ordered response choices*** present response options in a particular order or gradation. These questions are easy to code and less demanding for respondents. Examples of this type of question include:

Overall, how dissatisfied or satisfied were you with your visit to Smith Lakes State Park today? (Please check one)

☐ Very Dissatisfied
☐ Somewhat Dissatisfied
☐ Neither Satisfied nor Dissatisfied
☐ Somewhat Satisfied
☐ Very Satisfied

Which of the following broad categories best describes your current approximate annual household income before taxes? (Please check one)

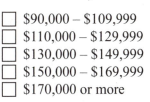

☐ Less than $10,000   ☐ $90,000 – $109,999
☐ $10,000 – $29,999   ☐ $110,000 – $129,999
☐ $30,000 – $49,999   ☐ $130,000 – $149,999
☐ $50,000 – $69,999   ☐ $150,000 – $169,999
☐ $70,000 – $89,999   ☐ $170,000 or more

To what extent do you oppose or support each of the following possible management actions at Smith Lakes State Park? (Please circle one number for each possible management action)

	Strongly Oppose	Oppose	Neither	Support	Strongly Support
Improve road access	1	2	3	4	5
Provide more parking	1	2	3	4	5
Provide more trash cans	1	2	3	4	5
Provide more toilets	1	2	3	4	5
Prohibit motorboats	1	2	3	4	5
Require dogs be kept on leash	1	2	3	4	5

Questions that are ***close-ended with unordered response choices*** are similar to those above with one exception—response choices are not in a particular order or gradation; people choose among discrete unordered response categories. With these types of response options, individuals completing the questionnaire are required to read the entire list, compare response categories, and process this information before selecting an answer. This task is progressively more challenging as more choices are added. These types of questions are also difficult for researchers who must ensure that all possible responses are provided and each category is mutually exclusive. Elicitation studies, focus groups, and pretests can help address these issues and improve response categories (see chapter 8). A *poor* close-ended question with unordered choices is:

What one type of deer hunting do you do in Arizona? (Please check one)
- [ ] Gun
- [ ] Rifle
- [ ] Archery
- [ ] Shotgun

This question is poor for three reasons. First, not all possible categories have been listed. Muzzleloading, for example, is a popular type of deer hunting, but was not included in the list. Second, categories are not mutually exclusive because "rifle" and "shotgun" are both forms of the more general "gun" hunting, which was also listed. Third, the question asks for just one type of deer hunting, but many hunters alternate between different types of hunting. For example, a bow hunter may also hunt with a shotgun for the same species. A more suitable response option is "check all that apply" instead of "check one." A *better* version of this question could be:

What types of deer hunting do you do in Arizona? (Please check all that apply)
- [ ] Gun (e.g., rifle, shotgun)
- [ ] Muzzleloading
- [ ] Archery

Questions with ***partially close-ended response choices*** offer a compromise between open-ended and close-ended questions. This type of question gives respondents flexibility to choose from a set of researcher-determined response options or create their own answers(s) by including, for example, an "other" category and asking respondents to write their answer. If the researcher has provided a relatively exhaustive list of mutually exclusive categories, few people will identify a different response, but at least they have the option of not being forced into a predefined category (Salant & Dillman, 1994). The following is an example of this type of question:

> What activities did you participate in today at this wildlife refuge? (Please check all that apply)
> ☐ Hunting
> ☐ Fishing
> ☐ Wildlife viewing
> ☐ Wildlife photography
> ☐ Other (Please write response) _____

Choosing to structure survey questions as open-ended, close-ended, or partially close-ended is never an easy decision. Each alternative has strengths and weaknesses, and should be evaluated within the context of project objectives and hypotheses, and how other studies have measured the same concepts. It is important to recognize, however, that many statistical techniques such as reliability, regression, and analysis of variance require independent and/or dependent variables to be measured on continuous scales (chapter 5). Five, seven, or nine-point close-ended ordered scales (e.g., strongly disagree [1], moderately disagree [2], slightly disagree [3], neither [4], slightly agree [5], moderately agree [6], strongly agree [7]) allow for these statistical procedures. In a recent human dimensions experiment; for example, standardized results for the same question did not differ between five and seven-point scales (e.g., slightly or strongly agree or disagree), but responses on these scales were different than those measured on three-point scales (e.g., agree, disagree; Vaske, Needham, Shelby, & Hummer, 2007). It is always possible to collapse and recode longer scales into categorical options (e.g., disagree, neither, agree) at a later time, but not vice versa. Continuous scales provide researchers and analysts with more options when analyzing data and reporting results.

Guideline 3:
Choose simple words and phrases over more specialized alternatives.
When writing questions, it is often effective to use words that are short, simple, and easy to understand. Researchers should never assume that all respondents will have an advanced education and/or a high level of reading comprehension. Respondents should never find themselves consulting a dictionary when completing a questionnaire. Asking people to review drafts of a questionnaire and pretesting the instrument are important for identifying problems with word and phrase choices. Table 7.5 shows examples of how to improve words and phrases.

Table 7.5   Examples of Using Simple Words and Phrases Instead of Specialized Words When Writing Survey Questions

	Worse	Better		Worse	Better
Words	Exhausted	Tired	**Phrases**	Occupants of this residence	People who live here
	Candid	Honest		Your responses in reply to this survey	Your answers
	Highest priority	Most important			
	Employment	Work		Post-school extra-curricular activities	What you do after school
	Leisure	Free time			
	Courageous	Brave		Work-related employment concerns	Job concerns
	Rectify	Fix			

Adapted from Dillman (2000)

Guideline 4:
Use as few words as possible to ask a question.

It is often not necessary to provide extra verbiage in a question. Long questions can confuse respondents and may cause them to simply skip over and not respond to the question or even stop filling out the questionnaire altogether. With long questions, people can give unequal attention to each word, important words get missed, and unimportant words may receive too much attention (Dillman, 2000). It is important to strive for brevity and clarity when writing questions. An example of a *poor* question would be:

Do you strongly oppose, somewhat oppose, neither oppose nor favor, somewhat favor, or strongly favor the National Park Service implementing and charging people fees to enter and visit National Parks? (Please check one)
- ☐ Strongly oppose
- ☐ Somewhat oppose
- ☐ Neither oppose nor favor
- ☐ Somewhat favor
- ☐ Strongly favor

A more succinct and *improved* version of this question would be:

To what extent do you oppose or favor National Park entrance fees? (Please check one)
- ☐ Strongly oppose
- ☐ Somewhat oppose
- ☐ Neither oppose nor favor
- ☐ Somewhat favor
- ☐ Strongly favor

Guideline 5:
Use complete sentences and avoid cryptic phrases when asking questions.

Incomplete sentences may save a small amount of space in surveys, but they never substitute for good questions. Fragments or cryptic questions may confuse respondents and provide answers that are unrelated to what the researcher was intending when writing the question. The following is an example of an incomplete and cryptic question:

How long in Colorado? (Please write response) _____

This question is an incomplete sentence, does not specify units of duration (e.g., days, years, decades), and does not specify what is "long" in Colorado (e.g., length of residence, length of winter season, length of employment). A possible revision for this question would be:

In total, about how many years have you lived in Colorado? (Please write response) Number of years _____

Guideline 6:
Avoid vague quantifiers if precise estimates can be obtained.

When selecting response categories for close-ended questions, it is important to be as precise as possible without being so specific that it is nearly impossible to answer (Schaeffer, 1991). Although broad categories make respondents' and researchers' jobs easier, categories that are too broad provide little, if any, useful information. Consider the following examples:

About how often did you go hiking during the past year? (Please check one)
- ☐ Never
- ☐ Rarely
- ☐ Occasionally
- ☐ Regularly

About how often did you go hiking during the past year? (Please check one)
- ☐ Never
- ☐ 1 to 12 times
- ☐ 13 to 24 times
- ☐ 25 to 52 times
- ☐ More than 52 times

The first question is problematic because "rarely," "occasionally," and "regularly" mean different things to different respondents. For one person, "rarely" might mean three to five times and "occasionally" might imply six to 10 times. For another person, however, "rarely" might mean once a month (i.e., 12 times in the past year) and "occasionally" may refer to twice a month (i.e., 24 times per year).

The second question is problematic because responses are so precise that it may be impossible to correctly answer the question. This level of precision may provide more detail than the researcher needs (Salant & Dillman, 1994). A problem with both questions is what is meant by "the past year?" If questions were answered in June 2007, for example, it is not clear if the last year refers to January 2007 to June 2007 or the last 12 months (i.e., June 2006 to June 2007). A possible revision for these questions would be:

About how often did you go hiking during the past 12 months? (Please check one)
- ☐ Not at all
- ☐ A few times
- ☐ About once a month
- ☐ Two or three times a month
- ☐ About once a week
- ☐ More than once a week

Guideline 7:
Use an equal number of positive and negative responses for scale questions.

Bias can be created when ordered response categories are weighted in one direction causing an imbalance in response choices. To illustrate, a problematic question would be:

Overall, how dissatisfied or satisfied were you with your river guide today?
(Please check one)
- ☐ Dissatisfied
- ☐ Neither Satisfied nor Dissatisfied
- ☐ Somewhat Satisfied
- ☐ Mostly Satisfied
- ☐ Completely Satisfied

This question has only one negative response ("dissatisfied") compared to three positive responses ("somewhat satisfied," "mostly satisfied," "completely satisfied"). The following question provides a more balanced response scale:

Overall, how dissatisfied or satisfied were you with your river guide today?
(Please check one)
- ☐ Completely Dissatisfied
- ☐ Somewhat Dissatisfied
- ☐ Neither Satisfied nor Dissatisfied
- ☐ Somewhat Satisfied
- ☐ Completely Satisfied

There is, however, an exception to this guideline. If most respondents are likely to check one extreme or a middle point (e.g., neither, neutral) does not make sense for the question, unequal numbers of positive and negative response choices may be appropriate. The nine-point crowding scale (e.g., Shelby & Vaske, 2007; Shelby, Vaske, & Heberlein, 1989; Vaske & Shelby, 2008; see chapter 4), for example, ranges from "not at all crowded" to "extremely crowded" with interior responses of "slightly crowded" and "moderately crowded." Similarly, survey items measuring importance of characteristics in motivating people to engage in a recreation activity (e.g., to be in nature, to be with friends/family, to get exercise) are often measured on a scale from "not important" to "extremely important."

Guideline 8:
Distinguish "neither" from "no opinion" response options for scale questions.

It is important to recognize that "neither" can mean something completely different than "no opinion" (e.g., Blasius & Thiessen, 2001; Dillman, 2000). A survey question, for example, may ask about the extent to which respondents oppose or support wolf reintroduction in Colorado. One respondent may never have given any thought to wolf reintroduction and knew little about the topic. For this individual, a correct answer is "no opinion." A second respondent who carefully researched the topic and weighed pros and cons of wolf reintroduction without coming to any resolution may say "neither support nor oppose." It is useful to consider providing both of these responses in addition to positive and negative choices:

To what extent do you oppose or support wolf reintroduction in Colorado? (Please check one)

☐ Strongly Oppose
☐ Somewhat Oppose
☐ Neither Support nor Oppose
☐ Somewhat Support
☐ Strongly Support
☐ No Opinion

Guideline 9:
Avoid double-negatives or asking people to say "yes" in order to mean "no."

Double-negatives almost always confuse respondents. Although this seems obvious, such questions are still commonly asked. The following question is an example of a double-negative:

Do you oppose or support not requiring catch-and-release fishing at Smith Lakes State Park? (Please check one)

☐ Oppose
☐ Support

If respondents quickly read or skim this question, they are likely to miss the word "not." The mental connection of supporting a "not" is challenging for respondents (Dillman, 2000). A revision of this question would be:

Do you oppose or support requiring all anglers to catch and release their fish at Smith Lakes State Park? (Please check one)

☐ Oppose requiring catch-and-release at Smith Lakes State Park
☐ Support requiring catch-and-release at Smith Lakes State Park

Guideline 10:
Do not write double-barreled questions.

A double-barreled question contains two different questions or components, but asks for only one answer. Respondents may feel differently about each component. The following example illustrates a double-barreled question:

When you go to work, do you walk or carry your lunch? (Please check one)

☐ No
☐ Yes

This question is double-barreled because a respondent may walk to work, but not carry his or her lunch. Another respondent may not walk to work, but carries his or her lunch with them when driving to work. It is unclear what part of the question to which a response of "no" or "yes" refers. The question contains two questions: (a) Do you walk to work? and (b) Do you carry your lunch to work? The questionnaire should be revised to include two separate questions:

Do you walk to work? (Please check one)

☐ No
☐ Yes

Do you carry your lunch to work? (Please check one)

☐ No
☐ Yes

A more subtle example of a double-barreled question was asked in a recent study of residents' attitudes toward selling timber harvested from a watershed near a small Oregon town. The question asked residents to read a belief statement and respond on a five-point scale from "strongly disagree" (1) to "strongly agree" (5). The statement was:

Plants and wildlife will benefit from the proposed timber sale. (Please circle one number)

This question is double-barreled because a respondent may agree that wildlife would benefit from the timber sale, but disagree that plants would benefit (or vice versa). It is unclear what part of the statement (plants or wildlife) to which people are agreeing or disagreeing. The statement should be split into two statements, each with their own response scale:

Plants will benefit from the proposed timber sale. (Please circle one number)

Wildlife will benefit from the proposed timber sale. (Please circle one number)

Guideline 11:
Make every question count.

Similar to Guideline 1, it is important to define exactly what information is needed and to make every question important. Otherwise, questions simply waste questionnaire space and respondent time. To illustrate, a survey was conducted with downhill skiers and asked:

Do you downhill ski? (Please check one)

☐ No
☐ Yes

Although this is a perfectly acceptable question, questionnaires were administered on-site in lineups of downhill skiers waiting to get on chairlifts. Snowboarding, cross-country skiing, and telemark skiing were prohibited at this downhill ski area at the time of the study. As a result, all respondents selected "yes." A more useful and informative question might be:

On average, about how often do you downhill ski during a typical season? (Please check one)

☐ Once
☐ Twice
☐ 3 to 5 times
☐ 6 to 10 times
☐ 11 to 20 times
☐ More than 20 times

Guideline 12:
Use an appropriate timeframe for questions and responses.

A common topic of interest in parks, recreation, and human dimensions research is how often people participate in a specific behavior during a particular period of time. Surveys of hunters, for example, often ask respondents how often they hunted a particular species (e.g., Needham, Vaske, Donnelly, & Manfredo, 2007). According to Dillman (2000), several issues should be considered when using time referents in questionnaires. First, when something is so common or mundane in a person's life (e.g., watching television, walking the dog), it is hard for them to quantify exactly how often they engaged in the behavior. Consequently, it may be more appropriate to ask for a general estimate (e.g., about once a day) rather than specific counts.

Second, memory tends to diminish over time and people may find it difficult to categorize information by precise time periods (e.g., month, year). An avid hiker, for example, may find it difficult to respond to a question asking how often they went hiking in the last five years. Depending on project objectives, it is typically appropriate to shorten the timeframe.

Third, some studies focus on specific short time periods such as engaging in a behavior in the last three days or one week (e.g., smoking, eating out, walking). Participation in the behavior, however, may differ substantially by day of week so different responses may be obtained depending on when respondents complete the questionnaire.

Finally, as mentioned in Guideline 6, questionnaires often ask people to report their participation in an activity "during the past year" or "this year." A problem with these phrases is that responses are likely to be higher later in the year. Respondents may also be confused with the timeframe. If questionnaires were administered in June 2007, for example, it is not clear if the last year refers to January 2007 to June 2007 (i.e., "this year") or the last 12 months (i.e., June 2006 to June 2007). An example of a poor question is:

> How many fishing trips have you taken in the last year? (Please write response)
>
> I have taken _____ fishing trips in the last year

This question could be improved by asking:

> How many fishing trips have you taken in the last 12 months? (Please write response)
>
> I have taken _____ fishing trips in the last 12 months

The revised question is better, but an avid angler may find it difficult to report a precise count of the number of times they went fishing in such a long period of time (i.e., 12 months). It may be more appropriate to ask the following question:

> About how many fishing trips have you taken in the last three months? (Please write response)
>
> I have taken _____ fishing trips in the last three months

Other alternatives for reducing item nonresponse for questions involving timeframes are to add phrases such as "provide your best estimate" or "your best estimate is fine," or to prelist responses in categories (e.g., 1 to 5 trips, 6 to 10 trips) instead of using open-ended response options. This latter approach, however, constrains the types of analyses that can be performed on data. Chapter 13 discusses strategies for analyzing categorical data.

Guideline 13:
Reduce impact of sensitive or objectionable questions.

Respondents may be reluctant to answer sensitive or potentially objectionable questions. This is especially problematic if the nonresponse reduces sample sizes and inflates social desirability bias (Tourangeau & Yan, 2007). Asking respondents about their income is one potentially objectionable question. Open-ended formats for income questions are especially problematic because people consider such specific personal information to be nobody else's business. In addition, few people can easily recall their exact annual income to the precise dollar amount. A problematic income question would be:

> What was your total household income before taxes in 2007? (Please write response)
>
> $_____ total income for 2007

Changing from an open-ended response option to broader categories can reduce nonresponse for this type of question. An alternative approach for measuring income is:

> Which of the following broad categories best describes your approximate annual household income before taxes in 2007? (Please check one)
>
> ☐ Less than $10,000   ☐ $90,000 – $109,999
> ☐ $10,000 – $29,999   ☐ $110,000 – $129,999
> ☐ $30,000 – $49,999   ☐ $130,000 – $149,999
> ☐ $50,000 – $69,999   ☐ $150,000 – $169,999
> ☐ $70,000 – $89,999   ☐ $170,000 or more

Researchers should consider response options for income questions in relation to research objectives and the target population. If the study is concerned with the impact of recreation fee increases on poor individuals, for example, finer distinctions at the low end of the response scale may be necessary. Alternatively, if the project examines recreation behaviors and attitudes of the extremely wealthy, more response options at the high end of the scale are likely appropriate.

Asking questions about behaviors in which people should or must engage (but many people do not) can also be objectionable to some respondents. In some areas, for example, it is mandatory for all hunters to submit all of their harvested deer or elk to be tested for chronic wasting disease (CWD). An objectionable question would be:

> Did you submit your deer or elk for CWD testing? (Please check one)
> ☐ No
> ☐ Yes

Hunters may feel offended by this question because if they said "no," they may be admitting to an illegal behavior. Hunters who did not submit their deer or elk are likely to say "yes" or skip over this question without providing an answer. One way to soften the impact of this type of objectionable question is:

For a variety of reasons, some hunters may not have had a chance to submit their deer or elk for CWD testing. Did you happen to submit your deer or elk for CWD testing? (Please check one)

☐ No
☐ Yes

Guideline 14:
Use terminology that makes sense to respondents and define terms that may be vague and unclear.

Some terminology can be unclear and may not make sense to respondents. Vague terms cause respondents to misunderstand questions, which can produce bias and error in responses (Fowler, 1992). Surveys examining participation in a recreation activity, for example, may ask "how many trips" people have taken. The definition of what constitutes a "trip" is potentially confusing. The following question uses potentially unclear terminology:

How many fishing trips have you taken in the last three months? (Please write response)

I have taken _____ fishing trips in the last three months

For this question, it is not clear what defines "a fishing trip." To some people, a fishing trip may simply involve walking a few blocks from their house to a nearby lake or stream. For other individuals, a fishing trip might constitute a multi-day excursion to hike-in lakes in another state or province. Researchers need to clarify or define potentially unclear terms. For example:

How many fishing trips have you taken in the last three months? (Please write response; a fishing trip is defined as a trip of more than 50 miles)

I have taken _____ fishing trips in the last three months

Other terms can confuse respondents. For a class assignment, for example, a student designed a questionnaire to be administered to skiers. One question in the instrument asked:

How many times did you go Nordic skiing in the last six months? (Please write response)

I went Nordic skiing _____ times in the last six months

This question is problematic because some skiers may not be familiar with the terminology "Nordic skiing." As discussed in Guideline 3 and Table 7.5 (p. 137), it is important to choose simple words that make sense for all respondents. This question could be improved by substituting "Nordic" with the more generic term "cross-country."

How many times did you go cross-country skiing in the last six months? (Please write response)

I went cross-country skiing _____ times in the last six months

Guideline 15:
Define abbreviations and acronyms that respondents may not understand.

Undefined abbreviations and jargon should never be used in questionnaires (Salant & Dillman, 1994). There is, however, an exception to this rule. Some abbreviations and jargon may be appropriate if the questionnaire is being completed by a specific group who use certain phrases or abbreviations frequently, and will definitely not be confused. A survey of professors, for example, may include the abbreviation "P&T" in questions because this group of respondents is likely to know that P&T refers to "Promotion and Tenure." An example where abbreviations would not be appropriate would be a survey of the general public asking:

> Do you believe that the EPA should continue funding CFC research? (Please check one)
> ☐ No
> ☐ Yes
> ☐ Unsure

Given that few people are likely to know what CFC and EPA mean, these abbreviations should be briefly defined. An alternative approach for asking the question is:

> Chlorofluorocarbons (CFCs) are compounds that have been used in the past by industry for such things as refrigeration and cleaning solvents. They are now banned from general use. The United States Environmental Protection Agency (EPA) has funded research on CFCs. Do you believe that the EPA should continue funding CFC research? (Please check one)
> ☐ No
> ☐ Yes
> ☐ Unsure

Guideline 16:
Avoid bias from unequal comparisons.

When asking close-ended questions with unordered response categories, it is possible to create bias when responses are skewed. Consider, for example, the following question:

> Who do you feel is most responsible for the litter at Smith Lakes State Park? (Please check one)
> ☐ Careless anglers
> ☐ Hikers
> ☐ Campers

The word "careless" adds a value connotation for anglers, which is not present for hikers or campers. This question should be revised to eliminate possible bias:

> Who do you feel is most responsible for the litter at Smith Lakes State Park? (Please check one)
> ☐ Anglers
> ☐ Hikers
> ☐ Campers

A subtle way to create unequal comparisons is to blame a small group by using two or more similar categories for the group. Salant and Dillman (1994) offer the following example:

Who do you feel is most responsible for the high cost of U.S. automobiles?
(Please check one)
☐ Autoworkers
☐ Auto company executives
☐ Consumers

The following revision helps to reduce bias and make comparisons more equal:

Who do you feel is most responsible for the high cost of U.S. automobiles?
(Please check one)
☐ Workers who produce automobiles
☐ Auto company executives who manage manufacturing plants
☐ Consumers who buy automobiles

Guideline 17:
Avoid using slanted / leading and loaded introductions and questions.

Questions can be biased when they are written in a way that makes it appear as though everyone shares the same opinion or participates in a certain behavior, and as a result, the respondent should too. Slanted or leading introductions introduce social desirability bias (i.e., respondents give answers that are consistent with perceived societal norms or shared viewpoints). An example of a slanted introduction is:

More Americans participate in wildlife viewing now than they did 10 years ago.
Do you participate in wildlife viewing? (Please check one)
☐ No
☐ Yes

This introduction should be revised by providing a simple, objective, and neutral question:

Do you participate in wildlife viewing? (Please check one)
☐ No
☐ Yes

Guideline 18:
State both sides of scales in question stems or introductions.

Researchers may try to reduce the length of questionnaires by minimizing the number of words in questions. One approach for reducing question length is to mention only one side of a response scale:

To what extent do you support lethal trapping of coyotes in urban areas? (Please check one)
☐ Strongly oppose
☐ Somewhat oppose
☐ Neither support nor oppose
☐ Somewhat support
☐ Strongly support

Leaving out any mention of disagreement or opposition in the question can potentially influence responses. Mentioning "support or oppose" conveys a greater range of response options and that opposition or disagreement is an acceptable answer. This question might be revised as:

> To what extent do you oppose or support lethal trapping of coyotes in urban areas?
> (Please check one)
> ☐ Strongly oppose
> ☐ Somewhat oppose
> ☐ Neither support nor oppose
> ☐ Somewhat support
> ☐ Strongly support

Guideline 19:
Minimize number of "check all that apply" questions to avoid "primacy" and "recency" effects.

For some topics, "check all that apply" questions are essential. For example, individuals can participate in multiple activities in a single day, so asking the following type of question is often necessary:

> Please check all of the activities in which you are participating at Copper Beach Park today. (Please check all that apply)
>
> ☐ Sunbathing   ☐ Snorkeling   ☐ Boating
> ☐ Swimming   ☐ SCUBA Diving ☐ Surfing
> ☐ Fishing   ☐ Beach Walking ☐ Windsurfing/Kitesurfing

There are, however, problems with "check all that apply" questions (Rasinski, Mingay, & Bradburn, 1994). Respondents may "*satisfice*" when answering these types of questions by checking answers and proceeding down the list until they believe that they have provided a "satisfactory" answer (Dillman, 2000). Although almost all respondents will read the first few options listed, some will not read the entire list. Options that are listed first are more likely to be checked. This is analogous to a *primacy effect* or a tendency to select from the first few answers, which is common in mail surveys and respondent-completed on-site surveys. These questions can also cause a *recency effect* or tendency to select among the last answers mentioned, which tends to be common in telephone and interviewer-completed on-site surveys (Dillman, 2000). An example where primacy and recency effects may occur is:

> People go deer hunting for many reasons. Listed below are several reasons why deer hunting may be important to you. Please select reasons that influence you to go deer hunting. (Please check all that apply)
>
> ☐ Harvesting a deer   ☐ Being with friends of family
> ☐ Bringing deer meat home to eat ☐ Experiencing the challenge of the hunt
> ☐ Harvesting only a trophy deer ☐ Testing hunting skills
> ☐ Being in nature   ☐ Getting physical exercise
> ☐ Experiencing solitude

To minimize primacy and recency effects from this type of "check all that apply" question, it is recommended that researchers use scale responses similar to the following example:

People go deer hunting for many reasons. Listed below are several reasons why deer hunting may be important to you. Please indicate how important each of these reasons is in influencing you to go deer hunting. (Please circle one number for each statement)

	Not at all Important	Slightly Important	Moderately Important	Extremely Important
Harvesting a deer	1	2	3	4
Bringing deer meat home to eat	1	2	3	4
Harvesting only a trophy deer	1	2	3	4
Being in nature	1	2	3	4
Experiencing solitude	1	2	3	4
Being with friends or family	1	2	3	4
Experiencing the challenge of the hunt	1	2	3	4
Testing hunting skills	1	2	3	4
Getting physical exercise	1	2	3	4

Guideline 20:
Use response categories that are mutually exclusive.

As noted in Guideline 2, all answers should be ***mutually exclusive***. If response categories overlap, there is potential for a respondent to select two or more answers for a "check one" question. This confuses respondents and complicates data entry and analysis. The following question, for example, asks respondents to choose one answer to a question that asks them how they learned about a recent attack on a human by a mountain lion.

> How did you first learn about the mountain lion attack on March 17, 2007?
> (Please check one)
> ☐ From a friend or family member
> ☐ From my spouse
> ☐ From the radio
> ☐ While at home
> ☐ While at work
> ☐ While attending a meeting

Problems with this question are: (a) choices combine sources and locations so someone could have heard about the attack from their spouse while at home, or from a friend who they work with while attending a meeting; (b) sources are not mutually exclusive because a spouse is also a friend and family member; and (c) locations are not mutually exclusive because a person could have heard about the attack while at work and attending a meeting. The question should be separated into two questions with revised choices:

> From whom or what did you first learn about the mountain lion attack on March 17, 2007? (Please check one)
> ☐ From my spouse
> ☐ From another friend or relative
> ☐ From the radio

Where were you when you first learned about the mountain lion attack on March 17, 2007? (Please check one)

☐ At home
☐ At work
☐ At a meeting at a place other than my work

These response items could be improved further by including other possible sources (e.g., television, newspaper, Internet) or locations (e.g., in car, at airport) to make options more exhaustive. Some items such as "at home" and "at work" may still not be mutually exclusive because some people work from home. Researchers may want to reconsider these types of lists and use scales or partially close-ended response choices (i.e., provide an "other" open-ended category) instead.

Guideline 21:
Make sure that each question or statement is accurate.

Statements, questions, or words that are inaccurate can reduce credibility of the survey, researcher, and even the organization funding the study. Errors in accuracy range from spelling or grammar mistakes to inaccurate or false information. An example of an *inaccurate* question is:

The ivory-billed woodpecker is considered by the National Conservation Union as a "threatened" species, meaning that it is vulnerable to extinction in the distent future. Should the U.S. federal government provide more funding for research on this species? (Please check one)

☐ No
☐ Yes
☐ Unsure

There are three major problems with this question; some are more subtle than others. First, the ivory-billed woodpecker is actually classified as "endangered," which means that it is at high risk of becoming extinct in the immediate future. Second, the organization that classifies species (e.g., threatened, endangered) is actually named the World Conservation Union, not the National Conservation Union. Third, "distent" is misspelled; it should be spelled "distant." A possible revision of this question could be:

The ivory-billed woodpecker is considered by the World Conservation Union as an "endangered" species, meaning that it is at high risk of becoming extinct in the immediate future. Should the U.S. federal government provide more funding for research on this species? (Please check one)

☐ No
☐ Yes
☐ Unsure

Asking experts to review the questionnaire and conducting a pretest of the instrument are critical to ensure technical accuracy (see chapter 8).

Guideline 22:
Select questions and responses that permit comparisons with existing information and / or previously collected data.

A benefit of conducting survey research is the ability to compare results to other studies. To compare data, researchers must ask for information in the same way as earlier studies.

Measurement consistency can allow for statistical approaches such as meta-analysis to examine generalizability, and longitudinal analysis to assess change over time. In addition, comparisons can be used to ensure that samples are representative of the larger population from which they were drawn, and assist with any necessary weighting procedures. In the 2000 U.S. Census, for example, responses for marital status were:

What is your marital status? (Please check one)
- ☐ Now married
- ☐ Widowed
- ☐ Divorced
- ☐ Separated
- ☐ Never married

Using these categories in a smaller study of the public allows researchers to use U.S. Census data to ensure that characteristics of participants in the sample are representative of the population. If not, the data may need to be weighted (see chapter 8).

Another example of measurement consistency is the nine-point scale used to measure perceived crowding in recreation settings (see chapter 4 and Vaske & Shelby, 2008):

To what extent did you feel crowded on the Black Butte trail today? (Please circle one number)

1	2	3	4	5	6	7	8	9
Not At All Crowded		Slightly Crowded			Moderately Crowded			Extremely Crowded

This scale has been used in at least 180 studies (see Vaske & Shelby, 2008, for a review), which allows for comparisons across time, settings, activity groups, geographical regions, and other contexts. It is important to consult the literature prior to survey writing and construction to examine how others have measured particular questions and concepts.

Guideline 23:
Provide information instead of assuming too much respondent knowledge.
Researchers should never assume that all respondents know enough to answer every question (Salant & Dillman, 1994). When asking about a specific topic that some respondents may not be aware of, it is useful to provide some background information before asking the question. An example of a question that assumes too much respondent knowledge is:

To what extent do you oppose or support the Oregon Department of Fish and Wildlife's new regulation on fishing for both salmon and steelhead in the Santiam River? (Please check one)
- ☐ Strongly oppose
- ☐ Somewhat oppose
- ☐ Neither support nor oppose
- ☐ Somewhat support
- ☐ Strongly support

This example assumes that all respondents are aware of the new regulation, which is unlikely. The question could be improved by: (a) providing respondents with more information about the regulation, (b) asking if they were aware of the regulation, and then (c) asking if they supported or opposed the regulation:

> Oregon Department of Fish and Wildlife has introduced a new regulation requiring all anglers to release wild (nonhatchery) salmon and steelhead caught in the Santiam River. Prior to receiving this survey, were you aware of this regulation? (Please check one)
> ☐ No, I was not aware of this regulation
> ☐ Yes, I was aware of this regulation
>
> To what extent do you oppose or support this new regulation? (Please check one)
> ☐ Strongly oppose
> ☐ Somewhat oppose
> ☐ Neither support nor oppose
> ☐ Somewhat support
> ☐ Strongly support

Guideline 24:
Avoid questions that are too difficult for respondents.

Asking respondents to report percentages or make other complex calculations should be avoided because errors are common, especially in on-site or telephone surveys where people are pressured to provide answers quickly (Dillman, 2000; Salant & Dillman, 1994). Although some people will attempt to report a precise number, most will make an estimate. Chapter 19 discusses impacts of numerical estimates (e.g., response heaping, digit preference). An example of a question asking for an unnecessary calculation is:

> What percent of days that you fished in the last three months were spent at Foster Lake? (Please write response)
>
> _____ % of days fishing in last three months spent at Foster Lake

This calculation is challenging, especially for avid anglers who may have fished many days at multiple locations. Asking for approximates and separating questions into: (a) total number of days fishing, followed by (b) number of days fishing at the specific site, reduces respondent burden and leaves the calculations to the researcher, not the respondent:

> Approximately how many days did you go fishing in the last three months? (Please write response)
>
> I fished approximately _____ days in the last three months
>
> Now, approximately how many of these days did you go fishing at Foster Lake? (Please write response)
>
> I fished approximately _____ days at Foster Lake in the last three months

These two questions allow the researcher to perform the calculation after the questionnaire has been completed. The SPSS `Compute` command (chapter 12) can perform these calculations.

Guideline 25:
Use multiple questions to measure complex concepts.

For questions about topics such as demographics (e.g., age), experiences (e.g., encounters with other visitors), and behavior (e.g., activity participation), respondents will usually attempt to give accurate estimates or correct answers. If asked the identical question in a questionnaire administered a day or two later, people are likely to provide the same responses because they possess many of these attributes. Questions about beliefs, norms, attitudes, or intentions, however, are more prone to measurement error and imprecision because we do not possess these characteristics in the same way as we possess things such as age and gender. Opinions can change from day to day and may not be well-thought-out before questionnaire completion (Salant & Dillman, 1994). For example, consider the following question:

> To what extent do you disagree or agree with the statement: "A moose hunt in Anchorage would benefit the future moose population in the area?" (Please check one)
> ☐ Strongly disagree
> ☐ Somewhat disagree
> ☐ Neither agree nor disagree
> ☐ Somewhat agree
> ☐ Strongly agree

Questions such as this may evoke uncertainty and take a while for respondents to think about before answering. As a result, people may give a different response if asked again at a later time.

No single question is a perfect measure of a complex concept such as an attitude or a belief. To improve reliability and validity of concepts measured in a survey, researchers typically use scales asking multiple questions about a single concept or issue. Statistical approaches such as reliability analysis (chapter 18) can be employed to examine patterns in how people answer questions, which can then be used to justify combining answers into a single numerical estimate of the concept being measured. The following example lists multiple questions that asked about Anchorage residents' attitudes toward a proposed urban moose hunt (modified from Whittaker, Manfredo, Fix, Sinnott, Miller, & Vaske, 2001):

> Please tell us whether you think each of the following outcomes of the proposed moose hunt would be good or bad. (Please circle one number for each item)

	Very Bad	Slightly Bad	Neither	Slightly Good	Very Good
Reducing number of accidents involving moose is…	1	2	3	4	5
Reducing number of potentially dangerous encounters between people and moose is…	1	2	3	4	5
Keeping moose from becoming overpopulated is…	1	2	3	4	5
Reducing number of moose in Anchorage is…	1	2	3	4	5
Providing more opportunities for moose hunters is…	1	2	3	4	5
Holding a hunt that might injure someone else is…	1	2	3	4	5
A hunt that costs a lot to administer is…	1	2	3	4	5
A hunt that generates a lot of conflict between people who favor and oppose the hunt is…	1	2	3	4	5
A hunt that prevents nonhunters from using the area is…	1	2	3	4	5
Being able to see moose as often as I like is…	1	2	3	4	5

Diagnosing Wording Problems: Questions to Ask Yourself

Writing good survey questions always takes several rounds of editing and rewriting. *The key to good writing is rewriting.* It is not uncommon to go through five, 10, or even 20 drafts before the final questionnaire is administered. Questionnaires require tremendous time and attention because multiple issues need to be considered when writing questions and designing the layout. Input from experts and one or more pilot tests help to diagnose problems. Questions to ask yourself when writing questions include:

- Can the question be misunderstood?
- To what extent would survey respondents have an accurate answer for the question?
- Can people accurately recall and report past behaviors?
- Is the respondent willing to reveal the requested information?
- Is the frame of reference clear and uniform for all respondents?
- Is the wording biased?
- Is the wording likely to be objectionable to respondents?
- Does the wording create a double-negative?
- Can the question be asked in a more direct or indirect form using simpler words?
- Is the question misleading because of unstated assumptions and implications?
- Is changing a question acceptable to the survey sponsor?

Diagnosing Content Problems Other Than Wording: Questions to Ask Yourself

Researchers should also ask themselves several questions about the content of questions (apart from specific wording), including:

- Is the question necessary and related to project objectives or hypotheses?
- How will the information be used?
- Are several questions necessary to examine the subject matter?
- Should the question be subdivided into narrower or more specific questions?
- Is information needed on respondents' intensity of conviction or degree of feeling?
- Is information on the importance of the issue to the respondent needed?
- Is information in the question accurate?
- Does the respondent have the information necessary to answer the question?
- Does the question need to be more specific?
- Are complete sentences used in the question?
- Is the question loaded or biased in one direction?
- Does the question contain two questions (i.e., double-barreled)?
- Have important terms and abbreviations been clearly defined?
- Has an appropriate timeframe been selected?
- Has the correct type of response scale been selected?
- Are all possible response options provided and mutually exclusive?

- Will the respondent offer the information that is being asked for?
- Has the literature been consulted to determine if comparisons are possible?

The First Draft: Constructing Good Surveys
General Recommendations for Constructing Surveys

Once the list of survey questions has been written and potential problems have been identified and corrected, the next step is to construct an attractive and professional questionnaire that is easy for respondents to follow and complete in a timely manner. Well-designed questionnaires take time to construct, but the payoff is large because people are more likely to respond (Dillman, 2000, 2007; Salant & Dillman, 1994).

Questionnaires should minimize *respondent burden*, which means: (a) keeping time required to complete the questionnaire to a minimum, (b) decreasing time that respondents need to think about questions, and (c) respecting respondents by ensuring that they will not be embarrassed by not understanding what is expected (Salant & Dillman, 1994). This section offers recommendations for constructing questionnaires and minimizing respondent burden.

Recommendation 1:
Start with an interesting, easy, and relevant question.

The first few questions receive more scrutiny than most, if not all, of the other questions. The first question should *never*:

- be boring or uninteresting,
- be unrelated to the topic of the study,
- embarrass a respondent,
- be difficult to answer,
- take a long time to answer,
- require an open-ended response,
- involve long scale responses,
- be something that does not apply to all respondents, and
- ask people about themselves (e.g., personal characteristics, demographics).

The first question should be simple to answer, short, related to the topic of the study, relevant to respondents, and should motivate respondents to complete the rest of the questionnaire. The first question should catch the interest of respondents and give them a context for more challenging questions later in the questionnaire. Examples of starting questions would be:

> There has not been a moose hunt in the state of New Hampshire since the early 1900s. Do you feel that there should be a moose hunt in New Hampshire again? (Please check one)
> - ☐ No
> - ☐ Yes
> - ☐ Unsure

Our records show that you purchased a license to hunt deer in Arizona during the 2007 deer hunting season (fall / winter 2007). Did you go deer hunting in Arizona during the 2007 deer hunting season? (Please check one)

☐ No
☐ Yes

Recommendation 2:
Never start with demographic questions.

Some respondents consider demographic questions to be asking for information that is none of the researcher's business. Demographic questions such as age, marital status, and income can be objectionable or sensitive. These questions should never be positioned at the beginning of a questionnaire. Respondents who find such questions objectionable may be reluctant to answer the question and any remaining questions, which reduces the sample size and response rate.

In the authors' experience, conducting parks, recreation, and human dimensions surveys, many demographic questions remain unanswered by at least 5% to 10% of respondents. Even when income is measured with broad categories, approximately 10% of participants avoid answering the question. It is recommended, therefore, that demographic questions be grouped together in a section at the end of the survey. To mitigate concerns regarding confidentiality and anonymity, this last section should be prefaced with a statement such as: "Finally, we would like to ask you a few questions about yourself to help us understand different characteristics of respondents and allow us to compare your answers with those of other people. You will remain anonymous and your answers will be confidential." If these demographic questions still go unanswered, respondents have probably already answered other questions earlier in the survey so useful information can still be salvaged.

Recommendation 3:
Segment a questionnaire by grouping similar questions into logical sections.

Questionnaires should be arranged logically. Questions at the *beginning* of the instrument should be simple and catch the interest of respondents. The section at the *end* of the questionnaire should include questions that are most likely to be objectionable. Questions in the *middle* should be those that are the most difficult but important for respondents to answer.

Questions examining the same specific subject or concept should be grouped together on the same page or in the same section. In a recent mail survey of hunters, for example, questions about hunters' motivations were on one page, items examining trust in wildlife agencies were on another page, and questions asking about demographic characteristics were on a separate page at the end of the questionnaire (Needham, Vaske, & Manfredo, 2005). This improves readability and flow, and reduces burden on respondents because they will not need to constantly switch from one topic to another and have their thought and response patterns disrupted.

Questions examining the same specific subject should also be grouped according to those that are similar in structure and response pattern. For example, questions about a topic using a five-point scale from "very unacceptable" to "very acceptable" should be grouped together, whereas "yes / no" questions examining a similar topic should be grouped together. This makes it easier for respondents to remember response scales, which can reduce survey completion time.

The order in which questions appear can occasionally influence how people answer. Although researchers may purposely want questions to build on each other, it is typically undesirable to have questions that may bias responses to other questions positioned near each other. Pairs of questions in which the first might have an influence on the second should be separated (Salant & Dillman, 1994). Chapter 19 discusses response patterns in greater detail.

Recommendation 4:
Use transitions to guide respondents through the questionnaire.
Questionnaires should be organized so that respondents proceed smoothly and expeditiously from question to question and section to section. One approach for improving flow is to periodically use transition phrases such as "Now, we would like to ask you…" or "Finally, we would like to ask you…" These kinds of transitions provide a conversational tone and act like a roadmap for respondents to signal changes in topic or types of questions that will come next in a questionnaire. Transitions are especially beneficial in telephone and on-site surveys, but can also be useful in mail and electronic surveys.

Salant and Dillman (1994) suggest using transitions: (a) *regularly* when beginning a new line of inquiry, (b) *sometimes* at the top of pages to catch the eye of a respondent flipping through the questionnaire to see what topics are addressed, and (c) *occasionally* to break the monotony of long lists of questions or statements and to increase respondent motivation.

Recommendation 5:
Short questionnaires are not always better.
Questionnaire layout is one of the most important factors influencing response rates and data quality, especially for mail, on-site, and electronic surveys. Some researchers believe that short questionnaires (e.g., one or two pages) are always best. This is not true. Condensing questions on pages can cause the questionnaire to look cluttered and makes it challenging to read and reply to questions. Respondents may be less motivated to complete the questionnaire.

There are several things to consider when structuring the layout of questions. First, questions should not appear on one page with their response categories on the next page. If items in a series or scale must be split between two or more pages, headings (e.g., questions, response scales) should be repeated on each page. Second, a questionnaire should never contain pages with large blank spaces while other pages are crammed with questions. Third, there should be adequate "white space" between each question to allow respondents to progress relatively quickly through the pages. Fourth, do not add extra questions that are somewhat irrelevant simply to fill space. Too many questions can increase respondent burden and item nonresponse, and decrease response rates (Heberlein & Baumgartner, 1978).

Adequate spacing within and between questions can create an attractive and professional looking questionnaire that will encourage people to respond. Compared to short questionnaires, slightly longer instruments can also convey a perception that the study is more important. Researchers, however, should consider a few things before adding more "white space" in questionnaires. First, questionnaires that are longer in terms of pages rather than questions can still be perceived as "too long" by respondents. Second, adding pages to mail and on-site questionnaires increases costs associated with purchasing more paper and printing more pages. Third, more pages add thickness and weight to mail surveys, which increase postage costs.

Side 1 of Postcard Questionnaire

New Hampshire Scenic Byways Survey

The New Hampshire Department of Transportation and the Office of State Planning are conducting this survey to learn more about those features that affect your trips to New Hampshire. It will be an important component of a scenic byways plan to be developed for the State in the near future. Thank you for taking the time to fill out this questionnaire.

1. Have you ever traveled along the Kancamagus Highway? ___no___yes___don't know
2. Prior to visiting New Hampshire, had you heard about the Kancamagus Highway?
   ___no   ___yes
3. How did you first hear about the Kancamagus Highway?
   ___Highway Signs___Newspaper or Magazine___Tourist Information Center
   ___Radio or TV___Friends / Family___ Brochure___Other_____
   ___I have not heard about the Kancamagus
4. In planning vacations, to what extent do you look for scenic byways?
   ___Never___Sometimes___Always
   5. When in New Hampshire, to what extent do you travel on scenic back roads as opposed to major highways?___Almost never___Sometimes___Always
6. In the designation of a scenic byway, which of the following would you consider important? (Check all that apply)
   ___Mountains___Covered Bridges___Backroads___Farms___Old Mills___Scenic Vistas
   ___Rivers___Historic Sites___Stonewalls___Camping Areas___Inns & Taverns
   ___State Parks___Lakes___Other_____

Side 2 of Postcard Questionnaire

7. When visiting New Hampshire do you *usually:* ___go to a single destination, or ___tour different parts of the state?
8. Do you have a *primary* destination on this trip?___no___yes; what is it: _____
9. On this particular visit are you:___vacationing in the area___on a day trip
10. On this trip, which of the following activities are you planning to do in New Hampshire? (CHECK ALL THAT APPLY)
    ___Personal or official business___Visiting scenic areas___Attending a cultural or sporting event___Driving for pleasure___Shopping___Visiting museums/historical sites___Outdoor recreation (Hiking, Camping, etc.)___Entertainment (Music or Theater)___Visiting family/friends ___Sports (Golfing, Tennis, etc.)___Other_____
11. About how many nights do you plan to spend in the area? (CHECK ONE)
    ___None___1 night___2 to 3___4 to 7___More than a week
    12. If you are staying overnight on this trip to New Hampshire, where are you staying? (CHECK ALL THAT APPLY)___I am not staying overnight___Condominium ___Hotel/Motel___Inn___with friends___Campground___other:_____
13. How many are in your travel party?___Number of adults___Number of children (Under 18)
14. For *each* of the following items, about how much money will you spend *per day* (on average) for this trip? $_____Lodging $_____Souvenirs $_____Entrance Fees $_____Transportation $_____Food $_____Entertainment
Thank you for your help!   Enjoy New Hampshire!

Note: Postcard questionnaire shown at 71% of original size

Figure 7.1   Example of Questionnaire with No "White Space"

Figure 7.1 is an example of an actual questionnaire that the State of New Hampshire was going to use to evaluate its scenic byways program. Questions were to be printed on both sides of a postcard. This is an example of how *not* to construct a questionnaire. The version in Figure 7.2

New Hampshire Scenic Byways Survey

The New Hampshire Department of Transportation and the Office of State Planning are conducting this survey to learn more about those features that affect your trips to New Hampshire. It will be an important component of a scenic byways plan to be developed for the State in the near future. Thank you for taking the time to fill out this questionnaire.

1. Have you ever traveled along the Kancamagus Highway? ____ no ____ yes ____ don't know

2. Prior to visiting New Hampshire, had you heard about the Kancamagus Highway? ____ no ____ yes

3. How did you first hear about the Kancamagus Highway?

   ____ Highway Signs   ____ Newspaper or Magazine
   ____ Tourist Information Center   ____ Radio or TV
   ____ Friends / Family   ____ Other _____
   ____ Brochure   ____ I have not heard about the Kancamagus

4. *In planning vacations*, to what extent do you look for scenic byways?

   ____ Never   ____ Sometimes   ____ Always

5. When in New Hampshire, to what extent do you travel on scenic back roads as opposed to major highways?

   ____ Almost never   ____ Sometimes   ____ Always

6. In the designation of a scenic byway, which of the following would you consider important (Check all that apply)

   ____ Mountains   ____ Covered Bridges
   ____ Backroads   ____ Farms
   ____ Old Mills   ____ Scenic Vistas
   ____ Rivers   ____ Historic Sites
   ____ Stonewalls   ____ Camping Areas
   ____ Inns & Taverns   ____ State Parks
   ____ Lakes   ____ Other _____

7. When visiting New Hampshire, do you *usually*:

   ____ go to a single destination, or   ____ tour different parts of the state

8. Do you have a *primary* destination on this trip? ____ no ____ yes; what is it? _____

9. On this particular visit are you: ____ vacationing in the area   ____ on a day trip

10. On this trip, which of the following activities are you planning to do in New Hampshire?
    (CHECK ALL THAT APPLY)

    ____ Personal or official business   ____ Visiting scenic areas
    ____ Attending a cultural or sporting event   ____ Driving for pleasure
    ____ Shopping   ____ Visiting museums/historical sites
    ____ Outdoor recreation (Hiking, Camping, etc.) ____ Entertainment (Music or Theater)
    ____ Visiting family and friends   ____ Other _____
    ____ Sports (Golfing, Tennis, etc.)

11. About how many nights do you plan to spend in the area? (CHECK ONE)

    ____ None   ____ 1 night   ____ 2 to 3   ____ 4 to 7   ____ More than a week

12. If you are staying overnight on this trip to New Hampshire, where are you staying?
    (CHECK ALL THAT APPLY)

    ____ I am not staying overnight   ____ Condominium   ____ Hotel/Motel
    ____ Inn   ____ with friends   ____ Campground
                                                                 ____ other: _____

13. How many are in your travel party? ____ Number of adults   ____ Number of children (Under 18)

14. For *each* of the following items, about how much money will you spend *per day* (on average) on this trip?

    $ _____ Lodging $ _____ Souvenirs

    $ _____ Entrance Fees $ _____ Transportation

    $ _____ Food $ _____ Entertainment

Thank you for your help!   Enjoy New Hampshire!

Note: Questionnaire shown at 67% of original size

Figure 7.2   Revised Version of Questionnaire in Figure 7.1, but with More "White Space"

was ultimately used for this project. The two versions of the questionnaire (i.e., Figures 7.1, 7.2) are identical in terms of questions asked. The revised version shown in Figure 7.2, however, is much easier to read and answer. These two versions clearly demonstrate the value of creating more "white" space and properly formatting a questionnaire.

Recommendation 6:
Minimize use of skip patterns.

A skip pattern asks a respondent who provided a particular answer to one question to skip over and not answer one or more questions that do not apply to him or her. Skip patterns tell respondents where to go next. An example of a skip pattern is:

1. Are you fishing at Lost Lake today? (Please check one)
    ☐ No   → If no, skip to question 3
    ☐ Yes

2. In total, about how many days have you fished at Lost Lake in the last three months?

    (Please write response) _____ days

3. What other activities are you participating in at Lost Lake today? (Please check all that apply)
    ☐ Picnicking   ☐ Having a campfire   ☐ Hunting
    ☐ Hiking   ☐ Mountain biking   ☐ Boating without fishing
    ☐ Overnight camping   ☐ Swimming   ☐ Other (please write response)
                                                 _____

People who answered "no" in question 1 skip over the other fishing-related question (i.e., question 2) and proceed to question 3.

Skip patterns are sometimes unavoidable, but researchers should try to minimize the number of skip patterns in a questionnaire. Multiple skip patterns create confusion among respondents and can be time consuming and cumbersome when entering data into SPSS. Although SPSS offers a module that resolves some data entry concerns, the module is not part of the base program. If the data entry module is unavailable, data-entry technicians must remember to distinguish answers that were purposefully not provided as directed by skip patterns (i.e., "does not apply") from questions that were voluntarily not answered (i.e., "respondent chose not to answer" or "missing"). In the above set of questions, for example, a respondent who answered "no" to question 1 would have the answer coded as "does not apply" for question 2. If another respondent answered "yes" to question 1, but failed to answer question 2, the answer would be coded by the researcher as "missing" for question 2.

Recommendation 7:
Use sequential numbering of questions within sections or throughout the questionnaire.

It is important to number questions so that respondents know which question to read and answer next. Numbering is also required for skip patterns. For relatively short questionnaires, questions should likely be numbered sequentially throughout the entire instrument. For longer questionnaires, however, it might be worthwhile to number questions only within individual sections or particular pages because respondents may be reluctant to complete a questionnaire where the last question is an extremely high number (e.g., question 172). There is no particular rule for numbering questions; researchers should simply be aware of any hidden message that may be communicated by numbering all questions sequentially in a long questionnaire.

Recommendation 8:
Be consistent when formatting response categories.

One of the most important things when designing a questionnaire is to be consistent, especially when formatting response categories. Salant and Dillman (1994) suggest using numbers for all close-ended answer categories rather than boxes or lines:

> What is your marital status? (Please circle the number of your answer)
> 1. Never Married
> 2. Married
> 3. Divorced
> 4. Separated
> 5. Widowed

Their rationale for this approach is that it "precodes" answers so the codes can be more easily and quickly entered directly as numbers into software packages such as SPSS. More recently, however, Dillman (2000, 2007) has used boxes for some close-ended response categories:

> What is your marital status? (Please check one)
> ☐ Never Married
> ☐ Married
> ☐ Divorced
> ☐ Separated
> ☐ Widowed

In the authors' recent studies using respondent-completed mail and on-site questionnaires, respondents have commented that it is easiest to answer questions when the following design guidelines have been followed throughout the instrument:

- Use *lines* (i.e., fill-in-the-blank) and "write response" commands for open-ended items:

  What is your age? (Please write response) _____ years old

- Use *boxes* and "check one" or "check all that apply" commands for close-ended questions with unordered or ordered responses that are not part of a scale or list of items:

  What types of deer hunting do you do in Wisconsin? (Please check all that apply)
  ☐ Gun (e.g., rifle, shotgun)
  ☐ Muzzleloading
  ☐ Archery

- Use *numbers* and "circle one number" commands for close-ended questions with ordered choices that are part of a scale or list of items. The authors' preference is to give the most negative response the lowest number (e.g., strongly disagree [1], very dissatisfied [1]) and most positive response the highest number (e.g., strongly agree [7], very satisfied [7]). Regardless of approach, it is important to be consistent throughout the questionnaire:

To what extent do you oppose or support each of the following possible management actions at Smith Lakes State Park? (Please circle one number for each action)

	Strongly Oppose	Oppose	Neither	Support	Strongly Support
Improve road access	1	2	3	4	5
Provide more parking	1	2	3	4	5
Provide more trash cans	1	2	3	4	5
Provide more toilets	1	2	3	4	5
Prohibit motorboats	1	2	3	4	5
Require dogs be kept on leash	1	2	3	4	5

There is no "perfect" way to format different types of response categories. It is crucial, however, that researchers maintain ***consistency*** throughout the entire questionnaire to minimize respondent confusion and maximize ease of questionnaire completion and data entry.

Constructing Mail and On-Site Surveys Completed by Respondents

Front Cover

Mail and respondent-completed on-site surveys (i.e., where respondents complete questionnaires on their own) rely on visual techniques to motivate people, which makes layout important when designing these questionnaires. One way to make multi-page questionnaires look interesting and professional is to use a graphic on the ***front cover***. Graphics not only help to stimulate interest, but also they convey a message that the survey is important and someone has worked hard to develop the questionnaire (Salant & Dillman, 1994). Covers should be free of clutter, *never* used as a cover letter (i.e., never include details about the study, how to respond, or researcher signatures), and should *not* include detailed instructions or the first few questions.

Covers should only include a few items. First, covers should have a short (i.e., one or two lines of text) ***title*** of what the survey is about. Subtitles of one or two additional lines of text can be added to provide more information about the survey or who is being surveyed. Titles should not be boring (e.g., "Smith Lakes State Park Survey"), biased (e.g., "Why You Should Vote in Favor of Wolf Reintroduction"), or academic (e.g., "A Stated-Choice Model for Examining Mutivariate Tradeoffs in Campers' Preferences"). Examples of acceptable titles would be "Public Responses to Wolf Reintroduction" or "Visitors' Experiences at Smith Lakes State Park."

Second, covers should contain an attractive and neutral ***graphic design, photograph, or illustration*** that generates interest in the study. Like titles, cover graphics should not be boring or suggest bias or controversy. A survey addressing urban wildlife management, for example, should not show a photograph of a collision between a deer and a vehicle. Figure 7.3 shows examples of acceptable cover graphics.

Third, the front cover should show ***names and logos*** (if available) of: (a) the funding or sponsoring agencies, and (b) the organizations or institutions conducting the survey. These names and logos demonstrate an objective and professional approach, and convey the importance of the study. For mail questionnaires, it might be useful to provide a return address on the cover, but this can be provided at the end of the questionnaire instead to reduce clutter on the cover. Figure 7.4 provides examples of acceptable cover pages for mail and on-site surveys.

Back Cover

If space permits, back covers of questionnaires can be used to give respondents an invitation to make additional open-ended comments. An appropriate question on the

Figure 7.3   Examples of Acceptable Cover Graphics for Questionnaires

back cover would be "Finally, do you have any other comments? If so, please write your comments below." If space is not available, the back cover could be used for asking objectionable or sensitive questions such as asking about demographic characteristics (e.g., age, income, marital status; Dillman, 2007). For mail surveys or on-site questionnaires that are handed to people and ask respondents to mail their completed form, the back cover should include a return address and directions for returning the completed questionnaire (e.g., "Please return your completed questionnaire in the enclosed self-addressed stamped envelope as soon as possible"). Back covers of printed questionnaires should always thank respondents for taking time to respond.

Figure 7.4   Examples of Cover Pages for Mail and On-Site Questionnaires

Formatting, Printing, and Length

Mail surveys should be printed in ***booklet format*** using paper folded and stapled down the fold. Placing a staple in the top left or right corner is not as professional, is more awkward for respondents when turning pages, and should never be considered when two-sided printing is used. Booklets can be created from 8 ½-by-14 inches (i.e., legal) or 11-by-17 inches paper folded in the middle and stapled down the fold. With this approach, questionnaire length will be in multiples of four when printed on both sides. A single sheet of paper, for example, creates four pages when folded, whereas two sheets create eight pages and three sheets create 12 pages. For mail surveys, always consult the postal service before designing print material.

On-site surveys should be shorter in number of questions and physical length. In the authors' experience conducting on-site surveys in recreation and tourism settings, a single sheet of legal (i.e., 8 ½-by-14 inches) paper printed on both sides, but *not* folded or stapled has been most effective. This format is easiest to use with a legal-size clipboard and does not require respondents to constantly flip pages (i.e., only once) when completing questionnaires on-site. With this approach, however, cover pages with graphics are not always possible because they take up an entire page, which may not be feasible for such a short questionnaire. In this case, the top of the first page should have text stating a title, brief (i.e., one or two sentences) introduction to the study, and agencies and organizations involved in funding and conducting the study.

For both mail and on-site surveys, questions should be printed on paper that is thick enough to prevent ink "bleed through." Color paper can sometimes improve attractiveness of questionnaires. Colors, such as light green, light blue, off-white or beige, pale yellow, tan or light brown, can be more unique and attractive than standard white paper. For on-site questionnaires that are completed outdoors, white paper can also create a glare that makes it difficult to read questions, so color paper may be more practical. If on-site questionnaires are administered in particularly rainy or damp locations, "Rite in the Rain" water-resistant paper may be useful.

When designing questionnaires, researchers should treat their word processor as a desktop publisher, not a typewriter. Default margins in word processing software, for example, are often larger (1 or 1 ½ inches) than necessary, so they should be adjusted. "Hanging" paragraphs can also be useful when numbering questions. Instead of double-spacing or hitting "enter" multiple times, "before" and "after" spacing capabilities can adjust the amount of space between questions and response categories. The "insert table" function instead of "tab" function should be used to create multi-item questions with scale responses (e.g., "strongly disagree" [1] to "strongly agree" [5]). Font sizes can be adjusted to fit the page and font styles can be changed to highlight text. Fonts should generally not be smaller than 10-point and font sizes may need to be larger for some audiences such as the elderly. Using bold, italics, capital letters, and underlining can also be useful for emphasizing and differentiating text. Finally, some word-processing software has the capability of translating questionnaires into different languages, which is critical if the target sample population does not speak English (e.g., Potaka & Cochrane, 2004). The software-generated translations should be checked by a speaker of the native language to ensure accuracy.

Constructing Telephone and On-Site Surveys Completed by Interviewers

Unlike mail surveys, telephone surveys and interviewer-completed on-site surveys (i.e., interviewers read questions and record answers) must sound rather than look good. Layout is less important because respondents seldom see the questionnaire, but layout should be consistent to make the interviewer's job as straightforward and routine as possible. Recommendations discussed earlier for designing mail and respondent-completed on-site questionnaires should be followed when constructing telephone or other interviewer-completed questionnaires (e.g., short, easy, relevant, and close-ended first question; use transition phrases; place difficult questions in the middle and objectionable questions at the end; group questions on the same topic). Salant and Dillman (1994), however, offer additional suggestions for these types of surveys:

- Select one font type for text that is always read, another font type (e.g., italics) for words or phrases that are sometimes read (e.g., *"feel free to provide your best guess if you are unsure"*), and a third font type (e.g., capital letters) for instructions to the interviewer that are not read to respondents (e.g., CODE ANSWER FROM CATEGORIES BELOW).

- Ensure that interviewers do not turn pages in the middle of questions or responses.

- In addition to answer categories that are read to respondents, include possible additional response categories that are not read to respondents but may be needed (e.g., Does not apply, Refused).

- Place response categories toward the right side of the page instead of the left side.

- The best check for a telephone questionnaire is whether it can be read to respondents exactly as it is written.

When writing questions for these surveys, it is important to remember that respondents are unable to see the questionnaire, so communicating response options is more tedious (Gad, 2000). Answer categories and response scales that are listed separately in mail questionnaires must now be incorporated into the question and read aloud by the interviewer:

> Which of the following activities did you participate in during your most recent visit to Findlay National Wildlife Refuge: hunting, fishing, wildlife viewing, wildlife photography, or something else? [CHECK ANSWER FROM CATEGORIES BELOW]
> Hunting ☐
> Fishing ☐
> Wildlife viewing ☐
> Wildlife photography ☐
> Other (write response) ☐ _____
> Refusal / No answer ☐

The task of communicating longer scales is even more challenging. If a seven-point response scale is used, for example, it would be cumbersome for interviewers and confusing for respondents if the question asked "Do you strongly oppose, moderately oppose, slightly oppose, neither support nor oppose, slightly support, moderately support, or strongly support reintroducing wolves to Colorado?" This can be even more challenging and time-consuming if multiple items are measured using these scales. Two steps are needed for these questions:

1. Ask if the respondent supports, opposes, or neither supports nor opposes (or agree/disagree; satisfied/unsatisfied, depending on response scale).

2. Then ask for the extent of support or opposition (i.e., slightly, moderately, strongly).

Some of the most important aspects of telephone or other in-person surveys are the interviewer's introduction, tone, and pace. The introduction sets the stage for the questionnaire and can make the difference between whether a respondent answers questions or refuses and hangs up the telephone (i.e., telephone survey) or walks away from the interviewer (i.e., on-site survey). Introductions should be short, simple, and include: (a) the interviewer's first name, (b) the organization and city from which they are calling, (c) a summary of the purpose of the survey, (d) a statement that their responses are confidential, (e) an estimate of how long the interview will take, and (f) permission to continue and ask questions (e.g., Houtkoop-Steenstra & van den Bergh, 2000; Salant & Dillman, 1994). An example of an acceptable introduction is:

> Hello, may I please speak with _____? My name is _____. I'm calling from Colorado State University in Fort Collins where we have been asked by the Colorado Division of Wildlife to talk with hunters about their opinions regarding deer management in the state. Would you be willing to answer a few quick questions, which will take less than 10 minutes to complete? Your responses will be completely confidential.

Throughout the introduction and remainder of the interview, the interviewer should set a neutral and professional tone and should maintain a moderate pace when asking questions. Once all questions are completed, the interviewer should thank the respondent with a statement such as "That is all the questions that I have. Thank you for your time and have a wonderful day."

Constructing Electronic Surveys

Email Surveys

It would seem that constructing an email survey simply involves writing a series of questions on the computer, sending the email to a selected group of email addresses, and asking people to answer in the spaces provided and hit the reply function (Dillman, 2007). Many recommendations for constructing mail surveys, however, should also be followed when designing email surveys. Dillman (2007) offers additional tips for constructing email surveys:

- Use multiple contacts (e.g., prenotice email, follow-up emails to nonrespondents) to improve response rates and leave a positive impression of the importance of the survey.
- Personalize each email contact so emails do not appear to be part of a bulk or mass mailing (e.g., multiple recipient addresses, listserv).
- Keep the cover letter short so respondents can see the first question without having to scroll down the page.
- Provide and inform respondents of alternative ways to respond (e.g., print and mail, call).
- Include a replacement electronic version of the questionnaire with reminder messages.
- Limit column width to approximately 70 characters to minimize likelihood of wrap-around text.
- Ask respondents to place an "X" inside brackets or boxes to indicate their answers to close-ended questions.

Although email surveys increase the speed at which data may be collected, they have many limitations that can make them somewhat inferior to other survey methods. Email surveys, for example, can have low response rates because using the delete key makes disposing of the questionnaire easy. The questionnaire must be short and the questions simplified due to formatting constraints of many email software packages. Using the Internet to distribute electronic surveys offers more flexibility and power than email (Dillman, 2007).

Internet Surveys

Unlike email surveys where questionnaires are sent to email addresses, Internet questionnaires are constructed on a website that is accessed by respondents. These types of questionnaires can be designed so that a new page appears for each question or respondents can scroll through questions on a single webpage. "Click here" boxes, drop-down menus, animation, sound, and color graphics can be used to improve interactive design beyond what is capable for most paper questionnaires (e.g., Couper et al., 2001; Dillman, 2007).

Gains in creative and advanced design tools, however, must be balanced against costs of making it difficult or impossible for some people to respond because of: (a) hardware and software performance or incompatibility, and (b) different levels of computer literacy among respondents (Dillman, 2007; Gaede & Vaske, 1999; Sills & Song, 2002). Researchers often need to restrain from using advanced and complex approaches for designing Internet questionnaires, and opt for simpler and more generic questionnaires that can be accessed by most respondents. Many recommendations for constructing mail and on-site questionnaires still apply in much the same way for Internet questionnaires (e.g., short, easy, relevant, and close-ended first question; difficult questions in the middle; objectionable questions at the end; group questions on same topic). Dillman (2007), however, discusses additional considerations for Internet questionnaires:

- Use a welcome screen to introduce the questionnaire, emphasize ease of responding, and provide instructions on how to proceed through the questionnaire.

- Provide a personalized identification number (PIN) to limit access only to people in the sample.

- Restrain use of color to maintain and not interfere with consistency, readability, navigational flow, and measurement properties. If colors are used, use high-contrast colors to improve readability.

- Avoid differences in visual appearance of questions that result from different screen configurations, operating systems, Internet browser software, partial screen display, and wrap-around text.

- Give precise instructions on how to use a computer to respond to the questionnaire, and give necessary instructions at the point where they are needed (e.g., use floating windows to show how to respond to types of questions, although this can introduce technical problems with some Internet browsers and software packages).

- Use drop-down menus sparingly and identify each with a "click here" instruction.

- Do not require all respondents to give an answer for each question before being allowed to proceed further in the questionnaire because it can frustrate respondents who may have a legitimate reason for not answering a particular question.

- Design Internet questionnaires so respondents scroll from question to question instead of having a new question appear on each page.

- Use symbols, a task bar, or text (e.g., percent complete) to give people an idea of where they are in the completion process.

- Always thoroughly test and debug your survey on the server before going live.

Internet surveys offer tremendous potential for little cost. However, there are limitations to this data collection method (e.g., coverage errors because not everybody has computer access; lack of control over who responds; issues related to anonymity, security, and confidentiality of responses; Couper, 2000). Although technological advances will continue to improve flexibility and power of Internet surveys, it is unreasonable to assume that everyone will have access to computers with the most recent and powerful technology (Dillman, 2007; Gaede & Vaske, 1999). As a result, researchers should consider their target population when deciding whether an Internet survey or other form of survey is appropriate for addressing project objectives.

Chapter Summary

This chapter discussed advantages, disadvantages, and guidelines for conducting different types of surveys (e.g., mail, on-site, telephone, electronic). Several suggestions for writing questions and constructing questionnaires were provided. It should be clear after reading this chapter that writing and constructing questionnaires are complex tasks. Researchers and funding agencies should not treat these tasks as afterthoughts. Questionnaires should never be finalized in a single sitting; experienced researchers often need 10, 15, or even 20 or more drafts and revisions of a single questionnaire before guidelines discussed in this chapter have been addressed and the instrument is ready to administer.

This chapter discussed advantages and disadvantages of survey research. Advantages of surveys are that they can describe characteristics of a larger population, large sample sizes can be obtained in a short period of time, they facilitate comparisons among groups, and numerous questions can be asked in a single instrument. Disadvantages of surveys are that all questions must be understandable to all respondents, and some questionnaires are not flexible and may not be changed once they are administered. Questionnaires may also seem artificial to respondents and may not always provide rich enough data to address particular topics. If surveys are not likely to provide the information desired, alternative methodologies should be considered (e.g., interviews, diaries, Delphi approach, document analysis, personal observation).

Several steps should be followed if the researcher decides survey research would be the best method for completing the study. The researcher must start by identifying the problem, objectives, and/or hypotheses that the project is trying to solve and information needs for addressing these issues. Following this, he or she should review the relevant literature to identify knowledge gaps and inform questions to be included in the questionnaire. The next step is to select the most appropriate type of survey for attaining project goals. This chapter discussed advantages and disadvantages of mail, on-site, telephone, electronic (i.e., email, Internet), drop-off, and mixed-mode surveys. Once the researcher has selected the type of survey to be used, he or she should proceed by writing questions and constructing a first draft of the questionnaire.

This chapter discussed 25 guidelines to consider when writing survey questions. Researchers, for example, should avoid double-barreled questions, vague quantifiers, double-negatives, leading or loaded questions, and questions that are too difficult or require unnecessary calculations. Questions should also include accurate and complete sentences with as few words as possible, an appropriate timeframe, and simple words and phrases that make sense to respondents. Response categories should be mutually exclusive, fixed or close-ended whenever possible, use an equal number of positive and negative response options, and ask respondents to provide a single answer rather than "check all that apply" whenever possible. Finally, researchers should strive to make every question count, reduce the impact of sensitive or objectionable questions, define abbreviations, select items that allow for comparisons with existing information or data, and use multiple questions to measure a complex theory or concept.

Once questions have been written, the researcher must construct the instrument. When designing questionnaires, it is important to start with easy, relevant questions that do not ask for demographic information. Questionnaires should be segmented by grouping similar questions into sections and numbering questions sequentially. Transitions should be included to guide respondents, and skip patterns should be avoided whenever possible. Response categories should be consistent; formatting should be used to provide adequate "white space." In addition to these guidelines, this chapter also provided specific recommendations for designing particular types of surveys such as respondent-completed mail and on-site surveys (e.g., booklet, cover graphics, title, formatting), interviewer-completed telephone and on-site surveys (e.g., layout, interviewer introduction, communicating response options), and electronic surveys (e.g., brief introduction or cover letter, personalized message or identification number).

Writing and designing questionnaires is just an initial step in survey research. Next steps include pretesting the instrument, asking and encouraging a sample of people to respond, establishing procedures for coding responses and entering data, analyzing data, and reporting findings. Chapter 8 provides details regarding sampling potential respondents and administering questionnaires to these individuals. Chapters 9 and 10 discuss procedures for coding responses and entering data into software to assist in data analysis. Chapter 11 through the end of this book presents various statistical approaches for analyzing data and reporting results using SPSS.

Review Questions

1. Discuss two advantages and two disadvantages of survey research.

2. List three alternative data collection techniques other than survey research.

3. What are two important questions to ask *before* deciding on the type of survey to administer and focusing on mechanics of constructing and implementing a survey?

4. Provide an example of a *vague* research question and suggest ways for improvement.

5. Define and differentiate *elicitation surveys* and *focus groups*.

6. Discuss three criteria that you might use when deciding whether to use a mail, on-site, telephone, or electronic survey.

7. What is *social desirability bias*?

8. Discuss one strength and one weakness for *each* of the following types of surveys: mail, on-site, and telephone.

9. Discuss one strength and one weakness of open-ended questions.

10. Give one example of *each* of the following types of questions: close-ended with ordered response choices, close-ended with unordered response choices, and partially close-ended response choices.

11. Discuss five general guidelines for improving question wording.

12. Why should a researcher distinguish *neither* from *no opinion* in response scales?

13. What does it mean when a question is *double-barreled*? Give an example of a double-barreled question.

14. Define and differentiate *primacy* and *recency* effects.

15. Response categories and answers should be *mutually exclusive*. What does this mean?

16. Why should multiple questions be used to measure a single complex concept or theory?

17. Discuss three general recommendations for constructing surveys.

18. List three things that should be on the cover of a mail survey.

19. Discuss the two steps that should be used when communicating long scale responses in telephone surveys.

20. Discuss two specific ways to improve design of Internet surveys.

8

survey implementation, sampling, and weighting data[1]

Chapter 7 discussed procedures for writing and designing questionnaires. Once a first draft of a questionnaire has been constructed, steps that follow in the survey research process include asking experts to review the questionnaire, pretesting the instrument, finalizing sampling procedures, administering the final questionnaire, and conducting a nonresponse bias check if necessary. This chapter discusses these steps and examines various approaches for selecting samples of potential respondents and administering questionnaires to these individuals. The chapter concludes with a discussion about weighting survey data.

Expert Advice, Pretesting, and Final Checks

Before administering a questionnaire, it is important to learn whether the instrument works satisfactorily or has any major problems. Pretesting a questionnaire adds more time to the survey research process, but it is an essential task (Krosnick, 1999; Salant & Dillman, 1994). *Pretesting* involves at least three phases: (a) seeking advice from experts such as academicians or representatives of organizations supporting the project, (b) administering the questionnaire to a small group of people who are typical of likely respondents (i.e., pilot testing), and (c) performing a final check of the instrument to ensure that no major errors are present.

Expert Advice

When writing and designing a questionnaire, it is important to allow input at various stages from policymakers, agency administrators, or other representatives of organizations supporting the project. These individuals have a vested interest in the project and substantial practical knowledge of topics being investigated and populations being surveyed. Having these individuals review drafts of the questionnaire can help identify technical problems that the researcher might miss, especially questions and statements that may not be technically accurate (see guideline 21, chapter 7). Expert advice is also important to identify if all necessary questions have been asked in the questionnaire, any questions that can be eliminated, and whether questions and response categories will allow comparisons to other existing data.

---

[1] This chapter was coauthored with Dr. Mark D. Needham, Oregon State University

Pilot Tests

After receiving expert advice and making any revisions to the questionnaire based on this input, the next step is to administer the instrument to a relatively small number of individuals who are similar to those who will likely be sampled in the larger data collection effort (Babbie, 2003; Krosnick, 1999). To pilot test a survey examining anglers' attitudes toward catch-and-release policies, for example, the questionnaire should be given to a group of anglers who represent the diversity of anglers in the population (e.g., young, old; fly anglers, bait anglers; male, female).

Researchers should not be overly concerned about obtaining large sample sizes for pilot tests. Dillman (2000) suggests that a sample of 100 to 200 respondents should be drawn for a pilot test, but this will vary considerably depending on project resources (e.g., time, budget) and population characteristics. For a study of hikers in a relatively low-use backcountry setting, for example, a realistic and feasible pilot test sample may consist of only 30 to 50 hikers.

When conducting a pilot test, it is desirable to watch or listen to individuals complete the questionnaire to check for signs indicating problems such as respondents being confused, misreading or misunderstanding instructions, being unable to answer questions, or straining to maintain focus due to questionnaire length and completion time (Salant & Dillman, 1994). It is also informative to debrief people after completing the questionnaire and ask questions such as:

- Were there any questions or statements that you did not understand or were confusing?
- Were any questions too difficult to answer?
- Were any questions double-barreled (i.e., two questions, but only one answer choice)?
- Were there any questions that you thought were overly sensitive or objectionable?
- Were there any questions or statements that may have biased your answers?
- Were any questions or statements factually inaccurate?
- Were there any questions that you think should have been asked but were not?
- Was the formatting of response categories easy to follow?
- Were all possible response categories included for each close-ended question?
- Were skip patterns (if any) easy to follow?
- Was the questionnaire too long?
- Did the flow or organization of the questionnaire make sense, or did it seem disorganized?
- Was the questionnaire cluttered, or was the appearance distracting?
- Did the questionnaire create a positive impression that motivated you to respond?
- Did you notice any spelling or grammatical errors?

Pilot testing questionnaires with small groups helps to identify problems that were not obvious to the researcher such as issues causing low response rates, entire pages or sections being skipped, questions not being answered, and items not correlating in a way that allows scales to be built.

Final Checks

A last step before administering a questionnaire to a larger sample is to perform a final check of the instrument to ensure that no errors are present. A few people who have not been involved in any stages of project development or questionnaire construction should be asked to read and answer the questionnaire as both respondents and proofreaders. Researchers who are closely involved with questionnaire design and revisions often read questions and response options so many times that they lose their ability to detect obvious problems (Dillman, 2000).

A final check can reveal subtle but important errors. In one of the authors' studies, for example, a final check showed that one scale response option was written as "slightly impotent" instead of "slightly important." Word processing software that automatically checks spelling would not have detected this embarrassing error. In the same questionnaire, a five-point scale was written as: "very unacceptable," "unacceptable," "neither," "acceptable," and "very unacceptable." Obviously, "very unacceptable" should not have been listed twice. These errors went unnoticed even after the questionnaire had already gone through 23 revisions based on expert advice at various stages, multiple reviews by three investigators, and a pilot test of over 200 respondents!

Taken together, objectives of pilot tests, expert advice, and final checks are to obtain feedback about questionnaire wording and design, and test validity and reliability of questions and scales measuring complex or multidimensional concepts (see chapter 18). Questionnaires should be revised based on input and results from these preliminary but important steps before selecting a larger sample from a population and proceeding with the main data collection effort.

Minimizing Error in Survey Research

Survey research involves administrating questionnaires to a sample of respondents selected from a larger population. Samples are used for making inferences about the population of interest. Unlike a census where everybody is surveyed, responses from a sample of people almost never perfectly match the population. Survey sampling is the art and science of "coming close" and producing "good estimates" of what people think or do (Salant & Dillman, 1994).

When conducting a survey, the researcher must start by identifying the *element* or unit about which information will be collected. Examples of elements include people, households, families, social clubs, corporations, and organizations. In random samples (discussed later), elements are the units of analysis and provide the basis for analysis of results. The theoretically specified aggregation of these elements forms a *population*. The *survey population* consists of the aggregation of elements from which the sample is actually selected and to which results will be generalized. The element or set of elements considered for selection in a sampling stage is the *sampling unit*. Single-stage samples consist of primary sampling units, which are the same as elements (e.g., random sample of hunters; every fifth person at trailhead). Multistage samples may employ different levels of sampling units such as primary (e.g., census blocks in a city) and secondary (e.g., individuals at select households in these blocks) sampling units. The *sampling frame* is the list from which a sample or some stage of the sample will be drawn to represent the survey population, whereas a *sample* consists of all *observation units* that are selected for inclusion in the survey. Finally, a *completed sample* consists of units that participated in the survey by completing a questionnaire (Dillman, 2000, 2007).

Before administering questionnaires, researchers need to address questions such as:

- How many completed questionnaires (i.e., completed sample) are needed, and how many people need to be selected in a sample to attain this many completed questionnaires?
- Should everyone in the sampling frame and sample have an equal chance to complete the questionnaire, or should it be targeted only to select groups of individuals?
- What is the most appropriate way to select the sample from the sampling frame given project constraints (e.g., cost, time, personnel) and desired accuracy and precision?
- How high should the response rate be?
- How accurate will the results be?

Each of these questions should be addressed to minimize errors. Common sources of problems in survey research include errors in coverage, measurement, nonresponse, and sampling.

Coverage Error

A completed sample can only be used to provide information about the sample, sampling frame, and survey population (Babbie, 2003; Salant & Dillman, 1994). *Coverage error* occurs with a discrepancy between the target population and subset of individuals who are included in the sampling frame. This error occurs, for example, when the list of individuals from which the sample is selected is not inclusive of all elements of the population of interest (Dillman, 2000). If there is error in coverage, all elements of the target population do not have an equal or known chance of being included in the sample. If the sample is not representative of the population, it is difficult to use survey results to generalize to the broader target population.

Coverage error can occur in all types of surveys. For example, if a mail survey was commissioned to examine Colorado residents' attitudes toward wolf reintroduction and questionnaires were only sent to residents of Colorado's urban east slope (e.g., Denver, Colorado Springs, Fort Collins), findings would likely show support for wolf reintroduction. Research shows that positive attitudes toward wolves are more prevalent among urban than rural residents and among people who live far from wolf reintroduction sites than those who live close to sites (e.g., Bright & Manfredo, 1996). This methodology, however, represents an error in coverage and as a result, this finding would not be representative of or generalizable to all Colorado residents. To ensure adequate coverage of the population, questionnaires should also be mailed to individuals living in Colorado's rural west slope region (e.g., Kremmling, Craig, Meeker).

One way to overcome coverage error is to get an accurate up-to-date list of everybody in the target population. This may be a simple task if the population is relatively small and easily identifiable (e.g., students in a class, clients at a hunting camp). General population lists or information about other large or diffuse groups, however, pose a greater challenge. Tax records, telephone directories, lists of utility hookups, voter registration lists, and lists from private firms such as Survey Sampling International (SSI) can be useful for obtaining contact information for the general public. There are several texts discussing strengths and weaknesses of various sources of sample lists (Babbie, 2003; Dillman, 2000, 2007; Fowler, 1993; Salant & Dillman, 1994). Researchers should evaluate a list and assess whether it is updated and maintained regularly, contains everyone in the population, does not include people who are not in the study population, and does not contain entries listed more than once (Dillman, 2007). Lists must be considered individually; a list used for one survey may not be suitable for another survey.

In parks, recreation, and human dimensions research, lists for more specific populations can also be obtained from sources such as hunting and fishing license sales or reservation/registration data (e.g., trail or campground permits). These lists, however, do not always guarantee perfect coverage because not everybody complies with requirements such as completing a trailhead registration card or purchasing a fishing license. For many studies, population lists such as these may also be unavailable. Many backcountry recreation areas, for example, contain multiple entry points (e.g., trailheads) and people show up at a particular location without being required to complete a registration card or other method for recording contact information. One strategy, therefore, would be to ask people to complete the questionnaire on-site, or ask people for their contact information and then follow up with a mail, telephone, or electronic survey.

Coverage error does not always occur because of incorrect or incomplete sampling lists. As illustrated earlier in the Colorado wolf reintroduction example, coverage error can occur when spatial differences are present in the population (e.g., east vs. west slope residents). Coverage error can also occur when researchers have not ensured adequate coverage across time and among subgroups of the population. In many recreation studies, for example, surveys should be administered in different seasons (e.g., high, shoulder, low seasons), at various times of the week (e.g., weekday, weekend), and with multiple activity groups (e.g., anglers, hikers) to account for differences in recreationists' characteristics and visitation patterns (Mitra & Lankford, 1999).

Measurement Error

Unlike coverage error, which is related to lists of samples or populations, *measurement error* occurs when data are collected and a respondent's answers are imprecise, inaccurate, or cannot be compared to answers provided by other respondents (Beimer, 1991; Dillman, 2000; Krosnick, 1999). Measurement error is the difference between a respondent's answer and the "correct" answer and can occur because of poor questionnaire wording and construction, type of survey, influence of the interviewer, or behavior of the respondent (Salant & Dillman, 1994).

Chapter 7 provided the following example of a question with vague quantifiers:

About how often did you go hiking during the past year? (Please check one)

☐ Never
☐ Rarely
☐ Occasionally
☐ Regularly

These response options can generate measurement error because they may not be understood in the same way by all respondents. One person, for example, may interpret "rarely" to mean three to five times and "occasionally" to imply six to ten times. Another person may think that "rarely" means once a month (i.e., 12 times in the past year) and "occasionally" refers to twice a month (i.e., 24 times per year). In addition to question wording, design of the questionnaire can also influence measurement error. If the questionnaire is cluttered and it is difficult to read and reply to questions (see Figure 7.1, p. 158), people may answer incorrectly or skip questions altogether.

As discussed in chapter 7, different types of surveys place different demands on respondents. In telephone surveys, for example, interviewers have control over the speed in which questions are asked and answered, and respondents rely on information conveyed by interviewers. Conversely, mail surveys give respondents more control over the order and speed in which questions are read and answered. For some questions, different types of surveys may provide different results than other types, thus inflating measurement error (see Tables 7.3, 7.4, p. 132).

Interviewers can also be a source of measurement error (Groves & McGonagle, 2001). In telephone surveys and interviewer-completed on-site surveys, for example, interviewers can bias respondents' answers through actions such as shortening questions that unintentionally change their meaning or adding phrases such as "This is an easy question for which everybody says yes" or "You oppose this strategy, right?" Even subtle interviewer behavior such as wearing a hat embroidered with "Save the Whales" when conducting an in-person survey about environmental issues can bias responses. Interviewers should remain as neutral and objective as possible.

Measurement error also occurs when respondents inadvertently or deliberately provide incorrect answers (Beimer, 1991). Parks, recreation, and human dimensions studies, for example, often ask people to report their willingness to pay for nonmarket goods such as access to a hiking trail or overnight stays at a wilderness campsite. People may strategically report low numbers so that they do not have to pay a high fee or they may report high numbers so that they will be the only person who could afford the fee and will have the area to themselves. Clearly, neither answer is "correct." To avoid these various sources of measurement error, it is important to carefully select the most appropriate survey method, write clear and unambiguous questions and response options, and train personnel to the fullest extent possible (Salant & Dillman, 1994). Consulting the literature, seeking expert advice, and pilot testing of questionnaires also help minimize measurement error.

Nonresponse Error

People without training in survey research often believe that if a large sample size is obtained, data will always be representative of and generalizable to the population of interest (Dillman, 2007). This is not true. *Nonresponse error* occurs when "a significant number of people in the survey sample do not respond to the questionnaire *and* are different from those who do in a way that is important to the study" (Salant & Dillman, 1994, p. 20). For example, if a questionnaire about residents' attitudes toward increasing fees in national parks was mailed to 100,000 people across the country and 5,000 questionnaires were completed and returned, this relatively large sample size might look impressive to the untrained observer. The low response rate (5%), however, should be a warning sign for problems associated with nonresponse error. Results from the 5,000 respondents may show support for a fee increase, but careful examination of these people may show that they have never visited a national park so may be unaffected by a fee increase. People who visit parks may be underrepresented in this sample, so despite the large sample size, results would not be representative of the 95% of people who did not respond. It is not always the sample size that counts most; the response rate may be more important.

One way to help minimize nonresponse error is to aim for a high response rate (Bailar, 1987; Krosnick, 1999; Pearl & Fairley, 1985). If a high response rate is not achieved, a nonresponse bias check should be conducted to compare those who responded to the questionnaire to those who did not respond. If results differ between respondents and nonrespondents, data may need to be weighted. Methods for encouraging high response rates, conducting nonresponse bias checks, and weighting data are discussed later in this chapter.

Sampling Error and Selecting Sample Sizes

When conducting a survey and having a sample from a larger population complete a questionnaire, there is always some degree of sampling error because sample statistics are rarely equal to population parameters (Bailar, 1987; Krosnick, 1999). *Sampling error* is the extent to which a sample is limited in its ability to perfectly describe a population because only some, and not all, elements in the population are sampled (Dillman, 2000). One way to avoid sampling error is to conduct a census (i.e., survey the entire population). Given costs in time, personnel, and financial resources, a census is often not realistic or feasible for most studies. Sampling error, however, can be minimized by increasing sample size.

Survey research allows investigators to estimate with precision the extent to which a population has a particular attribute simply by obtaining data from only a small sample of the total population. To minimize sampling error, it is usually advantageous to select a relatively large sample size. If a large sample size is obtained and potential problems related to coverage, nonresponse, and measurement errors have been minimized, the sample data may be representative of and generalizable to the target sample population. The sample data, however, may not estimate the entire population. If a mail survey about hunting regulations was completed by a large random sample of deer hunters in Utah, for example, results may allow fairly precise estimates for the population of Utah deer hunters. It would be a bold and incorrect claim, however, to say that these data are representative of *all* Utah hunters because deer hunters may feel differently about regulations than people hunting waterfowl, elk, bear, or other species.

Deciding on how large a sample should be depends on answering several questions:

- How much sampling error can be tolerated?
- How small or large is the size of the target population?
- How varied is this population with respect to characteristics of interest to the project?
- What is the smallest subgroup within the sample for which estimates are needed?

Sampling error is often calculated and communicated in terms of a level of confidence (i.e., confidence interval; see chapter 6) that results are within plus or minus some margin of error. In most parks, recreation, and human dimensions studies, it is desirable to obtain enough completed questionnaires to allow the researcher to be 95% confident that estimates from the data are within ±5% (or points) of the sample population. This means that 95 out of 100 times (95% of the time) that there is a random sample from a population the estimate ±5% will contain the population value assuming no nonresponse, measurement, or coverage errors. In other words, chances are 19 out of 20 that the population value is within 5% of the estimate in either direction. For example, if a random sample of 400 hikers in Sky Lakes Wilderness in Oregon showed that 63% of hikers supported requiring dogs be kept on leash, researchers can be 95% confident that between 58% and 68% of all hikers in this wilderness area would support this action if all hikers in the area had been surveyed.

Table 8.1   Completed Sample Sizes Needed for Population Sizes and Characteristics at Three Levels of Precision

	Sample size for the 95% confidence level					
	± 3% sampling error		± 5% sampling error		± 10% sampling error	
	50/50 split	80/20 split	50/50 split	80/20 split	50/50 split	80/20 split
100	92	87	80	71	49	38
200	169	155	132	111	65	47
400	291	253	196	153	78	53
600	384	320	234	175	83	56
800	458	369	260	188	86	57
1,000	517	406	278	198	88	58
2,000	696	509	322	219	92	60
4,000	843	584	351	232	94	61
6,000	906	613	361	236	95	61
8,000	942	629	367	239	95	61
10,000	965	640	370	240	95	61
20,000	1,013	661	377	243	96	61
40,000	1,040	672	381	244	96	61
100,000	1,056	679	383	245	96	61
1,000,000	1,066	683	384	246	96	61
1,000,000,000	1,067	683	384	246	96	61

Sources: Dillman (2000, 2007), Salant and Dillman (1994)

Table 8.1 is from Dillman (2007) and Salant and Dillman (1994), and lists sample sizes needed to estimate population percentages for various population sizes and levels of sampling error. In this table, a *50/50 split* means that the population is completely divided in their responses. The researcher would expect 50% of the population to answer one way (e.g., support, agree) and 50% to answer the other way (e.g., oppose, disagree). A 50/50 split is the most conservative value possible. An *80/20 split* means that answers are less variable; many people respond one way or have a certain characteristic, whereas a few do not. If researchers have little or no knowledge about the diversity of characteristics and opinions among the population, the conservative 50/50 split approach is recommended (Salant & Dillman, 1994). For most parks, recreation, and human dimensions studies, therefore, a sample size of approximately 400 is often considered to be suitable for generalizing to a population at a 95% confidence level with a ±5% margin of error.

Dillman (2007) provides the following formula for estimating desired sample sizes:

$$N_s = \frac{(N_p)(p)(1-p)}{(N_p-1)(B/C)^2 + (p)(1-p)}$$

Equation 8.1

where:

N_s = completed sample size needed (notation often used is *n*)
N_p = size of population (notation often used is *N*)
p = proportion expected to answer a certain way (50% or 0.5 is most conservative)
B = acceptable level of sampling error ($0.05 = ±5\%$; $0.03 = ±3\%$)
C = Z statistic associate with confidence interval ($1.645 = 90\%$ confidence level; $1.960 = 95\%$ confidence level; $2.576 = 99\%$ confidence level)

To illustrate, for a question with a 50/50 split in a population that consisted of 4,200 people, a sample size of 352 is needed to be 95% confident that the sample estimate is within ±5% of the true population value. The formula for this example is:

$$N_s = \frac{(4,200)(0.5)(1-0.5)}{(4,200-1)(0.05/1.96)^2 + (0.5)(1-0.5)} = 352$$

If the sample size and population size are known, a margin of error is calculated from:

$$B = C\sqrt{\frac{p(1-p)}{N_s} - \frac{p(1-p)}{N_p}}$$ Equation 8.2

To illustrate, if the completed sample size (N_s) is 1,126 and the population size (N_p) is 1,812,374, the margin of error (i.e., sampling error) at the 95% confidence level with a 50/50 split would be 0.029 or ±2.9% of the true population value. The formula for this example is:

$$B = 1.96\sqrt{\frac{0.5(1-0.5)}{1,126} - \frac{0.5(1-0.5)}{1,812,374}} = 0.029$$

There are some useful websites that will quickly perform calculations to estimate sample size and margin of error (e.g., http://www.custominsight.com/articles/random-sample-calculator.asp).

With large population sizes (e.g., over 100,000), there is little difference in sample sizes needed to achieve a small amount of sampling error. As a result, most statewide or national polls are based on 1,100 to 1,200 completed questionnaires to allow estimates of the population within a ±3% margin of error at the 95% confidence level (Salant & Dillman, 1994). Just because so few responses are needed for estimating such a large population, however, does not mean that only a small fraction of that number is needed for generalizing to a much smaller group (e.g., small town, recreation site). With smaller population sizes, a much greater proportion of the population needs to be sampled and complete a questionnaire to achieve a given margin of error. This does not imply that a census (i.e., survey everyone) must be conducted if the population is small. For example, doing a poor job surveying all 1,000 members of a population so that 350 people reply (i.e., 35% response rate; discussed later) is less cost-effective and increases chances of nonresponse error compared to doing a good job sampling only 500 people and encouraging a high response rate that produces the same number of responses (e.g., 350 people, 70% response rate). Strategies for improving response rates are discussed later in this chapter.

When approximating sample sizes and sampling error, it is also important to consider the smallest subgroup within the sample for which estimates are needed. If 1,000 resident deer hunters in Colorado, for example, completed a questionnaire asking about their participation in this activity, the sampling error would be approximately ±3% with a confidence level of 95% (population of Colorado resident deer hunters is approximately 60,000 per year). If these hunters were segmented into three relatively equal sized subgroups based on a characteristic (e.g., low, medium, and high skill level; young, middle age, older), however, the margin of error would increase to approximately ±5% for each subgroup when examining each third of the sample at a time. Segmenting samples into subgroups for analysis increases sampling error, so if it is important to understand characteristics and opinions of different subgroups, sample sizes should be increased.

Obtaining large sample sizes may not always be possible because of circumstances such as project budget, timeline, availability of personnel, and complexity of sampling methodology. Tradeoffs in the desired margin of error and precision with which estimates about the population can be made must be weighed against these factors as well as any additional expenditures that may be necessary for minimizing other sources of error (i.e., coverage, measurement, nonresponse).

Types of Sampling Approaches

In any survey, the first step to collecting data is to define in precise terms the population or community of individuals whose opinions are sought (Babbie, 2003; Mitra & Lankford, 1999). In parks, recreation, and human dimensions of natural resources, populations may be as broad as the general population in a state or country, or as specific as hikers on a particular section of trail. Once the population has been defined, it is necessary to obtain a list of the entire group so that a sample can be selected. As discussed earlier, there are various outlets for obtaining survey lists (e.g., tax records, telephone directories, lists of utility hookups, voter registration lists), but when lists are unavailable, on-site survey methods may be the only alternative. Lists should be checked for accuracy including whether there are any duplicates, omissions, and ineligible members.

Once the population has been defined and a list of members has been obtained, it is necessary to choose a method for selecting a sample that represents the population from which it was drawn. ***Sampling*** is the process of selecting observations, which gives social scientists the capability of describing a larger population based on only a selected portion of that population. ***Representativeness*** involves a process where all constituencies in the population have a known chance of being selected in the sample and the sampling procedure ensures that the sample contains the same characteristics as the population (Mitra & Lankford, 1999). A sample is representative of the population from which it was selected if characteristics of the sample closely approximate the same characteristics in the population for issues that are of interest in the study. Unless the sample is at least moderately representative of the population, it is difficult to make predictions about the population from which the sample was selected. Making statements such as "we are 95% confident that this estimate is within ± 5% of the true population" requires a degree of randomness to be built into the sampling design. This means that every unit or person in the population has a known nonzero chance of being selected for inclusion in the sample.

Sampling designs that strive for representativeness and are based on randomness are called probability samples. ***Probability sampling*** involves random samples, requires relatively few observations, and allows results to generalize to the larger target population. A probability sample will be representative of the population from which it was selected if all members of the population have a known nonzero chance of being selected (Morgan & Harmon, 1999). There are two main advantages of probability sampling. First, probability theory allows researchers to estimate accuracy or representativeness of a sample (e.g., sampling error). Second, probability samples are more representative than other types of samples because biases are avoided. ***Bias*** in connection with sampling occurs when units or individuals in the sample are not representative of the population. Bias would occur, for example, if the researcher avoided including certain types of people in the sample (e.g., only selected male hikers for an on-site trailhead survey).

If a sample is selected where the researcher makes a subjective judgment to include or exclude certain individuals, the integrity of the selection process may be compromised and it may be difficult to generalize results to a larger population. This is called ***nonprobability*** or ***purposive*** sampling. Convenience samples and focus groups are examples of nonprobability samples because some members of the population have a high chance be included in the sample, whereas others may have little or no chance of being selected. Nonprobability samples are useful for elicitation or exploratory studies that may generate new ideas to be systematically tested later using probability sampling techniques. After collecting data from nonprobability or convenience samples, researchers may examine demographic characteristics of their sample and conclude that respondents are similar to those in the larger population. Although this indicates an attempt to check for representativeness, similarities do not prove that the sample is representative of the population (Morgan & Harmon, 1999). Nonprobability samples should not be used to make inferences about the population because they may introduce bias and researchers are limited in their ability to determine the accuracy of nonprobability estimates (Salant & Dillman, 1994).

Given that this book focuses on asking a sample of people to complete a questionnaire and using results to generalize to the sample population, it examines probability as opposed to nonprobability samples. There are several methods of probability sampling (see Fowler, 1993; Lohr, 1999; Scheaffer, Mendenhall, & Ott, 1996, for reviews). ***Single stage sampling*** approaches (i.e., single set of primary sampling units) include simple random, systematic, stratified, and cluster samples. ***Multistage sampling*** approaches may use both primary (e.g., census blocks in a city) and secondary (e.g., individuals at select households in these blocks) sampling units and a combination of different sampling techniques (e.g., cluster sample combined with a stratified sample). Decisions about what type of approach to choose depend on the purpose of the study, type of population being surveyed, and availability of resources (e.g., personnel, time, budget).

Simple Random Sampling

Perhaps the most common and basic sampling method is ***simple random sampling*** (SRS), which consists of selecting a group of sampling units (e.g., people) in such a way that each member of the target population or each sample of a specific size has an equal chance of being selected (Scheaffer et al., 1996). For example, if a target population consisted of 100,000 hikers, a simple random sample of 1,000 hikers means that every member of this population has a 1 in 100 chance of being selected. Simple random samples are reasonably unbiased, but they require that all members of the target population be included in the list; if some members are missing, they do not all have the same chance of being selected (Morgan & Harmon, 1999).

To select a simple random sample, researchers might choose ***haphazard sampling*** by using their own judgment to "randomly" select a sample. A second method called ***representative sampling*** involves selecting a sample that the researcher considers to be "representative" or "typical" of the population (Scheaffer et al., 1996). Both haphazard and representative methods are subjective and prone to researcher bias so they are not "random" by definition and are not appropriate for probability samples. There are several more rigorous methods for selecting simple random samples such as using lotteries, random number tables, or statistical software.

Lottery techniques simply involve using approaches such as picking numbers out of a hat that contain sampling units (i.e., individual names, contact information) written on thoroughly mixed pieces of paper (Salant & Dillman, 1994). A more appropriate method for drawing a random sample, however, is to use tables of random numbers. A ***random numbers table*** is a long set of integers generated so that the table contains all 10 integers (i.e., 0, 1, ... , 9) in relatively equal proportions with no trends in the pattern in which digits were generated. If a number is selected from any point on the table, it has a relatively equal chance of being any digit from 0 through 9 (Scheaffer et al., 1996). Table 8.2 lists the first 10 lines of a random numbers table; almost all sampling and statistics books provide complete tables of random numbers.

Table 8.2   The First Ten Lines in a Random Number Table

Line / Col.	(1)	(2)	(3)	(4)	(5)	(6)	(7)	(8)	(9)	(10)	(11)	(12)	(13)	(14)
1	10480	15011	01536	02011	81647	91646	69179	14194	62590	36207	20969	99570	91291	90700
2	22368	46573	25595	85393	30995	89198	27982	53402	93965	34095	52666	19174	39615	99505
3	24130	48360	22527	97265	76393	64809	15179	24830	49340	32081	30680	19655	63348	58629
4	42167	93093	06243	61680	07856	16376	39440	53537	71341	57004	00849	74917	97758	16379
5	37570	39975	81837	16656	06121	91782	60468	81305	49684	60672	14110	06927	01263	54613
6	77921	06907	11008	42751	27756	53498	18602	70659	90655	15053	21916	81825	44394	42880
7	99562	72905	56420	69994	98872	31016	71194	18738	44013	48840	63213	21069	10634	12952
8	96301	91977	05463	07972	18876	20922	94595	56869	69014	60045	18425	84903	42508	32307
9	89579	14342	63661	10281	17453	18103	57740	84378	25331	12565	58678	44947	05585	56941
10	85475	36857	53342	53988	53060	59533	38867	62300	08158	17983	16439	11458	18593	64952

The first step for choosing numbers from a random numbers table is to allocate an identification number (ID) to each person who appears on a clean and complete population list that is free of errors (discussed earlier in this chapter). The second step is to determine the number of digits needed for the random numbers selected. Only use as many digits in the numbers table as what are contained in the highest ID number (e.g., if 2,000 members of a population, select four-digit numbers; if 975 members, select three-digit numbers). The third step is to randomly select a starting point in the table. Any starting point can be used because numbers in the table are entirely random. The fourth step is to create *n*-digit numbers out of the five-digit numbers in the table. If, for example, the population size is 975, the first three digits, last three digits, or middle three digits could be used. Make a plan and be consistent through the selection process. The final step is to proceed consistently through the random numbers table in any direction (e.g., vertically down or up columns, horizontally across rows from left to right or right to left, diagonally) and select entries that match numbers written on the list until the desired sample size is achieved. If a number is reached that is larger than the population size, ignore it and move on to the next number. The same solution applies if the same number appears more than once.

To illustrate, assume that a population list contains names and contact information for 950 bird watchers from which a random sample of 20 is to be drawn. The first step is to number each bird watcher on the list with numbers such as 001, 002, …, 950 so that the list contains 950 three-digit numbers where 001 represents the first person on the list and 950 is the last person. The second step is to determine the number of digits needed for random numbers. Given that the largest number is 950, only three-digit numbers are needed. The third step is to randomly select a starting point, which for this example will be column 10, line 1 in Table 8.2 (36207). The fourth step would be to drop, for example, the last two digits of each number in the table so that only the first three digits will be used to correspond to the 950 bird watchers. The final step is to proceed through the table and select numbers. Proceeding horizontally across the table, the first three-digit number is 362, the second is 209, the third is 995, the fourth is 912, and so on. Because 995 exceeds the number of cases in the population (950), it does not match and is, therefore, skipped. A simple random sample of 20 individuals would create the sample of numbers shown in Table 8.3.

Statistical software packages such as SPSS (see chapters 9 and 10) and even Microsoft Excel can also be used to rapidly generate a simple random sample. Population lists containing names or contact information can often be imported from other programs into these software packages. In SPSS, a random sample can be generated using drop-down menus (**Data > Select cases... > Random Sample of Cases...**) or simply typing and running syntax (e.g., `Sample 20 from 950. Execute`). Chapters 9 and 12 provide more information about SPSS commands.

Table 8.3   Bird Watchers to be Included in the Sample of 20

362	465	279	191
209	255	534	396
912	853	939	241
907	309	340	483
223	891	526	225

Systematic Sampling

Simple random sampling techniques can be cumbersome, especially when combined with long lists or applied to on-site survey research (Salant & Dillman, 1994). An alternative method is *systematic sampling*, which involves randomly selecting the first unit (i.e., person) in a sample population, choosing an appropriate fixed interval, and systematically selecting subsequent units (Fowler, 1993; Morgan & Harmon, 1999). For example, if a sample population list contained 10,000 anglers and a sample of 1,000 anglers is desired, it is possible to choose every 10th person on the list. To guard against any bias, it is critically important to select the first unit (i.e., person) at random. For an on-site study such as a trailhead survey, a person can be selected at random to be the first to complete the questionnaire followed by every n^{th} (e.g., 15th) person. Compared to simple random samples, this systematic approach to on-site surveys is easier to perform in the field and is less subject to selection errors by field researchers, especially if a good sampling frame is unavailable (Babbie, 2003; Scheaffer et al., 1996; Thompson, 1992).

In addition to being easier to perform and less susceptible to researcher error, systematic sampling can provide more information per unit cost than simple random sampling because the sample tends to be more uniformly spread over the entire population (Scheaffer et al., 1996). To illustrate, assume that a population list contained 1,000 boat-based whale watchers and a 1-in-5 systematic sample was desired so that the sample size would be $n = 200$. The first whale watcher is randomly selected from among the first few on the list (e.g., fourth person on the list) and every fifth person thereafter is selected for inclusion in the sample. Suppose, however, that the list is arranged so that most of the first 500 people on the list had gone whale watching with one particular company and the remaining 500 had participated with another company. If simple random sampling had been used, there is a possibility that most, if not all, of the 200 whale watchers chosen for the sample could have been selected just from the first 500 people or just the second 500 people. Results, therefore, would only be representative of whale watchers who had participated with a single company; findings would not be representative of all whale watchers across both companies included in the sample. A systematic procedure would have selected equal numbers of whale watchers from the two companies and may have increased the likelihood of achieving a more representative and generalizable sample (Scheaffer et al., 1996).

Two terms are frequently used in connection with systematic sampling. First, *sampling interval* is the standard distance between units (e.g., people) selected in the sample (e.g., five in the preceding whale watching example). The sampling interval is calculated as follows:

$$\text{sampling interval} = \frac{\text{population size}}{\text{sample size}}$$

Equation 8.3

Second, *sampling ratio* is the proportion of units in the population that are selected (e.g., ⅕ in the whale watching example). Sampling ratio is expressed with Equation 8.4.

$$\text{sampling ratio} = \frac{\text{sample size}}{\text{population size}}$$

Equation 8.4

To select a systematic sample, the researcher must choose the sampling ratio needed to obtain a specific sample size. The ratio could, for example, be 1 in 3, 1 in 5, 1 in 10, 1 in 100, or in general 1 in k. For a systematic sample of n (or N_s) units (e.g., people) from a population of size N (or N_p), k must be less than or equal to N / n. For example, if the population of interest was $N = 30,000$ and the required sample size to achieve a ± 5% margin of error at the 95% confidence level was $n = 400$, k would be 75; the researcher would select every 75th person after randomly selecting the first individual. If $k < 75$, the sample size would be greater than 400 people.

It is challenging to determine a value for k when the size of the sampling population is unknown. In outdoor recreation settings, for example, agencies may not have accurate data on total use levels for particular activities. In this case, researchers must determine a desired sample size and margin of error (see Table 8.1), and then estimate the value of k needed to reach this sample size. It may be prudent to select a conservative value for k because if it is too large, the required sample size may not be obtained through a systematic sample (Scheaffer et al., 1996).

Arrangements in a population list can make systematic sampling dangerous and unwise. Such an arrangement is often called *periodicity*. If the list of elements is arranged in a cyclical pattern that coincides with the sampling interval, a biased sample may be drawn. Assume that in a study of World War II soldiers, for example, researchers selected every 10th soldier on the roster. The rosters, however, were arranged by squad according to rank with privates listed first, followed by corporals, and then sergeants. Each squad had 10 members. As a result, every 10th person on the roster was a sergeant and the systematic sample contained only sergeants. Before drawing a systematic sample from a list, therefore, researchers should examine the nature of that list. If elements are arranged in any particular order, the researcher must determine whether that order will bias the sample and then take steps necessary to counteract any possible bias.

Stratified Random Sampling

Stratified random sampling involves: (a) dividing the sample population into different non-overlapping groups (i.e., strata) that are of interest or deserve special attention because of project objectives or hypotheses, and then (b) selecting a simple random sample from each stratum (Fowler, 1993; Morgan & Harmon, 1999; Scheaffer et al., 1996; Thompson, 1992). The resulting stratification helps to determine any differences among subgroups.

Stratified samples are useful for two primary reasons. First, many populations contain subgroups that are of particular interest to parks, recreation, and human dimensions researchers. For example, if a park manager was interested in the extent to which visitors would support and be willing to pay a user fee to enter the park, it would be useful to examine people in distinct income brackets (e.g., high, low). Opinions of visitors in a high income bracket may differ from those in a lower bracket.

Second, homogenous populations produce samples with less sampling error than heterogeneous populations. If 99% of the population agrees with a certain issue, for example, it is extremely unlikely that a probability sample will greatly misrepresent the extent of agreement. If the population is split (e.g., 50% agree, 50% disagree), however, sampling error will be much greater. Rather than selecting a sample from the total population at large, it would be more informative to select appropriate samples from more homogeneous subgroups of the population.

To obtain accurate information about populations of interest, it is important to ensure an adequate sample size of people in each subgroup. An assumption of stratified samples is that sample sizes of subgroups are reasonably comparable (i.e., relatively equal) and allow for tests of statistical differences among groups (Mitra & Lankford, 1999). Chapters 14 (means and *t*-tests) and 15 (analysis of variance) introduce statistical tests for examining differences among groups.

The ultimate objective of stratification is to organize the population into more homogeneous and meaningful subgroups (with heterogeneity between subgroups), and to select the appropriate number of people from each group. If there are two levels to the stratification variable (e.g., men, women), for example, recall from the sample size determination (see equation 8.1) and Table 8.1 (p. 180), that a final sample size of at least 768 (e.g., 384 men, 384 women) would be required to discuss findings in terms of the 95% confidence level with a ± 5% margin of error.

Table 8.4 (p. 188) shows a stratified sampling design used in a study of public values toward forests (Vaske & Donnelly, 1999). This study was interested in the extent to which newcomers to Colorado differed from long-time residents in terms of their views on how national forests should be managed and their value orientations toward forests. Notice that the simple random sample method yields a dramatically different solution than the stratified sample. In this study, the stratification dimension was length of time a person had lived in the state (i.e., short vs. long). Researchers should select stratification variables that they want to represent accurately.

One limitation of stratified sampling is that the ability of obtaining aggregate results for the total sample population irrespective of subgroups may be compromised (Mitra & Lankford, 1999; Scheaffer et al., 1996). Suppose, for example, that an objective of a hypothetical study about wolf reintroduction in Colorado is to examine differences in attitudes between rural farm/ranch owners and the rest of the state's population. A stratified design is implemented and 1,000 rural

Table 8.4   Comparison Between Simple Random Sampling and Stratified Random Designs

County	Post office name	Survey group (Strata)	Zip	Population size	% of pop	SRS [1] (n)	% of strata	Stratified sample (n)
Montezuma	Lewis	Oldtimers	81327	1,074	1.53%	14	2.22%	7
Montezuma	Yellow Jacket	Oldtimers	81335	349	0.50%	4	0.72%	2
Montezuma	Towaoc	Oldtimers	81334	1,146	1.64%	15	2.37%	7
Montezuma	Pleasant View	Oldtimers	81331	349	0.50%	4	0.72%	2
Rio Grande	Del Norte	Oldtimers	81132	2,792	3.99%	36	5.77%	17
Rio Grande	Monte Vista	Oldtimers	81144	6,159	8.79%	79	12.74%	38
Alamosa	Alamosa	Oldtimers	81101	13,617	19.44%	175	28.17%	84
Conejos	Sanford	Oldtimers	81151	4,080	5.83%	52	8.44%	25
Conejos	La Jara	Oldtimers	81140	1,149	1.64%	15	2.38%	7
Conejos	Antonito	Oldtimers	81120	2,294	3.28%	29	4.74%	14
Costilla	San Pablo	Oldtimers	81153	624	0.89%	8	1.29%	4
Costilla	San Luis	Oldtimers	81152	345	0.49%	4	0.71%	2
Montrose	Nucla	Oldtimers	81424	1,536	2.19%	20	3.18%	10
Montrose	Redvale	Oldtimers	81431	1,064	1.52%	14	2.20%	7
Montrose	Olathe	Oldtimers	81425	4,421	6.31%	57	9.14%	27
La Platta	Ignacio	Oldtimers	81137	5,129	7.32%	66	10.61%	32
Montrose	Crawford	Oldtimers	81415	1,200	1.71%	15	2.48%	8
Saguache	Saguache	Oldtimers	81149	1,019	1.45%	13	2.11%	7
Dolores	Cahone	Newcomers	81320	200	0.29%	3	1.55%	5
Hinsdale	Lake City	Newcomers	81235	467	0.67%	6	3.62%	11
San Miguel	Telluride PO Boxes	Newcomers	81435	2,421	3.46%	31	18.75%	56
Ouray	Ridgeway	Newcomers	81432	1,295	1.85%	17	10.03%	30
Gunnison	Carbondale	Newcomers	81623	8,527	12.18%	110	66.05%	198
Costilla	San Acacio	Mixed New&Old	81150	996	1.42%	13	11.35%	34
San Juan	Silverton	Mixed New&Old	81433	745	1.06%	10	8.49%	25
Montrose	Montrose	Mixed New&Old	81401	1,730	2.47%	22	19.71%	59
Archuleta	Pagosa Springs	Mixed New&Old	81147	227	0.32%	3	2.59%	8
Saguache	Center	Mixed New&Old	81125	5,081	7.25%	65	57.88%	174

Totals	Strata	Desired sample size	Population size	Simple random sample		Stratified sample
Population		900	70,036	100%	900	900
Oldtimers	1	300	48,347		620	300
Newcomers	2	300	12,910		167	300
Mixed Old & New	3	300	8,779		113	300

[1] SRS = Simple random sample

Example calculations:

% of population = 1,074 / 70,036 = 1.53% $SRS_{(n)}$ = .0153 * 900 = 14

% of strata = 1,074 / 48,347 = 2.22%   Stratified Sample $_{(n)}$ = .0222 * 300 = 7

farm/ranch owners and 1,000 other residents are sampled. Statistical comparisons between the two groups show that farm/ranch owners strongly oppose wolf reintroduction, whereas other residents are more supportive of this strategy. If data were to be aggregated across both groups (i.e., all 2,000 people sampled), results would be split (e.g., 50% oppose, 50% support), but this is not representative of the entire population in Colorado because it does not account for differences in population proportions of each group. There are many rural farm/ranch owners in

Colorado, but they are a small minority compared to the rest of the state's population. If the two samples were aggregated, there would be an overrepresentation of the minority group (i.e., rural farm/ranch owners) and an underrepresentation of the majority group (i.e., all other residents). Estimates for the total based on this sample would be incorrect unless data were weighted accordingly (Mitra & Lankford, 1999). Weighting is discussed later in this chapter.

It is possible to avoid some of these problems when aggregating data with stratified samples by estimating population proportions of each group in advance and using these estimates to determine the proportion of the sample needed for each stratum. If a researcher knew from other data sources (e.g., census data), for example, that 60% of the target population was male and 40% was female, proportionate sample sizes could be selected where 600 males are randomly selected in one stratum and 400 females are chosen in the second stratum. This would minimize the need for weighting data, but requires advance knowledge of population subgroups. In addition, researchers must select large enough samples for each group and address sources of error discussed earlier (e.g., coverage, nonresponse) to allow generalizations about populations.

When deciding to use stratified sampling, it is important to consider project goals, objectives, and hypotheses. Selection of a stratified sample also requires prior knowledge of the population. It is important to have a method for identifying different subgroups and categorizing them into their own lists before selecting random samples from each list. If this information is not available in advance, complicated screening questions would be needed before sampling.

Cluster Sampling

There are some studies where random, systematic, and stratified sampling approaches are not economical in terms of time or budget. In urban areas, for example, it may be more effective to sample specific families, buildings, districts, or city blocks rather than selecting a random sample of people. *Cluster sampling* involves conducting a simple random sample of *groups* or *clusters* and then sampling units (e.g., people) within the selected groups or clusters (Fowler, 1993; Scheaffer et al., 1996). This approach differs from stratified sampling where a random sample is drawn *within* each group; cluster sampling involves a random sample *of* groups.

Cluster sampling can be effective when: (a) a good sample list of population units is unavailable or expensive to obtain, but a listing of potential clusters is easily obtainable; and (b) the cost of obtaining completed questionnaires increases as distance separating population and sampling units increases (Rocco, 2003; Scheaffer et al., 1996). A goal of cluster sampling is to identify specific groups of similar types of people. It is assumed that there are geographic areas or other clusters where a greater probability exists for sampling desired units or individuals. If these areas or clusters can be identified in advance, cost and time to complete data collection can be less than other approaches (e.g., simple random). For example, if a study examines recreation participation among Hispanics in an urban area where only 5% of the population is Hispanic, and the researcher wants a sample size of 2,000 Hispanics, 40,000 questionnaires would need to be completed just to obtain a sample of 2,000 Hispanics. Given that most urban areas contain neighborhoods that are largely populated by specific minority groups (Mitra & Lankford, 1999), it may be more efficient to use cluster sampling by identifying areas that are predominantly Hispanic, conducting a random sample of these areas, and then sampling within selected areas.

The first step in cluster sampling is to identify appropriate clusters. Units (e.g., people) within a cluster are often physically close together and may share similar characteristics. Once clusters have been specified, the second step is to develop a sampling frame listing these clusters and then conduct a simple random sample of clusters. The final step in a cluster sample is to select a sample from within each cluster (Rocco, 2003). To illustrate, the example earlier focuses on recreation participation among Hispanics in urban areas. To conduct a cluster sample, assume that the researcher identifies six communities that are predominantly Hispanic. For simplicity, these communities will be named A, B, C, D, E, and F. Assume that communities A, C, and F were selected through a simple random sample of the six communities. To identify respondents for inclusion in this study, the researcher may then proceed to randomly select streets within each of the three clusters, then randomly select a certain number of households along these streets.

Multistage Sampling

Sampling can be complex, especially when several single-stage approaches are combined into a multistage design. A stratified-cluster sampling approach (i.e., cluster combined with stratification), for example, can be useful for on-site studies when a list of potential elements in the population is unavailable and researchers do not know in advance who is in the population.

To illustrate, assume that a goal of an on-site survey is to examine summer recreationists' reasons for visiting a large backcountry area with three access points: (a) Big Lake Trail, (b) Middle Park Trail, and (c) Little Basin Trail. Researchers know from previous data (e.g., trail counters) that use distribution differs among these access points with 50% of visitors accessing this backcountry on Big Lake Trail, 30% using Middle Park Trail, and 20% accessing via Little Basin Trail. At all three sites, 60% of weekly visitation occurs on weekdays and 40% occurs on weekends. Given that the study focuses solely on summer visitors, there are only 91 days (i.e., 13 weeks) available in the summer for contacting visitors. In addition, the researchers have only budgeted for two full-time (i.e., 40 hours per week) people to administer questionnaires. Given that few people enter or exit the area before 8:00 a.m. or after 8:00 p.m., a decision is made to sample visitors during three different time blocks (i.e., clusters): (a) 8:00 a.m. to noon, (b) noon to 4:00 p.m., and (c) 4:00 p.m. to 8:00 p.m. The goal is to conduct a representative survey of all people at each site during these times, accounting for differences in use distribution among sites.

The first step is to determine the proportion of effort to allocate to each stratum because the goal is to sample proportional to use distribution. In this example, there are two criteria for stratification: (a) three trailheads, and (b) two times during the week (i.e., weekdays, weekends). This stratification design generates six separate strata (e.g., Big Lake Trail on weekdays, Big Lake Trail on weekends, Little Basin Trail on weekdays, Little Basin Trail on weekends). The percent of person power to allocate to each stratum is calculated from two equations:

1. *Weekend Sampling for Trailhead X:*

Percent of total effort spent sampling on *weekends* at Trailhead X	=	Percent of total use that occurs at Trailhead X	*	The proportion of use that occurs on *weekends*

2. Weekday Sampling for Trailhead X:

| Percent of total effort spent sampling on *weekdays* at Trailhead X | = | Percent of total use that occurs at Trailhead X | * | The proportion of use that occurs on *weekdays* |

These equations produce the proportion of effort to allocate to each stratum shown in Table 8.5 (e.g., Big Lake Trail total use: 0.50 * Big Lake Trail weekday visitation: 0.60 = 0.30 or 30%).

Table 8.5   Percent of Person Power to Allocate to Each Stratum

Strata		% of total use occurring at trailhead	Proportion of use at time of week (weekday, weekend)	% of total effort to allocate
Trailhead	Time of week			
Big Lake	Weekday	50%	60%	30%
Big Lake	Weekend	50%	40%	20%
Middle Park	Weekday	30%	60%	18%
Middle Park	Weekend	30%	40%	12%
Little Basin	Weekday	20%	60%	12%
Little Basin	Weekend	20%	40%	8%

The second step is to determine the number of time blocks (i.e., clusters) to be sampled for each stratum given the proportion of effort allocated to each stratum. Given that only two people are available to administer questionnaires and they are only allowed to work a maximum of eight hours per day and 40 hours per week, the most likely scenario is that each person would work an eight hour day (i.e., two of the three time blocks) for five days a week for the 13-week summer period. This means that each person can work for 65 of the 91 days (i.e., 91 days in summer – 13 weeks * 2 days off a week = 65 days of work per person). The total number of time blocks that can be sampled is determined from the following equation:

$$2 \text{ people} * \frac{8 \text{ hrs per day}}{4 \text{ hrs per time block}} * 65 \text{ days per person} = 260 \text{ total time blocks to be sampled}$$

Results of this equation, when multiplied by the proportion of effort for each stratum (Table 8.5), produce the number of time blocks (i.e., clusters) to be sampled for each stratum, as shown in Table 8.6 (e.g., Big Lake Trail weekday proportion: 0.30 * 260 total blocks = 78 time blocks).

Table 8.6   Number of Time Blocks (Clusters) to be Sampled from Each Stratum

Strata		Proportion of effort	Total sample blocks	Sample blocks per stratum [1]
Trailhead	Time of week			
Big Lake	Weekday	.30	260	78
Big Lake	Weekend	.20	260	52
Middle Park	Weekday	.18	260	47
Middle Park	Weekend	.12	260	31
Little Basin	Weekday	.12	260	31
Little Basin	Weekend	.08	260	21

[1] Sample Blocks per Strata = Proportion of Effort * Total Sample Blocks.

Now that strata (i.e., three access points; two times per week) and clusters (i.e., three time blocks per day) are defined, the third step requires randomly selecting time blocks (i.e., clusters) to be sampled. To do this, all elements in each stratum should be arrayed, which involves listing every time block that can be sampled in the summer for each trail/time of week stratum. Each element for each stratum should be consecutively numbered with an identification number (ID) and then a trail sampling schedule should be randomly selected using a random numbers table or statistical software package. For *Middle Park Trail* on *weekdays*, for example, Table 8.7 shows how time blocks for the first 15 days were allocated ID numbers. A total of 47 time blocks will need to be selected randomly for this stratum (Table 8.6). Using a random numbers table, numbers are randomly selected and matched to those in Table 8.7. Days and time periods for the first 15 days that were selected for sampling are shown with "X" in Table 8.8. During each of these times, all people will be contacted and asked to complete a questionnaire. This process must be repeated for each of the six strata (e.g., Big Lake Trail on weekdays, Big Lake Trail on weekends, Little Basin Trail on weekdays, Little Basin Trail on weekends).

Table 8.7   Array of All Time Block Clusters for *Middle Park Trail* on *Weekdays*

Month	Day	8 a.m.-noon	noon-4 p.m.	4 p.m.-8 p.m.
June	1	1	2	3
	2	4	5	6
	3	7	8	9
	4	10	11	12
	5	13	14	15
	6	Weekend	Weekend	Weekend
	7	Weekend	Weekend	Weekend
	8	16	17	18
	9	19	20	21
	10	22	23	24
	11	25	26	27
	12	28	29	30
	13	Weekend	Weekend	Weekend
	14	Weekend	Weekend	Weekend
	15	31	32	33
	etc.	etc.	etc.	etc.

Table 8.8   Sampling Schedule for *Middle Park Trail* on *Weekdays*[1]

Month	Day	8 a.m.-noon	noon-4 p.m.	4 p.m.-8 p.m.
June	1		X	
	2		X	
	3	X		X
	4		X	
	5			X
	6	Weekend	Weekend	Weekend
	7	Weekend	Weekend	Weekend
	8			
	9		X	
	10			
	11			
	12			X
	13	Weekend	Weekend	Weekend
	14	Weekend	Weekend	Weekend
	15		X	
	etc.	etc.	etc.	etc.

[1] X = selected time for administering questionnaires.

There are many ways to set up complex sampling designs. In the earlier example, a systematic method where every n^{th} (e.g., 10th) person is sampled could be substituted for the final step instead of asking all people to complete questionnaires. This would have made this a stratified-cluster-systematic sample. Readers should consult texts and articles focusing solely on sampling for more information about these and other approaches (e.g., Cochran, 1977; Kelly & Cumberland, 1990; Kish, 1965; Rocco, 2003; Scheaffer et al., 1996; Thompson, 1992).

Survey Implementation

Once a sampling approach has been selected and the questionnaire has been written, designed, reviewed by experts and pretested, it is time to carry out the survey. Surveys should be implemented to encourage high response rates and sample sizes, and minimize nonresponse error. Strategies such as multiple contacts, design and content of a questionnaire, appearance of accompanying materials (e.g., envelopes), sponsorship, personalization, and other aspects of the communication process have the capability of generating interest in a study (Dillman, 2007). According to Salant and Dillman (1994), "people are more likely to respond when they think the benefits outweigh the costs, when they think they—or a group with which they identify—will get more in return than they are asked to give in the first place" (p. 137). This section summarizes issues to consider when implementing various types of surveys (e.g., mail, telephone, on-site). These considerations are based on various sources (e.g., Dillman, 2000, 2007; Mitra & Lankford, 1999; Salant & Dillman, 1994) and the authors' own research in parks, recreation, and human dimensions of natural resources.

Implementing Mail Surveys

Mail surveys require respondents to answer questions, then mail the questionnaire back to the researcher or agency. Given that there is no direct interaction between the researcher and respondent like there is in telephone and on-site surveys, there may be little incentive for people to cooperate. To obtain a good response rate, therefore, it is imperative to produce a well-written and attractive questionnaire, use personalized correspondence, and conduct repeat mailings (Kwak & Radler, 2002; Mitra & Lankford, 1999; Salant & Dillman, 1994).

Before administering a mail survey, it is important to have the sampling list in electronic format so that names and addresses can be quickly transferred to appropriate software to print mailing labels. Respondent names and addresses will be printed several times because multiple mailings are almost always necessary for achieving a high response rate (Dillman, 2000). The list must also be sorted between mailings to delete information about people who have responded and do not need to be contacted again. Having electronic information streamlines the process of preparing questionnaires for mailing, thereby saving time and reducing administrative costs.

In addition to storing sampling lists in computer software, it is important to prepare survey materials as far in advance as possible. For example, all materials for multiple mailings (e.g., letters, questionnaires, postcards, envelopes) should be printed and envelopes for the first mailing should be addressed before the first round of packets is mailed. Advance preparation can allow personnel to devote more time to other project tasks, such as responding to inquiries from respondents, checking names off mailing lists as questionnaires come in, and entering responses into statistical software packages (Salant & Dillman, 1994).

It may also be useful to publicize the survey in advance because this can help to demonstrate its legitimacy and improve overall response rates (Salant & Dillman, 1994). Brief alerts in outlets such as magazines, newspapers, or association newsletters would be appropriate for publicizing a survey. It is important, however, to be cautious when providing advanced notice because any negative coverage can be detrimental to response rates.

Mail surveys should almost always use multiple mailings (e.g., Dillman, 2000, 2007; Krosnick, 1999; Kwak & Radler, 2002; Salant & Dillman, 1994). According to Dillman (2000, 2007), multiple contacts are more effective than any other technique for increasing mail survey response rates. In Dillman's (2000, 2007) "Tailored Design Method," multiple contacts include:

- prenotification letter,
- first questionnaire packet,
- thank you/reminder postcard, and
- replacement questionnaire packet.

A brief *prenotification letter* of less than one page should be sent to the entire sample a few days before the questionnaire is mailed, notifying people: (a) about the purpose of the study, (b) that the questionnaire will arrive shortly, and (c) that their participation would be appreciated. Letters should contain letterhead or logos of organizations conducting/sponsoring the survey, signatures and contact information of lead investigators, personalized addresses, and a date. Prenotification letters should be brief, personally addressed, positively worded, emphasize importance of the study, and build anticipation; this is not the place for precise details about conditions for participation (e.g., anonymity, confidentiality, voluntary; Dillman, 2007).

Letters should be mailed using first-class postage with the label and letter specifying the respondent's name, not "resident of…" Compared to bulk-rate postage, first class allows items to be: (a) processed by the postal service faster, (b) returned or forwarded for invalid addresses, and (c) perceived as more important by potential respondents (Salant & Dillman, 1994).

When a government agency contracts a private company or another organization (e.g., university) to design and/or administer the survey, it is useful to print letters on appropriate government stationary (e.g., letterhead) and explain that the survey is being conducted for the agency by another organization and then name that organization (Heberlein & Baumgartner, 1978). This can improve response rates and show legitimacy and transparency (Dillman, 2007). Figure 8.1 provides an example of a prenotification letter for a recent survey of hunters.

The *first questionnaire packet* contains the: (a) envelope in which documents are contained, (b) personalized and signed cover letter, (c) questionnaire, and (d) addressed and postage-paid return envelope. This mailing should occur a few days to one week after the prenotification letter. The mailing envelope will vary in size depending on the size of paper used for the questionnaire booklet (see chapter 7), but should still contain logos and addresses of organizations or agencies conducting the study, be labeled with the respondent's name and address, and be mailed using stamped or metered first-class postage. Envelopes should not include statements such as "your response required," "open now," or "important documents inside" and should not be brightly colored (e.g., yellow, blue, red) because they convey a marketing image and are likely to be treated as junk mail by many recipients (Dillman, 2007). Before sending a survey

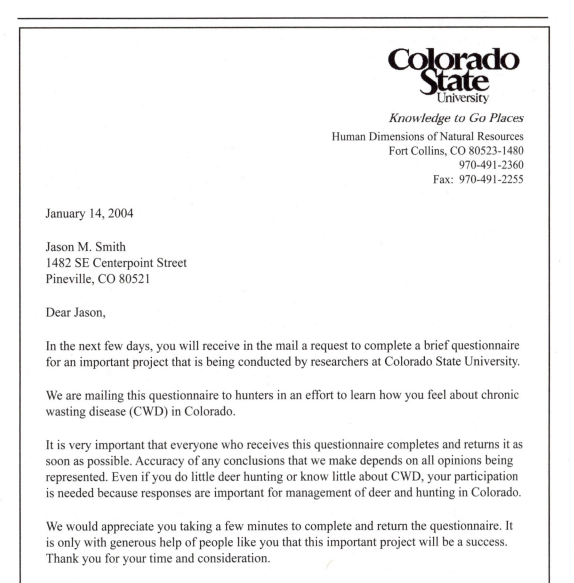

Figure 8.1   Example of a Prenotification Letter

mailing, the researcher should always contact the postal service for information about current postage rates and procedures that avoid complications with automated scanning and sorting equipment (e.g., use capital letters, avoid punctuation, label placement).

The cover letter is important for persuading respondents to take the questionnaire and project seriously. Like prenotification letters, cover letters should contain letterhead or logos of agencies conducting and sponsoring the survey, signatures and contacts of lead investigators, personalized addresses, and a date. Salutations such as "Dear Bill" or "Dear Mr. Jones" should be used to personalize letters because statements such as "Dear Resident" or "Dear Colorado Hunter" convey that a form letter is being sent and packets are likely to be tossed into the trash can or recycling bin. If it is difficult to determine gender from names, avoid offending recipients by not using salutations starting with "Mr., "Mrs.," "Ms.," or Miss." Sometimes it may be necessary to avoid names on a cover letter. If a household survey is being conducted, for example, it may be useful to ask in the cover letter for the adult who most recently celebrated a birthday, as most telephone directories can introduce bias because listings are still dominated by males (e.g., husbands; Binson, Canchola, & Catania, 2000; Dillman, 2007). Salutations such as "To residents at this address" or "To residents at 583 5th Avenue" are slightly more personable than "Dear Resident."

Cover letters should be no longer than a single page and should start by briefly stating what the letter is about, what is being requested, why they were among a small group of people selected, and why the request is important (e.g., Dillman, 2000; Porter & Whitcomb, 2003). Statements about the survey being voluntary, anonymous, and confidential may then be included because they are often required by human subject/regulatory compliance protocols (e.g., Office of Management and Budget [OMB], University Institutional Review Board [IRB]). Surveys are *voluntary* because people must be allowed to not partake in a study. Researchers can try to convince people of a project's importance and the value of their contribution, but must not be excessively coercive or offensive. *Confidentiality* means that responses will remain private through methods such as not discussing particular respondents with people uninvolved with the project, removing identification numbers and destroying mailing lists when they are no longer needed, and ensuring that people remain *anonymous* so that personal and contact information cannot be associated with specific questionnaires or answers (Salant & Dillman, 1994; Sobal, 1984; Wildman, 1977). The final section of a cover letter should provide directions for returning the questionnaire, contact information for inquiries, and a statement of appreciation. Letters should be personable, but professional and businesslike. They should also be free of complex language and technical jargon. Figure 8.2 is an example of a mail survey cover letter.

The main component of the packet is the questionnaire booklet. Chapter 7 provides several suggestions for writing and designing questionnaires. For mail surveys, it is important to provide an identification number in a corner of the questionnaire and on mailing labels that correspond to the mailing list. This allows researchers to track who has returned questionnaires and who should be included in follow-up mailings. This procedure reduces mailing and administrative costs by avoiding inserting and assembling duplicate packets, and sending reminders to people who have already responded. Identification numbers have little, if any, negative effect on response rates (Salant & Dillman, 1994), but they should be placed in a corner of the questionnaire so that if respondents tear them out, they do not tear through questions and answers. Trying to hide identification numbers on questionnaires (e.g., invisible ink, incorporate into an approval or processing number such as "Approved Form 426") is unethical and should be discouraged because it may convey a message that the researcher is trying to hide something or trick respondents (Dickson et al., 1977; Dillman, 2000). In the authors' research, it has been useful

Knowledge to Go Places
Human Dimensions of Natural Resources
Fort Collins, CO 80523-1480
970-491-2360
Fax: 970-491-2255

January 17, 2004

Jason M. Smith
1482 SE Centerpoint Street
Pineville, CO 80521

Dear Jason,

We are contacting you to ask for your help in a study of hunters that is very important for management of deer and hunting in Colorado. This study is part of an effort to learn how hunters feel about chronic wasting disease (CWD) in Colorado.

You are one of a small number of deer hunters chosen at random and invited to participate in this study by completing the enclosed questionnaire. Accuracy of any conclusions that we make depends on all opinions being represented. Even if you do little deer hunting or know little about CWD, your participation is needed.

The purpose of this study is to learn how CWD has affected, if at all, your hunting experiences and how you think your future hunts may be affected by CWD. By understanding hunters' opinions and attitudes about CWD, state wildlife agencies can work to prevent and control CWD.

Please complete the enclosed questionnaire, which will take less than 20 minutes to complete. This survey is voluntary and there are no risks associated with your participation. When you return your completed questionnaire, your name will be deleted from the mailing list and will never be connected to your answers, thus you will remain anonymous and your responses will be confidential. Responses will take the form of statistical data. If you have questions about your rights as a participant, please contact the Colorado State University Human Research Committee at (970) 491-1563.

Once you have completed the questionnaire, please place it in the enclosed addressed and postage-paid envelope and mail it back to us as soon as possible. If you have any questions regarding this questionnaire or study, please feel free to contact us at (970) 491-2360 or jerryv@cnr.colostate.edu.

Thank you very much for completing and returning the enclosed questionnaire. Your input is very important.

Sincerely,

Jerry J. Vaske, Ph.D.
Professor

Figure 8.2   Example Cover Letter for Mail Surveys

to add identification numbers to both the questionnaire and return envelope because respondents seldom notice these numbers in multiple locations.

An envelope should be provided in the packet so that respondents can return their completed questionnaires to the researcher or agency. This envelope should be printed with the researcher or agency address and should provide first-class postage. Expecting respondents to pay postage increases respondent burden and is likely to reduce overall response rates (Salant & Dillman, 1994). According to Dillman (2000, 2007), return envelopes should be personally stamped and use first-class postage because: (a) response rates can be improved, (b) responses tend to come back more quickly, (c) it conveys a message that a monetary value has been given to the respondent so it is likely to be seen as a positive gesture that will help the sender be viewed more positively, (d) it encourages trust in the respondent and questionnaire, and (e) it is culturally difficult for many people to discard something with monetary value. Adding stamps to return envelopes, however, increases postage costs and personnel time when inserting and assembling survey packets. For large projects or studies constrained by budget, business reply envelopes may be more practical because postage is only paid for envelopes that are returned. Research shows, however, that response rates from studies using business reply envelopes can be up to 10% lower than response rates from first-class postage (e.g., Armstrong & Lusk, 1987).

When selecting a date for mailing questionnaires, researchers may want to avoid certain holiday periods such as Thanksgiving and Christmas because people are more likely to be busier or away from home, and extra volume at the postal service during these times may increase the likelihood of delivery mistakes (Dillman, 2007; Weeks, Jones, Folsom, & Benrud, 1980). It is useful to tailor mailing times to characteristics of the population. If a study was interested in hunter participation rates in the most recent deer hunting season, for example, questionnaires should be mailed shortly after the hunting season so that memories of the hunt can be recalled easily by respondents. Dillman (2000, 2007) suggests that January to March appears to be the most conducive period for obtaining completed mail questionnaires, but there is little evidence to suggest that time of week or month of year has any substantial effect on response rates.

Without follow-up contacts, response rates will usually be between 20% and 40% lower irrespective of how well-designed, interesting, or attractive the questionnaire and mail packet (Dillman, 2000). The first follow-up contact should be a ***thank you/reminder postcard***, which expresses gratitude to those who responded and mailed back the completed questionnaire, and reminds those who have not responded that it would be appreciated if they could complete and return the questionnaire soon. The purpose of this mailing is to thank those who have responded and encourage those who have not. Most people who answer questionnaires will respond within a few days after receiving the questionnaire packet, but as each day passes without looking at the questionnaire, it becomes a lower priority until is it forgotten, lost, or discarded. Postcards are a relatively inexpensive and unique way to remind nonrespondents because they offer a different stimulus than opening an envelope or letter, and can be quickly turned over and read instead of remaining unopened with other mail items (Dillman, 2007; Heberlein & Baumgartner, 1981).

Postcards should briefly state when the questionnaire was sent, why it is important, thank those who responded and ask those who have not responded to do so today, and give respondents the option of calling for a replacement questionnaire. Final items should include a statement of appreciation, signature, and contact information of investigators. All of this text is printed on the back of the postcard. Name and address of the respondent should appear in a mailing label on the front of the postcard, but not on the back because it takes up too much space.

Postcards should be mailed using first-class postage approximately two weeks after the prenotification letter and ten days following the first questionnaire packet. However, postcards should be printed and labeled before the first mailing to allow personnel ample time to answer inquiries and process returned questionnaires. Figure 8.3 provides an example of a postcard.

Last week, we sent you a questionnaire seeking your opinions about chronic wasting disease (CWD) and how CWD may affect, if at all, your current and future hunting experiences in Colorado. You are one of a small number of deer hunters chosen at random and invited to participate in this important study.

If you have already completed the questionnaire and mailed it back to us, please accept our sincere thanks. If not, please do so today. Your response is important because future strategies for preventing or controlling CWD may be based on the opinions and attitudes of hunters like yourself.

If you did not receive the questionnaire or it was misplaced, please ask for another copy by contacting us at (970) 491-2360 or jerryv@cnr.colostate.edu.

Thank you for your cooperation!

Sincerely,

Jerry Vaske

Jerry J. Vaske, Ph.D.
Professor
Human Dimensions of Natural Resources
Colorado State University
Fort Collins, CO, USA 80523-1480

Figure 8.3   Example Postcard for Mail Surveys

Approximately four weeks after the prenotification letter and two weeks after the postcard, a second complete mailing should be sent to nonrespondents indicating that their completed questionnaire has not been received. This *replacement questionnaire packet* should contain a: (a) reminder cover letter, (b) questionnaire, and (c) addressed and postage-paid return envelope. Like the first questionnaire packet, this replacement packet should be sent using first-class postage. Timing for sending this packet is somewhat delayed compared to the shorter time frame among the prenotification letter, first questionnaire, and postcard because it allows the potential for more questionnaires to be received, especially those that have been delayed by the postal service. This timing also reduces costs associated with another complete mailing.

This questionnaire packet is identical to the first packet sent to respondents with one major exception—a different cover letter informing nonrespondents that their questionnaire has not been received and urging respondents to complete and return the instrument. This cover letter should be more insistent, but still maintain a professional and businesslike tone. The most important sentence in this cover letter is "As of today, we have not received your completed questionnaire" (Salant & Dillman, 1994, p. 146). This phrase attempts to convince people that their individual responses are critical for success of the study and that other people have already responded. An example of this type of cover letter is shown in Figure 8.4. It is important to include with this cover letter a replacement questionnaire and stamped return envelope because many respondents will have misplaced or discarded the first questionnaire packet.

If the response rate or number of completed questionnaires is still low after all of these mailings, a *final contact* may be necessary where special procedures such as priority or certified mail, special delivery, or telephone (if the sample list contains telephone numbers) are used to contact nonrespondents. An objective of this final contact is not to send the same envelope and cover letter again, but rather to emphasize the importance and legitimacy of the request by providing a different stimulus in terms of packaging, mode and speed of delivery, and appearance. Alternative methods such as final contacts can be cost prohibitive, but have been found to increase response rates (see Dillman, 2007; Gitelson & Drogin, 1992 for reviews).

Given constraints of most mail survey projects, tradeoffs between response rate, project cost, number of mailings, timing, and other implementation issues must almost always be made. There are other details that should also be considered when implementing mail surveys such as type and size of stationary for questionnaires and envelopes, incentives to encourage higher response rates, and how to properly insert and assemble materials in mail packets. Due to space constraints in this book, readers should consult other texts and articles that discuss these issues in more detail (e.g., Dillman, 2000, 2007; Mitra & Lankford, 1999; Salant & Dillman, 1994).

Implementing Telephone Surveys

As discussed in chapter 7, telephone surveys are advantageous because they can rapidly generate data, allow researchers a high degree of control over sequence in which questions are asked, and ensure that all questions are answered. There are, however, weaknesses of telephone surveys such as low response rates, incomplete samples, and difficulty of asking complex questions. Although telephone surveys are less sensitive to design layout because respondents seldom see the instrument, researchers must plan in advance and everything must come together efficiently because issues always arise as soon as dialing begins (Salant & Dillman, 1994).

The first step to conducting a telephone survey is to select the sample. Telephone numbers for specific populations may be available in population and sample lists. In many states, for example, hunters and anglers record their telephone number on applications for hunting or fishing licenses. Many other sources of telephone numbers, however, are problematic because of coverage errors (see Keeter, 1995 for a review). Telephone directories, for example, are often outdated because they are published once or twice per year and do not account for numbers that are issued, changed, or cancelled during the year (Salant & Dillman, 1994). Given that telephone directories often do not list cellular telephone numbers or unlisted numbers, and some people may not own a telephone or have telephone service, it is difficult to generate a random sample where all members of the population have an equal or known chance of being selected. In addition, telephone directories may introduce systematic bias in that certain segments of the population may be less likely to list their telephone numbers (e.g., single females, wealthy).

Simple random digit dialing (RDD) may seem like an alternative for overcoming these problems. In RDD, the telephone directory is first used to determine area codes and prefixes that are in use. In Colorado, for example, area codes include 970, 303, and 719. In the Fort Collins area

---

Knowledge to Go Places
Human Dimensions of Natural Resources
Fort Collins, CO 80523-1480
970-491-2360
Fax: 970-491-2255

February 7, 2004

Jason M. Smith
1482 SE Centerpoint Street
Pineville, CO 80521

Dear Jason,

About three weeks ago, we sent you a questionnaire seeking your opinions about management of chronic wasting disease (CWD) and how CWD may affect your current and future hunting experiences. As of today, we have not received your completed questionnaire. If you have completed the questionnaire in the last few days and mailed it back to us, please accept our sincere thanks.

We are writing to you again because every questionnaire is important. You are one of a small number of Colorado deer hunters chosen through a random sampling process in which every Colorado deer hunter had an equal chance of being selected to participate in this study. For results to represent opinions of Colorado deer hunters, it is important that every questionnaire be completed and mailed back to us. Without your help, conclusions that we draw from questionnaires that we have already received from other hunters *may be wrong*.

Even if you do little deer hunting or know little about CWD, your opinions are still important and must be considered. Results will be used to inform strategies for preventing or controlling CWD and the enclosed questionnaire is your chance to have a say in what happens with respect to this issue.

We want to assure you that this survey is voluntary and there are no risks associated with your participation. You will remain anonymous and your responses will be confidential. An identification number is printed on the questionnaire so that we can check your name off the mailing list when it is returned. This list is then destroyed so that individual names can never be connected to results in any way. Protecting confidentiality of your answers is important to us and the university.

We have enclosed another copy of the questionnaire in case you did not receive the first copy or it was misplaced. Please place your completed questionnaire in the enclosed addressed and postage-paid envelope, and mail it back to us as promptly as possible. If you have questions, please contact us at (970) 491-2360 or jerryv@cnr.colostate.edu.

Thank you for completing and returning the enclosed questionnaire. Your input is very important.

Sincerely,

Jerry J. Vaske, Ph.D.
Professor

Figure 8.4   Example of Second Cover Letter for Mail Surveys

of Colorado, prefixes include 377, 491, 498, and 495. The next four digits are then selected randomly using a random number table or statistical software package. RDD may seem like an acceptable process, but it is rarely used because any randomly generated number could be a: (a) working household number, (b) working nonresidential number, or (c) nonworking number. RDD methods (e.g., four-digit, two-digit) are inefficient because telephone companies generally assign numbers to residences and businesses in blocks, and often large blocks of numbers are left unassigned or do not contain residences (e.g., Brick, Waksberg, Kulp, & Starer, 1995; Kvitz, 1978). Given that few assigned numbers are residential, chances of selecting a nonresidential number are large (Mitra & Lankford, 1999). Two sampling designs that attempt to overcome these problems are the Waksberg (1978) method and plus-one sampling directory design.

The *Waksberg (1978) method of random digit dialing* involves a two-stage cluster design aimed at reducing the number of unproductive calls. In the first stage, the researcher obtains a recent listing of all telephone area codes and existing prefix numbers in the area of interest. For each area code and prefix combination, the researcher adds all possible choices for the next two numbers (e.g., 970-491-00 through 970-491-99) and thereby constructs a list of all possible eight-digit numbers of the 10 digits in telephone numbers. These combinations of eight digits represent primary sampling units (PSU; e.g., 970-491-23). Software or a random number table is then used to assign two additional digits to a randomly selected PSU (e.g., 970-491-2343). This process so far is analogous to a two-digit RDD. After the number is dialed, however, the PSU is retained for additional calls if it is a residential number. If the number is not a working residential number, the PSU is eliminated from further sampling consideration.

In the second stage of Waksberg's methodology, additional last two digits are selected randomly within each valid PSU until a set number of residential telephones is reached and this process is repeated until the desired sample size is reached. One disadvantage of this method involves the amount of clerical time needed to identify elements in the sampling unit.

The Waksberg method is a nondirectory sampling design that attempts to eliminate bias associated with selection straight from telephone directories. The *plus-one method*, however, is a directory-based sampling design with an identical objective. This sampling design involves adding a number between zero and nine to the last digit of a selected telephone number. The number selected may be a constant for all telephone numbers or may be assigned randomly for each selected number. If the chosen number, for example, was 862-4069 and the constant was one, the actual number called would be 862-4070 (i.e., *add-a-digit dialing*).

The plus-one method involves using a random start for selecting pages within a given telephone directory. Once a page has been identified, one column on that page is randomly selected. The position on the page from which a number is drawn is randomly selected to the inch on the identified column of telephone numbers and the first residential number within the selected inch of text is chosen. After the aggregate sample is identified, a constant is added to each number to capture unlisted numbers or numbers that were added after directory publication.

The plus-one technique is advantageous because it is a relatively straightforward method of including unlisted numbers or numbers that were added since the directory was published. In theory, numbers can be added to the last two or three digits, not just the last digit. Substituting more numbers increases the probability of including unlisted or new telephone numbers. Using this method also eliminates the need for preliminary screening required by the Waksberg method because numbers that are initially selected from the telephone directory are within a residential block. Another advantage is that if the population distributions relative to telephone directories can be identified, a sample proportional to the population distribution of an area can be selected.

There are, however, disadvantages of the plus-one method. If the working residential numbers are not assigned in definable groups, plus-one will not appreciably improve efficiency over what can be expected in other RDD designs. In addition, if an area has an unusually high proportion of unlisted numbers, plus-one may underrepresent this group because it is based on initial assignment of working numbers. Finally, equal probability of selection may be reduced because for a number to be included in the sample, its predecessor must be listed in the directory.

When selecting a sample size for a telephone survey, it is important to estimate the time needed to complete this many questionnaires and financial resources available to pay for costs associated with achieving this sample size. It would take an experienced interviewer an average of at least 30 to 40 minutes, for example, to complete a 15-minute interview because of time taken up by no-answers, invalid telephone numbers, respondents not at home, and double-checking answered questionnaires for completeness and accuracy (Salant & Dillman, 1994). If 400 completed questionnaires are required, approximately 267 hours of interviewing time are necessary (i.e., 400 interviews * 40 minutes / 60 minutes per hour). If five telephones are in use four hours per evening, it will take 13 to 14 days to achieve this sample size. Given the demands of telephone interviewing, Salant and Dillman (1994) recommend that interviewers be given occasional days off so approximately one and a half times as many people as there are telephones should be hired (e.g., seven or eight interviewers on staff if there are five telephones).

Once a telephone sample has been selected, the researcher must make arrangements for facilities and equipment. Telephone surveys can be more successful when administered from a single centralized location because it gives interviewers and supervisors the opportunity to work together, and allows supervisors to support and monitor interviewers when they are conducting interviews. Using a central location also allows interviewers to work together instead of on their own and increases efficiency because supervisors can redistribute uncompleted questionnaires to interviewers who finished their calls ahead of schedule (Salant & Dillman, 1994).

Centralized locations for telephone surveys can be as extravagant as a custom designed call center or simple room that is typically used for another purpose and is temporarily equipped with additional telephone lines and telephones borrowed from other offices. Rooms may also be equipped with computers and headsets if computer-assisted telephone interviewing (CATI) systems are to be used and the project budget permits. Instead of the interviewer recording answers on a hardcopy questionnaire, most CATI systems generate a telephone number from the sample (and may dial the number), guide the interviewer through the questionnaire, alert the interviewer if a mistake or inconsistent response is made, and record and store responses for data analysis. The CATI process decreases time required for conducting telephone interviews and entering data into software packages for statistical analysis (see Frankel & Frankel, 1987; Groves & Magilavy, 1986; Groves & Mathiowetz, 1984; Lynn, 1998 for reviews).

Before placing any telephone calls, it is useful to send notification letters to potential respondents if their addresses are available in the sample list. This letter minimizes any element of surprise that may occur with such an unexpected telephone call and improves legitimacy by introducing the survey and distinguishing it as a genuine research effort (Salant & Dillman, 1994). This letter should summarize in less than one page what the study is about, how people were selected, when they should expect to receive a call and how to arrange a more convenient time if necessary, how long the interview will last, and then thank respondents in advance for participating in the survey. Like cover letters for mail surveys, these advance notification letters should be written on letterhead and include researcher signatures and contact information.

Researchers must also hire and train interviewers before any calls are placed. Success of telephone interviews is dependent on interviewers being able to read fluently, communicate in a clear and pleasant manner without hesitating or stumbling with word pronunciation, and respond to inquiries without losing composure or focus (e.g., Groves & McGonagle, 2001; Oksenberg, Coleman, & Cannell, 1986; Singer, Frankel, & Glassman, 1983; Tucker, 1983). Interviewers should have a voice that is distinct and well-articulated, but will not interfere with other interviewers who work in close proximity. Interviewers should also have the ability to generate comradeship with respondents so that they stay on the telephone and complete all questions (Groves & McGonagle, 2001; Mitra & Lankford, 1999).

Many people have been "oversurveyed" to the point where they screen calls with call display technologies or belong to national "do not call" lists. To obtain high response rates with telephone surveys, interviewers must quickly convey professionalism and legitimacy (e.g., Mangoine, Fowler, & Louis, 1992). These skills must be taught; training interviewers is not optional. Some issues that should be covered when training interviewers include:

- background information about the project
- procedures for dialing telephone numbers (e.g., local, international)
- keeping an interviewer record log of all calls (e.g., busy, disconnected, call back)
- dealing with abusive or aggressive respondents (e.g., be nice, keep cool, be professional)
- tone and pace when reading questions (e.g., clear, neutral, enthusiastic, loud enough to hear, slow pace, consistency, sensitive to respondents)
- probing for more complete answers (e.g., "which would be closer to the way you feel")
- reading every question in order and reading the entire question before accepting response
- reading response scales (e.g., 5, 7, or 9 point; see chapter 7)
- repeating the entire question unless only one part was misunderstood
- providing feedback (e.g., "I see," "Thank you," "That is useful," "Let me get that down," "I want to make sure that I have it right")
- recording answers on questionnaire forms
- answering inquiries (e.g., who is study sponsor, what is study purpose, how many people sampled, who are you, who is conducting survey, how did you get my name)
- completing interviews (e.g., recording time, coding, checking responses)

It may be useful to prepare a help sheet addressing these issues and then post this sheet at interviewer workstations and/or provide this sheet directly to interviewers.

Once interviewers have been trained and a sample has been selected, questionnaires can start being administered. Chapter 7 offers guidelines on writing and constructing telephone surveys. One document that needs to be added, however, is an interviewer record form (IRF) or cover sheet for each questionnaire that identifies individuals using their name or an identification number, and records information about each contact. Given that it may take several calls each day for multiple days to reach intended people and ensure a high response rate, it is important to maintain a call record on this form so that different interviewers know what occurred during previous calls and when would be the best time to reach each individual. Researchers suggest that up to 15 call attempts per telephone number is the best approach, but cost efficiency of cutoffs with as few as five or six attempts is nearly as good (e.g., Kalsbeek, Botman, Massey, & Liu, 1994). Disposition of each call is also important for calculating response rates (discussed later). Figure 8.5 (p. 206) provides an example of an interviewer record form for a telephone survey.

For work-related surveys, telephone calls should occur during business hours (e.g., 9 a.m.–5 p.m.). For most parks, recreation, and human dimensions surveys, however, weekday or weekend evenings between 5:00 p.m. and 9:00 p.m., and occasional afternoons on weekends are most productive (Dillman, 2000; Salant & Dillman, 1994; Weeks, Kulka, & Pierson, 1987). Daytime hours on weekdays are less productive because many households will not have anybody at home (Weeks et al., 1987). If a RDD sample is being used, however, some daytime calls will be needed to eliminate working nonresidential numbers from the sample (Mitra & Lankford, 1999).

Interviewers encounter challenges with telephone surveys. It is important, therefore, to ensure that a supervisor is present when calls are made to overcome problems. One challenge is how to handle refusals where a person hangs up as soon as the interviewer introduces himself or herself without hearing what the study is about or answering any questions. To improve response rates, it may be useful to call back a few days later and attempt a ***refusal conversion*** by using a polite tone and beginning the interview differently such as "one of our interviewers attempted to call your household the other night, but we may have called at a bad time so I wanted to check back with you. We would like to ask a few quick questions about [topic] and would appreciate hearing your opinion" (e.g., Salant & Dillman, 1994; Snijkers, Hox, & de Leeuw, 1999).

Implementing On-Site Surveys

Common examples of on-site surveys in parks, recreation, and human dimensions of natural resources include trailhead surveys of hikers, questionnaires administered to wildlife viewers in parking areas or on viewing platforms, on-site surveys of skiers in warming huts or on-mountain restaurants, and questionnaires given to boaters at take-out or put-in points (see Manning, 1999 for a review). Door-to-door on-site household surveys tend to be less popular. On-site surveys are often the only solution when a population list is unavailable or people will not or are unable to respond accurately to another type of survey (Salant & Dillman, 1994).

As discussed earlier in this chapter, systematic, cluster, and multistage sampling designs can be effective when conducting on-site surveys because population lists are often unavailable. Although on-site questionnaires are typically shorter in length (e.g., one legal-size piece of paper printed on both sides; chapter 7), interviewers should estimate that they will only obtain approximately three or four completed questionnaires per hour. For example, if a goal is to achieve a

Respondent ID Number: _____

PSU Number: ____ ____ ____ ____

Phone Number:　　Area Code　　　　Prefix　　　　　　Suffix

　　　　　　　　____ ____ ____　____ ____ ____　____ ____ ____ ____

Disposition:

Date	Time	Disposition Code	Time	Disposition Code	Time	Disposition Code	Interviewer ID	Comments
___	___	___	___	___	___	___	___	_____
___	___	___	___	___	___	___	___	_____
___	___	___	___	___	___	___	___	_____
___	___	___	___	___	___	___	___	_____
___	___	___	___	___	___	___	___	_____

Appointments:

Today's Date	Current Time	Spoke With	Ask For	Call Back Date	Call Back Time	Interviewer ID	Comments
___	___	_____	_____	___	___	___	_____
___	___	_____	_____	___	___	___	_____
___	___	_____	_____	___	___	___	_____

Refusals:

Today's Date	Current Time	Spoke With	Interviewer ID	Comments
_____	_____	_____	___	_____

Final Disposition: _____

Disposition Codes:

01 = Completed interview　　　　　　　　　07 = No eligible respondent could be reached during time period
02 = Refused interview　　　　　　　　　　08 = Language barrier prevented completion of interview
03 = Nonworking number　　　　　　　　　09 = Interview terminated within questionnaire
04 = No answer (multiple tries)　　　　　　10 = Line busy (multiple tries)
05 = Business phone　　　　　　　　　　　11 = Selected respondent unable to respond
06 = No eligible respondent at this number

Figure 8.5　Sample Interviewer Record Form for Telephone Surveys

sample size of 400 completed questionnaires and an interviewer obtains four questionnaires per hour, it will take 100 hours or 12 to 13 days of full-time interviewing time. It is important to recognize, however, that use levels in natural resource settings vary considerably so some surveys may average less than one or more than ten questionnaires per hour. Given that many natural settings are relatively remote, it is also advisable to have more than one interviewer working on the project so that they can work together as a safety precaution.

On-site and telephone surveys are similar in that both require advance planning in terms of sampling, survey materials, and hiring and training personnel. One difference between these survey types, however, is that interviewers are sent out on their own to administer questionnaires on-site. As a result, it is important to ensure that interviewers are trained. Interviewers should be friendly, direct, honest, and professional. They should also wear modest clothing and be nicely groomed so that they make a good impression (e.g., Singer et al., 1983). Interviewers must be willing and able to work independently, and should be outgoing and personable when contacting and communicating with strangers. Several of the issues discussed for training telephone interviewers apply to on-site surveys (Groves & McGonagle, 2001). When an individual refuses to complete a questionnaire, for example, the interviewer must maintain his or her composure, be professional, and respond with a statement such as "I am sorry to bother you; have a nice day." Interviewers must also be prepared to address any inquiries about the project or questionnaire.

Before starting data collection, it is important to inform public officials and resource managers when and where questionnaires are being administered, and also provide officials with names and contact information of interviewers and supervisors. Interviewers may also want to carry a formal letter written on letterhead from resource managers and/or public agencies to demonstrate the study's legitimacy to potential respondents (Salant & Dillman, 1994).

When administering on-site questionnaires, interviewers should wear a nametag that identifies their name and organization, and shows a photograph of the individual. Interviewers should also carry: (a) clipboards; (b) pens or pencils; (c) signed letters from the researcher explaining the purpose of the study and issues related to confidentiality and anonymity (similar to cover letters for first questionnaire packet in a mail survey; Figure 8.2, p. 197); (d) questionnaires; (e) interviewer forms to record number of contacts, refusals, and completed questionnaires; and (f) a waterproof bag to carry materials and completed questionnaires. Salant and Dillman (1994) also recommend that interviewers carry a full manual or set of instructions about the survey and who should be sampled, but this may be too heavy and cumbersome to carry long distances in natural resource settings, and may be unnecessary if effective training is provided in advance.

Supervisors should be available on-site to address questions or problems that arise during data collection. Supervisors should also frequently consult with each interviewer to ensure that everything is proceeding smoothly and check a sample of completed questionnaires for legibility, consistency, and completeness. Meetings allow supervisors to identify any errors that may be recurring during sampling or questionnaire completion. Researchers should also consider having interviewers ask each respondent for their telephone number so that a sample of respondents can be contacted at a later time to confirm that they were actually interviewed. This technique minimizes the possibility of interviewers cheating and completing questionnaires on their own without ever contacting an individual (Mitra & Lankford, 1999; Salant & Dillman, 1994).

Implementing Electronic Surveys

Chapter 7 provided guidelines for constructing email and Internet surveys. Like other surveys (e.g., mail, telephone), multiple contacts are essential to the success of electronic surveys (Porter & Whitcomb, 2003). According to Dillman (2007), a prenotification email is of utmost importance for electronic surveys because questionnaires are easy to discard simply by deleting them. If the email is boring or too long, it will often go unread by many individuals. The prenotification letter should be short (e.g., two or three short paragraphs) and enthusiastically discuss what the study is about, when the survey will be sent, who to contact with questions, and a statement of appreciation. Email letters should fit on the screen so readers are not required to scroll through the message. Finally, email letters should be personalized so that it does not appear that they were part of a mass mailing (e.g., listserv, multiple recipient addresses).

Time intervals between repeated contacts should be shorter for electronic surveys than they are for mail surveys (Dillman, 2007; Kwak & Radler, 2002). Prenotification emails, for example, should be sent just one to three days before the questionnaire is first emailed to recipients. Each time a message is sent to respondents, a replacement questionnaire or website link should be provided in the body of the email. This approach is somewhat different than mail surveys where postcard reminders are sent without a replacement questionnaire.

The most effective implementation strategy for electronic surveys will depend on available alternatives (Gaede & Vaske, 1999). If telephone numbers or mailing addresses are available in the sample list, for example, mixed mode surveys (e.g., email with telephone follow-up) may be useful for improving response rates. If alternative contact information is unavailable, researchers should consider a multiple contact strategy similar to that used in mail surveys.

It is important to be cautious when using advanced tools for designing and implementing electronic surveys because some of these techniques make it difficult or impossible for some people to respond because of: (a) hardware and software performance or incompatibility, and (b) different levels of computer literacy among respondents (Dillman, 2007; Gaede & Vaske, 1999). Researchers should restrain from using advanced methods for implementing electronic surveys and opt for simpler and more generic questionnaires that can be accessed by most respondents.

Response Rates

The main reason for following these implementation strategies is to achieve the highest possible response rate. A *response rate* is commonly defined as the proportion of completed interviews to the total number of eligible respondents, and it indicates how successful the researcher was in gaining cooperation of potential respondents in a sample. As discussed earlier, a poor response rate may increase the likelihood of introducing nonresponse error. When a response rate for a random sample of a population is low, the researcher may not know whether those who completed a questionnaire are similar to those who did not complete a questionnaire. Low response rates, therefore, may weaken the ability to generalize to the target population.

There is disagreement on what constitutes an acceptable response rate. Babbie (2003), for example, considers a 50% response rate adequate, a response of at least 60% as good, and a return of 70% as very good. Salant and Dillman (1994) state that a response rate less than 60% for a general population survey and less than 70% for specific groups should be a red flag. Some recreation researchers (e.g., Dolson & Machlis, 1991) recommend response rates of at least 65%, whereas tourism researchers (e.g., Woodside & Ronkainen, 1984) suggest that response rates less than 80% can result in bias. Conversely, Mitra and Lankford (1999) suggest that response rates of 25% to 35% are within acceptable industry standards for leisure and recreation mail surveys.

Research shows that survey response rates tend to be declining over time for many social science studies and parks, recreation, and human dimensions of natural resources studies (e.g., Connelly, Brown, & Decker, 2003; Cook, Heath, & Thompson, 2000; Krosnick, 1999; Steeh, 1981; Steeh, Kirgis, Cannon, & DeWitt, 2001). Issues such as saliency of the topic to respondents, number and personalization of contacts, time of survey administration, question complexity, and questionnaire design all influence response rates. In addition, some people have been surveyed so much that they have started using tactics such as call screening, national "do not call lists," and junk mail filters to avoid being contacted by telemarketers and other survey firms. Although response rates tend to be declining, they vary considerably depending on sampling technique, type of survey, type of target population, and other data collection methods used (Figure 8.6).

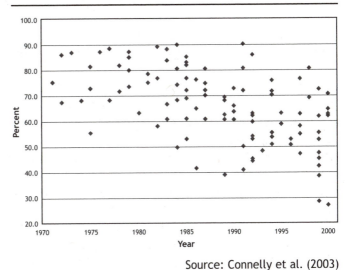

Source: Connelly et al. (2003)

Figure 8.6   Response Rates to Mail Surveys for 105 Studies Between 1971 and 2000

Calculating Response Rates

Response rates are typically calculated with the following equation:

$$\text{Response Rate} = \frac{C}{E}$$

Equation 8.5

where:

C = number of completed questionnaires
E = total number of eligible respondents

When multiplied by 100, this rate can be expressed as a percentage. For a questionnaire to be considered "completed" (i.e., C in equation 8.5), at least some portion of it must be completed or a set of predetermined and strategically chosen questions must be answered (Mitra & Lankford, 1999). The total number of "eligible" respondents (i.e., E in equation 8.5) depends on the number of categories of dispositions, which differ among survey types (e.g., mail, telephone).

In mail surveys, the number of eligible respondents is equal to the original sample size minus the number of questionnaires returned because they could not be delivered. For example, assume that questionnaires were mailed to 2,000 anglers in North Dakota. In total, 173 questionnaires were undeliverable (e.g., incorrect address information, moved) and after multiple mailings, 1,274 completed questionnaires were returned. The formula would be:

$$\text{Response Rate} = \frac{1,274}{2,000-173} = 69.7\%$$

Simply dividing the number of completed questionnaires (1,274) by the total sample (2,000) would yield a lower response (63.7%), which would be an incorrect calculation of response rate.

Researchers may also want to consider those people who recently moved out of the geographical region of the study (e.g., moved from North Dakota to Minnesota in the example) as undeliverables, but this may be difficult to track if first-class postage forwards the envelopes to new addresses and respondents complete and mail back the questionnaire.

It is important for researchers to estimate possible response rates before printing mail surveys. Table 8.9, for example, shows a hypothetical estimate of how many questionnaire packets (1,363) and postcards (409) may need to be printed and mailed to achieve a 59% overall response rate and total sample size of $n = 400$ for a survey with four mailings. Response rates and expected returns in Table 8.9, however, are estimates and may not be applicable to a specific population or project. Consulting recent research, therefore, is useful for anticipating response rates for different mailings and estimating how many documents may need to be printed.

Multiple contacts are important for achieving adequate response rates. The hypothetical estimate in Table 8.9, for example, shows that the expected response rate for the first mailing is 40%; three additional mailings are needed to achieve a 59% overall response rate. The variable response rates for each mailing (i.e., 40%, 10%, 15%, 10%) are estimates and may not be realistic for specific populations being studied in a particular project. It should also be noted that these response rates for each mailing do not sum to 59%; a final response rate is calculated by dividing the total number of questionnaires returned across all mailings by the number sent in the first questionnaire packet (i.e., 400 / 682 = 59%).

Table 8.9   Hypothetical Response Rates and Number of Questionnaires for a Mail Survey

	Number mailed	Expected response rate	Expected number returned
First mailing (first questionnaire packet)	682	40%	273
Second mailing (postcard)	409	10%	41
Third mailing (replacement questionnaire packet)	368	15%	55
Fourth mailing (certified or registered mail)	313	10%	31
Total	1,772[1]	59%[2]	400

[1] Total of 1,363 questionnaire packets and 409 postcards.
[2] Assumes no undeliverables (e.g., incomplete address, moved)

Multiple contacts are also important for minimizing nonresponse error. Consider the following hypothetical example. Many states conduct tourism conversion surveys where a goal is to examine the effectiveness of promotional brochures for attracting visitors to the state. Table 8.10

shows that with just one mailing and a response rate of 35%, 87% of respondents had visited the state and 13% had not visited. If no additional mailings were conducted, it can be assumed that the brochures were effective at attracting visitors. This conclusion is premature because of potential for nonresponse bias. By the fourth mailing, an 80% overall response rate is achieved and results show that only 11% of respondents had visited the state, suggesting that perhaps the brochures were actually not highly effective at attracting visitors to the state.

Table 8.10 Hypothetical Response Rates and Results by Mailing for State Tourism Conversion Survey

	Total response rate after mailing	Results by mailing: Visited state?	
		Yes	No
First mailing (first questionnaire packet)	35%	87%	13%
Second mailing (postcard)	45%	67%	33%
Third mailing (replacement questionnaire packet)	65%	53%	47%
Fourth mailing (certified or registered mail)	80%	11%	89%

In some other types of surveys such as telephone surveys, the general response rate calculation (i.e., C / E) fails to account for the variety of possible outcomes or dispositions of a telephone call. How does a researcher, for example, treat numbers that are not answered or remain busy even after repeated callbacks? Should these numbers be considered eligible or ineligible? Frankel (1982), in a special report for the Council of American Survey Research Organizations (CASRO), proposed a solution to the problem known as the ***CASRO estimator***.

$$\text{Response rate} = \frac{C}{E + \left[\dfrac{E}{I+E}\right]U}$$

Equation 8.6

where:

C = the number of completed interviews
E = the total number of eligible respondents
I = the number of ineligible
U = the number of unknown final dispositions (i.e., no answer, line busy)

The CASRO estimator apportions dispositions with unknown eligibility status (e.g., no answer, busy) to dispositions representing eligible respondents in the same proportion as exists among calls of known status (Table 8.11, p. 212). The resulting estimate reflects telephone sampling efficiency and degree of cooperation among eligible respondents contacted. Based on disposition codes provided in Table 8.11, the CASRO formula would be:

$$\text{Response Rate} = \frac{01}{(01+02+07+09) + \left[\dfrac{(01+02+07+09)}{(03+05+06+08+11)+(01+02+07+09)}\right] * (04+10)}$$

Table 8.11   CASRO Disposition Codes for Calls in a Telephone Interview

Final disposition of call	Status	Code
Completed interview	Eligible	01
Refused interview	Eligible	02
Nonworking number	Ineligible	03
Ring, no answer	Unknown	04
Business phone	Ineligible	05
No eligible respondent at this number	Ineligible	06
No eligible respondent could be reached in time period	Eligible	07
Language barrier	Ineligible	08
Interview terminated	Eligible	09
Line busy	Unknown	10
Respondent unable to respond due to impairment	Ineligible	11

The CASRO estimator is just one approach for calculating response rates for telephone surveys. There are many other methods for estimating more liberal or conservative response rates for telephone surveys and other types of surveys (see Frey, 1989; Gripp, Luloff, & Yonkers, 1994; Lavrakas, 1987; McCarty, 2003 for reviews). The American Association for Public Opinion Research (AAPOR), for example, provides a spreadsheet that can be downloaded (http://www.aapor.org/uploads/Response_Rate_Calculator.xls) to calculate telephone survey response rates based on their formula.

There have been studies presenting predictive models for calculating anticipated survey response rates based on factors such as who is conducting the study (e.g., agency, university), type of population (e.g., general, specific group), saliency of topic, number of pages or length of survey, and number of mailings or contacts (e.g., Baruch, 1999; Connelly et al., 2003; Cook et al., 2000; Heberlein & Baumgartner, 1978; Krosnick, 1999). These approaches, which are often based on regression models (see chapter 16), are useful when anticipating or predicting future events such as final response rates when conditions such as questionnaire length, personalization and number of contacts, complexity of questions, and type of population are known in advance.

Nonresponse Bias Checks

One concern in survey research is that individuals who completed the questionnaire may be different from those who did not complete the questionnaire. In other words, respondents may not be representative of the population or sample of which they are a member. One way to address this issue is to conduct a nonresponse bias check. A nonresponse check can involve contacting a sample of original nonrespondents and asking questions from the questionnaire. Number of questions asked will depend on length of the original questionnaire. If a questionnaire was 12 pages in length, for example, it would be advisable to only ask a subset of important questions from each major section to minimize respondent burden. If a questionnaire was only one or two pages, it might be feasible to ask all questions in a nonresponse check.

According to Babbie (2003), a demonstrated lack of response bias is more important than a high response rate. Nonresponse bias may exist even with a relatively high response rate such as 70%; a low response rate such as 30% may be acceptable if there are no differences between those who responded to a survey and those who did not respond (Crompton & Tian-Cole, 2001; Krosnick, 1999). Given that some studies of relatively homogeneous groups have found few differences among multiple contacts (e.g., first contact, postcard, final contact), some researchers have argued that going to the expense of obtaining high response rates and extensive contacts may not be necessary to avoid nonresponse error (e.g., Becker & Iliff, 1983; Dolsen & Machlis, 1991; Hammitt & McDonald, 1982). Other studies of heterogeneous samples (e.g., general public), however, have found substantial differences between respondents and nonrespondents of multiple contacts (e.g., Brown & Wilkens, 1978; Manfredo, Teel, & Bright, 2003; Woodside & Ronkainen, 1984). Regardless, a nonresponse check is an important step in survey research and it may be even more important than high response rates and sample sizes for allowing researchers to be confident in the representativeness of their results (Crompton & Tian-Cole, 2001).

It can be useful to use a different type of survey method for nonresponse bias checks (Dillman, 2000). A nonresponse bias check should emphasize the importance and legitimacy of the request, and one way to do this is to provide a different survey mode and appearance. After conducting multiple mailings for a mail survey, for example, it can be effective to conduct a nonresponse bias check using telephone contacts and asking a sample of original nonrespondents a subset of questions from the mail questionnaire (e.g., Manfredo, Teel et al., 2003; Needham, Vaske, & Manfredo, 2005; Needham, Vaske, Donnelly, & Manfredo, 2007). Using another form of contact may not always be possible because full contact information may not be available for all members of the sample (Mitra & Lankford, 1999). A telephone nonresponse check for an original mail survey, for example, assumes that valid telephone numbers are available for all sample members. Alternating types of surveys also requires researchers and personnel to have sufficient training in each survey methodology.

Weighting

Weighting by Nonresponse Checks

If results of a nonresponse bias check show differences between people in the sample who completed a questionnaire and those who did not complete it, data may need to be weighted for sample results to be representative of the target population. Assume, for example, that the response rate for a random mail survey was only 10% and results showed that 30% of these respondents were males and 70% were females. A nonresponse check with a random sample of the 90% of people who did not respond showed that 60% were male and 40% were female. Although the original sample was selected at random, this suggests that responses to the mail survey may not be truly representative of the population because far more women responded to the mail survey than men, so there was an underrepresentation of males. Given the low response rate and this substantial disparity in results between the mail survey and nonresponse check, it may be prudent to weight the data from the mail survey, as follows:

$$\text{Weight} = \frac{\text{Population \%}}{\text{Sample \%}} \qquad\qquad \text{Equation 8.7}$$

$$\text{Weight}_{(males)} = \frac{0.60}{0.30} = 2.0 \qquad\qquad \text{Weight}_{(females)} = \frac{0.40}{0.70} = 0.57$$

Weighting by Population Proportions: Single Variable

Weighting may also be necessary if population proportions are known in advance and survey results reveal that specific groups or segments are overrepresented or underrepresented. In a recent mail survey of resident and nonresident deer hunters in eight states and elk hunters in three states, for example, more questionnaires were received from nonresident hunters in each state (e.g., Needham et al., 2007). For the year in which the study was conducted, however, hunting license sales showed that many more residents than nonresidents purchased a license to hunt deer or elk in each state. Given that more questionnaires were received from nonresident hunters, data were weighted to reflect the population proportions of hunters as follows:

$$\text{Weight} = \frac{\text{Population \%}}{\text{Sample \%}}$$

where:

$$\text{Population \%} = \frac{\text{Number of hunters in stratum}}{\text{Number of hunters across strata}}$$

$$\text{Sample \%} = \frac{\text{Number of respondents in stratum}}{\text{Number of respondents across strata}}$$

Among Arizona deer hunters, for example, there were 32,502 resident and 1,079 nonresident hunters in the population. Completed questionnaires were received from 396 resident and 443 nonresident hunters. To combine residents and nonresidents, and generalize to the total population of Arizona deer hunters, the following weight would need to be applied for *residents*:

$$\text{Population \%}_{\text{(residents)}} = \frac{32,502}{33,581} = 0.968 \qquad \text{Sample \%}_{\text{(residents)}} = \frac{396}{839} = 0.472$$

therefore: $\text{Weight}_{\text{(residents)}} = \dfrac{0.968}{0.472} = 2.051$

In addition, the following weight would need to be applied for *nonresidents*:

$$\text{Population \%}_{\text{(nonresidents)}} = \frac{1,079}{33,581} = 0.032$$

$$\text{Sample \%}_{\text{(nonresidents)}} = \frac{443}{839} = 0.528$$

therefore: $\text{Weight}_{\text{(nonresidents)}} = \dfrac{0.032}{0.528} = 0.061$

This gives a higher weight to the underrepresented group (i.e., residents) and a lower weight to the overrepresented group (i.e., nonresidents) of Arizona hunters. With nonresidents coded as "0" and residents coded as "1" in SPSS statistical software, the SPSS syntax (see chapter 12) for applying these weights to the Arizona dataset was a series of "if" statements:

```
if residency = 0 weight = 0.061.
```

```
if residency = 1 weight = 2.051. execute.
WEIGHT BY weight.
```

Generalizing results to a more macro or higher level requires a different set of weights. To generalize to the population of all hunters across all eight states irrespective of state, residency (i.e., resident, nonresident), or species hunted (i.e., deer, elk), 22 different weights would be needed (i.e., resident and nonresident deer hunters across eight states = 16 weights, plus resident and nonresident elk hunters across three states = 6 weights, so [2 * 8] + [2 * 3] = 22). The total population from all licenses was 1,329,464 hunters and the total sample size was 9,567. The weight for Arizona resident deer hunters, for example, was calculated as follows:

$$\text{Population \%}_{(\text{AZ res. deer})} = \frac{32,502}{1,329,464} = 0.024$$

$$\text{Sample \%}_{(\text{AZ res. deer})} = \frac{396}{9,567} = 0.041$$

therefore: $\text{Weight}_{(\text{AZ res. deer})} = \frac{0.024}{0.041} = 0.59$

These calculations were repeated for the 22 strata. State (Arizona [1], Colorado [2], North Dakota [3], Nebraska [4], South Dakota [5], Utah [6], Wisconsin [7], Wyoming [8]), residency (nonresident [0], resident [1]), and species (deer [0], elk [1]) were coded in SPSS, and syntax for applying weights was:

```
if state = 1 and residency = 1 weight = 0.59.
if state = 1 and residency = 0 weight = 0.02.
if state = 2 and residency = 1 and deerelk = 0 weight = 1.00.
if state = 2 and residency = 0 and deerelk = 0 weight = 0.31.
if state = 2 and residency = 1 and deerelk = 1 weight = 2.02.
if state = 2 and residency = 0 and deerelk = 1 weight = 0.88.
if state = 3 and residency = 1 weight = 1.56.
if state = 3 and residency = 0 weight = 0.05.
if state = 4 and residency = 1 weight = 1.10.
if state = 4 and residency = 0 weight = 0.05.
if state = 5 and residency = 1 weight = 0.92.
if state = 5 and residency = 0 weight = 0.05.
if state = 6 and residency = 1 and deerelk = 0 weight = 1.15.
if state = 6 and residency = 0 and deerelk = 0 weight = 0.08.
if state = 6 and residency = 1 and deerelk = 1 weight = 0.74.
if state = 6 and residency = 0 and deerelk = 1 weight = 0.05.
if state = 7 and residency = 1 weight = 10.30.
if state = 7 and residency = 0 weight = 0.51.
if state = 8 and residency = 1 and deerelk = 0 weight = 1.17.
if state = 8 and residency = 0 and deerelk = 0 weight = 0.48.
if state = 8 and residency = 1 and deerelk = 1 weight = 0.84.
if state = 8 and residency = 0 and deerelk = 1 weight = 0.15. execute.
WEIGHT BY weight.
```

Weighting by Population Proportions: Multiple Variables

Although proportions are sometimes known for populations of interest in parks, recreation, and human dimensions of natural resources through sources such as hunter or angler license sales, there are instances such as general population surveys where it is difficult to know "correct" population ratios and multiple variables must be used to weight data. In these situations, Census data is one helpful source of information about populations that can be used for weighting survey data.

A study of public attitudes toward the desert tortoise, for example, surveyed a sample of the general public in five California counties (Vaske & Donnelly, 2007). To reflect the actual population of individuals living in each county, the sample was weighted by U.S. Census 2000 data. Four weighting variables were used: (a) county (Imperial, Kern, Los Angeles, Riverside, San Bernardino), (b) ethnicity (Hispanic, Non-Hispanic), (c) sex (male, female), and (d) age (18–29, 30–39, 40–49, 50–59, 60–69, 70+ years). The combination of these four variables and their associated levels resulted in 120 cells (i.e., 5 counties * 2 levels of ethnicity * 2 levels of sex * 6 age groups = 120) in a set of crosstabs (see chapter 13). Population size and percent for these 120 cells were based on Census data. Percent of the sample in these cells was based on survey data. Weights were calculated using the formula presented earlier (weight = population % / sample %). Table 8.12 provides an example of calculations and weights for one of the five counties.

Normalizing Weights

For analyses, the weighted overall number of cases (i.e., weighted sample size) should equal the unweighted overall number of cases (i.e., unweighted sample size) and the mean of the weights should be 1 (Glynn, 2004). If the weighted number of cases differs dramatically from the unweighted number of cases, tests of statistical significance may be invalid. To address this issue, weights should be adjusted by dividing the weight by the mean of the weights:

$$\text{Adjusted Weight} = \frac{\text{Weight}}{\text{Mean of the Weights}}$$

Equation 8.8

Using this strategy, relative values of weights are unchanged, but they are normalized to have a mean of 1 and the sum of weights equals the number of cases. In general, if the weighted number of overall cases differs dramatically from the unweighted number of cases, normalized weighting is the recommended approach because it retains the original sample size. Appendix 1 in chapter 17 provides more weighting examples, including an example of normalizing weights.

Other Considerations for Weighting Data

The weighting strategies discussed involve adjusting sample data after it is collected so that it is more reflective of the larger target population. There are, however, strategies for weighting samples to adjust for unequal chances of selection when drawing a sample prior to data collection (e.g., Salant & Dillman, 1994, p. 70). There are also more complex approaches for weighting data, including weighting based on multiple sources of population information such as combining data from nonresponse checks with Census information (see Beaman & Redekop, 1990; Kalton & Flores-Cervantes, 2003; Manfredo, Teel et al., 2003; Valliant, 2004 for reviews on various weighting approaches).

Table 8.12   Sampling Weights for One of Five Counties Based on Multiple Variables from Census Data [1]

County	Population	Category	Hispanic Population	% Hispanic Population	% Hispanic Sample	Hispanic Weight
Total Population	1,709,434					
% 18 and over	0.677					
Total Population 18+	1,157,287					
		Male 18–29	71,871	0.062	0.023	2.700
		Male 30–39	55,711	0.048	0.027	1.783
		Male 40–49	38,600	0.033	0.045	0.741
		Male 50–59	18,964	0.016	0.042	0.390
		Male 60–69	9,450	0.008	0.025	0.327
		Male 70+	7,094	0.006		
		Female 18–29	65,623	0.057	0.02	2.835
		Female 30–39	53,291	0.046	0.048	0.959
		Female 40–49	38,129	0.033	0.045	0.732
		Female 50–59	19,706	0.017	0.038	0.448
		Female 60–69	11,436	0.010	0.025	0.395
		Female 70+	10,050	0.009	0.015	0.579
			Non-Hispanic Population	% Non-Hispanic Population	% Non-Hispanic Sample	Non-Hispanic Weight
		Male 18–29	80,993	0.070	0.037	1.891
		Male 30–39	75,968	0.066	0.055	1.194
		Male 40–49	83,455	0.072	0.08	0.901
		Male 50–59	58,634	0.051	0.116	0.437
		Male 60–69	34,983	0.030	0.103	0.293
		Male 70+	34,769	0.030	0.01	3.004
		Female 18–29	75,071	0.065	0.037	1.753
		Female 30–39	79,301	0.069	0.037	1.852
		Female 40–49	86,123	0.074	0.07	1.063
		Female 50–59	59,006	0.051	0.045	1.133
		Female 60-69	37,863	0.033	0.06	0.545
		Female 70+	51,296	0.044		

[1] Some cells are empty because no individual in the demographic category completed and returned a questionnaire.

There are two major issues that should be considered before weighting data. First, the researcher must be comfortable with how data used for weighting the sample were collected. For example, if data used for weighting were collected with nonprobability methods or were collected many years before the sample data, it may be unwise to use it as a basis for establishing weights because it may not be representative of the current population. Second, the sample size of data used for weighting should not be too small or substantially lower than the main sample. Assume, for example, that the number of completed questionnaires for a random survey was 14,510 with a 65% response rate, but a nonresponse check of 125 nonrespondents showed that respondents' and nonrespondents' answers differed for a few questions. Should the researcher assume that answers from 125 nonrespondents are more representative of the population than answers from 14,510 respondents? This is a researcher decision, but given the high sample size and response rate, it can be argued that the larger sample is likely to be more representative.

Chapter Summary

This chapter discussed various approaches for checking and pretesting a questionnaire, selecting samples of potential respondents, and administering questionnaires to individuals. Response rates, nonresponse checks, and approaches for weighting data were also examined.

This chapter discussed steps that should be taken before administering a questionnaire to determine whether the instrument works satisfactorily or has any major problems. These steps include: (a) seeking expert advice from academicians or representatives of organizations supporting the project, (b) administering a pilot test of the questionnaire to a small group of people who are typical of likely respondents, and (c) performing a final check of the instrument to ensure that no errors are present. Questionnaires should be revised based on input and results from these steps before selecting a larger sample and proceeding with data collection.

Questionnaires should be administered to reduce errors in coverage, measurement, nonresponse, and sampling. Coverage error occurs with a discrepancy between the population and subset of individuals who are included in the sampling frame (e.g., incomplete population list). If there is error in coverage, all elements of the population do not have an equal or known chance of being included in the sample, which makes it difficult to use survey results to generalize to the larger population. Measurement error occurs when answers are imprecise, inaccurate, or cannot be compared to those of other respondents. This error occurs because of poor questionnaire wording and construction, type of survey used, influence of the interviewer, or behavior of the respondent. Nonresponse error occurs when some people in the sample do not respond to the questionnaire and are different from those who do in a way that is important to the study. One way to minimize this error is to use techniques for improving response rates. Sampling error is the extent to which a sample is limited in its ability to perfectly describe a population because only some elements in a population are sampled. When conducting a survey, there is always sampling error because sample data are rarely equal to population parameters. One way to avoid sampling error is to conduct a census (i.e., survey entire population), but this is often not realistic or feasible. Most human dimensions studies should at least obtain enough questionnaires to minimize sampling error to just $\pm 5\%$ of the population at the 95% confidence level. Formulas for calculating sampling error and necessary sample sizes were provided in this chapter.

Once the population has been defined and a list of members has been obtained, it is necessary to choose a method for selecting a sample that represents the population from which it was drawn. This chapter discussed five sampling approaches. First, simple random sampling involves selecting a group of sampling units (e.g., people) where each member of the population has an equal nonzero chance of selection. Lottery techniques, tables of random numbers, and statistical software facilitate selection of random samples. Second, systematic samples require randomly selecting the first unit (i.e., person) in a sample population, choosing an appropriate fixed interval (i.e., every n^{th} person), and systematically selecting units. Third, stratified random sampling involves dividing the sample population into different nonoverlapping groups (i.e., strata) that are of interest or deserve particular attention because of project objectives or hypotheses, and then selecting a random sample from each stratum. Fourth, cluster sampling involves conducting a simple random sample of groups or clusters, then sampling units (e.g., people) within selected groups or clusters. This approach differs from stratified sampling where a random sample is drawn within each group; cluster sampling involves a random sample of groups. Fifth, multistage sample designs are more complex because they combine several single stage approaches into a multistage design (e.g., stratified-cluster approach).

This chapter discussed survey implementation strategies for encouraging high response rates and minimizing nonresponse error. Strategies such as multiple contacts, appearance of accompanying materials (e.g., envelopes), sponsorship, personalization, and other aspects of the communication process were discussed. Mail surveys, for example, should use multiple contacts (e.g., prenotification, first questionnaire packet, thank you/reminder postcard, replacement questionnaire packet). Samples for telephone surveys should be selected using approaches such as the Waksberg methodology or plus-one method. Before conducting telephone surveys, it is important to estimate time needed to complete questionnaires and financial resources available to pay for associated costs, make arrangements for facilities and equipment, and hire and train interviewers. When conducting on-site surveys, it is important to estimate time necessary to achieve a specific sample size, ensure that interviewers are properly trained, inform public officials and agencies when questionnaires are being administered, and supply interviewers with appropriate materials (e.g., clipboards, pens, questionnaires, interviewer forms). Like mail surveys, electronic surveys should use prenotification letters and multiple contacts, but timing between contacts should be shorter. This chapter reviewed these and other techniques for implementing mail, telephone, on-site, and electronic surveys.

One reason for following implementation strategies outlined in this chapter is to achieve a high response rate. Response rate is the proportion of completed interviews to the total number of eligible respondents, and it indicates how successful the researcher was in gaining cooperation of respondents. This chapter reviewed several possible approaches for calculating response rates including the CASRO estimator for telephone surveys. One concern with low response rates is that individuals who completed a questionnaire may differ from those who did not complete a questionnaire. Nonresponse bias checks should be conducted with a sample of nonrespondents to ensure that they are not different from respondents. If nonrespondents are different, data may need to be weighted for sample results to represent the target population. This chapter provided several approaches, formulas, and syntax for weighting data based on nonresponse checks, population proportions, and Census data.

Review Questions

1. Discuss three approaches for determining in advance if a questionnaire works satisfactorily or has any major problems.

2. Define each of the following terms: element, population, survey population, sampling unit, sampling frame, sample, observation unit, and completed sample.

3. Define and give an example of coverage error. What is one way to overcome this error?

4. Questionnaires are mailed to 50,000 hunters and 2,500 are completed and returned. Despite this large sample size, what is an obvious potential problem or error with this sample?

5. Define sampling error and suggest one way to avoid this type of error.

6. What does it mean when we say that the margin of error was ±5% and confidence was 95%?

7. In most parks, recreation, and human dimensions studies, what sample size is considered to be suitable? Why?

8. When segmenting samples into subgroups, what happens to sampling error? What is one way to avoid this happening?

9. Define and differentiate probability sampling from nonprobability sampling. List advantages and disadvantages of both types of sampling.

10. Describe simple random sampling (SRS); list three rigorous methods for selecting a SRS.

11. Define and differentiate haphazard and representative sampling.

12. Summarize the steps involved in using a table of random numbers to select a random sample.

13. Describe systematic sampling, using the concepts of sampling interval, sampling ratio, and periodicity in your description.

14. Describe how to conduct a stratified random sample and discuss two primary reasons why stratified samples are useful.

15. Define cluster sampling, summarize the steps involved in selecting a cluster sample, and explain how cluster sampling differs from stratified sampling.

16. Identify advantages of a multistage stratified-cluster sampling approach and describe how this strategy could be executed in a backcountry recreation area.

17. Explain in detail characteristics of four types of contacts when conducting a mail survey.

18. When conducting a mail survey, list three reasons why first-class postage is preferred.

19. What is a difference between *voluntary* and *confidential*?

20. Briefly describe how the Waksberg two-stage sampling design is implemented.

21. Describe the plus-one sampling methodology and list one advantage and one disadvantage of this methodology.

22. List five things that all interviewers should carry when administering on-site questionnaires.

23. Define *response rate* and explain why the response rate is important for survey research.

24. Using examples, explain how you would calculate response rates for both mail and telephone surveys. Include formulas in your response.

25. What is a nonresponse bias check? Using an example and the appropriate formula, show how data can be weighted based on results of a nonresponse check.

9

an introduction to SPSS for Windows

The Statistical Package for the Social Sciences (SPSS) is an integrated system of computer programs that allows users to easily perform statistical analysis. The software provides a comprehensive set of procedures for data transformation and file manipulation as well as common social science statistical tests.

SPSS runs on computers ranging from large mainframes to PCs. This chapter discusses SPSS for Windows version 15 as adapted for Microsoft Windows operating systems. Version 15 uses menus and dialog boxes that do most of the work for the analyst. Although many tasks can be accomplished by simply pointing and clicking, the use of a program file (or *syntax file* in SPSS terminology) when conducting analyses is recommended. The rationale for this argument is described later in the chapter.

The basics of SPSS for Windows are easy to learn. Like any software application, however, it takes practice to become familiar and comfortable with the functionality of the software. This chapter provides an introduction to SPSS.

Starting SPSS

There are at least three ways to start SPSS:

1. To open SPSS from the Windows Start menu, choose:

   > Start > Programs > SPSS for Windows > SPSS 15 for Windows

2. To open SPSS from the desktop (if there is an SPSS icon on the desktop), double click the icon.

SPSS 15.0 for Windows

3. To open SPSS with an existing file (i.e., data, syntax or output) from Windows Explorer, go to:
   a. The directory where the file is located (e.g., C:\My Documents\ )
   b. Double click on the desired file (e.g., NH - State Parks - Report card.sav)
   c. SPSS will open the selected file

File Types Used by SPSS for Windows

Although SPSS uses a variety of file types, three are common to most analyses:

1. *Data Editor files*. The responses from a survey are stored in data files. Any file with an extension of *.sav* is a data file in SPSS. The contents of a data file are displayed in the Data Editor window.

2. *Syntax Editor files*. Syntax or program files tell SPSS what kinds of actions should be performed on the data. Included among these tasks are: (a) defining or describing variables, (b) consolidating the values of an existing variable, (c) computing new variables, (d) selecting specific cases (i.e., respondents) for analysis, and (e) running statistical procedure commands. Files with an extension of *.sps* are syntax files and are displayed in the Syntax window.

3. *Output Viewer files*. Output files contain the output from an SPSS procedure (e.g., a FREQUENCIES analysis). Files with an extension of *.spo* are output files and are displayed in the Output Viewer window. In SPSS version 16, output files have an extension of *.spv*.

SPSS Windows

There are four basic windows in SPSS:

1. *SPSS application window.*
   This window contains the menu bar, which is used to open files, choose statistical procedures, and select other features of the system (see items 2–4, description of menu choices).

2. *Data Editor window.*
   The Data Editor window displays the contents of the data file. The researcher can create new data files or modify existing files with the Data Editor. A blank or empty Data Editor window opens automatically when you launch an SPSS session from the Start menu. To open an existing data file.

   From the menu,
   - (a)   Choose: File > Open > Data...
   - (b)   File name: (specify the directory where the file is located)
   - (c)   Files of type: [SPSS (*filename*.sav)]
   - (d)   Select the desired data file
   - (e)   Click OK

3. *Syntax Editor window.*
   The Syntax window is a text window that runs SPSS commands. By default, SPSS does not open a Syntax window when the software is started. During an SPSS session, one or more existing Syntax windows can be opened.

   From the menu,
   - (a)   Choose: File > Open > Syntax...
   - (b)   File name: (specify the directory where the file is located)

    (c)   Files of type: [Syntax (*filename*.sps)]

    (d)   Select the desired syntax file

    (e)   Click OK

4. *Output (Viewer) window.*

An Output or Viewer window displays the results of an SPSS analysis. An output window opens automatically when you start a new SPSS session from the Start Menu in Windows. The contents of an output window can be edited when the SPSS processor is not running commands.

To open an existing Output window from the menu:

    (a) Choose **File > Open > Output...**

    (b) File name: (specify the directory where the file is located)

    (c) Files of type: [Viewer document (*filename*.spo)]

    (d) Select the desired output file

    (e) Click OK

Designated versus Active Window

If more than one Output Viewer window is open, the results of an analysis are sent to the *designated* Viewer window. If more than one Syntax window is open, commands (syntax) are pasted into the *designated* Syntax Editor window. The designated windows are indicated by a plus sign in the title bar (Figure 9.1).

Figure 9.1   SPSS Designated and Active Syntax Editor

The designated window should not be confused with the *active* (or currently selected) window. The active window is in the foreground and may or may not be the designated window as in Figure 9.1. Syntax will be automatically pasted into the designated window, which may not be the window on top. If a new Syntax Editor or Viewer window is opened, that window automatically becomes the active window *and* the designated window. You can change the designated windows at any time by: (a) making the window that you want to designate the active window (click anywhere in the window) and (b) clicking the plus sign icon on the menu bar (i.e., the Designate Window button).

Understanding the distinction between designated and active windows helps avoid frustration and questions like "Where did my syntax (or output) go?" Note: Sometimes this question is worded more strongly. All computer programs, including SPSS, operate in a logical sequence; humans sometimes don't follow perfect logic.

Menus

Most tasks in SPSS start with menu selections. Each SPSS window has its own menu bar with menu selections appropriate for that window type. For example, the Data Editor (Figure 9.2) and Syntax Editor (Figure 9.3) menus both have *File, Edit, View, Data, Transform, Analyze, Graphs, Utilities, Add-ons, Window*, and *Help* as choices. The *Data* and *Transform* options are tasks appropriate for data manipulation. The Syntax Editor menu (but not the Data Editor menu) includes a selection called *Run* (i.e., running SPSS commands). The Output (Viewer) window (Figure 9.4) is identical to Data Editor menu, but has two more options, *Insert* and *Format*. These options allow you control the way your output looks (e.g., add a title, insert a page break). Similar to the designated versus active window distinction, understanding what menu choices are available on different menus helps to minimize frustration levels.

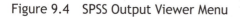

Figure 9.2   SPSS Data Editor Menu

Figure 9.3   SPSS Syntax Editor Menu

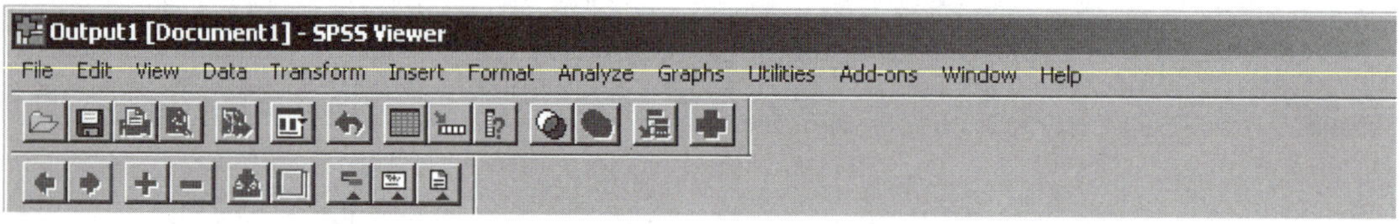

Figure 9.4   SPSS Output Viewer Menu

The available options within each drop-down menu of the Data Editor are shown in Figure 9.5 with the exeption of *Add-ons*, which are not discussed in this text. The list of options appears overwhelming, because it is. However, you do not need to understand every component in SPSS to analyze survey data. Many people routinely use Microsoft Word, Excel, and PowerPoint and do not understand (or even need) all of the functionality in these programs.

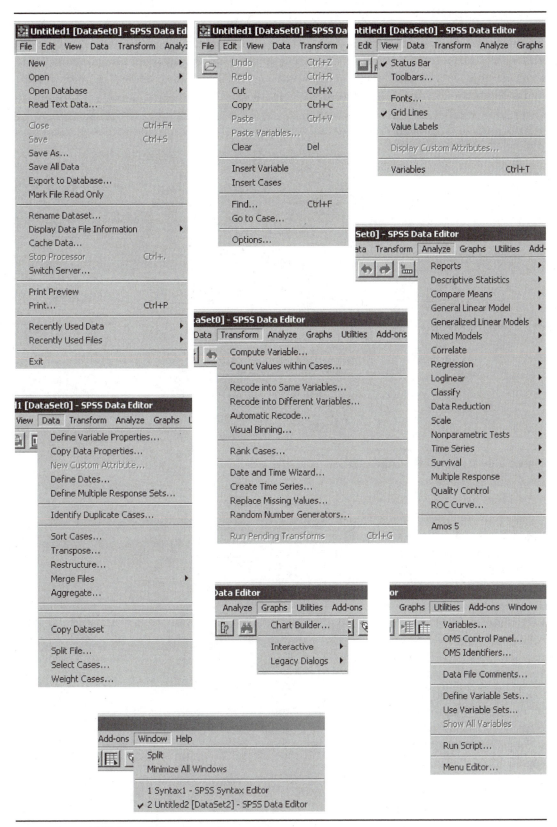

Figure 9.5   SPSS Data Editor Drop-Down Menus

Useful "Optional" Settings

SPSS is installed with a number of default settings that can be changed to suit your needs and preferences. These settings control, among other things, what appears when results are displayed (e.g., variable "labels" vs. variable "names and labels"). The default settings can be accessed and changed by selecting Edit > Options... (Figure 9.6).

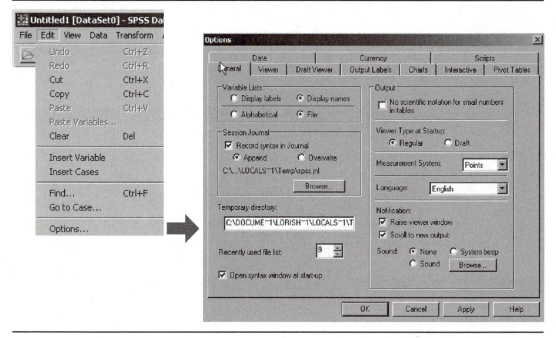

Figure 9.6   Optional Settings in SPSS

Across the top of the Options dialog box are a series of tabs. Within the Viewer tab under the subheading Initial Output State is an option to "Display commands in the log" (Figure 9.7). It is often convenient to "check" this option. For example, if you Recode an existing variable or Compute a new variable, displaying the syntax commands in the output file provides a reference for what syntax commands were used to perform a specific task.

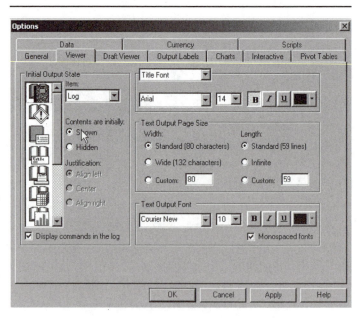

Figure 9.7   The Viewer Tab in the Options Dialog box

By default, SPSS displays only variable "labels" in the output file (Figure 9.8). Showing both "names and labels" and "values and labels" is helpful when the variables have been recoded.

Default Settings **Alternative Settings**

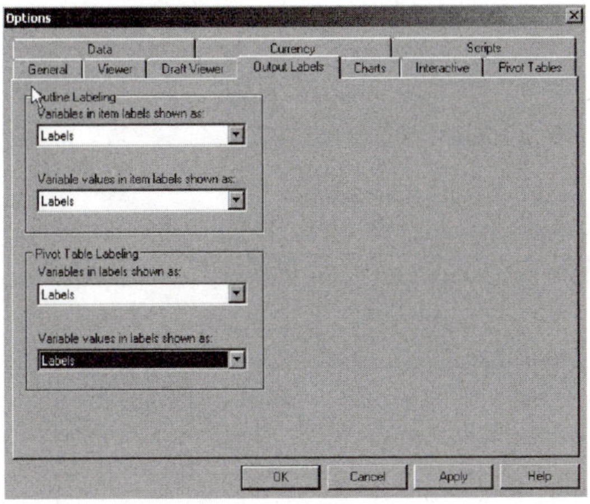

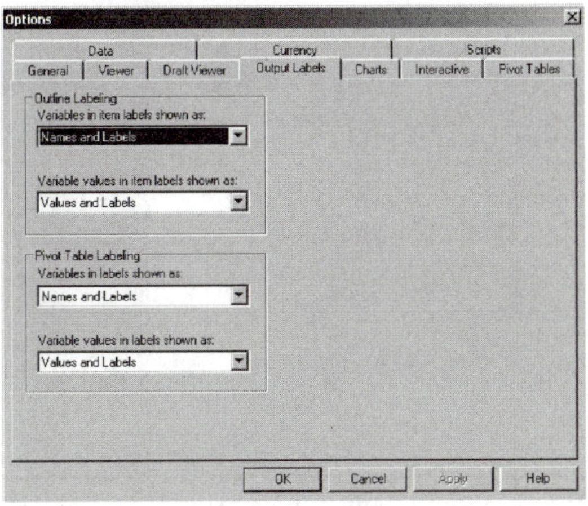

Figure 9.8   Output Labels: Default and Alternative Settings

The remaining tabs (Figure 9.8) control other aspects of the way an analyst interacts with SPSS. You should experiment with these settings to determine which options best meet your preferences. These suggested changes to the default settings under the Viewer and Output Label tabs, however, will help avoid problems that can arise when analyzing data and interpreting output.

Statistical Analysis with the Dialog Box Interface

There are four basic steps to analyzing data with SPSS:

1. Select a data file.
2. Select a statistical test.
3. Select variables for analysis.
4. Select additional statistics and options.

These steps apply to *all* analyses (e.g., FREQUENCIES, CROSSTABS, INDEPENDENT-SAMPLES T-TESTS, ONE-WAY ANOVA, CORRELATION, REGRESSION).

Step 1. Select a Data File

To select a data file,
      (a) Click on: File > Open > Data...
      (b) File name: (specify the directory where the file is located)
      (c) Files of type: [SPSS (*filename*.sav)]
      (d) Select the desired data file
      (e) Click OK

This sequence of actions is diagrammed in Figure 9.9 (p.230).

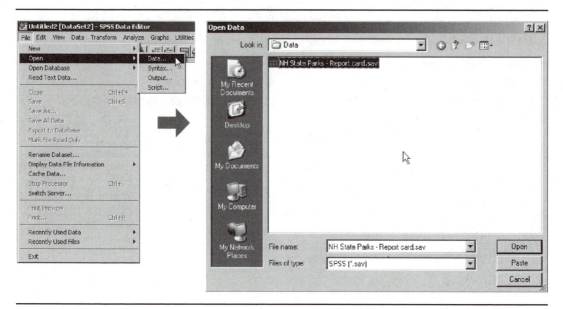

Figure 9.9   Opening an Existing SPSS Data File

Step 2. Select a Statistical Test

SPSS contains numerous statistical tests (e.g., FREQUENCIES, CROSSTABS, INDEPENDENT-SAMPLES T-TESTS, ONE-WAY ANOVA). Figures 9.10 through 9.13 illustrate how the four basic steps apply to each of these analyses. Although not shown, the same steps apply to all other SPSS analyses (e.g., CORRELATION, REGRESSION, RELIABILITY). When learning any software package, especially a statistics program, it is easy to be overwhelmed by the details. For the moment, *the key message is that the same basic steps always apply to all tests.* Details on the specifics will be discussed in later chapters.

Figure 9.10 applies the basic analysis steps to a FREQUENCIES analysis. The majority of statistical tests are under the **Analyze** menu. To run a FREQUENCIES test, click on:

Analyze > Descriptive Statistics > Frequencies...

The ellipsis (i.e., the three dots "…") after the command FREQUENCIES… signifies that there dialog boxes under this option. Selecting FREQUENCIES… brings up a window of variables associated with this analysis.

Step 3. Select Variables for Analysis

The dialog box (Step 3 in Figure 9.10) displays all of the variables contained in the data file in the left window. Variables that are to be analyzed in a given session are transferred to the window on the right by clicking on the arrow between the two windows. The analysis can include all of the variables or only a subset of the variables.

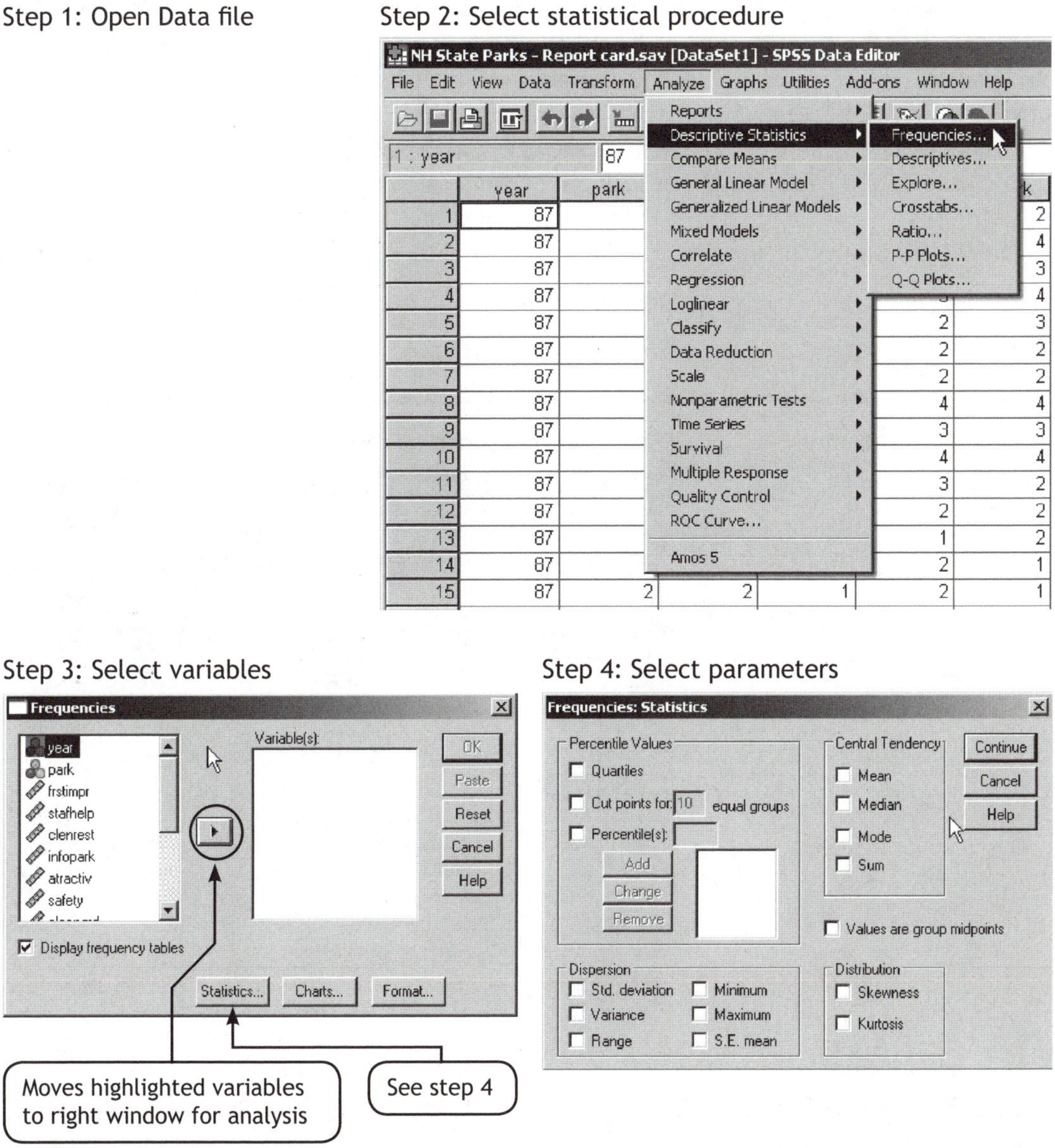

Step 1: Open Data file   Step 2: Select statistical procedure

Step 3: Select variables   Step 4: Select parameters

Moves highlighted variables to right window for analysis

See step 4

Figure 9.10   Applying the Steps to a Frequencies Analysis

Step 4. Select Additional Statistics and Options

Because SPSS procedures contain numerous analytical options, not all of possible choices can be included in a single dialog box. The initial dialog boxes (e.g., Step 3 in Figure 9.10) contain the minimum information required to run a procedure. Additional statistics and options (e.g., formatting) are found in subdialog boxes.

In an SPSS dialog box, push buttons with an ellipsis (i.e., "…") after the name indicate a subdialog box. For example, the FREQUENCIES… main dialog box has three subdialog boxes: STATISTICS…, CHARTS…, AND FORMAT… (Step 3 in Figure 9.10).

The FREQUENCIES: STATISTICS subdialog box contains the available summary statistics. To select one or more of these statistics, click on the check box next to the statistic. A ✓ is displayed in the box. For convenience, the statistics are grouped by measures of percentile values (e.g., quartiles, cut points), central tendency (e.g., mean, median, mode), dispersion (e.g., standard deviation, variance), and distribution (i.e., skewness, kurtosis). There are no restrictions on how many (or few) of the statistics from each group can be selected.

Figure 9.11 illustrates the four basic steps for a CROSSTABS... analysis. From the menu choose:

Analyze > Descriptive Statistics > Crosstabs...

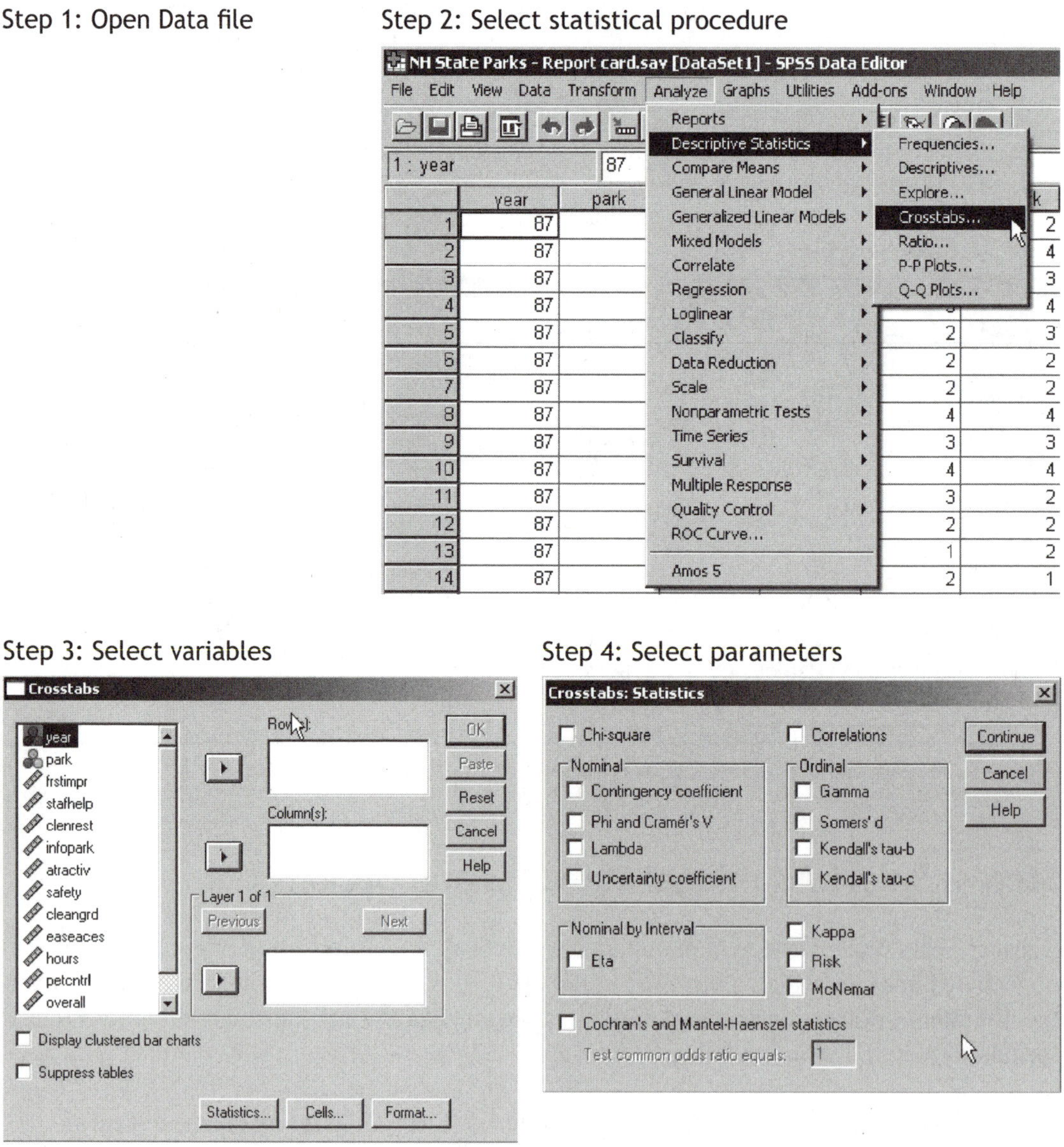

Step 1: Open Data file

Step 2: Select statistical procedure

Step 3: Select variables

Step 4: Select parameters

Figure 9.11   Applying the Steps to a Crosstabulation Analysis

The general four-step process of selecting variables in a CROSSTABS analysis is identical to the procedures described for a FREQUENCIES. Because a CROSSTABS analysis involves at least two variables, you must specify which variable(s) should be in the rows of the resulting matrix and which variables should be displayed in the columns (Figure 9.11, Step 3). Details regarding this procedure are discussed in chapter 13.

The additional options in a CROSSTABS procedure are STATISTICS…, CELLS…, and FORMAT… (see Figure 9.11, Step 3). For example, STATISTICS… includes chi-square hypothesis tests and several effect size measures (e.g., Phi, Cramer's *V*). CELLS… determines what is displayed in the resulting crosstabulation matrix: (a) *Counts* (i.e., observed and expected) of the number of survey respondents in each cell, and (b) *Percentages* (e.g., row, column) that are associated with each cell. FORMAT… controls whether the results are displayed in *ascending* or *descending* order.

Figures 9.12 and 9.13 (p. 234) apply the four basic steps to an INDEPENDENT-SAMPLES T-TEST and a ONE-WAY ANOVA.

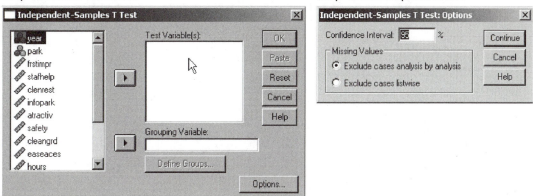

Figure 9.12   Applying the Steps to an Independent-Samples T Test

Step 1: Open Data file   Step 2: Select statistical procedure

Step 3: Select variables   Step 4: Select parameters

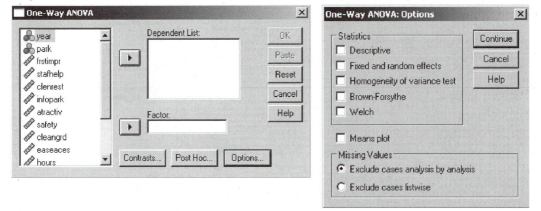

Figure 9.13   Applying the Steps to a One-Way ANOVA

Running a Procedure

After selecting a data file, statistical analysis, variables, and any additional statistics, there are two ways to run an SPSS procedure.

1. Click on OK in the dialog box. The results appear in the Output Viewer window.

2. Click on Paste. This approach copies SPSS command syntax generated by the dialog box selections into the Designated Syntax (see Figure 9.15) window, automatically opening one if necessary. The syntax can be edited, saved, or run without modification.

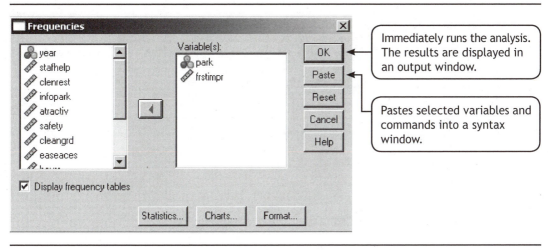

Figure 9.14   Alternative Strategies for Running an SPSS Procedure

Although the second method seems like an unnecessary extra step, there are several advantages to this approach:

1. When all of the analyses have been completed, there is a record of the steps that were followed. If you later change your mind (or have made a mistake in your logic) about a particular step, the syntax file can be edited and the analyses re-run without having to rethink all of the logic.

2. Survey research typically produces data files with hundreds of variables. When the analysis requires computing new variables (e.g., a multiple-item index reflecting an underlying concept, chapter 18), syntax files prevent having to remember which variables are associated with what concepts every time an analysis is conducted.

3. With practice, typing commands such as `Recode`, `If,` and `Compute` into a syntax window is actually easier than using the menu system and dialog boxes. Experienced SPSS users often prefer the efficiency and speed of the syntax command language.

4. Most SPSS commands are accessible from the SPSS menus and dialog boxes. Some commands and options, however, are available only by using the SPSS syntax command language.

Running Commands in a Syntax Window

After the commands have been typed or pasted (from the dialog boxes) into the syntax window:

1. Use the mouse or keyboard to select the desired commands for an analysis. To run a single command, the entire command does not need to be highlighted; just click the cursor anywhere inside the command. To run multiple commands at one time, select as much of the syntax as needed.

2. Click *Run* on the menu bar to execute the selected command syntax.

3. The results are output into the Designated Output window.

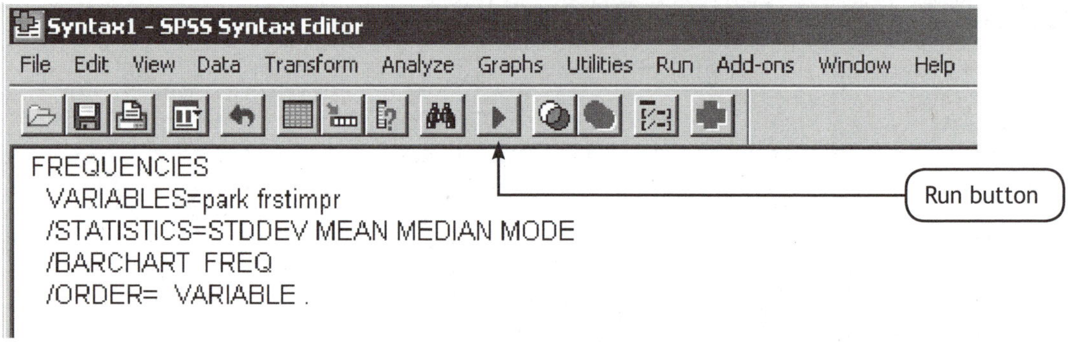

Figure 9.15   Running Commands from a Syntax Window

General Comments about SPSS Syntax Files

If SPSS commands are manually typed into a syntax file (as opposed to letting SPSS generate the commands using the Paste button), keep the following in mind:

1. Every command must end with a command terminator to tell SPSS that the command is complete. The command terminator is the period (.).

2. Subcommands are separated from one another with a slash (/).

3. Variables, commands, and subcommands can be typed in uppercase, lowercase, or a mixture of uppercase and lowercase letters.

4. Keywords are words defined by SPSS to minimize what has to be typed. For example, the keyword ALL refers to all user-defined variables in the file. Rather than typing every variable into the syntax file, this keyword selects all of the variables and runs the analysis on every variable. Note, however, that if there are hundreds of variables in the data file, the output file can become quite large. Other useful keywords include: (a) THRU, which specifies a range of *values* associated with a variable, and (b) TO, which specifies a range of *variables*. The use of keywords is illustrated in Box 9.1 and described in detail in chapter 12.

5. Sometimes it is helpful to write notes in a syntax file that describe the objectives of an analysis. For example, "This analysis combines three variables into a multiple-item index." Lines beginning with an asterisk (*) are comments that are not analyzed by SPSS.

Many of the statistical examples in this book use a data file from a survey of New Hampshire State Parks visitors. An example syntax file for analyzing these data is shown in Box 9.1. The notes in the second column overview some general points regarding the commands and subcommands. The specifics are explained in later chapters.

Box 9.1   Example Syntax File

Syntax	Explanation
```* Note the data file for this * program is NH State Parks – * Report card.sav```	The * indicates that this is comment line. SPSS ignores the text after a *. Comments can facilitate understanding the analysis objectives.
```Value Labels YEAR 87 '1987' 88 '1988' 89 '1989' /```	This command adds value labels to the variables.
```PARK 1 'Monadnock Camp' 2 'Moose Brook Camp' 3 'Miller Day Use' 4 'Mt Washington' 5 'Hampton Beach' 6 'Silver Lake Beach' 7 'Robert Frost' 8 'Dan Webster' 9 'Franconia Flume' 10 'Franconia Tram' /```	A slash is used to separate the value labels for the variable YEAR and the variable PARK. The words inside the single quotes (e.g., Monadnock Camp) define the label associated with each value of the variable. Periods should not be used in variable names or it will terminate the procedure (`Mt Washington` not `Mt. Washington`).
```FRSTIMPR TO OVERALL 0 'F' 1 'D' 2 'C' 3 'B' 4 'A' 9 'No Response'.```	The keyword `TO` is used a specify a range of variables from FRSTIMPR to OVERALL. This range of variables will all receive the same labels. The command terminator is a period (.)
```Frequencies variables = ALL / Statistics = mean stddev.```	This command produces a frequency distribution. The keyword `ALL` implies that all variables in the data file will be analyzed. The subcommand `Statistics` requests: (a) one measure of central tendency (i.e., `mean`), and (b) one measure of dispersion (i.e., standard deviation or `stddev`) for each of the variables.
```Crosstabs / Tables = PARK by YEAR / Statistics = Chisq Phi / Cells = Count Column```	This command examines the bivariate relationship between (a) PARK (the row variable) and (b) YEAR (the column variable). Two statistics are requested: (a) a chi-square hypothesis test (`Chisq`) and (b) the effect size measure phi (`Phi`). The `Cells` subcommand asks for: (a) a frequency `Count` of the number of respondents in each cell (b) the percentages for the `Column` variable.

Saving Files

Output and syntax files are usually saved before exiting SPSS.

> To save either type of file,
> > (a) Choose from the menu: File > Save As...
> > (b) Designate the directory where the file should be saved
> > (c) Give the file a name
> > (d) Click *Save*

With most spreadsheets (e.g., Microsoft Excel) and databases (e.g., Microsoft Access), any changes to the data are saved before exiting the program. When exiting SPSS for Windows, however, there are times when you may not want to save the data. For example, if a series of seven-point scales ("Strongly Agree" to "Strongly Disagree") were recoded into three-point scales ("Agree-Neutral-Disagree") with the same variable names and the file is saved, the data file will contain only the three-point version of the scales (not the original 7-point versions). Because there is no way to go back to the original coding, you should be cautious about saving SPSS data. This problem can be avoided by recoding the variables into new variables (chapter 12). The best way to avoid this problem is to ***always work with a backup copy of your data.***

Chapter Summary

This chapter provides an introduction to the Statistical Package for the Social Sciences (SPSS), version 15.0. Most, if not all, of the analyses survey researchers conduct can be performed in SPSS. Compared to some statistical programs, SPSS is easy to learn. For example: (a) data, syntax and output files are opened and saved using menu selections common to Windows-based programs, and (b) the program will automatically generate the syntax necessary for running an analysis.

There are three basic types of files in SPSS: (a) data files containing respondents' answers to survey questions, (b) syntax files containing instructions that tell SPSS what analyses or data manipulations are to be performed, and (c) output files displaying the results of an analysis.

Most tasks in SPSS begin by making selections from a menu. There are three primary menus in SPSS (i.e., Data Editor, Syntax, and Output [or Viewer] menu). Although these menus share much of the same functionality (i.e., *File, Edit, View, Data, Transform, Analyze, Graphs, Utilities, Add-ons, Window, Help*), each menu bar has selections that are only appropriate for that window. For example, only the Syntax Editor contains the menu choice *Run*.

Each menu has numerous options. Although the list of options can be daunting, an immediate understanding of all SPSS components is not necessary to analyze survey data. As noted earlier, people routinely use Microsoft Word, Excel, and PowerPoint and do not understand (or even need) all of the functionality in these programs.

Changing some of the default settings in SPSS is useful: (a) turning on "Display commands in the log" and (b) changing the way the output is displayed from "Labels" and "Names" to "Values and Labels" and "Names and Labels." These modifications are made through the Edit menu and only need to be done once if SPSS is installed on an individual user's PC. If the software is installed on a network, these settings may have to be modified at beginning of each session. These modifications often facilitate understanding of the output generated by SPSS.

There are four basic steps to analyzing data in SPSS: (a) selecting a data file, (b) selecting a statistical test, (c) selecting variables for analysis, and (d) selecting additional statistics and options. Although the specifics for each analysis differ, the key point is that *the basic steps apply to all statistical tests*.

After these four steps have been completed, an SPSS procedure can be run by either clicking "OK" or "Paste" on the test statistic's dialog box. Pasting the commands into a syntax window is the recommended approach. This approach creates a record of what steps were taken in the analysis. If you later change your mind about the analysis strategy or made a mistake in logic, the syntax file can be edited and the analyses re-run. Because survey research can yield data files with hundreds of variables, syntax files facilitate recall; for example: (a) What variables were combined to create new measures reflecting the underlying concept, and (b) How the values of variables were collapsed (recoded) for particular analyses (e.g., collapsing a 7-point "strongly agree" to "strongly disagree" to a 3-point "agree" to "disagree" scale).

Caution should be exercised when saving SPSS data files. For example, if seven-point variables are recoded into three-point variables with the same names and the data file is saved, the file will contain the three-point scales (not the 7-point scales).

Review Questions

1. Briefly describe the general contents of the three types of files used by SPSS for Windows.

2. What is the difference between a designated window and an active window in SPSS for Windows?

3. Describe four basic steps in performing statistical analysis with SPSS for Windows.

4. What are the advantages to using syntax windows when running SPSS for Windows?

5. Why is it important to be cautious about saving data in SPSS for Windows?

10

constructing SPSS data files

Before analyses can be performed, the information obtained from a survey must be converted to a format that SPSS understands. Questions are the foundation of any survey, but data analysis is based on variables. A given survey may contain more variables than questions. Assume, for example, that a researcher has developed the wildlife viewer survey shown in Figure 10.1 and has administered the instrument to 1,200 individuals.

Ten of these variables come directly from the questions on the survey. Questions 1, 3, 4, and 5 represent one variable each. Question 2, however, contains six different variables because respondents were asked to check all of the activities that they participated in during their visit. Five of these variables are the checkmarks for each activity (i.e., hiking, camping, wildlife viewing, wildlife photography, other). The sixth variable is the actual "other activity" the individual specified on the survey.

Two remaining variables might be an identification number for each respondent and the date the individual completed the survey. The identification number is useful if the researcher needs to re-examine a given respondent's answers on the actual survey. The DATE variable allows the researcher to compare respondents who visited on weekends as opposed to weekdays.

This survey is designed to better understand your wildlife refuge experience. Your participation is totally voluntary and your responses are voluntary. Your answers will be anonymous.

1. Including this visit, about how many times have you visited this refuge in the last 3 months?

_____ Number of visits

2. What activities did you participate in during this visit? (Check all that apply)

____ Hiking   ____ Wildlife viewing

____ Camping   ____ Wildlife photography

____ Other (please specify): _____

3. How crowded did you feel by the number of visitors? (Circle one number)

| 1 | 2 | 3 | 4 | 5 | 6 | 7 | 8 | 9 |

Not at all Crowded   Slightly Crowded   Moderately Crowded   Extremely Crowded

4. What is an acceptable number of other visitors to see while you are visiting this refuge? (Please fill in a number or check one of the other two options)

It is OK to see as many as _____ other visitors

❏ It doesn't matter to me

❏ It matters to me, but I cannot specify a number

5. What is your zipcode? _____

Figure 10.1   Wildlife Viewer Survey

Data analysis typically begins with the preparation of a *codebook* to describe the variables on the survey as well as any additional variables of interest to the researcher. Although the survey in Figure 10.1 contains only five questions, 12 different variables might be coded.

The codebook associated with this hypothetical survey is shown in Table 10.1. Each variable is described using six characteristics:

1. Variable name
2. Variable type
3. Variable width
4. Variable label
5. Value label
6. Missing value codes

Table 10.1   Codebook for Wildlife Viewer Survey

Variable Name	Variable Type	Variable Width	Variable Label	Value Label	Missing Value
ID	Numeric	4	Respondent ID		
DATE	Date	Date	Date survey completed		
VISITS	Numeric	2	Number of prior visits		99
HIKING	Numeric	1	Hiking	0 = No 1 = Yes 9 = Missing	9
CAMPING	Numeric	1	Camping	0 = No 1 = Yes 9 = Missing	9
VIEWING	Numeric	1	Wildlife viewing	0 = No 1 = Yes 9 = Missing	9
PHOTO	Numeric	1	Wildlife photography	0 = No 1 = Yes 9 = Missing	9
OTHER	Numeric	1	Other activity indicated	0 = No 1 = Yes 9 = Missing	9
OTHERS	String	24	Specific other activity		
CROWDED	Numeric	1	Perceived crowding	1 = Not at all crowded 2 = Not at all crowded 3 = Slightly crowded 4 = Slightly crowded 5 = Moderately crowded 6 = Moderately crowded 7 = Moderately crowded 8 = Extremely crowded 9 = Extremely crowded 0 = Missing	0
NORM	Numeric	3	Tolerance for others	777 = Does not matter 888 = Matters—cannot specify 999 = Missing	777 888 999
ZIPCODE	String	10	Respondent zipcode		

Understanding Variables in SPSS

Variables in SPSS have six characteristics: names, label, type, width, values, and labels.

Variable Names

- In version 15 of SPSS, variable names can be up to 64 characters length. Variable names in earlier versions of the program were constrained to eight characters.

- Variable names cannot contain spaces or special characters (e.g., !, ?, ', *).

- The first character must be a letter or the @ symbol. Subsequent characters can be any letter, digit, or the symbols @, _, $, or #.

- Variable names cannot end with a period. Variable names that end with an underscore should be avoided as such names conflict with variables automatically created by some procedures.

- Each variable name must be unique; duplication is not allowed.

- Variable names are not case sensitive. For example, the names NEWVAR, NewVar and NEWVAR are considered equivalent.

Although some researchers might name the first variable in a file "V1," using names that have more meaning avoids confusing variables during analysis. For example, the respondent's ID number is named ID in Table 10.1.

Variable Labels

- The variable label is optional, but highly recommended. The *variable label* provides a more complete description of the variable. For example, the variable named VISITS might have the following label: "Number of prior visits" (Table 10.1).

- A variable label can contain up to 256 characters. Not all SPSS procedure commands, however, will print all 256 characters.

Variable Types

- *Variable type* specifies the data type for each variable. All new variables are assumed to be numeric. The contents of the Variable Type dialog box depend on the data type selected (Figure 10.2; see also Figure 10.5 later in the chapter). Some data types have text boxes for entering the width and

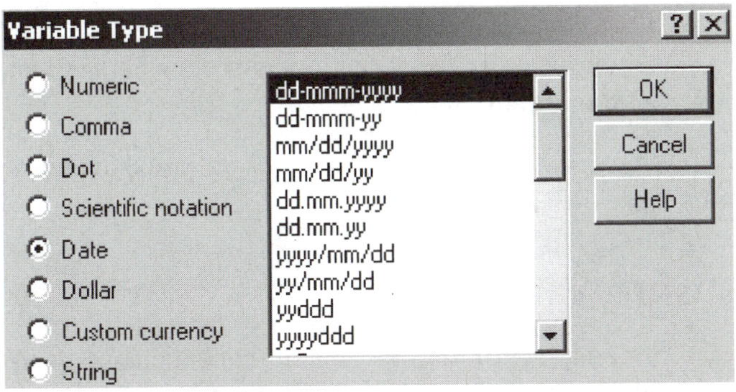

Figure 10.2   Date Format Dialog Box in SPSS

number of decimals; for others (e.g., Date), the researcher selects a format from a scrollable list of examples.

- Version 15 of SPSS offers eight different data types: numeric, comma, dot, scientific notation, date, dollar, custom currency, and string. With survey research, you are most likely to use *numeric* or *string* and occasionally *date*. *Numeric variables* only contain numbers (e.g., 0, 1, 2, …). *String variables* may contain letters (e.g., A, B, C), numbers or other characters (e.g., @, !, ?). Upper and lower case letters are considered distinct in a string variable. For the variable OTHERS in Table 10.1, if one respondent's "other activity" is coded as "Backpacking" and another respondent's other activity is coded as "backpacking," SPSS would treat these as two distinct activities. To avoid this problem, data entry personnel should be instructed to always use uppercase or lowercase when typing the responses to string variables.

- Because string variables cannot be used in calculations, *define your variables as numeric whenever possible*. For example, for the variable like SEX, use 0 for males and 1 for females, rather than M and F. One exception to this general rule is the variable ZIPCODE. This variable should be defined as a string variable for three reasons:

  1. You will never want to perform any calculations on the variable. For example, it does not make sense to calculate an average zip code.

  2. International zip codes contain letters. In Canada, for example, a postal code might be M4K 3N2.

  3. If you ever want to use the data file to produce mailing labels and some respondents live on the east coast, SPSS does not save the initial zeros in numeric variables. For example, the zip code 00019 becomes 19. The U.S. Post Office recognizes a zip code of 00019 (i.e., the string variable), but not a zip code of 19 (i.e., the numeric variable).

Variable Width

- *Variable width* specifies the number of positions needed to display values of the variable.
- The maximum length of a numeric variable is 20 characters.
- The maximum practical length of a string variable is 80 characters.
- If the variable has fractional or negative values, leave space for the decimal point and minus sign (i.e., the variable width must be large enough to accommodate the decimal point or minus sign).

The variables in the wildlife viewer survey varied in their width (Table 10.1). Table 10.2 explains why these differences occur.

Missing Values

- For a variety of reasons, not all respondents may answer a given question. Some may simply skip the question, or they may not understand the question. For others, the question may not apply.

Table 10.2   Explanation for Differences in Variable Width in the Wildlife Viewer Survey

Variable	Width	Reason
ID	4	Researcher surveyed 1,200 individuals (coded as 1200).
VISITS	2	The survey asked for number of visits during the last 3 months. Even if respondents visited every day, the highest possible response would be 93 (i.e., 3 months * 31 days per month = 93).
HIKING TO OTHER	1	Responses are either "Yes" (1) or "No" (0) (participated or not; checked or not checked).
CROWDED	1	The response scale ranges from 1 (not at all crowded) to 9 (extremely crowded). As long as the missing value for this variable is coded as 0, only one position is required. If the researcher had opted to use "99" as a missing value code, the width would be 2.
NORM	3	If the wildlife refuge is a frontcountry location, a respondent might be willing to tolerate 100 or more other visitors. Thus, the variable width is 3.
ZIPCODE	10	A researcher may want to use the 10-digit version of U.S. zip codes (12345-6789).

- When analyzing data using SPSS, user-defined missing values indicate that a case should not be included in an analysis. For example, a code of 9 might be used to indicate that a respondent did not answer a question. As a general rule of thumb, the variable width often determines the missing value code; for example:

Variable Width	Missing Value code
1	9
2	99
3	999
4	9999
5	99999

These rules, however, do not always apply. For the variable CROWDED, the researcher opted to use a missing value code of "0" because the value "9" is a valid response to this question (i.e., extremely crowded).

- Not all of the variables in Table 10.1 had missing value codes. This occurs for several reasons:

  1. There are no missing value codes for the variable ID because the researcher (not the respondent) added this identification code to each survey.

  2. SPSS does not allow the user to assign missing value codes for date variables (e.g., DATE) or long string variables (e.g., OTHERS, ZIPCODE). A *long string variable* is longer than eight characters. All string values, including null or blank values, are considered valid values unless explicitly defined as missing. To define null or blank values as missing for a string variable, enter a single space in one of the fields for "discrete" missing values (see Figure 10.5 later in the chapter).

- In SPSS for Windows, up to three discrete (specific) values may be declared as missing. This allows you to distinguish between data missing because a respondent refused to answer the question, and data missing because the question did not apply to that respondent. For example, the variable NORM in Table 10.1 had three missing value codes:

```
777 = Does not matter
888 = Matters - cannot specify
999 = Missing
```

- For numeric variables, a range of missing values, or a range plus one discrete value, can be specified. For example, the variable VISITS, where the maximum possible value is 93 (i.e., 3 months * 31 days per month), any value between 94 and 99 might be defined as missing.

Value Labels

- *Value labels* define the meaning of a variable's attributes. For example, for the variable HIKING, the researcher assigned the label "No" for the value 0, and the label "Yes" for the value 1.

- Value labels do not affect the analysis, but they greatly facilitate the interpretation and should always be used, especially when recoding data (chapter 12). For example, if the variable CROWDED is recoded:

```
Recode CROWDED (1, 2     = 0)
               (3 thru 9 = 1).
```

to distinguish those who felt "Not at all crowded" from those who indicated some degree of crowding, adding value labels helps you remember how the variable was modified.

Having collected the data and developed a codebook that describes how the information on the survey will be entered into an SPSS data file (i.e., *filename*.sav), the next step is building the Data Entry form that will be used for coding the data.

One of the products available from SPSS is called SPSS Data Entry Builder®. Although this tool offers considerable flexibility for building custom data entry forms, entering data, and checking data for accuracy using researcher-defined rules, not all users may have access to this software. The specifications outlined above, however, can be accomplished with the basic version of SPSS.

Defining Variables in SPSS

When SPSS is started, an empty Data Editor window is displayed (see chapter 9 for details on starting SPSS). The Data Editor is a spreadsheet-like window for creating and editing data files. The window has two views: (a) Data View (Figure 10.3) and (b) Variable View (Figure 10.4). To switch between the two views click on the tabs in lower left of the window.

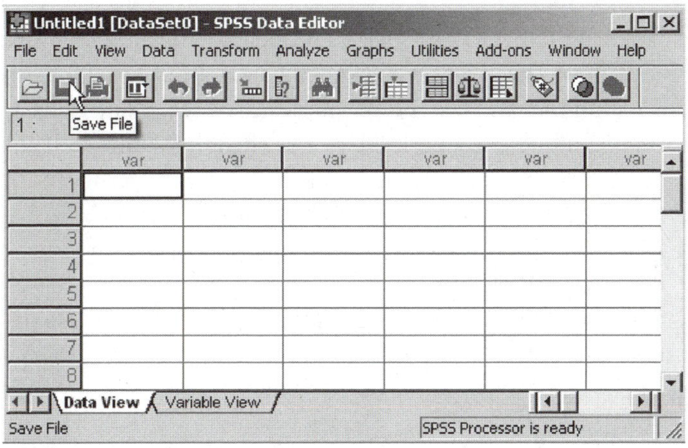

Figure 10.3   The SPSS Data Editor: Data View

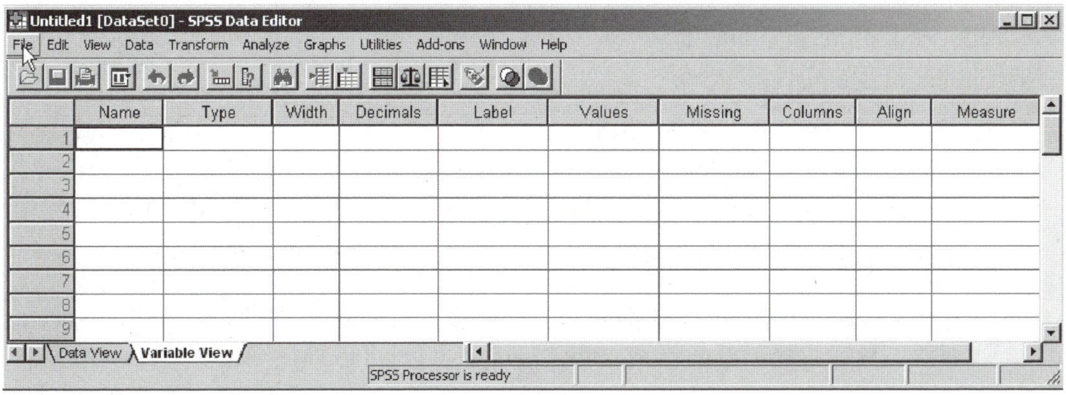

Figure 10.4   The SPSS Data Editor: Variable View

Data View

Many of the features of the Data View are similar to those in spreadsheet applications. There are, however, several important distinctions:

- The rows represent cases. In survey research, each respondent to the questionnaire is a case. In the wildlife viewer survey with a sample size of 1,200, the researcher would have 1,200 rows in the file; one row for each respondent.

- The columns in the Data View are variables. Each column represents a different variable. For the wildlife viewer survey, there would be 12 columns corresponding to the 12 variables in Table 10.1.

- The cells contain values or the answers given by a respondent for each variable. Each cell contains a single value of a variable for a case. The cell is the intersection of the case (i.e., a respondent) and a variable (e.g., VISITS, HIKING, CAMPING). Cells contain only data values. Unlike spreadsheet programs, cells in the Data Editor cannot contain formulas.

- The data file is rectangular. The dimensions of the data file are determined by the number of cases (i.e., 1,200) and variables (i.e., 12). Data can be entered into any cell. There are no empty cells within the data file. For numeric variables, blank cells are converted to the system-missing value (i.e., a period [.]). For string variables, a blank is considered a valid value.

Variable View

The Variable View is used to define variables and their attributes before the data are entered into the file. In the Variable View:

- Rows are variables.
- Columns are variable attributes.

You can add or delete variables and modify attributes of variables, including:

- Variable name
- Data type
- Number of digits or characters
- Number of decimal places
- Descriptive variable and value labels
- User-defined missing values
- Column width (see discussion that follows)
- Measurement level (see discussion that follows)

Once a variable's attributes have been defined, the attributes can be copied and applied to one or more variables. Basic copy and paste operations are used to apply variable definition attributes. You can:

- Copy a single attribute (e.g., value labels), and paste it to the same attribute cell(s) for one or more variables.

- Copy all the attributes from one variable, and paste them to one or more other variables.

- Create multiple new variables with all of the attributes of a copied variable.

Figure 10.5 illustrates the completed Variable View for the wildlife viewer survey. Dialog boxes for some of the procedures have been added to visually clarify this discussion. Two "Variable Type" dialog boxes are shown. For numeric variables (e.g., ID), both the width and the number of decimal places are specified. Since the ID variable does not need decimal places, the decimal value has been set to 0. For string variables (e.g., ZIPCODE), the number of "characters" for the variable width is specified.

The Value Labels dialog box shows that three labels have been added for the variable HIKING. Although the label "Missing" was assigned for values of 9 in this dialog box, the label per se does not tell SPSS to treat 9s as missing. Rather, SPSS knows that 9s are missing for this variable because of the specification in the Missing column. Three "Missing Values" (i.e., 777, 888, 999) have been assigned to the variable NORM.

Three columns in Figure 10.5 (i.e., Columns, Align, Measure) have not been discussed. *Columns* is used to modify the number of characters displayed in Data View of the Data Editor. Column widths can also be changed in the Data View by clicking and dragging the column borders (similar method as is used in an Excel spreadsheet). Column formats affect *only* the display of values in the Data Editor. Changing the column width does not change the defined width of a variable. If the defined and actual width of a value is wider than the column, asterisks (*) are

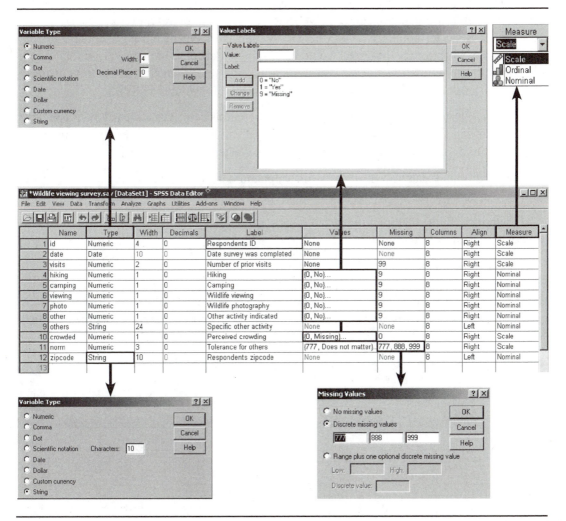

Figure 10.5   SPSS Data Editor: Variable View for the Wildlife Viewer Survey

displayed in the Data View. Expanding the column width in the Data View is useful for displaying the contents of long string variables.

Align controls the display of data values and/or value labels in the Data View. The default alignment is right for numeric variables and left for string variables. This setting affects only the display in the Data View.

Measure refers to the level of measurement. Chapter 5 detailed the similarities and differences between the terminology used in this book, by other researchers, and by SPSS. In SPSS terms:

- *Scale:* Numeric data measured on a continuous scale.

- *Ordinal:* Data values represent categories with some intrinsic order (e.g., low, medium, high). Ordinal variables can be either string (alphanumeric) or numeric values that represent distinct categories (e.g., low [1], medium [2], high [3]). For ordinal string variables, the alphabetic order of string values is assumed to reflect the true order of the categories. For example, for a string variable with the values of low, medium, and high, the order of the categories is interpreted as high, low, medium—which is not the correct order. In general, it is better to use numeric codes (in SPSS terms, *scale*) to represent ordinal data.

  In SPSS terminology, a variable with response options of "strongly agree, agree, disagree, and strongly disagree" would be considered ordinal. In this book, as long as the variable approximates a normal distribution, the variable is considered continuous (not ordinal), and as a result should be designated as a scale variable in SPSS.

- *Nominal:* Data values represent categories with no intrinsic order (e.g., actual OTHER activity or ZIPCODE in the wildlife viewer survey). Nominal variables can be either string (alphanumeric) or numeric values that represent distinct categories (e.g., MALE [0], FEMALE [1]).

Nominal and ordinal data can be either string (alphanumeric) or numeric. Regardless of how a variable is defined, measurement specification in SPSS is relevant *only for*:

- Chart procedures that identify variables as scale or categorical. Nominal and ordinal are both treated as categorical.

- SPSS-format data files used with AnswerTree®.

Having defined all of the variables in the wildlife viewer survey, the Data View of the wildlife viewer survey looks like Figure 10.6. The variables are shown as columns across the top. Each

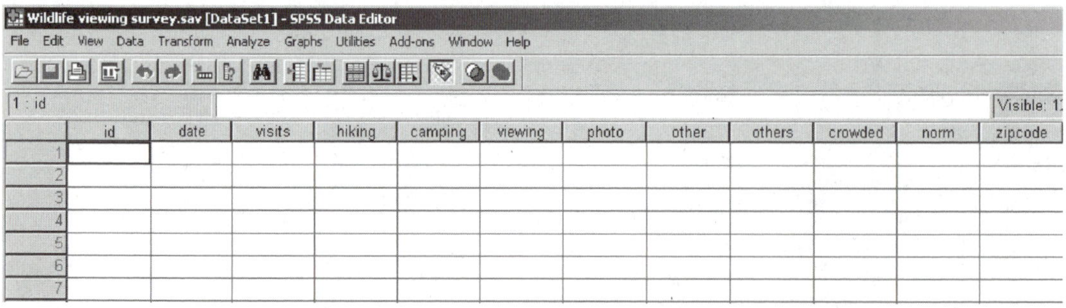

Figure 10.6   SPSS Data Editor: Data View for the Wildlife Viewer Survey

row in the matrix represents a respondent to the survey. All of the cells are currently empty because none of the respondents' answers have been entered.

Entering Data

The Data View window in the Data Editor is used to enter and/or change data. Data can be entered in any order (i.e., by case or by variable). With most data entry tasks, all of the variables for a given survey respondent (i.e., by case) would be entered before moving onto the next respondent's answers.

To enter a value:
- Use the cursor keys or the mouse to highlight a cell. The variable name and row number of the active cell are displayed in the top left corner of the Data Editor.
- Type a value (e.g., a respondent's answer to a question). The value is displayed in the cell editor at the top of the Data Editor. Data values are not recorded until you press ENTER, TAB, or select another cell with the mouse.
- Press ENTER to accept the value and move down one row.
- Press TAB to accept the value and move right one column.

To delete a case or variable:
- Select the row or column heading and clear it by choosing the Edit > Clear, or simply press the DELETE key.

To change the name, type, column width, missing values, or labels of a variable:
- Double-click the variable name in the column heading, or
- Select the Variable View tab in the lower left corner of the data matrix.

In the hypothetical wildlife viewer survey example, there would be 1,200 rows (i.e., the sample size for the study) in the matrix when the data entry process is complete.

Saving a Data File

Saving a data file in SPSS parallels the steps used in other Windows based applications:

> (a) Choose File > Save As...
> (b) Specify the directory where you want the file to be saved
> (c) Name of file (e.g., Hypothetical - wildlife viewing survey.sav)

The ".sav" extension indicates that the file is an SPSS data file, as opposed to a syntax file (*filename*.sps) or an output file (*filename*.spo).

As noted in Chapter 9, saving a data file saves all of the data transformation commands that have been run during the session. If the nine-point CROWDED variable was recoded into a dichotomous variable (e.g., NOT CROWDED [0] vs. CROWDED [1]), the two-category variable will be saved. Since the two-level variable may not be appropriate for all analyses, caution should be used when saving SPSS data files. As a rule of thumb, *always have backups of your original data.*

Primary Sample Data for Book

In this book we will analyze data from a New Hampshire State Parks visitor "report card" study. Figure 10.7 shows the report card and Table 10.3 provides a codebook for the data. This survey was used for monitoring visitor satisfaction and was developed in the late 1970s (LaPage & Bevins, 1981). The instrument was initially tested in a number of state parks in Massachusetts, Vermont, and New Hampshire. Subsequent verification was conducted in private campground facilities nationwide.

The report card asked visitors to evaluate the services and facilities at the state park they had visited. Eleven evaluation variables were included on the survey (Figure 10.8, p. 254). The letter grades (i.e., A, B, C, D, F) have an intuitive appeal because such scales are commonly used in North America to assess a student's performance across all education levels (e.g., grade school, high school, colleges and universities).

Park employees at over 30 units managed by the State Parks distributed report cards each year. These included campgrounds, day-use areas, beaches, and historic sites. Random samples of individuals were handed the report card as they entered the park and were asked to return the completed survey when they left.

Vaske, Donnelly, and Williamson (1991) summarized the report card data for three years (1987–1989). Their analyses were based on a sample of 4,282 respondents. The data used in this book are based on a subset of these individuals (*n* = 300), with 100 respondents

---

State of New Hampshire
Division of Parks and Recreation

No. 0700

Park Visitor Report Card

Date of visit: _____

Name of Park: _____

Please rate us on the following. Give us an:

A (for excellent)
B (if better than average)
C (average)
D (below average)
F (poor)

	A	B	C	D	F
Your first impression	4	3	2	1	0
Helpfulness of staff	4	3	2	1	0
Cleanliness of restrooms	4	3	2	1	0
Attractiveness of park	4	3	2	1	0
Safety and security	4	3	2	1	0
Cleanliness of grounds	4	3	2	1	0
Ease of access	4	3	2	1	0
Hours of operation	4	3	2	1	0
Control of pets	4	3	2	1	0
Your overall satisfaction	4	3	2	1	0

Comments:

Please leave at park office or mail to:

P.O. Box 856, Concord, NH 03301
Thank You!

Figure 10.7   The New Hampshire State Parks Report Card

from each year of data collection. In addition, the sample data were restricted to 10 New Hampshire State Parks. Ten individuals were selected at random from each State Park in the sample data set used here.

Table 10.3   Codebook for the Variables for New Hampshire State Parks Report Card Data Set

Variable Name	Variable Type	Variable Width	Variable Label	Missing Value	Value Labels	
YEAR	Numeric	2	Year of Visit	99	87	1987
					88	1988
					89	1989
PARK	Numeric	2	Park Visited	99	01	Monadnock Campground
					02	Moose Brook Campground
					03	Miller Day Use Area
					04	Mt. Washington Day Use
					05	Hampton Beach
					06	Silver Lake Beach
					07	Robert Frost Historic Site
					08	Daniel Webster Historic Site
					09	Franconia Notch Flume
					10	Franconia Tramway
FRSTIMPR	Numeric	1	First Impression	9	0	Poor (F)
					1	Below Average (D)
					2	Average (C)
					3	Better than Average (B)
					4	Excellent (A)
					9	No response
STAFHELP	Numeric	1	Helpfulness of Staff	9	Same as First Impression	
CLENREST	Numeric	1	Cleanliness of Restrooms	9	Same as First Impression	
INFOPARK	Numeric	1	Information at Park	9	Same as First Impression	
ATRACTIV	Numeric	1	Attractiveness of Park	9	Same as First Impression	
SAFETY	Numeric	1	Safety and Security	9	Same as First Impression	
CLEANGRD	Numeric	1	Cleanliness of Grounds	9	Same as First Impression	
EASEACES	Numeric	1	Ease of Access	9	Same as First Impression	
HOURS	Numeric	1	Hours of Operation	9	Same as First Impression	
PETCNTRL	Numeric	1	Control of Pets	9	Same as First Impression	
OVERALL	Numeric	1	Overall Satisfaction	9	Same as First Impression	

The New Hampshire State Parks Data
(NH – State Parks – Report card.sav)

Figure 10.8 (p. 254) shows the Data Editor – Variable View – for the NH State Parks report card data. The Variable View shows:

1. All 13 numeric variables in the data file.

2. The variables YEAR and PARK are two columns wide, while the remaining variables are one column wide. All of the variables are whole numbers (i.e., 0 decimal places).

3. Because everyone may not have version 15 of SPSS, the variable names have been limited eight characters. The longer variable labels provide more information on what the variable measures.

4. The value labels for FRSTIMPR to OVERALL are 'F' (0), 'D' (1), 'C' (2), 'B' (3) and 'A' (4).

5. YEAR and PARK use 99 as a missing value code, while the remaining variables use the code of 9.

6. The variables YEAR and PARK are nominal level variables (SPSS terminology). The remaining variables are treated as scale variables.

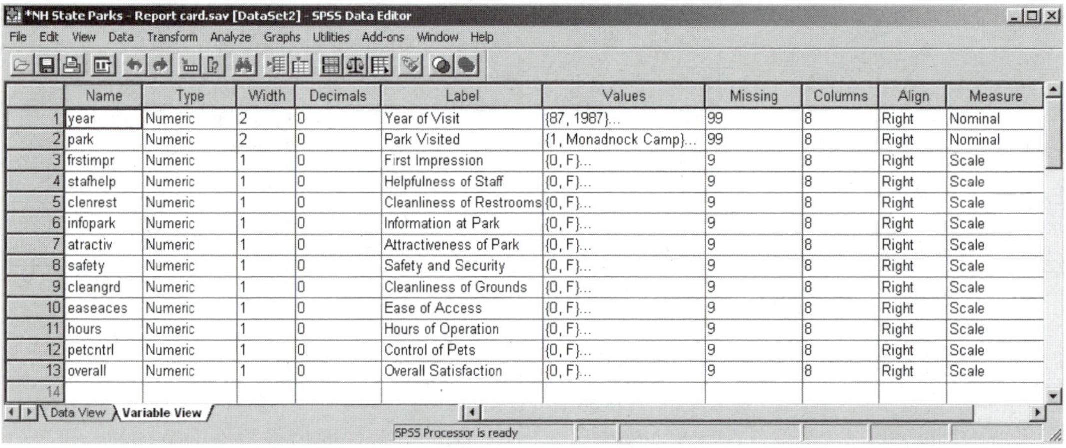

	Name	Type	Width	Decimals	Label	Values	Missing	Columns	Align	Measure
1	year	Numeric	2	0	Year of Visit	{87, 1987}...	99	8	Right	Nominal
2	park	Numeric	2	0	Park Visited	{1, Monadnock Camp}...	99	8	Right	Nominal
3	frstimpr	Numeric	1	0	First Impression	{0, F}...	9	8	Right	Scale
4	stafhelp	Numeric	1	0	Helpfulness of Staff	{0, F}...	9	8	Right	Scale
5	clenrest	Numeric	1	0	Cleanliness of Restrooms	{0, F}...	9	8	Right	Scale
6	infopark	Numeric	1	0	Information at Park	{0, F}...	9	8	Right	Scale
7	atractiv	Numeric	1	0	Attractiveness of Park	{0, F}...	9	8	Right	Scale
8	safety	Numeric	1	0	Safety and Security	{0, F}...	9	8	Right	Scale
9	cleangrd	Numeric	1	0	Cleanliness of Grounds	{0, F}...	9	8	Right	Scale
10	easeaces	Numeric	1	0	Ease of Access	{0, F}...	9	8	Right	Scale
11	hours	Numeric	1	0	Hours of Operation	{0, F}...	9	8	Right	Scale
12	petcntrl	Numeric	1	0	Control of Pets	{0, F}...	9	8	Right	Scale
13	overall	Numeric	1	0	Overall Satisfaction	{0, F}...	9	8	Right	Scale
14										

Figure 10.8   SPSS Data Editor Variable View: New Hampshire State Parks Report Card

Figure 10.9 illustrates the Data View of the file. The rows represent individuals who responded to the survey. The columns are the variables in the study. The cells in Figure 10.9 show the numerical values that were coded for the variables YEAR, PARK and each of the eleven evaluation questions on the survey (FIRSTIMPR to OVERALL).

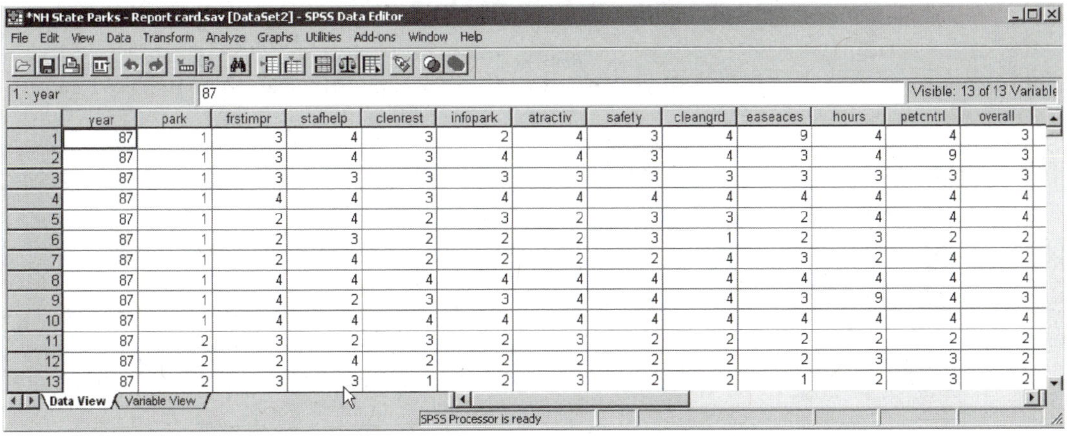

	year	park	frstimpr	stafhelp	clenrest	infopark	atractiv	safety	cleangrd	easeaces	hours	petcntrl	overall
1	87	1	3	4	3	2	4	3	4	9	4	4	3
2	87	1	3	4	3	4	4	3	4	3	4	9	3
3	87	1	3	3	3	3	3	3	3	3	3	3	3
4	87	1	4	4	3	4	4	4	4	4	4	4	4
5	87	1	2	4	2	3	2	3	3	2	4	4	4
6	87	1	2	3	2	2	2	3	1	2	3	2	2
7	87	1	2	4	2	2	2	2	4	3	2	4	2
8	87	1	4	4	4	4	4	4	4	4	4	4	4
9	87	1	4	2	3	3	4	4	4	3	9	4	3
10	87	1	4	4	4	4	4	4	4	4	4	4	4
11	87	2	3	2	3	2	3	2	2	2	2	2	2
12	87	2	2	4	2	2	2	2	2	2	3	3	2
13	87	2	3	3	1	2	3	2	2	1	2	3	2

Figure 10.9 SPSS Data Editor Data View: New Hampshire State Parks Report Card

The Data View of the Data Editor can display the value labels instead of the actual values. From the main menu of the Data Editor, click View and then Value Labels (Figure 10.10).

Figure 10.11 shows the value labels (as opposed to the actual values) in the report card data set. The "column width" for the displayed labels has been increased for the variables PARK, EASEACES, and PETCONTRL to make it easier to read the entire label. Changing the width of what is displayed, however, did not change the physical width of the actual variable. The variables EASEACES and PETCONTRL are still one column wide.

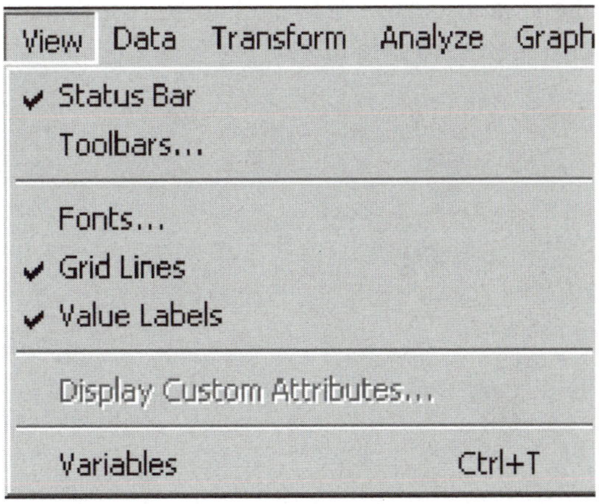

Figure 10.10 Displaying Value Labels in the Data Editor

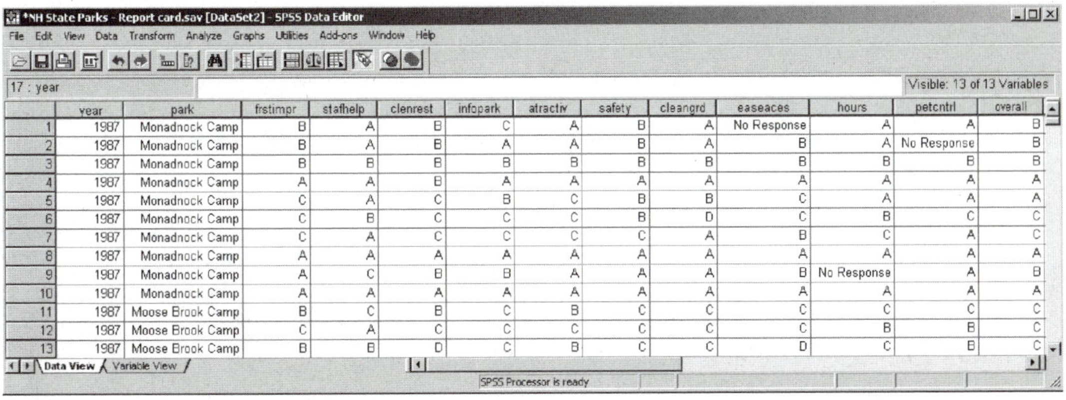

	year	park	frstimpr	stafhelp	clenrest	infopark	atractiv	safety	cleangrd	easeaces	hours	petcntrl	overall
1	1987	Monadnock Camp	B	A	B	C	A	B	A	No Response	A	A	B
2	1987	Monadnock Camp	B	A	B	A	A	B	A	B	A	No Response	B
3	1987	Monadnock Camp	B	B	B	B	B	B	B	B	B	B	B
4	1987	Monadnock Camp	A	A	B	A	A	A	A	A	A	A	A
5	1987	Monadnock Camp	C	A	C	B	C	B	B	C	A	A	A
6	1987	Monadnock Camp	C	B	C	C	C	B	D	C	B	C	C
7	1987	Monadnock Camp	C	A	C	C	C	C	A	B	C	A	C
8	1987	Monadnock Camp	A	A	A	A	A	A	A	A	A	A	A
9	1987	Monadnock Camp	A	C	B	B	A	A	A	B	No Response	A	B
10	1987	Monadnock Camp	A	A	A	A	A	A	A	A	A	A	A
11	1987	Moose Brook Camp	B	C	B	C	B	C	C	C	C	C	C
12	1987	Moose Brook Camp	C	A	C	C	C	C	C	C	B	B	C
13	1987	Moose Brook Camp	B	B	D	C	B	C	C	D	C	B	C

Figure 10.11 SPSS Data Editor Data View: Value Labels Displayed

Chapter Summary

This chapter outlined the process of constructing an SPSS data file. Variables in SPSS have six characteristics:

1. Variable name
2. Variable type
3. Variable width
4. Variable label
5. Value label
6. Missing value codes

A hypothetical wildlife viewer survey was used to describe and illustrate each of these characteristics. We will primarily be using data from a New Hampshire State Parks visitor "report card" study (LaPage & Bevins, 1981; Vaske, Donnelly, & Williamson, 1991) to illustrate statistical analyses discussed in later chapters. This chapter described the structure and characteristics of the report card data file.

Review Questions

1. Explain the statement: "Questions are the foundation of any survey, but data analysis is based on variables. A given survey may contain more variables than questions."

2. List the six characteristics of an SPSS variable.

3. How many characters can be used to name a variable in SPSS version 15?

4. Define the distinction between a *value label* and a *variable label* in SPSS. Give an example of each.

5. In SPSS, a *variable type* can be defined as either *numeric* or *string*. Why should variables normally be defined as numeric?

6. Give an example of a variable that should be defined as a string and explain why it is appropriate to define the variable as a string.

7. In the SPSS Data Editor – Variable View, explain the difference between *width* and *columns*.

8. In the hypothetical wildlife viewer survey, why was the variable width for the variable ID set at a value of 4.

9. What does the *missing value* command in SPSS do? Give an example of where you might use this command.

10. How many discrete values for a variable can be declared as missing in SPSS?

11. In the Data View of the Data Editor, what do the rows and columns represent?

12. SPSS uses three terms—scale, ordinal, nominal—to describe a variable's level of measurement. Describe each of these terms and compare them to the terminology used in this book.

13. One of the variables in the New Hampshire data set refers to the visitors' evaluations of the "helpfulness of the staff." The values for this variable are: 'F' (0), 'D' (1), 'C' (2), 'B' (3) and 'A' (4). Would you consider this variable to be nominal, ordinal, or scale variable? Explain your reasoning.

14. Why should caution be exercised when saving an existing SPSS data file?

11

frequencies and descriptive statistics

Data analysis usually begins by examining the basic distributional characteristics of the variables in the survey. A variable's central tendency (e.g., mean, mode, median), dispersion (e.g., standard deviation, variance), and shape (i.e., skewness, kurtosis) provides the researcher with information required for selecting subsequent statistical techniques. SPSS offers several programs for exploring information about how variables are distributed. In this chapter, two of these programs (i.e., FREQUENCIES, DESCRIPTIVES) will be used. They are illustrated by the variables in the New Hampshire Report Card data file (NH - State Parks - Report card.sav). The potential for conflict index (PCI) is introduced in the last section of this chapter as an alternative to traditional summary statistics.

Frequency Distributions

To obtain a frequencies distribution of one or more variables in the New Hampshire State Parks data file:

1. Open the data file   See chapter 9

2. Click on Analyze > Descriptive Statistics > Frequencies...   See Figure 11.1

3. Select variables to be included in the analysis   See Figure 11.2

4. Select additional statistical procedures   See Figure 11.3
   Select charts   See Figure 11.4
   Select format of output   See Figure 11.5

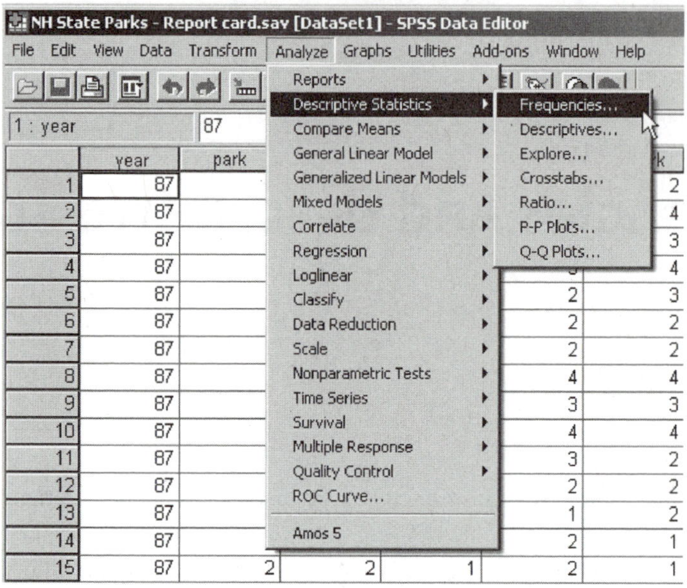

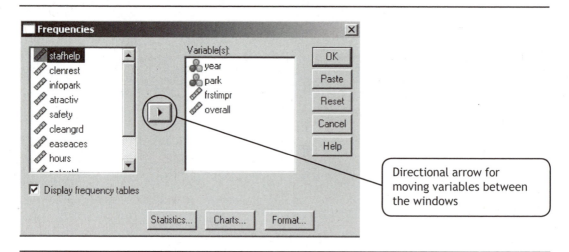

Figure 11.1   Selecting the SPSS Frequencies Procedure

Four variables (i.e., YEAR, PARK, FRSTIMPR, OVERALL) will be selected for this analysis. To select these variables:

1. Click on the variables in the left window (Figure 11.2).
   (To select more than one variable at a time, hold down the Control key or Shift key while selecting variables).

2. Click the directional arrow and move the variables to the right window.

3. Once the variables are selected, specify the desired statistics by clicking on the Statistics… button, which will bring up the window shown in Figure 11.3.

Figure 11.2   Selecting Variables for a Frequencies Analysis

In this analysis, three measures of central tendency (i.e., mean, median, mode) and three measures of dispersion (i.e., standard deviation, variance, range) will be used. Click on the Continue button once the statistics have been selected.

Most of the statistics available from the FREQUENCIES analysis are defined in Box 11.1 (p. 270).

Clicking on Charts… (Figure 11.2) will display the available chart types in a FREQUENCIES

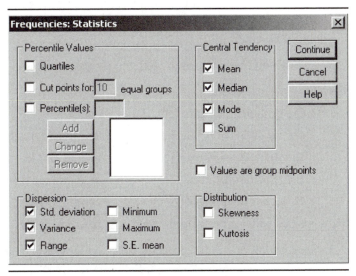

Figure 11.3   Selecting Statistics for a Frequencies Analysis

analysis (Figure 11.4). Bar, pie and histograms can be produced for the selected variables. If bar or pie are selected, the chart values can be displayed as frequencies or percentages. If histogram is selected, the output can be shown with or without the normal curve overlaying the distribution. Including the normal curve provides a visual indication of the extent to which the data are skewed. Skewness in relation to the normal curve is discussed later in this chapter (see p. 274).

SPSS allows the user to control how the output will be presented by clicking the Format… button (Figure 11.2). Clicking the Format… button displays the dialog box in Figure 11.5.

The defaults for this dialog box are:

1. Display the values for each variable in "Ascending values" (lowest to highest values). This default will be accepted for the current analysis.

2. Display the statistics (e.g., mean, median) for all the variables selected for this analysis in a single location in the output

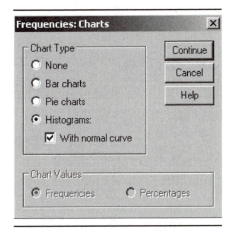

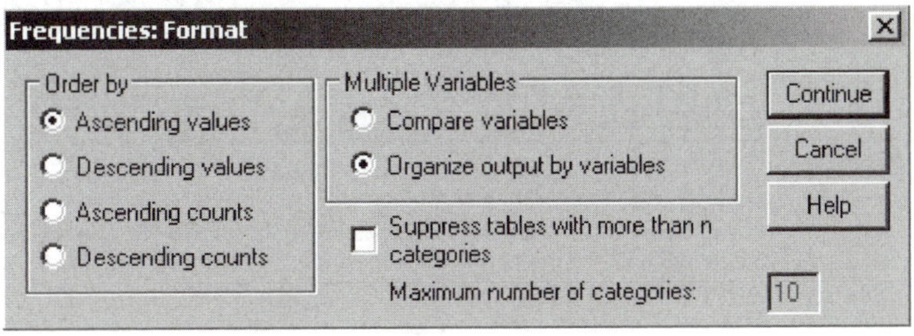

Figure 11.4   Selecting Charts for a Frequencies Analysis

Figure 11.5   Frequencies Format Dialog Box

file (i.e., "Compare variables"). In this analysis, this default is changed to "Organize output by variables."

3. Click Continue to return to the FREQUENCIES window.

Therefore, after selecting:

- the desired procedure (e.g., FREQUENCIES),
- the variables to be analyzed (e.g., YEAR, PARK, FRSTIMPR, OVERALL),
- the statistics of interest (e.g., mean, median, mode, stabdard deviation, variance, range),
- the appropriate graphs (e.g., bar chart, histogram, pie chart), and
- how the output should look (e.g., ascending values, organize output by variables)

there are two ways to perform the analysis (refer to Figure 11.6):

1. Click on OK to run the procedure and options (e.g., statistics and format) that were selected and generates an output file containing the results of the analysis.

2. Click on Paste to generate the command line syntax for the procedure and associated statistics and pastes the syntax into a Syntax file. As discussed in chapter 9, this is the preferred method. SPSS will generate the syntax shown in Figure 11.7 and paste the program commands into the designated Syntax window (see chapter 9 for a discussion of Designated vs. Active windows).

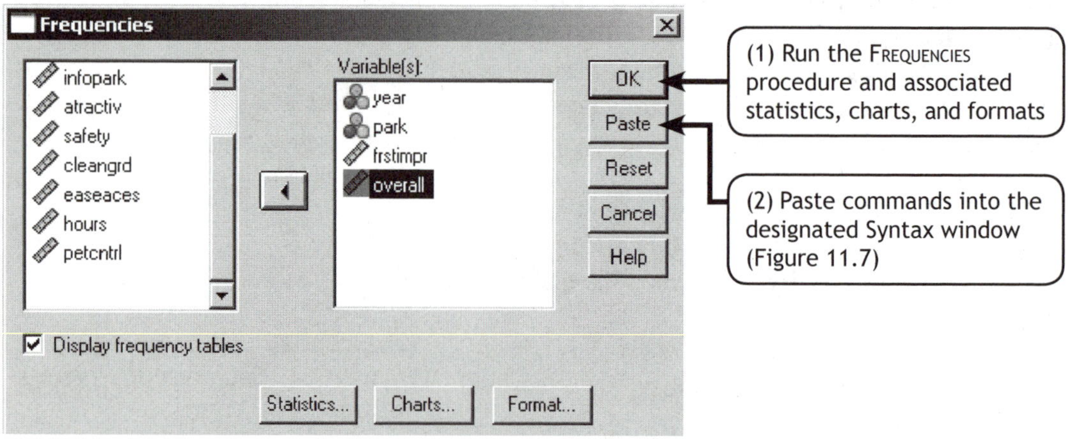

Figure 11.6   Running the SPSS Frequencies Procedure

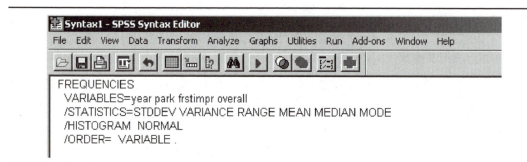

Figure 11.7   SPSS Commands for Running a Frequencies

The SPSS syntax commands shown in Figure 11.7 perform the following actions:

Line	Command	Action
1	Frequencies	Runs the "FREQUENCIES"
2	Variables=year...	Identifies the variables to be included in the analysis
3	/Statistics=stddev...	Identifies the statistics to calculate for each variable selected
4	/Histogram normal	Creates a histogram graph and overlays a normal curve
5	/Order=Analysis	Specifies how the output should look

To run this procedure from a syntax window, highlight the syntax to be included in this analysis and click on the *Run* button (See Figure 11.8). There are two ways to highlight the text:

1. Using the arrow keys, position the cursor where the highlighting should begin. Hold down the shift key and select the syntax to be included in the analysis by moving the cursor over the text.

2. Click on where highlighting should begin. Hold down the left mouse button and drag the cursor to the end of the desired syntax.

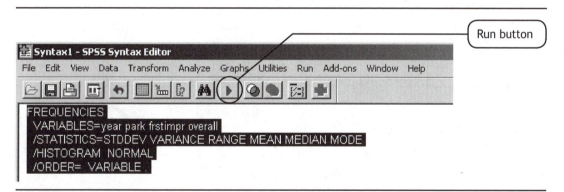

Figure 11.8   Running a Procedure from a Syntax Window

The output from this analysis is shown in Outputs 11.1 through 11.4 (pp. 264–267). Due to space considerations, the histogram is only shown in Output 11.4.

Output 11.1   Frequency Analysis of the Variable YEAR

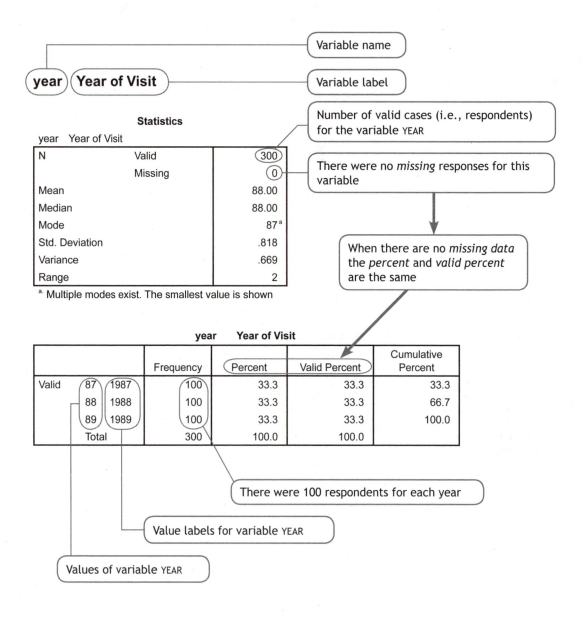

Output 11.2   Frequency Analysis of the Variable PARK

park   Park Visited

Statistics

park   Park Visited

N	Valid	300
	Missing	0
Mean		5.50
Median		5.50
Mode		1[a]
Std. Deviation		2.877
Variance		8.278
Range		9

a. Multiple modes exist. The smallest value is shown

> Since PARK is a categorical level variable, these statistics are totally meaningless. For example, an average of 5.50 implies that the person visited somewhere between Hampton Beach (value = 5) and Silver Lake (value = 6).

park   Park Visited

			Frequency	Percent	Valid Percent	Cumulative Percent
Valid	1	Monadnock Camp	30	10.0	10.0	10.0
	2	Moose Brook Camp	30	10.0	10.0	20.0
	3	Miller Day Use	30	10.0	10.0	30.0
	4	Mt Washington Day	30	10.0	10.0	40.0
	5	Hampton Beach	30	10.0	10.0	50.0
	6	Silver Lake Beach	30	10.0	10.0	60.0
	7	Robert Frost Hist	30	10.0	10.0	70.0
	8	Dan Webster Hist	30	10.0	10.0	80.0
	9	Franconia Flume	30	10.0	10.0	90.0
	10	Franconia Tram	30	10.0	10.0	100.0
	Total		300	100.0	100.0	

> There were 30 respondents from each park

> *Value labels* for the variable PARK

> *Values* of the variable PARK

Output 11.3   Frequency Analysis of the Variable FRSTIMPR

frstimpr   First Impression

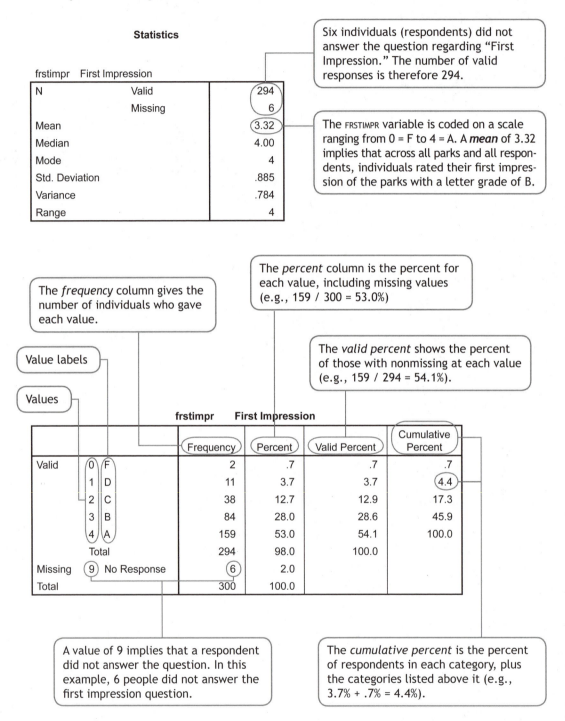

Statistics

Six individuals (respondents) did not answer the question regarding "First Impression." The number of valid responses is therefore 294.

frstimpr   First Impression

N	Valid	294
	Missing	6
Mean		3.32
Median		4.00
Mode		4
Std. Deviation		.885
Variance		.784
Range		4

The FRSTIMPR variable is coded on a scale ranging from 0 = F to 4 = A. A *mean* of 3.32 implies that across all parks and all respondents, individuals rated their first impression of the parks with a letter grade of B.

The *percent* column is the percent for each value, including missing values (e.g., 159 / 300 = 53.0%)

The *frequency* column gives the number of individuals who gave each value.

The *valid percent* shows the percent of those with nonmissing at each value (e.g., 159 / 294 = 54.1%).

Value labels

Values

frstimpr   First Impression

		Frequency	Percent	Valid Percent	Cumulative Percent
Valid	0 F	2	.7	.7	.7
	1 D	11	3.7	3.7	4.4
	2 C	38	12.7	12.9	17.3
	3 B	84	28.0	28.6	45.9
	4 A	159	53.0	54.1	100.0
	Total	294	98.0	100.0	
Missing	9 No Response	6	2.0		
Total		300	100.0		

A value of 9 implies that a respondent did not answer the question. In this example, 6 people did not answer the first impression question.

The *cumulative percent* is the percent of respondents in each category, plus the categories listed above it (e.g., 3.7% + .7% = 4.4%).

Output 11.4   Frequency Analysis of the Variable OVERALL

OVERALL   Overall Satisfaction

Statistics

overall   Overall Satisfaction

N	Valid	291
	Missing	9
Mean		3.33
Median		4.00
Mode		4
Std. Deviation		.917
Variance		.841
Range		4

overall   Overall Satisfaction

		Frequency	Percent	Valid Percent	Cumulative Percent
Valid	0 F	2	.7	.7	.7
	1 D	12	4.0	4.1	4.8
	2 C	42	14.0	14.4	19.2
	3 B	68	22.7	23.4	42.6
	4 A	167	55.7	57.4	100.0
	Total	291	97.0	100.0	
Missing	9 No Response	9	3.0		
Total		300	100.0		

Histogram

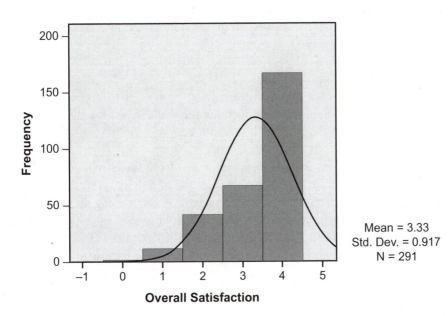

Mean = 3.33
Std. Dev. = 0.917
N = 291

Based on the FREQUENCIES analysis, 291 individuals gave valid responses for the overall satisfaction question. Over half of the respondents (57%) gave a letter grade of "A" and approximately one quarter (23%) evaluated their experience with a "B." The mean response was 3.33 (a B+), with a standard deviation of .92 (see Box 11.1 and the section on the normal curve later in the chapter). The mode and median were 4 (see Box 11.1).

Interpreting the Measures of Central Tendency and Dispersion

Measures of Central Tendency

The ***mean*** (or average) is the sum of the individual values for each respondent divided by the number of cases. The formula is shown in Box 11.1.

The ***median*** divides the distribution in half. In Output 11.3, approximately half (54%) of the respondents gave a letter grade of A for the variable FRSTIMPR; the other half (46%) rated their first impression as less than a grade of A. Since there were only five possible response options, the median does not reflect a perfect 50-50 split.

The ***mode*** is the most frequently occurring response. For the first impression variable (Output 11.3), the value of 4 (a letter grade of A) was given more often than any other response.

Measures of Dispersion

The ***standard deviation*** is defined as the square root of the mean of the square deviations from the mean. Box 11.1 gives the formula for calculating a standard deviation. In words, the calculation steps involve (a) subtracting an individual's response to a question from the mean, (b) squaring each difference, (c) summing the results, (d) dividing by the number of cases, and (e) taking the square root.

The ***variance*** is the square of the standard deviation.

The ***range*** is the highest number minus the lowest number. For the variable FRSTIMPR this equals 4 (or $4 - 0 = 4$).

To illustrate the calculation of these measures of dispersion, consider the two hypothetical examples in Table 11.1. Both examples are based on a sample size of five individuals. In Example 1, the first respondent gave an answer of 4 for the variable X. Subtracting the mean ($M = 3$) from this response results in a difference of 1. The sum of these individual response differences from the mean will always be 0. The sum of the squared differences in Example 1 is 4. Taking the square root of 4 divided by 5 (i.e., the sample size) produces a standard deviation of .89. By comparison, the same calculations for Example 2 resulted in a standard deviation of .4. The larger standard deviation for Example 1 occurred because there was more variability in the respondents' answers (i.e., maximum – minimum = range; or $4 - 2 = 2$). In Example 2, all of the respondents gave an answer of 4 to variable X, with the exception of respondent 5 who had a 3 on this variable. If all five values on this variable had been the same, the standard deviation would have been zero. In general, the greater the spread about the mean, the larger the standard deviation.

Table 11.1   Hypothetical Example of Standard Deviation Calculations ($n = 5$)

Example 1			Example 2		
X_i	$(X_i - M)$	$(X_i - M)^2$	X_i	$(X_i - M)$	$(X_i - M)^2$
4	1	1	4	.2	.04
2	-1	1	4	.2	.04
4	1	1	4	.2	.04
2	-1	1	4	.2	.04
3	0	0	3	-.8	.64
$M = 3$	$\Sigma = 0$	$\Sigma = 4$	$M = 3.8$	$\Sigma = 0$	$\Sigma = .8$

$$s = \sqrt{\frac{\sum_i^N (X_i - M)^2}{n}} = \sqrt{\frac{4}{5}} = .89 \qquad\qquad s = \sqrt{\frac{\sum_i^N (X_i - M)^2}{n}} = \sqrt{\frac{.8}{5}} = .4$$

Box 11.1	Statistics Available from SPSS Frequencies
Mean	M (or average) is the sum of the individual values for each case divided by the number of cases. $$Mean = M = \frac{\sum_{i}^{N} X_i}{n}$$
Median	The numerical value of the middle case or the case lying exactly on the 50th percentile, once all the cases have been rank ordered from highest to lowest.
Mode	The value of the variable which occurs most often.
Minimum	The smallest value of a variable.
Maximum	The largest value of a variable.
Range	The minimum subtracted from the maximum.
Variance	The variance (s^2) is a measure of the dispersion of the data about the mean of a variable. This statistic is one way of measuring how closely the individual scores of the variable cluster around the mean. Mathematically, it is the average squared deviation from the mean. $$Variance = s^2 = \frac{\sum_{i}^{N}(X_i - M)^2}{n}$$ Squaring the deviations from the mean takes into account all differences from the mean, including negative differences, and it gives additional weight to extreme cases. The variance will be small when there is a great deal of homogeneity in the data.
Standard Deviation	The standard deviation is the square root of the variance. The advantage of the standard deviation is that it has a more intuitive interpretation, being based on the same units as the original variable. $$StdDev = s = \sqrt{\frac{\sum_{i}^{N}(X_i - M)^2}{n}}$$
Standard Error	If we were to draw an infinite number of equal-size samples from a given population, the mean of each sample would be an estimate of the true population mean, but not all of them would be identical. The pattern of these means would constitute a normal distribution and would have a standard deviation. The standard deviation of this distribution is the standard error. The standard error helps us to determine the potential degree of discrepancy between the sample mean and the (usually) unknown population mean. The measure is used in tests of statistical significance and for creating confidence intervals. Note that the standard error cannot be computed exactly, but can be estimated by dividing the standard deviation by the square root of the number of cases.
Skewness	Skewness measures deviations from symmetry (the degree to which a distribution of cases approximates a normal curve). The measure will take on a value of 0 when the distribution is a completely symmetric bell-shaped curve. A positive value indicates that the cases are clustered more to the left of the mean. A negative value indicates clustering to the right.
Kurtosis	A measure of the relative peakedness or flatness of the curve defined by the distribution of cases. A normal distribution will have a kurtosis of 0. If the kurtosis is positive, the distribution is more peaked (narrow) than would be true for a normal distribution, while a negative value means that it is flatter.

Descriptives in SPSS

Basic descriptive information about the variables in a data file can also be obtained by running the program DESCRIPTIVES.

1. Click on Analyze > Descriptive Statistics > Descriptives...   See Figure 11.9

2. Select variables to be included in the analysis.   See Figure 11.10
   In this analysis select the variables FRSTIMPR through OVERALL.

3. Select Options…   See Figure 11.11

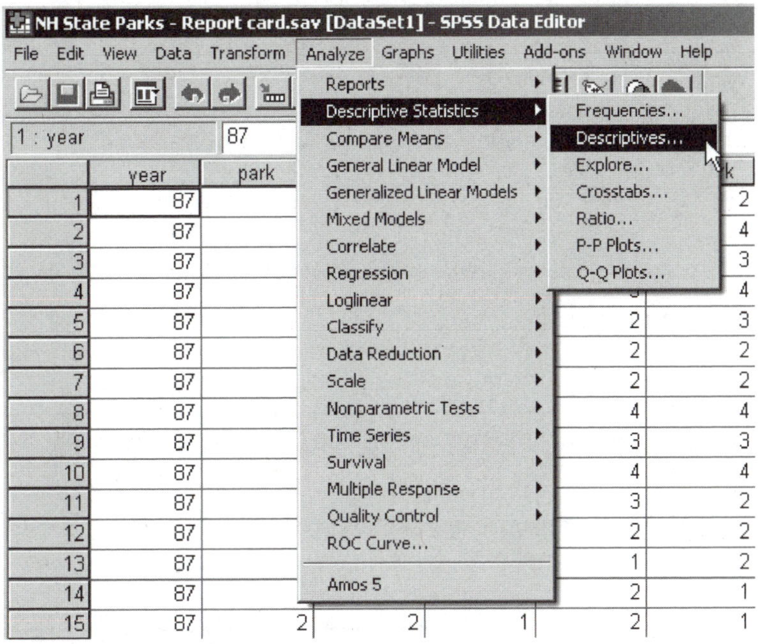

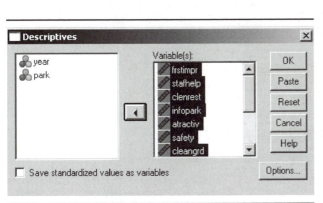

Figure 11.9   Selecting the SPSS Descriptives Procedure

Figure 11.10   Selecting the Variables for the Descriptives Analysis

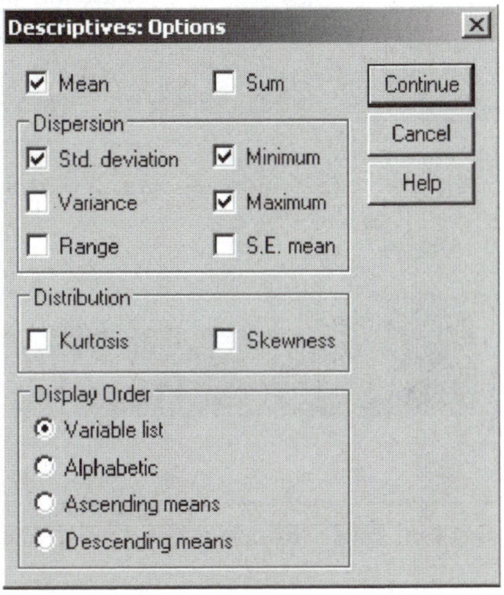

Figure 11.11   Descriptives: Options

The SPSS selected defaults for the Descriptives: Options dialog box are:

- Statistics: Mean, Standard deviation, Minimum, Maximum
- Display Order: Variable list

For this exercise, accept these defaults by clicking the Continue button.

When the dialog box for DESCRIPTIVES appears (Figure 11.10), click the Paste button. Given the FREQUENCIES syntax from the previous exercise, the syntax window should look like Figure 11.12.

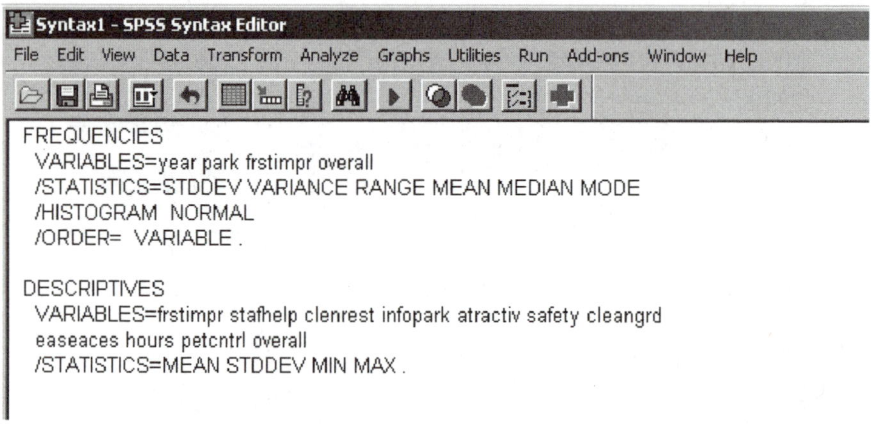

Figure 11.12   Syntax Window with Frequencies and Descriptive Commands

Highlight the DESCRIPTIVES commands and run this procedure by clicking the Run button (Figure 11.13).

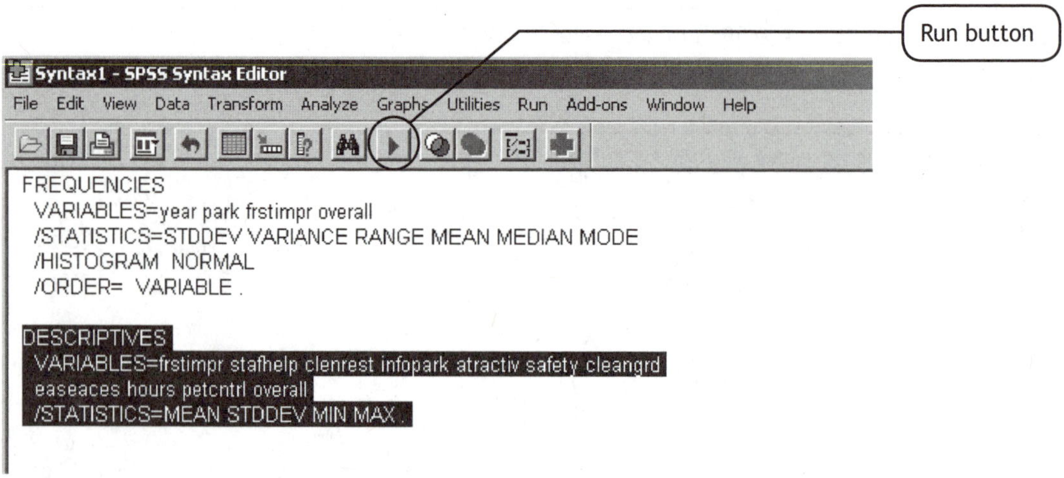

Figure 11.13   Running the Descriptives Procedure

The output file should now show the following results:

Output 11.5　Descriptives results

Descriptives

Descriptive Statistics

	N	Minimum	Maximum	Mean	Std. Deviation
frstimpr　First Impression	294	0	4	3.32	.885
stafhelp　Helpfulness of Staff	296	0	4	3.33	.969
clenrest　Cleanliness of Restrooms	269	0	4	3.01	1.044
infopark　Information at Park	288	0	4	3.10	1.083
atractiv　Attractiveness of Park	298	0	4	3.30	.936
safety　Safety and Security	277	0	4	3.17	1.021
cleangrd　Cleanliness of Grounds	298	0	4	3.36	.954
easeaces　Ease of Access	289	0	4	3.17	1.072
hours　Hours of Operation	269	0	4	3.25	.951
petcntrl　Control of Pets	254	0	4	3.22	.917
overall　Overall Satisfaction	291	0	4	3.33	.917
Valid N (listwise)	220				

Across all 11 evaluation questions in this sample, the "Valid N" was 220. This sample size is based on a *listwise* deletion. With listwise deletion, only respondents who have answered *all* of the questions are included in the analysis. Chapter 16 discusses the distinction between listwise and *pairwise* deletion.

The responses for each of the variables ranged from 0 (the *minimum*) to 4 (the *maximum*). This implies that at least one person for each variable gave a grade of "F" (i.e., 0) and at least one person on each variable gave a grade of "A."

The mean scores ranged from 3.01 (i.e., cleanliness of the restrooms) to 3.36 (i.e., cleanliness of the grounds). The substantive conclusion is that, on average, visitors rated their New Hampshire State Park experience as a "B." This initial analysis, however, was based on all three study years in the data set (1987–1989) and across all ten parks. Whether or not these positive evaluations differ by study year and specific parks remains a topic for future chapters.

As noted in the introduction to this chapter, any continuous variable can be described using measures of central tendency (e.g., mean, mode, median), dispersion (e.g., standard deviation, variance), and shape (i.e., skewness, kurtosis). The preceding concentrated on central tendency and dispersion. The next section addresses issues associated with a distribution's shape. Skewness and kurtosis are discussed relative to the normal curve.

A Distribution's Shape

Normal Curve Distributions

Frequency distributions for many parks, recreation, and human dimensions variables approximate the distribution of a normal curve (Figure 11.14). Chapter 6 provided a general introduction to the normal curve. This section further discusses some basic properties inherent to every normal curve:

1. The normal curve is unimodal with a single "hump," in the middle of the distribution. The most frequent value (i.e., the mode) is in the middle.

2. The mean, median, and mode are equal in a normal distribution.

3. The curve is symmetric. If a normal curve is folded in half vertically, the right side would fit perfectly with the left side (i.e., the curve is not **skewed**).

4. The range is infinite; meaning that the extreme ends of the distribution approach but never touch the x axis.

5. The curve is not too peaked or too flat; the tails are not too short or too long (i.e., **kurtosis** = 0).

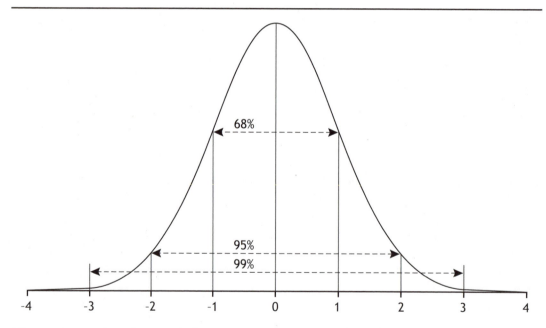

All normal curves have two population parameters: mean (μ) and standard deviation (σ). Although different values of μ and σ yield different normal curves, all normal curves share the 68% - 95% - 99% rule:

68% of the observations lie within 1 standard deviation of the mean (i.e., between $\mu - \sigma$ and $\mu + \sigma$)

95% of the observations lie within 2 standard deviations of the mean (i.e., between $\mu - 2\sigma$ and $\mu + 2\sigma$)

99% of the observations lie within 3 standard deviations of the mean (i.e., between $\mu - 3\sigma$ and $\mu + 3\sigma$)

Figure 11.14   The Normal Curve

As noted in chapter 6, researchers typically use a probability or *p*-value of 0.05 for determining statistical significance. This judgment is based on the 95% rule. In other words, the difference between 100% and 95% is the 5% needed for statistical significance. Values not falling within two standard deviations of the mean are seen as relatively rare events.

Finally, if we assume an infinite number of equal-size samples from a given population, the mean of each sample would be an estimate of the population mean, but not all of the means would be identical. The pattern of these means would constitute a normal distribution and this distribution would have a standard deviation. The standard deviation of this distribution is the ***standard error***. In other words, the standard error of a statistic (e.g., a mean) is the standard deviation of the sampling distribution of that statistic. Standard errors are important because they reflect how much sampling fluctuation a statistic will show. The inferential statistics involved in the construction of confidence intervals and significance testing (chapter 6) are based on standard errors. The standard error of a statistic depends on the sample size. In general, the larger the sample size, the smaller the standard error.

Non-Normally Shaped Distributions

Skewness

If one tail of a frequency distribution is longer than the other, and if the mean and median are different, the curve is skewed (Morgan, Gliner, & Harmon, 2006). Skewness measures deviations from symmetry. A normal curve has a skewness of zero (0.0). Because most common inferential statistics assume that the dependent variable is normally distributed (i.e., the data are normal), it is important to know whether the variables are highly skewed.

A positive skewness implies that the distribution is skewed to the left of the mean (Figure 11.15a), while a negative skewness implies that the distribution is skewed to the right of the mean (Figure 11.15.b).

If the skewness is more than +1.0 or less than −1.0, the distribution is markedly skewed (Morgan et al., 2006). In these situations the researcher might consider using a nonparametric

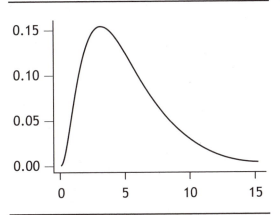

Figure 11.15a
A positively skewed distribution

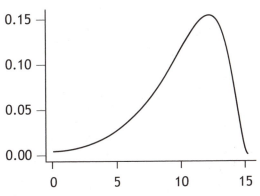

Figure 11.15b
A negatively skewed distribution

statistic. As noted in chapter 5, however, parametric statistics are robust and yield valid conclusions even when the assumption of normality has been violated.

Kurtosis

Kurtosis measures the relative peakedness or flatness of a distribution. A distribution that is more peaked than the normal curve is called *leptokurtic* and has a positive kurtosis. If a frequency distribution is relatively flat, the curve is called *platykurtic* and has negative kurtosis. Similar to all descriptive statistics, measures of kurtosis and skewness are designed to help the researcher think about how the data are distributed. Although there are no hard-and-fast rules for interpretation, Morgan, Gliner, and Harmon (2006) suggest that if a distribution has a large kurtosis relative to the standard error, the variable deviates from the normal curve.

In SPSS, skewness and kurtosis can be calculated with either the FREQUENCIES (see Figure 11.4) or DESCRIPTIVES (see Figure 11.11) commands by checking the appropriate boxes. Output 11.6 shows a plot of the variable FRSTIMPR in the New Hampshire State Park data set and gives the standard error of the mean, the skewness and kurtosis statistics for the variable. The distribution has a negative skew. Since the skewness statistic is less than 1.0, the distribution is skewed. Given that the kurtosis is large relative to the standard error of the mean, the distribution deviates from the normal curve.

Output 11.6   Standard Error of the Mean, Skewness, and Kurtosis for the Variable FRSTIMPR

Statistics

frstimpr   First Impression

N	Valid	294
	Missing	6
Std. Error of Mean		.052
Skewness		−1.230
Kurtosis		.988

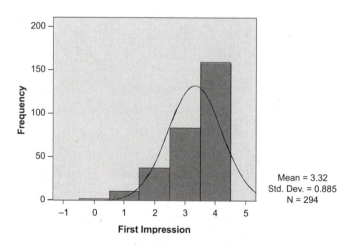

Histogram

Mean = 3.32
Std. Dev. = 0.885
N = 294

Table 11.2 summarizes the types of descriptive statistics that can be used given dichotomous, categorical, and continuous data.

Table 11.2   Selection of Appropriate Descriptive Statistics[1]

	Dichotomous	Categorical	Continuous
Frequency Distribution			
Counts	Yes	Yes	Yes
Percents	Yes	Yes	Yes
Bar graphs/Histograms	Yes	Yes	Yes
Central Tendency			
Mean	Yes	No	Yes
Median	No	No	Yes
Mode	Yes	Yes	Yes
Variability			
Standard deviation	Yes	No	Yes
Variance	Yes	No	Yes
Range	Yes	No	Yes
Shape			
Skewness	No	No	Yes
Kurtosis	No	No	Yes

[1] "Yes" means a good choice with this level of measurement; "No" means not appropriate at this level of measurement.

The Potential for Conflict Index: An Alternative to Traditional Summary Statistics

A goal of parks, recreation, and human dimensions research is to provide input that will improve decision making. When communicating results to managers and other nonstatistical audiences, it is imperative that researchers provide clear statistical information and convey the practical implications of their findings. Basic summary statistics describe variables in terms of central tendency (e.g., mean), dispersion (e.g., standard deviation), and shape (e.g., skewness). Although these statistics can efficiently convey meaning, an accurate understanding of a variable's distribution requires consideration of all three indicators simultaneously. The potential for conflict index (PCI) was developed to facilitate understanding and interpreting statistical data (Manfredo, Vaske, & Teel, 2003; Vaske, Needham, Newman, Manfredo, & Petchenik, 2006).

Surveys often use response scales with an equal number of response options surrounding a neutral center point. Numerical ratings are typically assigned with the neutral point being 0 (e.g., $-3, -2, -1, 0, 1, 2, 3$ where highly unacceptable [-3], neutral [0], and highly acceptable [3]). The PCI describes the ratio of responses on either side of a rating scale's center point. The greatest possibility for conflict (PCI = 1) occurs when there is a bimodal distribution between the two extreme values of the response scale (e.g., 50% highly unacceptable, 50% highly acceptable, 0% neutral). A distribution with 100% at any one point on the response scale yields a PCI of 0 and suggests no potential for conflict. Computation of the PCI uses a frequency distribution and follows the formula:[1]

$$
PCI = \left[1 - \left| \frac{\sum\limits_{i=1}^{na} |X_a|}{Xt} - \frac{\sum\limits_{i=1}^{nu} |X_u|}{Xt} \right| \right] * \frac{Xt}{Z}
$$

Equation 11.1

where:

X_a = an individual's "acceptable" (or "favor" or "likely") score

na = all individuals with acceptable scores

X_u = an individual's "unacceptable" (or "oppose" or "unlikely") score

nu = all individuals with unacceptable scores

$$
Xt = \sum_{i=1}^{na} |X_a| + \sum_{i=1}^{nu} |X_u|
$$

Z = the maximum possible sum of all scores = n * *extreme score on scale* (e.g., $Z = 3n$ for scale with 7 response options); n = total number of subjects.

Following computation of the PCI, results are displayed as bubble graphs to visually and simultaneously describe a variable's form, dispersion, and central tendency (see Figures 11.16, p. 280, and 11.17, p. 283, for examples). The size of the bubble depicts the PCI and indicates degree of dispersion (e.g., extent of potential conflict regarding the acceptability of a management strategy). A small bubble suggests little potential conflict; a larger bubble suggests more potential conflict.

The center of the bubble is plotted on the y axis and indicates the mean response (e.g., central tendency) to the measured variable. With the neutral point of the response scale highlighted on the y axis, it is apparent that respondents' average evaluations are situated above or below the neutral point (i.e., the action, on average, is acceptable or unacceptable). Information about a distribution's skewness is reflected by the position of the bubble relative to the neutral point (i.e., bubbles at the top or bottom of the graph suggest high degrees of skewness).

A Univariate PCI Illustration

Manfredo, Vaske, and Teel (2003) used data from the Western Association of Fish and Wildlife Agencies "Wildlife Values in the West" Demonstration Project to illustrate the computation and display of the PCI. The larger project assessed wildlife value orientations (chapter 2), management action acceptability and wildlife-associated recreation behaviors in six western states (i.e., Alaska, Arizona, Colorado, Idaho, North Dakota, South Dakota). For illustration purposes, results were presented for the state of Alaska on a series of items dealing with bear management. Before responding to the items, subjects were presented with the following scenario:

---

[1] Instructions for calculating the PCI in Excel can be found at http://www.warnercnr.colostate.edu/NRRT/people/ jerryj.htm This web page also contains Excel spreadsheets for 5- and 7-point scales, and a PowerPoint template for generating the associated graphic display. The Excel and PowerPoint templates can be downloaded.

In some areas and during certain times of the year, bears have been known to wander into residential areas where they get into trash cans, storage sheds, and bird feeders. They can destroy vegetation and can pose a threat to both pets and humans. Some people feel the bears should be left alone or simply chased away. Others think the bears should be caught and relocated or destroyed. Still others feel that people who live near bear habitat should be educated about how to avoid problems with bears.

Respondents were then asked to rate the acceptability of five different management responses (e.g., leave the bear alone, capture and destroy the bear).

Table 11.3 shows Alaskan respondents' evaluations of the acceptability of "leave the bear alone" after it has been seen in residential areas. Frequencies and percentages as well as indicators of the distribution's central tendency, dispersion and shape are displayed. Using data from the frequency distribution, the potential for conflict index was computed as follows:

$$\sum_{i=1}^{nu}|X_u| = (|-3| * 26) + (|-2| * 31) + (|-1| * 20) = 160$$

$$\sum_{i=1}^{na}|X_a| = (3 * 108) + (2 * 90) + (1 * 52) = 556$$

$$Xt = 160 + 556 = 716$$

$$n = \text{total number of subjects} = 342$$

$$\text{PCI for "Leave the Bear Alone"} = \left[1 - \left|\frac{556}{716} - \frac{160}{716}\right|\right] * \frac{716}{(3*342)} = .31$$

Table 11.3 Alaskan Respondents' Ratings of Acceptability of "Leave the Bear Alone"

Response Scale	Scoring	Frequency	Percent
Highly Unacceptable	−3	26	8
Moderately Unacceptable	−2	31	9
Slightly Unacceptable	−1	20	6
Neutral	0	15	4
Slightly Acceptable	1	52	15
Moderately Acceptable	2	90	26
Highly Acceptable	3	108	32
Total		342	100
Descriptive statistics			
Mean	1.16		
Median	2.00		
Mode	3.00		
Standard Deviation	1.96		
Variance	3.83		
Skewness	−.93		
Kurtosis	−.45		

The potential for conflict index for "leave the bear alone" was approximately .31. Similar computations for the other four management actions revealed the following indices: .39 for "capture and destroy the bear," .18 for "capture and relocate the bear," .10 for "use techniques designed to frighten the bear away," and .04 for "educate people who live near bear habitat on how to avoid problems with bears" (Table 11.4, p. 280). Because the PCI ranges from 0 to 1, the results clearly indicate that "leave the bear alone" and "destroy the bear" are likely to be the most controversial among the actions presented to this sample of Alaskan residents.

Frightening the bear was far less controversial, and education showed virtually no potential for conflict.

Table 11.4   Potential for Conflict Indices and Mean Scores for Alaskan Respondents' Ratings of Acceptability of Bear Management Actions[1]

Management Action...	Conflict Index	Mean Score[2]
Leave the bear alone.	.31	1.16
Capture and destroy the bear.	.39	−0.91
Capture and relocate the bear to a new location in hopes that it will NOT return.	.18	1.54
Use techniques (e.g., loud noises, rubber bullets) designed to frighten the bear away.	.10	2.02
Educate people who live near bear habitat on how to avoid problems with bears.	.04	2.62

[1] Data for this example were taken from the WAFWA "Wildlife Values in the West" Demonstration Project and used only the responses from individuals living in Alaska.

[2] The following scoring was used in the computation of means for this variable: Highly Unacceptable (−3), Moderately Unacceptable (−2), Slightly Unacceptable (−1), Neither (0), Slightly Acceptable (1), Moderately Acceptable (2), and Highly Acceptable (3).

Figure 11.16 displays the conflict indices and variable means graphically. Visually, it is apparent that "leaving the bear alone" and "destroying the bear" have higher potential for conflict than the other actions (i.e., the bubbles are bigger). Leaving the bear alone is, on average, acceptable,

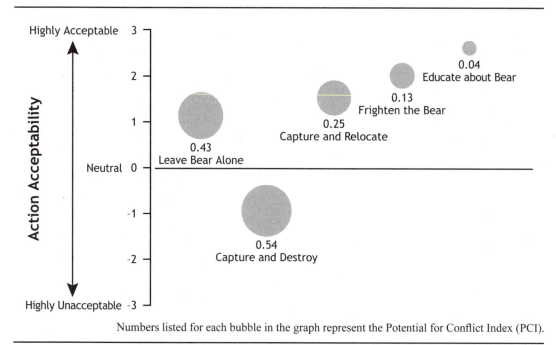

Numbers listed for each bubble in the graph represent the Potential for Conflict Index (PCI).

Figure 11.16   Univariate Measures Using the PCI and the Graphic Technique: Alaskans' Ratings of Acceptability of Bear Management Actions

while destroying the bear is not. Among the other actions, education and frightening are far more acceptable, and there is relatively little disagreement about these actions. Their distribution is very positively skewed. Relocation, overall, is acceptable, but this action has a higher conflict potential than either education or frightening techniques.

A Bivariate PCI Illustration

A recent study by Vaske and Taylor (2006) used the PCI to understand the acceptability of alternative management actions for addressing human-wolf conflict in the Greater Yellowstone Area (GYA). Gray wolves (*Canis lupus*) appeared in Grand Teton National Park (GTRE) northern boundary in October of 1998, two years after being reintroduced to Yellowstone National Park. Over 300 wolves are currently estimated to reside in the GYA. Human populations in the area have also increased in recent years. The population of Teton County, Wyoming, for example, increased 73% from 1990 to 2005. Park visitation for GTRE now averages 2.5 million visitors annually. In addition, unlike other national parks, grazing rights in the GTRE are protected, and livestock and wolf conflicts have increased. Livestock depredations by wolves within the Greater Yellowstone Area resulted in the deaths of approximately 150 cattle, sheep, and goats during 2003. Two thirds of these depredations occurred on public grazing allotments and 34% on private property. The U.S. Fish and Wildlife Service responded to these depredations by killing 38 wolves in 2003.

Vaske and Taylor (2006) sampled local resident ($n = 604$, response rate = 51%) and park visitor ($n = 596$, response rate = 81%) populations during 2003. The local resident sample included individuals who live within a 100-mile radius of Jackson, Wyoming. Park visitors were initially surveyed on-site to collect basic information and addresses for the follow-up mail survey. A total of 1,200 mail surveys were used in our analyses. A telephone nonresponse check for the resident sample did not identify any statistical differences between respondents and nonrespondents to the mail survey.

The survey described four hypothetical situations depicting possible human-wolf encounters (Table 11.5). Factors that might affect respondents' evaluation of the acceptable management actions were experimentally manipulated in the scenarios, including: the location of the encounter (on park property or private land); the type of encounter (e.g., hikers seeing wolves on trail, wolves harassing cattle, or pets and cattle being depredated by wolves); and the endangered species status of the wolves (listed as "endangered population" or as delisted).

Table 11.5   Description of Scenarios Depicting Possible Human-Wolf Encounters

Scenario	Status of wolves	Encounter type	Location of encounter
1	Endangered population	Wolves chase cattle	Public land
2	Endangered population	Wolves kill cattle	Private land
3	Delisted	Pet killed by wolves	Private land
4	Delisted	Wolves kill cattle	In GTRE

Respondents evaluated the acceptability of several management options designed to remedy or prevent the conflict in the hypothetical situation (e.g., monitor the situation, frighten the wolves away, capture and relocate the wolves, destroy the wolves). Acceptance of management actions were coded on seven-point scales ranging from highly unacceptable (–3) to highly acceptable (+3).

Table 11.6 provides summary statistics for the management action of destroying the wolves involved in the situation. Findings are presented for both the local residents and National Park visitors. In general, local residents rated "destroy the wolves involved" as acceptable, whereas park visitors rated this management option as unacceptable. Although these descriptive statistics detail the differences between the two samples of respondents, the findings are easier to interpret when the data are displayed graphically with the potential for conflict index (Figure 11.17). Across all four scenarios, the visitors' acceptability ratings are consistently below the neutral line, whereas the local residents were above the neutral line in 3 of the 4 scenarios. The visitors PCI bubbles were consistently smaller (i.e., more consensus) than those for the local visitors. The residents' PCI value (.60) for scenario 1 is approximately five times larger than the PCI for visitors (.13), and the residents' bubble straddles the neutral line, suggesting destroying the wolf in this situation would be controversial.

Table 11.6   Descriptive Statistics for Local Residents and National Park Visitors Regarding the Acceptability of Destroying the Wolf in Four Hypothetical Scenarios

	Management Action: Destroy the wolves involved			
	Scenario 1	Scenario 2	Scenario 3	Scenario 4
Status of wolf	Endangered	Endangered	Delisted	Delisted
Land type	Public	Private	Private	Public
Encounter with wolf	Chasing cattle	Kills cattle	Kills pet	Kills cattle
Local residents				
Mean	–.48	.39	.71	.36
Standard error of mean	.10	.10	.10	.10
Median	–1.00	1.00	2.00	1.00
Mode	–3.00	3.00	3.00	3.00
Standard Deviation	2.42	2.46	2.36	2.41
Variance	5.83	6.03	5.59	5.82
Skewness	.35	–.26	–.52	–.25
Kurtosis	–1.54	1.64	–1.38	–1.61
National Park visitors				
Mean	–2.19	–1.35	–.91	–1.30
Standard error of mean	.06	.09	.09	.09
Median	–3.00	–2.00	–2.00	–2.00
Mode	–3.00	–3.00	–3.00	–3.00
Standard Deviation	1.55	2.08	2.13	2.08
Variance	2.39	4.32	4.56	4.31
Skewness	2.16	1.00	.59	.92
Kurtosis	3.76	–.47	–1.13	–.65

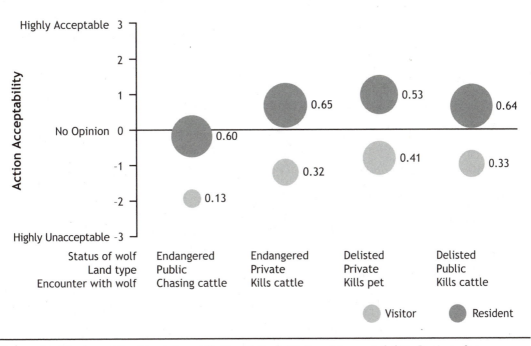

Figure 11.17   Local Residents' and National Park Visitors' Acceptability Ratings for Destroying Wolves in Four Hypothetical Situations

Chapter Summary

This chapter outlined the steps involved in running two SPSS programs — FREQUENCIES and DESCRIPTIVES — that can be used for describing variables. Four variables (i.e., YEAR, PARK, FRSTIMPR, OVERALL) from the New Hampshire State Parks data set were used to illustrate measures of central tendency (e.g., mean, mode, median), dispersion (e.g., standard deviation, variance), and shape (i.e., skewness, kurtosis). The distributional properties of the normal curve were also discussed.

An alternative to these traditional summary statistics, the potential for conflict index (PCI), was introduced and illustrated with data from Alaska and the Greater Yellowstone Area. The PCI and associated graphical display offers an intuitive approach to summarizing statistical results.

Review Questions

1. In an SPSS FREQUENCIES analysis, what does the *Frequency* column tell you?

2. If there are 500 respondents in a data file and 25 people did not answer one of the questions, what is the *Valid N* for this variable?

3. In an SPSS FREQUENCIES analysis, what is the difference between the *Percent* and the *Valid Percent* columns?

4. When a variable has no missing data and the *Percent* for a value equals 35%, what is the percent for the *Valid Percent* on this value?

5. How is the *Cumulative Percent* calculated?

6. Identify three measures of central tendency and three measures of dispersion.

7. Compare the mode, median, and mean in terms of interpretation.

8. Explain *listwise deletion* in a DESCRIPTIVES analysis.

9. List three properties inherent to every normal curve.

10. In a normal distribution, if the mean equals 35, what is the value of the median?

11. If a variable's maximum value is 75 and the minimum value is 25, what is the variable's range?

12. If the standard deviation for a variable equals 2, what is the variance?

13. Define the concept of *standard error*.

14. If your measure of skewness equals 0, what is the shape of the distribution?

15. Explain the 68%-95%-99% rule in a normal distribution.

16. Why is the potential for conflict index (PCI) and associated graphical display more intuitive to understand than traditional summary statistics (e.g., mean, standard deviation, skewness)?

17. What does the size of a potential for conflict (PCI) bubble indicate?

18. Describe a situation where the potential for conflict index (PCI) equals 0.

19. Describe a situation where the potential for conflict index (PCI) equals 1.

12

data manipulation techniques

The complexities of parks, recreation, and human dimensions concepts and research questions typically necessitate manipulating the raw data file. SPSS contains a variety of data transformation procedures; for example: (a) creating new variables (i.e., the Compute command), (b) rearranging or consolidating values of an existing variable (i.e., Recode command), (c) conditional transformations of existing or new variables (i.e., the If command), or (d) selecting specific respondents for analysis (i.e., Select if command). Box 12.1 (pp. 313–314) briefly describes data manipulation commands that are commonly used in survey research.

This chapter describes these techniques using data from surveys of visitors to New Hampshire State Parks (Vaske, Donnelly, & Williamson, 1991), and the Columbia Icefield in Jasper National Park, Canada (Vaske, Donnelly, Doctor, & Petruzzi, 1994). Specific hypotheses and research questions are advanced for each study to illustrate why the data manipulations were necessary.

Compute Command

Summated Rating-Scales

Summated rating scales that combine multiple variables into a new index are commonly used in survey research (chapter 18). There are at least three ways of computing an additive scale. The first two approaches assume that there are *no missing data*.

1. The simplest approach merely adds the variables together. For example, a researcher may want to know a group of respondents' total participation across a range of recreation activities (ACTV1, ACTV2, ACTV3, ACTV4), where participation is coded as Yes (value = 1) or No (value = 0).

   ```
   Compute totlactv = (actv1 + actv2 + actv3 + actv4).
   ```
   OR
   ```
   Compute totlactv = sum(actv1, actv2, actv3, actv4).
   ```

   For example, if a respondent plays basketball (ACTV1) and baseball (ACTV2), but does not swim (ACTV3) or jog (ACTV4), the individual's combined value on the new computed variable is 2:

```
totlactv = (1 + 1 + 0 + 0) = 2.
```

2. Since it is often useful to convert the total score (or value) back to the original metric to make the interpretation easier (e.g., grade point averages or average scores from a 5-point agree to disagree scale), a researcher can divide the total by the number of items in the scale; for example:

```
Compute gpa = (grade1 + grade2 + grade3 + grade4) / 4.
```
or
```
Compute gpa = sum(grade1, grade2, grade3, grade4) / 4.
```

Thus, if a person received an "A" in a research methods course (GRADE1 = 4), an "A" in a theory course (GRADE2 = 4), a "B" in a statistics course (GRADE3 = 3), and a "C" in a chemistry course (GRADE4 = 2), the grade point average would be:

```
gpa = (4 + 4 + 3 + 2) / 4 = 13 / 4 = 3.25.
```

Both methods 1 and 2 are acceptable if there are no missing data. When *any* of the data are missing on variables from which the scale is being constructed, SPSS deletes that case (e.g., a respondent's survey) from the analysis (see chapter 19 for a discussion on handling missing data).

3. Method 3 is the recommended approach for computing a variable in SPSS because the researcher controls how much missing data will be tolerated. The general syntax for this method:

```
Compute avgbelief = mean(grade1, grade2, grade3, grade4).
```

Note the variables within the parentheses must be separated with a comma.

With this command, if a respondent answers at least one of the questions, the scale will be computed. SPSS, however, allows more stringent criteria for a person to be included in the scale. For example, a researcher could decide that a respondent should have answered at least two of the questions. The syntax in this situation would be:

```
Compute avgbelief = mean.2 (grade1, grade2, grade3, grade4).
```

To require 3 respondent provided answers for inclusion in the scale, the syntax is:

```
Compute avgbelief = mean.3 (grade1, grade2, grade3, grade4).
```

Once the scale is computed with any of the above methods, the calculations should be checked by running a LIST CASES and/or a FREQUENCIES analysis.

Empirical Example: `Compute` Commands

The following illustrates Methods 2 and 3 using the New Hampshire State Parks - Report Card data. Three of the satisfaction variables in this data file concerned the day-to-day operations of running and maintaining a State Park (i.e., Cleanliness of the Restrooms, Cleanliness of the Grounds, Hours of Operation). These three items might be combined into a scale reflecting the concept of "operations." The frequency distributions for these three variables are as follows:

```
FREQUENCIES
  VARIABLES=clenrest cleangrd hours
  /STATISTICS=STDDEV MEAN MEDIAN MODE
  /ORDER=  ANALYSIS .
```

Statistics

		clenrest Cleanliness of Restrooms	cleangrd Cleanliness of Grounds	hours Hours of Operation
N	Valid	269	298	269
	Missing	31	2	31
Mean		3.01	3.36	3.25
Median		3.00	4.00	4.00
Mode		4	4	4
Std. Deviation		1.044	.954	.951

For the variables Cleanliness of the Restrooms and Hours of Operation, 31 visitors did not answer the questions. Two individuals did not answer the Cleanliness of the Grounds question.

clenrest Cleanliness of Restrooms

			Frequency	Percent	Valid Percent	Cumulative Percent
Valid	0	F	4	1.3	1.5	1.5
	1	D	23	7.7	8.6	10.0
	2	C	52	17.3	19.3	29.4
	3	B	78	26.0	29.0	58.4
	4	A	112	37.3	41.6	100.0
	Total		269	89.7	100.0	
Missing	9	No Response	31	10.3		
Total			300	100.0		

The values for each of these 3 variables ranged from 0 to 4.

The user-defined missing value code for each of these variables is a value of 9.

cleangrd Cleanliness of Grounds

			Frequency	Percent	Valid Percent	Cumulative Percent
Valid	0	F	3	1.0	1.0	1.0
	1	D	15	5.0	5.0	6.0
	2	C	38	12.7	12.8	18.8
	3	B	59	19.7	19.8	38.6
	4	A	183	61.0	61.4	100.0
	Total		298	99.3	100.0	
Missing	9	No Response	2	.7		
Total			300	100.0		

hours Hours of Operation

			Frequency	Percent	Valid Percent	Cumulative Percent
Valid	0	F	1	.3	.4	.4
	1	D	17	5.7	6.3	6.7
	2	C	39	13.0	14.5	21.2
	3	B	69	23.0	25.7	46.8
	4	A	143	47.7	53.2	100.0
	Total		269	89.7	100.0	
Missing	9	No Response	31	10.3		
Total			300	100.0		

Scale Construction (Method 2)

```
Compute OPER1 = (CLENREST + CLEANGRD + HOURS)/3.
```

> This command computes a new variable called OPER1 by summing the values for the three variables (i.e., CLENREST, CLENGRD and HOURS) and then dividing by 3 (the number of variables in the scale).

```
List Variables = CLENREST CLEANGRD HOURS OPER1 /cases = from 1 to 10.
```

> This command checks the computations by listing the values for the original three variables and the new computed variable (OPER1) for the first 10 individuals in the data set. The SPSS output produced by the List command is shown below.

> The first individual in the data set gave a grade of B (i.e., a value of 3) for the variable Cleanliness of the Restrooms).

CLENREST	CLEANGRD	HOURS	OPER1
3	4	4	3.67
3	4	4	3.67
3	3	3	3.00
3	4	4	3.67
2	3	4	3.00
2	1	3	2.00
2	4	2	2.67
4	4	4	4.00
3	4	9	.
4	4	4	4.00

> Grades of A (i.e., values of 4) were given for the variables CLEANGRD and HOURS.

> The sum of these values (i.e., 3 + 4 + 4) divided by 3 (the number of variables in the index) equals 3.67.

> The computed value for the variable OPER1 equals system missing (i.e., a period) because the respondent did not answer the question Hours of Operation.

A second way to check the calculations is to run a FREQUENCIES on the computed variable.

```
Frequencies variables = OPER1
/STATISTICS=MEAN.
```

Statistics

OPER1

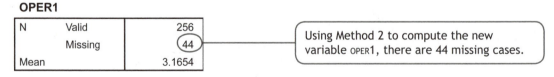

N	Valid	256
	Missing	44
Mean		3.1654

> Using Method 2 to compute the new variable OPER1, there are 44 missing cases.

The original values for the three variables used to compute the OPER1 variable ranged from 0 to 4. A value of .33 can occur if the respondent gave a grade of D (i.e., 1) on all three variables. A value of 4 could occur if the person gave an "A" on all three variables.

The FREQUENCIES for the computed index (OPER1) range from .33 to 4.00. Because the values on the computed variable are within the range of the values for the original variables, we have one check that the computation is correct.

In general, this variable could have ranged from 0 to 4. A zero would occur if a respondent gave all 0 (i.e., F) on all three variables. A 4 occurs when a respondent gives all As.

Park operations grades

		Frequency	Percent	Valid Percent	Cumulative Percent
Valid	.33	1	.3	.4	.4
	1.00	7	2.3	2.7	3.1
	1.33	6	2.0	2.3	5.5
	1.67	9	3.0	3.5	9.0
	2.00	16	5.3	6.3	15.2
	2.33	19	6.3	7.4	22.7
	2.67	19	6.3	7.4	30.1
	3.00	27	9.0	10.5	40.6
	3.33	33	11.0	12.9	53.5
	3.67	42	14.0	16.4	69.9
	4.00	77	25.7	30.1	100.0
	Total	256	85.3	100.0	
Missing	System	44	14.7		
Total		300	100.0		

Scale Construction (Method 3)

```
Compute OPER2 = mean(CLENREST,CLEANGRD,HOURS).
```

> With this method, a respondent only has to answer one of the questions to be included in the index (i.e., OPER2).

```
List variables = CLENREST CLEANGRD HOURS OPER2 /cases = from 1 to 10.
```

List

CLENREST	CLEANGRD	HOURS	OPER2
3	4	4	3.67
3	4	4	3.67
3	3	3	3.00
3	4	4	3.67
2	3	4	3.00
2	1	3	2.00
2	4	2	2.67
4	4	4	4.00
3	4	9	3.50
4	4	4	4.00
3	2	2	2.33

> This respondent answered CLENREST and CLEANGRD variables, but did not answer the HOURS variable. Using Method 3, the value for the computed variable (OPER2) is 3.50. In other words, (3 + 4) / 2 = 3.50.
>
> With Method 3, SPSS automatically changes the denominator to the appropriate value.

```
Frequencies variables = OPER2.
```

Statistics

OPER2

N	Valid	298
	Missing	2

> Using Method 3 and not specifying a number after the command mean on the Compute statement results in only two missing cases.

```
Compute OPER3 = mean.3(CLENREST,CLEANGRD,HOURS).

Frequencies Variables = OPER3.
```

Statistics

OPER3

N	Valid	256
	Missing	44

> Using Method 3 and specifying the number 3 after the command mean on the Compute statement results in 44 missing cases. OPER3 thus required the respondent to answer all three questions in the three-item scale. This is simply another way of saying if any of the questions are not answered (same as OPER1), delete the case.

A decision to use mean.2 or mean.3 (or some other number) depends on: (a) the number of variables that are to be included in the index and (b) the amount of missing data. It is generally advisable to run the Compute command multiple times and examine the amount of missing that results with stricter (e.g., mean.3) or more lenient (e.g., mean.1) solutions.

Recode Command

The Recode command changes, rearranges, or consolidates the values of an existing variable. To illustrate the Recode command, consider the following example from the New Hampshire State Parks database. In this data set, the variable PARK originally had 10 values.

```
Frequencies Variables = PARK.
```

park   Park Visited

			Frequency	Percent	Valid Percent	Cumulative Percent
Valid	1	Monadnock Camp	30	10.0	10.0	10.0
	2	Moose Brook Camp	30	10.0	10.0	20.0
	3	Miller Day Use	30	10.0	10.0	30.0
	4	Mt Washington Day	30	10.0	10.0	40.0
	5	Hampton Beach	30	10.0	10.0	50.0
	6	Silver Lake Beach	30	10.0	10.0	60.0
	7	Robert Frost Hist	30	10.0	10.0	70.0
	8	Dan Webster Hist	30	10.0	10.0	80.0
	9	Franconia Flume	30	10.0	10.0	90.0
	10	Franconia Tram	30	10.0	10.0	100.0
	Total		300	100.0	100.0	

The first two parks (Monadnock and Moose Brook) referred to campgrounds (values = 1 and 2). The next two parks (Miller and Mt Washington) represented day use areas (values = 3 and 4). Parks coded as 5 (Hampton) and 6 (Silver Lake) were beaches. Robert Frost (value = 7) and Dan Webster (value = 8) were historic sites. The last two parks (Franconia Flume [value = 9] and Franconia Tramway [value = 10]) were attraction sites. Thirty respondents were obtained from each of these 10 parks.

A researcher might be interested in examining how individuals from these general categories of parks (i.e., campgrounds, day-use areas, beaches, historic sites, attraction areas) differed on each of the satisfaction statements (e.g., First impression, Helpfulness of the staff). To perform this analysis, the values on the PARK variable need to be collapsed into the more general categories using the Recode command.

```
Recode PARK (1,2  = 1)
            (3,4  = 2)
            (5,6  = 3)
            (7,8  = 4)
            (9,10 = 5).
```

> This Recode collapses specific parks into general park categories.

```
Value Labels PARK 1 'Campground'
                  2 'Day Use'
                  3 'Beach'
                  4 'Historic'
                  5 'Attraction'.
```

> Always add new value labels after recoding a variable.

Frequencies Variables = PARK.

> Always check the computations.

park   Park Visited

			Frequency	Percent	Valid Percent	Cumulative Percent
Valid	1	Campground	60	20.0	20.0	20.0
	2	Day Use	60	20.0	20.0	40.0
	3	Beach	60	20.0	20.0	60.0
	4	Historic	60	20.0	20.0	80.0
	5	Attraction	60	20.0	20.0	100.0
		Total	300	100.0	100.0	

The Recode statement collapsed specific parks into general categories of parks. There were two campgrounds: Monadnock ($n = 30$) and Moose Brook ($n = 30$). The number of cases for the recoded campground category should equal 60 (i.e., $30 + 30$). Running the FREQUENCIES provided a check on the accuracy of the Recode statement.

There are two ways to recode variables in SPSS: (a) into Same Variables... and (b) into Different Variables... (Figure 12.1). Recode commands can either be typed directly into a syntax window (as illustrated by the previous example) or specified via the menu system.

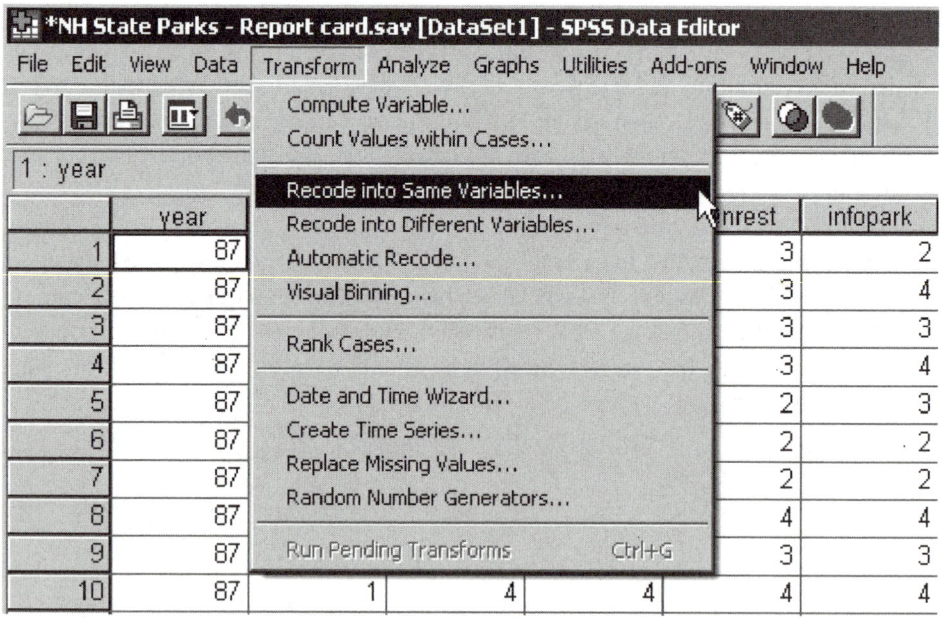

Figure 12.1   Selecting Recode from the Main SPSS Menu

The RECODE INTO SAME VARIABLES... dialog box reassigns the values of existing variables or collapses ranges of existing values into new values (See Figure 12.2). *A word of caution is necessary here.* If the researcher saves the data file after collapsing the specific parks into the general categories of parks, only the collapsed five-level version of the variable will exist in the data **and** there is no way to return to the original 10-level categorical variable.

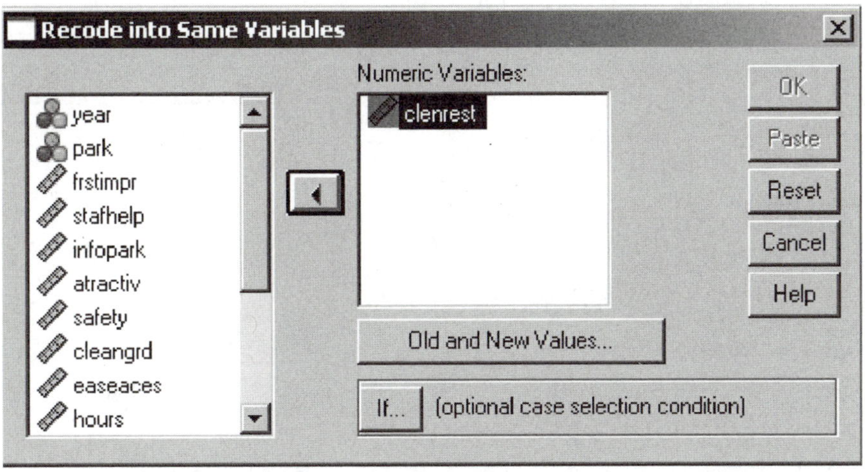

Figure 12.2   Recode into Same Variables Dialog Box

The RECODE INTO DIFFERENT VARIABLES… dialog box reassigns the values of existing variables or collapses ranges of existing values into new values for a *new variable* (Figure 12.3).

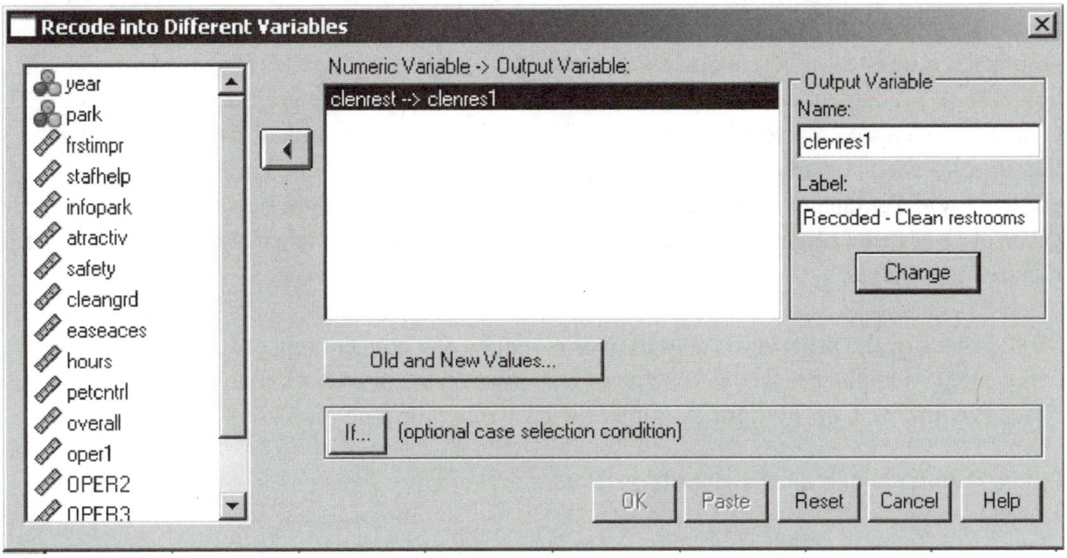

Figure 12.3   Recode into Different Variables Dialog Box

With either RECODE INTO SAME VARIABLES… or RECODE INTO DIFFERENT VARIABLES…, click the Old and New Values button to specify how to recode the values (Figure 12.4).

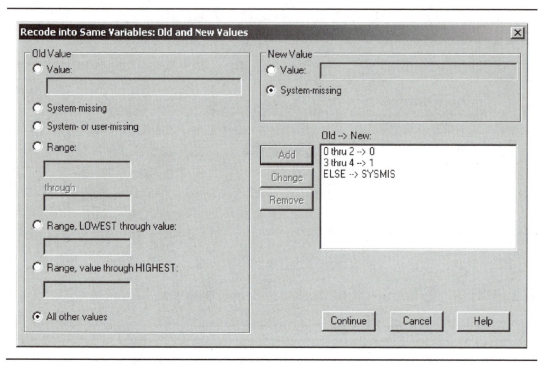

Figure 12.4   Specifying Values to Recode

Figures 12.2 through 12.4 used the Cleanliness of the Restroom (CLENREST) variable for illustration purposes. This satisfaction variable was originally coded: 4 = A, 3 = B, 2 = C, 1 = D, and 0 = F. The Recode statement collapses the continuous variable into a dichotomous variable where 0 = a response of C, D, or F, and 1 = A or B. Such a recode might of interest if the researcher is interested in how many respondents gave a "passing" grade. The word *passing*, however, is a judgment call. In many universities, a passing grade for graduate students is A or B. Graduate students who receive a C or less are considered to have "failed" the course. Changing the rules for what constitutes a passing grade will influence the results. For example, a passing grade for undergraduates who are taking courses in their major might be a C or better. A letter grade of D or better might be considered a passing grade for undergraduates in general university requirement courses.

More generally, the procedures used to operationalize any concept (e.g., satisfaction with an experience) will influence the distribution of responses on the indicator variables (e.g., Cleanliness of the Restroom). Consider, for example, the crowding variable discussed in chapter 4.

Did you feel crowded on the river today?

1	2	3	4	5	6	7	8	9
Not At All Crowded		Slightly Crowded			Moderately Crowded		Extremely Crowded	

Two of the nine scale points for this question label the situation as uncrowded (1 and 2), while the remaining seven points label it as crowded to some degree (3 through 9). When describing a wilderness experience, where the goal is to provide an opportunity for low-density recreation, researchers have traditionally collapsed the scale into a dichotomous variable (i.e., two categories — not crowded vs. some degree of crowding). This provides a conceptually meaningful break-point between those who label the situation as not at all crowded (scale points 1 and 2, a positive evaluation), and those who label the situation as slightly, moderately, or extremely crowded (scale points 3 through 9, a negative evaluation). When describing a frontcountry experience, however, individuals often accept, expect, and can tolerate higher densities of people. Collapsing the scale into not at all crowded versus some degree of crowding may be too strict a definition for what constitutes crowding in these situations. For frontcountry settings, the crowding scale might be collapsed into "not at all" or "slightly crowded" (scale points 1 through 4) versus "moderately or extremely crowded" (scale points 5 through 9; Vaske, Donnelly, & Petruzzi, 1996). If this variable is used to inform management standards regarding acceptable levels of crowding (Vaske & Shelby, 2008), the researchers' decision about how to recode the variable is likely to influence whether or not the resource in question has a crowding problem.

The original distribution for the Cleanliness of Restrooms (CLENREST) in the New Hampshire data set is shown below.

clenrest   Cleanliness of Restrooms

			Frequency	Percent	Valid Percent	Cumulative Percent
Valid	0	F	4	1.3	1.5	1.5
	1	D	23	7.7	8.6	10.0
	2	C	52	17.3	19.3	29.4
	3	B	78	26.0	29.0	58.4
	4	A	112	37.3	41.6	100.0
		Total	269	89.7	100.0	
Missing	9	No Response	31	10.3		
Total			300	100.0		

Recoding the variable such that 0 = C, D, or F, and 1 = A or B yields the following distribution. The rectangles and ovals have been added to the output to demonstrate that the correct values resulted from the RECODE command (i.e., 4 + 23 + 52 = 79 and 78 + 112 = 190). Note that the value labels have been changed based on the new values for this variable.

clenrest   Cleanliness of Restrooms

			Frequency	Percent	Valid Percent	Cumulative Percent
Valid	0	Fail	79	26.3	29.4	29.4
	1	Pass	190	63.3	70.6	100.0
		Total	269	89.7	100.0	
Missing		System	31	10.3		
Total			300	100.0		

The actual syntax of this recode might look like:

```
Recode CLENREST
        (0 thru 2 = 0)
        (3, 4     = 1)
        (ELSE = SYSMIS).
```

It is important to note that the Recode *syntax should not be run twice in the same SPSS session.* The top of Output 12.1 displays the distribution of the Cleanliness of the Restrooms variable after running the Recode syntax the first time. At this stage, the values associated with the variable are 0 and 1. Given the RECODE command instructs SPSS to collapse the values between 0 and 2 into 0, running the command a second time changes all of the values to 0.

Output 12.1   Caution: Do Not Run the Same Recode **Twice**

1st Recode

clenrest   Cleanliness of Restrooms

		Frequency	Percent	Valid Percent	Cumulative Percent
Valid	0 Fail	79	26.3	29.4	29.4
	1 Pass	190	63.3	70.6	100.0
	Total	269	89.7	100.0	
Missing	System	31	10.3		
Total		300	100.0		

2nd Recode

```
recode CLENREST (0 thru 2=0) (3 thru 4=1) (ELSE=SYSMIS).
```

clenrest   Cleanliness of Restrooms

		Frequency	Percent	Valid Percent	Cumulative Percent
Valid	0 Fail	269	89.7	100.0	100.0
Missing	System	31	10.3		
Total		300	100.0		

Select if Command

Using the PARK variable that was recoded into general categories (e.g., campgrounds, day-use areas) and the computed operations scale (OPER3), a researcher might ask the question: Are New Hampshire State Park campgrounds providing a quality experience in terms of visitor satisfaction with the operation of the park? There are multiple ways to examine this research question. For example, since PARK is a categorical level variable (5 levels) and OPER3 is a continuous level variable, a one-way analysis of variance could be run to compare the average scores among parks categories (chapter 15 discusses one-way analysis of variance). Alternatively, the researcher could select only people who visited campgrounds and run a FREQUENCIES analysis on the operations scale. The following illustrates the use of the Select if command.

```
Select if (PARK = 1).
```

Selects only respondents (cases) who visited campgrounds.

```
Frequencies Variables = OPER3 / statistics = mean median.
```

Statistics

OPER3

N	Valid	57
	Missing	3
Mean		3.3918
Median		3.6667

Consistent with the previous FREQUENCIES, 60 individuals are included in this analysis; 57 gave valid responses, 3 were missing

Frequencies

OPER3   Park operations grades

		Frequency	Percent	Valid Percent	Cumulative Percent
Valid	1.67	2	3.3	3.5	3.5
	2.00	3	5.0	5.3	8.8
	2.33	5	8.3	8.8	17.5
	2.67	2	3.3	3.5	21.1
	3.00	4	6.7	7.0	28.1
	3.33	7	11.7	12.3	40.4
	3.67	13	21.7	22.8	63.2
	4.00	21	35.0	36.8	100.0
	Total	57	95.0	100.0	
Missing	System	3	5.0		
Total		60	100.0		

There are several points to consider when looking at this output:

1. The analysis is based on 60 cases (respondents). This is consistent with the previous analyses showing 60 people in the sample had visited New Hampshire campgrounds.

2. Relatively few people ($n = 12$) gave a grade less than 3.00 (i.e., B). While this represents 21% of the sample, the overall sample size for campground visitors is relatively small ($n = 60$).

3. The mean score on the scale is 3.39, suggesting that, on average, respondents gave a grade of B for the operations aspect of New Hampshire State Parks campgrounds.

4. The median score is 3.67. This implies that half of the respondents rated campground operations as a B+ and half were below this grade.

5. The values for this variable range from 1.67 (i.e., D) to 4.00 (i.e., A).

6. When the three variables (i.e., CLENREST, CLEANGRD, HOURS) were combined, the values for the computed index reflect the continuous concept underlying the observed variables and cast further doubt on Stevens's (1951) assertion regarding the manipulation of social science data.

Putting It All Together: Columbia Icefield Examples

The goals of this section are to:

1. Show the connection between norm theory and research (chapters 2 and 3).

2. Test three hypotheses using two different statistical procedures (CROSSTABS and T-TESTS).

3. Illustrate the use of four SPSS data transformation commands:
   - `Compute`
   - `Temporary. Select if`
   - `Recode`
   - `If`

4. Demonstrate the process of converting SPSS printouts into journal-style tables.

Study Background

The importance of developing evaluative standards for judging the acceptability of impacts caused by recreation is common to all recent natural resource management frameworks (e.g., Visitor Impact Management – Kuss, Graefe, & Vaske, 1990). A normative model has been advanced as a useful way to conceptualize, collect and organize empirical data representing standards for resource management issues (Vaske & Whittaker, 2004). Most existing work has focused on backcountry areas with respondents from North America. The Columbia Icefield study provides data for examining encounter norms from a frontcountry experience (Vaske, Donnelly, Doctor, & Petruzzi, 1994).

The data were collected during the summer of 1993 at the Columbia Icefield; one of the most heavily visited day-use areas in Jasper National Park, Canada. Of the 425,000 Icefield visitors during 1990, 330,000 visited the adjacent Athabasca Glacier on one of the commercial Snocoach tours. Respondents to the one-page survey evaluated the Snocoach experience in terms of their perceptions of the number of visitors on the glacier (variable = CONTACTS), their tolerance limits for other visitors (variable = NORM), and their perceptions of crowding (variable = CROWDED). The survey also asked for the respondents' country of origin. To simplify the analyses, respondents were grouped into three broad categories (i.e., North America, Japan, and Europe). The question wording for these variables is shown in Box 12.2.

Hypotheses

1. The proportion of people reporting a norm varies among the countries of origin (i.e., North America, Japan, and Europe).

2. Among those who have an encounter norm, the median tolerance limit will vary by the countries of origin.

3. Among those who have an encounter norm, when contacts exceed the visitors' tolerance limits (i.e., norms), crowding will increase for each of the three countries of origin.

Each of these hypotheses are stated as "alternative" as opposed to "null" hypotheses (chapter 5).

Box 12.2   Columbia Icefield Survey Questions

1. While you were walking on the glacier at the turn-around point, about how many other **visitors** were within eyesight?

   I saw about _____ other visitors walking on the glacier at the turn-around point.

2. What is an acceptable number of other **visitors** to be within eyesight while you are walking on the glacier at the turn-around point?

   It is OK to have as many as _____ other visitors within eyesight while on the glacier.

   _____ It doesn't matter to me

3. Did you feel crowded by the number of visitors while you were walking on the glacier today?

1	2	3	4	5	6	7	8	9
Not At All Crowded		Slightly Crowded			Moderately Crowded		Extremely Crowded	

4. Where are you from?   Country: _____

Basic Descriptive Findings

```
FREQUENCIES  VARIABLES=country contacts norm crowded
                / STATISTICS=STDDEV MEAN
                / ORDER= VARIABLE .
```

country   Visitors' Country

			Frequency	Percent	Valid Percent	Cumulative Percent
Valid	1	North America	124	24.8	26.2	26.2
	2	Japan	234	46.7	49.5	75.7
	3	European	115	23.0	24.3	100.0
		Total	473	94.4	100.0	
Missing	9	Missing	28	5.6		
Total			501	100.0		

About half of the respondents were from Japan

CONTACTS Reported contacts with other visitors

Statistics

contacts   Reported contacts with other visitors

N	Valid	480
	Missing	21
Mean		121.03
Std. Deviation		67.462

contacts   Reported contacts with other visitors

		Frequency	Percent	Valid Percent	Cumulative Percent	
Valid	8	3	.6	.6	.6	Six individuals saw 10 or fewer other visitors.
	10	3	.6	.6	1.3	
	12	1	.2	.2	1.5	
	15	3	.6	.6	2.1	
	20	3	.6	.6	2.7	
	23	1	.2	.2	2.9	
	25	1	.2	.2	3.1	
	30	10	2.0	2.1	5.2	
	35	1	.2	.2	5.4	
	40	11	2.2	2.3	7.7	
	45	1	.2	.2	7.9	
	50	47	9.4	9.8	17.7	
	52	1	.2	.2	17.9	
	56	1	.2	.2	18.1	
	60	28	5.6	5.8	24.0	
	65	1	.2	.2	24.2	
	67	1	.2	.2	24.4	
	70	11	2.2	2.3	26.7	
	75	10	2.0	2.1	28.8	
	80	21	4.2	4.4	33.1	
	90	1	.2	.2	33.3	
	100	119	23.8	24.8	58.1	
	105	1	.2	.2	58.3	
	110	1	.2	.2	58.5	
	120	15	3.0	3.1	61.7	
	125	1	.2	.2	61.9	
	140	3	.6	.6	62.5	
	150	61	12.2	12.7	75.2	
	160	5	1.0	1.0	76.3	
	180	4	.8	.8	77.1	
	190	1	.2	.2	77.3	
	200	76	15.2	15.8	93.1	
	210	1	.2	.2	93.3	
	225	1	.2	.2	93.5	
	230	1	.2	.2	93.8	
	239	1	.2	.2	94.0	
	240	1	.2	.2	94.2	
	250	12	2.4	2.5	96.7	
	270	1	.2	.2	96.9	
	280	2	.4	.4	97.3	
	300	12	2.4	2.5	99.8	Thirteen individuals reported seeing 300 or more other visitors.
	400	1	.2	.2	100.0	
	Total	480	95.8	100.0		
Missing	System	21	4.2			
Total		501	100.0			

NORM Normative tolerance limit for seeing others

Statistics

norm   Normative tolerance limit for seeing others

N	Valid	467
	Missing	34
Mean		335.36
Std. Deviation		362.581

> The mean tolerance limit (NORM) is 335.36. This average, however, includes individuals who did not specify a norm (i.e., a value of 888). Consequently, this average is incorrect.

norm   Normative tolerance limit for seeing others

		Frequency	Percent	Valid Percent	Cumulative Percent
Valid	1	2	.4	.4	.4
	2	1	.2	.2	.6
	5	2	.4	.4	1.1
	9	1	.2	.2	1.3
	10	4	.8	.9	2.1
	15	1	.2	.2	2.4
	20	12	2.4	2.6	4.9
	25	2	.4	.4	5.4
	30	20	4.0	4.3	9.6
	40	4	.8	.9	10.5
	45	1	.2	.2	10.7
	50	66	13.2	14.1	24.8
	60	11	2.2	2.4	27.2
	70	4	.8	.9	28.1
	75	4	.8	.9	28.9
	79	1	.2	.2	29.1
	80	13	2.6	2.8	31.9
	90	1	.2	.2	32.1
	100	86	17.2	18.4	50.5
	120	3	.6	.6	51.2
	130	1	.2	.2	51.4
	140	1	.2	.2	51.6
	150	23	4.6	4.9	56.5
	160	2	.4	.4	57.0
	180	2	.4	.4	57.4
	200	43	8.6	9.2	66.6
	225	1	.2	.2	66.8
	250	5	1.0	1.1	67.9
	300	9	1.8	1.9	69.8
	400	1	.2	.2	70.0
	500	3	.6	.6	70.7
	888 No Norm	137	27.3	29.3	100.0
	Total	467	27.3	29.3	100.0
Missing	System	34	6.8		
Total		501	100.0		

> Two individuals indicated they could tolerate seeing only one other visitor.

> These individuals gave a numerical estimate of other people they could tolerate. In other words, they reported a "NORM."

> These individuals checked the response "It does not matter to me" for this survey item. In other words, they did not have a NORM for this situation.

CROWDED Perceived crowding

Statistics

crowded   Perceived crowding

N	Valid	470
	Missing	31
Mean		2.97
Std. Deviation		2.032

> For the crowding variable, an average score of 2.97 equals "Slightly crowded."

park   Park Visited

			Frequency	Percent	Valid Percent	Cumulative Percent
Valid	1	Not at all crowded	131	26.1	27.9	27.9
	2	Not at all crowded	115	23.0	24.5	52.3
	3	Slightly crowded	86	17.2	18.3	70.6
	4	Slightly crowded	47	9.4	10.0	80.6
	5	Moderately crowded	26	5.2	5.5	86.2
	6	Moderately crowded	30	6.0	6.4	92.6
	7	Moderately crowded	12	2.4	2.6	95.1
	8	Extremely crowded	13	2.6	2.8	97.9
	9	Extremely crowded	10	2.0	2.1	100.0
	Total		470	93.8	100.0	
Missing	System		31	6.2	100.0	
Total			501	100.0		

> Over half of the respondents said "Not at all crowded"

> Approximately 5% indicated "Extremely crowded"

Testing Hypothesis 1

H₁ The proportion of people reporting a norm varies among the countries of origin (i.e., North America, Japan, and Europe)

```
Recode NORM (1 thru 500 = 1)
             (888 = 0).
```

> To test the first hypothesis, the NORM variable must first be recoded into two categories (i.e., those who had a norm vs. those who did not).

```
Value labels NORM 0 'No Norm'
                  1 'Reported a norm'.
```

```
Frequencies Variables = NORM.
```

> Numbers are consistent with initial FREQUENCIES analysis.

norm   Normative tolerance limit for seeing others

		Frequency	Percent	Valid Percent	Cumulative Percent
Valid	0 No norm	137	27.3	29.3	29.3
	1 Reported a norm	330	65.9	70.7	100.0
	Total	467	93.2	100.0	
Missing	System	34	6.8		
Total		501	100.0		

```
Crosstabs COUNTRY by NORM
        /cells = count row
        /statistics = chisq.
```

> With the NORM variable recoded as a dichotomous level variable (reported a norm vs. did not), we now have one dichotomous and one categorical variable and the appropriate analysis strategy is a chi-square. In SPSS, the chi-square statistic is obtained from a CROSSTABS procedure (chapter 13).

country visitors' country* norm   Normative tolerance limit for seeing others Crosstabulation

			norm Normative tolerance limit for seeing others		Total
			0 No norm	1 Reported a norm	
country visitor's country	1 N. American	Count	50	59	109
		% within country visitors' country	45.9%	54.1%	100.0%
	2 Japan	Count	52	173	225
		% within country visitors' country	23.1%	76.9%	100.0%
	3 European	Count	22	85	107
		% within country visitors' country	20.6%	79.4%	100.0%
Total		Count	124	317	441
		% within country visitors' country	28.1%	71.9%	100.0%

> Row percents sum to 100 going across the table

Chi-Square Tests

	Value	df	Asymp. Sig. (2-sided)
Pearson Chi-Square	22.812[a]	2	.000
Likelihood Ratio	21.596	2	.000
Linear-by-Linear Association	17.206	1	.000
N of Valid Cases	441		

a. 0 cells (.0%) have expected count less than 5. The minimum expected count is 30.09.

> SPSS produces a variety of chi-square statistics. The differences in these statistics will be discussed in chapter 13.

When summarizing these findings for a journal article, the table might look like:

Table 12.1   Norm Existence by Country of Origin

	Reported Encounter Norm	
Country of Origin	Yes	No
North America	54%	46%
Europe	79	21
Japan	77	23

$\chi^2 = 21.60, p < .001$

Testing Hypothesis 2

H_2 Among those who have an encounter norm, the median tolerance limit will vary by the countries of origin.

Testing this hypothesis requires several steps:

1. Because the NORM variable was recoded into the same variable, the original data set must be reopened to get back to our initial values for the NORM variable.

2. Eliminate those individuals who did not specify a norm from the analysis. There are several ways to accomplish this task. One approach is shown below.

   ```
   Missing values NORM (888, 999).
   ```

3. Obtain the medians for each of the three countries or origin.

North America

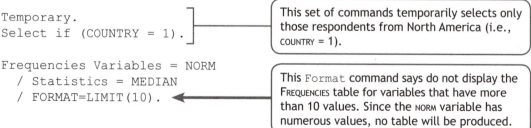

```
Temporary.
Select if (COUNTRY = 1).
```

> This set of commands temporarily selects only those respondents from North America (i.e., COUNTRY = 1).

```
Frequencies Variables = NORM
   / Statistics = MEDIAN
   / FORMAT=LIMIT(10).
```

> This Format command says do not display the FREQUENCIES table for variables that have more than 10 values. Since the NORM variable has numerous values, no table will be produced.

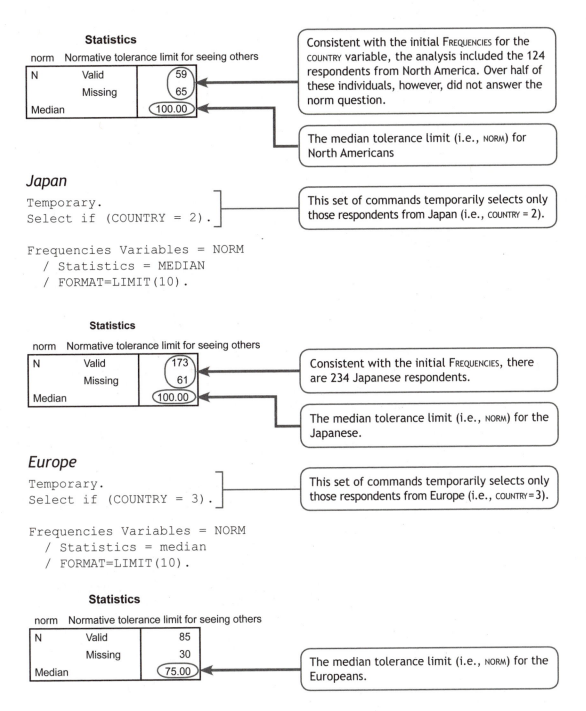

Statistics

norm Normative tolerance limit for seeing others

N	Valid	59
	Missing	65
Median		100.00

Consistent with the initial FREQUENCIES for the COUNTRY variable, the analysis included the 124 respondents from North America. Over half of these individuals, however, did not answer the norm question.

The median tolerance limit (i.e., NORM) for North Americans

Japan

```
Temporary.
Select if (COUNTRY = 2).

Frequencies Variables = NORM
  / Statistics = MEDIAN
  / FORMAT=LIMIT(10).
```

This set of commands temporarily selects only those respondents from Japan (i.e., COUNTRY = 2).

Statistics

norm Normative tolerance limit for seeing others

N	Valid	173
	Missing	61
Median		100.00

Consistent with the initial FREQUENCIES, there are 234 Japanese respondents.

The median tolerance limit (i.e., NORM) for the Japanese.

Europe

```
Temporary.
Select if (COUNTRY = 3).

Frequencies Variables = NORM
  / Statistics = median
  / FORMAT=LIMIT(10).
```

This set of commands temporarily selects only those respondents from Europe (i.e., COUNTRY = 3).

Statistics

norm Normative tolerance limit for seeing others

N	Valid	85
	Missing	30
Median		75.00

The median tolerance limit (i.e., NORM) for the Europeans.

The results of these three separate FREQUENCIES analyses (along with some additional statistics) are summarized in Table 12.2 (p. 306). Consistent with prior research (Donnelly, Vaske, Whittaker, & Shelby, 2000), the amount of missing data on these variables suggests that compared to backcountry visitors, frontcountry visitors are less likely to report a norm.

Table 12.2   Norm Tolerance Limits by Country of Origin

Country of Origin	Mean[1]	Median	Mode	Range
North America	99.07	100	100	1–250
Europe	95.53	75	50	5–500
Japan	114.57	100	100	2–500

[1] $F = 1.97$, $p < .14$

Testing Hypothesis 3

H_3 Among those who have an encounter norm, when contacts exceed the visitors' tolerance limits (norms), crowding will increase for each of the three countries of origin.

Testing this hypothesis again requires a series of data manipulation steps.

```
Recode NORM (888 = 999).
Missing values NORM (999).
```

> **Step 1:** Eliminates respondents who did not specify an encounter norm tolerance limit.

> **Step 2:** Computes a new variable for contrasting those who saw more than their norm versus those who saw less than or equal to their norm. This requires a series of sub-steps.

```
Compute CONTNORM = 9.
Missing Values CONTNORM (9).
Formats CONTNORM (F1).
```

> **Step 2a:** This sequence of commands computes the new variable (name = CONTNORM) and sets all of the values equal to 9, which are then declared to be missing. The Formats command sets the new variable's width to 1.

```
If (contacts le norm) CONTNORM = 0.
If (contacts gt norm) CONTNORM = 1.
```

> **Step 2b:** The values for the new variable (CONTNORM) are then selectively changed to either 0 or 1 (using If commands) depending on whether the person saw less than (or equal to) or greater than his/her norm.

```
Value Labels CONTNORM 0 'Saw LE Norm'
                      1 'Saw GT Norm'.
```

> **Step 2c:** These commands add value labels and variables labels.

```
Variable Labels CONTNORM 'Number of contacts versus norm tolerance'.
Frequencies variables = CONTNORM.
```

CONTNORM Number of contacts versus norm tolerance

		Frequency	Percent	Valid Percent	Cumulative Percent
Valid	0 Saw LE Norm	181	36.1	55.0	55.0
	1 Saw GT Norm	148	29.5	45.0	100.0
	Total	329	65.7	100.0	
Missing	9	172	34.3		
Total		501	100.0		

Step 3: The hypothesis suggests separate analyses for respondents from each of the three countries of origin. This can be accomplished through a series of `Temporary. Select if` commands.

Step 4: Given a dichotomous level independent variable (CONTNORM: saw less or equal to their norm vs. saw more than their norm) and a continuous level dependent variable, the appropriate analysis strategy is an independent samples *t*-test (chapter 14).

North America

```
Temporary.
Select if (COUNTRY = 1).
T-Test Groups CONTNORM (0,1)/ Variables = CROWDED.
```

T-Test

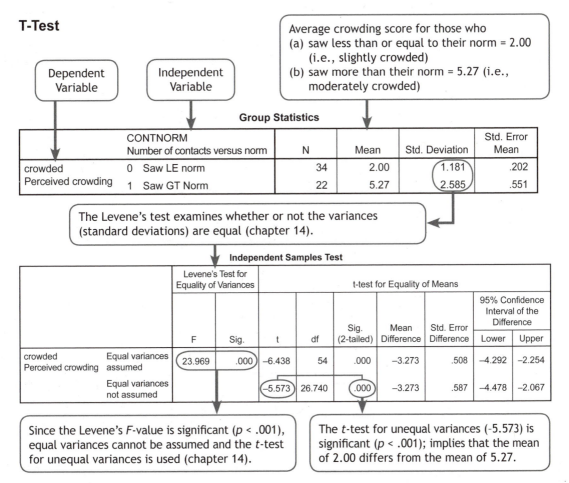

Dependent Variable

Independent Variable

Average crowding score for those who
(a) saw less than or equal to their norm = 2.00 (i.e., slightly crowded)
(b) saw more than their norm = 5.27 (i.e., moderately crowded)

Group Statistics

	CONTNORM Number of contacts versus norm	N	Mean	Std. Deviation	Std. Error Mean
crowded Perceived crowding	0 Saw LE norm	34	2.00	1.181	.202
	1 Saw GT Norm	22	5.27	2.585	.551

The Levene's test examines whether or not the variances (standard deviations) are equal (chapter 14).

Independent Samples Test

		Levene's Test for Equality of Variances		t-test for Equality of Means					95% Confidence Interval of the Difference	
		F	Sig.	t	df	Sig. (2-tailed)	Mean Difference	Std. Error Difference	Lower	Upper
crowded Perceived crowding	Equal variances assumed	23.969	.000	−6.438	54	.000	−3.273	.508	−4.292	−2.254
	Equal variances not assumed			−5.573	26.740	.000	−3.273	.587	−4.478	−2.067

Since the Levene's *F*-value is significant ($p < .001$), equal variances cannot be assumed and the *t*-test for unequal variances is used (chapter 14).

The *t*-test for unequal variances (−5.573) is significant ($p < .001$); implies that the mean of 2.00 differs from the mean of 5.27.

Japan

```
Temporary.
Select if (COUNTRY = 2).
T-Test Groups CONTNORM (0,1)/ Variables = CROWDED.
```

Group Statistics

	CONTNORM Number of contacts versus norm	N	Mean	Std. Deviation	Std. Error Mean
crowded Perceived crowding	0 Saw LE norm	92	2.32	1.016	.106
	1 Saw GT Norm	76	4.07	1.886	.216

Independent Samples Test

		Levene's Test for Equality of Variances		t-test for Equality of Means						
									95% Confidence Interval of the Difference	
		F	Sig.	t	df	Sig. (2-tailed)	Mean Difference	Std. Error Difference	Lower	Upper
crowded Perceived crowding	Equal variances assumed	28.355	.000	−7.663	166	.000	−1.751	.228	−2.202	−1.300
	Equal variances not assumed			−7.269	110.043	.000	−1.751	.241	−2.228	−1.273

Europe

```
Temporary.
Select if (COUNTRY = 3).
T-Test Groups CONTNORM (0,1)/ Variables = CROWDED.
```

Group Statistics

	CONTNORM Number of contacts versus norm	N	Mean	Std. Deviation	Std. Error Mean
crowded Perceived crowding	0 Saw LE norm	43	2.00	1.496	.228
	1 Saw GT Norm	36	5.11	2.572	.429

Independent Samples Test

		Levene's Test for Equality of Variances		t-test for Equality of Means						
									95% Confidence Interval of the Difference	
		F	Sig.	t	df	Sig. (2-tailed)	Mean Difference	Std. Error Difference	Lower	Upper
crowded Perceived crowding	Equal variances assumed	13.838	.000	−6.698	77	.000	−3.111	.465	−4.036	−2.186
	Equal variances not assumed			−6.407	54.022	.000	−3.111	.486	−4.085	−2.138

The findings from these *t*-tests are summarized in columns 4 through 6 of Table 12.3. As predicted by hypothesis 3, mean differences in perceived crowding were significantly higher for individuals indicating more contacts than their norm ($t > 5.57$, $p < .001$, for respondents from all three countries of origin). For those who saw fewer other visitors than their norm, the average crowding score was approximately 2 (i.e., not at all crowded). When encounters exceeded the norm tolerance limit, crowding increased to 4.07 or higher.

Table 12.3   Norms and Perceived Crowding by Country or Origin

Country of Origin	Reported Contacts Compared to Norm		Mean Crowding Scores		
	More Contacts	Fewer Contacts	More Contacts	Fewer Contacts	*t*-value
North America	39%	61%	5.27	2.00	5.57*
Japan	45	56	4.07	2.32	7.27*
Europe	48	52	5.11	2.00	6.41*

* *p* < .001

Although not asked for in hypothesis 3, Table 12.3 also shows the percentages of each group (i.e., countries of origin) who indicated more or fewer contacts than their norm (columns 2 and 3). These results were obtained from a crosstabulation (chapter 13).

```
CROSSTABS /TABLES=COUNTRY BY CONTNORM
          /FORMAT= AVALUE TABLES
          /CELLS= COUNT row.
```

country   visitors' country * CONTNORM Number of contacts versus norm tolerance Crosstabulation

			CONTNORM Number of contacts versus norm tolerance		
			0 Saw LE Norm	1 Saw GT Norm	Total
country visitors' country	1 North American	Count	36	23	59
		% within country visitors' country	61.0%	39.0%	100.0%
	2 Japan	Count	96	77	173
		% within country visitors' country	55.5%	44.5%	100.0%
	3 European	Count	44	40	84
		% within country visitors' country	52.4%	47.6%	100.0%
Total		Count	176	140	316
		% within country visitors' country	55.7%	44.3%	100.0%

Chapter Summary

This chapter illustrated the use of several data manipulation commands (e.g., `Compute`, `Recode`, `If`, `Select if`) using data from surveys of visitors to New Hampshire State Parks, and the Columbia Icefield in Jasper National Park, Canada. Specific hypotheses and research questions were advanced for each study to illustrate why the data manipulations were necessary.

The `Compute` command creates a new numeric variable. Three methods were described for computing summated rating scales. The first two methods assume that there are no missing data. Method 3 was the recommended approach because the researcher controls how much missing data will be tolerated. The general syntax for Method 3 is: `Compute newvar = mean.2(Var1,Var2,Var3)`. The number (e.g., 2) after the command `mean` (or `sum`) determines how many questions (variables) the respondent has to answer to be included in the computed index. The decision to use `mean.2` or `mean.3` (or some other number) depends on: (a) the number of variables that are to be included in the index and (b) the amount of missing data. It is generally advisable to run the `Compute` command multiple times and examine the amount of missing data that results with stricter (e.g., `mean.3`) or more lenient (e.g., `mean.2`) solutions. Although not illustrated here, `Compute` commands can be requested through dialog boxes in SPSS. Typing `Compute` commands directly into a syntax window, however, is often easier and is, therefore, the recommended approach.

The `Recode` command changes, rearranges, or consolidates the values of an existing variable. There are two ways to recode variables in SPSS: (a) **into Same Variables...** and (b) **into Different Variables...** . If the variables are recoded into the same variable, caution should be exercised when saving the data file because it is impossible to return to the variables' initial codes once the data have been recoded and saved. `Recode` commands can either be typed directly into a syntax window or specified via the menu system and dialog boxes. In most situations, a given set of `Recode` commands should only be run once during a given SPSS session. Running the same recodes a second time will recode the recoded values.

The `If` command conditionally executes a single transformation based upon the logical conditions found in the data. The transformation can create a new variable or modify the values of an existing variable for each case in the working data file.

The `Select if` command permanently selects cases (i.e., respondents) for analysis based upon logical conditions found in the data. The selection stays in effect for the duration of the analysis session or until a new data file is opened. If the data file is saved with the `Select if` in effect, only the selected cases will be saved. The `Temporary.` `Select if` command provides the same functionality as the `Select if` command, except the selection stays in effect only for the next command.

Other commonly used SPSS data transformation commands are outlined in Box 2.1 (pp. 313–314).

After running any of these data manipulation commands, the results should always be checked (e.g., a Frequencies analysis, List Cases) to verify that the transformation resulted in the desired outcome.

Data from a Columbia Icefield survey were used to: (a) show the connection between norm theory and research, (b) test three hypotheses using two different statistical procedures (CROSSTABS and T-TESTS), (c) illustrate the use of four SPSS data transformation commands (i.e., `Compute`, `Recode`, `Temporary. Select if`, and `If`), and (d) demonstrate the process of converting SPSS printouts into journal-style tables.

Review Questions

1. Describe the function of each of the following SPSS commands and give an example where each command may prove useful:
   - Compute
   - Count
   - Recode
   - If
   - Select if **versus** Temporary. Select if
   - Auto recode
   - Missing Values
   - Value Labels
   - Variable Labels
   - List

2. Why should caution be exercised when saving a file after recoding variables?

3. Why should the same Recode command not be run twice in a given SPSS analysis session?

Box 12.1	Commands in SPSS
Command	**Overview / Example**

Compute	Compute creates new numeric variables. Examples:
	`Compute newvar = mean.2(Var1,Var2,Var3).`
	`Compute Var4 = 9.`

Count	Count creates a numeric variable that, for each case, counts the occurrences of the same value (or list of values) across a list of variables. Examples:
	`Count cntscale = belief1 belief2 belief3 belief4 (1 thru 7).`
	`Count newvar = V1 V2 V3 (2).`

Recode	Recode changes, rearranges, or consolidates the values of an existing variable. Examples:
	`Recode Days (366 thru 999 = sysmis).`
	`Recode belief1 to belief4 (1,2 = 1) (3 = 2) (4,5 = 3).`

If	If conditionally executes a single transformation command based upon the logical conditions found in the data. The transformation can create a new variable or modify the values of an existing variable for each case in the working data file. Examples:
	`If (Sex = 1) pregnant = 8.`
	`If (age > 20 and sex = 1) group = 2.`

Select if	Select if permanently selects cases for analysis based upon logical conditions found in the data. The selection stays in effect for the duration of the analysis session or until a new data file is opened. (Note: If the data file is saved with the select if in effect, only the selected cases will be saved). Examples:
	`Select if (Park = 1).`
	`Select if (income gt 10000 or income le 25000).`

Temporary.
Select if
	Same as the above command, except the selection stays in effect only for the next command; for example:
	`Temporary.`
	`Select if (Park = 1).`
	`Frequencies variables = crowding / statistics = median.`
	`Temporary.`
	`Select if (Park = 2).`
	`Frequencies variables = crowding / statistics = median.`

Auto recode	Auto recode recodes the values of string variables to consecutive integers and puts the recoded values into a new variable called a *target variable*. The values of the original variable are used as value labels for the target variable. This is convenient when recoding, for example, states (e.g., CO, WY, UT) into regions of the country. Example: `Auto recode variables = state / into state1.`
	continued >>

Box 12.1 Commands in SPSS (continued)	
Command	**Overview / Example**
Mult Response	Example: A respondent on a survey is asked to identify three recreation activities he/she participated in during the last year. Some respondents may list canoeing first (variable = Activit1), others may list it second (variable = Activit2). As a researcher, it may not matter whether canoeing was listed first or second, but rather was it listed at all. Mult Response provides the capability to examine this latter type of situation. Format: Mult Response Groups = Activity (Activit1 to Activit3).
Missing values	Missing values declares values for numeric variables as *user missing*. These missing values are not included in the calculation of statistics. Up to three missing values can be defined for a given variable. Examples: Missing values Var1 (77, 88, 99). Missing values all (9).
Value labels	Value labels deletes all existing value labels for the specified variables and assigns new value labels. For example, new value labels should be added after variable(s) are recoded: Recode Var1 to Var5 (1,2 = 1) (3 = 2) (4,5 = 3). Value Labels Var1 to Var5 1 'Agree' 2 'Neutral' 3 'Disagree'.
Variable labels	Variable labels assigns descriptive labels to variables in the working data file. This is convenient when a new variable has been computed: Compute Expenses = sum(gas, food, lodge). Variable labels Expenses 'Sum of all trip expenses'.
List	List displays case values for variables in the working data file. This is convenient for checking computations. Example: List variables = Var1 Var2 Var3 Avgvar / cases from 1 to 50.
Sample	Sample draws a random sample of cases for processing in all subsequent procedures. The following example randomly selects 400 cases (e.g., individuals) from a larger data file containing 3420 cases. Sample 400 from 3420. This next command samples approximately 25% of the cases in the data file. Sample .25.

13

crosstabulations

A *crosstabulation* (a.k.a. *contingency table*) is a joint frequency distribution of cases based on two or more variables. This chapter focuses on contingency table analysis using the SPSS CROSSTABS procedure. A CROSSTABS computes two-way to *n*-way crosstabulation tables, tests of significance, and effect size measures. The CROSSTABS procedure is appropriate when the variables are dichotomous or categorical. Crosstabs are **not** appropriate for continuous level variables.

Bivariate Crosstabulations

Consider the following hypothetical bivariate example. A researcher might be interested in whether individuals who are of college age (18–24 years old) differ from older individuals (25+) in their support or opposition to an environmental program. Both of these variables are measured at the dichotomous level. In Table 13.1, age is the column variable and attitude toward the environmental program (support vs. opposition) is the row variable. The cells of the table contain the number and percent of individuals who are in each of the respective categories (e.g., 18–24 years old and support the program, 25+ and oppose the program).

Table 13.2 shows the same two variables with the order reversed. Support or opposition to the environmental program is now the column variable and age is the row variable.

The order in which variables are displayed (i.e., environmental program support by age vs. age by environmental program support) is in some ways irrelevant. For example, the order will

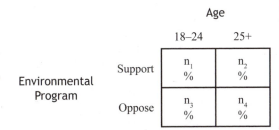

Table 13.1
Environmental Program Support by Age

	Age 18–24	Age 25+
Environmental Program / Support	n_1 %	n_2 %
Environmental Program / Oppose	n_3 %	n_4 %

Table 13.2
Age by Environmental Program Support

	Environmental Program Support	Environmental Program Oppose
Age 18–24	n_1 %	n_2 %
Age 25+	n_3 %	n_4 %

not influence the *n*s in each of the cells (i.e., n_1, n_2, n_3, n_4), nor will it affect the calculation of the test statistic (i.e., chi-square or symbolically, χ^2). The order of variable specification, however, is important for determining what percentages should be computed. In other words, should the percentages sum to 100 down the column, or should the percents sum to 100 across the rows? More generally, the order of variable specification in a contingency table influences what research question is asked. For example, if column percentages are calculated, the research question in Table 13.1 is: what percent of college age individuals compared to older individuals support the environmental program? If column percents are computed for Table 13.2, the research question becomes: what percent of environmental program supporters are college age individuals as opposed to older people?

Although either question is legitimate, Table 13.1 is more logical. Age might influence support or opposition for the environmental program. Support (or opposition) for the environmental program cannot influence the person's age. In this sense, age can be thought of as the ***independent variable***, whereas the support for the environmental program is the ***dependent variable***. To differentiate the independent from the dependent variable, remember that:

- The dependent variable depends on the other variable.

- The independent variable does not depend on the other variable; it goes its own way, independently.

As a general rule of thumb, the independent variable should be the column variable. In this situation, column percentages are computed.

n-way Crosstabulations

Tables 13.1 and 13.2 are two-way contingency tables. If other variables are included in the analysis, the analysis becomes an *n*-way crosstabulation. For example, the respondents' sex (male vs. female) might influence the relationship between support for the environmental program and age. Instead of a single table, two partial tables or ***subtables*** are analyzed (Table 13.3).

Table 13.3   Environmental Program by Age by Sex

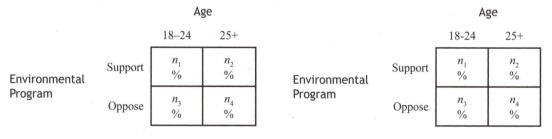

When a table is split into a separate subtable for each category of a third variable, the third variable is called a ***control***. In this example, sex is the control variable. Controlling for variables is an important concept that applies to a variety of data analysis strategies (e.g., analysis of variance, regression). The primary interest in this analysis is the relationship between attitude toward the environmental program and age, but the third variable (SEX) was suspected to influence this relationship. The impact of this third variable in the crosstabulation is controlled by producing a separate subtable of the main relationship (i.e., environmental program by age) for each category of the control variable (i.e., SEX). Even if sex affects the main relationship, it does not affect it in the subtables because everyone in a subtable is the same sex.

Subtables could be constructed for several control variables (e.g., sex, education, income). Such a large table, however, would be difficult to read and interpret, especially since most of the cells would have few respondents. SPSS allows for as many as ten of these classifications, but whenever another variable is included, the same number of respondents are split into more and more cells. Building subtables is most useful when there are a small number of variables that will be examined simultaneously, and there are a large number of respondents.

Crosstabulation Statistics

Although examination of the percentages in a crosstabulation is a useful first step in examining the relationship between variables, the percentages do not test the statistical significance of the relationship or measure the strength of the association (i.e., the effect size, chapter 6).

The Chi-square Test of Independence

The ***Pearson chi-square*** (χ^2) is often used to test the hypothesis that the row and column variables are independent of each other. The χ^2 test for independence evaluates statistically significant differences between proportions for two or more groups. The test statistic compares the ***observed*** cell counts (i.e., frequencies) against what would be ***expected*** if no relationship is evident given the row and column totals. The formula for the χ^2 test of independence is:

$$\chi^2 = \sum \frac{(f_o - f_e)^2}{f_e}$$

Equation 13.1

where:

f_o = the observed frequency in each cell
f_e = the expected frequency for each cell

Small deviations between the observed and expected counts produce a small chi-square value and suggest that the relationship can be attributed to chance. As the deviations between the observed and expected counts increase, the distributions are likely to differ statistically. The greater the discrepancies between the actual (i.e., observed) and expected cell frequencies, the larger the chi-square.

Table 13.4 (p. 318) gives a hypothetical example of observed counts for the attitude toward the environmental program by age. The ***null*** and ***alternative*** hypotheses are:

H_0 College age individuals do not differ from older individuals in their support for the environmental program.

H$_1$ College age individuals differ from older individuals in their support for the environmental program.

Table 13.4   Observed Counts (Frequencies) Between Environmental Program Support and Age

		Age		
		18–24	25+	Total
Environmental Program	Support	126	99	225
	Oppose	71	162	233
	Total	197	261	458

The sample includes 458 respondents. Of these, 225 supported the environmental program and 233 opposed the program. These observed counts (i.e., 225 and 233) are the row totals or marginals in the matrix. The word ***marginals*** simply means that the totals are in the margins of the table. The observed column marginals are 197 and 261 for the 18–24 and 25+ age groups, respectively.

To obtain the expected counts in a 2×2 contingency table, label each of the cells and marginals with letters (Table 13.5).

Table 13.5   Generalized Procedure for Computing Expected Counts

		Age		
		18–24	25+	Total
Environmental Program	Support	a	b	a + b
	Oppose	c	d	c + d
	Total	a + c	b + d	N

For a 2×2 matrix, the expected counts can be computed by multiplying the two marginals corresponding to a cell in question and dividing by N. The expected counts for each cell in this example would be:

Cell a = $(a + b)(a + c) / N$ = $(225)(197) / 458$ =   96.8
Cell b = $(a + b)(b + d) / N$ = $(225)(261) / 458$ = 128.2
Cell c = $(c + d)(a + c) / N$ = $(233)(197) / 458$ = 100.2
Cell d = $(c + d)(b + d) / N$ = $(233)(261) / 458$ = 132.8

The expected counts computations assume that the variables are unrelated, whereas the observed counts indicate the extent to which this assumption is violated. If two variables are statistically independent, knowing the value of one does not facilitate predicting the other. For example, if the observed and expected counts were exactly equal, knowing a person's age group (i.e., 18–24 vs. 25+) would not help in predicting his or her attitude toward the environmental program. By convention, the expected cell counts are shown in parentheses below the observed counts (Table 13.6).

Table 13.6   Observed and Expected Counts between Environmental Program Support and Age

		Age[1]		
		18–24	25+	Total
Environmental Program	Support	126 (96.8)	99 (128.2)	225
	Oppose	71 (100.2)	162 (132.8)	233
	Total	197	261	458

[1.] Cell entries are observed and expected counts. The expected counts are in parentheses.

If no relationship exists between the attitude and age in the sample data, any deviations from the expected values that occur in the table are based on chance. Although some small deviations can be reasonably expected due to chance, large deviations (i.e., large values of chi-square) are unlikely. Given that the researcher only has a sample of respondents, the actual relationship in the population is unknown. Small values of chi-square are interpreted to indicate the absence of a relationship in the population, often referred to as *statistical independence*. A large chi-square implies that a systematic or statistical relationship exists between the variables.

Using Equation 13.1 and the observed and expected counts in Table 13.6, the computations for a Pearson χ^2 are shown in Table 13.7. In a 2×2 matrix, the $f_o - f_e$ will always have the same numerical value, but this does not hold in general. Squaring this difference eliminates any negative values. The denominator in Equation 13.1 is the expected frequencies (f_e) and not the observed frequencies (f_o). The observed frequencies will vary from sample to sample and in some cases may be zero. Based on these computations, the Pearson $\chi^2 = 30.389$.

Table 13.7   Computing the Pearson x^2

Cell	Observed Frequency f_o	Expected Frequency f_e	Observed - Expected $(f_o - f_e)$	Observed - Expected)[2] $(f_o - f_e)^2$	$(f_o - f_e)^2 / f_e$
a	126	96.8	29.2	852.6	8.810
b	99	128.2	−29.2	852.6	6.650
c	71	100.2	−29.2	852.6	8.508
d	162	132.8	29.2	852.6	6.421
N	458	458			$\chi^2 = 30.389$

To determine the statistical significance of the relationship between the attitude toward the environmental program and age, the *computed chi-square* (i.e., 30.389) is compared against the *critical value* (chapter 6) from the *theoretical chi-square distribution*. This comparison produces an estimate of how likely or unlikely (i.e., the *p*-value) this calculated value is if the two variables are in fact independent. The *p-value* is the probability of obtaining a value of chi-square as large or larger than the one calculated from the sample. This depends, in part, on the degrees of freedom. In a crosstabulation, ***degrees of freedom*** refers to the number of cells in a table that can be *arbitrarily* filled, when the row and column totals (marginals) are fixed before the numbers in the remaining cells are determined (Box 13.1). The degrees of freedom vary with the number of rows and columns in the table and are important because the probability of obtaining a specific chi-square value depends on the number of cells in the table. In general, degrees of freedom for an $r \times c$ *table* (row-by-column table) are calculated as:

$$df = (r - 1) \times (c - 1)$$

In a 2 x 2 table, the degrees of freedom are:

$$df = (2 - 1) \times (2 - 1) = 1$$

Box 13.1   Understanding Degrees of Freedom (*df*)

The degrees of freedom in a crosstabulation are defined as the number of cells in a table that can be *arbitrarily* filled, when the row and column totals (marginals) are fixed, before the numbers in the remaining cells are determined. Consider the following 2x2 table. The column marginals are 200 and 500. The row marginals are 400 and 300.

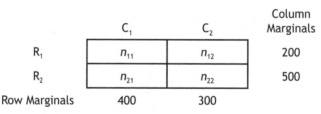

For a 2x2 table, there is only 1 degree of freedom ($df = [2 - 1] \times [2 - 1]$), because once one cell is filled, frequencies in the remaining row and column cells must be chosen so that the marginal totals are maintained. For example, if $n_{11} = 100$, n_{21} must $= 300$, n_{22} must $= 200$, and $n_{12} = 100$.

The theoretical chi-square distribution estimates the probability that two variables are statistically related for different degrees of freedom and levels of significance (e.g., .05, .01, .001). Statistics and methodology books often include tables of these theoretical chi-square values. A portion of that table is shown in Table 13.8. To illustrate the mechanics of using this table, a chi-square of at least 6.635 would be expected by chance 1% of the time ($p < .01$). If the calculated value of the chi-square is larger than this theoretical value (6.635), the relationship is statistically significant at $p < .01$.

Table 13.8   Theoretical Distribution of Chi-square[1]

	\multicolumn{4}{c}{Probability (Significance Level)}			
df	.10	.05	.01	.001
1	2.706	3.841	6.635	10.827
2	4.605	5.991	9.210	13.815
3	6.251	7.815	11.341	16.268

[1.]   Tables similar to this can be found in the back of most statistics books. The table shows a portion of the *df* and significance levels associated with the chi-square distribution.

The Pearson chi-square calculated for the relationship between attitude toward the environmental program and age was 30.389. The probability of obtaining a chi-square of this magnitude is less than .001 (Table 13.8), because 30.389 is greater than the theoretical value (10.827) at the .001 significance level. This finding would be reported by saying that the relationship is statistically significant at the $p < .001$ level. Because it is so improbable that the observed relationship could have resulted from sampling error alone, the null hypothesis (i.e., no relationship) is rejected, and a statistical relationship is assumed to exist between the two variables in the population.

Similar to other statistical tests (e.g., t, F), the calculated value of the χ^2 is compared to the value in the theoretical chi-square distribution. Statistical programs like SPSS eliminate the need for looking up theoretical values in tables like Table 13.8 when comparing the computed test statistic against the critical values. SPSS does the comparison and reports the ***actual observed significance level***. SPSS labels this p-value "**Sig.**" This Sig. level is the probability of a Type-I error or the probability of rejecting the null hypothesis when it is actually true (chapter 6). For any specific statistic (e.g., χ^2, t, F), if the Sig. or p is small (.05, .01, .001), the finding is *statistically* significant and the null hypothesis is rejected.

Significance tests provide a yardstick for estimating the significance of differences and/or associations between variables. They assist in ruling out relationships that do not represent genuine relationships in the population under study. There are, however, at least three cautionary notes that are important to emphasize in regard to the interpretation of tests of significance. First, significance tests make sampling assumptions that are often not satisfied by the actual sampling design. Second, tests of significance depend on the absence of nonsampling errors—a questionable assumption in some empirical studies. Third, statistical significance is often incorrectly interpreted as "strength of association" or "practical significance" (see chapter 6 on effect size).

This latter point is especially true for chi-square statistics because the χ^2 is heavily influenced by sample size. If the ***proportions in the cells remain unchanged***, chi-square varies directly with the number of survey respondents. If the number of respondents doubles, the chi-square doubles. If the sample size is tripled, the chi-square triples. More generally, if the number of respondents increases by a factor of k, the value of the chi-square is k times larger.

Consider the results obtained from two hypothetical studies examining the relationship between attitude toward the environmental program and sex (Table 13.9). Study 1 had a sample size of 100, whereas the sample size for study 2 was 10,000 (i.e., 100 times larger). In both studies, 52% of the males and 48% of the females supported the environmental program. The chi-square for study 1, however, was .16 (i.e., not significant); the chi-square for study 2 was 16.0, (i.e., significant, see Table 13.8).

Table 13.9   Two Hypothetical Studies Illustrating the Impact of Sample Size on Chi-square [1]

Environmental Program	Study 1		Study 2	
	Males	Females	Males	Females
Support	26	24	2,600	2,400
Oppose	24	26	2,400	2,600
χ^2	.16		16.0*	

[1.] Cell entries are observed counts;   * $p < .001$ (see Table 13.8)

A difference may be statistically significant without being significant in any other sense. Tests of statistical significance are **not** tests of practical significance. Practical significance means that an observed association is strong, important, and meaningful. Although there are no objective tests of substantive significance, effect sizes are commonly reported as one indicator of practical significance.

Effect Sizes in Crosstabulations

The statistics that are used to quantify the strength of the relationship between two variables in a crosstabulation are called **measures of association** in SPSS, or more generally, **effect sizes** (see also chapter 6). A variety of different measures of association exist because there are different ways to define association. The measures differ in their interpretation and how they define perfect and intermediate levels of association. For dichotomous and categorical data, two general categories of effect sizes exist: (a) measures of proportional reduction in error (a.k.a., PRE measures), and (b) measures based on chi-square.

Effect size measures based on proportional reduction in error (PRE) were introduced by Goodman and Kruskal (1954). All of these measures essentially compare two error rates: (a) the error when one variable is used to predict the values of another, and (b) the error when no additional information is available. The general formula of a PRE measure is:

$$\text{PRE coefficient} = \frac{\text{Error without X} - \text{Error with X}}{\text{Error without X}}$$

Equation 13.2

PRE coefficients have a clear interpretation. Goodman and Kruskal's **lambda (λ)**, for example, always ranges between 0 and 1. A value of 0 implies that the independent variable provides no assistance in predicting the dependent variable. A value of 1 means that the independent variable perfectly predicts the categories of the dependent measure. As an illustration, a λ of .40 implies a 40% reduction in error when the independent variable is used to predict a dependent variable.

Effect size measures based on chi-square attempt to modify the statistic to eliminate the influence of sample size. In general, the values of these measures range from 0 to 1 (a value of 0 corresponds to no association; a value of 1 corresponds to perfect association). Normalizing the coefficients to fall within the 0 to 1 range allows for comparisons of chi-square values from contingency tables with different sample sizes and different dimensions. The larger the absolute value of these measures, the stronger the relationship. Three common chi-square–based measures of association are: the phi (ϕ) coefficient, Cramer's V, and the contingency coefficient. Each of these measures is discussed below.

In a 2×2 crosstabulation, the appropriate effect size is **phi (ϕ)**:

$$\phi = \sqrt{\frac{\chi^2}{N}}$$

Equation 13.3

In general, values of ϕ range between 0 and 1. If a table has more than two rows or two columns, however, ϕ can be greater than 1 — an undesirable result.

In the attitude toward the environmental program by age group example, the $\chi^2 = 30.389$ and sample size $= 458$, so $\phi = .258$.

$$\phi = \sqrt{\frac{\chi^2}{N}} = \sqrt{\frac{30.389}{458}} = .258$$

Phi is a product-moment correlation (chapter 16) and, as an effect size, is interpreted the same as Pearson r (Cohen, 1988). As discussed in chapter 6, a phi of .258 would be interpreted as somewhere between a "minimal" (i.e., $\phi = .1$) and a "typical" (i.e., $\phi = .3$) relationship. If phi is greater than .5, the relationship is interpreted as "substantial."

Cramer's V measures the strength of association between of two categorical variables when one or both of the variables have three or more levels. Cramer's V ranges between 0 and 1 and can attain a value of 1 for tables of any dimension. The formula for a Cramer's V is:

$$V = \sqrt{\frac{\chi^2}{N(k-1)}}$$

Equation 13.4

where:
    k is the smaller of the number of rows and columns

Applied to the attitude toward the environment by age example, the Cramer's V is:

$$V = \sqrt{\frac{30.389}{458\,(2-1)}} = .258$$

In a 2 x 2 table, the phi and Cramer's V coefficient will always be the same.

The **contingency coefficient (C)** is appropriate for two categorical variables. The values of this coefficient always ranges between 0 and 1, but can never attain a value of 1. The largest value depends on the number of rows and columns in the table. In a 4 x 4 table, for example, the largest possible C coefficient is .87. The formula for this chi-squared–based contingency coefficient is:

$$C = \sqrt{\frac{\chi^2}{\chi^2 + N}}$$

Equation 13.5

Applied to the above example, the resulting C coefficient is:

$$C = \sqrt{\frac{30.389}{30.389 + 458}} = .249$$

Different effect size measures produce different estimates of the strength of association. In a crosstabulation, the choice of one effect size over another depends on the dimensions of the table. A phi, for example, is appropriate for a 2 x 2 table. A Cramer's V is appropriate for larger tables (e.g., 2 x 3, 3 x 5). *Do not simply select the effect size that gives the largest value.*

Crosstabulations in SPSS

The New Hampshire State Parks Report Card data file (chapter 10) will be used to illustrate the CROSSTABS procedure in SPSS. To obtain a crosstabulation of two or more variables the four basic steps in conducting statistical analysis discussed in chapter 9 apply:

1. Open the data file: NH - State Parks - Report card.sav
   (see chapter 9 – Introduction to SPSS – for assistance in opening a data file)

2. Click on: **Analyze > Descriptive Statistics > Crosstabs...**   See Figure 13.1

3. Select the variables to be included in the analysis   See Figure 13.2

4. Select additional statistical procedures   See Figures 13.3 through 13.5

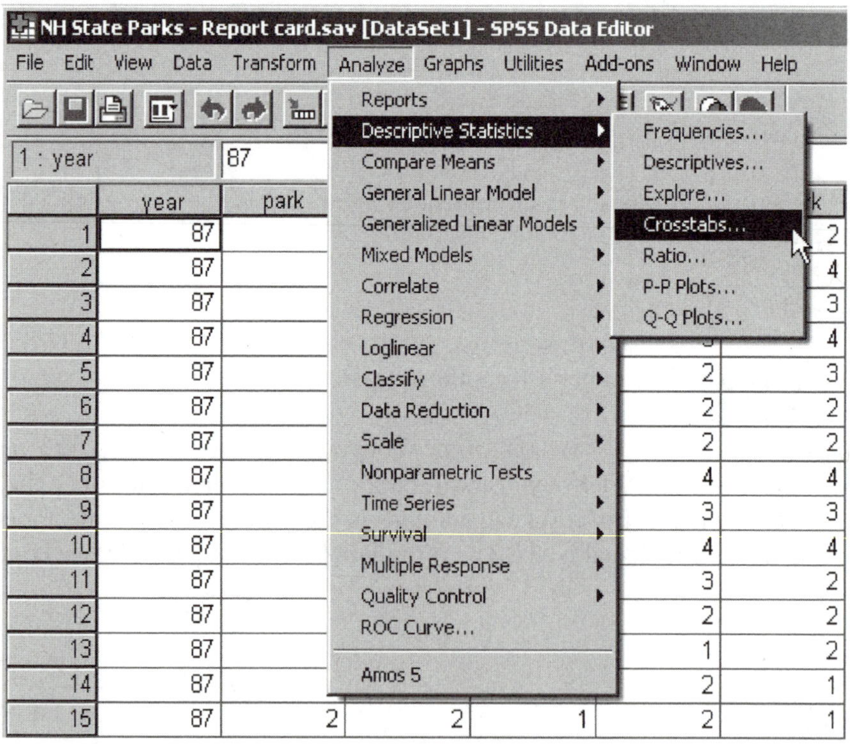

Figure 13.1   Selecting the SPSS Crosstabs Procedure

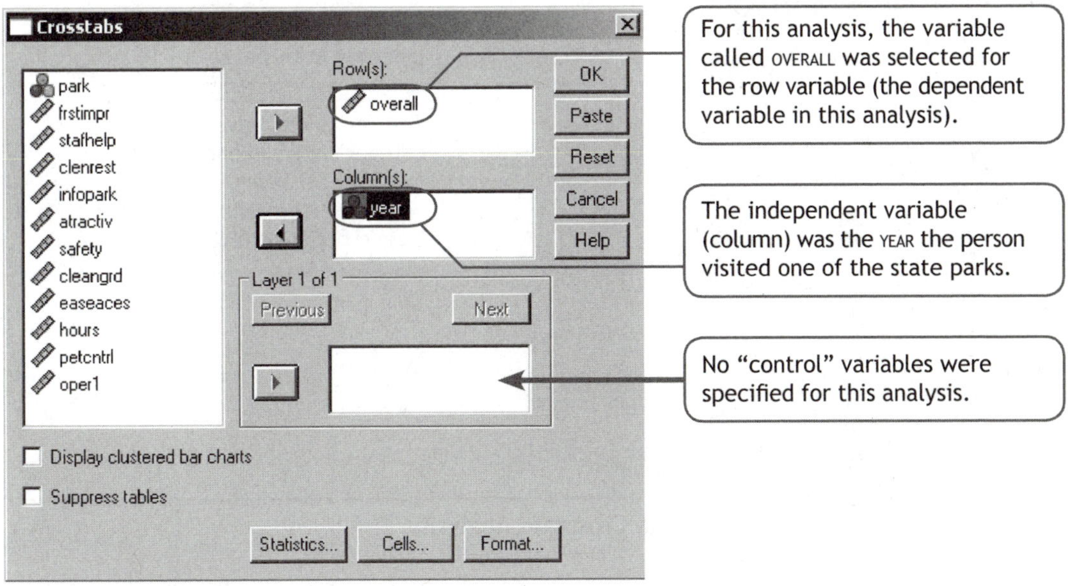

Figure 13.2   Selecting Variables for a Crosstabs Analysis

The overall satisfaction variable (OVERALL) is the dependent variable and the year the respondent visited the state park (YEAR) is the independent variable. Due to management changes in the years the data were collected, it is reasonable to assume that YEAR influences the respondents' satisfaction. A person's satisfaction, however, cannot influence the year of the trip.

For this analysis, overall satisfaction was recoded into a dichotomous variable where a 0 implies that the respondent gave a "failing" grade (i.e., F, D, C) and 1 equals a "passing" grade (i.e., B, A). As discussed in chapter 12, operationalizing satisfaction with this set of recodes is a researcher-based judgment call.

The YEAR variable might be considered a continuous variable given that the values could theoretically span a wide range of years. The New Hampshire data set, however, only includes the years 1987, 1988, and 1989. Chapter 5 defined a continuous variable as: (a) an *ordered* variable with at least five levels, and (b) a distribution that is approximately normally distributed in the population sampled. Given that the YEAR variable in this exercise has only three levels, YEAR will be considered a categorical variable. Because the YEAR variable represents three separate studies, it could have been named STUDY, with value labels of study 1, study 2, and study 3. The name YEAR was chosen because it has a more intuitive meaning.

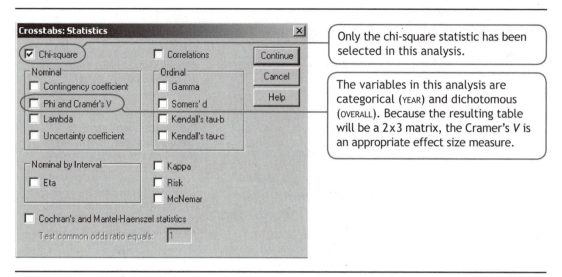

Only the chi-square statistic has been selected in this analysis.

The variables in this analysis are categorical (YEAR) and dichotomous (OVERALL). Because the resulting table will be a 2×3 matrix, the Cramer's *V* is an appropriate effect size measure.

Figure 13.3   Selecting Statistics for a Crosstabs Analysis

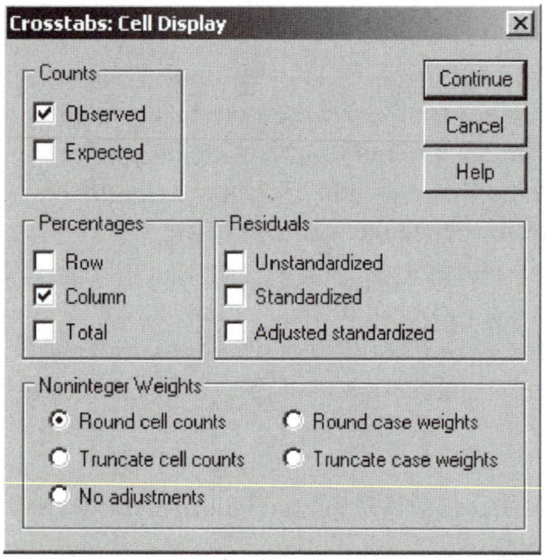

Figure 13.4   Selecting the Cells of the Crosstab Matrix

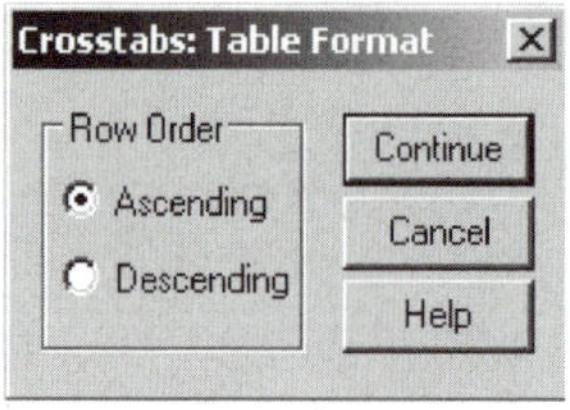

Figure 13.5   Crosstabs Format Dialog Box

With the variables and statistics selected for the analysis, the next step is to specify what should be included in the cells of the crosstabulation matrix (Figure 13.4). Of interest is the number and percent of respondents who reported a passing or failing grade *for each year* (the independent variable). Check the "observed" count and the "column" percent, and then click the Continue button.

The Format button on the main CROSSTABS dialog box (Figure 13.2) controls how the output will be presented (Figure 13.5). The default for this option is "Ascending" order for the values of the row variable (i.e., OVERALL). This means that the lowest values (i.e., 0 or a failing grade) will be presented first and the highest values (i.e., 1 or a passing grade) will be presented last.

Click the Continue button and main dialog box appears (Figure 13.2). At this point, click the Paste button and SPSS generates the CROSSTABS syntax in Figure 13.6. Figure 13.6 also shows the syntax for recoding the overall satisfaction variable and adds new value labels for the recoded variable. Run the analysis by highlighting the commands and clicking the Run button. Output 13.1 shows the results.

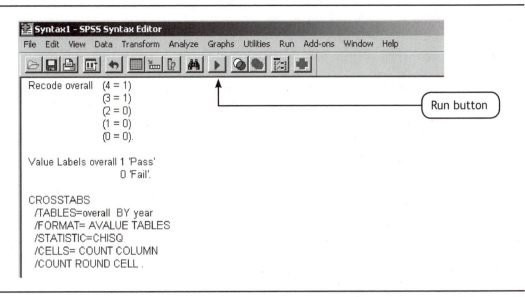

Figure 13.6   SPSS Syntax for Running a Crosstabs with Overall Satisfaction Recoded

Output 13.1a   Crosstabs: Overall Satisfacton by Year of Visit

Case Processing Summary

	Cases					
	Valid		Missing		Total	
	N	Percent	N	Percent	N	Percent
overall Overall Satisfaction * year Year of Visit	291	97.0%	9	3.0%	300	100.0%

For the combination of these two variables, 291 respondents (97%) gave valid answers (i.e., 0 or 1) to the question about overall satisfaction; 9 individuals (3%) were excluded from the analysis.

A value for the variable YEAR

overall   Overall Satisfaction * year Year of Visit Crosstabulation

A value label

			year Year of Visit			
			87 1987	88 1988	89 1989	Total
overall Overall Satisfaction	0 Fail	Count	33	14	9	56
		% within year Year of Visit	33.3%	14.9%	9.2%	19.2%
	1 Pass	Count	66	80	89	235
		% within year Year of Visit	66.7%	85.1%	90.8%	80.8%
Total		Count	99	94	98	291
		% within year Year of Visit	100.0%	100.0%	100.0%	100.0%

The dependent variable in this analysis

Because "column" percents were requested, percentages sum to 100 going down the table.

The Total observed counts (marginals) vary due to missing data.

The crosstabulation table indicates that the percent of respondents giving a passing grade increased from 66.7% in 1987, to 85.1% in 1988, and to 90.8% in 1989. The chi-square statistic can be used to determine whether these distributions differ statistically (Output 13.1b).

Output 13.1b   Chi-square: Overall satisfaction by Year of Visit

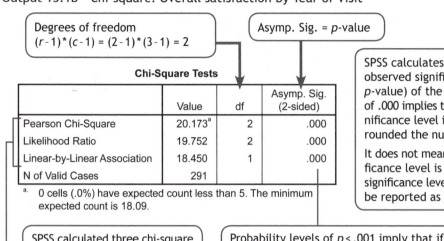

Degrees of freedom
$(r-1)*(c-1) = (2-1)*(3-1) = 2$

Asymp. Sig. = *p*-value

Chi-Square Tests

	Value	df	Asymp. Sig. (2-sided)
Pearson Chi-Square	20.173[a]	2	.000
Likelihood Ratio	19.752	2	.000
Linear-by-Linear Association	18.450	1	.000
N of Valid Cases	291		

a.   0 cells (.0%) have expected count less than 5. The minimum expected count is 18.09.

SPSS calculates the actual observed significance level (or *p*-value) of the test. A *p*-value of .000 implies the observed significance level is < .0005 (SPSS rounded the number to .000). It does not mean that the significance level is 0. An observed significance level of .000 should be reported as *p* < .001.

SPSS calculated three chi-square statistics (see Understanding Chi-Square Statistics in SPSS).

Probability levels of *p* < .001 imply that if the null hypothesis (H_0) is true, chi-squares as large as these would be expected less than 1 time in a 1,000 (Reject the H_0)

Understanding Chi-square Statistics in SPSS

The hypothetical example at the beginning of this chapter:

1. Calculated a Pearson chi-square for the environmental support by age relationship.

2. Determined the degrees of freedom.

3. Compared the computed test statistic to the value in the theoretical chi-square distribution for a given level of significance (e.g., .05, .01, .001) by referring to Table 13.8 (p. 320).

4. Made a decision to reject or fail-to-reject the null hypothesis of statistical independence.

The SPSS program did roughly the same thing. For example, the program automatically:

1. Calculated the chi-squares for the relationships in the data.

2. Determined the degrees of freedom.

3. Compared the calculated chi-square value against the theoretical value.

4. Displayed the actual observed significance level. *With SPSS, there is no need to manually compare the computed test statistic against the theoretical value.* A *p*-value of .000, however, should not be interpreted 0. Rather, the observed significance level was less than .0005; SPSS rounded the *p*-value to .000. An observed significance should never be reported as 0; the probability should be reported as *p* < .001.

5. The decision to reject or fail-to-reject the null hypothesis was made by simply looking at the observed significance level. If this probability is less than the predetermined p-value (e.g., .05, .01, .001), reject the null hypothesis (chapter 6).

The SPSS printout calculated three chi-square statistics: (a): Pearson, (b) Linear-by-Linear Association, and (c) Likelihood Ratio (see Output 13.1b).

Pearson Chi-square

The low probability level ($p < .001$) associated with the Pearson χ^2 (20.173) indicates that it is unlikely that the two variables are independent in the population. In other words, there is a statistical relationship between the YEAR of the survey (1987, 1988, 1989) and the respondents' overall satisfaction (variable = OVERALL). In this example, the null hypotesis is rejected. The pattern of percentages of individuals who gave a passing grade for their overall satisfaction with the park experience increased over the three-year time span.

Linear-by-Linear Association

The linear-by-linear association statistic is also known as the Mantel-Heanszel chi-square. This statistic is based on the Pearson correlation (chapter 16) and tests whether there is a linear association between two variables. The test is not appropriate for dichotomous or categorical variables.

Likelihood Ratio (LR) Chi-square

The SPSS output also displays the likelihood ratio (LR) chi-square. This test is based on maximum likelihood theory and is often used in the analysis of dichotomous and categorical data. For large samples, the Pearson and LR chi-square statistics give similar results. In the above analysis, for example, the Pearson chi-square was 20.173 and the LR was 19.752. Both chi-squares often lead to the same conclusion.

The steps in the calculation of an LR, however, differ from those used with the Pearson chi-square. This section: (a) demonstrates how a LR chi-square is calculated and (b) describes the process of decomposing a LR chi-square.

The steps used for calculating the LR chi-square are outlined in Table 13.10 (p. 330). In general, these steps involve multiplying the observed frequencies (e.g., cell, row, column, total) by the *natural log* of the frequency. A logarithm transforms a nonlinear model into a linear model that allows for the use of regression techniques (see chapter 17). For a positive number, n, the logarithm of n is the power to which some number b (the base of the logarithm) must be raised to yield n. For example, if $b^x = n$, then $log_b n = x$. This means that if x is the logarithm of n, then you must raise the base b to the power of x to get n.

Two types of logarithms—common and natural logarithms—are discussed in the literature. The two types differ in what is used as the base. With common logarithms, the base is 10. For example, the common logarithm of 100 is 2, because $10^2 = 100$ and $log_{10} 100 = 2$. For natural logarithms, the base = e = 2.718. This base is used in logistic regression analysis (chapter 17).

Table 13.10   Steps in the Calculation of Likelihood Ratio Chi-square

			Save the product as:
1	Multiply each observed frequency in the table by the natural log of the frequency	Add up the products	Cell Sum
2	Multiply each row total by the natural log of the row total	Add up the products	Row Sum
3	Multiply each column total by the natural log of the column total	Add up the products	Column Sum
4	Multiply the table n by the natural log of the number		Total N

The LR chi-square is then calculated by the following equation:

$$LR = 2 * (cell\ sum - row\ sum - column\ sum + total\ N) \qquad \text{Equation 13.5}$$

The observed counts from the New Hampshire database for the relationship between overall satisfaction and study year are shown in Table 13.11. Plugging these numbers into the equations shown in Box 13.2 yields a LR chi-square of 19.752 (identical to the SPSS output).

Table 13.11   Observed Counts for the Relationship between Overall Satisfaction and Study Year

	Study Year			
Satisfaction Grade	1987	1988	1989	Row Totals
Fail	33	14	9	56
Pass	66	80	89	235
Column Totals	99	94	98	291

Decomposing the LR Chi-square

Both the Pearson and LR chi-squares revealed a statistically significant relationship between YEAR and OVERALL satisfaction. Not indicated by these results is whether specific years differed from one another. For example, were the satisfaction scores in 1988 statistically higher than those in 1987? Were the scores from 1989 statistically higher than those for the first two years of the study?

One way to address these questions is to decompose the LR chi-square statistic. For example, any 2 x 3 table can be decomposed into two 2 x 2 tables. In general, the rules for decomposing a 2 x 3 are:

1. Each frequency in the original table must appear once and only once as a frequency of the same type in one of the component tables.

2. Each frequency that is in a component table, but not in the original table, must appear in another component table as a frequency of the other type.

Box 13.2 Computing the Likelihood Ratio (LR) Chi-square

Satisfaction Grade		Study Year			Total
		1987 C_1	1988 C_2	1989 C_3	
Fail	R_1	n_{11}	n_{12}	n_{13}	n_{1+}
Pass	R_2	n_{21}	n_{22}	n_{23}	n_{2+}
Total		n_{+1}	n_{+2}	n_{+3}	N

Cell	Observed Frequency f_o	$f_o * \ln(f_o)$
n_{11}	33	115.38
n_{12}	14	36.95
n_{13}	9	19.78
n_{21}	66	276.52
n_{22}	80	350.56
n_{23}	89	399.49
Cell Sum	291	**1198.68**
Row Total		
n_{+1}	56	225.42
n_{+2}	235	1283.00
Row Sum	291	**1508.42**
Col Total		
n_{+1}	99	454.92
n_{+2}	94	427.07
n_{+3}	98	449.33
Col Sum	291	**1331.32**
Total N	291	**1650.94**
LR	*19.75*	

LR = 2 * (1198.67 – 1508.42 – 1331.31 + 1650.94) = 19.75

Using these rules, the overall LR chi-square can be decomposed into two separate LR chi-square statistics:[1]

- LR1 compares 1987 against 1988

- LR2 compares 1987 and 1988 against 1989

---

[1] The decomposition rules only apply to the Likelihood Ratio chi-square, not the Pearson chi-square.

In SPSS, the commands for this analysis are:

```
MISSING VALUES Year (89).
```
> Eliminates 1989 respondents for purposes of this analysis (1987 vs. 1988).

```
CROSSTABS /TABLES=overall BY year /STATISTIC=CHISQ /CELLS= COUNT
COLUMN .
```

Output 13.2   Crosstabs: Overall Satisfaction by 1987 versus 1988

Chi-Square Tests

	Value	df	Asymp. Sig. (2-sided)
Likelihood Ratio	9.120	1	.003

> Satisfaction was statistically higher in 1988 than 1987.

overall   Overall Satisfaction * year   Year of Visit Crosstabulation

			year Year of Visit		
			87 1987	88 1988	Total
overall Overall Satisfaction	0 Fail	Count	33	14	47
		% within year Year of Visit	33.3%	14.9%	24.4%
	1 Pass	Count	66	80	146
		% within year Year of Visit	66.7%	85.1%	75.6%
Total		Count	99	94	193
		% within year Year of Visit	100.0%	100.0%	100.0%

The LR chi-square is 9.12 ($p < .003$), suggesting that respondents from 1987 differ statistically from those in 1988 in terms of overall satisfaction.

The next step is to compare respondents from 1987 and 1988 (combined) against those from 1989. The corresponding SPSS syntax and output follow:

```
MISSING VALUES YEAR ().
```
> Indicates that none of the values for the variable YEAR should be treated as missing.

```
RECODE YEAR (87,88 = 88).
VALUE LABELS YEAR
            88 '1987 and 1988'
            89 '1989'.
```
> Combines the respondents from 1987 and 1988 into a single group for purposes of this analysis.

```
CROSSTABS
  /TABLES=OVERALL BY YEAR
  /FORMAT= AVALUE TABLES
  /STATISTIC=CHISQ
  /CELLS= COUNT COLUMN .
```

The output from this analysis is shown below.

Output 13.3   Crosstabs: Overall Satisfaction by (1987 & 1988) versus 1989

Chi-Square Tests

	Value	df	Asymp. Sig. (2-sided)
Likelihood Ratio	10.632	1	.001

Suggests that 1989 respondents reported statistically higher satisfaction levels than those in 1987 and 1988.

overall   Overall Satisfaction * year   Year of Visit Crosstabulation

			year Year of Visit		
			88 1987 and 1988	88 1989	Total
overall Overall Satisfaction	0 Fail	Count	47	9	56
		% within year Year of Visit	24.4%	9.2%	19.2%
	1 Pass	Count	146	89	235
		% within year Year of Visit	75.6%	90.8%	80.8%
Total		Count	193	98	291
		% within year Year of Visit	100.0%	100.0%	100.0%

One way to check the calculations with the LR decomposition process is to add up the separate chi-square statistics. If the computations were correct, LR1 and LR2 should sum to the overall LR statistic (Table 13.12).

Table 13.12   Check on Likelihood Ratio Computations[1]

Likelihood Ratio Chi-square	Comparison	Chi-square Value
LR1	1987 vs. 1988	9.12
LR2	1987 & 1988 vs. 1989	10.63
Overall LR	1987 vs. 1988 vs. 1989	19.75

[1.] Check demonstrates that LR1 + LR2 = LR.

In summary, the percentages in these crosstabulation tables suggest that satisfaction with the New Hampshire State Park experiences increased each year during the three-year study period. The overall Pearson and LR chi-squares provided evidence that at least one of the three distributions (1987, 1988, 1989) differed statistically from the others. Decomposing the LR chi-square and examining separate subgroups of respondents (e.g., 1987 vs. 1988) further supported the positive progression in satisfaction ratings. The examination of these subgroups is *conceptually* similar to the post hoc tests (e.g., least significant difference [LSD], Scheffé) used in analysis of variance (chapter 15). The LR chi-square will be also be examined in the logistic regression chapter (chapter 17).

Effect Sizes in SPSS Crosstabulations

As noted earlier, chi-square statistics and associated *p*-values provide little information about the strength of an association between two variables. SPSS, however, provides a number of effect size measures that estimate the strength of variable relationships. In a crosstabulation analysis, these statistics are accessed from the CROSSTABS main dialog box (Figure 13.7).

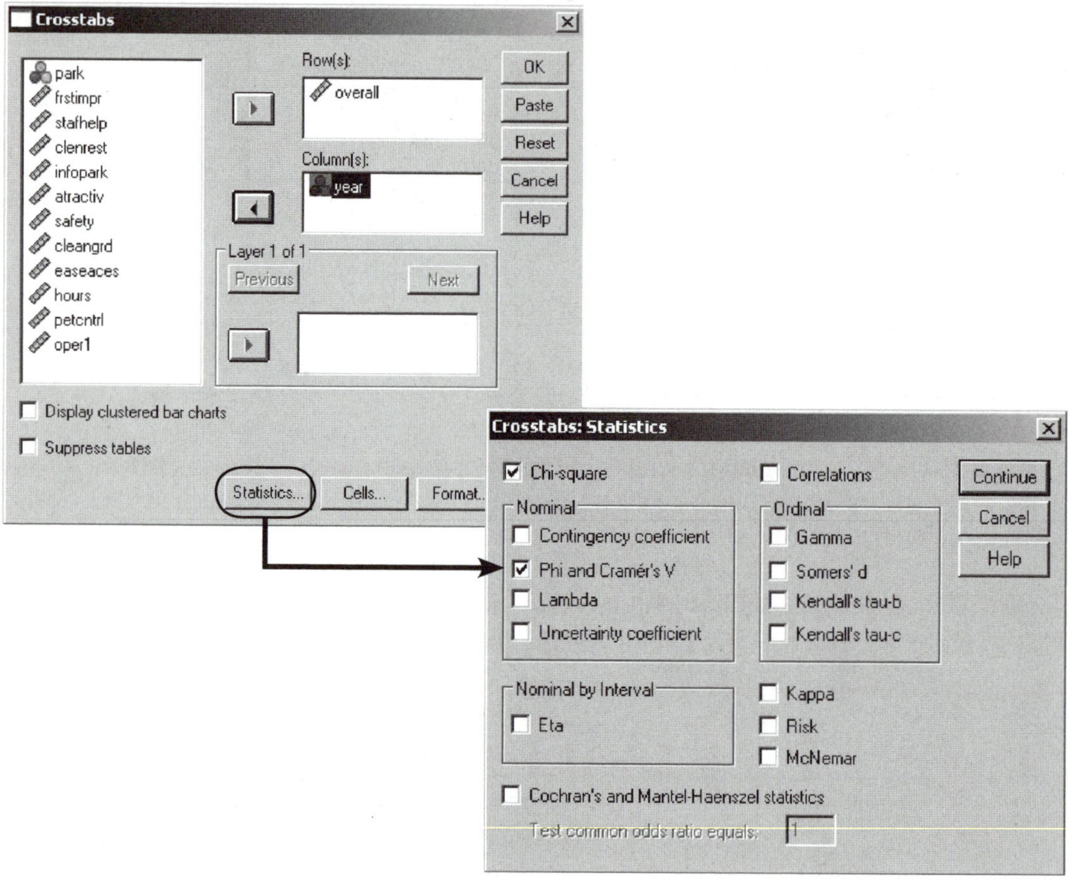

Figure 13.7   Effect Size Measures in Crosstabs

For the overall satisfaction analysis (2-levels; fail [0] and pass [1]) by year (3-levels; 1987, 1988, and 1999), a Cramer's *V* is an appropriate effect size measure (Figure 13.7). Given the previous analysis, the syntax is:

```
CROSSTABS / TABLES = OVERALL BY YEAR
          / CELLS = COUNT COLUMN
          / STATISTIC = CHISQ PHI.
```

Output 13.4   Effect Size Statistics

Symmetric Measures

		Value	Approx. Sig.
Nominal by	Phi	.263	.000
Nominal	Cramer's V	.263	.000
N of valid cases		291	

> Implies that the effect size statistics are significant at $p < .001$

The phi (ϕ) and Cramer's V from this analysis were .263 implying a "minimal" (.1) to "typical" (.3) relationship (chapter 6). In a 2×2 crosstabulation, the ϕ and V will always be equal. This analysis was based on a 2×3 table (OVERALL by YEAR) and the two statistics had identical values. Such similarities will not necessarily hold for all analyses.

Crosstabulations with Larger Tables

All of the crosstabulations examined in this chapter have focused on contingency tables with relatively few dimensions (e.g., 2 x 3, 2 x 2). When larger tables are analyzed, the researcher must address other statistical considerations. This section examines the relationship between the five-level overall satisfaction variable (i.e., A, B, C, D, F) and the five-level general category PARK variable (chapter 12).

The syntax for this analysis is:

```
CROSSTABS / TABLES = OVERALL BY PARK
           / CELLS = COUNT COLUMN
           / STATISTIC = CHISQ PHI.
```

Output 13.5a   Crosstabs: 5 x 5 Table

overall   Overall Satisfaction * park   Park Visited Crosstabulation

			park Park Visited					
			1 Campgrounds	2 Day use areas	3 Beaches	4 Historic sites	5 Attractions	Total
overall Overall Satisfaction	0 F	Count	1	1	0	0	0	2
		% within park Park Visited	1.7%	1.7%	.0%	.0%	.0%	.7%
	1 D	Count	0	0	11	0	1	12
		% within park Park Visited	.0%	.0%	19.0%	.0%	1.7%	4.1%
	2 C	Count	9	6	17	0	10	42
		% within park Park Visited	15.5%	10.3%	29.3%	.0%	16.9%	14.4%
	3 B	Count	10	16	17	2	23	68
		% within park Park Visited	17.2%	27.6%	29.3%	3.4%	39.0%	23.4%
	4 A	Count	38	35	13	56	25	167
		% within park Park Visited	65.5%	60.3%	22.4%	96.6%	42.4%	57.4%
Total		Count	58	58	58	58	59	291
		% within park Park Visited	100.0%	100.0%	100.0%	100.0%	100.0%	100.0%

The column percentages highlight differences in the satisfaction distributions among the five park types. Nearly all (97%) of the historic site visitors rated their experience with a letter grade of A. About two thirds of the campground respondents and 60% of the day-use visitors gave similar evaluations. Only 22% of the beach visitors, however, reported this level of satisfaction.

The output from this analysis for effect sizes includes both the Phi and the Cramer's V. The Cramer's V is the appropriate effect size measure given the 5 x 5 table—avoid the temptation to report the Phi (appropriate for a 2 x 2 table).

Output 13.5b   Crosstabs: Effect Size Statistics

Symmetric Measures

		Value	Approx. Sig.
Nominal by Nominal	Phi	.613	.000
	Cramer's V	.307	.000
N of valid cases		291	

The output for the Pearson and LR chi-square tests indicate that both statistics result in the same conclusion (reject the null hypothesis).

Output 13.5c   Crosstabs: Chi-square Statistics

Chi-Square Tests

	Value	df	Asymp. Sig. (2-sided)
Pearson Chi-Square	109.455[a]	16	.000
Likelihood Ratio	115.139	16	.000
Linear-by-Linear Association	.023	1	.880
N of Valid Cases	291		

> Implies that all of the χ^2 statistics are significant at $p < .001$

[a]. 10 cells (40.0%) have expected count less than 5. The minimum expected count is .40.

Approximately 40% of the cells for the crosstabulation of satisfaction (OVERALL) and PARK, however, have expected count cells less than 5 (see footnote on Output 13.5c). When the expected frequencies are too low, the p-value based on the chi-square distribution may not be correct. Some statisticians have suggested that the expected count should always be 5 or more in all cells of a 2×2 table, and 5 or more in 80% of cells in larger tables. The topic, however, is controversial. Everitt (1992), for example, suggests that the requirement of at least 5 expected observations per cell is probably too stringent and can be relaxed.

For a 2×2 contingency table, an adjusted value of the chi-square statistic (the **Yates corrected chi-square**) is sometimes used to correct for expected counts less than 5. The Yates formula reduces the absolute value of each difference between observed and expected frequencies by 0.5 before squaring:

$$\chi^2 = \sum \frac{(|f_o - f_e| - 0.5)^2}{f_e}$$

Equation 13.6

Subtracting 0.5 from each observed minus expected count reduces the computed chi-square and increases the p-value. The approach prevents overestimating statistical significance when the sample size is small. The Yates's correction, however, can yield an overly conservative result that fails to reject the null hypothesis when it should. SPSS labels the Yates correction as **continuity corrected chi-square** in the output.

To understand which specific cells have an expected count less than 5, click on **Cell...** on the main CROSSTABS dialog box and then check Observed and Expected on the Cell Display dialog box (Figure 13.8, p. 338).

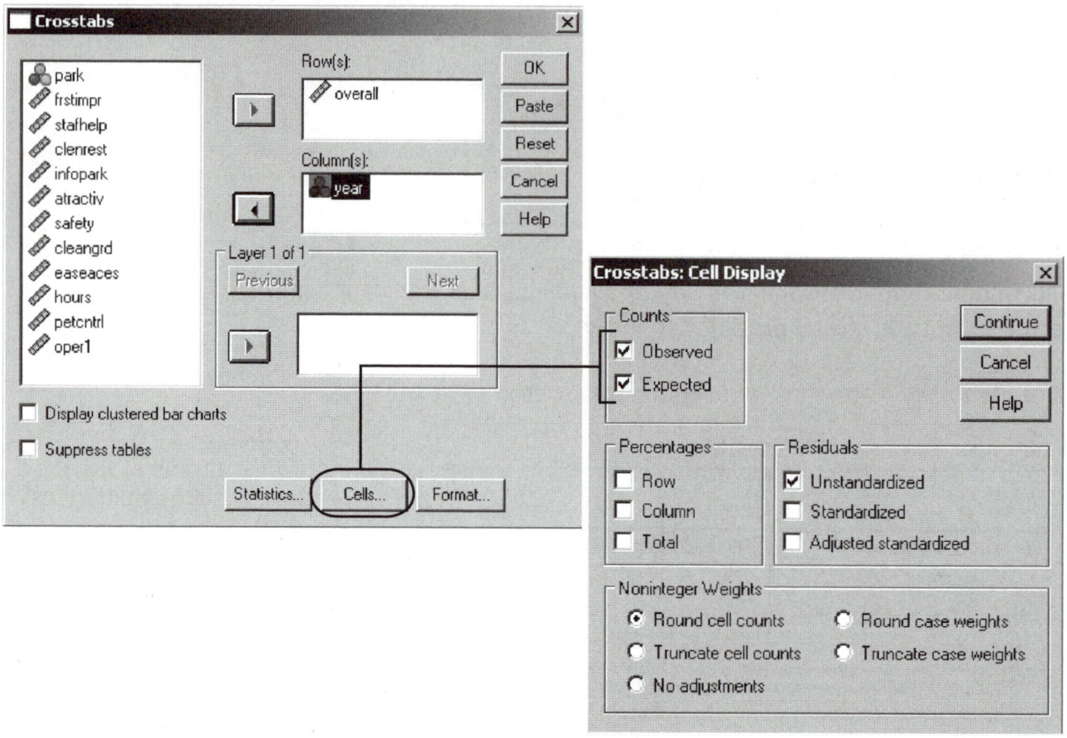

Figure 13.8   Observed and Expected Cell Counts in SPSS

The syntax for the analysis shown in Figure 13.8 analysis is:

```
CROSSTABS
  /TABLES=OVERALL BY YEAR
  /FORMAT= AVALUE TABLES
  /CELLS= COUNT EXPECTED RESID
  /COUNT ROUND CELL .
```

Results are shown in Output 13.5d.

Output 13.5d   Crosstabs: Observed and Expected Counts

overall   Overall Satisfaction * park   Park Visited Crosstabulation

| | | | park   Park Visited | | | | | |
			1 Campgrounds	2 Day use areas	3 Beaches	4 Historic sites	5 Attractions	Total
overall Overall Satisfaction	0 F	Count	1	1	0	0	0	2
		Expected Count	.4	.4	.4	.4	.4	2.0
		Residual	.6	.6	−.4	−.4	−.4	
	1 D	Count	0	0	11	0	1	12
		Expected Count	2.4	2.4	2.4	2.4	2.4	12.0
		Residual	−2.4	−2.4	8.6	−2.4	−1.4	
	2 C	Count	9	6	17	0	10	42
		Expected Count	8.4	8.4	8.4	8.4	8.5	42.0
		Residual	.6	−2.4	8.6	−8.4	1.5	
	3 B	Count	10	16	17	2	23	68
		Expected Count	13.6	13.6	13.6	13.6	13.8	68.0
		Residual	−3.6	2.4	3.4	−11.6	9.2	
	4 A	Count	38	35	13	56	25	167
		Expected Count	3.3	33.3	33.3	33.3	33.9	167.0
		Residual	4.7	1.7	−20.3	22.7	−8.9	
Total		Count	58	58	58	58	59	291
		Expected Count	58.0	58.0	58.0	58.0	59.0	291.0

The ten cells with expected counts less than 5 all occurred for the letter grades of D and F (numbers circled in the output). The *Residual = Observed – Expected* and suggests where departures from independence exist.

Chapter Summary

This chapter focused on contingency (or crosstabulation) table analysis using the SPSS CROSSTABS procedure. CROSSTABS computes two-way to *n*-way crosstabulation tables, tests of significance, and effect size measures. The CROSSTABS procedure is appropriate when the variables are dichotomous or categorical. Crosstabs are *not* appropriate for continuous level variables.

A two-way crosstabulation examines the relationship between two dichotomous or categorical variables. The order in which variables are displayed in a two-way crosstabulation (variable X by variable Y vs. variable Y by variable X) does not influence the *n*s in each of the cells or the chi-square test statistic (χ^2). The order of variable specification, however, is important for determining the appropriate percentages. In general, the independent variable should be the column variable and column percentages should be computed.

An *n*-way crosstab examines three or more variables at the same time. In an *n*-way crosstab, the third variable is called a *control*. Only a limited number of control variables should be included in a given analysis.

The Pearson χ^2 tests the hypothesis that the row and column variables are independent of each other. The test statistic compares the observed cell counts against what would be expected if no relationship is evident given the row and column totals. Small deviations between the observed and expected counts produce a small chi-square value and suggest that the relationship can be attributed to chance. Large deviations between the observed and expected counts result in a large chi-square and suggest that the distributions differ statistically.

The likelihood ratio (LR) chi-square is computed by multiplying the observed frequencies by the natural log of the frequencies. The LR statistic can be decomposed into separate LR chi-squares that facilitate understanding which specific distributions differ from each other in contingency tables larger than 2 x 2.

Statistical significance is determined by comparing the computed chi-square against the theoretical chi-square distribution. In a crosstabulation, this comparison partially depends on the degrees of freedom. The degrees of freedom are defined as the number of cells in a table that can be *arbitrarily* filled before the numbers in the remaining cells are determined. The degrees of freedom are important because the probability of obtaining a specific chi-square value depends on the number of cells in the table.

Most statistical tests (e.g., χ^2, *t*, *F*) can be evaluated by comparing the calculated test statistic to the theoretical distribution (e.g., the chi-square distribution, *t* distribution, or the normal distribution). Regardless of the specific statistic, if the *p*-value is small (.05, .01, .001), the finding is *statistically* significant and the null hypothesis is rejected. In SPSS terminology, the *p*-value is called "Sig."

Chi-square statistics are heavily influenced by sample size. If the proportions in the cells remain unchanged and the number of respondents increases by a factor of *k*, the value of the chi-square is *k* times larger. For this reason, tests of statistical significance do not measure the strength of the relationship. Effect size measures are often used as one indicator of substantive or practical significance. For dichotomous and categorical data, two general categories of effect sizes exist: (a) measures of proportional reduction in error (e.g., lambda [λ]), and (b) measures based on chi-square (e.g., phi, Cramer's *V*, contingency coefficient).

Review Questions

1. What levels of measurement are appropriate for variables in a crosstabulation?

2. Explain the concepts of *independent* and *dependent* as they apply to variables used in a contingency table analysis.

3. Explain the concept of a *control variable* when used in an *n*-way crosstabulation.

4. Explain the concept of *degrees of freedom* for a contingency table.

5. SPSS calculates a variety of chi-square statistics (e.g., Pearson, linear-by-linear association, likelihood ratio). Of these chi-square statistics, which are appropriate for dichotomous and categorical data?

6. Explain why you might want to decompose an overall LR chi-square statistic.

7. Why is a chi-square statistic not very useful for examining the strength of a relationship between two variables?

8. Discuss the statement "Test of statistical significance are not tests of substantive significance."

9. Define the term *effect size*.

10. What is an appropriate effect size measure for a 2 x 2 contingency table?

11. What is an appropriate effect size measure for a 2 x 3 contingency table?

means and *t*-tests

Most universities in the United States record students' grades from courses taken during a semester. Grades are typically coded on a five-point scale with responses of F (0), D (1), C (2), B (3), and A (4). For example, an individual might receive a "B" (3) in English, and "A*s*" (4) in chemistry, statistics, calculus, and psychology. Using these data, this student's grade point average (GPA) for the semester is 3.80 (i.e., $3 + 4 + 4 + 4 + 4 / 5 = 3.80$). University administrators, professors, the student, and the parents would all interpret this GPA as somewhere between an "A" and "A–" average and are likely to be pleased with the student's performance.

Calculation of a GPA assumes that the variables are measured as continuous variables. As discussed in chapter 5, a *continuous variable* is an ordered variable with at least five levels and a distribution that is approximately normally distributed in the population. University grades meet each of these assumptions. A grade is an ordered variable with five categories. The middle of the scale (2) is considered a "C" or "average" and there are relatively few students at the extremes of the distribution (i.e., a GPA of 4.00 or 0.00). In other words, the distribution is approximately normally distributed.

The same logic can be applied to the New Hampshire State Park report card study (see chapter 10), where the evaluation variables (e.g., first impression of the park, overall satisfaction with the experience) were coded as grades (F [0] through A [4]). Chapter 11 examined the frequency distributions and univariate means for these variables. This chapter focuses on SPSS procedures for computing bivariate means: means and *t*-tests. Two types of *t*-tests are explored: independent samples *t*-tests and paired sample *t*-tests.

The Means Command in SPSS

Unlike the FREQUENCIES command that describes one variable at a time, the MEANS command allows for an examination of the relationship between two variables. The New Hampshire State Parks Report Card data file (chapter 10) will be used to illustrate the MEANS procedure in SPSS. The four basic steps in conducting statistical analysis discussed in chapter 9 apply to the MEANS command:

1. Open the data file: NH - State Parks - Report card.sav
   (see chapter 9 – Introduction to SPSS – for assistance in opening a data file).

2. Click on Analyze > Compare Means > Means...   See Figure 14.1

3. Select the variables to be included in the analysis   See Figure 14.2

4. Select additional Options…   See Figure 14.3

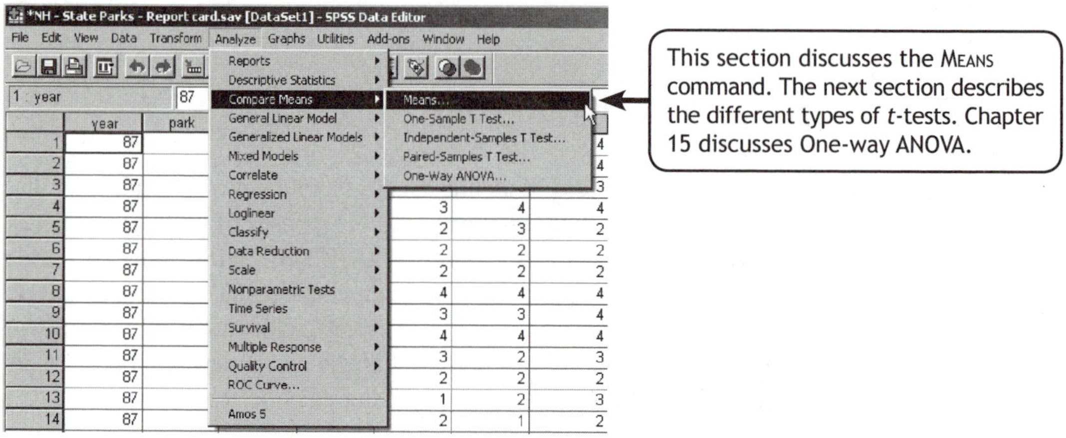

This section discusses the MEANS command. The next section describes the different types of *t*-tests. Chapter 15 discusses One-way ANOVA.

Figure 14.1   Selecting the Means Procedure

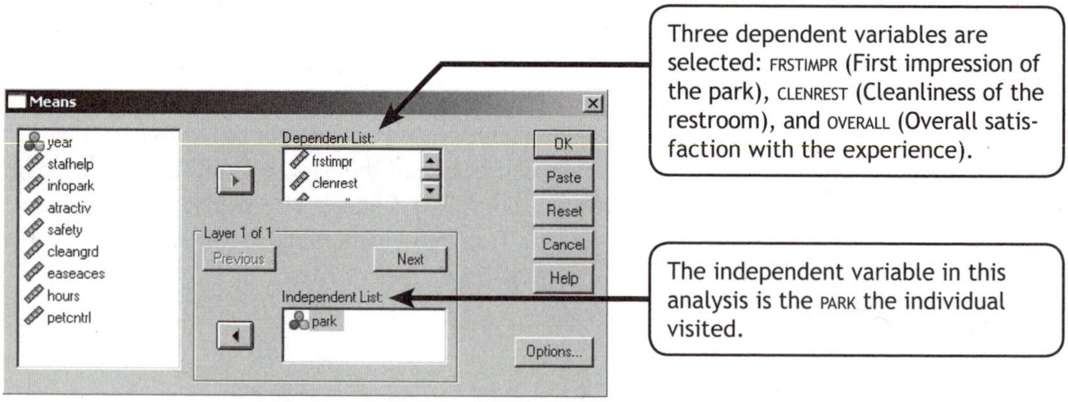

Three dependent variables are selected: FRSTIMPR (First impression of the park), CLENREST (Cleanliness of the restroom), and OVERALL (Overall satisfaction with the experience).

The independent variable in this analysis is the PARK the individual visited.

Figure 14.2   Selecting Variables for a Means Analysis

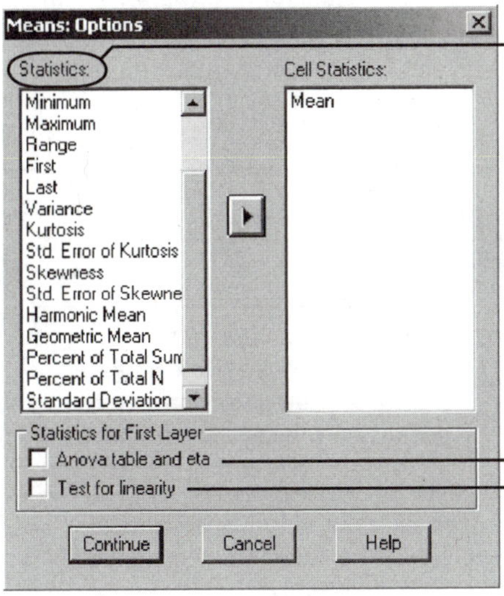

A variety of statistics can be generated by the MEANS command (see Box 14.1). For this analysis, only the mean is selected.

Checking this box displays an analysis of variance table and calculates eta and eta^2 (displayed in the Measures of Association table).

"Test for linearity" displays additional statistics in the tables created by the ANOVA keyword: the sums of squares, degrees of freedom, and mean square associated with linear and nonlinear components, the F-ratio, and significance level for the ANOVA table and Pearson's r and r^2 for the Measures of Association table.

Figure 14.3   Selecting Options in a Means Analysis

Box 14.1   Statistics Available from the Options Menus in the Means Command

Statistic	Description	Statistic	Description
DEFAULT	Means, standard deviations, and cell counts	SESKEW	Standard error of cell skewness
		FIRST	First value
MEAN	Cell means	LAST	Last value
STDDEV	Cell standard deviations	NPCT	Percentage of the total number of cases
COUNT	Cell counts		
MEDIAN	Cell median	SPCT	Percentage of the total sum
GMEDIAN	Grouped median	NPCT(var)	Percentage of the total number of cases within the specified variable. The specified variable must be one of the control variables.
SEMEAN	Standard error of cell mean		
SUM	Cell sums		
MIN	Cell minimum		
MAX	Cell maximum	SPCT(var)	Percentage of the total sum within the specified variable. The specified variable must be one of the control variables.
RANGE	Cell range		
VARIANCE	Variances		
KURT	Cell kurtosis	HARMONIC	Harmonic mean
SEKURT	Standard error of cell kurtosis	GEOMETRIC	Geometric mean
SKEW	Cell skewness	ALL	All cell information

Click the Continue button (Figure 14.3) and the main dialog box appears (Figure 14.2). At this point, click the Paste button and SPSS generates the MEANS syntax in Figure 14.4 (p. 346). Figure 14.4 also shows the syntax for recoding the ten-level categorical PARK variable[1] into five

---

[1] See chapter 10 for a description of the categories in the original PARK variable.

types of parks (i.e., campgrounds, day-use areas, beaches, historic sites, and attractions), and adds new value labels for the recoded variable. Run the analysis by highlighting the commands, then clicking the Run button.

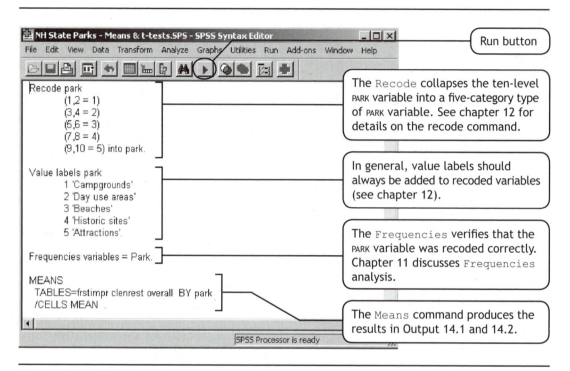

Figure 14.4   SPSS Syntax for Running a Means with Park Recoded

The means output from this analysis is shown in Output 14.1.

The Case Processing Summary (Output 14.1) indicates that for the combination of the "First Impression" and "Park" type visited variables, 2% of the cases were missing. The combination of "Cleanliness of the Restrooms" and "Park" resulted in 10% missing. Given that there were no missing values on the variable PARK (see chapter 11), all of the missing cases are the result of nonresponse on the evaluation variables (FRSTIMPR, CLENREST, OVERALL).

Output 14.1   Case Processing Summary

Means

Case Processing Summary

	Cases					
	Included		Excluded		Total	
	N	Percent	N	Percent	N	Percent
frstimpr Firsr Impression * park Park Visited	294	98.0%	6	2.0%	300	100.0%
clenrest Cleanliness of Restrooms * park Park Visited	269	89.7%	31	10.3%	300	100.0%
overall Overall Satisfaction * park Park Visited	291	97.0%	9	3.0%	300	100.0%

The Report (Output 14.2) from this analysis suggests that across the three evaluation variables, respondents who visited historic sites consistently gave the most positive grades (i.e., $M = 3.79$, $M = 3.77$, and $M = 3.97$, respectively). These mean scores can be interpreted as letter grades of "A." Conversely, the means for visitors to the beaches reflected "B–" grades (i.e., $M = 2.67$ for first impression, $M = 2.47$ for cleanliness of the restrooms, $M = 2.55$ for overall satisfaction).

Output 14.2   Means Report

Report

Mean

park Park Visited	frstimpr First Impression	clenrest Cleanliness of Restrooms	overall Overall Satisfaction
1 Campgrounds	3.40	3.23	3.45
2 Day use areas	3.38	3.00	3.45
3 Beaches	2.67	2.47	2.55
4 Historic sites	3.79	3.77	3.97
5 Attractions	3.36	2.81	3.22
Total	3.32	3.01	3.33

The means examined up to this point have considered the evaluation variables (e.g., FRSTIMPR, CLENREST, OVERALL) separately. A researcher might be interested in how the parks were evaluated when all the scores from all of the variables are combined into a single index. Chapter 18 details procedures for creating an index and testing the reliability of the scale. Chapter 12 describes the techniques for computing a summated index. The specific SPSS syntax for: (a) computing the grade point average (GPA) scale, (b) adding a variable label, and (c) running a Frequencies check on the new index is shown below. The ".5" in the Compute command indicates that a respondent must answer at least five of the evaluation questions to be included in the scale.

```
COMPUTE GPA = MEAN.5(FRSTIMPR,STAFHELP,CLENREST,INFOPARK,
                     ATRACTIV,SAFETY,CLEANGRD,EASEACES,
                     HOURS,PETCNTRL,OVERALL).

VARIABLE LABELS GPA 'Overall Grade Point Average'.

FREQUENCIES VARIABLES = GPA
                / STATISTICS = MEAN, STDDEV.
```

Using the .5 option on the Compute command, resulted in only two respondents who had not answered at least 5 of the evaluation items (Output 14.3, p. 348). The mean for the grade point average (GPA) variable across all parks and years of data collection was 3.25 (i.e., slightly better than a B average).

Output 14.3   Frequencies Analysis for the GPA Computed Indices

Frequencies

Statistics

gpa   Overall Grade Point Average

N	Valid	298
	Missing	2
Mean		3.2547
Std. Deviation		.81330

The syntax for running a Means for GPA by PARK is:

```
MEANS
   TABLES=GPA BY PARK
   /CELLS MEAN COUNT STDDEV .
```

Across all parks, the Total Mean (i.e., 3.25 in Output 14.4) from the Means analysis equals the mean from the Frequencies analysis (Output 14.3). The historic sites received the highest grade point average ($M = 3.87$) from the New Hampshire State Parks visitors, whereas the beaches had the lowest GPA ($M = 2.51$).

Output 14.4   Means Report for GPA by PARK

Means

Report

gpa   Overall Grade Point Average

park Park Visited	Mean	N	Std. Deviation
1 Campgrounds	3.4282	60	.67456
2 Day use areas	3.2710	60	.69664
3 Beaches	2.5148	59	.97799
4 Historic sites	3.8696	59	.29908
5 Attractions	3.1880	60	.63263
Total	3.2547	298	.81330

Defining Subgroups in SPSS Means

The GPA means specific to park type visited suggest that managers may want to concentrate on improving the services and experiences offered at state park beaches where the overall grade point average was low. These analyses (Output 14.4), however, do not take into account the year that the respondents visited the state park. To control for a second independent variables in a MEANS analysis, the Layer option in the MEANS window is used (Figure 14.5).

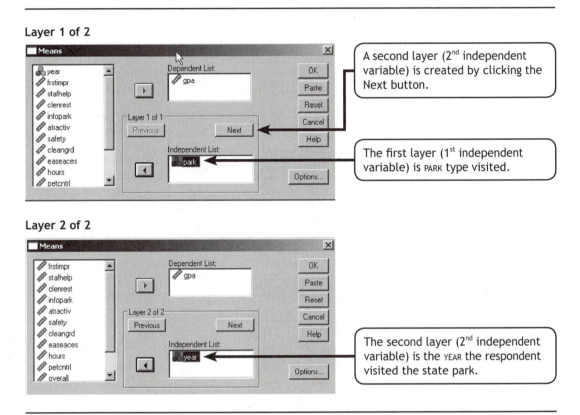

Layer 1 of 2

A second layer (2nd independent variable) is created by clicking the Next button.

The first layer (1st independent variable) is PARK type visited.

Layer 2 of 2

The second layer (2nd independent variable) is the YEAR the respondent visited the state park.

Figure 14.5   Controlling for a Second Independent Variable Using the Layer Option

The SPSS syntax generated from the above dialog boxes is:

```
MEANS
  TABLES=GPA BY PARK BY YEAR
  /CELLS MEAN COUNT STDDEV .
```

Each TABLES subcommand can contain a maximum of 10 BY variable lists. Remember, however, that same number of respondents will be divided into more tables. With the two independent variables in this analysis, there were approximately a total of 20 individuals per cell. Output 14.5 (p. 350) shows the grade point averages for each park type by each study year. In contrast to the Output 14.4 that signaled a potential problem at the beaches, this view of the data suggests visitor evaluations at the beaches increased dramatically from 1987 ($M = 1.56$) to 1989 ($M = 3.41$). Respondents evaluations at the attractions, on the other hand, declined from an average of 3.72 (1987) to 2.82 (1989).

Output 14.5 Means Report for GPA by PARK by YEAR

Report

gpa   Overall Grade Point Average

park Park Visited	year Year of Visit		Mean	N	Std. Deviation
1 Campgrounds	87	1987	2.8605	20	.76824
	88	1988	3.6890	20	.48497
	89	1989	3.7352	20	.27841
	Total		3.4282	60	.67456
2 Day use areas	87	1987	2.7666	20	.76521
	88	1988	3.5050	20	.44733
	89	1989	3.5413	20	.56481
	Total		3.2710	60	.69664
3 Beaches	87	1987	1.5591	20	.58492
	88	1988	2.5789	19	.69711
	89	1989	3.4095	20	.5585
	Total		2.5148	59	.97799
4 Historic sites	87	1987	3.9426	20	.13361
	88	1988	3.7671	19	.46660
	89	1989	3.8939	20	.17942
	Total		3.8696	59	.29908
5 Attractions	87	1987	3.7186	20	.33513
	88	1988	3.0227	20	.66600
	89	1989	2.8227	20	.47051
	Total		3.1880	60	.63263
Total	87	1987	2.9695	100	1.01663
	88	1988	3.3154	98	.70907
	89	1989	3.4805	100	.56645
	Total		3.2547	298	.81330

> Although the visitors' average GPA at the beaches in 1987 was only 1.56, visitors in 1988 (*M* = 2.58) and 1989 (*M*=3.41) gave more positive evaluations.

> The visitors' average GPA at the attraction areas declined from 3.72 (1987) to 2.82 (1989).

As noted in Figure 14.3, an analysis of variance table and effect size statistics (eta [η] and eta^2 [η^2]) can also be requested in a MEANS analysis. Building on the previous example, the SPSS syntax is:

```
MEANS
  TABLES=gpa BY park BY year
  /CELLS MEAN COUNT STDDEV
  /STATISTICS ANOVA .
```

If two or more independent variables are specified, the second and subsequent dimensions are ignored in the analysis of variance table produced by the means command. To obtain a two-way and higher analysis of variance, use the ANOVA procedure (chapter 15). The ANOVA table and effect size statistics generated from the above syntax are shown in Output 14.6. Details regarding the interpretation of an *F*-value are described in chapter 15. For the moment, simply recognize that the $F = 29.72$, $p < .001$ (i.e., the Sig. = .000) implies that at least one of the means listed in Output 14.4 statistically differs from another mean in the output. A visual inspection of the means suggests that the average GPA from respondents who visited beaches ($M = 2.51$) was lower than that reported by visitors to other types of state parks sites. The one-way ANOVA procedure in SPSS provides a systematic way of comparing which specific means differ from one another (i.e., multiple contrast and post hoc tests).

The eta or effect size (chapter 15) provides a measure of strength of association. In this example, the eta of .537 suggests that park type has a "substantial" (chapter 6) influence on respondents' reported grade point average. The eta^2 can be interpreted as the amount variance (i.e., 28.9%) in the GPA index that is explained by the park type variable. The unsquared version of eta should be used when eta is being reported as the effect size measure.

Output 14.6 ANOVA Table and Effect Size Statistics from a MEANS Analysis

> The overall F-ratio is significant at $p < .001$.

ANOVA Table

			Sum of Squares	df	Mean Square	F	Sig.
gpa Overall grade Point Average * park Park Visited	Between Groups	(Combined)	56.698	4	14.174	29.717	.000
	Within Groups		139.756	293	.477		
	Total		196.454	297			

> Remember that a Sig. of .000 does not imply 0 probability. The actual observed significance level was < .0005 and SPSS rounded the Sig. to .000. This should be reported as $p < .001$.

Measures of Association

	Eta	Eta Squared
gpa Overall Grade Point Average * park Park Visited	.537	.289

> The eta is a measure of strength of association (effect size). An eta of .537 reflects a "substantial" relationship (chapter 6).

> The eta^2 is interpreted as the amount of variance in the dependent variable that is explained by the independent variable.

Statistical Inference from Sample Means

There are three types of *t*-tests in SPSS. A ***one sample t-test*** examines the null hypothesis that a sample comes from a population with a specified mean. For example, the average age of hunters as determined by a random sample survey of hunters in a given state could be compared against the mean age of hunters based on license sales in that state. Assuming that all individuals who hunt in the state are required to purchase a license, the mean based on the license sales reflects the population mean. For general population surveys, the mean age based on a survey could be compared against census data to determine differences between the sample and the population. For many of the psychological variables (e.g., attitudes, norms) of interest to social scientists, however, the population mean is not known. Consequently, use of the one sample *t*-test is not commonly seen in the parks, recreation, and human dimensions literature.

An *independent samples t-test* addresses the hypothesis that the difference between means of two independent random samples differ statistically (e.g., Do the 1987 and 1988 samples differ in their overall grade point average [GPA]?). Because individuals who visited New Hampshire State Parks in 1987 were not in the sample of individuals who visited in 1988, an independent samples *t*-test is referred to as a *between respondent* design.

Paired samples t-tests test differences within the same respondent (i.e., a *within respondent* or *repeated measures design* [Chapter 15]). For example, as measured on a pretest survey, an individual may oppose trapping wildlife. The person then watches a video (i.e., treatment) arguing in favor of trapping and completes the survey a second time (i.e., the posttest). The empirical question is: does the individual become more favorable toward trapping after watching the video?

Independent Samples *t*-tests

Variables and Assumptions

Independent samples *t*-tests are appropriate when the independent variable (X) is *dichotomous* and the dependent variable (Y) is *continuous* (see chapter 5). For the New Hampshire State Parks data, the independent variable might be the YEAR the person visited the state park (e.g., 1987 vs. 1988), and the dependent variable(s) could be the respondents' evaluations of their experience (e.g., first impressions of the park, cleanliness of the restrooms, overall satisfaction).

Three *assumptions* are required for an independent sample *t*-test. First, the test assumes that the respondents in each group of the independent variable were obtained from independent random samples. In the New Hampshire data, the assumption implies that individuals who were randomly surveyed in 1987 were not included in the 1988 random survey. Second, an independent sample *t*-test assumes that the dependent variable (e.g., overall satisfaction) is normally distributed. This normality assumption, however, can be relaxed when the sample sizes for the two groups are large (e.g., both over 50), as is typically the case in survey research. Third, the test assumes that the two population standard deviations for the dependent variable are equal. In the New Hampshire data, for example, the assumption implies the population standard deviation for overall satisfaction (the dependent variable) in 1987 equals the population standard deviation for overall satisfaction in 1988. This relationship can be represented symbolically as $\sigma_{1987} = \sigma_{1988}$ where σ is the *population standard deviation*. As demonstrated below, the assumption that $\sigma_{1987} = \sigma_{1988}$ (or more generally, $\sigma_1 = \sigma_2$) can be tested separately using an F test (i.e., the Levene test).

Hypothesis Testing Steps

Chapter 6 described the general steps used in null hypothesis significance testing (NHST). When applied to the comparison of two means, the steps are:

1. State hypotheses.

   H_0: $\mu_1 = \mu_2$
   H_1: $\mu_1 \neq \mu_2$

The null (H_0) and alternative (H_1) hypotheses state the expected relationship for the population means (μ). As is always the case, the null hypothesis indicates that there is no statistical relationship between the two population means. The alternative hypothesis in this example, says the two population means are not equal (a nondirectional hypothesis). If the researcher had reason to believe that one population mean is larger than the other population mean, a directional alternative hypothesis could be advanced (i.e., $\mu_1 > \mu_2$, or $\mu_1 < \mu_2$).

2. Select a significance level (e.g., .05, .01, .001).
   The choice of one significance level (*p*-value or Sig. in SPSS terminology) over another is somewhat arbitrary. By convention in the social sciences, the *p*-value is usually set at .05. For large samples, the *p*-value might be set at .01 or .001 because sample size influences the probability of finding a statistically significant outcome.

3. Test the equality of the sample variances. Two different population level models are hypothesized and tested:

   Model 1: $\sigma_1^2 = \sigma_2^2$
   Model 2: $\sigma_1^2 \neq \sigma_2^2$

   These models test the third assumption of an independent samples *t*-test noted earlier.

4. Calculate the appropriate *t*-test (equal variance assumed vs. equal variance not assumed).

5. Compare the computed value of the *t* statistic against the theoretical ***t distribution*** or ***Student's t distribution***. The *t* distribution was first introduced by William Sealy Gosset (1908). Gosset worked at the Guinness Brewery and developed the *t* statistic as a method for monitoring the quality of beer brews. Because he was not allowed to publish under his own name, the 1908 article was written under the pseudonym ***Student***. The *t*-test and the associated theory were popularized by Fisher (1925), who called the distribution "Student's distribution."

   Student's distribution applies when the population standard deviation is unknown. Hypothesis tests rely on Student's *t* distribution to cope with the uncertainty of estimating the standard deviation from a sample. If the population standard deviation is known, a normal distribution is used.

6. Make a decision regarding the null hypothesis (reject or fail-to-reject H_0). If the calculated *t*-value is as large or larger than the *t*-value in the theoretical distribution for a given level of significance (e.g., .05), the null hypothesis is rejected.

7. Estimate the strength of association (***effect size***).
   As noted in chapter 6, tests of statistical significance do not estimate the strength of the relationship. Step 7 involves calculating an appropriate effect size (e.g., Pearson *r*, Hedge's *g*, Glass's Δ) as a measure of strength of association.

Testing the Equality of the Variances

The statistical inference problem in an independent samples *t*-test involves determining whether a difference between two sample means implies a true difference in the populations. Before this difference in the means can be examined, the equality (or inequality) of variances must be determined (Step 3 in hypothesis testing steps). An ***F test (Levene's)*** is used to test whether the two populations have the same variance.

Model 1: $\sigma_1^2 = \sigma_2^2$
Model 2: $\sigma_1^2 \neq \sigma_2^2$

Given that the population variances are typically unknown, the F is computed from the sample variances:

$$F = \frac{\text{Larger } s^2}{\text{Smaller } s^2}$$

Equation 14.1

If the results of this test indicate that the variances are equal (model 1 above), the *t-test for equal variances* is used to compare the sample means. If the variances are not equal (model 2), the *t-test for unequal variances* is used for comparing the sample means.

Model 1: $\sigma_1^2 = \sigma_2^2$

Model 1 is based on the assumption that the variances between the two samples are equal. Because it is impractical to compute a mean based on all members in a population, the researcher must use a sample. The true but unknown population mean (μ) is estimated by the *sample mean (M)*. The difference between two independent sample means can be referred to as *between sample (or groups) variability*. Testing this difference involves examining the ratio of the variability between two samples divided by the variability within the samples:

$$t = \frac{\text{Variability}_{\text{Between Samples}}}{\text{Variability}_{\text{Within Samples}}}$$

Equation 14.2

The between samples variability is determined by differences in the sample means. The *variability within samples (or groups)* is determined by differences in the standard deviations within each group. When the variances are equal, the equation is:

$$t = \frac{M_1 - M_2}{\sqrt{s_p^2 \left(\dfrac{1}{n_1} + \dfrac{1}{n_2} \right)}}$$

Equation 14.3

where:

M = sample means
n = sample sizes
s_p^2 = pooled sample variances = $\dfrac{(n_1 - 1)s_1^2 + (n_2 - 1)s_2^2}{n_1 - n_2 - 2}$

Equation 14.4

If the ratio in Equation 14.3 is large (i.e., large t-value): (a) the variability between the sample means is greater than the variability within the samples, (b) the t-value is likely to be statistically significant, and (c) the null hypothesis is rejected. If the ratio is small (i.e., a small t-value), the relationship between the two sample means is not likely to be statistically significant and a fail-to-reject the null hypothesis decision is made.

Similar to the discussion on the chi-square statistic (chapter 13), determining statistical significance for a *t*-test depends, in part, on the degrees of freedom. Degrees of freedom for a chi-square are based on the number of cells in a contingency table. In a *t*-test, ***degrees of freedom (df)*** refer to a count of the number of pieces of ***independent*** information contained within a particular analysis. Crawley (2005) provides an excellent illustration for understanding independent pieces of information. To paraphrase, assume a sample of 6 numbers with an average of 5. The sum of these numbers must be 30 otherwise the mean would not be 5. There are thus six pieces of information (i.e., |_| |_| |_| |_| |_| |_|). If each box is filled with a positive or negative number, the first number might be a 3 (i.e., (|3| |_| |_| |_| |_| |_|). The next number could be a 9 (i.e., |3| |9| |_| |_| |_| |_|). The next numbers could also be anything, say 4, 0 and 6. (i.e., |3| |9| |4| |0| |6| |_|). The last value, however, must be an 8 because the numbers must add up to 30. In this example, there is total freedom in selecting the first five numbers, but no choice when selecting the sixth. There are thus five degrees of freedom when selecting six numbers. In general, there are $(n-1)$ degrees of freedom when estimating the mean from a sample of size n.

For a *t*-test, when equal variances are assumed, there are two sample means so the degrees of freedom are:

$$df = (n_1 - 1) + (n_2 - 1)$$

Equation 14.5

Model 2: $\sigma_1^2 \neq \sigma_2^2$

Given populations with unequal variances (model 2), a *t*-value cannot be computed for the differences in sample means. Instead, an approximation of *t* may be computed.

$$t = \frac{M_1 - M_2}{\sqrt{\dfrac{s_1^2}{n_1} + \dfrac{s_2^2}{n_2}}}$$

Equation 14.6

This test statistic is not distributed as Student's *t*, but the probability for *t* can be approximated by treating it as *t*. The degrees of freedom for this test statistic are:

$$df = \frac{\left[(s_1^2/n_1) + (s_2^2/n_2)\right]^2}{\left[(s_1^2/n_1)^2/(n_1-1) + [(s_2^2/n_2)^2/(n_2-1)]\right]}$$

Equation 14.7

This number is usually not an integer, but a reasonably accurate probability is obtained by rounding the number to the nearest integer.

The only difference between model 1 and model 2 is the assumption regarding the equality of variances. Because the variances for each sample in model 1 are equal, an overall estimate of variance can be made by pooling the two variances (Equation 14.4). For model 2 the variances are not equal and must be treated separately (Equation 14.6). For large samples, the two models will usually yield similar results. This idea of ***pooled*** versus ***separate*** variance will be reexamined in chapter 15 on analysis of variance.

With the appropriate *t*-value and degrees of freedom calculated, the next step (step 5, p. 253) in null hypothesis significance testing is to compare the computed value of *t* against the theoretical ***t* distribution**. Similar to the chi-square distribution, tables for the critical values of the *t* distribution are found in the back of statistics books. The degrees of freedom in these tables typically range from 1 to 120, with a final *df* for infinity. Given that sample sizes in survey research often exceed 120 respondents, only the row for infinity is shown in Table 14.1.

Table 14.1   Distribution of *t*

	Level of significance for one-tailed test		
	.025	.005	.0005
	Level of significance for two-tailed test		
	.05	.01	.001
df ∞	1.960	2.576	3.291

If the calculated value of *t* is as large or larger than theoretical value of *t* for a given significance level (.05, .01, .001), the relationship is statistically significant at that probability level. For example, if the computed *t* was 5.89, the relationship would be statistically significant $p < .001$ because the calculated value (5.89) is larger than the critical value (3.291) at a significance level of .001. In SPSS, this is a two-tailed probability and it is appropriate if the alternative hypothesis is nondirectional. In other words, the alternative hypothesis does not assume that *t* will be either positive or negative. If the alternative hypothesis is directional, the one-tailed level of significance should be used. Note that the one-tailed *p*-value is exactly one half of the two-tailed significance level (Table 14.1).

As noted in chapter 13, SPSS eliminates the need for looking up theoretical values in tables like Table 14.1 when comparing the computed test statistic against the critical values. SPSS output automatically does the comparison and reports the ***actual observed significance level***. This *p*-value is called "**Sig.**" in SPSS terminology and refers to the probability of a Type I error (i.e., rejecting the null hypothesis when it is actually true, see chapter 6). If the Sig. or *p* is small ($< .05, < .01, < .001$), the finding is *statistically* significant and the null hypothesis is rejected.

Effect Sizes in Independent Samples *t*-tests

The last step in null hypothesis significance testing involves estimating the strength of the relationship or an effect size statistic. As described in chapter 6, effect size statistics are generally referred to as the *d* family of indices and the *r* family of indices (Rosenthal, 1994). The *d* effect size indices are expressed in standard deviation units and computed by finding the difference between the means of two groups and then dividing by the appropriate standard deviation. The *r* family of indices is the effect size expressed as a correlation coefficient, *r* (Rosenthal, Rosnow, & Rubin, 2000). In an independent samples *t*-test, the *r* is a point biserial correlation because the independent variable is dichotomous (chapter 16).

If equality of variances can be assumed, Hedge's *g* or Cohen's *d* can be used as the effect size:

$$\text{Hedge's } g = \frac{M_1 - M_2}{S_{Pooled}}$$

Equation 14.8

$$\text{Cohen's } d = \frac{M_1 - M_2}{\sigma}$$

Equation 14.9

If equality of variances cannot be assumed, Cohen (1988) suggests replacing the σ in Equation 14.9 with the square root of the mean of the two variances (note that d' is my notation, not Cohen's):

$$\textit{Cohen's } d' = \frac{M_1 - M_2}{\sqrt{\dfrac{s_1^2 + s_2^2}{2}}}$$

Equation 14.10

If the original means and standard deviations are not available (e.g., as might occur in a meta-analysis based of the published literature), an effect size in an independent samples *t*-test can be computed *indirectly*. Equations 14.11 and 14.12 can be used when equality of variances can be assumed; equation 14.13 is more appropriate when equality of variances cannot be assumed:

$$\text{Hedge's } g = \frac{2t}{\sqrt{N}} \text{ for equal sample sizes}$$

Equation 14.11

$$r = \sqrt{\frac{t^2}{t^2 + df}} \text{ for equal sample sizes}$$

Equation 14.12

$$\text{Hedge's } g = \frac{t\sqrt{n_1 + n_2}}{\sqrt{n_1 n_2}} \text{ for unequal sample sizes}$$

Equation 14.13

Independent Samples *t*-tests in SPSS

The New Hampshire State Parks data set will be used to illustrate INDEPENDENT-SAMPLES T TESTS in SPSS. The four basic steps in conducting statistical analysis discussed in chapter 9 apply to the independent samples *t*-test command:

1. Open the data file: NH - State Parks - Report card.sav
   (see chapter 9 – Introduction to SPSS – for assistance in opening a data file).

2. Click on Analyze > Compare Means > Independent-Samples T Test...   See Figure 14.6

3. Select the variables to be included in the analysis   See Figure 14.7

4. Select additional options   See Figure 14.8

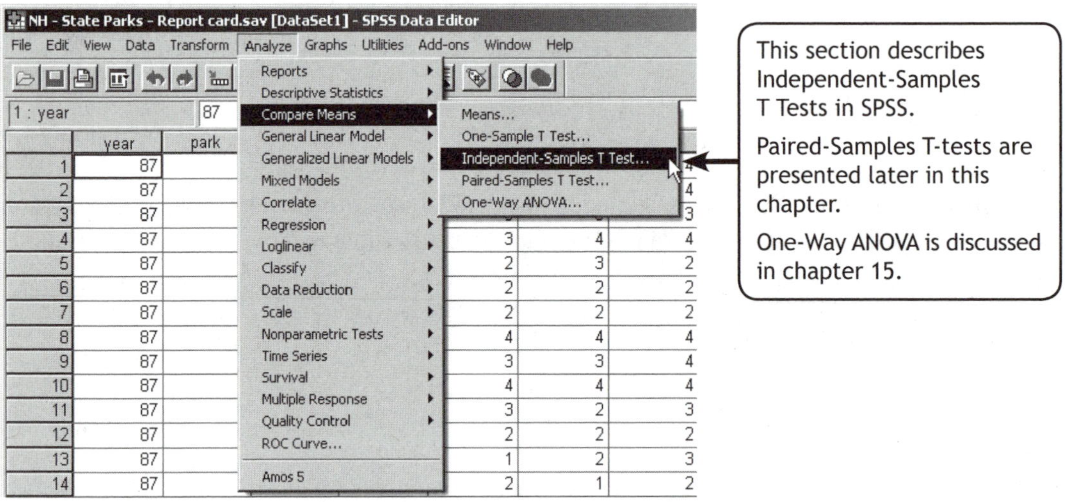

Figure 14.6   Selecting an Independent-Samples T Test in SPSS

For this example, two dependent variables were selected (OVERALL, GPA). The variable OVERALL refers to the respondents' overall satisfaction with the experience. As described earlier in this chapter, the GPA variable is a computed index that combines all 11 evaluation items on the survey (chapter 10). In an independent samples *t*-test, SPSS calls the dependent variables ***Test variables*** (Figure 14.7). The independent variable in an independent samples *t*-test is called the ***grouping variable***. For this illustration, the grouping variable is the year the respondent visited the state park. This categorical variable has three levels (i.e., 1987, 1988, 1989). For this *t*-test, the years 1988 and 1989 are compared. To declare these two years for this analysis, click on the Define Groups... button (Figure 14.7). The values of 88 (Group 1) and 89 (Group 2) are the values in the variable YEAR.

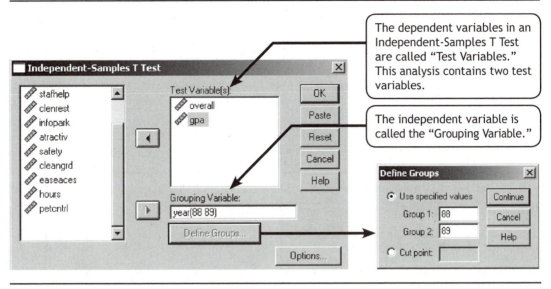

The dependent variables in an Independent-Samples T Test are called "Test Variables." This analysis contains two test variables.

The independent variable is called the "Grouping Variable."

Figure 14.7   Selecting Variables in an Independent Samples T Test

Figure 14.8 displays the available Options in an independent samples *t*-test. By default, a 95% confidence interval for the difference in means is displayed. This default can be changed to any value between 1 and 99. When more than one dependent variable is specified in the test variable list (Figure 14.7), missing values can be excluded on either: (a) an analysis by analysis basis or (b) listwise. When ***exclude cases analysis by analysis*** is selected, each *t*-test uses all cases that have valid data for the tested variables. The sample sizes for

Figure 14.8   Selecting Options in an Independent-Samples T Test

different *t*-tests may vary from test to test, depending on the amount of missing associated with the variables. When ***exclude cases listwise*** is selected, only cases that have valid data for all variables included in the analysis will be used (i.e., both OVERALL and GPA in this example). The sample size in this situation will remain constant across all tests.

The syntax generated from the options selected in this analysis is:

```
T-TEST
  GROUPS=year(88 89)
  /MISSING=ANALYSIS
  /VARIABLES=overall gpa
  /CRITERIA=CIN(.95) .
```

Two independent samples *t*-tests were requested—OVERALL BY YEAR and GPA BY YEAR. The Group Statistics from this analysis (Output 14.7) displays the sample sizes, means, standard deviations, and standard errors of the mean (see chapter 11 for definitions of these statistics). The sample sizes for the different groups vary because exclude cases analysis by analysis was selected (Figure 14.8). The ultimate objective of this independent samples *t*-test is to test for differences in the two study years (1988 vs. 1989) for the test variables: (a) overall satisfaction ($M = 3.40$ vs. $M = 3.53$, respectively) and (b) overall grade point average ($M = 3.32$ vs. $M = 3.48$, respectively). Before these mean comparisons can be made, however, differences in the standard deviations must be examined (i.e., $SD = .821$ vs. $SD = .735$ for OVERALL, $SD = .709$ vs. $SD = .566$ for GPA). As described above, an F test (Levene's) is used to test whether the two populations have the same variance (Figure 14.8).

Output 14.7   Group Statistics from an Independent Samples *t*-test

Group Statistics

	year Year of Visit	N	Mean	Std. Deviation	Std. Error Mean
overall Overall Satisfaction	88 1988	94	3.40	.821	.085
	89 1989	98	3.53	.735	.074
gpa Overall Grade Point Average	88 1988	98	3.3154	.70907	.07163
	89 1989	100	3.4805	.56645	.05665

For the overall satisfaction variable, the Levene's test for equality of variances was not statistically significant ($p = .125$, Output 14.8). This suggests that equal variance can be assumed (i.e., model 1: $\sigma_1^2 = \sigma_2^2$ above) and the *t*-test for equal variances is used (Equation 14.3). The *t*-value for the overall satisfaction variable was not statistically significant, $t(190) = -1.125$, $p = .262$. Substantively, this implies that the mean for 1988 ($M = 3.40$) does not differ from the mean for 1989 ($M = 3.53$). On the five-point scale used to measure overall satisfaction, New Hampshire State Park visitors rated their experiences in both years as a B+. Because the variances were equal, Equation 14.5 is used to calculate the degrees of freedom:

$$df = (n_1 - 1) + (n_2 - 1) = (94 - 1) + (98 - 1) = 190$$

Output 14.8   Significance Tests from an Independent Samples *t*-test

Independent Samples Test

		Levene's Test for Equality of Variances		t-test for Equality of Means						
									95% Confidence Interval of the Difference	
		F	Sig.	t	df	Sig. (2-tailed)	Mean Difference	Std. Error Difference	Lower	Upper
overall Overall Satisfaction	Equal variances assumed	2.375	.125	−1.125	190	.262	−.126	.112	−.348	.095
	Equal variances not assumed			−1.122	185.743	.263	−.126	.113	−.348	.096
gpa Overall Grade Point Average	Equal variances assumed	5.952	.016	−1.812	196	.071	−.16514	.09111	−.34483	.01455
	Equal variances not assumed			−1.808	185.270	.072	−.16514	.09132	−.34530	.01501

For the overall grade point average (GPA) variable, the Levene's test for equality of variances was significant ($p = .016$). For this analysis, the *t*-value for "equal variances not assumed" (model 2: $\sigma_1^2 \neq \sigma_2^2$ and Equation 14.6) is used to compare the means for 1988 ($M = 3.315$) and 1989 ($M = 3.480$). The *t*-value for GPA is also not statistically significant—$t(185.27) = -1.808$ and

$p = .072$—suggesting that the mean scores for the two years on the composite GPA index are not statistically equivalent. The degrees of freedom (185.27) for this analysis is based on Equation 14.7.

Effect Sizes in Independent Samples *t*-tests

In the previous independent samples *t*-test example, the years 1988 and 1989 were compared as an illustration. In this example the years 1987 and 1988 are compared to illustrate the calculation of an effect size for independent samples *t*-tests. Output 14.9 shows an independent samples *t*-test where the independent variable is YEAR (1987 vs. 1988) and the dependent variable is GPA. The syntax for this analysis is:

```
T-TEST
  GROUPS=year(87 88)
  /MISSING=ANALYSIS
  /VARIABLES=gpa
  /CRITERIA=CIN(.95) .
```

The standard deviations on GPA are 1.02 (1987) and .71 (1988) as seen in Output 14.9. Given that the Levene's test comparing these variances was statistically significant ($F = 25.68$, $p < .001$), the *t*-test for equal variances not assumed is used to compare the means ($M = 2.97$ vs. $M = 3.32$). This *t*-value (–2.78) with 177.133 degrees of freedom is significant at $p = .006$.

Output 14.9   Data for Calculating an Effect Size from an Independent Samples *t*-test

Group Statistics

	year Year of Visit	N	Mean	Std. Deviation
gpa Overall Grade Point Average	87 1987	100	2.9695	1.01663
	88 1988	98	3.3154	.70907

Independent Samples Test

		Levene's Test for Equality of Variances		t-test for Equality of Means		
		F	Sig.	t	df	Sig. (2-tailed)
gpa Overall Grade Point Average	Equal variances assumed	25.676	.000	–2.772	196	.006
	Equal variances not assumed			–2.782	177.133	.006

Given that the variances in this example are not equal, Cohen's d' could be used to estimate the effect size:

$$\text{Cohen's } d' = \frac{2.9695 - 3.3154}{\sqrt{\dfrac{(1.01663)^2 + (.70907)^2}{2}}} = .395$$

Equation 14.14

In this example, a d' of .395 is interpreted as somewhere between a minimal and a typical relationship. For the d family of effect size statistics (chapter 6), a value of .2 is interpreted as a "minimal" relationship, .5 is a "typical" relationship, and .8 is considered a "substantial" relationship. If an *r* family effect size is used the comparable guidelines for interpreting minimal, typical and substantial are .1, .3, and .5 respectively.

When using either a *d* family or an *r* family effect size statistic, the choice is dependent on whether or not the variances are equal. In this illustration using Output 14.9, the variances are not equal. If equation 14.12 is used to calculate the effect size, the *t*-value is –2.78, the degrees of freedom are 177.13 and the resulting *r* = .205:

$$r = \sqrt{\frac{t^2}{t^2 + df}} = \sqrt{\frac{(-2.78)^2}{(-2.78)^2 + 177.13}} = .205 \quad \text{Equal variances not assumed}$$

Equation 14.15

Equation 14.12, however, is not appropriate in this situation because the variances are not equal. To illustrate the problem that can arise, consider for the moment that the equality of variances assumption had not been violated, and the researcher used the data from Output 14.9 to calculate the effect size. The *t*-value equals –2.77, but the degrees of freedom are 196. The resulting correlation is:

$$r = \sqrt{\frac{t^2}{t^2 + df}} = \sqrt{\frac{(-2.77)^2}{(-2.77)^2 + 196}} = .194 \quad \text{Equal variances assumed}$$

Equation 14.16

This can be verified by running a Pearson correlation between year of visit (coded as a dichotomous variable, 1987 [0], 1988 [1]) and overall grade point average (Output 14.10). The point biserial correlation assumes equality of variances in the two samples.

Output 14.10   Pearson Correlation between Year of Visit and GPA

Correlations

		year	gpa
year Year of visit	Pearson Correlation	1	.194**
	Sig. (2-tailed)		.006
	N	200	198
gpa Overall Grade Point Average	Pearson Correlation	.194**	1
	Sig. (2-tailed)	.006	
	N	198	298

**. Correlation is significant at the 0.01 level (2-tailed).

The only major difference between equations 14.15 and 14.16 is the degrees of freedom (i.e., *df* = 177.13 for equal variances not assumed; *df* = 196 for equal variances assumed). Use of the incorrect equation (i.e., equation 14.15), tends to inflate the effect size statistic (i.e., *r* = .205 from equation 14.15 vs. *r* = .194 from equation 14.16).

Confidence Intervals in Independent Samples *t*-tests

If a null hypothesis is rejected at $p < .05$, the probability is less than 5 times in 100, given the null hypothesis, that the result could have occurred by chance. A 95% confidence interval (CI) around a difference in sample means says that the researcher is 95% confident that the true population mean is within the interval. In other words, if 100 samples were selected and a confidence interval was computed for each sample, the true population mean would be in the CI range 95 times and not in the CI range 5 times.

Constructing a confidence interval requires: (a) the difference between sample means, (b) the estimated standard error for the difference between the means, and (c) the *t*-value associated with the two-tailed significance level (e.g., the *p*-value or $\alpha = .05$ or $.01$ or $.001$). The formula for a confidence interval is:

$$(M_1 - M_2) - t_{critical}[\alpha, df]s_{M_1} - s_{M_2}$$

and

$$(M_1 - M_2) + t_{critical}[\alpha, df]s_{M_1} - s_{M_2}$$

Equation 14.17

where:

M_1 and M_2 = the means for the two groups

$t_{critical}$ = the critical *t*-value for the desired level of statistical significance (e.g., for $p < .05$, the critical value of t is 1.96 [see Table 14.1, p. 356])

α = the desired *p*-value (e.g., .05)

df = degrees of freedom

s_{M_1} and s_{M_2} = the standard deviations for the two groups

To illustrate confidence intervals from an independent samples *t*-test in SPSS, Output 14.11 displays the results of an analysis where type of park visited (historic site [0], attractions [1]) is the independent variable and overall satisfaction is the dependent variable. The syntax for this analysis is:

```
Recode park
        (7,8 = 0)
        (9,10 = 1)
        (1 thru 6 = 9).

Missing values park (9).

Value labels park
        0 'Historic sites'
        1 'Attractions'.

T-TEST
   GROUPS=park (0 1)
   /MISSING=ANALYSIS
   /VARIABLES=overall
   /CRITERIA=CIN(.95)  .
```

> This recode collapses the 10-level categorical PARK variable into a dichotomous variable where 0 = historic sites and 1 = attractions.

The average overall satisfaction rating reported by historic site visitors is 3.97 (i.e., a letter grade of A). The mean satisfaction score from visitors to attractions (i.e., the Franconia Flume and Tram) is 3.22 (i.e., a letter grade of B). The difference between these two means is .75. Using equation 14.17, SPSS calculates the 95% lower bound as .534 and the upper bound as .956 (Output 14.11). This indicates that the true mean difference lies somewhere between .53 and .96.

Output 14.11   Confidence Intervals from an Independent Samples *t*-test

Group Statistics

			N	Mean	Std. Deviation	Std. Error Mean
Overall Satisfaction	park Park Visited	0 Historic sites	58	3.97	.184	.024
		1 Attractions	59	3.22	.789	.103

Independent Samples Test

		t-test for Equality of Means					95% Confidence Interval of the Difference	
		t	df	Sig. (2-tailed)	Mean Difference	Std. Error Difference	Lower	Upper
Overall satisfaction	Equal variances not assumed	7.059	64.393	.000	.750	.106	.534	.956

Paired Samples *t*-tests

In some analyses, instead of selecting the observations for the two groups independently, the observations are paired. The paired *t*-test is frequently used in experiments involving a pre-post design. For example, the effect of a drug on blood pressure could be examined by measuring blood pressure before and after taking the drug. The statistic, however, can also be used in surveys that ask respondents to evaluate two different groups of items. In general, a paired *t*-test is referred to as a within-subjects design.

As will be empirically illustrated here, a survey of Colorado State Parks visitors ($n = 929$) were asked to evaluate the importance of different types of interpretive services (Table 14.2). In general these interpretation techniques can be conceptualized as either "personal" (e.g., involving a human interpreter such as a park ranger) or "nonpersonal."

Since all respondents evaluated all interpretation techniques, the researcher could conduct multiple paired *t*-tests; one for each potential pair of variables (INTERP1 to INTERP7). Alternatively, separate reliability analyses of the three personal (INTERP1 to INTERP3) and the four nonpersonal interpretation (INTERP4 to INTERP7) variables were conducted (Table 14.3). Details regarding reliability analysis and more specifically, Cronbach's alpha (a measure of internal consistency) are discussed in chapter 18. In general, however, the Cronbach's alpha coefficients for both sets of personal and nonpersonal items were acceptable (i.e., .76). Deleting any of the items from either the personal or the nonpersonal scales did not improve the reliability.

Table 14.2   Personal and Nonpersonal Interpretation Techniques

Concept	Question on survey[1]	Variable
Personal Interpretation	Campfire programs	INTERP1
	Lectures and workshops	INTERP2
	Guided nature walks	INTERP3
Nonpersonal Interpretation	Self-guided nature trails	INTERP4
	Visitor center displays	INTERP5
	Signs along roads and trails	INTERP6
	Books, pamphlets, and brochures	INTERP7

[1]   The survey asked respondents to rate the importance of each interpretation technique on a three-point scale: not at all important (1), somewhat important (2), very important (3).

Table 14.3   Reliability of Personal and Nonpersonal Interpretation Techniques

Interpretation Techniques[1]	Inter-Item Correlation	Alpha if Item Deleted	Cronbach's Alpha
Personal Interpretation			.76
Campfire programs	.54	.74	
Lectures and workshops	.63	.64	
Guided nature walks	.62	.65	
Nonpersonal Interpretation			.76
Self-guided nature trails	.51	.73	
Visitor center displays	.53	.72	
Signs along roads and trails	.66	.65	
Books, pamphlets, and brochures	.55	.71	

[1]   The survey asked respondents to rate the importance of each interpretation technique on a three-point scale: not at all important (1), somewhat important (2), very important (3).

Using the techniques described in chapter 12, the three personal and the four nonpersonal interpretation variables were combined into two composite indices—one for personal and one for nonpersonal interpretation. The syntax for these Compute statements is:

```
COMPUTE personal = mean.2(interp1,interp2,interp3).
VARIABLE LABELS personal 'Personal Interpretation'.

COMPUTE nonper = mean.2(interp4,interp5,interp6,interp7).
VARIABLE LABELS nonper 'Non-Personal Interpretation'.
```

There are two advantages to adopting this strategy for conducting the paired-samples *t*-test in this example. First, the original variables were coded on three-point scales (not at all important [1], somewhat important [2], very important [3]). Ordered variables with only three categories do not constitute continuous variables (see chapter 5), an assumption of a paired *t*-test. The computed scales, however, are approximately normally distributed variables with at least eight levels (see Appendix 14.1). Second, a single paired *t*-test can be used to compare the two computed scales. The null and alternative hypotheses are:

H_0: Personal = Nonpersonal
H_1: Personal ≠ Nonpersonal

To compute a *t* for paired samples, SPSS creates a paired difference variable, $D = X_1 - X_2$, where X_1 is the respondent's score on the personal interpretation scale and X_2 is the same individual's score on the nonpersonal index. *D* is normally distributed with a mean δ. The sample mean and variance (*d'* and $s_{d'}^2$) are computed, and the formula for a paired-samples *t*-test is:

$$t = \frac{d' - \delta}{s_{d'}^2}$$

Equation 14.18

Paired Samples *t*-tests in SPSS

The four basic steps in conducting statistical analysis discussed in chapter 9 apply to the PAIRED-SAMPLES T TEST… command:

1. Open the data file: CO – State Parks – Paired Samples t-test.sav
   (see chapter 9, Introduction to SPSS, for assistance in opening a data file)

2. Click on: Analyze > Compare Means > Paired-Samples T Test…   See Figure 14.9

3. Select the variables to be included in the analysis   See Figure 14.10

4. Select additional options   See Figure 14.11

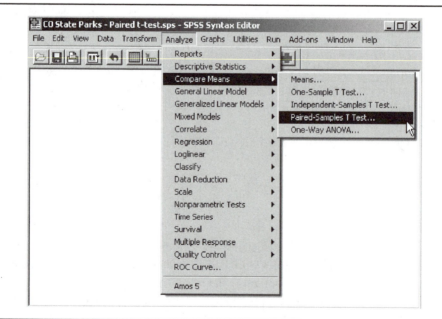

Figure 14.9   Selecting the Paired-Samples T Test

Selecting variables in a paired samples *t*-test is a two-step process. Step 1 involves selecting the variables that are to be paired (dialog box on the left of Figure 14.10). In this example, the computed index called PERSONAL is paired with the index for nonpersonal interpretation (i.e., NONPER). Select two variables at the same time by holding the Control key when selecting with the mouse. Clicking the directional arrow moves both variables as a pair to the window pane on the right.

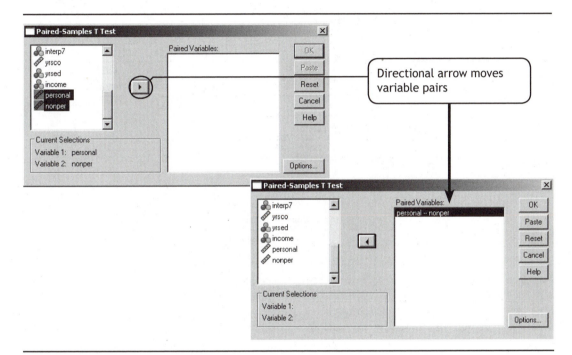

Figure 14.10   Selecting Variables in a Paired-Samples T Test

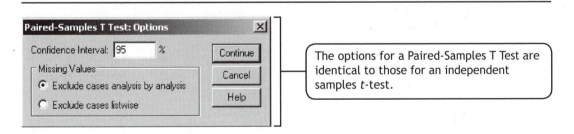

Figure 14.11   Selecting "Options" in a Paired-Samples T Test

The SPSS syntax for the paired samples *t*-test is:

```
T-TEST PAIRS= personal WITH nonper (PAIRED)
  /CRITERIA=CIN(.95)
  /FORMAT=LABELS
  /MISSING=ANALYSIS.
```

The paired sample statistics output from this analysis (Output 14.12) displays the means, sample sizes, standard deviations, and standard errors of the mean. On average, nonpersonal interpretation services were rated more positively ($M = 2.41$) than the personal interpretation services ($M = 1.89$). This difference is statistically significant, $t(915) = 28.705, p < .001$. The Pearson correlation between the two paired scores is .542, $p < .001$.

Output 14.12   Paired Samples Statistics, Correlations and Significance Tests

Paired Samples Statistics

		Mean	N	Std. Deviation	Std. Error Mean
Pair 1	personal Personal Interpretation	1.8934	916	.62325	.02059
	nonper Nonpersonal Interpretation	2.4136	916	.50037	.01653

Paired Samples Correlations

		N	Correlation	Sig.
Pair 1	personal Personal Interpretation & nonper Nonpersonl Interpretation	916	.542	.000

Paired Samples Test

	Paired Differences							
				95% Confidence Interval of the Difference				
	Mean	Std. Deviation	Std. Error Mean	Lower	Upper	t	df	Sig. (2-tailed)
Pair 1 personal Personal Interpretation & nonper Nonpersonl Interpretation	−.52020	.54847	.01812	−.55576	−.48463	−28.705	915	.000

Table 14.4 summarizes this overall paired *t*-test analysis, along with similar analyses (SPSS results not shown) for specific subgroups of visitors. Across all subgroups (Colorado residents: Yes or No; income level: < $50,000 or ≥ $50,000; education level: high school or less and college degree), nonpersonal interpretive services are rated as more important than activities involving a human interpreter. ·

Table 14.4   Colorado State Park Visitors Preferences for Personal and Nonpersonal Interpretation

Independent Variable	Type of Interpretation[1]		t-value	p-value
	Personal	Nonpersonal		
Overall evaluation	1.89	2.41	28.71	.001
Resident of Colorado				
Yes	1.90	2.42	27.46	.001
No	1.74	2.20	3.48	.004
Income				
< $50,000	1.93	2.42	22.83	.001
$50,000 +	1.83	2.44	16.27	.001
Education				
High School or less	1.91	2.39	12.61	.001
College degree	1.89	2.42	25.90	.001

[1] Personal interpretation services included (a) campfire programs, (b) lectures and workshops, and (c) guides nature walks. Nonpersonal interpretation included: (a) self-guided nature trails, (b) visitor center displays, (c) signs along roads and trails, and (d) books, pamphlets, and brochures.

Variables coded on three-point composite scales: not at all important (1), somewhat important (2), very important (3). (See Appendix 14.1)

Chapter Summary

This chapter focused on SPSS procedures for computing bivariate means: Means and *t*-tests. Two types of *t*-tests were explored: independent samples *t*-tests and paired sample *t*-tests.

The MEANS command can be used to compute the averages for continuous dependent variables by one or more dichotomous or categorical variables. Tables can be produced for up to ten independent variables. When multiple independent variables are used, however, the same number of respondents are split into multiple tables. This can result in small sample sizes for specific cells. The *F*-ratio from a MEANS command provides an omnibus test of whether at least one of the means differs statistically from another mean. In SPSS, the MEANS command is used to generate effect size statistics (e.g., eta) in an analysis of variance. The unsquared version of eta should be used as the effect size statistic. The squared version (eta^2) provides a measure of the amount of variance in the dependent variable that is explained by the independent variable.

There are three types of *t*-tests in SPSS: (a) one sample *t*-test, (b) independent samples *t*-test, and (c) paired samples *t*-test. The *one sample t-test* examines the null hypothesis that a sample comes from a population with a specified mean. An *independent samples t-test* addresses the hypothesis that the difference between means of two independent random samples differ statistically. A *paired samples t-test* tests differences in the means within the same respondent (e.g., a pre-post experimental design). An independent samples *t*-test is called a *between respondent design*, whereas the paired samples *t*-test is referred to as a *within respondent design*.

Independent sample *t*-tests are appropriate when the independent variable is *dichotomous* and the dependent variable is *continuous*. Three assumptions are required for an independent samples *t*-test. First, the test assumes that the respondents in each group of the independent variable were obtained from independent random samples. Second, an independent samples *t*-test assumes that the dependent variable is approximately normally distributed. Third, the test assumes that the two population standard deviations for the dependent variable are equal.

As applied to an independent samples *t*-tests, there are seven steps associated null hypothesis significance testing:

1. State the hypotheses (e.g., $H_0: \mu_1 = \mu_2$; $H_1: \mu_1 \neq \mu_2$).

2. Select a significance level (e.g., $p < .05$ or $p < .01$ or $p < .001$).

3. Test the equality of the sample variances. Two different population level models are hypothesized and tested (model 1: $\sigma_1^2 = \sigma_2^2$; model 2: $\sigma_1^2 \neq \sigma_2^2$). The Levene's *F* test is used to test whether the two populations have the same variance.

4. Calculate the appropriate *t*-test (equal variance assumed vs. equal variance not assumed).

5. Compare the computed value of the *t* statistic against the theoretical *t* distribution or Student's *t distribution*.

SPSS eliminates the need for looking up theoretical values in a statistics book when comparing the computed test statistic against the critical values. SPSS output automatically does the comparison and reports the *actual observed significance level*. The *p*-value is called "Sig." in SPSS terminology and refers to the probability of a Type I error (i.e., rejecting the null hypothesis when it is actually true).

6. Make a decision regarding the null hypothesis (reject or fail-to-reject H$_0$). If the ratio of between group variability to the within group variability is large (i.e., a large *t*-value), the null hypothesis is rejected. If the ratio is small (i.e., a small *t*-value), the relationship between the two sample means is not statistically significant and a fail-to-reject the null hypothesis decision is made.

Determining statistical significance for a *t*-test depends, in part, on the degrees of freedom. In a *t*-test, *degrees of freedom* (*df*) refers to a count of the number of pieces of independent information contained within a particular analysis.

7. Estimate the strength of association (*effect size*). For an independent samples *t*-test, the effect size can be calculated from the original data or from the computed *t*-value.

In an independent samples *t*-test, SPSS calls the dependent variables *test variables*. The independent variable in an independent samples *t*-test is called the *grouping variable*. If the sample variances are equal (model 1), the *t*-test for "equal variances assumed" is used to test for differences in the means. If sample variances are *not* equal (model 2), the *t*-test for "equal variances not assumed" is used.

If a null hypothesis is rejected at $p < .05$, the probability is less than 5 times in 100, given the null hypothesis, then the result could have occurred by chance. A 95% confidence interval (CI) around a difference in sample means says that the researcher is 95% confident that the true population mean is within the interval. Constructing a confidence interval requires: (a) the difference between sample means, (b) the estimated standard error for the difference between the means, and (c) the *t*-value associated with the two-tailed significance level (e.g., the *p*-value or $\alpha = .05$ or .01 or .001).

The paired *t*-test is commonly used in experiments involving a pre-post design. The statistic, however, can also be used in surveys that ask respondents to evaluate two different groups of items. In general, a paired *t*-test is referred to as a *within-subjects design*. Data from a survey of Colorado State Parks visitors was used to illustrate the paired samples *t*-test.

Review Questions

1. What level of measurement is appropriate for an *independent* variable in a MEANS analysis?

2. What level of measurement is appropriate for the *dependent* variable in a MEANS analysis?

3. How is an *F*-ratio in a MEANS test interpreted?

4. What is an appropriate effect size statistic in an analysis of variance?

5. Give an example of a null hypothesis in a one-sample *t*-test?

6. Discuss the distinction between *independent samples* and *paired samples* when conducting a *t*-test.

7. How many categories can the independent variable have when conducting an independent samples *t*-test?

8. What level of measurement is appropriate for the dependent variables in an independent samples *t*-test?

9. List three assumptions of an independent samples *t*-test.

10. Explain the concept of *degrees of freedom* in an independent samples *t*-test.

11. In SPSS terminology, what is the *dependent* variable in an independent samples *t*-test called?

12. In SPSS terminology, what is the *independent* variable in an independent samples *t*-test called?

13. In SPSS, if Sig. = .054, do you reject or fail-to-reject the null hypothesis?

14. How should a Sig. of .000 be reported?

15. If the Levene's test for equality of variances is $F = 11.737$, $p = .001$, do you report the *t*-test value for equal or unequal variances?

16. If the Levene's test for equality of variance is *significant*, what is an appropriate effect size statistic in an independent samples *t*-test?

17. If the Levene's test for equality of variance is *not significant*, what is an appropriate effect size statistic in an independent samples *t*-test?

18. What does a 95% confidence interval around the difference in means imply?

Appendix 14.1
Scale Construction for Personal and Nonpersonal Interpretation Techniques

SPSS syntax for computing the personal and nonpersonal interpretation scales:

```
Compute personal = mean.2(interp1,interp2,interp3).
Variable labels personal 'Personal Interpretation'.

Compute nonper = mean.2(interp4,interp5,interp6,interp7).
Variable labels nonper 'Non-Personal Interpretation'.

Frequencies variables = personal nonper
         / statistics = mean median mode stddev.
```

Statistics

		personal Personal Interpretation	nonper Nonpersonal Interpretation
N	Valid	916	918
	Missing	13	11
Mean		1.8934	2.4149
Median		2.0000	2.5000
Mode		2.00	3.00
Std. Deviation		.62325	.50057

personal Personal Interpretation

			Frequency	Percent	Valid Percent	Cumulative Percent
Valid	1.00	Not at all important	164	17.7	17.9	17.9
	1.33		113	12.2	12.3	30.2
	1.50		2	.2	.2	30.5
	1.67		132	14.2	14.4	44.9
	2.00	Somewhat important	190	20.5	20.7	65.6
	2.33		159	17.1	17.4	83.0
	2.67		67	7.2	7.3	90.3
	3.00	Very important	89	9.6	9.7	100.0
	Total		916	98.6	100.0	
Missing	System		13	1.4		
Total			929	100.0		

nonper   Nonpersonal Interpretation

		Frequency	Percent	Valid Percent	Cumulative Percent
Valid	1.00 Not at all important	24	2.6	2.6	2.6
	1.25	13	1.4	1.4	4.0
	1.50	29	3.1	3.2	7.2
	1.75	55	5.9	6.0	13.2
	2.00 Somewhat important	134	14.4	14.6	27.8
	2.25	131	14.1	14.3	42.1
	2.50	151	16.3	16.4	58.5
	2.67	2	.2	.2	58.7
	2.75	183	19.7	19.9	78.6
	3.00 Very important	196	21.1	21.4	100.0
	Total	918	98.8	100.0	
Missing	System	11	1.2		
Total		929	100.0		

15

analysis of variance[1]

Analysis of variance (ANOVA) can be thought of as an extension of an independent samples *t*-test (chapter 14). With an independent samples *t*-test, the independent variable is dichotomous (e.g., males vs. females) and dependent variable is continuous (e.g., participation rates in a recreation activity). With a one-way ANOVA, the independent variable can be either a dichotomous or a categorical level variable and the dependent variable is continuous. Both independent samples *t*-tests and the ANOVA are concerned with comparing means among different groups. If the independent variable in a one-way ANOVA is dichotomous, an ANOVA and an independent samples *t*-test will yield exactly the same results.

This chapter focuses on ANOVA as a technique for comparing means and variances. When there is one independent variable the SPSS program ONE-WAY ANOVA can be used to compare means and variances. When there is more than one independent variable, the SPSS program GENERAL LINEAR MODEL is used for conducting an ANOVA. In general, such models are referred to as *n*-way ANOVA. If there are two independent variables, the analysis is called a two-way ANOVA; three independent variables result in a three-way ANOVA. This chapter provides an overview of analysis of variance and illustrates the procedures for running both one-way and *n*-way ANOVAs in SPSS.

Similar to an independent samples *t*-test (chapter 14), there are three key assumptions in an ANOVA. First, the test assumes that the respondents in each category of each independent variable were obtained from independent random samples. Second, an ANOVA assumes that the dependent variable is approximately normal distributed for each category of the independent variable(s) in the population. ANOVA is sufficiently robust for handling moderate violations of this assumption. Third, the test assumes that the groups formed by the independent variable(s) have equal variances on the dependent variable. ANOVA is robust for this assumption, especially when the sample sizes for each group are equal. As was demonstrated in the means and *t*-test chapter (chapter 14), this assumption can be tested using the Levene's *F* test.

---

[1] This chapter was coauthored with Dr. Lori B. Shelby, George Mason University.

One-way Analysis of Variance

Overview

Although the assumptions for ANOVA are similar to an independent samples t-test, the test itself is different. An ANOVA involves working directly with the variances rather than the means. Because the populations are assumed to have the same standard deviation, two independent estimates of common variance (σ^2) can be computed. One estimate is analogous to the pooled variance in an independent samples t-test. This estimate is a weighted average of the variances within each of the separate groups formed by the independent variable. A second estimate of common variance involves the variance of the separate groups treated as individual scores. For this estimate, deviations of the sample means about the grand mean are used in the calculating the variance.

The test used in ANOVA involves comparing the two separate estimates of the population variance. Rather than taking a difference between the two estimates, however, the ratio of the second estimate to the first is calculated. If the null hypothesis is correct, this ratio should be approximately 1. If the population means actually differ, however, the second estimate will be larger than the first and the ratio will be larger than 1. The ratio of the two estimates has a known sampling distribution, F, which is used to gauge statistical significance.

Hypothesis Testing

The null (H_0) and alternative (H_1) hypotheses for a one-way ANOVA state the expected relationship for the population means (μ). In the New Hampshire State Parks data, the independent variable might be the year the person visited a given park (i.e., 1987 vs. 1988 vs. 1989), and the dependent variables could be the respondents evaluations of their experience (chapter 10). For a one-way ANOVA where the independent variable has three groups (e.g., 1987, 1988, 1989), the null and alternative hypotheses are:

H_0: $\mu_1 = \mu_2 = \mu_3$
H_1: At least 2 of the population means differ (e.g., $\mu_1 \neq \mu_2$)

Nondirectional ($\mu_1 \neq \mu_2$) or directional ($\mu_1 > \mu_2$) alternative hypotheses can be advanced for the suspected relationships between the means. Depending on an analysts prior knowledge for a given research topic, combinations of nondirectional and directional hypotheses might be advanced ($\mu_1 \neq \mu_2 > \mu_3$).

Decomposing the Total Variation

Consider a one-way ANOVA with a continuous dependent variable (i.e., Y) and a categorical independent variable (i.e., X). The ultimate goal of an ANOVA is the computation of two independent estimates of variance. The analysis is based on the amount of "variation" among the groups. *Variation* is distinct from variance and is defined as the sum of the squared differences from the mean. Total variation about the grand mean across all individuals is:

$$SS_y = \sum_{i=1}^{N}(\text{each individual's score on the dependent variable} - \text{grand mean})^2$$

Equation 15.1

Several important points should be noted about equation 15.1:

1. The term is labeled "SS" because it is the "sum" of the "squared" differences.

2. The *total variation* (SS_y) does not divide by the number of cases in the sample as would be done for a true measure of variance. Thus, SS_y is not trying to create variance estimation but is intended to see how much variation there is among the individuals.

3. Third, the *grand mean* is calculated by averaging the means for each category of the independent variable.

The total sum of squares in Y (SS_y) can be decomposed into two independent components (two sources of variation) that will be used to estimate the two variance components. One of these components is referred to as the $SS_{Between}$. The $SS_{Between}$ is the portion of the sum of squares in Y (the dependent variable) due to the independent variable X. In other words, the $SS_{Between}$ is based on how much the group means vary among themselves (i.e., based on the means). The formula for computing the $SS_{Between}$ is:

$$SS_{Between} = \sum \left[n * \left(\text{group mean} - \text{grand mean}\right)^2 \right] \quad \text{Across all groups}$$

Equation 15.2

The second component (or source of variation) is called the SS_{Within}. The SS_{Within} is the variation in the dependent variable Y that is not accounted for by the independent variable X and is often expressed as SS_{error}. The SS_{Within} is determined by how much the observations within each category of the independent variable varies (i.e., based on the standard deviations). The formula for computing this component is:

$$SS_{Within} = \sum \left[(n-1) * \left(\text{standard deviation}\right)^2 \right] \quad \text{Across all groups}$$

Equation 15.3

Overall, an ANOVA is based on SS_y with the variation decomposed into $SS_{Between}$ and SS_{Within}. The formula is equivalent to a regression model (chapter 15):

$$SS_y = SS_{Between} + SS_{Within}$$

Equation 15.4

Hypothetical Example

Suppose that 300 students are randomly assigned to one of three different classes, each of which employs a different teaching method (e.g., lecture only, hands-on exercises only, or combination of lecture and hands-on exercises). After a certain period of time the students are tested on a common set of questions. The examination score (Y) is the dependent variable and teaching method (X) is the experimental independent variable (or factor). Table 15.1 (p. 378) provides hypothetical data for this example:

Table 15.1   Hypothetical Test Scores from Three Different Teaching Methods

Teaching Method (X)	Number of Students	Examination Results (Y)	
		Mean	Standard Deviation
Lecture only	100	70	5.6
Hands-on exercises only	100	79	6.2
Combination of lecture and exercises	100	92	5.3
Total	300	80	5.7

Although an ANOVA is typically considered to compare means, what we are interested in is the inference that the means of the populations are equal to each other (Figure 15.1). Practically, we use the means obtained from samples of the population (i.e., Groups 1, 2, and 3) to make these inferences.

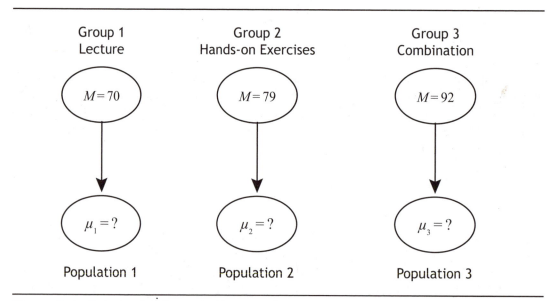

Group 1 Lecture	Group 2 Hands-on Exercises	Group 3 Combination
$M = 70$	$M = 79$	$M = 92$
$\mu_1 = ?$	$\mu_2 = ?$	$\mu_3 = ?$
Population 1	Population 2	Population 3

Figure 15.1   Relationship between Means and μ in Analysis of Variance

As shown in Table 15.1 the overall average (i.e., grand mean) is 80, the three groups have respective means (*M*) of 70, 79, and 92, and the respective standard deviations are 5.6, 6.2, and 5.3. Plugging these numbers into equations 15.2 through 15.4, results in:

$$
\begin{aligned}
SS_{Between} &= \Sigma[n * (group\ mean - grand\ mean)^2]\ across\ all\ groups \\
&= [100 * (70 - 80)^2] + [100 * (79 - 80)^2] + [100 * (92 - 80)^2] \\
&= 10{,}000 + 100 + 14{,}400 \\
&= 24{,}500
\end{aligned}
$$

$$
\begin{aligned}
SS_{Within} &= \Sigma[(n - 1) * (standard\ deviation)^2]\ across\ all\ groups \\
&= [(100 - 1) * (5.6)^2] + [(100 - 1) * (6.2)^2] + [(100 - 1) * (5.3)^2] \\
&= 3{,}104.64 + 3{,}805.56 + 2{,}780.91 \\
&= 9{,}691.11
\end{aligned}
$$

$$SS_y = SS_{Between} + SS_{Within}$$
$$= 24,500 + 9,691.11$$
$$= 34,191.11$$

The statistical test for the null hypothesis that all groups have the same mean is the F-ratio. The degrees of freedom (df) for the F test are calculated using the number of cases (N) and the number of categories in the independent variable (k).

For the *between* category variations, the degrees of freedom are:

$$df_{Between} = k - 1$$

Equation 15.5

For the *within* category variations, the degrees of freedom are:

$$df_{Within} = N - k$$

Equation 15.6

Thus, for the classroom example:
$$df_{Between} = 3 - 1 = 2$$
$$df_{Within} = 300 - 2 = 298$$

Because $SS_{Between}$ and SS_{Within} are summed values, they can be influenced by the number of summed quantities. Dividing the SS by the df eliminates this influence and creates the ***mean square (MS)***. $MS_{Between}$ represents the average amount of variation accounted for by the independent variable X, whereas the MS_{Within} represents the average amount of variation not accounted for by X.

The estimate of population variance based on *between* category variations is:

$$MS_{Between} = \frac{SS_{Between}}{(k-1)}$$

Equation 15.7

The estimate of population variance based on *within* category variations is:

$$MS_{Within} = \frac{SS_{Within}}{(N-k)}$$

Equation 15.8

For the classroom example:

$$MS_{Between} = \frac{24,500}{2} = 12,25$$

$$MS_{Within} = \frac{9,691.11}{298} = 32.52$$

The ***F-ratio*** follows the F sampling distribution and measures the variations explained by $SS_{Between}$ and SS_{Within} with $(k-1)$ and $(N-k)$ degrees of freedom. The test statistic can be directly calculated by dividing the $MS_{Between}$ by the MS_{Within}:

$$F = \frac{SS_{Between} / (k-1)}{SS_{Within} / (N-k)} = \frac{MS_{Between}}{MS_{Within}}$$

Equation 15.9

For the classroom example:

$$F = \frac{MS_{Between}}{MS_{Within}} = \frac{12250}{32.52} = 376.69$$

Similar to other statistical tests (e.g., χ^2, t), the calculated value of the F (i.e., 376.69) is compared to the value in the theoretical F distribution. Tables for these critical values of the F distribution are found in the back of statistics books. Separate tables are presented for different desired probability levels (e.g., .05, .01, .001). Table 15.2 shows a portion of an F distribution table for $p = .001$. The cell entries are the critical values for the F distribution. Values for different degrees of freedom (df) for the between-group variation (e.g., $n_1 = 1, 2, 3, 4, 5$) are displayed across the table. The degrees of freedom for the within-group variation (n_2) are shown down the table. The degrees of freedom for n_2 typically range from 1 to 120, with a final df for infinity. The last three rows of the critical values for an F distribution associated with $p = .001$ are shown in Table 15.2.

Table 15.2   Theoretical F Distribution for p = .001[1]

n_2 \ n_1	1	2	3	4	5
			$p = .001$		
60	11.97	7.76	6.17	5.31	4.76
120	11.38	7.31	5.79	4.95	4.42
∞	10.83	6.91	5.42	4.62	4.10

[1].   Tables similar to this can be found in the back of most statistics books.

For the classroom example, there were 2 degrees of freedom (n_1) for the between-group variation, and 298 df for the within-group variation (n_2). Under these conditions, the critical value of the F distribution is 6.91 for a p-value of .001. Given that the calculated F-ratio was 376.69 (i.e., larger than the critical value), the relationship between teaching method and performance on the exam was statistically significant at $p < .001$.

Statistical programs like SPSS eliminate the need for looking up theoretical values in tables like Table 15.2 when comparing the computed test statistic against the critical values. SPSS does the comparison and reports the ***actual observed significance level***. SPSS labels this p-value "**Sig.**" This Sig. level is the probability of a Type I error or the probability of rejecting the null hypothesis when it is actually true (chapter 6). For any specific statistic (e.g., χ^2, t, F), if the Sig. or p is small ($< .05, < .01, < .001$), the finding is *statistically* significant and the null hypothesis is rejected.

When the overall F-ratio is not significant the means for the groups being compared are statistically equal to each other, and researcher fails-to-reject the null hypothesis. If the overall F-ratio is statistically significant at least one of the means for the groups being compared is different from the other group means. To determine which specific means differ from one another, additional analysis is needed (e.g., contrasts, post hoc tests).

Contrasts

One method for determining where the differences are when there is a statistically significant F-ratio is contrasts. A ***contrast*** between two means is simply the difference between the means disregarding whether the difference is positive or negative. For example, with three groups (or categories) in an independent variable, three pairwise contrasts are possible:

$M_1 - M_2$	Contrasts the 1st group and the 2nd group
$M_1 - M_3$	Contrasts the 1st group and the 3rd group
$M_2 - M_3$	Contrasts the 2nd group and the 3rd group

In the classroom example, $M_1 - M_2$ is an independent samples t-test comparing the mean performance on the exam for the "lecture only" sample and "hands-on exercise only" sample. The $M_1 - M_3$ comparison contrasts the means for the "lecture only" sample against the "combined lecture and exercises" sample. The third contrast ($M_2 - M_3$) compares the "hands-on exercises only" sample and the "combined lecture and exercises" sample.

Computationally, a contrast between means involves a weighted sum of means in which the weights (W_js) sum to 0. Practically, for pairwise comparisons weights are either 1, –1, or 0. For the classroom example with three categories to the independent variable, three pairwise contrasts are possible. Table 15.3 illustrates how the weights are assigned for this example. The mean for the first sample (M_1) is assigned a weight of 1, M_2 is assigned a weight of –1, and M_3 has a weight of 0. The sum of these weights is 0. (i.e., $[1] + [-1] + [0] = 0$). Multiplying any number by 0 results in a value of 0, so M_3 drops out of the comparison for the first contrast. Multiplying M_1 by 1 does not change mean. Multiplying M_2 by –1 does not change the mean, only the sign. In other words, the weights of 1, –1, and 0 do not change the results of the contrast, but are used only to set up the contrasts. The result of contrast 1 is an independent samples t-test between M_1 and M_2. Similar logic is applied to contrasts 2 and 3 in Table 15.3.

Table 15.3   Setting Up Pairwise Contrasts

Contrast	$W_1 M_1$	$W_2 M_2$	$W_3 M_3$	Test
1	1 (M_1)	–1 (M_2)	0 (M_3)	$= M_1 - M_2$
2	1 (M_1)	0 (M_2)	–1 (M_3)	$= M_1 - M_3$
3	0 (M_1)	1 (M_2)	–1 (M_3)	$= M_2 - M_3$

Nonpairwise contrasts may be used to answer other specific research questions. The following contrast examines if individuals in a control group (M_0; e.g., another class) differ from those in the three experimental groups (M_1, M_2, M_3).

$$M_0 = \frac{M_1 + M_2 + M_3}{3}$$

The contrast for this comparison is: $1 -.333 -.333 -.334 = 0$.

Although contrasts provide valuable information, there are also problems. The number of possible pairwise comparisons among the means increases dramatically as the number of groups in the independent variable increases. For example, with four groups associated with the independent variable, six pairwise contrasts result:

$M_1 - M_2$ Contrasts the 1st group and the 2nd group
$M_1 - M_3$ Contrasts the 1st group and the 3rd group
$M_1 - M_4$ Contrasts the 1st group and the 4th group
$M_2 - M_3$ Contrasts the 2nd group and the 3rd group
$M_2 - M_4$ Contrasts the 2nd group and the 4th group
$M_3 - M_4$ Contrasts the 3rd group and the 4th group

Depending on the research question, multiple nonpairwise comparisons (C) are also possible. As the number of comparisons of means (or contrasts) increase, the probability of obtaining at least one significant comparison by chance increases. More formally, this can be expressed as:

$1 - (1 - \alpha)^C$, which is approximately equal to $C\alpha$ Equation 15.10

where:

     C = the number of contrasts
     α = p-value or probability level

For example, the probability (α or p-value) for three contrasts increases to:

     $C\alpha = 3(.05) = .15$

This implies that rather than testing the differences between the means at $p = .05$, the test is based on $p = .15$. Two strategies for compensating for this situation and keeping the desired probability (e.g., .05 or .01 or .001) for all multiple comparisons are the Bonferroni correction and post hoc comparisons.

Bonferroni Correction

The simplest approach for determining an appropriate p-value is called the Bonferroni correction (see also chapter 16). The **Bonferroni** correction divides the desired p-value by the number of contrasts that are performed:

$$\text{Bonferroni Correction} = \frac{p\text{-value}}{\text{number of tests}}$$
         Equation 15.11

For the three pairwise contrasts associated with the classroom example, the Bonferroni correction is:

$$\text{Bonferroni Correction} = \frac{.05}{3} = .0167$$

With the Bonferroni correction in the classroom example where the independent variable was a three-level categorical variable, a given contrast would be statistically significant if the p-value was less than .0167. If there were four categories associated with the independent variable, six pairwise contrasts are possible, and the appropriate p-value for testing statistical significance at $p < .05$ is .008:

$$\text{Bonferroni Correction} = \frac{.05}{6} = .008$$

Post Hoc Comparisons

In general, ***post hoc comparisons*** attempt to keep the p-value (α) at some desired level (e.g., $\alpha = .05$, or $\alpha = .01$, or $\alpha = .001$) for all contrasts when conducting multiple comparisons. Table 15.4 (p. 384) lists eight common post hoc comparison tests and provides short descriptions for each test (see Kirk, 1968, for more information). The tests differ in how they go about achieving the goal of keeping the p-value at some desired level and in their ability to detect differences between categories (i.e., liberal vs. conservative tests). For example, the *least significant difference* (LSD) uses t-tests to perform all pairwise comparisons between category means. LSD is the most liberal post hoc comparisons since it is most likely to find that categories differ (Type I error, Table 15.4). When the overall F-ratio is significant, the LSD between two means is:

$$\text{LSD} = t_{\alpha/2,v}\sqrt{\frac{2\text{MS}_{Within}}{n}}$$

Equation 15.12

where:
  $t_{\alpha/2,v}$ = the upper percentage point from Student's t distribution for v degrees of freedom
     v = the degrees of freedom associated with the denominator of the F-ratio

The Scheffé's S Method uses a more demanding critical value for the F-ratio. Scheffé's S controls for Type I error and thus provides a conservative post hoc comparison. As a result, the method tends to err on the side of Type II errors (underestimates statistical significance). The Scheffé test controls for the fact that multiple comparisons are being made to maintain an $\alpha = .05$, but as a result it loses statistical power (Type II errors). If the overall F-ratio is significant, the Scheffé's S between two means is:

$$S = \sqrt{(k-1)F_{\alpha;v_1,v_2}}\sqrt{MS_{error}\left[\sum_{j=1}^{k}\frac{(C_j)^2}{n_j}\right]}$$

Equation 15.13

where:
  $F_{\alpha;v_1,v_2}$ = tabled value for F for v_1 and v_2 df
     k = number of groups
    C_j = coefficient of the contrast
    n_j = number of scores for the jth group

The choice of one post hoc comparison over another depends in part on sample size. When the sample size for given categories of the independent variables is small, the LSD comparison is commonly reported. A cautionary note, however, is that LSD is the most likely post hoc test to find that the categories differ. Generally, researchers analyze more than one post hoc test in order to compare the results between liberal and conservative tests. If the sample sizes are large, the Scheffé's S method is more common. In addition, similar to independent samples *t*-tests where the appropriate test depends on whether or not the variances are equal (chapter 14), the researcher's decision to use a particular post hoc test in an ANOVA is dictated by the equality of the variances (Table 15.4). Post hoc comparisons such as LSD, Bonferroni, or Scheffé's S are appropriate when equality of variances can be assumed. When this assumption is not supported by the Levene's test (see chapter 14 and discussion below), post hoc tests such as Games-Howell or the Tamhane's T2 post hoc test can be used.

Table 15.4   Comparison of Commonly Used Post Hoc Comparison Tests

Test	Description
Equal Variances Assumed	
LSD	The *least significant difference* pairwise comparison test uses multiple *t*-tests between all possible pairs of categories. It is a liberal post hoc test (most likely to find that the categories differ).
Bonferroni	The Bonferroni correction (also called *Bonferroni adjusted test* or *Dunn's test*) uses *t*-tests to perform pairwise comparisons, but adjusts the observed significance level for the fact that multiple comparisons are made. This test is generally used when there are few comparisons, since it is difficult to show significance when there are many comparisons.
Sidak	A variation of the Bonferroni correction approach, which is more conservative (less likely to find that the categories differ).
Dunnett	A pairwise multiple comparison *t*-test used to compare the means of treatment groups with the mean of a control group.
Tukey[1]	Tukey's *honestly significant difference* test (HSD) uses the studentized range statistic (i.e., q statistic[2]) to make the pairwise comparisons between categories. The test is a conservative post hoc test (less likely to find that the groups differ). It is adjusted for multiple comparisons and is preferred over Bonferroni correction when the number of categories is large.
Scheffé's S	Scheffé's S method performs simultaneous pairwise comparisons for all possible pairs using the F sampling distribution. This test is widely used, and is very conservative (more conservative than Bonferroni correction or Tukey). It is particularly useful for conducting a large number of comparisons.
Equal Variances Not Assumed	
Games-Howell	Pairwise comparison test that is slightly liberal and appropriate for unequal variances.
Tamhane's T2	A conservative pairwise comparisons test based on a *t*-test, which is appropriate when the variances are unequal.

[1]   Not to be confused with Tukey-b, which is a less common post hoc test that ranks group means and computes a range variable.

[2]   Similar to the *t* statistic which tests for differences between two means, the q statistic tests that the largest and smallest means were sampled from the same population (see Kirk, 1968, for more information).

Effect Sizes in ANOVA

As discussed in chapter 6 on effect sizes, whether the overall differences are to be considered substantial or trivial depends on the degree of overall variation in the whole sample (e.g., 300 students in the classroom example), and, in particular, on the variation within each category of X. The most popular effect size statistic for ANOVA measuring the strength of the effect of X on Y is eta^2 (or symbolically, η^2) and is defined as the ratio:

$$\text{eta}^2 = \eta^2 = \frac{SS_x}{SS_y} = \frac{SS_y - SS_{\text{Within}}}{SS_y}$$ Equation 15.14

The value of eta^2 will be 1.0 if and only if there is no variability within each category of X and there is some variability between categories. The index will be 0 if and only if there is no difference among the means of the three categories in the classroom example. An eta$^2 = 0$ indicates there is no effect of X on Y. For the classroom example:

$$\text{eta}^2 = \frac{SS_y - SS_{\text{Within}}}{SS_y} = \frac{34,191.11 - 9,691.11}{34,191.11} = .717$$

Eta^2 is analogous to R^2 in regression analysis (chapter 16) and can be interpreted as the proportion of variance in the dependent variable explained by differences among the categories of the independent variable. When reporting an eta as effect size the non-squared eta is used. For the classroom example, eta $= \sqrt{.717} = .847$ which indicates that there is "substantial" (chapter 6) variability between classrooms. Eta is not available in the ONE-WAY ANOVA procedure in SPSS; instead it can be produced using the MEANS command (chapter 14).

One-way ANOVA in SPSS

The New Hampshire State Parks Report Card data file (chapter 10) will be used to illustrate the ONE-WAY ANOVA procedure in SPSS. Similar to chapter 14, an overall GPA was calculated.

```
Compute GPA = Mean.5(frstimpr,stafhelp,clenrest,infopark,
                     atractiv,safety,cleangrd,easeaces,hours,
                     petcntrl,overall) .

Variable Labels GPA 'Overall Grade Point Average'.
```

To obtain a ONE-WAY ANOVA the four basic steps in conducting statistical analysis discussed in chapter 9 apply:

1. Open the data file: NH - State Parks - Report card.sav
   (see chapter 9, Introduction to SPSS, for assistance in opening a data file)

2. Click on **Analyze > Compare Means > One-Way ANOVA...**   see Figure 15.2

3. Select the variables to be included in the analysis   see Figure 15.3

4. Select additional statistical procedures   see Figures 15.4 through 15.6

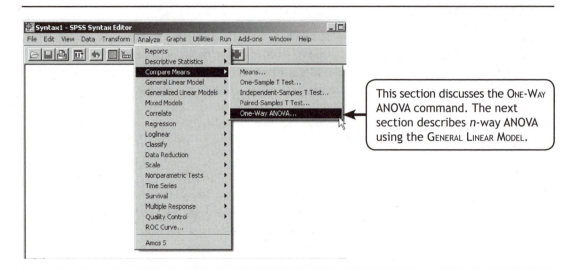

Figure 15.2 Selecting the SPSS One-Way ANOVA Procedure

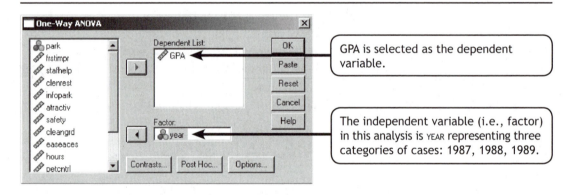

Figure 15.3 Selecting Variables for a One-Way ANOVA Analysis

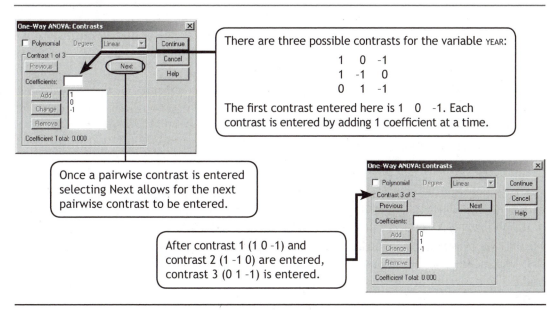

Figure 15.4   Obtaining Contrasts in One-Way ANOVA

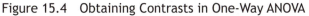

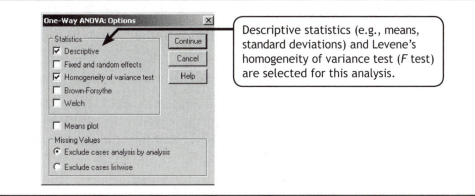

Figure 15.5   Selecting Post Hoc Comparisons for a One-Way ANOVA

Figure 15.6   Selecting Additional Options for a One-Way ANOVA

The syntax generated from the options selected in this analysis is:

```
ONEWAY
  GPA BY year
  /CONTRAST= 1 -1  0
  /CONTRAST= 1  0 -1
  /CONTRAST= 0  1 -1
  /STATISTICS DESCRIPTIVES HOMOGENEITY
  /MISSING ANALYSIS
  /POSTHOC = T2 GH ALPHA(.05).
```

The DESCRIPTIVES output from this analysis is shown in Output 15.1. GPA is the dependent variable and YEAR of visit to a New Hampshire State Park is the independent variable. The goal of the ANOVA was to test for differences in the means for each of the three study years (1987 vs. 1988 vs. 1989) for the dependent variable GPA. The DESCRIPTIVES output displays the sample sizes, means, standard deviations, and standard errors of the mean (see chapter 11 for definitions of these statistics) for the three years.

Output 15.1   Descriptives from a One-Way Analysis of Variance

Descriptives

GPA   Overall Grade Point Average

		N	Mean	Std. Deviation	Std. Error	95% Confidence Interval for Mean		Minimum	Maximum
						Lower Bound	Upper Bound		
87	1987	100	2.9695	1.01663	.10166	2.7678	3.1712	.64	4.00
88	1988	98	3.3154	.70907	.07163	3.1732	3.4576	1.00	4.00
89	1989	100	3.4805	.56645	.05665	3.3681	3.5929	1.50	4.00
Total		298	3.2547	.81330	.04711	3.1620	3.3475	.64	4.00

For the overall grade point average index (GPA), the Levene's test for equality of variances was significant ($p < .001$) indicating that equal variances should not be assumed (Output 15.2).

Output 15.2   Test of Homogeneity of Variances

Test of Homogeneity of Variances

GPA   Overall Grade Point Average

Levene Statistic	df1	df2	Sig.
31.607	2	295	.000

Indicates that the variances differ statistically at $p < .001$ and that a post hoc test for "equal variances not assumed" should be used.

The overall F-ratio for the one-way ANOVA is used to compare the means for 1987 ($M = 2.97$), 1988 ($M = 3.32$), and 1989 ($M = 3.48$). The F-value for GPA is statistically significant ($F = 10.97$, $p < .001$), suggesting that there is a difference between at least two of the mean scores (Output 15.3).

Output 15.3 ANOVA Table

> Indicates that the overall *F*-ratio is statistically at *p* < .001 (i.e., at least two of the means differ from each other).

ANOVA

GPA Overall Grade Point Average

	Sum of Squares	df	Mean Square	F	Sig.
Between Groups	13.597	2	6.798	10.968	.000
Within Groups	182.857	295	.620		
Total	196.454	297			

The degrees of freedom for this analysis are based on equations 15.5 and 15.6:

$$df_{Between} = k - 1 = 3 - 1 = 2$$
$$df_{Within} = N - k = 298 - 3 = 295$$

Computation of the *F*-ratio is based on equations 15.7, 15.8, and 15.9:

$$MS_{Between} = \frac{SS_{Between}}{(k-1)} = \frac{13.597}{2} = 6.798$$

$$MS_{Within} = \frac{SS_{Within}}{(N-k)} = \frac{182.857}{295} = .620$$

$$F = \frac{MS_{Between}}{MS_{Within}} = \frac{6.798}{.620} = 10.968$$

Because the overall *F*-ratio is significant ($p < .001$), it is appropriate to explore which specific means differ from one another. The SPSS output reiterates the contrast coefficients that were used in this analysis (Output 15.4).

Output 15.4 Contrast Coefficients and Contrast Tests

Contrast Coefficients

	year Year of VIsit		
Contrast	87 1987	88 1988	89 1989
1	1	−1	0
2	1	0	−1
3	0	1	−1

> The contrast coefficients (weights) specified by the researcher in Figure 15.4.

Given the results of the Levene's *F* test (31.607; Output 15.2), the appropriate contrasts are found under "Does not assume equal variances" (Output 15.5, p. 390). The contrasts perform a series of independent samples *t*-tests. As noted above, for each *t*-test the mean associated with each level of the independent variable is first multiplied by the coefficients in Output 15.4 (e.g., 1, −1, or 0). Multiplying a number by 1 or −1 does not change the actual value, only the sign. Multiplying the value by 0 sets the mean to 0 (i.e., it drops out of the contrast). As a result, contrast 1 compares 1987 versus 1988, contrast 2 compares 1987 versus 1989, and contrast 3 compares 1988 versus 1989 on the GPA variable. Contrasts 1 and 2 are significant ($p < .05$). This indicates that the means for 1987 ($M = 2.97$) versus 1988 ($M = 3.32$), and 1987 ($M = 2.97$) versus 1989 ($M = 3.48$) are significantly different ($p < .05$). Contrast 3 is not significant indicating that there is not a difference between the 1988 ($M = 3.32$) versus 1989 ($M = 3.48$) respondents.

Output 15.5   Contrast Tests in an One-Way Analysis of Variance

Contrast Tests

		Contrast	Value of Contrast	Std. Error	t	df	Sig. (2-tailed)
GPA Overall Grade Point Average	Assume equal variances	1	−.3459	.11191	−3.091	295	.002
		2	−.5111	.11134	−4.590	295	.000
		3	−.1651	.11191	−1.476	295	.141
	Does not assume equal variances	1	−.3459	.12436	−2.782	177.133	.006
		2	−.5111	.11638	−4.391	155.133	.000
		3	−.1651	.09132	−1.808	185.270	.072

> This set of *p*-values would be reported because the variances were not equal (Output 15.2)

Post hoc tests were also specified in the SPSS command syntax for this analysis (Output 15.6). Two post hoc tests were requested (Tamhane's T2 and Game-Howell). In this example, both tests lead to the same conclusion. The first line in the Tamhane's T2 test, for example, compares 1987 against 1988. After controlling for multiple tests, the difference in the means (−.34592) is statistically significant at $p = .018$. The second line in the Tamhane's T2 test contrasts the mean scores for 1988 against 1989. The difference (−.51106), after controlling for multiple tests is statistically significant, $p < .001$.

Notice that the comparison of 1988 versus 1987 is redundant with the comparison of 1987 versus 1988. The only thing that changes is the direction of the difference (i.e., −.34592 vs. .34592).

Output 15.6   Post Hoc Tests / Multiple Comparisons

Multiple Comparisons

Dependent Variable: GPA   Overall Grade Point Average

	(I) year Year of Visit	(J) year Year of Visit	Mean Difference (I-J)	Std. Error	Sig.	95% Confidence Interval Lower Bound	Upper Bound
Tamhane	87 1987	88 1988	−.34592*	.12436	.018	−.6457	−.0461
		89 1989	−.51106*	.11638	.000	−.7920	−.2301
	88 1988	87 1987	.34592*	.12436	.018	.0461	.6457
		89 1989	−.16514	.09132	.201	−.3852	.0549
	89 1989	87 1987	.51106*	.11638	.000	.2301	.7920
		88 1988	.16514	.09132	.201	−.0549	.3852
Games-Howell	87 1987	88 1988	−.34592*	.12436	.016	−.6399	−.0520
		89 1989	−.51106*	.11638	.000	−.7865	−.2357
	88 1988	87 1987	.34592*	.12436	.016	.0520	.6399
		89 1989	−.16514	.09132	.170	−.3809	.0506
	89 1989	87 1987	.51106*	.11638	.000	.2357	.7865
		88 1988	.16514	.09132	.170	−.0506	.3809

The results from the multiple comparison post hoc tests support the contrast results in this example. For both the Tamhane's T2 and Game-Howell tests 1987 versus 1988, and 1987 versus 1989 are significantly different ($p < .05$). There is not a significant difference between 1988 and 1989 for Tamhane's T2 test ($p = .201$) or the Games-Howell test ($p = .170$). The difference in the *p*-values occurs due to the way the two tests calculate the comparison. The Tamhane's T2 test is more conservative and the resulting *p*-value is slightly higher (.201) than the more liberal Games-Howell (.170) test.

Table 15.5 illustrates how these results might be displayed in a journal article. The superscripts on the means indicate where the differences between the specific means occur. Means with different superscripts signify statistical differences after controlling for multiple comparisons based on the Tamhane's T2 method. For example, the mean of 2.97 for 1987 has a superscript of [a] and the mean of 3.48 has a superscript of [c]. This indicates that the 2.97 is statistically different than 3.48. The mean for 1988 (3.32) has two superscripts (i.e., [bc]). The superscript [b] is an indication that 3.32 statistically differs from 2.97, which has a superscript of [a]. The [c] associated with the mean of 3.32 implies that the average for 1988 is statistically equivalent to the mean for 1989 (3.48), which also has a superscript of [c].

Table 15.5   Grade Point Average by Year for New Hampshire State Parks

	Year of Visit[1]				
	1987	1988	1989	*F*-value	*p*-value
GPA[2]	2.97[a]	3.32[bc]	3.48[c]	10.97	.001

1. Means with different superscripts are significant at *p* < .05 based on Tamhane's T2 method.

2. GPA is the overall grade point average obtained from a scale of survey questions measured on five-point scales (F [0], D [1], C [2], B [3], and A [4]).

n-way ANOVA

In an *n*-way ANOVA (also referred to as a ***factorial ANOVA***), there is more than one independent variable and one continuous dependent variable. The independent variables are referred to as *factors* (or *main effects*) and can be either dichotomous or categorical. A two-way ANOVA involves two factors, a three-way ANOVA involves three factors. Each factor consists of two or more levels. This notation can be more specific to designate the number of factors as well as the number of levels for each factor. For example, a 2 x 4 ANOVA is a two-way ANOVA including one factor with two levels and one factor with four levels. A 3 x 2 x 4 ANOVA is a three-way ANOVA which has one factor with three levels, one with two levels, and one with four levels.

The assumptions for an *n*-way ANOVA are similar to those for a one-way ANOVA. First, the respondents in each category of each independent variable are assumed to come from independent random samples. Second, the dependent variable is assumed to have an approximately normal distribution for each category of the independent variables in the population. Third, the groups associated with each independent variable are assumed to have equal variances on the dependent variable. Similar to the independent samples *t*-test and one-way ANOVA, this third assumption can be tested with the Levene's test.

n-way ANOVA Example

An endangered fish experiment was designed to evaluate the message effectiveness of a video entitled *Survivors: Endangered Fish in the Upper Colorado River Basin*. The video was produced by the U.S. Fish and Wildlife Service. Elaboration likelihood theory (see Eagly & Chaiken, 1993 for details) was used to predict that the extent to which one can elaborate on a message as a function of two general classes of variables: (a) motivation and (b) ability. Figure 15.7 shows the elaboration likelihood theory model as it relates to the endangered fish experiment. Motivation (i.e., level of involvement) and ability (i.e., length of video) are the independent variables, and elaboration (i.e., total number of reasons listed for fish being endangered) is the dependent variable.

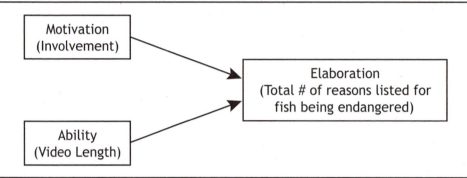

Figure 15.7   Elaboration Likelihood Theory Model for Endangered Fish Experiment

To examine the model shown in Figure 15.7, a sample of Colorado State University students (*n* = 90) was randomly assigned to six experimental groups (*n* = 15 in each group). Table 15.6 shows the experimental design. This is referred to a *factorial ANOVA* (or an *n*-way ANOVA). There are two types of factorial ANOVA designs: full factorial and fractional factorial. This experiment is considered a *full factorial ANOVA* because the design: (a) contains two independent factors (involvement and video length), (b) each factor has discrete possible values or "levels" associated with it, and (c) all possible combinations of these levels across all such factors are included. With a factorial design, the researcher can test for main effects of each independent variable and for interaction effects between the predictors (see discussion below).

Table 15.6   Experimental Design for Endangered Fish Example

Video Length (in minutes)	Involved[1]	Not Involved[1]
2	15	15
7	15	15
15	15	15

[1] Cell entries are sample sizes.

It is desirable to have equal sample sizes within each cell (i.e., *n* = 15 in this example). If a third or fourth independent variable is added to the design, the required number of respondents (or subjects) increases dramatically. For example, for a 3 x 3 x 3 x 3 design (i.e., four independent variables, each with three levels), there are 81 cells. If a researcher wants an *n* of 15 in each cell, a total of 1,215 subjects are required. Reducing the number of respondents to 10 per cell would still necessitate an overall sample of 810.

To compensate for the cost and effort associated with a full factorial design when multiple independent variables are examined, some experiments do *not* include all possible combinations of the levels associated with the factors. This type of experiment is referred to as a *fractional factorial design*. The subset (or fraction) of the experimental conditions selected are chosen to highlight information about the most important features of the problem under investigation while using a fraction of the effort required by a full factorial. Such designs can be quite complex and are beyond the scope of this book (see Box, Hunter, & Hunter, 2005 for a discussion of fractional factorial designs).

In the 3 x 2 full factorial experiment in this section (Table 15.6), involvement (an indicator of a person's motivation to elaborate) was operationalized through role playing. The experimenter told half of the subjects (involved group, $n = 45$) they would have to make a verbal presentation (after the watching the video) to their peers that described the reasons the fish had declined. The other subjects (not involved group, $n = 45$) were simply asked to watch the video. The variable was coded "1" (involved) or "0" (not involved). After watching the video both groups completed a survey.

Video length was operationalized by using three versions of the video that varied in length (2 minutes [$n = 30$], 7 minutes [$n = 30$], and 14 minutes [$n = 30$]). The longer versions of the video provided more reasons for the decline of the fish and thus, enhanced the subject's ability to elaborate on the reasons.

The dependent variable was operationalized as the total number of reasons for the decline of the endangered fish that respondents listed on the survey (i.e., an open-ended, fill-in-the blank question).

The research questions and hypotheses of interest here are:

1. Is there a significant main effect for *each* factor (video length and involvement) on the number of reasons given for the decline of the endangered fish? The corresponding null and alternative hypotheses for these research questions are:

   H_0: $\mu_{involved} = \mu_{not\ involved}$
   H_1: $\mu_{involved} \neq \mu_{not\ involved}$

   H_0: $\mu_{2\ min.} = \mu_{7\ min.} = \mu_{14\ min.}$
   H_1: At least 2 of the population means differ (e.g., $\mu_{2\ min.} \neq \mu_{7\ min.}$).

2. Is there a significant interaction between the independent factors? Do video length and involvement interact to influence number of reasons given for the decline in endangered fish? More specifically, does the difference between the involved group and the not involved group change across videos of different length?

   H_0: No interaction between involvement and video length
   H_1: There is an interaction

An *interaction* means that the effect of one independent variable has on a dependent variable is not the same for all levels of the other independent variable. A significant interaction requires caution in interpreting main effects. Interactions can be examined through the use of marginal means and profile plots, which are discussed next.

n-way ANOVA in SPSS

The Colorado Endangered Fish Experiment data file will be used to illustrate a two-way ANOVA in SPSS. A two-way ANOVA is performed in SPSS through the GENERAL LINEAR MODEL UNIVARIATE procedure. Similar to the other tests discussed in this book, the four basic steps in conducting statistical analysis apply:

1. Open the data file: CO – Endangered Fish Experiment.sav

2. Click on: **Analyze > General Linear Model > Univariate...**   see Figure 15.8

3. Select the variables to be included in the analysis   see Figure 15.9

4. Select additional statistical procedures   see Figures 15.10 through 15.15

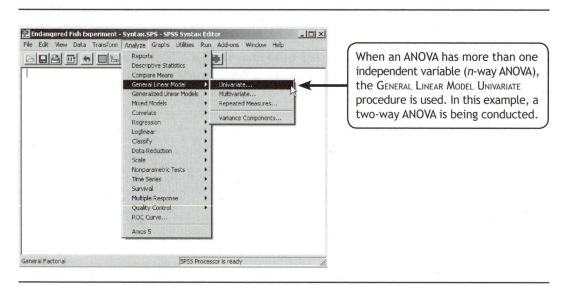

Figure 15.8   Selecting the SPSS General Linear Model Univariate Procedure

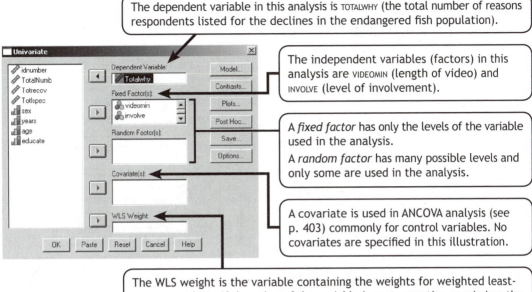

The dependent variable in this analysis is TOTALWHY (the total number of reasons respondents listed for the declines in the endangered fish population).

The independent variables (factors) in this analysis are VIDEOMIN (length of video) and INVOLVE (level of involvement).

A *fixed factor* has only the levels of the variable used in the analysis.

A *random factor* has many possible levels and only some are used in the analysis.

A covariate is used in ANCOVA analysis (see p. 403) commonly for control variables. No covariates are specified in this illustration.

The WLS weight is the variable containing the weights for weighted least-squares analysis. If the value of the variable is zero, negative or missing, the case is excluded from the analysis. This option is more frequently used in regression analysis (chapter 16).

Figure 15.9   Selecting Variables for a General Linear Model Univariate Procedure

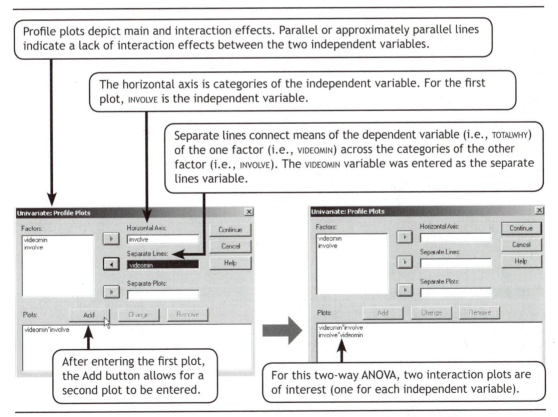

Profile plots depict main and interaction effects. Parallel or approximately parallel lines indicate a lack of interaction effects between the two independent variables.

The horizontal axis is categories of the independent variable. For the first plot, INVOLVE is the independent variable.

Separate lines connect means of the dependent variable (i.e., TOTALWHY) of the one factor (i.e., VIDEOMIN) across the categories of the other factor (i.e., INVOLVE). The VIDEOMIN variable was entered as the separate lines variable.

After entering the first plot, the Add button allows for a second plot to be entered.

For this two-way ANOVA, two interaction plots are of interest (one for each independent variable).

Figure 15.10   Selecting Plots for a General Linear Model Univariate Procedure

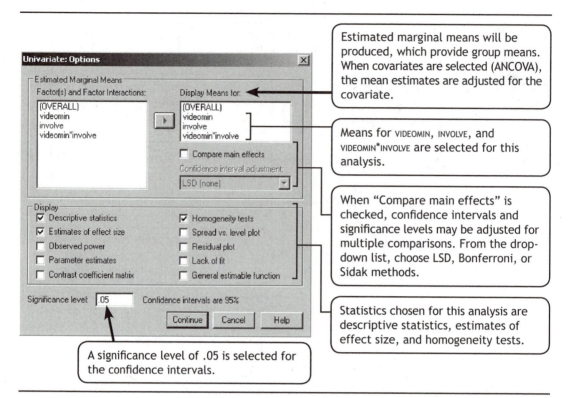

Estimated marginal means will be produced, which provide group means. When covariates are selected (ANCOVA), the mean estimates are adjusted for the covariate.

Means for VIDEOMIN, INVOLVE, and VIDEOMIN*INVOLVE are selected for this analysis.

When "Compare main effects" is checked, confidence intervals and significance levels may be adjusted for multiple comparisons. From the drop-down list, choose LSD, Bonferroni, or Sidak methods.

Statistics chosen for this analysis are descriptive statistics, estimates of effect size, and homogeneity tests.

A significance level of .05 is selected for the confidence intervals.

Figure 15.11   Selecting Statistics for a General Linear Model Univariate Procedure

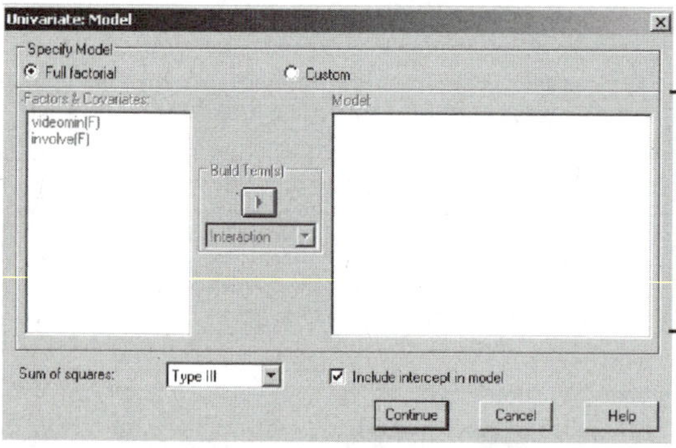

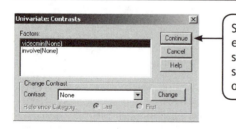

Allows a model to be defined containing a subset of possible factor-by-factor inter-actions or factor-by-covariate interactions (ANCOVA). None are selected for this example. This model is a full factorial design.

Figure 15.12   Univariate Model

Standard contrasts using the *t*-statistic are available for each factor, which tests whether the categories are significantly different from one another. None are selected for this example. Because INVOLVE variable has only two levels, contrasts are not necessary.

Figure 15.13   Univariate Contrasts

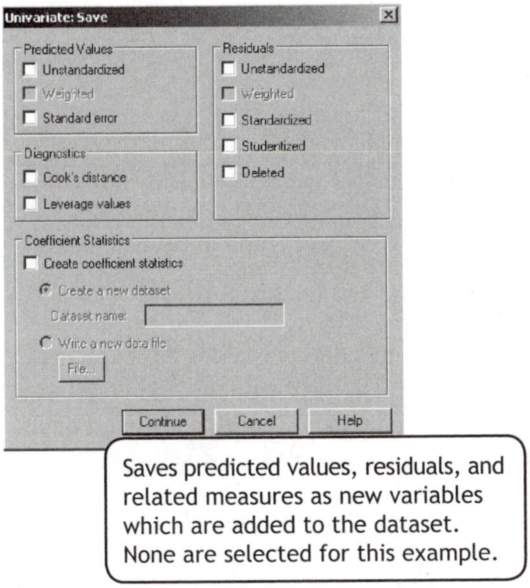

Figure 15.14   Saving Univariate Variables 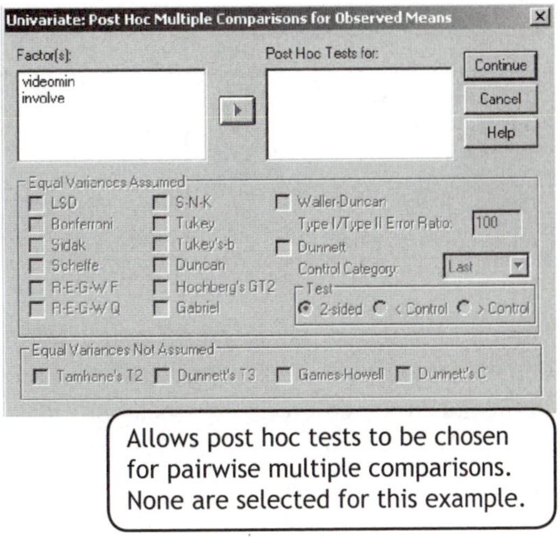   Figure 15.15   Univariate Post Hoc Tests

The syntax generated from the options selected in this analysis is:

```
UNIANOVA
  Totalwhy  BY videomin involve
  /METHOD = SSTYPE(3)
  /INTERCEPT = INCLUDE
  /PLOT = PROFILE( videomin*involve involve*videomin )
  /EMMEANS = TABLES(OVERALL)
  /EMMEANS = TABLES(videomin)
  /EMMEANS = TABLES(involve)
  /EMMEANS = TABLES(videomin*involve)
  /PRINT = DESCRIPTIVE ETASQ HOMOGENEITY
  /CRITERIA = ALPHA(.05)
  /DESIGN = videomin involve videomin*involve .
```

A two-way ANOVA was requested (TOTALWHY by VIDEOMIN and INVOLVE). The between-subjects factors shown in Output 15.6 (p. 398) describe the how the variables were coded, value labels and sample sizes for the two independent variables. This is a between-subjects design because each respondent was in one and only one cell of the experimental design.

Output 15.6   Between-Subjects Factors

Between-Subjects Factors

			Value Label	N
videomin Independent	1		2 min	30
variable – Video length	2		7 min	30
	3		14 min	30
involve Independent	0		No involvement	45
variable – Involvement	1		Involvement	45

Output 15.7 shows the descriptive statistics for the two independent variables based on the dependent variable. For example, for respondents who watched the 2-minute video who were in the not-involved group, the mean number of reasons listed was 3.73 with a standard deviation of .961.

Output 15.7   Descriptive Statistics

Descriptive Statistics

Dependent Variable: Totalwhy   Total number of reasons listed

videomin Independent	involve Independent	Mean	Std. Deviation	N
1 2 min	0 No Involvment	3.73	.961	15
	1 Involvement	3.60	1.121	15
	Total	3.67	1.028	30
2 7 min	0 No Involvment	3.93	.961	15
	1 Involvement	6.00	2.000	15
	Total	4.97	1.866	30
3 14 min	0 No Involvment	4.67	1.447	15
	1 Involvement	5.13	1.246	15
	Total	4.90	1.348	30
Total	0 No Involvment	4.11	1.191	45
	1 Involvement	4.91	1.781	45
	Total	4.51	1.560	90

The Levene's test of equality of error variances uses a F test to determine if the variance of error for the dependent variable is equal across groups (Output 15.8). In other words, that each category of the independent variables have the same variance. The Levene's test is not significant ($p = .103$) indicating that equal variances can be assumed.

Output 15.8   Levene's Test of Equality of Error Variances

Levene's Test of Equality of Error Variances[a]

Dependent Variable: Totalwhy   Total number of reasons listed

F	df1	df2	Sig.
1.897	5	84	.103

Because the Levene's test was not significant ($p = .103$) equality of variances is assumed.

Tests the null hypothesis that the error variance of the dependent variable is equal across all groups.

[a.] Design: Intercept+videomin+involve+videomin * involve

In the ANOVA table (Output 15.9) each term in the model, in addition to the model as a whole, is tested for its ability to account for variation in the dependent variable. All of the terms are statistically significant for this example ($p < .05$).

Output 15.9   Tests of Between-Subjects Effects

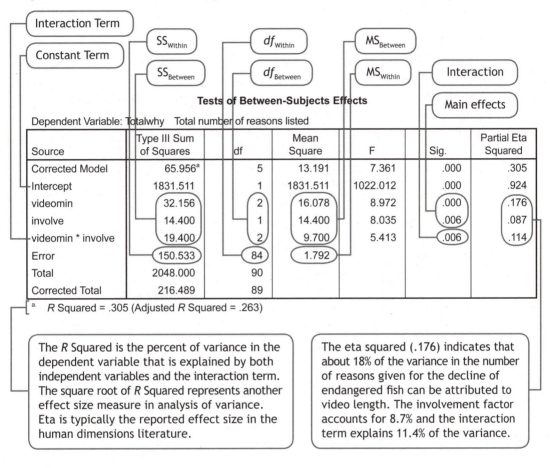

Tests of Between-Subjects Effects

Dependent Variable: Totalwhy   Total number of reasons listed

Source	Type III Sum of Squares	df	Mean Square	F	Sig.	Partial Eta Squared
Corrected Model	65.956[a]	5	13.191	7.361	.000	.305
Intercept	1831.511	1	1831.511	1022.012	.000	.924
videomin	32.156	2	16.078	8.972	.000	.176
involve	14.400	1	14.400	8.035	.006	.087
videomin * involve	19.400	2	9.700	5.413	.006	.114
Error	150.533	84	1.792			
Total	2048.000	90				
Corrected Total	216.489	89				

a.   R Squared = .305 (Adjusted R Squared = .263)

The *R* Squared is the percent of variance in the dependent variable that is explained by both independent variables and the interaction term. The square root of *R* Squared represents another effect size measure in analysis of variance. Eta is typically the reported effect size in the human dimensions literature.

The eta squared (.176) indicates that about 18% of the variance in the number of reasons given for the decline of endangered fish can be attributed to video length. The involvement factor accounts for 8.7% and the interaction term explains 11.4% of the variance.

The *F*-value is computed by using sums of squares (SS), degrees of freedom (*df*) and mean squares (MS) values for the Between and Within components of the model. More specifically:

$$F_{video\,min} = \frac{SS_{Between} / (k-1)}{SS_{Within} / (N-k)} = \frac{32.156/2}{150.533/84} = \frac{MS_{Between}}{MS_{Within}} = \frac{16.078}{1.792} = 8.972$$

$$F_{involve} = \frac{SS_{Between} / (k-1)}{SS_{Within} / (N-k)} = \frac{14.400/1}{150.533/84} = \frac{MS_{Between}}{MS_{Within}} = \frac{14.400}{1.792} \doteq 8.035$$

$$F_{video\,min\,x\,involve} = \frac{SS_{Between} / (k-1)}{SS_{Within} / (N-k)} = \frac{19.400/2}{150.533/84} = \frac{MS_{Between}}{MS_{Within}} = \frac{9.700}{1.792} = 5.413$$

The overall mean of the dependent variable for all of the students indicates that, on average, students listed 4.511 reasons for the decline in endangered fish populations (Output 15.10, p. 400).

Output 15.10   Estimated Marginal Means – Grand Mean

1. Grand Mean

Dependent Variable: Totalwhy   Total number of reasons listed

| Mean | Std. Error | 95% Confidence Interval | |
		Lower Bound	Upper Bound
4.511	.141	4.230	4.792

For the independent variable video length the means appear to be different for the 2-minute video than either the 7-minute or 14-minute video based on the means and confidence intervals (Output 15.11). Note that the means for the 7-minute video and the 14-minute video are similar and that the confidence intervals overlap indicating that there may be no difference in the number of reasons listed based for these two video lengths.

Output 15.11   Estimated Marginal Means – Independent Variable – Video Length

2. Independent variable - Video length

Dependent Variable: Totalwhy   Total number of reasons listed

| Independent variable - Video length | Mean | Std. Error | 95% Confidence Interval | |
			Lower Bound	Upper Bound
1 2 min	3.667	.244	3.181	4.153
2 7 min	4.967	.244	4.481	5.453
3 14 min	4.900	.244	4.414	5.386

There does appear to be a difference for the independent variable involvement based on the means and confidence intervals (Output 15.12).

Output 15.12   Estimated Marginal Means – Independent Variable – Involvement

3. Independent variable - Involvement

Dependent Variable: Totalwhy   Total number of reasons listed

| Independent variable - Involvement | Mean | Std. Error | 95% Confidence Interval | |
			Lower Bound	Upper Bound
0 No involvement	4.111	.200	3.714	4.508
1 Involvement	4.911	.200	4.514	5.308

The estimated marginal means also suggest an interaction effect between video length and involvement for the 2-minute and 14-minute videos. For example, for the independent variable video length, if there were not an interaction one would expect the means to remain relatively constant for the 2-minute, 7-minute, and 14-minute versions of the video for the total number of reasons listed. The output shows that the means for the 2-minute and 14-minute videos based on involvement are similar and their confidence intervals overlap.

Output 15.13   Estimated Marginal Means Video Length * Involvement Interaction

4.   Independent variable - Video length * Independent variable - Involvement

Dependent Variable: Totalwhy   Total number of reasons listed

Independent variable - Video length	Independent variable - Involvement	Mean	Std. Error	95% Confidence Interval	
				Lower Bound	Upper Bound
1 2 min	0 No involvement	3.733	.346	3.046	4.421
	1 Involvement	3.600	.346	2.913	4.287
2 7 min	0 No involvement	3.933	.346	3.246	4.621
	1 Involvement	6.000	.346	5.313	6.687
3 14 min	0 No involvement	4.667	.346	3.979	5.354
	1 Involvement	5.133	.346	4.446	5.821

The interaction can be seen more easily in the profile plots (Output 15.14 and 15.15, p. 402). The profile plots are visual representations of the marginal means tables. For Output 15.14, the factor levels of video length are along the horizontal axis (2 min., 7 min., 14 min.). Separate lines are produced for each level of involvement (i.e., no involvement, involvement).

Output 15.14   Profile Plot with Video Length on Horizontal Axis

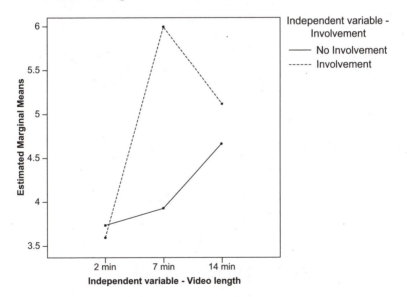

Estimated Marginal Means of Total numberof reasons listed

Output 15.15 (p. 402) shows an additional plot with involvement on the horizontal axis and the lines produced for each video length. When there are not interaction effects, the lines in the plots are parallel. For Output 15.14, the difference in involvement for the different video lengths is greater for the 7-minute video than the 2-minute video. There is an interaction effect that is unlikely to be due by chance, based on this plot. Output 15.14 and 15.15 supports the assumption that there is an interaction effect between the two independent variables (i.e., factors).

Output 15.15   Profile Plot with Involvement on Horizontal Axis

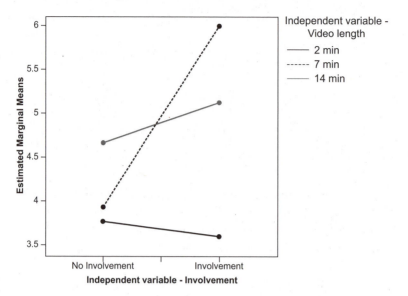

Estimated Marginal Means of Total number of reasons listed

Table 15.7 illustrates how the results from this two-way ANOVA might be presented in journal article. The information for this table is shown in Output 15.9.

Table 15.7   Two-Way ANOVA for Video Length and Involvement

	df	MS	*F*-value	*p*-value	η^2
Video length[1]	2	16.08	8.97	<.001	.18
Involvement[2]	1	14.40	8.04	<.006	.09
Video length x Involvement	2	9.70	5.41	.006	.11

[1] Video length 1 "2 minutes", 2 "7 minutes", and 3 "14 minutes".
[2] Involvement was measured as 0 "No involvement" and 1 "Involvement".

Other Types of ANOVA

There are a variety of types of ANOVA. All versions of ANOVA are similar in that they focus on the means. They differ, however, in four areas: (a) number of independent variables, (b) number of dependent variables, (c) the inclusion of one or more covariates, and (d) whether samples are independent or correlated (Table 15.8). As discussed in this chapter, a one-way ANOVA is the simplest analysis with one dichotomous or categorical independent variable and one continuous dependent variable. The *n*-way ANOVA involves one or more dichotomous and/or categorical independent variables, each with independent categories and one continuous dependent variable. Other types of ANOVA are not discussed in this chapter but consist of: (a) analysis of covariance (ANCOVA), (b) multiple analysis of variance (MANOVA), (c) multiple analysis of covariance (MANCOVA), and (d) repeated measures ANOVA.

Table 15.8   Types of Analysis of Variance

| | Number of Variables | | | |
Analysis Strategy	Independent Variable	Dependent Variable	Covariate	Sample
1-way ANOVA	1	1	No	Independent
n-way ANOVA	2+	1	No	Independent
ANCOVA	2+	1	Yes	Independent
MANOVA	2+	2+	No	Independent
MANCOVA	2+	2+	Yes	Independent
Repeated measures ANOVA	Cases	2+	No	Correlated

Note: The word "Cases" in the above table refers to the sample of respondents.

*Analysis of covariance (**ANCOVA**)* is typically used to control for differences between groups based on another variable called a *covariate*. The covariate is typically measured as a continuous variable. The differences in the groups in the endangered fish experiment, for example, could have occurred because some respondents were frequent anglers (a continuous variable) and were more knowledgeable about the fish. ANCOVA allows the researcher to control for the influence of this third variable.

*Multiple analysis of variance (**MANOVA**)* is used to examine the main and interaction effects of dichotomous or categorical factors on multiple continuous dependent variables. An *n*-way ANOVA tests the differences in means of a single continuous dependent for various categories of the independents. MANOVA tests the differences in the centroid (i.e., vector) of means of multiple continuous dependents for various categories of the independents.

*Multiple analysis of covariance (**MANCOVA**)* is a combination of ANCOVA and MANOVA. The test allows for multiple independent variables, multiple dependent variables and multiple covariates. In SPSS, MANOVA and MANCOVA are found under GENERAL LINEAR MODEL.

Repeated measures ANOVA can be thought of as an extension of a paired samples *t*-test (chapter 14). For example, a paired samples *t*-test might compare a student's exam scores before and after a given lecture. A repeated measures ANOVA adds a third (or fourth) testing period to determine the extent to which the information presented in the lecture is retained over time. Because the same individuals are tested multiple times, the samples are correlated. Huck and Cormier (1996) provide more information on these ANOVA procedures.

Chapter Summary

In an independent samples *t*-test (chapter 14), the independent variable is dichotomous and dependent variable is continuous. A one-way analysis of variance extends the *t*-test model to include either a dichotomous or categorical independent variable and a continuous dependent variable. If the independent variable in a one-way ANOVA is dichotomous, a one-way ANOVA and an independent samples *t*-test will produce identical results (see chapter 16 for an illustration of this relationship). An *n*-way ANOVA extends the logic of a one-way analysis by allowing for more than one independent variable. A two-way ANOVA, for example, has two independent variables.

This chapter examined one-way and two-way analysis of variance as techniques for comparing means and variances. If there is one independent variable, the SPSS program ONE-WAY ANOVA or the SPSS MEANS program (discussed in chapter 14) can be used to compare means and variances. When there is more than one independent variable, the SPSS program GENERAL LINEAR MODEL is used for conducting an analysis of variance.

Similar to an independent samples *t*-test (chapter 14), an analysis of variance is based on three key assumptions:

1. The respondents in each category of each independent variable were obtained from independent samples (i.e., a between-subjects design)

2. The dependent variable has an approximately normal distribution for each category of the independent variable(s) in the population.

3. The categories (groups) associated with the independent variable(s) have equal variances on the dependent variable. As illustrated in the means and *t*-test chapter, as well as in this chapter, this assumption can be tested using the Levene's *F* test.

Unlike an independent samples *t*-test, however, an ANOVA involves working directly with the variances rather than the means. Two independent estimates of common variance are computed. One estimate is similar to the pooled variance in an independent samples *t*-test. The second estimate of common variance involves the variance of the separate group means treated as individual scores. The statistical test in an analysis of variance compares the two separate estimates of the population variance. Rather than taking a difference between the two estimates, however, the ratio of the second estimate to the first is computed. If the null hypothesis is correct, this ratio is approximately 1. If the population means actually differ, however, the second estimate will be larger than the first and the ratio will be larger than 1. The ratio of the two estimates has a known sampling distribution, *F*, which is used to gauge statistical significance.

The null (H_0) and alternative (H_1) hypotheses for a one-way ANOVA state the expected relationship for the population means (μ). For example, if there are three categories in the independent variable, the null hypothesis is $\mu_1 = \mu_2 = \mu_3$. The alternative can be stated as either a nondirectional (e.g., $\mu_1 \neq \mu_2 \neq \mu_3$) or a directional (e.g., $\mu_1 > \mu_2 > \mu_3$) hypothesis. Depending on an analysts prior knowledge for a given research topic, combinations of nondirectional and directional hypotheses might be advanced (e.g., $\mu_1 \neq \mu_2 > \mu_3$).

Similar to regression analysis (chapter 16), an analysis of variance decomposes the total sum of squares (SS_y) in the dependent variable (Y) into two independent components, two sources of variation.

1. The $SS_{Between}$ is the portion of the sum of squares in Y attributable to the independent variable X, and represents how much the group means vary among themselves.

2. The SS_{Within} is the variation that is not accounted for by X, and is determined by how much the observations within each category of the independent variable vary. In other words, the SS_{Within} is based on the standard deviations.

The statistical test for the null hypothesis that all groups have the same mean is the F-ratio. The degrees of freedom (df) for the F test are calculated using the number of cases (N) and the number of categories (k). For the *between* category variations, the degrees of freedom are $df_{Between} = k - 1$. For the *within* category variations, the degrees of freedom are $df_{Within} = N - k$.

The $SS_{Between}$ and SS_{Within} are influenced by the number of summed quantities. To eliminate this influence, the SS are divided by the degrees of freedom to create two mean square (MS) terms in a one-way ANOVA. $MS_{Between}$ is the average amount of variation accounted for by X, whereas the MS_{Within} reflects the average amount of variation not accounted for by X. The F test is calculated by dividing the $MS_{Between}$ by the MS_{Within}. When this ratio results in a small value (i.e., a small F-value), the independent variable does not account for much of the variability in the dependent variable. In this situation, the results are attributed to chance and the researcher fails to reject the null hypothesis. When the ratio of $MS_{Between} / MS_{Within}$ is large (i.e., a large F-value), the findings suggest that means of the dependent variable differ statistically for at least two of the categories of the independent variable.

To determine statistical significance, the calculated value of the F-ratio is compared to the value in the theoretical F distribution. SPSS does the comparison, reports the actual observed significance level, and labels this p-value "**Sig.**" This Sig. level is the probability of a Type I error or the probability of rejecting the null hypothesis when it is actually true (chapter 6). For any specific statistic (e.g., χ^2, t, F), if the Sig. or p is small (.05, .01, .001), the finding is *statistically* significant and the null hypothesis is rejected.

If the overall F-ratio is not significant, the means for the groups being compared are statistically equal to each other. If the overall F-ratio is statistically significant, at least one of the means for the groups being compared is different from the other group means. To determine which specific means differ from one another requires additional analysis (e.g., contrasts, post hoc tests).

A contrast is simply an independent samples t-test for the difference between the means. With three groups (or categories) in an independent variable, three pairwise contrasts can be conducted. With four groups associated with an independent variable, six pairwise contrasts are possible. The probability of obtaining at least one significant comparison by chance increases as multiple contrasts are evaluated. For example, the probability (α or p-value) for three contrasts increases to $C\alpha = 3(.05) = .15$. There are two strategies for compensating for this situation and keeping the desired probability (e.g., .05, .01) for all multiple comparisons: Bonferroni correction and post hoc comparisons.

The Bonferroni correction divides the desired *p*-value by the number of contrasts that are performed. Post hoc comparisons attempt to keep the *p*-value or α equal to .05 (or $\alpha = .01$ or $\alpha = .001$) for all contrasts when conducting multiple comparisons. Eight different post hoc comparisons were defined. These tests simply differ in how they adjust the *p*-value. For example, the least significant difference (LSD) uses *t*-tests to perform all pairwise comparisons between category means. LSD is the most liberal post hoc comparison since it is most likely to find that categories differ (Type I error). The Scheffé's S method uses a more demanding critical value for the *F*-ratio, and thus provides a conservative post hoc comparison. Scheffé's S method tends to err on the side of Type II errors (i.e., underestimates statistical significance).

The choice of a specific post hoc comparison depends in part on: (a) sample size, and (b) the assumption of equality of variances. Post hoc comparisons such as LSD, Bonferroni, or Scheffé's S are appropriate when equality of variances can be assumed. When this assumption is not supported by the Levene's test, the Games-Howell or the Tamhane's T2 post hoc tests are appropriate.

In an ANOVA, eta^2 (η^2) or eta (η) are commonly used as a measure of strength of association between the independent and dependent variable. Eta^2 is analogous to R^2 in regression analysis (chapter 16) and represents the proportion of variance in the dependent variable explained by differences among the categories of the independent variable. When reporting an eta as an effect size the nonsquared eta is used. Eta is not available in the ONE-WAY ANOVA SPSS procedure; the SPSS MEANS command is used to calculate eta (chapter 14).

An *n*-way ANOVA contains more than one independent dichotomous and/or categorical variable, but still has a single continuous dependent variable. With an *n*-way ANOVA, the researcher is interested in both the main effects for each factor (i.e., independent variable) and the interaction between the factors. An *interaction* means that the effect of one independent variable has on a dependent variable is not the same for all levels of the other independent variables. If the interaction is significant, caution should be exercised in interpreting main effects. Profile plots provide a useful strategy for visualizing interaction effects.

Other types of ANOVA (not discussed here) represent further extensions of the basic ANOVA model. All versions of ANOVA are similar in that they focus on the means. They differ, however, in four areas: (a) number of independent variables, (b) number of dependent variables, (c) the inclusion of one or more covariates, and (d) whether samples are independent or correlated. MANOVA, for example, has multiple dependent variables in addition to multiple independent variables. A repeated measures ANOVA extends a PAIRED-SAMPLES T TEST (chapter 14) to allow for comparisons of the same individual across multiple time periods.

Review Questions

1. What levels of measurement are appropriate for the *independent* variable in a one-way ANOVA?

2. What levels of measurement are appropriate for the *dependent* variable in a one-way ANOVA?

3. List two assumptions for conducting a one-way ANOVA.

4. What does a significant F-ratio in a one-way ANOVA tell you?

5. If the overall F-ratio is statistically significant, list two techniques for determining which means differ from each other.

6. If there are three groups in an independent variable, how many pairwise contrasts are possible?

7. What problem occurs if you conduct multiple contrasts in a one-way ANOVA?

8. In a one-way ANOVA, if the Levene's test shows that the variances are equal, list two appropriate post hoc tests.

9. In a one-way ANOVA, if the Levene's tests show that the variances are not equal, list two appropriate post hoc tests.

10. If the Levene's test equals 12.83 ($p < .001$), would you use Scheffé's S or Tamhane's T2 for post hoc comparisons?

11. How does a researcher decide which post hoc test is appropriate?

12. In a one-way ANOVA, what is an appropriate effect size measure?

13. What is an eta^2 telling you in a one-way ANOVA?

14. How many *independent* variables are there in three-way ANOVA?

15. How many *dependent* variables are there in a three-way ANOVA?

16. In a 3 x 2 x 4 ANOVA, how many levels are associated with each independent variable?

17. What does an R^2 in an n-way ANOVA tell you?

18. What does a significant interaction term in an n-way ANOVA tell you?

19. How do profile plots facilitate understanding interaction effects in a two-way ANOVA?

20. When would an ANCOVA be used?

21. Explain the phrase: A repeated measures ANOVA extends a paired samples t-test.

16

bivariate correlation and regression

The early chapters of this book referenced the application and interpretation of correlation and regression analyses. Chapter 3, for example, presented data from over 20 studies that examined the correlations between variables such as reported encounters with others in recreation settings, perceptions of crowding, and visitor satisfaction. Chapter 4 presented results from a series of regression models predicting New Hampshire residents' level of approval for a proposed moose hunt. Chapter 6 discussed the interpretation of correlation coefficients as effect size indicators. Chapter 13 illustrated that a phi (ϕ) coefficient from a crosstabulation can be interpreted as a correlation. This chapter focuses on bivariate correlations and three types of regression models: (a) bivariate, (b) multiple, and (c) dummy variable. The calculation and interpretation of these analytical procedures is emphasized.

Correlation

A correlation coefficient indicates the strength of the linear association between two variables. It measures how closely the data points cluster around a straight line. The most commonly used measure is the ***Pearson correlation coefficient***, which is abbreviated as ***r***. Glass and Hopkins (1996), for example, estimate that social scientists select the Pearson correlation 95% of the time for describing the strength of relationships or inferring population correlations.

The choice of correlation coefficient is partially dependent on the variables' level of measurement (Chen & Popovich, 2002). Pearson correlations are appropriate when both variables are continuous and approximately normally distributed (Table 16.1). The ***point-biserial correlation (r_{pb})*** is used when one of the variables is continuous (e.g., days of participation in a recreation activity) and the other variable represents a natural dichotomy (e.g., a respondents' sex). The ***biserial correlation (r_{bis})*** is similar, except that one of the variables is continuous and the second variable is a constructed dichotomy. For example, age is typically measured as a continuous variable but might be recoded into a dichotomous measure for some analyses (e.g., < 45 vs. ≥ 45 years of age). A ***tetrachoric correlation (r_{tet})*** is the relationship between two continuous variables that have been recoded into dichotomous variables. As noted by Cohen (1983, p. 253), however, the dichotomization of one or more continuous variables results in a reduction of predicted variance and the approach should generally not be used.

The *phi* (ϕ), *Cramer's V*, and *contingency coefficient* (*C*) were discussed in chapter 13 (crosstabulation). In general, these correlations involve the relationship between dichotomous and/or categorical variables. The *eta* (η) coefficient is a correlation between a categorical variable and a continuous variable. Details regarding this correlation were discussed in chapter 15 (analysis of variance).

The *Spearman correlation* (r_{rank} *or* r_s) is a nonparametric (see chapter 1) correlation that is based on the ranks of the data rather than the actual values. In other words, the variables are arranged in rank order. The r_{rank} is appropriate for ordinal variables (Stevens's 1951 terminology) or for continuous variables (terminology used in this book) that are not normally distributed. *Kendall's tau* (τ) is also a nonparametric measure of association for ordinal or ranked variables that accounts for ties in the ranks. There are two types of Kendall's tau available in SPSS. *Kendall tau-b* is used for square tables (e.g., 2 x 2) or nonsquare tables (e.g., 2 x 3), while *Kendall's tau-c* is used for nonsquare tables and includes an adjustment for the size of the table.

Overall, the point-biserial, biserial, tetrachoric, phi, eta, and Spearman rank-ordered correlations can be thought of as special cases of the Pearson *r* (Cohen & Cohen, 1983). All of the null hypothesis tests discussed in chapter 6 apply to these correlations. The computations of these statistics are primarily simplified versions of the Pearson *r* equation. The absolute values of these correlations, however, tend to be smaller than the Pearson correlation due to differences in the shapes of the distributions (Chen & Popovich, 2002).

The column headers in Table 16.1 are labeled "1st variable" and "2nd variable." The order of 1st versus 2nd does not matter in a correlation analysis. If the variables are named X and Y, then $r_{xy} = r_{yx}$. The generic labeling also emphasizes the common dictum that "correlation does not prove causation" (Pedhazur & Schmelkin, 1991). For example, using the measurement procedures promoted by Fishbein and Ajzen (1975), attitudes (A) are often highly correlated with behaviors (B). Given the cross-sectional (i.e., single study) and temporally bound nature of most empirical demonstrations of this relationship, however, establishing a causal link is typically impossible. Did the attitude cause the behavior (A→B) or did the behavior cause the attitude (B→A)? Scholars have debated this causal sequence from both perspectives (e.g., Bem, 1970). Thus, although the distinction between the independent variable and dependent variable is not relevant in a correlation context (Hays, 1994), Pedhazur and Schmelkin (1991) argue that a causal sequence is indispensable in research and practice when attempting to explain a phenomenon.

Computing correlations in SPSS is not always straightforward. Table 16.1 shows the SPSS procedures to be used for each correlation. For example, a point-biserial correlation is computed by using the bivariate correlation procedure and requesting a Pearson correlation. This method works because the formula for the Pearson correlation will compute a point-biserial correlation when a naturally dichotomous variable and a continuous variable are being analyzed.

Table 16.1   Correlation Coefficients

Correlation Coefficient	Measurement Level		SPSS Procedure	SPSS Terminology
	1ˢᵗ Variable	2ⁿᵈ Variable		
Pearson r	Continuous	Continuous	Bivariate Correlation	Pearson
Point Biserial (r_{pb})	Dichotomous (Natural)	Continuous	Bivariate Correlation	Pearson
Biserial (r_{bis})	Dichotomous (Recoded Continuous)	Continuous	Bivariate Correlation	Pearson
Tetrachoric (r_{tet})	Dichotomous (Recoded Continuous)	Dichotomous (Recoded Continuous)	Not Available	Not Available
Phi (ϕ)	Dichotomous (Natural)	Dichotomous (Natural)	Crosstabs	Phi
Cramer's V	Dichotomous or Categorical	Categorical	Crosstabs	Cramer's V
Contingency Coefficient C	Categorical	Categorical	Crosstabs	Contingency Coefficient
Eta (η)	Categorical	Continuous	Means or Crosstabs	Eta
Spearman (r_{rank})	Ranked Ordinal	Ranked Ordinal	Correlation	Spearman
Kendall's τ-b	Ranked Ordinal	Ranked Ordinal	Bivariate Correlation or Crosstabs	Kendall's tau-b
Kendall's τ-c	Ranked Ordinal	Ranked Ordinal	Crosstabs	Kendall's tau-c

The Pearson Correlation (*r*)

Given the popularity of the Pearson correlation (Glass & Hopkins, 1996), and the fact that many of the correlations in Table 16.1 are special cases of the Pearson *r*, this chapter primarily focuses on this statistic. The values of the Pearson coefficient can range from +1 to –1 (Figures 16.1a and 16.1b, p. 412), with a value of 0 indicating no linear relationship (Figures 16.1c and 16.1d, p. 412). The sign of the coefficient indicates the direction of the relationship. The absolute value of a correlation indicates the strength of the association, with larger absolute values indicating stronger relationships. If one pair of variables has a correlation of +.8 and another pair has a coefficient of –.8, the strength of the relationship is the same for both; only the direction of the relationship differs.

In Figure 16.1a, every time the value on VAR_1 increases 1 unit, the value of VAR_2 increases 1 unit, indicating a perfect linear relationship between these two variables ($r = +1.0$). Similarly, Figure 16.1b reflects a perfect negative relationship ($r = -1.0$). A correlation coefficient of 0, however, does not necessarily mean that there is no relationship between the two variables; only that there is no *linear* relationship. The relationship between the two variables could be curvilinear (Figure 16.1d).

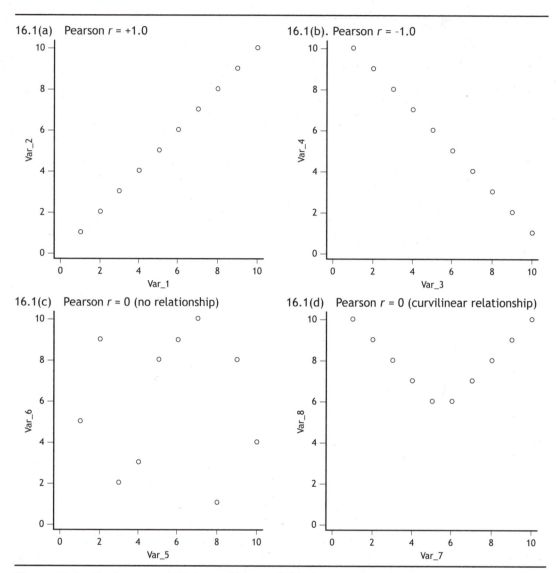

Figure 16.1   Maximum and Minimum Values of the Pearson Correlation

The size of a correlation reflects how much the observed values of the variables deviate from a straight line. With a correlation of .75 and a *small sample size*, the linear trend between the two variables is readily apparent in a scatterplot. Figure 16.2a, for example, illustrates a Pearson *r* of .75 for a sample of 10. As the values of VAR_9 increase, the values of VAR_10 increase although not in a lockstep manner. Correlations of .50 and .25 are displayed in Figures 16.2b and 16.2c, respectively. When correlations decrease in absolute value, the dispersion from the straight line increases. Scatterplots provide a useful visual strategy for examining the relationship between two continuous variables when the sample size is relatively small. The three graphs in Figure 16.2 were based on a sample size of 10. With large sample sizes (e.g., 1,000 respondents), detecting a pattern is less obvious because the number of data points in the plot obscures the linear trend. Because extreme values (i.e., outliers, see chapter 19) can underestimate or exaggerate the strength of the relationship, scatterplots should be used to visually inspect the data whenever possible. Scatterplots are also useful in detecting curvilinear relationships.

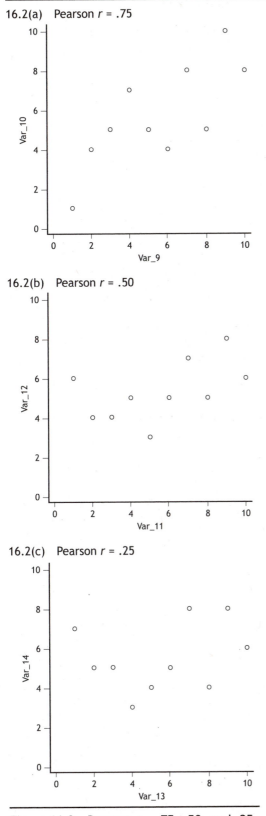

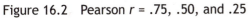

Figure 16.2   Pearson *r* = .75, .50, and .25

Calculating the Pearson Correlation Coefficient

The data used to calculate the Pearson r of .50 in Figure 16.2b are shown in Table 16.2. Respondent 1 had a value of 1 on variable X and a value of 6 on variable Y. The second respondent gave an answer of 2 on X and 4 on Y.

Table 16.2   Hypothetical Data for a Pearson r = .50

Respondent	X	Y	$X_i - M_X$	$Y_i - M_Y$	$(X_i - M_X) \cdot (Y_i - M_Y)$
1	1	6	−4.50	0.70	−3.15
2	2	4	−3.50	−1.30	4.55
3	3	4	−2.50	−1.30	3.25
4	4	5	−1.50	−0.30	0.45
5	5	3	−0.50	−2.30	1.15
6	6	5	0.50	−0.30	−0.15
7	7	7	1.50	1.70	2.55
8	8	5	2.50	−0.30	−0.75
9	9	8	3.50	2.70	9.45
10	10	6	4.50	0.70	3.15
Mean	5.50	5.30			
Std Dev	3.03	1.49			
					$\sum$ = 20.50

One formula for calculating a Pearson correlation coefficient is Equation 16.1:

$$r_{xy} = \frac{\sum_{i=1}^{n}(X_i - M_x)(Y_i - M_y)}{(n-1)S_x S_y}$$

Equation 16.1

where:
r_{xy} = Pearson correlation coefficient
X_i = Values on variable X
Y_i = Values on variable Y
M_x = Mean of variable X
M_y = Mean of variable Y
n = Sample size
S_x = Standard deviation of X
S_y = Standard deviation of Y

Replacing the symbols in Equation 16.1 with the data in Table 16.2 produces the Pearson correlation:

$$r_{xy} = \frac{20.50}{(10-1)(3.03)(1.49)} = \frac{20.50}{40.63} = .504$$

The Pearson *r* is also called a ***product-moment correlation*** because the coefficient can be computed by: (a) converting the initial values on two variables, X and Y, to standardized scores, z_x and z_y, (b) multiplying the two *z* scores (i.e., the product) and (c) calculating the average (i.e., the moment).[1] Using this approach, the Pearson correlation is Equation 16.2 (Cohen & Cohen, 1983):

$$r_{xy} = \frac{\sum z_{X_i} z_{Y_i}}{n}$$

Equation 16.2

where:

$$z_{X_i} = \frac{X_i - M_x}{s_X} \text{ and } z_{Y_i} = \frac{Y_i - M_Y}{s_Y}$$

and

X_i = values on variable X
Y_i = values on variable Y
M_X and M_Y = the means of the variables X and Y
s_x and s_Y = the standard deviations of X and Y

Correlations in SPSS

Data from a survey of residents' attitudes toward wolf reintroduction in Colorado (Bright & Manfredo, 1996) are used to illustrate bivariate correlations in SPSS. Three survey questions asked about wolf reintroduction. Each of these questions was coded on seven-point scales. For example, "Do you think reintroducing the Gray Wolf into Colorado would be good, bad, or neither?" Responses to this question were coded as "extremely bad" (1), "neither" (4), and "extremely good" (7). A second question asked: "Do you like or dislike the prospect of reintroducing wolves into Colorado?" with response categories ranging from "strongly dislike" (1) to "strongly like" (7). A third survey question was: "Do you approve, disapprove, or neither approve or disapprove of reintroducing the Gray Wolf into Colorado?" The responses were coded: "strongly disapprove" (1), "neither" (4), "strongly approve" (7). Using the procedures described in chapters 12 and 18, a summated rating index was computed as the average of respondents' answers to these three questions. The computed scale had values ranging from 1.00 to 7.00 and reflected the individuals' specific attitude toward wolf reintroduction.[2] Larger values on this index represented greater support for wolf reintroduction. The SPSS variable name assigned to this index was Spec_Att_Reint (see chapter 18 for information on indices and computed scales).

For illustration purposes, the "attitude toward wolf reintroduction" summated rating scale was correlated with three demographic variables (i.e., education, age, sex) that were asked in the

---

[1] In the mathematics of a distribution, the 1st moment is the mean, the 2nd moment is the variance, the 3rd moment is the skewness, and the 4th moment is the kurtosis.

[2] Because correlations are standardized (i.e., not expressed in any particular unit of measurement), the correlation coefficient between variables will be the same regardless of how the variables are coded. For example, the correlation between X and Y measured on a seven-point scale where strongly disagree is coded as 1 and strongly agree is 7 will equal the correlation between the same two variables in the same data set where the codes for X and Y range from –3 for strongly disagree to +3 for strongly agree.

Bright and Manfredo (1996) study. Education was coded as a continuous variable ranging from 7 (i.e., grade 7) to 22 (i.e., an advanced college degree such as a Ph.D.). The values for the age variable ranged from 13 to 95. The sex variable was coded 0 = males and 1 = females. SPSS produces Pearson correlations for the relationships between attitude and education, and between attitude and age (i.e., the continuous variables). The relationship between the attitude and sex is measured by a point-biserial correlation (i.e., one continuous and one dichotomous variable).

Three null and alternative hypotheses are advanced for the relationships between these variables (Table 16.3). As discussed in chapter 6, a ***statistical hypothesis*** is a statement about population parameters. The null hypothesis always states that there is no relationship between the variables in the population (i.e., $\rho_0 = 0$). A population correlation is symbolized as ρ *(rho)*. The alternative hypothesis states that there is a relationship in the population. In this example, the subscripts on the ρ (i.e., ρ_1, ρ_2, ρ_3) are used to differentiate the three alternative hypotheses. Each of these alternative hypotheses predicts a directional (e.g., $\rho_1 > 0$ or $\rho_2 < 0$) as opposed to a nondirectional ($\rho_1 \neq 0$) relationship.

The statistical hypotheses in Table 16.3 should be differentiated from the ***substantive hypotheses*** that are statements involving concepts (e.g., specific attitude toward wolf reintroduction) that predict or explain the phenomena in question. The substantive null hypothesis for the relationship between attitude and education would be phrased: "There is no relationship between education and attitude toward wolf reintroduction in the population." The substantive alternative hypothesis for this correlation is: "As education increases, support for wolf reintroduction will increase." The direction of this hypothesis could be rationalized by arguing that individuals with more formal education are likely to view wolves as part of the larger ecosystem and believe that wolves represent a symbol of wilderness that should be preserved for future generations. If the researcher is not willing to accept this logic and/or past research does not support the predicted relationship, the alternative hypothesis could be nondirectional (i.e., $\rho_1 \neq 0$, or "The attitude toward wolf reintroduction will vary by education level"). For each of these analyses, $p < .05$ was used for gauging statistical significance. Note the distinction between the population correlation (the Greek letter ρ) and the significance level (a lower case, italized English letter p); the two symbols appear similar in print.

Table 16.3 Hypothesized Relationships

Correlation between:	Null hypothesis	Alternative hypothesis
Attitude and education	$\rho_0 = 0$	$\rho_1 > 0$
Attitude and age	$\rho_0 = 0$	$\rho_2 < 0$
Attitude and sex	$\rho_0 = 0$	$\rho_3 > 0$

To obtain a bivariate correlation between two variables the four basic steps in conducting statistical analysis in SPSS discussed in chapter 9 apply:

1. Open the data file: Wolf Reintroduction.sav
   (see chapter 9 – Introduction to SPSS – for assistance in opening a data file)

2. Select the statistic: **Analyze > Correlate > Bivariate…**   See Figure 16.3

3. Select the variables to be included in the analysis   See Figure 16.4

4. Select additional options   See Figure 16.5

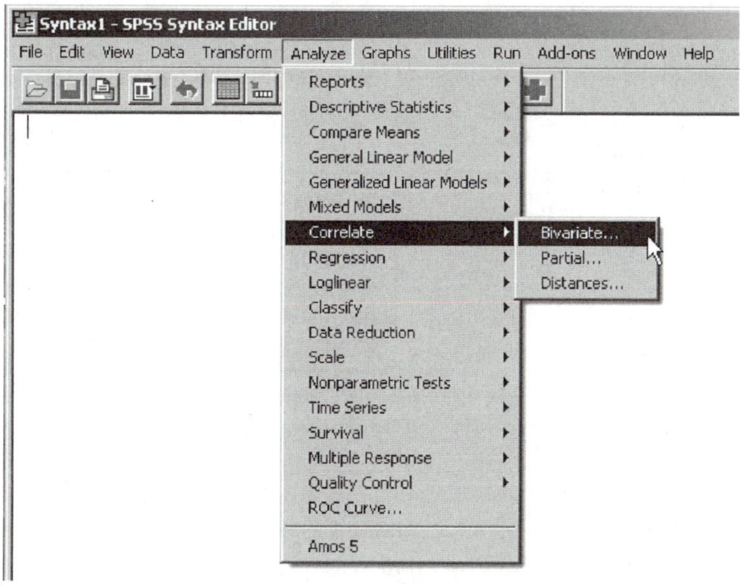

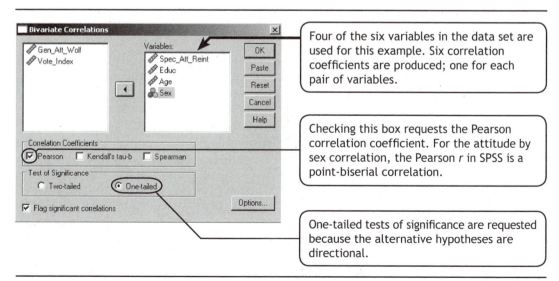

Figure 16.3   Selecting the SPSS Bivariate Correlation Procedure

Figure 16.4   Selecting Variables and Statistics in a Bivariate Correlation

One-tailed and Two-tailed Significance Probabilities

If the researcher is unsure whether a pair of variables should be positively or negatively correlated, a ***two-tailed significance level*** is used (see chapter 6). The null hypothesis is rejected for either large positive or large negative values of the correlation coefficient. If a logical argument can be advanced for a directional relationship between the variables or if past research suggests that the relationship is directional, the ***one-tailed significance level*** is used. For a one-tailed test, the null hypothesis is rejected only if the value of the correlation coefficient is large *and* in the direction specified. With a one-tailed test, the observed significance level is one-half of the two-tailed value.

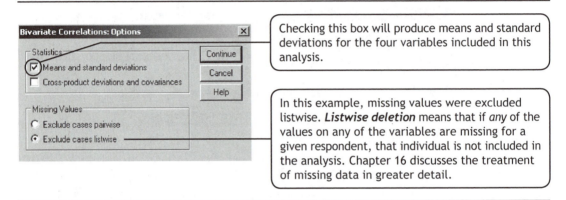

Figure 16.5   SPSS Options for Bivariate Correlations

With the variables and options selected, click the Paste button on the bivariate correlations dialog box (Figure 16.4). The SPSS generated syntax is:

```
CORRELATIONS
   /VARIABLES=Spec_Att_Reint Educ Age Sex
   /PRINT=ONETAIL NOSIG
   /STATISTICS DESCRIPTIVES
   /MISSING=LISTWISE .
```

The output from this analysis is shown in Output 16.1.

Output 16.1   Descriptive Statistics

Descriptive Statistics

	Mean	Std. Deviation	N
Spec_Att_Reint Specific attitude toward wolf reintroduction	5.0746	1.92466	1388
Educ Respondent education in years	14.41	2.559	1388
Age Respondent age in years	44.81	15.693	1388
Sex Respondent sex	.53	.499	1388

The descriptive statistics from this correlation analysis included the mean, standard deviation, and sample size after listwise deletion. The researcher-computed index (chapter 18) for specific attitude was coded on a seven-point scale ranging from strong disapproval (1) to strong approval (7), with a neutral point of 4. The mean of 5.07 for this summated rating index suggests that respondents' slightly approved of wolf reintroduction in Colorado. On average, this sample of individuals had completed two years of college ($M = 14.41$) and were 44.81 years old. The mean of .53 for the sex variable implies that 53% of the respondents were female. The mean of a dichotomous variable coded as 0 (males) and 1 (females) equals the percent of individuals with a value of 1. With listwise deletion, a total of 1,388 responses were analyzed for each of the variables.

A correlation matrix is symmetric (Output 16.2). All of the values on the diagonal of the matrix are 1; any variable correlated with itself equals 1. The correlation coefficients in the upper half of the matrix are identical to the coefficients in the lower half of the matrix. By requesting all possible pairs of bivariate correlations among the four variables, a total of six unique correlations were generated.

Output 16.2   All Bivariate Correlations between Four Variables

Correlations[a]

		Spec_Att_Reint	Educ	Age	Sex
Spec_Att_Reint	Pearson Correlation	1	.061*	−.260**	.017
	Sig. (1-tailed)		.011	.000	.267
Educ	Pearson Correlation	.061*	1	.013	−.089**
	Sig. (1-tailed)	.011		.316	.000
Age	Pearson Correlation	−.260**	.013	1	−.042
	Sig. (1-tailed)	.000	.316		.061
Sex	Pearson Correlation	.017	−.089**	−.042	1
	Sig. (1-tailed)	.267	.000	.061	

*. Correlation is significant at the 0.05 level (1-tailed)
**.Correlation is significant at the 0.01 level (1-tailed)
a. Listwise N = 1388

The Pearson correlation can be used as a descriptive statistic similar to the mean or standard deviation. When viewed as a descriptive statistic, no sampling distribution assumptions are required. To test the hypotheses in Table 16.3 (p. 416), however, inferential statistics are necessary (chapter 6). Similar to other test statistics (e.g., χ^2, F), the calculated value of the Pearson r is compared to the critical value in the theoretical sampling distribution of ρ. When $\rho = 0$, the sampling distribution of a Pearson correlation is distributed as a t distribution (chapter 14; see also Chen & Popovich, 2002, for an expanded discussion of the theoretical distribution). If the calculated value of r is as large or larger than the critical value of ρ for the predetermined level of statistical significance (i.e., $p < .05$ in this example), the null hypothesis is rejected. As demonstrated in the crosstabulation chapter (chapter 13), SPSS eliminates the need for manually looking up the theoretical values and making the comparison. Rather, SPSS does the comparison and reports the ***actual observed significance level***, which is labeled as ***Sig.*** in the output. If the Sig. value is small (typically less than .05), the relationship is statistically significant and the null hypothesis is rejected.

The Pearson correlation between the specific attitude index and education was .061 and was statistically significant at $p < .011$ (Output 16.2). Because the first alternative hypothesis had predicted a positive correlation ($\rho_1 > 0$, Table 16.3), the null hypothesis is rejected. Statistical significance for this relationship was determined by simply looking at the Sig. value. Because the Sig. (.011) was less than the predetermined significance level (.05), the null hypothesis was rejected.

Although the correlation between the attitude measure and the education variable was statistically significant, the Pearson *r* would be characterized as only a "minimal" relationship. As noted in chapter 6, a minimal relationship is evident for correlations of about .1; a typical relationship would require a correlation of .3 and a substantial relationship exists when the Pearson *r* is .5 or greater. The observed statistical significance in this example can largely be attributed to sample size ($n = 1,388$). As sample size increases, the probability of finding a statistically significant relationship increases (Gliner, Vaske, & Morgan, 2001).

The Pearson *r* between attitude and age (Output 16.2) was larger (−.260) than that observed for attitude and education (.061). Remember that the strength of a relationship is determined by the absolute value of the correlation. The correlation was in the predicted negative direction ($\rho < 0$, Table 16.3) and was statistically significant (Sig = .000). For these reasons, the null hypothesis would be rejected. The *p*-value of .000, however, should not be interpreted 0. Rather, the observed significance level was less than .0005. SPSS rounded the *p*-value to .000. The researcher would report this relationship between attitude and age as statistically significant at $p < .001$.

The correlation between attitude and sex was .017 and the Sig. was .267. Because .535 is greater than the predetermined significance level of .05, the researcher would fail-to-reject the null hypothesis ($\rho = 0$). Substantively, this means that the respondents' sex *did not influence* their attitude toward wolf reintroduction. As noted earlier, the labels' independent variable and dependent variable are technically not relevant to correlations because correlations do not prove causation (Hays, 1994; Pedhazur & Schmelkin, 1991). In this example, however, sex would be considered the independent variable and attitude the dependent variable. The respondent's attitude toward wolf reintroduction could not influence whether or not the person was a male or female, but the reverse is a possibility.

The syntax for this example generated six correlation coefficients (Output 16.2). Only three of these correlations were needed to test the hypothesized relationships. In a relatively small correlation matrix, the coefficients of interest are easy to identify. If the correlation matrix contains numerous rows and columns, identifying the appropriate coefficients can take more time. To generate only the correlations needed to test the three hypotheses, edit the SPSS syntax:

```
CORRELATIONS
  /VARIABLES=Educ Age Sex WITH Spec_Att_Reint
  /PRINT=ONETAIL NOSIG
  /STATISTICS DESCRIPTIVES
  /MISSING=LISTWISE
```

Variable lists joined by the keyword "WITH" produce a rectangular correlation matrix. Variables before WITH define the rows of the matrix; variables after WITH define the columns.

This syntax generates three correlations:

1. Educ WITH Spec_Att_Reint
2. Age WITH Spec_Att_Reint
3. Sex WITH Spec_Att_Reint

The results from this analysis are shown in Output 16.3.

Output 16.3 Bivariate Correlations: Education, Age, Sex WITH Specific Attitude

Correlations[a]

		Spec_Att_Reint
Educ	Pearson Correlation	.061*
	Sig. (1-tailed)	.011
Age	Pearson Correlation	−.026**
	Sig. (1-tailed)	.000
Sex	Pearson Correlation	.017
	Sig. (1-tailed)	.267

*· Correlation is significant at the 0.05 level (1-tailed).
**· Correlation is significant at the 0.01 level (1-tailed).
[a]· Listwise N=1388

The three correlations and observed significance levels in Output 16.3 are identical to the comparable coefficients in Output 16.2. The keyword WITH constrained the number of correlations to those necessary for testing the three hypotheses. Simplifying the results can reduce errors when transcribing numbers from SPSS output into tables constructed using a word processor for journal articles or theses.

Examining Many Correlation Coefficients

Parks, recreation, and human dimensions surveys often have hundreds of variables. The researcher may be tempted to compute all possible correlation coefficients among the variables, but this temptation should be resisted. The more significance tests that are performed, the more likely the null hypothesis will be rejected when it is true (i.e., a Type I error, chapter 6). This problem is referred to as inflation of the p-value and can be corrected by using a more stringent p-value (i.e., smaller) when performing multiple tests (Abdi, 2007). As was discussed in chapter 15 on analysis of variance, a variety of such corrections can be found in the statistical literature. The simplest approach for determining an appropriate p-value, however, is called the Bonferroni correction. The ***Bonferroni correction*** is based on the logic that if n independent hypotheses are examined in a given data set, the statistical significance level that should be used for each hypothesis separately is $1/n$ times what it would be if only one hypothesis was tested. Equation 16.3 is the formula for calculating the Bonferroni correction:

$$\text{Bonferroni Correction} = \frac{p\text{-value}}{\text{number of tests}} \qquad \text{Equation 16.3}$$

For the three hypotheses examined in this section, the Bonferroni correction is:

$$\text{Bonferroni Correction} = \frac{.05}{3} = .0167$$

With the Bonferroni correction in this example, a given hypothesis test would be statistically significant if the observed Sig. was less than .0167.

Regression

A Pearson correlation coefficient provides a measure of the strength of linear association between two continuous variables. All it measures, however, is how *closely* the points cluster together about a straight line. The coefficient says nothing about the line itself. In many situations it is useful to obtain information about the actual line that is drawn through the data points. For example, if there is a linear relationship between two variables, one variable can be used to predict values of the other variable. This section describes the procedures for calculating a *regression line* and interpreting the findings.

Overview

Regression is a general statistical technique for analyzing the relationship between a dependent variable and one or more independent (i.e., predictor) variables. This section examines (a) **bivariate regression** (i.e., one continuous dependent and one continuous independent variable), (b) **multiple regression** (i.e., one continuous dependent and two or more continuous independent variables), and (c) **dummy variable regression** (i.e., one continuous dependent and one or more dichotomous independent variables). Chapter 17 describes more complex multiple regression techniques. Similar to a correlation analysis, regression can be viewed either as a **descriptive tool** that summarizes the linear dependence of one variable on another or as an **inferential tool** that makes statistical inferences about the population parameter based on the sample data. Although these two aspects of the statistical technique are closely related, it is convenient to treat each separately, at least at the conceptual level.

Regression analysis can be used to: (a) find the best linear prediction equation, (b) evaluate the equation's predictive accuracy, (c) control for other confounding predictors, or (d) find structural relations that provide explanations for complex relationships, such as is done in path analysis (chapter 20).

Choosing the Best Line

When the correlation coefficient is +1 or –1, all the data points fall exactly on a straight line (Figures 16.1a and 16.1b, p. 412). The regression line in this situation is obtained by simply drawing a line through the points. When the observations are not perfectly correlated, many different lines can be drawn through the data. The line should be as close as possible to all the data points. Although there are a variety of ways to define "as close as possible," the most commonly used method for determining the line is called the *method of least squares* (a.k.a. ordinary least squares or OLS). Consider the relationship between crowding and reported contacts examined in chapter 3. Of the 20 studies examining this relationship, the average correlation was .34. As the number of reported contacts with others increased, perceived crowding increased. Figure 16.6 displays the least squares regression line for a scatterplot of 20 observations. For any two variables (X and Y), the variable plotted on the vertical axis is called Y (the dependent variable, crowding in this example), the variable plotted on the horizontal axis is called X (the independent variable, reported contacts in this example). The **least squares line** has the smallest sum of squared vertical distances from the observed points to the line. In general, computing a least squares line involves three basic steps:

1. Calculate the vertical distances to the line from all points.

2. Square the vertical distances (squaring removes negative values).

3. Sum the squared differences.

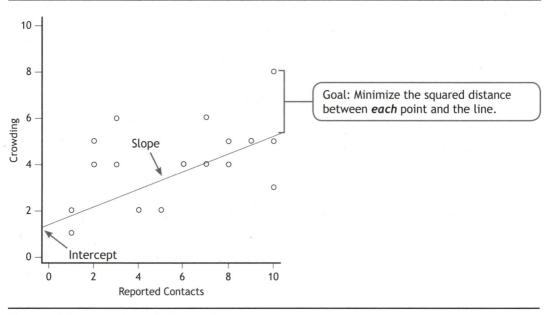

Figure 16.6   Least Squares Regression Line

The Equation of a Line

The three basic steps for computing a straight line can be stated more formally. Equation 16.4 is the equation for a straight line:

$$Y = A + B(X)$$ Equation 16.4

A and B are just numbers. The value of A is called the *intercept*, and the value of B is called the *slope* (see Figure 16.6). The intercept (i.e., A) refers to where the regression line crosses the *y* axis. The intercept is a constant that is added to all cases. The slope (i.e., B) refers to the steepness of the regression line. B is a constant by which all values of the independent variable (i.e., X) are multiplied.

In a bivariate regression (i.e., 1 dependent and 1 independent variable), values of the dependent variable are predicted from a linear function of the form:

$$Y' = A + B(X)$$
Equation 16.5

where Y' is the estimated value of the dependent variable Y. The difference between the actual and estimated value of Y for each case is called the *residual* (i.e., the error in prediction) and may be represented by the expression:

$$\text{Residual} = Y - Y'$$
Equation 16.6

The regression strategy involves the selection of A and B in such a way that the sum of the squared residuals are smaller than any possible alternative values. In other words:

$$\sum(Y - Y')^2 = SS_{res} = \text{minimum}$$
Equation 16.7

The optimum values for B and A are obtained from the following formulas:

$$B = \frac{\sum(X_i - M_X)(Y_i - M_Y)}{\sum(X_i - M_X)^2}$$
Equation 16.8

$$A = M_Y - B(M_X)$$
Equation 16.9

Summary Points

- The constant A (intercept) is the point at which the regression line crosses the *y* axis and represents the predicted value of Y when X = 0.

- The constant B usually referred to the unstandardized regression coefficient is the slope of the regression line and indicates the expected change in Y with a change of one unit in X.

- The predicted Y' values fall on the regression line.

- The vertical distances (Y − Y') of the points from the line represent the residuals (or errors in prediction).

- Because the sum of the squared residuals is minimized, the regression line is called the *least squares line* or the *line of best fit*.

Partitioning of Sum of Squares

The total sum of squares in Y (i.e., the variability of the dependent variable Y) can be partitioned into two components: (a) the variability that is explained or accounted for by the regression line (denoted SS_{reg}), and (b) the unexplained variability or the sum of squared residuals (denoted by SS_{res} or ε). Since the least squares solution guarantees that the residuals are independent of the predictor (Y'), this partitioning of the sum of squares can be written as Equation 16.10. This formula is identical to the equation used in the analysis of variance (chapter 15):

$$SS_y = SS_{reg} + SS_{res}$$

Equation 16.10

Given this partitioning, a measure of prediction accuracy and strength of linear association is the ratio of explained variation in the dependent variable to the total variation in Y:

$$r_{xy}^2 = \frac{SS_{reg}}{SS_y} = \frac{SS_y - SS_{res}}{SS_y}$$

Equation 16.11

This ratio is called the ***coefficient of determination*** and represents that amount of variability in the dependent variable that is explained by the independent variable(s). The square root of the coefficient of determination is equal to the Pearson correlation between X and Y. Although the correlation coefficient always has the same sign as the unstandardized regression coefficient, these two coefficients will not be equal except in the special case where the variances of X and Y are equal (i.e., when X and Y are standardized variables).

Standardized Regression Coefficients

In simple bivariate regression (i.e., one dependent and one independent variable), values of the dependent variable are predicted from a linear function of Equation 16.5. When both X and Y are standardized to have a variance of 1, the standardized regression coefficient will be equal to the Pearson correlation:

$$\beta_{xy} = r_{xy}$$

Equation 16.12

The symbol β (a.k.a., beta or beta weights) is used to indicate that the coefficients have been computed on standardized X and Y values rather than the original unstandardized values (Bring, 1994). The relationship between beta weights and unstandardized regression coefficients is shown in Equations 16.13 and 16.16:

$$\beta_{xy} = B_{xy}\left(\frac{SD_x}{SD_y}\right)$$

Equation 16.13

$$B_{xy} = \beta_{xy}\left(\frac{SD_y}{SD_x}\right)$$

Equation 16.14

where:

   β_{xy} = the standardized regression coefficient (i.e., beta)
   B_{xy} = the unstandardized regression coefficient
   SD_x = the standard deviation of X
   SD_y = the standard deviation of Y

Unstandardized versus Standardized Regression Coefficients

In a linear regression model the unstandardized regression coefficient (B) is interpreted as the change in value in the predicted value of the dependent variable for a one unit increase in the independent variable. An unstandardized coefficient of 1.0 implies that for every unit increase in the independent variable, the predicted value of the dependent variable also increases one unit. Because the B coefficient is the slope of the regression line, the larger the B, the steeper the slope (i.e., the more the dependent variable changes for each unit change in the independent variable).

Standardized regression coefficients (β) cannot be used to estimate Y values in the original raw value units, but the standardized regression coefficients can be more convenient to use. For example, because standardization places all variables on the "same" scale, it is easier to compare the effects of different independent variables when standardized coefficients are used. If two or more independent variables are measured in different units (e.g., income in dollars and education in years), standardized coefficients may provide the only sensible way to compare the relative effect of each independent variable on the dependent variable. In addition, standardized coefficients are sometimes easier to interpret than unstandardized coefficients. In a simple bivariate regression, the standardized coefficient is equivalent to the Pearson correlation coefficient (Equations 16.12), and the square of this coefficient is interpreted as the *proportion of variance explained* in the dependent variable.

Despite these advantages, the use of standardized regression coefficients has been controversial in the social sciences (Bring, 1994; Darlington, 1990; Hargens, 1976; Kim & Ferree, 1981; Wright, 1960). The debate over standardized versus unstandardized coefficients is partially a matter of the types of variables examined in different social science disciplines. Psychologists, for example, who deal with arbitrary scaled attitude items tend to standardize the coefficients. Economists who deal with dollars tend to use unstandardized coefficients.

The controversy, however, is more than the researcher's personal preference. Consider the equations used to transform the coefficients (Equations 16.13 and 16.14). This transformation is helpful when the variables do not have intuitive scales (e.g., attitude indices) or when the metrics have widely different scales of measurement (e.g., eduation and income). Comparability between the variables is achieved by standardizing each variable according to common characteristics (i.e., mean and standard deviation). When dealing with a single sample, the decision to use or not use standardized variables is based on the relative convenience in interpretation provided by standardization.

This situation, however, changes when more than one sample or group are compared. Assume, for example, that the researcher is interested in predicting the annual incomes of people living in rural Colorado versus Denver based on the respondents' education level. Even if the analyst decides to use the usual standardization equation (Equation 16.13), two options must be considered: (a) use the means and standard deviations of the entire sample (i.e., all Colorado respondents), or (b) use the group specific means and standard deviations (i.e., rural vs. urban Colorado residents). If the variables are standardized on the means and standard deviations of the entire sample, the resulting transformed variables in one group (e.g., rural Colorado residents) may or may not be comparable to the transformed variables in the other group (e.g., urban Colorado residents) because the same linear transformations were applied to both groups. If the variables are standardized based on the means and standard deviations of each subgroup, different transformations are used for the different groups.

The use of standardized regression coefficients implicitly assumes that the standard deviation of the variable X (or Y) for one group is equivalent to the standard deviation of the same variable for the other group. This assumption is sometimes not valid. For example, the standard deviation of income may be $5,000 for sample 1 and $2,000 for sample 2. The assumption that these two standard deviations (i.e., $5,000 vs. $2,000) are equivalent is at best tenuous in this example.

As with many controversies, common sense serves as the best guide for how to proceed. A rule of thumb for choosing one coefficient over another is the kind of statement the researcher wants to make. If the goal is to make comparisons between subsets of data (e.g., rural vs. urban Colorado residents), unstandardized coefficients are preferable because they are immune to the effects of the different variances in the same variable. Thus, when making comparisons *between samples*, the unstandardized estimates should be used. Alternatively, if the goal is to make statements about the relative importance of variables *within a sample*, the standardized coefficient is more appropriate because it adjusts for the different measurement scales of the variables. A useful practice is to report both coefficients, or if only one coefficient is reported, present the standard deviations of the variables so that the reader can calculate the other coefficient (see equations 16.13 and 16.14).

Regression in SPSS

Bivariate Regression

The data for this exercise use the public's attitudes toward wolf reintroduction (Bright & Manfredo, 1996) presented earlier in this chapter. One regression model in this study suggested that attitudes toward wolf reintroduction predict voting intentions (i.e., behavior) on a ballot initiative to allow wolf reintroduction in Colorado. The behavior variable was a multiplicative index (chapter 18) computed by combining the respondent's reported behavior (i.e., voted "for" [coded as +1] vs. "against" [coded as –1] wolf reintroduction) with the certainty of his or her decision. The response categories for the three-point certainty variable ranged from 0 "not at all certain" to 3 "extremely certain." The combination of these two variables produced a continuous behavior variable that ranged from –3 (voted against and extremely certain) to +3 (voted for and extremely certain).

Mathematically, this attitude-behavior regression model can be written as:

$$Y = A + B_1(X_1) + \varepsilon$$

Equation 16.15

where:
    Y = Voting intention (i.e., dependent variable)
    A = The intercept and constant added to each case
    B_1 = The slope and constant by which all values of "Attitude toward wolf reintroduction"
        are multiplied
    X_1 = Attitude toward wolf reintroduction (i.e., independent variable)
    ε = Error term or residual

Running a regression analysis in SPSS involves the four basic steps discussed in chapter 9:

1. Open the data file: Wolf Reintroduction.sav

2. Select the statistic. Click on: **Analyze > Regression > Linear...**   See Figure 16.7

3. Select the variables to be included in the analysis   See Figure 16.8

4. Select additional options   See Figures 16.9 to 16.12

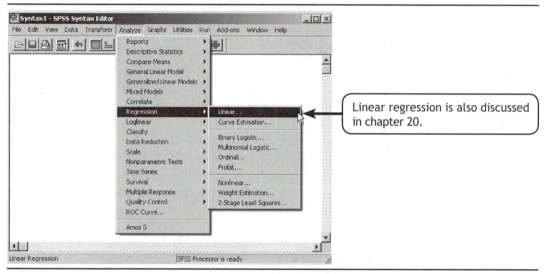

Figure 16.7   Selecting the Regression Procedure in SPSS

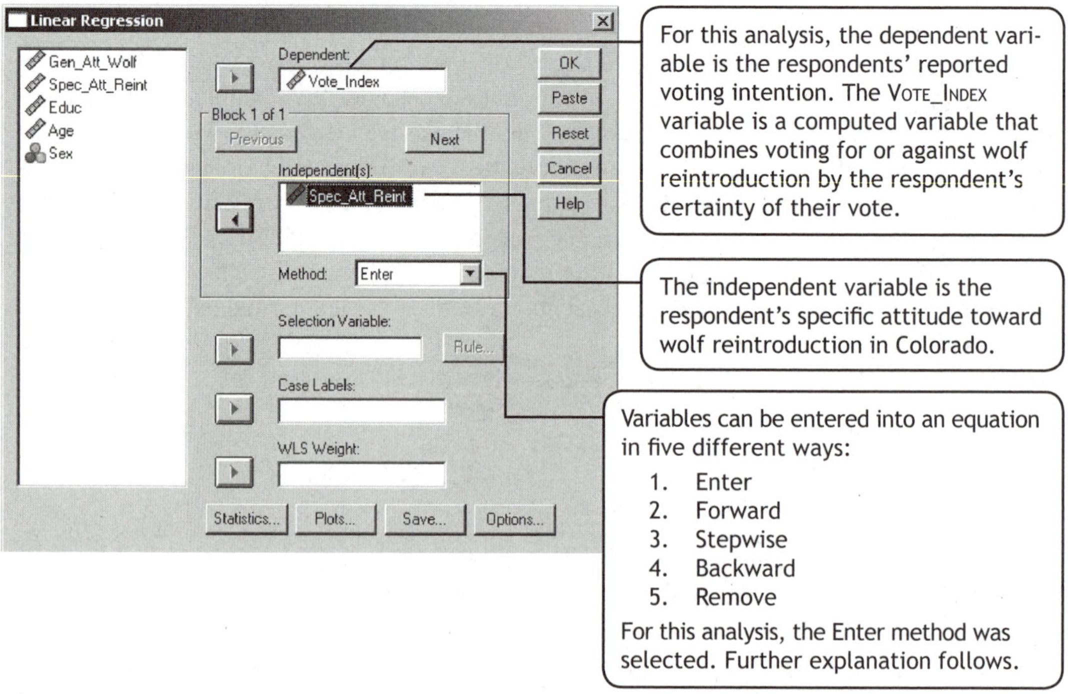

Figure 16.8   Selecting Variables in a Regression Analysis

Entering Variables into a Regression Equation

In SPSS regression analysis, the Method option (Figure 16.8) allows the researcher to specify how independent variable(s) will be entered into the equation. There are five alternatives available:

1. With the ***Enter*** method, all variables are entered into the equation simultaneously. This option was selected in Figure 16.8 because there is only one independent variable in the regression model. When there is more than one independent variable in the model, the *Enter method is still the recommended choice.* Variables should be included in an analysis based on their theoretical importance, not because of their empirical strength in a given data set.

2. The ***Forward*** method begins with no independent variables in the model and includes variables sequentially (one at a time). The first independent variable entered into the model has the strongest (+ or −) correlation with the dependent variable. At step 2 (and each subsequent step) the variable with the strongest partial correlation enters the equation. A ***partial correlation*** is the variance in the dependent variable that is explained by the independent variable after controlling for the other variables in the model. A variable is entered into the model only if it satisfies the criterion for entry (see Figure 16.12, p. 431). The procedure stops when there are no variables that meet the entry criterion.

3. The ***Stepwise*** method is similar to Forward stepping. Variables are sequentially entered into the equation based on the size of the correlation between the dependent and independent variable (step 1) or the size of the partial correlation in subsequent steps. The Stepwise method, however, also examines the statistical significance of all variables included in the model at a given step. This implies that a given variable could be entered into the model at one step and be removed at a later step. This additional checking is *not* performed with the Forward procedure.

4. The ***Backward*** method begins with all variables in the model. At each step, independent variables that explain the least amount of variance in the dependent variable (i.e., the smallest partial correlation) are sequentially removed. Similar to the Forward method, the process of removing variables stops when the criterion for removal is no longer satisfied.

5. The ***Remove*** method removes all variables in a block (e.g., demographic variables) in single step.

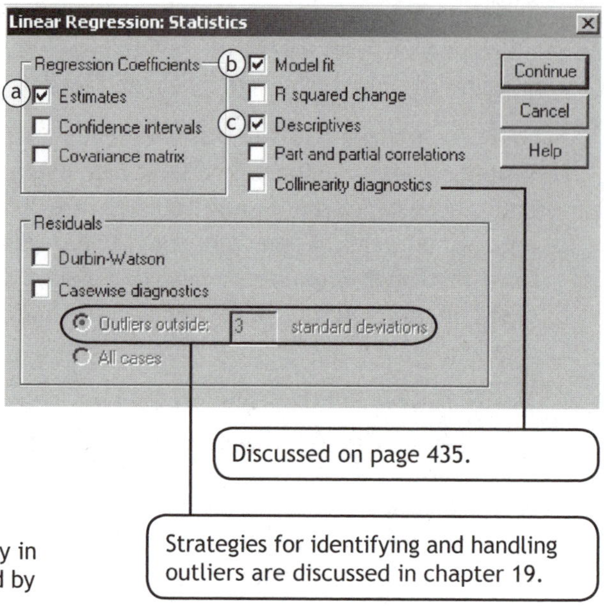

The **"Statistics..." option** in a regression analysis controls what statistics will be displayed in the output. In this example, three types of statistics were selected:

(a) *Regression coefficient estimates*

- Unstandardized (B) & standardized (*B*) coefficients
- Standard error of B
- the *t*-value for B
- two-tailed significance level of *t*.

(b) *Model fit*

- Multiple *R* if there is more than one independent variable; or the bivariate Pearson correlation if there is only one independent variable.
- R^2 or the coefficient of determination is interpreted as the percent of variability in the dependent variable that is explained by the independent variable(s).
- Adjusted R^2 — The percent of variability in the dependent variable that is explained by the independent variable(s) after adjusting for sample size.
- *Standard error of the estimate* measures the spread of the residuals about the fitted line.

Linear Regression: Statistics

Regression Coefficients
- (a) ☑ Estimates
- ☐ Confidence intervals
- ☐ Covariance matrix
- (b) ☑ Model fit
- ☐ R squared change
- (c) ☑ Descriptives
- ☐ Part and partial correlations
- ☐ Collinearity diagnostics

Residuals
- ☐ Durbin-Watson
- ☐ Casewise diagnostics
- ⦿ Outliers outside: 3 standard deviations
- ○ All cases

Continue | Cancel | Help

Discussed on page 435.

Strategies for identifying and handling outliers are discussed in chapter 19.

- ANOVA summary table (chapter 15)

(c) *Descriptives* (i.e., number of valid cases, the mean and standard deviation for each variable in the analysis, and a correlation matrix).

Figure 16.9   Selecting Statistics in the Linear Regression Analysis Window

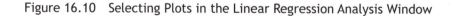

Linear Regression: Plots

Scatter 1 of 1

DEPENDNT
*ZPRED
*ZRESID
*DRESID
*ADJPRED
*SRESID
*SDRESID

Previous | Next

Y: [ ]
X: [ ]

☐ Produce all partial plots

Standardized Residual Plots
- ☐ Histogram
- ☐ Normal probability plot

Continue | Cancel | Help

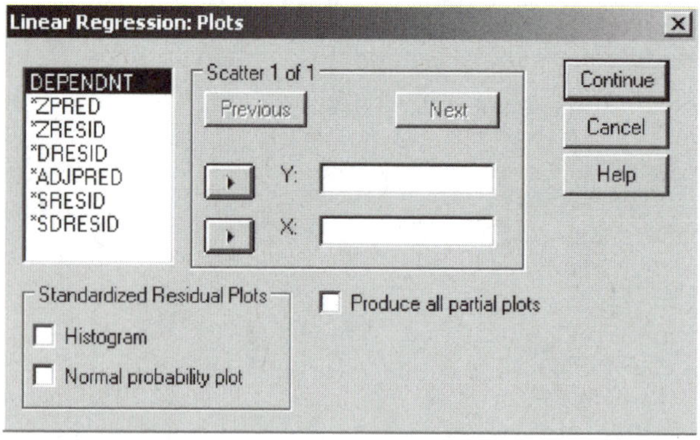

The **"Plots..." option** can aid in the validation of the assumptions of normality, linearity, and equality of variances. When the sample size is small, plots are also useful for detecting outliers (see chapter 19).

In this example, the procedure:

Graphs > Interactive > Scatterplot...

was used to display the relationship between the independent (i.e., attitude) and dependent (i.e., behavior) variables (see Figure 16.13).

Figure 16.10   Selecting Plots in the Linear Regression Analysis Window

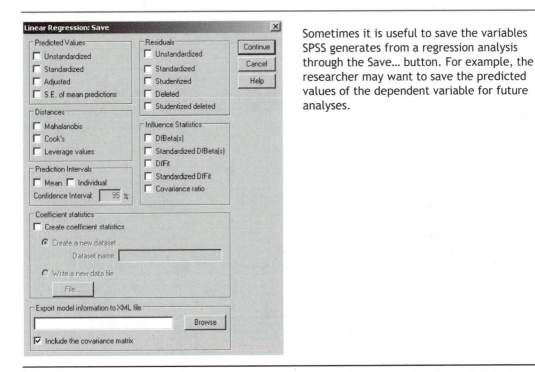

Sometimes it is useful to save the variables SPSS generates from a regression analysis through the Save... button. For example, the researcher may want to save the predicted values of the dependent variable for future analyses.

Figure 16.11   Selecting Variables to be Saved in the Linear Regression Analysis Window

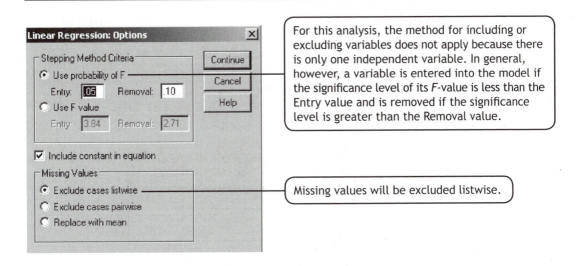

For this analysis, the method for including or excluding variables does not apply because there is only one independent variable. In general, however, a variable is entered into the model if the significance level of its *F*-value is less than the Entry value and is removed if the significance level is greater than the Removal value.

Missing values will be excluded listwise.

Figure 16.12   Available Options in the Linear Regression Analysis Window

With the variables and options selected, click the Paste button on the main Linear Regression dialog box (Figure 16.8, p. 428). The SPSS generated syntax is:

```
REGRESSION
  / DESCRIPTIVES MEAN STDDEV CORR SIG N
  / MISSING LISTWISE
  / STATISTICS COEFF OUTS R ANOVA
  / NOORIGIN
  / DEPENDENT Vote_Index
  / METHOD=ENTER Spec_Att_Reint .
```

The results from this analysis are shown in Output 16.4.

Output 16.4   Regression Analysis:
            Dependent Variable = Voting index
            Independent Variable = Specific attitude toward wolf reintroduction

Descriptive Statistics

	Mean	Std. Deviation	N
Vote_Index	1.4093	2.33910	1400
Spec_Att_Reint	5.0750	1.93380	1400

Model Summary

Model	R	R Square	Adjusted R Square	Std. Error of the Estimate
1	.918[a]	.843	.843	.92789

a. Predictors: (constant), Spec_Att_Reint   Specific attitude toward wolf reintroduction

> With one independent and one dependent, Multiple R = Pearson r = Standardized B.

> The R^2 = Adjusted R^2 because the sample size is large (n = 1,400)

Correlations

		Vote_Index	Spec_Att_Reint
Pearson Correlation	Vote_Index	1.000	.918
	Spec_Att_Reint	.918	1.000
Sig. (1-tailed)	Vote_Index	.	.000
	Spec_Att_Reint	.000	.
N	Vote_Index	1400	1400
	Spec_Att_Reint	1400	1400

> A Sig. of .000 implies that the observed significance level was < .0005. This p-value would typically be reported as $p < .001$.

ANOVA[b]

Model		Sum of Squares	df	Mean Square	F	Sig.
1	Regression	6450.823	1	6450.823	7492.379	.000[a]
	Residual	1203.656	1398	.861		
	Total	7654.479	1399			

a. Predictors: (Constant), Spec_Att_Reint   Specific attitude toward wolf introduction
b. Dependent Variable: Vote_Index   Vote index

> The F-value and Sig. is the statistical significance of the entire regression model. With only one independent variable, the square root of the F-value ($\sqrt{7492}$) = the t-value (86.56) for the independent variable.

The *F*-value is computed using the sums of squares, degrees of freedom (*df*) and mean squares values for the regression and residual components in the regression model. More specifically:

$$\text{Mean Square}_{\text{Regression}} = \frac{\text{Sum of Squares}_{\text{Regression}}}{df} = \frac{6450.823}{1} = 6450.823 \qquad \text{Equation 16.16}$$

$$\text{Mean Square}_{\text{Residual}} = \frac{\text{Sum of Squares}_{\text{Residual}}}{df} = \frac{1203.656}{1398} = .861 \qquad \text{Equation 16.17}$$

$$F = \frac{\text{Mean Square}_{\text{Regression}}}{\text{Mean Square}_{\text{Residual}}} = \frac{6450.823}{.861} = 7492.379 \qquad \text{Equation 16.18}$$

Coefficients[a]

Model		Unstandardized Coefficients		Standardized Coefficients	t	Sig.
		B	Std. Error	Beta		
1	(Constant)	−4.226	.070		−60.660	.000
	Spec_Att_Reint	1.110	.013	.918	86.559	.000

a. Dependent variable: Vote_Index   Vote index

The constant term (the intercept) is the point at which the regression line crosses the *y* axis and represents the predicted value of Y when X = 0. The unstandardized regression coefficient (B) of 1.110 implies that for every unit increase in the independent variable, the predicted value of the dependent variable increases by 1.110 units.

As predicted by Equation 16.12, the standardized regression coefficient (β = .918) equals the Pearson correlation of .918 and the Multiple *R* of .918. This equivalence works in this situation because there is only one dependent and one independent variable in the model. With standardized regression coefficients (β), the constant term is always 0.

Figure 16.13 graphs the relationship between the specific attitude toward wolf reintroduction and the voting intentions index. Both the ordinary least squares regression line and the scatterplot are displayed. The regression line reflects the "substantial" magnitude of this relationship (β = .918). Because the scatterplot

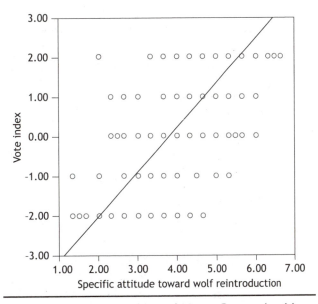

Vote index = -4.23 + 1.11 * Spec_Att_Reint
R-Square = 0.84

Figure 16.13   Scatterplot and Linear Regression Line

is based on an *n* of 1,400, detecting the linear trend is not as obvious as the earlier examples. Overall, the findings from this analysis imply that individuals who hold a positive attitude toward wolf reintroduction will be more likely to vote in favor of the wolf reintroduction if presented with the opportunity to vote on a ballot initiative.

Multiple Regression

A regression model that includes more than one independent variable is called a ***multiple regression***. For example, a researcher might be interested in the combined influence of respondents' "specific attitude toward wolf reintroduction" *and* their "general attitude toward wolves" on the voting intentions index. As discussed in chapter 4, both of these attitudes represent a positive or negative evaluation of an object. The two concepts differ in terms of the specificity of the object. When the object is "wolves," the evaluation reflects general cognitions such as "like or dislike" or "beneficial or harmful" that form a general attitude. When the object is "wolf reintroduction in Colorado during 1996," the evaluation represents a narrower context and time frame, and thus a specific attitude. The two concepts are likely to be correlated, although the Pearson *r* is probably less than 1.00. For example, a person may feel that wolves symbolize the natural beauty of the world and should be protected (i.e., the general attitude), but not want them reintroduced into Colorado where they might kill cattle and sheep (i.e., the specific attitude). This distinction is sometimes referred to NIMBY (i.e., Not In My Back Yard).

In the Bright and Manfredo (1996) study, the respondents' general attitude toward wolves was measured with three variables. Similar to the specific attitude in that investigation, each of these questions was coded on a seven-point scale. For example, "In general, do you dislike or like wolves?" Responses to this question were coded as "strongly dislike" (1) through "strongly like" (7) with "neutral" (4) as the midpoint. A second question asked: "In general, do you think wolves are harmful or beneficial animals?" with response categories ranging from "extremely harmful" (1) to "extremely beneficial" (7). A third survey question was: "Would you say your general attitude toward wolves is negative, positive, or neutral?" The responses were coded: "extremely negative" (1) through "extremely positive" (7) with "neither" (4) as the midpoint. The procedures described in chapters 12 and 18 were used to compute a summated rating index that was the average of respondents' answers to these three questions. The computed scale had values ranging from 1.00 to 7.00 and reflected the individuals' general attitude toward wolves.

The logic of the cognitive hierarchy (chapter 2) would predict that the specific attitude should be a better predictor of the voting behavior than the general variable. Both variables when considered simultaneously, however, might contribute to an understanding of respondents' reported voting intentions. To address the combined influence of these two predictors, the regression model is restated as:

$$Y = A + B_1(X_1) + B_2(X_2) + \varepsilon$$

Equation 15.19

where:
   Y = voting intention (i.e., dependent variable)
   A = the intercept and constant added to each case. With two variables in the model, the
        intercept is a plane (see Figure 16.14, p. 439)

B$_1$ = the constant by which all values of the "specific attitude toward wolf reintroduction" are multiplied

X$_1$ = specific attitude toward wolf reintroduction (i.e., one independent variable)

B$_2$ = the constant by which all values of the "general attitude toward wolves" are multiplied

X$_2$ = general attitude toward wolves (i.e., a second independent variable)

ε = error term

The SPSS syntax for this multiple regression is:

```
REGRESSION
  / DESCRIPTIVES MEAN STDDEV CORR SIG N
  / MISSING LISTWISE
  / STATISTICS COEFF OUTS R ANOVA COLLIN TOL CHANGE
  / NOORIGIN
  / DEPENDENT Vote_Index
  / METHOD=ENTER Spec_Att_Reint
  / METHOD=ENTER Gen_Att_Wolf .
```

This syntax is similar to the regression model examining the relationship between the specific attitude and voting behavior, but there are some important differences. The command line / STATISTICS now includes COLLIN, TOL, and CHANGE. The COLLIN and TOL commands provide collinearity diagnostics for the relationship between the two independent variables. These statistics are generated by checking the Collinearity Diagnostics box in Figure 16.9. Testing for collinearity in the two variable regression model is warranted because the specific and general attitudes are likely to be highly correlated.

Collinearity and Multicollinearity Diagnostics

With two independent variables in the model, ***collinearity*** exists when there is substantial correlation ($r > .90$) between the independent variables (Belsley, Kuh, & Welsch, 1980). Collinear variables are problematic because they provide very similar information, and it is difficult to separate out the effect of the individual variables. ***Multicollinearity*** occurs in a regression model that includes three or more independent variables, and there is a substantial intercorrelation among the predictors. As a rule of thumb, collinearity is a problem if the Pearson r between two independent variables is greater than .90 or there are several correlations greater than .7 among the predictor variables. Two common approaches for examining multicollinearity are the tolerances for individual variables and the *variance inflation factor* (VIF).

The ***tolerance*** of a variable is defined as:

$$\text{Tolerance} = 1 - R^2 \hspace{4cm} \text{Equation 15.20}$$

where:

R = multiple correlation coefficient when an independent variable is predicted from the other independent variables

If the tolerance of a variable is low ($< 1 - R^2$), it is almost a linear combination of the other independent variables. There will be as many tolerance coefficients as there are independent variables. The higher the intercorrelation among the predictor variables, the more the tolerance will approach zero. As a rule of thumb, if tolerance is less than .20, a multicollinearity problem is indicated. When tolerance is close to 0 there is high multicollinearity of that variable with other independents, and the B and beta coefficients will be unstable. In general, as multicollinearity increases, tolerance decreases and the standard error of the regression coefficients increases.

The **variance inflation factor (VIF)** is defined as the reciprocal of the tolerance:

$$\text{VIF} = \frac{1}{1 - R^2}$$

Equation 15.21

This quantity is called the *variance inflation factor* because the term is used in the calculation of the variance of the regression coefficient. As the variance inflation factor increases, the variance of the regression coefficient increases. When an independent variable is nearly a linear combination of other predictor variables in the model, the estimates of the unstandardized and standardized coefficients in the regression model are unstable and have high standard errors.

Table 16.4 shows the inflationary impact on the standard error of the regression coefficient (B) of an independent variable for various levels of multiple correlation (R), tolerance, and VIF. In the Impact on Standard Error of B column, 1.0 corresponds to no impact. The Standard Error is doubled when the VIF is 4.00 and the tolerance is .25, corresponding to $R = .87$.

Table 16.4   Multicollinearity Diagnostics

Multiple R	Tolerance	VIF	Impact on Standard Error of B
.00	1.00	1.00	1.00
.40	.84	1.19	1.09
.60	.64	1.56	1.25
.75	.44	2.25	1.50
.80	.36	2.78	1.67
.87	.25	4.00	2.02
.90	.19	5.26	2.29

Adapted from Fox (1991)

VIF ≥ 4 is an arbitrary but common cut-off criterion for deciding when a given independent variable displays "too much" multicollinearity; values above 4 suggest a multicollinearity problem. Some researchers use the more lenient cutoff of 5.0 or even 10.0 to signal when multicollinearity is a problem. The researcher may wish to drop the variable with the highest VIF if multicollinearity is indicated and theory warrants.

Multiple Regression Models

The syntax for the two independent variable regression model also includes the command CHANGE on the / STATISTICS line and indicates that two models will be examined:

```
/ STATISTICS COEFF OUTS R ANOVA COLLIN TOL CHANGE

/ METHOD=ENTER Spec_Att_Reint
/ METHOD=ENTER Gen_Att_Wolf .
```

CHANGE refers to the extent to which the R^2 changes when the general attitude variable is included in the model. By declaring two /METHOD statements, SPSS will calculate two regression models. Model 1 is identical to the earlier regression analysis (independent variable = specific attitude). Model 2 includes both independent variables (i.e., specific and general attitude).

The results from this analysis are shown in Output 16.5.

Output 16.5   Regression Analysis:
Dependent Variable = Voting index
Independent Variable = Specific attitude toward wolf reintroduction
Independent Variable = General attitude toward wolves

Descriptive Statistics

	Mean	Std. Deviation	N
Vote_Index	1.4214	2.33045	1386
Spec_Att_Reint	5.0838	1.92741	1386
Gen_Att_Wolf	5.3568	1.54415	1386

The means for the specific (*M* = 5.08) and general (*M* = 5.36) attitudes suggest favorable evaluations for reintroduction and wolves in general. The mid-point of each scale is 4 (neutral). Values greater than 4 imply positive attitudes.

Correlations

		Vote_Index	Spec_Att_Reint	Gen_Att_Wolf
Pearson Correlation	Vote_Index	1.000	.917	.752
	Spec_Att_Reint	.917	1.000	.819
	Gen_Att_Wolf	.752	.819	1.000
Sig. (1-tailed)	Vote_Index	.	.000	.000
	Spec_Att_Reint	.000	.	.000
	Gen_Att_Wolf	.000	.000	.
N	Vote_Index	1386	1386	1386
	Spec_Att_Reint	1386	1386	1386
	Gen_Att_Wolf	1386	1386	1386

Both of the attitude indices were correlated with the behavior index (*r* = .917 and .752, *p* < .001).

The Pearson *r* = .819 suggests a potential collinearity problem.

Model Summary

Model	R	R Square	Adjusted R Square	Std. Error of the Estimate	Change Statistics R Square Change	F Change	df1	df2	Sig. F Change
1	.917[a]	.841	.841	.92903	.841	7330.987	1	1384	.000
2	.917[b]	.841	.841	.92936	.000	.021	1	1383	.885

[a] Predictors: (Constant), Spec_Att_Reint
[b] Predictors: (Constant), Spec_Att_Reint, Gen_Att_Wolf

Model 1 included only the specific attitude index and explained 84% of the variability in the voting behavior index. Model 2 included both attitude measures. The addition of the general attitude scale did not increase the R^2 (i.e., R^2 change = .00 for model 2). Thus, although both attitude measures indicated substantial bivariate correlations with the voting behavior (*r* = .917 and .752), the collinearity between the two independent variables resulted in no additional explanatory power when the general attitude was included in model 2.

ANOVA[c]

Model		Sum of Squares	df	Mean Square	F	Sig.
1	Regression	6327.394	1	6327.394	7330.987	.000[a]
	Residual	1194.534	1384	.863		
	Total	7521.928	1385			
2	Regression	6327.412	2	3163.706	3662.911	.000[b]
	Residual	1194.516	1383	.864		
	Total	7521.928	1385			

[a.] Predictors: (Constant), Spec_Att_Reint
[b.] Predictors: (Constant), Spec_Att_Reint, Gen_Att_Wolf
[c.] Dependent Variable: Vote_Index

The *F*-value for model 1 (1 independent variable) was 7,330.99, whereas the *F*-value for Model 2 (2 independent variables) was 3,662.91. This dramatic reduction occurred for two reasons: (a) the inclusion of the general attitude did not increase the R^2 and (b) the way an *F*-value is calculated (see Equations 16.16 to 16.18). The sum of squares remained roughly the same in both models (i.e., 6,327.394 and 6,327.412), but the degrees of freedom (*df*) double. There was 1 *df* in model 1 because only one regression coefficient was estimated. In model 2 there were 2 *df* because two regression parameters were computed—one for specific attitude and one for general attitude.

Coefficients[a]

Model		Unstandardized Coefficiants		Standardized Coefficients	t	Sig.	Collinearity Statisitics	
		B	Std. Error	Beta			Tolerance	VIF
1	(Constant)	−4.216	.070		−59.879	.000		
	Spec_Att_Reint	1.109	.013	.917	85.621	.000	1.000	1.000
2	(Constant)	−4.225	.091		−46.637	.000		
	Spec_Att_Reint	1.106	.023	.915	49.040	.000	.330	3.032
	Gen_Att_Wolf	.004	.028	.003	.144	.885	.330	3.032

[a.] Dependent Variable: Vote_Index

With both attitude variables in the model, the coefficient for the general attitude index was not statistically significant ($\beta = .003, p = .855$). Consistent with the Pearson *r* between the two independent variables ($r = .819$), the tolerance = .33 and the VIF = 3.03 highlight the collinearity problem between the specific attitude and the general attitude.

As a final step in this analysis, Figure 16.14 graphs the relationship between the two attitudinal predictor variables and the voting behavior index. This graph was produced by selecting:

Graphs > Interactive > Scatterplot...

The intercept for the two independent variable model is now a plane, as opposed to a line when there was only one independent variable (Figure 16.14).

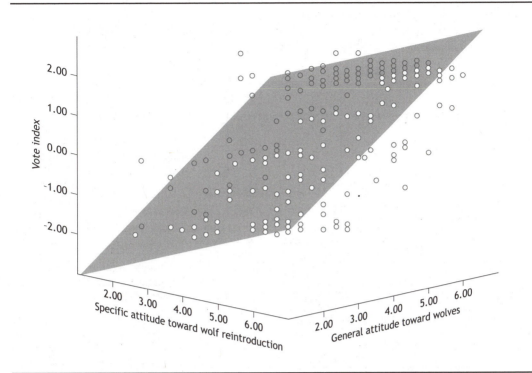

Figure 16.14 The Relationship between Two Attitudinal Predictor Variables and Voting Behavior

Dummy Variable Regression

In the regression models examined thus far, all of the variables (i.e., both independent and dependent) were continuous measures. *Dummy variable regression* refers to an analysis where one or more of the independent variables are dichotomous and the dependent variable is continuous.[3] The distinction between ordinary least squares (OLS) regression and dummy variable regression can be illustrated using two variables—specific attitude toward wolf reintroduction and age—from the Bright and Manfredo (1996) study. Both of these variables are continuous measures. For the OLS model predicting the respondents' attitude based on their age, the SPSS OLS syntax is:

```
REGRESSION
  /DESCRIPTIVES MEAN STDDEV CORR SIG N
  /MISSING LISTWISE
  /STATISTICS COEFF OUTS R ANOVA
  /NOORIGIN
  /DEPENDENT Spec_Att_Reint
  /METHOD=ENTER Age   .
```

The results from this syntax are shown in Output 16.6.

---

[3] Chapter 17 on logistic regression considers the opposite situation where the dependent variable is dichotomous and the independent variable(s) are continuous.

Output 16.6   Ordinary Least Squares Regression:
Dependent Variable = Specific attitude toward wolf reintroduction
Independent Variable = Respondents' age

Correlations

		Spec_Att_Reint	Age
Pearson Correlation	Spec_Att_Reint	1.000	−.262
	Age	−.262	1.000
Sig. (1-tailed)	Spec_Att_Reint	.	.000
	Age	.000	.
N	Spec_Att_Reint	1396	1396
	Age	1396	1396

The bivariate correlation ($r = -.262$) from the OLS regression approximates the correlation ($r = -.260$) produced from the correlation analysis (Output 16.2). The difference at the 3rd decimal point occurs due to differences in the sample sizes. The regression model was based on an n of 1,396. The earlier correlation analysis was based on $n = 1,388$ (Output 16.1).

Model Summary

Model	R	R Square	Adjusted R Square	Std. Error of the Estimate
1	.262[a]	.068	.068	1.86228

a. Predictors: (Constant), Age   Respondent age in years

The absolute value of the Pearson r = Multiple R because there is only one independent and one dependent variable.

ANOVA[b]

Model		Sum of Squares	df	Mean Square	F	Sig.
1	Regression	355.425	1	355.425	102.484	.000[a]
	Residual	4834.524	1394	3.468		
	Total	5189.950	1395			

a. Predictors: (Constant), Age   Respondent age in years
b. Dependent Variable: Spec_Att_Reintr   Specific attitude toward wolf reintroduction

The F-value (102.484) is the square of the t-value (-10.123) associated with the predictor age. This relationship holds when there is one independent and one dependent variable.

Coefficients[a]

Model		Unstandardized Coefficients		Standardized Coefficients		
		B	Std. Error	Beta	t	Sig.
1	(Constant)	6.514	.151		43.200	.000
	Age	−.032	.003	−.262	−10.123	.000

a. Dependent Variable: Spec_Att_Reint   Specific attitude toward wolf reintroduction

Dummy Variable Example

Most statistics books, including this textbook, discuss topics such as dummy variable regression, *t*-tests, and analysis of variance in separate chapters. This section illustrates the relationships among these various approaches to analyzing data.

Assume that the researcher is interested in whether younger individuals (as a group) differ from older individuals (as a group). To address this question, the continuous age could be recoded into a dichotomous (dummy) variable. An arbitrary cut-point is the respondents' mean age ($M = 45$). The SPSS syntax for recoding AGE into a dichotomous variable (AGE1) and running a dummy variable regression is:

```
* Regression - Independent (Dummy) - Dependent (Continuous)

RECODE age
       (12 thru 45=0)
       (46 thru 98=1)    into age1.
VALUE LABELS   age1
     0 '12 thru 45'
     1 '46 thru 98'.

REGRESSION
  /MISSING LISTWISE
  /STATISTICS COEFF OUTS R ANOVA
  /CRITERIA=PIN(.05) POUT(.10)
  /NOORIGIN
  /DEPENDENT Spec_Att_Reint
  /METHOD=ENTER age1 .
```

The results of this dummy variable regression are shown in Output 16.7.

Output 16.7   Dummy Variable Regression:
                Dependent Variable = Specific attitude toward wolf reintroduction
                Independent Variable = Respondents' age recoded in a dichotomous variable

Model Summary

Model	R	R Square	Adjusted R Square	Std. Error of the Estimate
1	.209ᵃ	.044	.043	1.88709

a. Predictors: (Constant), age1

> With the range of values on the independent variable is constrained to 0 (age = 12 thru 45) and 1 (46 thru 98), the Multiple R for AGE1 and the specific attitude decreased to r = .209. When the two variables were measured at the continuous level, the Multiple R was .262 (Output 16.6).

ANOVAᵇ

Model		Sum of Squares	df	Mean Square	F	Sig.
1	Regression	225.772	1	225.772	63.399	.000ᵃ
	Residual	4964.178	1394	3.561		
	Total	5189.950	1395			

a. Predictors: (Constant), age1
b. Dependent Variable: Spec_Att_Reintr   Specific attitude toward wolf reintroduction

> Identical to the OLS regression:
> $F = t^2$ and $t = \sqrt{F}$
> for the t-value associated with the independent variable (i.e., $63.399 = (-7.962)^2$)

Coefficientsᵃ

Model		Unstandardized Coefficiants		Standardized Coefficients		
		B	Std. Error	Beta	t	Sig.
1	(Constant)	5.426	.067		80.770	.000
	age1	−.811	.102	−.209	−7.962	.000

a. Dependent Variable: Spec_Att_Reint   Specific attitude toward wolf reintroduction

With only two variables in the model, the standardized coefficient ($\beta = -.209$) for the dummy variable equals the correlation coefficient ($r = -.209$, not shown) and the Multiple R ($R = .209$).

The unstandardized B coefficient in OLS is interpreted as the amount the dependent variable increases (or decreases) when the independent variable associated with the B increases by one unit. When dummy variables are used as the predictors, this interpretation changes. The B coefficient is how much the dependent variable increases (or decreases if B is negative) when the dummy variable goes from 0 (i.e., age = 12 thru 45) to 1 (age = 46 thru 98). The "constant" term in the equation equals the mean on the specific attitude variable ($M = 5.426$) for the individuals in the younger age group (coded as 0). The difference between the constant term and the unstandardized regression coefficient is the mean for individuals in the older group (i.e., $5.426 - .811 = 4.615$; see Output 16.8).

To demonstrate this relationship between the constant term and the unstandardized regression coefficient, a *t*-test (chapter 14) and an analysis of variance (chapter 15) were conducted. In these analyses the independent variable was the dichotomized age variable (AGE1) and the dependent variable was an index of continuous specific attitude variables.

The SPSS syntax for the *t*-test is:

```
* Comparison of Dummy Variable Regression with t-test

T-TEST
  GROUPS=age1(0 1)
  /MISSING=ANALYSIS
  /VARIABLES=Spec_Att_Reint
  /CRITERIA=CIN(.95)  .
```

The results from the *t*-test are shown in Output 16.8.

Output 16.8　*t*-test:
Dependent Variable = Specific attitude toward wolf reintroduction
Independent Variable = Respondents' age recoded in a dichotomous variable

T-Test

Group Statistics

	age1	N	Mean	Std. Deviation	Std. Error Mean
Spec_Att_Reint	0　12 thru 45	789	5.4263	1.68807	.06010
	1　46 thru 98	607	4.6150	2.11810	.08597

The mean for the 12 thru 45 group equals the constant term in the dummy variable regression. The mean for 46 thru 98 group equals the constant term minus the unstandardized regression.

Independent Sample Test

		Levene's Test for Equality of Variances		t-test for Equality of Means		
		F	Sig.	t	df	Sig. (2-tailed)
Spec_Att_Reint	Equal variances assumed	90.234	.000	7.962	1394	.000
	Equal variances not assumed			7.734	1134.600	.000

The *t*-value in the dummy variable regression was 7.962. The *t*-value from the *t*-test was also 7.962 under the assumption of equal variances. As was discussed in chapter 14, because the

Levene's test for equality of variances was significant ($F = 90.234$, $p < .001$), the appropriate *t*-value is 7.734 (i.e., equal variances not assumed) for this relationship. The *t*-value reported in the dummy variable regression assumes equal variances, and the *t*-test provides a test of this assumption.

The SPSS syntax for the analysis of variance (ANOVA) is:

```
* Comparison of Dummy Variable Regression with ANOVA

ONEWAY
  Spec_Att_Reint BY age1
  /CONTRAST= 1 -1
  /STATISTICS DESCRIPTIVES HOMOGENEITY
  /MISSING ANALYSIS .
```

The results from the ANOVA are shown in Output 16.9.

Output 16.9 Analysis of Variance:
            Dependent Variable = Specific attitude toward wolf reintroduction
            Independent Variable = Respondents' age recoded in a dichotomous variable

One-way

Descriptives

Spec_Att_Reint   Specific attitude toward wolf reintroduction

	N	Mean	Std. Deviation	Std. Error
0 12 thru 45	789	5.4263	1.68807	.06010
1 46 thru 98	607	4.6150	2.11810	.08597
Total	1396	5.0735	1.92883	.05162

> The means from the ANOVA equal the means from the *t*-test and the dummy variable regression's constant and unstandardized coefficient.

Test of Homogeneity of Variances

Spec_Att_Reint   Specific attitude toward wolf reintroduction

Levene Statistic	df1	df2	Sig.
90.234	1	1394	.000

> The Levene's statistic from the ANOVA is identical to the *t*-test.

ANOVA

Spec_Att_Reint   Specific attitude toward wolf reintroduction

	Sum of Squares	df	Mean Square	F	Sig.
Between Groups	225.772	1	225.772	63.399	.000
Within Groups	4964.178	1394	3.561		
Total	5189.950	1395			

> The *F*-value in the ANOVA table produced from the analysis of variance equals the *F*-value in the ANOVA table produced by the dummy variable regression (Output 16.7).

The syntax for the analysis of variance requested a contrast (*t*-test) between the two levels of the independent variable. Under the assumption of equality of variance, the *t*-value (7.962) is identical to the *t*-values generated by the *t*-test and absolute value of the dummy variable regression.

Contrast Tests

		Contrast	Value of Contrast	Std. Error	t	df	Sig. (2-tailed)
Spec_Att_Reint	Assume equal variances	1	.8112	.10188	7.962	1394	.000
	Does not assume equal	1	.8112	.10489	7.734	1134.600	.000

Multiple Dummy Variables in Regression

The previous dummy variable regression based the analysis on a single dichotomous variable where the continuous age variable was recoded into two categories. The arbitrary cut-point for these two categories was the mean. A researcher is not limited to a single dichotomous independent variable in a dummy variable regression. For example, rather than creating one dichotomous variable, three dummy variables might be computed by recoding the continuous age variable. There are a variety of ways to accomplish this task in SPSS. The syntax for one approach is:

```
RECODE   age
        (12 thru 36=0)
        (37 thru 50=1)
        (51 thru 98=2)   into age2.

VALUE LABELS   age2
     0 '12 thru 36'
     1 '37 thru 50'
     2 '51 thru 98'.

Frequencies variables = age2.
```

A frequencies analysis of AGE2 is shown in Output 16.10.

Output 16.10   Frequencies Analysis of Age2

age2

			Frequency	Percent	Valid Percent	Cumulative Percent
Valid	0	12 thru 36	471	32.2	33.3	33.3
	1	37 thru 50	472	32.3	33.4	66.6
	2	51 thru 98	472	32.3	33.4	100.0
	Total		1415	96.9	100.0	
Missing	System		46	3.1		
Total			1461	100.0		

The recode created a new variable (AGE2) and divided the age variable into three equal groups.

The syntax for computing three dummy variables based on AGE2 is:

```
Compute youth  = age2 = 0.
Compute midage = age2 = 1.
Compute over50 = age2 = 2.

Variable labels
        youth '12 thru 36 dummy variable'
      / midage '37 thru 50 dummy variable'
      / over50 'Over 50 dummy variable'.

Value labels youth midage over50
      0 'No'
      1 'Yes'.

Frequencies variables = youth midage over50.
```

A frequencies analysis of the three dummy variables is shown in Output 16.11.

Output 16.11   Frequencies Analyses of Three Dummy Variables

youth   12 thru 36 dummy variable

		Frequency	Percent	Valid Percent	Cumulative Percent
Valid	0 No	944	64.6	66.7	66.7
	1 Yes	471	32.2	33.3	100.0
	Total	1415	96.9	100.0	
Missing	System	46	3.1		
Total		1461	100.0		

The *n*s and %s for the "Yes" category for each of the three dummy variables equal the *n*s and %s for the three levels of the AGE2 variable (Output 16.10).

midage   37 thru 50 dummy variable

		Frequency	Percent	Valid Percent	Cumulative Percent
Valid	0 No	943	64.5	66.6	66.6
	1 Yes	472	32.3	33.4	100.0
	Total	1415	96.9	100.0	
Missing	System	46	3.1		
Total		1461	100.0		

over50   Over 50 dummy variable

		Frequency	Percent	Valid Percent	Cumulative Percent
Valid	0 No	943	64.5	66.6	66.6
	1 Yes	472	32.3	33.4	100.0
	Total	1415	96.9	100.0	
Missing	System	46	3.1		
Total		1461	100.0		

The syntax for a dummy variable regression predicting the specific attitude based on these dichotomous variables is:

```
REGRESSION
  /MISSING LISTWISE
  /STATISTICS COEFF OUTS R ANOVA
  /NOORIGIN
  /DEPENDENT Spec_Att_Reint
  /METHOD=ENTER midage over50.
```

With three dichotomous variables, only two dummy variables are entered into the equation (i.e., MIDAGE and OVER50 in this example). *The third dummy variable (i.e., youth) serves as the reference category.* The influence of this reference independent variable on the dependent variable is the constant term in the regression equation. A portion of the results from this regression analysis is shown in Output 16.12.

Output 16.12   A Three Variable Dummy Variable Regression

ANOVA[b]

Model		Sum of Squares	df	Mean Square	F	Sig.
1	Regression	279.867	2	139.934	39.699	.000[a]
	Residual	4910.082	1393	3.525		
	Total	5189.950	1395			

a. Predictors: (Constant), over50   Over 50 dummy variable, midage   37 thru 50 dummy variable
b. Dependent Variable: Spec_Att_Reintr   Specific attitude toward wolf reintroduction

Coefficients[a]

Model		Unstandardized Coefficiants B	Std. Error	Standardized Coefficients Beta	t	Sig.
1	(Constant)	5.591	.087		64.421	.000
	midage	−.467	.123	−.115	−3.811	.000
	over50	−1.096	.123	−.267	−8.883	.000

a. Dependent Variable: Spec_Att_Reint   Specific attitude toward wolf reintroduction

> All three dummy variables influenced the specific attitude ($p < .001$). The constant term is the mean on the specific attitude variable for the youth dichotomous variable ($M = 5.591$). The means for the other two dummy variables are computed by subtracting the unstandardized coefficients from the constant term.

The means for all three groups (i.e., youth, midage, over50) can be verified by running an analysis of variance. The syntax for this analysis is:

```
ONEWAY
  Spec_Att_Reint BY age2
  /STATISTICS DESCRIPTIVES
  /MISSING LISTWISE.
```

The results are presented in Output 16.13.

Output 16.13   One-way Analysis of Variance:
Independent Variable: Age2
Dependent Variable: Specific attitude toward wolf reintroduction

Descriptives

Spec_Att_Reint   Specific attitude toward wolf reintroduction

	N	Mean	Std. Deviation	Std. Error
0 youth	468	5.5908	1.56849	.07250
1 midage	469	5.1233	1.88329	.08696
2 over50	459	4.4953	2.14196	.09998
Total	1396	5.0735	1.92883	.05162

> The mean for the YOUTH category of AGE2 equals the constant term in the regression model.
>
> The mean for the MIDAGE category (M = 5.123) equals the constant minus the unstandardized coefficient for the MIDAGE dummy variable (i.e., 5.591 - .467 = 5.123).
>
> The mean for the OVER50 category equals 5.591 - 1.096 = 4.495.

ANOVA

Spec_Att_Reint   Specific attitude toward wolf reintroduction

	Sum of Squares	df	Mean Square	F	Sig.
Between Groups	279.867	2	139.934	39.699	.000
Within Groups	4910.082	1393	3.525		
Total	5189.950	1395			

> The F-value from the ANOVA equals the F-value from the dummy variable regression (Output 16.12).

Chapter Summary

This chapter examined bivariate correlations and three types of regression models: (a) bivariate, (b) multiple, and (c) dummy variable. The calculation and interpretation of these analytical procedures was emphasized.

A correlation coefficient measures the strength of the linear association between two variables. The Pearson correlation (r) is the most commonly reported correlation and is appropriate when both variables are continuous and approximately normally distributed. Examples of other types of correlations found in human dimensions research include: (a) point-biserial, (b) biserial, (c) tetrachoric, (d) phi, (e) eta, and (f) Spearman rank-order correlation. These correlations differ in their level of measurement requirements (i.e., dichotomous, categorical, continuous) and can be thought of as special cases of the Pearson r. The equations for computing these correlations are simplified versions of the Pearson r.

Because *correlations do not prove causation*, the distinction between independent and dependent variables is not relevant in a correlation context. Thinking about a causal sequence between the independent and dependent measures, however, is often useful when attempting to explain a phenomenon. For example, a respondent's sex (i.e., independent variable) might influence his or her attitude (i.e., the dependent variable). The attitude, however, cannot influence whether the person is male or female.

The values of the Pearson coefficient can range from +1 to –1, with a value of 0 indicating no linear relationship. The sign of the coefficient indicates the direction of the relationship. The absolute value of a correlation indicates the strength of the association with larger absolute values indicating stronger relationships. A correlation coefficient of 0, however, does not neces- sarily mean that there is no relationship between the two variables; only that there is no *linear* relationship. Because extreme values (i.e., outliers) can underestimate or exaggerate the strength of a correlation, scatterplots should be used to visually inspect the data whenever possible.

Data from a survey of residents' attitudes toward wolf reintroduction in Colorado were used to illustrate bivariate correlations in SPSS. Three null and alternative hypotheses were advanced for the relationships between respondents' attitude and their: (a) education, (b), sex, and (c) age. In hypothesis testing, a ***statistical hypothesis*** is a statement about population parameters. With correlations, the population parameter is symbolized as ρ *(rho)*. The null hypothesis always states that there is no relationship between the variables in the population (i.e., $\rho_0 = 0$). The alternative statistical hypotheses state there is either a directional ($\rho_1 > 0$ or $\rho_1 < 0$) or nondirectional ($\rho_1 \neq 0$) relationship. Statistical hypotheses should be differentiated from the ***substantive hypotheses***, which are statements involving concepts (e.g., specific attitude toward wolf reintroduction) that predict or explain the phenomena in question.

A ***two-tailed significance level*** is used if the researcher is unsure whether a pair of variables should be positively or negatively correlated. The null hypothesis is rejected for either large positive or large negative values of the correlation coefficient. If a directional relationship between the variables can be advanced, a ***one-tailed significance level*** is used. For a one-tailed test, the null hypothesis is rejected only if the value of the correlation coefficient is large *and* in the direction specified. With a one-tailed test, the observed significance level is one-half of the two-tailed value.

Similar to other test statistics (e.g., χ^2, F), the calculated value of the Pearson r is compared to the critical value in the theoretical sampling distribution of ρ. If the calculated value of r is as large or larger than the critical value of ρ for the predetermined level of statistical significance (e.g., $p < .05$), the null hypothesis is rejected. SPSS eliminates the need for manually looking up the theoretical values and making the comparison. Rather, SPSS does the comparison and reports the ***actual observed significance level***, which is labeled as ***Sig.*** in the output. If the Sig. value is small (typically less than .05), the relationship is statistically significant and the null hypothesis is rejected.

Although parks, recreation, and human dimensions surveys often include hundreds of variables, the researcher should avoid the temptation of computing all possible correlation coefficients among the variables. The more significance tests that are performed, the more likely the null hypothesis will be rejected when it is true (i.e., a Type I error). This problem is referred to as inflation of the p-value and can be corrected by using a more stringent p-value (i.e., smaller) when performing multiple tests. One approach for determining an appropriate p-value is called the Bonferroni correction. The Bonferroni correction is the ratio of the desired p-value to the number of significance tests conducted.

When two continuous variables are examined, correlation coefficients measure how *closely* the data points cluster together about a straight line, but say nothing about the line itself. Regression analysis can be used to describe the characteristics of the line. Regression analysis is useful for finding the best linear prediction equation and evaluating its prediction accuracy. This chapter examined (a) ***bivariate regression*** (i.e., one continuous dependent and one continuous independent variable), (b) ***multiple regression*** (i.e., one continuous dependent and two or more continuous independent variables, and (c) ***dummy variable regression*** (i.e., one dichotomous dependent and one or more continuous independent variables. Similar to a correlation analysis, regression can be viewed either as a ***descriptive tool*** that summarizes the linear dependence of one variable on another, or as an ***inferential tool*** that makes statistical inferences about the population parameter based on the sample data.

A common method for determining a regression line is called the *method of least squares* (a.k.a. ordinary least squares or OLS). There are three basic steps in computing a least squares line: (a) calculate the vertical distances to the line from all points, (b) square the vertical distances, and (c) sum the squared differences. In the bivariate regression equation:

- The constant A (intercept) is the point at which the regression line crosses the y axis and represents the predicted value of Y when X = 0.

- The constant B, usually referred to the unstandardized regression coefficient, is the slope of the regression line and indicates the expected change in Y with a change of one unit in X.

- The predicted Y' values fall on the regression line.

- The vertical distances (Y – Y') of the points from the line represent the residuals (or errors in prediction).

- Because the sum of the squared residuals is minimized, the regression line is called the *least squares line* or the *line of best fit*.

The ***coefficient of determination*** (***R^2***) provides a measure of how much variation in the dependent variable is explained by the independent variable(s).

A ***standardized regression coefficient*** (a.k.a. *β*, beta, or beta weight) converts all of the variables to the same scale, making it easier to compare the relative effects of different independent variables. If two or more independent variables are measured in different units (e.g., income in dollars and education in years), standardized coefficients provide a vehicle for comparing the relative effect of each independent variable on the dependent variable.

The use of standardized regression coefficients, however, has been controversial in the social sciences. As a general rule of thumb, when making comparisons *between samples*, the unstandardized estimates should be used. Alternatively, when making statements about the relative importance of variables *within a sample*, the standardized coefficient is more appropriate because it adjusts for the different measurement scales of the variables. A useful practice is to report both coefficients.

Data from a study of public attitudes toward wolf reintroduction in Colorado were used to illustrate regression analysis in SPSS. One bivariate model predicted respondents' voting intentions to allow wolf reintroduction (the dependent variable) based on their specific attitude toward wolf reintroduction. The multiple regression empirical example included two predictor variables (i.e., the specific attitude and respondents' general attitude toward wolves). The multiple regression example highlighted potential problems with collinearity. ***Collinearity*** exists when there is substantial correlation ($r > .90$) between the independent variables. ***Multicollinearity*** occurs in a regression model that includes three or more independent variables and there is a substantial intercorrelation among the predictors. As a rule of thumb, collinearity is a problem if the Pearson r between two independent variables is greater than .90 or there are several correlations greater than .7 among the predictor variables. Two common approaches for examining multicollinearity were discussed: (a) the tolerances for individual variables and (b) the ***variance inflation factor*** (VIF).

Dummy variable regression refers to an analysis where when one or more of the independent variables are dichotomous and the dependent variable is continuous. The distinction between ordinary least squares (OLS) regression and dummy variable regression was illustrated using two variables—specific attitude toward wolf reintroduction and respondents' age. The example regression analyses included models with: (a) one dichotomous independent variable, and (b) two dichotomous independent variables. The multiple dummy variable regression model was based on three dichotomous age variables (i.e., YOUTH, MIDAGE, OVER50). With three dichotomous variables, only two dummy variables are entered into the equation. The third dummy variable serves as the reference category, and the effect of the reference independent variable on the dependent variable is the constant term in the regression equation.

The findings from the dummy variable regression models were compared to results obtained from *t*-tests and analysis of variance to illustrate the connection between these different analytical procedures.

Review Questions

1. What does a Pearson correlation coefficient measure? What is the range of values associated with this coefficient? How do you interpret the values of this coefficient?

2. What is the difference between a Pearson r, a point-biserial, a biserial, and a tetrachoric correlation in terms of their level of measurement?

3. In correlation analysis, what is the difference between a *statistical* hypothesis and a *substantive* hypothesis?

4. When would you want to use a one-tailed versus a two-tailed test of significance with the Pearson correlation?

5. Would you reject or fail-to-reject the null hypothesis where there is no linear relationship between two variables in the population, if $r = .39$, $p < .049$.

6. What is the danger in examining many correlation coefficients at one time?

7. What does the Bonferroni correction do?

8. Briefly explain the difference between *correlation* and *regression*.

9. What are the differences between a: (a) bivariate regression, (b) multiple regression, and (c) dummy variable regression?

10. Briefly describe the distinction between the SPSS subcommands Enter and Stepwise methods when running a regression analysis.

11. What is an *intercept* in a regression analysis?

12. Explain the meaning of the *slope of a regression*.

13. What is a *coefficient of determination*?

14. What does *collinearity* mean?

15. Explain the difference between unstandardized and standardized regression coefficients. When is it appropriate to use an *unstandardized* regression coefficient? When is it appropriate to use a *standardized* regression coefficient?

16. In a simple regression (1 independent variable, 1 dependent variable), if $\beta = .75$:
    - What is the value of the multiple R?
    - What is the value of the coefficient of determination?

17. When examining standardized regression coefficients, what is the value of the intercept if the value of $\beta = .23$?

18. In a dummy variable regression where sex (males [0] and females [1]) is the independent variable and days of participation in a recreation activity for a period of one year (coded 0 through 365) is the dependent variable, if the constant term equals 9.83, how many days, on average, did the males participate in the activity during the year?

19. Under the assumption of equality of variances, if the t-value in the dummy variable regression equals 7.962, what is the t-value produced from a t-test?

20. If the F-value in an ANOVA table produced from the analysis of variance equals 14.98, what is the F-value in the ANOVA table produced by the dummy variable regression?

17

logistic regression and discriminant function analysis

Predicting the probability that an event will or will not occur (i.e., a dichotomous dependent variable) and identifying the variables useful in making the prediction (i.e., predictor variables, also considered independent variables) are important in parks, recreation, and human dimensions research. For example, why do some people support a management proposal and others not (see Donnelly & Vaske, 1995)? Why do some people hunt and others not (see Barro & Manfredo, 1996)? The last chapter discussed linear regression, where the dependent variable is continuous. Linear regression, however, is not appropriate when the dependent variable has only two values because the assumptions necessary for hypothesis testing are violated. For example, it is unreasonable to assume that the distribution of errors is normally distributed when the dependent variable is dichotomous.

A variety of statistical techniques can be used to predict a dichotomous dependent variable. This chapter considers two techniques—logistic regression and discriminant analysis—for estimating the probability that an event occurs. *Discriminant analysis* allows direct prediction of group membership, but the method requires several assumptions (e.g., multivariate normality of the independent variables, equal variance-covariance matrices in the two groups) for the predictions to be optimal (Silva & Stam, 1995). *Logistic regression* **(LR)** requires fewer assumptions than discriminant analysis, although logistic regression also performs well when the assumptions required for discriminant analysis are satisfied (Darlington, 1990; Morgan, Vaske, Gliner, & Harmon, 2003; Press & Wilson, 1978).

Logistic Regression

In logistic regression, the researcher directly estimates the probability of an event occurring. LR models include a dichotomous dependent variable and one or more independent variables that may be either dichotomous or continuous. Logistic regression should not be confused with *multinomial* logistic regression where the dependent variable has more than two categories (see Long, 1997). This chapter focuses on dichotomous outcome variables only.

In linear regression, the regression coefficient represents the amount of change in the dependent variable for one-unit change in the independent variable. The coefficients are estimated using the least-squares method. In other words, the regression coefficients represent the smallest sum of squared differences between the observed and the predicted values of the dependent variable (chapter 16). In logistic regression, the probability of an event occurring or not is estimated using the ***maximum-likelihood method***. The coefficients that make the observed results most likely are selected.

The probability of the event *not* occurring is estimated as:

$$\text{Prob(no event)} = 1 - \text{Prob(event)} \qquad\qquad \text{Equation 17.1}$$

Because logistic regression is nonlinear (Figure 17.1), an ***iterative algorithm*** (i.e., a step-by-step procedure for solving statistical problems that involves repetition of a process) is necessary for coefficient estimation. When there is a single independent variable in the model, the logistic regression model can be written as:

$$\text{Prob}(event) = \frac{e^{\beta_0 + \beta_1 X}}{1 + e^{\beta_0 + \beta_1 X}} \qquad\qquad \text{Equation 17.2}$$

where:

$\beta_0 = Exp(B)$ constant term
$\beta_1 = Exp(B)$ logistic coefficient
$X =$ independent variable
$e =$ the base of the natural logarithms, approximately 2.718

Exp(B) is explained in detail later in this chapter. For more than one independent variable, the model can be written as:

$$\text{Prob}(event) = \frac{e^{Z}}{1 + e^{Z}} \qquad\qquad \text{Equation 17.3}$$

where:

$$Z = \beta_0 + \beta_1 X_1 + \beta_2 X_2 + \ldots + \beta_p X_p$$

Figure 17.1 illustrates a logistic regression curve when the values of Z are between –6 and +6. The S-shaped curve resembles the curve obtained when the cumulative probability of the normal distribution is plotted (Agresti, 2002). The probability estimate for each respondent will always be between 0 and 1, regardless of the value of Z. In general, if the estimated probability of the event is < 0.5, the event is predicted to *not* occur for that person. If the probability is > 0.5, the event is predicted to occur. If the probability is exactly 0.5000, SPSS basically flips a coin to determine the individual's predicted group membership (Norusis, 2003).

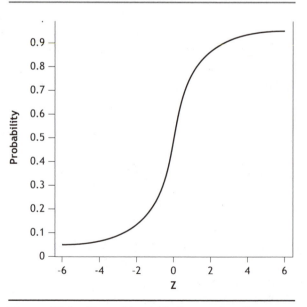

Figure 17.1   Plot of Logistic Regression Curve

Testing Hypotheses about the Coefficients

In logistic regression, significance tests are provided for each independent variable. The test that a coefficient is 0 can be based on the *Wald statistic*, which has a chi-square distribution with one degree of freedom. The Wald statistic is the square of the ratio of the unstandardized logistic regression coefficient to its standard error:

$$\text{Wald} = \left(\frac{B}{S.E.} \right)^2$$

Equation 17.4

where:

 B = unstandardized logistic regression coefficient
 S.E. = standard error of the coefficient

Unfortunately, the Wald statistic has an undesirable property. When the absolute value of the unstandardized logistic regression coefficient becomes large, the estimated standard error is too large (Morgan, Vaske, Gliner, & Harmon, 2003). This produces a Wald statistic that is too small, leading the researcher to fail-to-reject the null hypothesis where the coefficient is 0, when in fact the analyst should reject it (Hauck & Donner, 1977). Therefore, whenever the coefficient is large, the Wald statistic should be interpreted cautiously for hypothesis testing. As an alternative, significance can be examined using a confidence interval (see Wilson & Langenberg, 1999).

As is the case with multiple linear regression, the contribution of individual variables in logistic regression depends on the other variables in the model. A statistic that is used to examine the partial correlation between the dependent variable and each of the independent variables is the *R statistic*, which can range in value from –1 to +1. A positive value of R indicates that as the variable increases in value, the likelihood of the event occurring increases. If R is negative, the opposite is true. As the variable decreases in value, the likelihood of the event occurring decreases. Small values for R indicate that the variable has a small partial contribution to the model. The equation for the R statistic is:

$$R = \pm \sqrt{\left[\frac{\text{Wald statistic} - 2K}{-2LL} \right]}$$

Equation 17.5

where:

 K = degrees of freedom for the variable. The value $2K$ is an adjustment for the number of coefficients estimated. If the Wald statistic is less than $2K$, R is set to 0.
 $-2LL$ = –2 times the log likelihood (see discussion later) of a base model that contains only the intercept (i.e., constant).

The sign of the corresponding unstandardized logistic regression coefficient (i.e., B in the Wald formula) is attached to R.

Interpreting the Regression Coefficients

In multiple linear regression, the interpretation of the regression coefficient is straightforward. The coefficient indicates the amount of change in the dependent variable for one-unit change in the independent variable. Logistic regression coefficients, on the other hand, are expressed as either the log odds (i.e., unstandardized logistic coefficient) or the odds (*Exp[B]*) of an event occurring. The **odds** of an event is the ratio of the probability that the outcome occurs to the probability that it does not. For example, the odds of getting heads on a single flip of a coin are:

$$\text{odds (heads on coin flip)} = \left[\frac{p}{1-p}\right] = \left[\frac{.5}{1-.5}\right] = 1.0$$

Similarly, the odds of getting a diamond on a single draw from a card deck are:

$$\text{odds (diamond from single draw)} = \left[\frac{p}{1-p}\right] = \left[\frac{.25}{1-.25}\right] = \left[\frac{.25}{.75}\right] = \frac{1}{3}$$

The technical meaning of odds should not be confused with its informal usage that implies a probability. Thus, if the probability of an event occurring is .8, the odds of the event is .8 divided by the probability of it not occurring (.2) or .8 / .2 = 4.0. In everyday language, this means that the odds are 4 to 1.

Odds ratios are central to logistic regression, just as the correlation coefficient is central to linear regression. An **odds ratio** (**OR**) is simply the ratio of two odds. For example, if the odds of an event is 4 for males, and the odds of the same event is 3 for females, the odds ratio relating sex to the event is 4 / 3 = 1.33. The null value of an odds ratio is 1.0 (similar to a correlation coefficient of 0) and indicates random association. When a positive association increases, the correlation coefficient increases from 0 to 1 and the odds ratio increases from 1 to infinity. As a negative association increases, the correlation coefficient decreases from 0 to –1 and the odds ratio decreases from 1 to 0.

The null hypothesis is that the population odds ratio is equal to 1. If the null hypothesis were true (OR = 1), membership in the two categories of the dependent variable would be unrelated to the independent variable. Although some researchers (e.g., Epstein, 2003; McNutt, Holcomb, & Carlson, 2000) have raised questions about the value of the odds ratio, the odds ratio is an excellent indicator of nonrandomness. Thus, despite reservations about the odds ratio, logistic regression continues to be widely used (Morgan, Vaske, Gliner, & Harmon, 2003).

To understand the interpretation of the logistic coefficients, the logistic regression equation can be written in terms of the **log of the odds** (**ln[odds]**, a.k.a. a *logit*):

$$\ln(\text{odds}) \left[\frac{\text{Prob(event)}}{\text{Prob(no event)}} \right] = B_0 + B_1 X_1 + \cdots + B_p X_p$$

Equation 17.6

From equation 17.6, the logistic coefficient can be interpreted as the change in the log odds associated with one-unit change in the independent variable. For example, if the logistic coefficient for sex (the independent variable) is 0.024, when sex changes from 0 to 1 and the values of the other independent variables remain the same, the log odds increase by 0.024.

Because it easier to think of odds rather than log odds, the logistic regression equation can be written in terms of odds as:

$$\left[\frac{\text{Prob(event)}}{\text{Prob(no event)}} \right] = e^{\beta_0 + \beta_1 X_1 + \cdots + \beta_p X_p}$$

Equation 17.7

The e raised to the power β_i is the factor by which the odds change when a given independent variable increases by one-unit.

- If β_i is positive, this factor will be greater than 1, which means the odds are increased.

- If β_i is negative, this factor will be less than 1, which means the odds are decreased.

- If β_i is 0, this factor equals 1, which leaves the odds unchanged.

In SPSS terminology, odds are denoted as *Exp(B)*. ***Exp(B)*** represents odds rather than log odds. For example, if *Exp(B)* for an independent variable is greater than 1 (e.g., 1.5), when the independent variable increases by one-unit, the dependent variable increases by a factor of 1.5. Conversely, if *Exp(B)* is less than 1, a unit increase in the independent variable decreases the odds of the event occurring.

Assessing a Model's Goodness-of-Fit

There are various ways to assess whether the model fits the data in logistic regression (e.g., a classification table, goodness-of-fit tests). A ***classification table*** compares the predicted group membership to the observed outcomes. If the independent variables in a model correctly predicted all individuals in both categories of the dependent variable, the classification table would indicate that the model correctly classified 100% of the respondents. In linear regression terms this is equivalent to an R^2 of 1.00. On the other hand, if the model only correctly classified 50% of the individuals in the two groups, the findings suggest that the independent variables are not very useful. The researcher could have done equally as well by simply flipping a coin.

Another test for whether the *combination* of independent variables has a greater-than-chance ability to predict the status of people on the dependent variable in logistic regression is called a ***goodness-of-fit test***. The goal is to identify a set of independent variables (i.e., a model) that predicts or explains group membership on the dependent variable. The probability of the observed results, given the coefficient estimates, is known as the *likelihood*. Since the likelihood is a small number less than or equal to 1, it is customary to use *–2 **times the log of the likelihood** (–2LL)* as a measure of how well the estimated model fits the data. A good model is one that results in a high likelihood of the observed results. This translates into a small value of *–2LL*. If the model fits perfectly, the likelihood is 1, and –2 times the log likelihood is 0.

Additional Considerations with Logistic Regression

As is true of all regression models, logistic regression can be conducted in a simultaneous, hierarchical, or stepwise matter. For ***simultaneous logistic regression models***, all of the variables are included at the same time. In ***hierarchical logistic regression***, a set of independent variables is entered first. These are often the variables considered to be background variables and of less interest to the researcher. The remaining independent variables (those of primary interest to the researchers) are then added to determine if they increase the predictive power of the model (Hosmer & Lemeshow, 1989; King, 2003). In ***stepwise logistic regression***, each independent variable is entered (or removed) one at a time into the model, based on the level of statistical association between the independent and dependent variable. Similar to linear regression, stepwise methods in logistic regression are not recommended for two major reasons. First, variables should be included or excluded from models based on past research or theoretical arguments, not on their level of statistical significance. Second, from a statistical perspective, stepwise procedures often do not correctly identify the best set of predictors (Huberty, 1989; Thompson, 1989, 1995).

Finally, it is important to remember the distinction between statistical significance and practical significance (chapter 6). If the sample is large, a finding can be statistically significant and yet, be of trivial practical significance. The size of the odds ratio is an index of the strength of the relationship. The "strength of the effect," however, should not be interpreted as a *causal* link between the independent variables and the dependent variable. Causality cannot be inferred simply from effect size analyses.

Logistic Regression Example

It is often easier to understand the mechanics of logistic regression when applied to an empirical example such as hunters' responses to chronic wasting disease. Chronic wasting disease (CWD) is a fatal transmissible spongiform encephalopathy (TSE) found in deer (*Odocoileus* spp.), elk (*Cervus elaphus*), and moose (*Alces alces*; Gross & Miller, 2001; Joly et al., 2003; Schauber & Woolf, 2003). The disease is similar to scrapie in sheep, mad cow disease, and a variant of Creutzfeldt-Jakob disease (vCJD) in humans (Williams, Miller, Kreeger, Kahn, & Thorne, 2002). Although the probability of human infection from CWD is very low, the transmission of the disease to humans cannot be entirely dismissed (Belay, Maddox, Williams, Miller, Gambetti, & Schonberger, 2004; Bosque, 2002; Raymond et al., 2000).

Given the similarities between CWD and other TSE diseases that can cause human death (e.g., vCJD), wildlife agencies are concerned that the possible unknown risks associated with CWD will erode hunters' willingness to hunt in states where the disease is found (Needham, Vaske, & Manfredo, 2004, 2006). In Wisconsin, for example, the largest single-year decline in deer hunting license sales in the 20th century (10.7%) occurred in 2002, the year after the discovery of CWD in the state (Heberlein, 2004). Some of this attrition was attributed to hunters' perceived risks regarding CWD (Needham & Vaske, 2006 ; Stafford, Needham, Vaske, & Petchenik, 2006). Hunting participation rates in many states, however, have declined for a variety of reasons unrelated to CWD (e.g., aging of the deer hunting population, lack of hunting partners, access to hunting areas; Heberlein & Thomson, 1996; Miller & Vaske, 2003).

Theory suggests that hunters' behavior may be influenced by perceptions of risk regarding a hazard such as CWD, and these risk perceptions may be shaped by the extent to which hunters trust the managing agency (Needham & Vaske, 2008).[1] Shared goals, values, thoughts, and opinions (i.e., perceived similarity) are thought to constitute foundations of this trust. If the

---

[1] Most risk perception studies involve technologies or activities, which have both benefits and negative consequences (e.g., nuclear power provides electricity, but accidents harm humans). Hazards have no obvious benefits (Sjöberg, 2000; Slovic, 1993). Given that CWD is always fatal in animals and is similar to TSE diseases that can cause human death, few hunters would likely contend that CWD has benefits. CWD, therefore, is considered a hazard in this chapter.

agency is perceived as similar to the individual, trust increases and perceived risk declines (Siegrist, Cvetkovich, & Roth, 2000). Vaske, Timmons, Beaman, and Petchenik (2004) examined the extent to which CWD influenced 2001 Wisconsin deer hunters who did not participate in the 2002 season.

One of the empirical questions in the Vaske, Timmons, Beaman, and Petchenik (2004) study was how do 2002 deer hunters compare to those of 2001 hunters who dropped out of the activity based on: (a) perceptions of risk associated with CWD, and (b) social trust in the Wisconsin Department of Natural Resources (WDNR)? The indices measuring perceived CWD risk and overall social trust in the WDNR were used to predict the 2001 Wisconsin deer hunters who did not participate in the 2002 season due to CWD concerns versus non-CWD reasons. A logistic regression model was used in the analysis.

The data were obtained from a random sample of 2001 Wisconsin gun deer license holders. Questionnaires were mailed to 1,500 resident gun deer hunters statewide and an additional 600 resident gun deer hunters that lived in the counties where CWD had been detected. Of the 2,100 surveys initially mailed, 43 were undeliverable. A total of 1,373 usable questionnaires were returned, yielding a response rate of 67% (1,373 / 2,057).

The data were weighted to adjust for the oversampling of hunters who lived in the CWD affected counties (see chapter 8 for a general discussion of weighting data). Of the initial statewide random sample ($n = 1,500$ mailout), 154 respondents lived in CWD counties. In the oversampled CWD counties ($n = 600$), completed surveys were received from 389 individuals. The weight factor correcting for oversampling in CWD counties was computed as:

$$W = \frac{154}{154 + 389} = .28$$

The weight for respondents who did not live in counties where CWD had been detected was 1.00. There are a variety of ways to construct a weight variable in SPSS. Appendix 17.1 describes two of these alternatives.

Analysis Variables

Perceived constraints. The survey included 14 possible reasons for not hunting during the 2002 gun deer season. Three of these items involved perceived risks associated with CWD (e.g., I/my spouse has concerns about CWD and the safety of venison.). Two questions concerned WDNR management actions (e.g., "I disagree with the DNR management approach to CWD and did not hunt as a personal protest."). The remaining nine items were reasons for not hunting due to personal constraints (e.g., age, health, lack of hunting partners) unrelated to CWD and the WDNR. Each of these items was coded on a four-point scale: not at all important (0), not too important (1), somewhat important (2), and very important (3).

A cluster analysis (see Romesburg, 1990) of the 14 reasons for not hunting identified three distinct segments of individuals. The first cluster (37% of the nonhunter group) was "strongly" influenced by CWD concerns. The remaining reasons listed on the survey did not factor into this group's decision to not hunt. Cluster 2 (15%) contained individuals who were "moderately" concerned with CWD as well as constraints unrelated to CWD (e.g., not enough deer, no hunting partners, did not buy a license). The final cluster (48%) included nonhunters for whom

CWD was not a concern. These individuals did not participate in the 2002 deer hunting season due to lack of time for hunting, lack of a license, and conflicting responsibilities.

The distribution of responses from the cluster analysis suggested that the perceived risks associated with CWD either strongly or moderately influenced individuals in the first two clusters to not hunt deer in 2002. Given the small sample size for cluster 2 ($n = 21$), clusters 1 and 2 were combined into one cluster. This implies that about half (estimate = 52% ± 5%) of the 2001 Wisconsin hunters that did not participate in the 2002 season did not hunt because of CWD. The remainder dropped out of deer hunting for a variety of reasons unrelated to CWD. This dichotomous variable (No CWD influence vs. Yes CWD influence) served as the dependent variable in the logistic regression.

Perceived risk. Individuals' perceived risk regarding CWD was assessed using a three-item index. Two of the questions in the index asked respondents how concerned they would be about eating venison from a free-ranging deer that: (a) was not tested for CWD, and (b) tested positive for CWD. The third item asked how concerned they were about becoming ill from CWD. Responses were on a five-point scale from: not at all concerned (1) to very concerned (5). The Cronbach's alpha for the computed additive index was .81 (see chapter 18 for a discussion on psychological scales, Cronbach alpha, and reliability). Deleting any of the items from the scale did not improve the reliability.

Social trust. A multiple-item index of social trust was created from eight survey questions. Five of these items involved agency credibility: (a) WDNR information on CWD is believable, (b) WDNR provided enough information on CWD to make decisions on what actions to take regarding CWD, (c) WDNR can be trusted to make good deer management decisions regarding CWD in Wisconsin, (d) WDNR can be trusted to provide the best available information on CWD, and (e) WDNR provided adequate opportunities to listen to hunters' concerns. These items were measured on a five-point scale from: strongly disagree (1) to strongly agree (5). The Cronbach alpha reliability coefficient for this five-item credibility scale was .90.

Three other social trust items focused on the believability of the information provided by the WDNR. Respondents indicated how believable they felt the: (a) biological information, (b) human safety information, and (c) deer management strategies were regarding CWD. These items were measured on a five-point scale from: not at all believable (1) to highly believable (5). The Cronbach alpha reliability for these three items was .85. For purposes of this analysis, the two concepts (i.e., credibility, believability) were combined into a single "social trust" index with an overall Cronbach alpha reliability of .93.

The indices measuring perceived CWD risk and overall social trust in the WDNR were used as independent variables in a logistic regression to predict the 2001 Wisconsin deer hunters who did not participate in the 2002 season due to CWD concerns versus non-CWD reasons (i.e., dependent variable).

Logistic Regression in SPSS

To obtain a binary logistic regression, the four basic steps in conducting statistical analysis in SPSS discussed in chapter 9 apply:

1. Open the data file: WI – CWD Data – Nonhunters.sav
   (see chapter 9 – Introduction to SPSS – for assistance in opening a data file).

2. Select the statistic: **Analyze > Regression > Binary Logistic...**   See Figure 17.2

3. Select the variables to be included in the analysis   See Figure 17.3

4. Select additional options
   Define categorical variables   See Figure 17.4
   Save variables generated by the logistic regression   See Figure 17.5
   Options available in logistic regression   See Figure 17.6

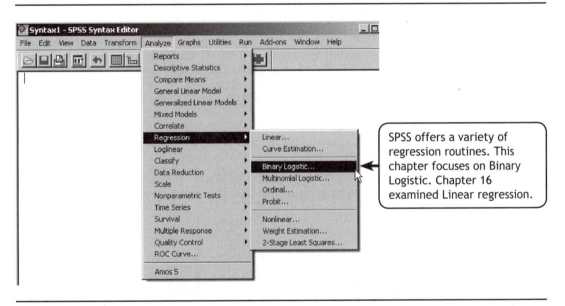

Figure 17.2   Selecting a Binary Logistic Regression

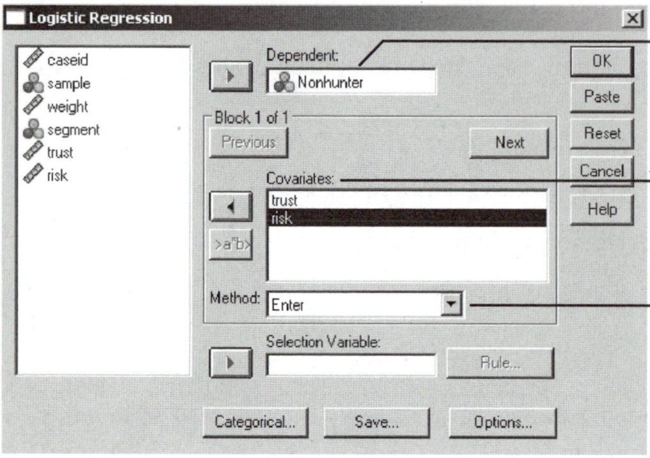

NONHUNTER is coded as:
0 = No CWD influence
1 = Yes CWD influence

Predictor variables (i.e., independent variables) are called *covariates*. Trust in the WDNR and perceived risks associated with CWD are the predictors.

Both predictors are entered simultaneously. The Methods for including variables are:

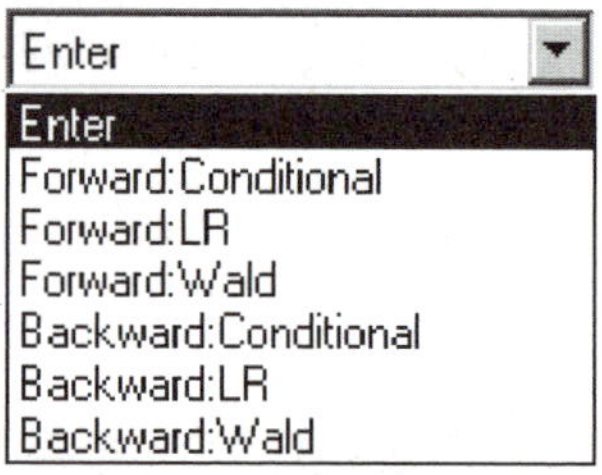

Enter
Enter
Forward:Conditional
Forward:LR
Forward:Wald
Backward:Conditional
Backward:LR
Backward:Wald

These methods are described in Box 17.1

Figure 17.3   Selecting Variables in a Logistic Regression

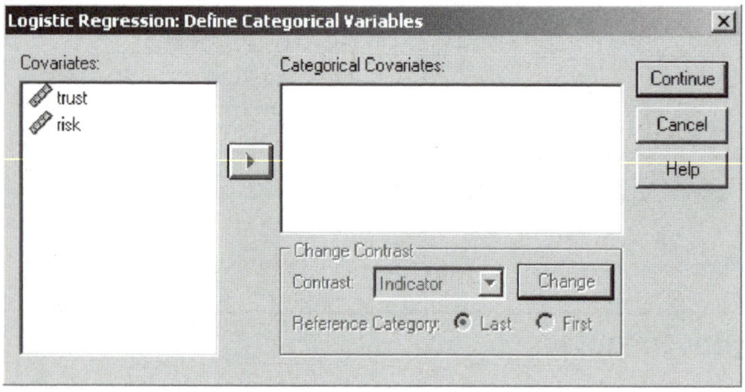

This dialog box does not apply in this example because both predictors are continuous level indices.

If TRUST (or RISK) had been recoded into low, medium and high categories, SPSS replaces the categorical variable with a set of contrast variables. With three levels to a categorical variable (low, medium, high), *n* – 1 contrast variables are generated. One of the dummy variables is treated as the reference category in the regression (see chapter 16, dummy variable regression).

Figure 17.4   Defining Categorical Variables in a Logistic Regression

Box 17.1	Methods for Entering Variables into a Logistic Regression
Method	**Description**
Enter	All variables are entered in a single step. This is the default setting.
Forward Stepwise	Variables are tested for entry into the model one by one, based on their significance level. The variable with the smallest significance is entered first. At each step, variables that are already in the model are tested for possible removal based on the significance of the conditional statistic (see Figure 17.6, Probability for Stepwise, p. 465), the Wald statistic, or the likelihood-ratio criterion. The variable with the largest probability is removed, and the model is re-estimated. Variables in the model are then evaluated again for removal. When no more variables satisfy the removal criterion, covariates that are not in the model are evaluated for entry. Model building stops when no more variables meet entry or removal criteria or when the current model is the same as a previous model.
Backward Stepwise	All of the variables that are specified as predictors are initially entered into the model together and then tested for removal one by one. Stepwise removal and entry follow the same process as described for Forward Stepwise until no more variables meet entry or removal criteria or when the current model is the same as a previous model.
Conditional	This setting is the default if Forward or Backward Stepwise is specified. A variable is added or removed at each step based on a probability level required for entry (SPSS default = .05) and a probability level for removal (SPSS default = .10; see Figure 17.6, p. 465).
Wald	The removal of a predictor from the model is based on the significance of the Wald statistic (see Equation 17.4, p. 455).
Likelihood Ratio (LR)	The removal of a predictor from the model is based on the significance of the change in the log-likelihood ratio (see discussion below). If LR is specified, the model is re-estimated without each of the variables in the model. Although this process increases computational time, the likelihood-ratio statistic is the best criterion for deciding which variables are to be removed if a stepwise procedure is used.

In general, the Save... command saves the variables that are created by logistic regression (Figure 17.5). If new variable names are not specified, SPSS generates default names.

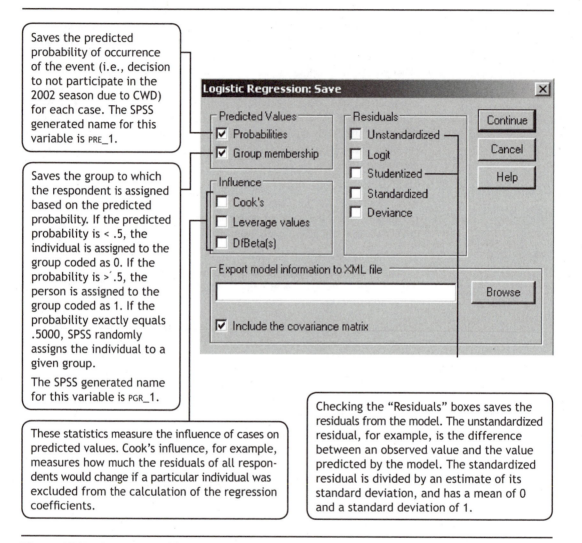

Saves the predicted probability of occurrence of the event (i.e., decision to not participate in the 2002 season due to CWD) for each case. The SPSS generated name for this variable is PRE_1.

Saves the group to which the respondent is assigned based on the predicted probability. If the predicted probability is < .5, the individual is assigned to the group coded as 0. If the probability is >´.5, the person is assigned to the group coded as 1. If the probability exactly equals .5000, SPSS randomly assigns the individual to a given group.

The SPSS generated name for this variable is PGR_1.

These statistics measure the influence of cases on predicted values. Cook's influence, for example, measures how much the residuals of all respondents would change if a particular individual was excluded from the calculation of the regression coefficients.

Checking the "Residuals" boxes saves the residuals from the model. The unstandardized residual, for example, is the difference between an observed value and the value predicted by the model. The standardized residual is divided by an estimate of its standard deviation, and has a mean of 0 and a standard deviation of 1.

Figure 17.5   Saving Variables Generated by a Logistic Regression

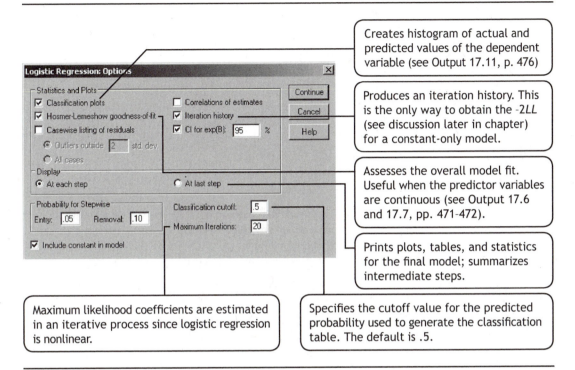

Figure 17.6   Options Available in a Logistic Regression

The SPSS syntax for the variables and options that have been selected in this example is:

```
LOGISTIC REGRESSION  Nonhunter
  /METHOD = ENTER trust risk
  /SAVE PRED PGROUP
  /CLASSPLOT
  /PRINT = GOODFIT ITER(1) SUMMARY CI(95)
  /CRITERIA = PIN(.05) POUT(.10) ITERATE(20) CUT(.5) .
```

Table 17.1 (p. 466) explains each of the commands in the SPSS logistic regression syntax for this example.

Table 17.1   Interpreting the Commands in the Syntax

Line	Command	Description
1	LOGISTIC REGRESSION Nonhunter	Runs the LOGISTIC REGRESSION analysis and specifies the dichotomous dependent variable.
2	/METHOD = ENTER trust risk	Identifies the METHOD for entering variables into the logistic regression. In this case, the ENTER method is used and all variables are entered in a single step, resulting in a simultaneous logistic regression model.
		Identifies the predictor variables (i.e., covariates) to be included in the analysis.
3	/SAVE PRED PGROUP	Saves variables generated by the logistic regression. In this example, the probabilities of occurrence of the event and group membership (i.e., the group to which the respondent is assigned based on the predicted probability).
4	/CLASSPLOT	Produces a classification plot (i.e., a histogram of actual and predicted values of the dependent variable).
5	/PRINT = GOODFIT ITER(1) SUMMARY CI(95)	Produces Hosmer-Lemeshow goodness-of-fit test, an iteration history, and the confidence interval for $Exp(B)$. Also summarizes the logistic regression output by producing only the last step.
6	/CRITERIA = PIN(.05) POUT(.10) ITERATE(20) CUT(.5).	PIN (.05) and POUT (.10) don't apply and don't influence the output, but is produced in the syntax by SPSS automatically.
		Specifies the maximum number of iterations (default is 20).
		Specifies the cutoff value for the predicted probability used to generate the classification table (default is .5).

Among those who completed the survey ($n = 1,373$), 1,151 (84%) participated in the 2002 gun deer hunting season in Wisconsin and 222 (16%) did not hunt during this season. This 16% dropout rate (i.e., unweighted data including the oversample of CWD affected counties) is relatively consistent with the WDNR's estimate that 19% of the individuals living in CWD counties did not participate in the 2002 season (Petchenik, 2003). After weighting, 90% of the 2001 hunters in the sample participated in the 2002 season and 10% dropped out (Output 17.1, p. 467). License sales data suggested that 10.7% of Wisconsin hunters did not purchase a license to hunt deer in 2002. The difference between the estimated 10% drop based on the survey data and the 10.7% decline in license purchases is within statistical probabilities of occurring by chance.

Output 17.1   Case Processing Summary from the Logistic Regression

Logistic Regression

Case Processing Summary

Unweighted Cases[a]		N	Percent
Selected Cases	Included in Analysis	137	10.0
	Missing Cases	1236	90.0
	Total	1373	100.0
Unselected Cases		0	0
Total		1373	100.0

a. If weight is in effect, see classification table for the total number of cases.

> Among the survey respondents, 10% did not participate in the 2002 deer hunting season. This estimate is statistically equivalent to the decline in license sales in the population (10.7%).

> 90% of respondents participated in the 2002 deer hunting season. Given the study's focus on people who dropped out of the 2002 hunting season, these individuals were not included in this analysis.

Dependent Variable Encoding

Original Value	Internal Value
0 No CWD influence	0
1 Yes CWD influence	1

> NONHUNTER is the dependent outcome variable and is coded as 0 and 1. A value of 0 implies that the respondent's decision to not participate in the 2002 hunting was *not* influenced by concerns with CWD. A value of 1 implies that the individual did not hunt at least in part because of CWD concerns.

In this analysis all variables were entered simultaneously using the ENTER command. In SPSS terminology, a ***Block*** refers to the number of variables being entered at one time. At Block 0 only the constant term is considered. At Block 1 both variables go into the equation.

Output 17.2   Classification Table at Block 0

Block 0: Beginning Block

> Beginning block includes only the constant term

Iteration History[a, b, c]

Iteration		-2 Log likelihood	Coefficients Constant
Step 0	1	122.337	-.049
	2	122.337	-.049

a.   Constant is included in the model.

b.   Initial -2 Log Likelihood: 122.337

c.   Estimation terminated at iteration number 2 because parameter estimates changed by less than .001.

> The test that all coefficients in the model are 0 is the *likelihood*. The likelihood statistic is the probability of the observed results given the coefficients in the model; -2 times the log of the likelihood (-2*LL*) is a measure of how well the estimated model fits the data. A good model has a small -2*LL*.

> This -2*LL* is for the model with only the constant term in the equation (i.e., the predictors have not been included at this stage).

Output 17.2   Classification Table at Block 0 (continued)

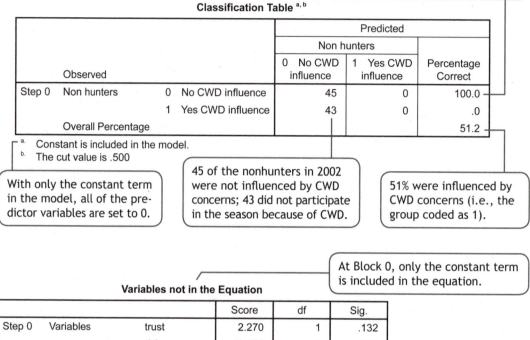

With all independent variables set to 0, the model correctly classifies 100% of those not influenced by CWD (i.e., the group coded as 0).

Classification Table [a, b]

Observed			Predicted		
			Non hunters		Percentage Correct
			0 No CWD influence	1 Yes CWD influence	
Step 0	Non hunters	0 No CWD influence	45	0	100.0
		1 Yes CWD influence	43	0	.0
	Overall Percentage				51.2

a. Constant is included in the model.
b. The cut value is .500

With only the constant term in the model, all of the predictor variables are set to 0.

45 of the nonhunters in 2002 were not influenced by CWD concerns; 43 did not participate in the season because of CWD.

51% were influenced by CWD concerns (i.e., the group coded as 1).

At Block 0, only the constant term is included in the equation.

Variables not in the Equation

			Score	df	Sig.
Step 0	Variables	trust	2.270	1	.132
		risk	42.156	1	.000
	Overall Statistics		42.756	2	.000

When considered separately, only the perceived risk of CWD is statistically significant (p < .001)

The **Score statistics** (a.k.a. Rao's [1973] efficient score) shown in Output 17.2 test whether the logistic regression coefficient for a given predictor variable is 0. These statistics are particularly useful when using the forward stepwise method of entering variables into the equation (see Box 17.1, p. 463), because they provide a computationally quick method for determining which variable should be entered first. If the likelihood ratio method is used for entering variables, score statistics are similar to the results after the first iteration.

Block 1: Method = Enter

Because logistic regression is nonlinear, a series of iterations are required to estimate the coefficients (Output 17.3). The iteration process stops when the coefficient (i.e., parameter) estimates change by less than .001. For the CWD data a final solution was determined after 5 iterations. The default number of iterations is 20 (Figure 17.6, p. 465). Although this default can be increased, a model that does not converge to a final solution prior to 20 iterations may signal that there is something wrong with the model.

Output 17.3   Iteration History

Iteration History[a, b, c, d]

Iteration		−2 Log likelihood	Coefficients		
			Constant	trust	risk
Step 1	1	74.279	−2.440	−.130	1.650
	2	69.075	−3.530	−.254	2.420
	3	68.582	−3.951	−.305	2.746
	4	68.574	−4.008	−.313	2.793
	5	68.574	−4.009	−.313	2.794

> The coefficients at Step 5 are the unstandardized regression coefficients (B) (i.e., log odds) in Output 17.9 (p. 473).

[a.] Method: Enter
[b.] Constant is not included in the model
[c.] Initial −2 Log likelihood: 122.337
[d.] Estimation terminatied at iteration number 5 because parameter estimates changed by less than .001.

> The -2LL of **68.574** is the likelihood statistic with both TRUST and RISK in the model.
>
> likelihood ratio = (constant only model) - (predictors included model)
>
> 53.763   =   122.337   -   68.574

The change in the likelihood statistic provides a measure of how well the data fit the model. The model containing only the constant term was 122.337 (footnote in Output 17.3). In logistic regression, the ***likelihood ratio statistic*** is used in hypothesis testing and is defined as:

likelihood ratio = (−2*LL* constant only model) − (−2*LL* model with predictors included)

Equation 17.8

or more generally:

likelihood ratio = (−2*LL* model 1) − (−2*LL* model 2)   **Equation 17.9**

Equation 17.8 is useful for comparing the constant only model against a model including all predictor variables simultaneously. Equation 17.9 is useful for examining the contribution of individual predictors to the equation. For example, one model containing the constant and RISK could be compared against a second model including the constant and both predictors (RISK and TRUST). The difference in the −2*LL* for the two models provides a test of the individual coefficients.

Using Equation 17.8 for the CWD data, the likelihood ratio is:

likelihood ratio = 122.337 − 68.574 = 53.763

This difference (53.763) is the chi-square shown in Output 17.4. The degrees of freedom associated with this chi-square is the difference between the number of coefficients in the two models. The constant only model included no (0) parameters; the second model included the two predictors (TRUST and RISK). Therefore, 2 − 0 = 2 degrees of freedom.

Because both predictors were entered simultaneously (i.e., ENTER command), the chi-square for the Step 1, Block and Model are the same (i.e., 53.763, Output 17.4). The chi-square omnibus test of model coefficients indicates that the *combination* of social trust and risk significantly predicts the reason for dropping out of the 2002 season (i.e., CWD influence – No vs. Yes). This chi-square test is comparable to the overall F test for ordinary least squares regression.

Output 17.4   Omnibus Test of Model Coefficients

Omnibus Tests of Model Coefficients

		Chi-square	df	Sig.
Step 1	Step	53.763	2	.000
	Block	53.763	2	.000
	Model	53.763	2	.000

> There are 2 degrees of freedom (*df*) because there are 2 predictors.

The model summary (Output 17.5) shows the –2*LL* and two R^2 statistics (i.e., Cox & Snell, Nagelkerke). The –2*LL* in this summary is the last iteration (step 5) in Output 17.3. The null hypothesis that all of the coefficients in the model are 0 is rejected because the chi-square associated with the difference between the –2*LL* models (constant only – model with predictors) was significant ($p < .001$, Output 17.4).

Output 17.5   Model Summary

> The *-2LL* of 68.574 is the likelihood statistic with both trust and risk in the model at the iteration step (Step 5) in Output 17.3.
>
> likelihood ratio = (constant only model) – (predictors included model)
>   53.763   =   122.337   –   68.574
>
> The 53.763 = the chi-square in Output 17.4.

Model Summary

Step	–2 Log likelihood	Cox & Snell R Square	Nagelkerke R Square
1	68.574[a]	.456	.608

> These are similar to R^2 and approximate the variance that can be predicted from the combination of the two predictors.

> If the model fits perfectly, the likelihood is 1 and -2 times the log likelihood is 0.

Researchers using linear regression are typically interested in the R^2 value, or the coefficient of determination. R^2 in linear regression is the proportion of the variance in the dependent variable that is explained by the independent variables. Although there is no such statistic in logistic regression with a comparable interpretation, a number of pseudo R^2 measures have been proposed. DeMaris (2002), for example, compared eight of these R^2 analogues. All of these pseudo R^2 type measures have advantages and disadvantages, and no one measure is universally accepted or employed (Achen, 1982; King, 1985). The recommendation here is to use these summary measures as approximations. In SPSS, the ***Cox & Snell R²*** and ***Nagelkerke R²*** provide a logistic analogy to R^2 in linear regression (Output 17.5).

The Cox & Snell R^2 is:

$$R^2 = 1 - \left[\frac{L(0)}{L(B)}\right]^{2/N}$$

Equation 17.10

where:

$L(0)$ = likelihood of the model with only the constant

$L(B)$ = likelihood of the model with the predictors in the equation

N = sample size

The Cox & Snell R^2, however, can never reach a value of 1.00 (King, 2003). The Nagelkerke (1991) R^2 is an adaptation of the Cox & Snell statistic and does vary from 0 to 1, similar to R^2 in ordinary least squares regression. The Nagelkerke R^2 is:

$$R^2 = \frac{R^2}{R^2_{MAX}}$$

Equation 17.11

where: $R^2_{MAX} = 1 - \left[L(0)\right]^{2/N}$

The values of the R^2 from logistic regression will usually be smaller than the R^2 from a linear regression. In the CWD example, the Cox & Snell $R^2 = .456$ and the Nagelkerke $R^2 = .608$.

The ***Hosmer and Lemeshow*** (2000) ***goodness-of-fit test*** evaluates the difference between observed and expected number. Respondents are divided into ten approximately equal groups based on the probability of the event (Output 17.6). The *Total* column, for example, shows that there were approximately nine individuals in each of the ten groups. The chi-square test is used to compare the observed and expected number of events. As noted in the crosstabulation chapter (chapter 13), the expected number of events in most cells should exceed 5 and none should have expected values less than 1. As shown in Output 17.6, this latter assumption is violated for 3 of the 10 cells in the "Yes CWD influence" column, and 2 of the 10 cells for the "No CWD influence" group. This suggests that this CWD data set is too small to have a practical application of the Hosmer and Lemeshow test.

Output 17.6   Hosmer and Lemeshow Goodness-of-Fit Test

Contingency Table for Hosmer Lemeshow Test

		No CWD influence		Yes CWD influence		
		Observed	Expected	Observed	Expected	Total
Step 1	1	9	8.810	0	.175	9
	2	8	8.150	1	.552	9
	3	7	7.434	2	.985	8
	4	8	6.922	1	1.779	9
	5	6	5.202	2	3.350	9
	6	3	3.718	6	4.416	8
	7	4	2.717	6	6.552	9
	8	0	1.450	9	7.819	9
	9	0	.596	9	8.673	9
	10	1	.226	8	8.760	9

Violates the chi-square assumption of no expected values less than 1.

For illustration purposes, Output 17.6 shows the observed and predicted number of respondents in each of the two levels of the dependent variable (No vs. Yes CWD influence). For example, in the 5th Hosmer and Lemeshow group there were nine respondents. Six individuals were observed in the "No CWD influence" category and two were observed in the "Yes CWD influence" category. Summing the predicted probabilities, the predicted number in the No group is 5.202 and the predicted number in the Yes group is 3.350.

The Hosmer-Lemeshow chi-square is the difference between the observed and predicted number of cases in each of the cells (Output 17.7). Using the equation from chapter 13, the chi-square is the $(O - E)^2 / E$ for each cell in the table. The degrees of freedom (df) for this chi-square is the number of groups (i.e., 10) minus 2. In the CWD data, the chi-square of 6.643, with 8 df was not statistically significant ($p = .576$). A nonsignificant Hosmer-Lemeshow chi-square test is desirable because it implies that: (a) the observed and predicted values do not differ, and (b) the logistic regression model appears to fit the data.

Output 17.7   Hosmer and Lemeshow Chi-square

Hosmer and Lemeshow Test

Step	Chi-square	df	Sig.
1	6.643	8	.576

> A nonsignificant Hosmer and Lemeshow goodness-of-fit test implies that the observed and predicted values do not differ and that the model fits the data.

Given that the weighted sample size for this CWD data set was small ($n = 91$, see p. 499) and violated the assumption of no expected values less than 1, the utility of this goodness-of-fit test is questionable in this example. Conversely, because chi-square is proportional to sample size (chapter 13), a large sample may result in a statistically significant Hosmer-Lemeshow test statistic. This would suggest that the observed and predicted probabilities differ from one another and that the logistic regression model does not fit the data very well. Although the researcher wants this goodness-of-fit test to be *not* significant, caution must be exercised in interpreting this statistic when the sample is small or very large.

The classification table (Output 17.8) tallies the correct and incorrect estimates for the model with the two independent variables (TRUST and RISK) and the constant. The columns are the predicted values of the dependent variable; the rows are the observed (actual) values of the dependent variable. Respondents who have a predicted probability of 0.5 or greater are classified as belonging to the "Yes CWD influenced" group (code = 1). Individuals with a predicted probability less than 0.5 are in the "No CWD influenced" group (code = 0). If a respondent was *not* influenced by CWD in his or her decision to dropout of the 2002 hunt (code = 0) and the model predicted that the person dropped out for non-CWD reasons (code = 0), a correct prediction was made. In a perfect model, all respondents are on the diagonal and the overall percent correct is 100%. This is analogous to an R^2 of 1.00 in linear regression. An R^2 of 1.00 implies that all of the variability in the dependent variable is accounted for by the independent variables.

Output 17.8 Logistic Regression Classification Table

Number predicted by the model.

Classification Table[a]

			Predicted		
			Non hunters		
			0 No CWD influence	1 Yes CWD influence	Percentage Correct
Observed					
Step 1	Non hunters	0 No CWD influence	(38)	8	83.0
		1 Yes CWD influence	6	(37)	86.4
	Overall Percentage				84.7

Number observed in the sample (i.e., 38 + 8 = 46 and 6 + 37 = 43).

Circled numbers are correct predictions.

The two predictors (TRUST and RISK) correctly classified 83% of the 2001 hunters who dropped out of the 2002 season for non-CWD reasons, and 86.4% of the hunters who did not participate for CWD reasons. Overall, 84.7% of the respondents were correctly classified ([83% + 86.4%] / 2 = 84.7). This implies that the model was successful in predicting both groups.

When evaluating the success of a model, it is important to consider all three percentages. For example, if the model had predicted 96% of the respondents in the group coded as 0, and 45% of the individuals in the group coded as 1, the overall correct percent classified is 70.5% (i.e., 96 + 45 / 2 = 70.5). This result implies that the logistic regression predictors do *not* do a very good job. The researcher could have better predicted those in the group coded as 1 by simply flipping a coin.

Output 17.9 shows the logistic regression coefficients and significance tests. The Bs are the unstandardized logistic regression coefficients (i.e., the log odds). The S.E.s are the standard errors associated with the coefficients. The Wald statistic (a.k.a. Wald χ^2, see Equation 17.4) is used to test the significance of individual logistic regression coefficients for each independent variable (i.e., the Wald statistic tests the null hypothesis that a given regression coefficient is 0). The *Exp(B)*s represent the odds rather than the log odds.

Output 17.9 Logistic Regression Coefficients and Significance Tests

Variables in the Equation

		B	S.E.	Wald	df	Sig.	Exp(B)
Step 1[a]	trust	−.313	.324	.934	1	.334	.731
	risk	2.794	.565	24.417	1	.000	16.346
	Constant	−4.009	1.499	7.152	1	.007	.018

a. Variable(s) entered on step 1: trust, risk.

In this model, trust in the WDNR is not statistically significant ($p = .334$), while perceived risk of CWD is significant ($p < .001$). Using Equation 17.4 and the data in Output 17.9, the Wald statistical significance test for the risk variables is calculated as:

$$\text{Wald} = \left(\frac{B}{S.E.}\right)^2 = \left(\frac{2.794}{.565}\right)^2 = 24.417$$

As noted by Menard (2002), however, when the unstandardized coefficient is large, the standard error is inflated and the Wald chi-square statistic is reduced. This can lead to an increase in Type II errors (chapter 6, concluding that there is no difference between the two groups, when there really was a difference). For this reason, it is better to use the likelihood ratio test (i.e., $-2LL$) of the difference between two models (Equation 17.9) when testing for individual parameters (Agresti, 1996).

The $-2LL$ can be used to assess the consequences of including additional predictors in a model, where each model builds on the previous equation by adding one new independent variable. For example, given that trust in the WDNR was not significant in Output 17.9 consider a simplified logistic regression equation with only risk in the model. Given the previous analyses and this reduced model, there are now three $-2LL$ statistics: (a) constant only, (b) constant and 1 predictor (risk), and (c) constant and 2 predictors (risk and trust). With only the constant in the equation, the $-2LL$ was 122.337 (Table 17.3 and Output 17.2). When risk is added to the constant only model, the $-2LL$ is 69.523. Because $-2LL$ is approximately distributed as a chi-square, subtracting these chi-squares (i.e., $-2LL$ [constant only] $- 2LL$ [constant & risk model]) results in a new chi-square ($\Delta\chi^2$). Numerically, this difference (122.337 − 69.523) is statistically significant ($\Delta\chi^2 = 52.814$, $p < .001$), meaning the model including risk is a better model. Models with smaller values of the $-2LL$ are better equations from a statistical perspective. Comparing this single predictor model to the one including both risk and trust (Output 17.5) yields a $\Delta\chi^2 = 0.949$, which is not significant ($p = .330$). Overall, this suggests that although perceived risk of CWD enhances our understanding of why the 2001 hunters did not participate in the 2002 season, information regarding the respondents' trust in the WDNR is less useful in this model.

Table 17.3   Comparison of Three Logistic Regression Models

Model	Variables in Equation	-2LL	$\Delta\chi^2$	df	p-value
1	Constant only	122.337			
2	Constant + 1 predictor (Risk)	69.523	52.814	1	< .001
3	Constant + 2 predictors (Risk & Trust)	68.574	0.949	1	.330

As noted above, the Bs in Output 17.9 are the unstandardized logistic regression coefficients (a.k.a., logit coefficients) and correspond to the Bs (unstandardized coefficients) in ordinary least squares regression. These coefficients are the natural log of the odds (ln[odds], Equation 17.6, p. 456). Similar to the Bs in linear regression, the logit coefficients can be used in a predictive model. For example, if the logit for a given independent variable is B_1, then a unit increase in the independent variable is associated with a B_1 change in the log odds of the dependent variable. The logistic regression coefficients from the model including the constant and risk index is shown in Output 17.10.

Output 17.10   Logistic Regression Coefficients for Perceived CWD Risk Model

Variables in the Equation

		B	S.E.	Wald	df	Sig.	Exp(B)	95% C.I. for EXP(B) Lower	Upper
Step 1[a]	risk	2.810	.554	25.707	1	.000	16.615	5.607	49.239
	Constant	−5.148	1.068	23.232	1	.000	.006		

a. Variable(s) entered on step1: risk.

The equation for predicting ln(odds) of a person not hunting during the 2002 Wisconsin deer season due to CWD concerns is:

$$\ln(\text{odds}) = \text{constant} + B_1(\text{risk})$$

If a respondent was concerned about the risk of CWD and had a score of 5 on the risk index (possible range for this index is 1 to 5 [no risk to high risk]), the predicted log odds and the predicted odds (*Exp[B]*) are:

Predicted log odds: $\ln(\text{odds}) = -5.148 + 2.810(5) = 8.902$

Predicted odds: $Exp(B) = \text{odds} = Exp^{\ln(\text{odds})} = e^{8.902} = 16.615$

This means that the odds of not hunting due to CWD, given a high level of perceived risk, are 16.6 to 1. These odds can be converted back to probabilities using Equation 17.2:

Predicted probability: $\text{Prob} = \dfrac{e^{\beta_0+\beta_1 X}}{1+e^{\beta_0+\beta_1 X}} = \dfrac{\text{odds}}{1+\text{odds}} = \dfrac{16.615}{1+16.615} = .943$

This implies that there is 94% probability that a person with a score of 5 on the perceived risk index did not participate in the 2002 season due to concerns about CWD.

The confidence interval around the logistic regression coefficient (Output 17.10) is ±1.96*ASE, where *ASE* is the *asymptotic standard error* of the logistic B. "Asymptotic" simply means the smallest possible value for the standard error (SE) when the data fit the model. The standard error that is used in most calculations is typically slightly larger than the asymptotic standard error. The SE is used if the errors in the data are systematic. The ASE is used if the errors are hypothesized to be random; a likely situation with logistic regression.

The last piece of output from the logistic regression is a classplot or histogram of predicted probabilities (Output 17.11, p. 476). *Classplots* are an alternative strategy for evaluating correct and incorrect predictions in logistic regression. The x-axis is the predicted probability and ranges from 0.0 to 1.0 of the dependent being classified "1" (i.e., Yes CWD influence). The y-axis is a frequency of the number of cases classified. The symbols (N or Y) plotted in the graph designate the group to which the person actually belongs (i.e., N = No CWD influence, Y = Yes CWD influence). If the model successfully differentiates the two groups, individuals who are to the right of the 0.5 probability should be mostly people in category 1 of the dependent variable (i.e., Yes CWD influence). Conversely, individuals with a value of 0 on the dependent variable (i.e., No CWD influence) should be to the left of the 0.5 probability.

Output 17.11   Histogram of Predicted Probabilities.

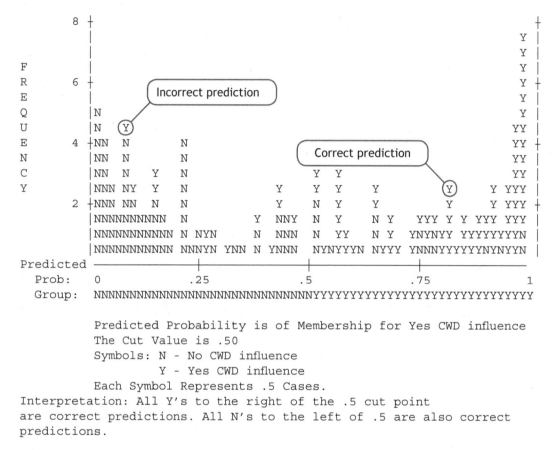

```
Step number: 1
Observed Groups and Predicted Probabilities

        8 +                                                              +
          |                                                          Y  |
          |                                                          Y  |
  F       |                                                          Y  |
  R       6 +                                                        Y  +
  E       |         ╭──────────────────────╮                        Y  |
  Q       |    N    │  Incorrect prediction │                       Y  |
  U       |    N   (Y)                                              YY  |
  E       4 +NN   N          N                                      YY  +
  N       |  NN   N          N                                      YY  |
  C       |  NN   N     Y    N                    ╭──────────────────────╮
  Y       |  NNN NY  Y       N              Y     │   Correct prediction │
          |  NNN NY  Y       N        Y   Y Y   Y          (Y)     Y YYY |
          2 +NNN NN   N       N        Y   N Y   Y           Y      Y YYY +
          |  NNNNNNNNNN   N          Y   NNY N  Y     N Y   YYY Y Y YYY YYY |
          |  NNNNNNNNNNN N NYN     N   NNN  N  YY    N Y   YNYNYY YYYYYYYYN |
          |  NNNNNNNNNNN NNNYN YNN N YNNN   NYNYYYN NYYY YNNNYYYYYYNYNYYN |
Predicted ──────────────────────────┼──────────────────┼──────────────────
   Prob:    0              .25              .5              .75            1
   Group:   NNNNNNNNNNNNNNNNNNNNNNNNNNNNNNNNNNNNNNNNNNYYYYYYYYYYYYYYYYYYYYYYYYYYYYYYYYYYYYY
```

Predicted Probability is of Membership for Yes CWD influence
The Cut Value is .50
Symbols: N - No CWD influence
         Y - Yes CWD influence
Each Symbol Represents .5 Cases.
Interpretation: All Y's to the right of the .5 cut point
are correct predictions. All N's to the left of .5 are also correct
predictions.

Discriminant Analysis

Similar to binary logistic regression, discriminant analysis (DA) can be used to classify and predict group membership using one or more continuous or dichotomous predictor variables (Huberty, 1994; Silva & Stam, 1995). The groups could be: (a) people who support versus oppose wolf reintroduction in the Colorado; (b) hiking boot treads that impact the environment versus those that leave little imprint; or (c) wildlife species that are tolerant of humans versus those who flee when people are near. Unlike binary logistic, however, the dependent variable in a discriminant analysis can be dichotomous or categorical; for example, predicting soils that are slightly, moderately, or extremely resistant to human impact. The comparable analysis with logistic is a multinomial logistic.

The goals of a discriminant analysis, regardless of whether the criterion variable is a dichotomous measure or a multilevel categorical variable are to: (a) classify cases (e.g., respondents) into groups using a discriminant prediction equation, (b) assess the relative importance of the independent variables in classifying the dependent variable, and (c) determine the percent of variance in the dependent variable explained by the independent variables.

Discriminant analysis involves two steps. First, an ***F test*** (***Wilks' lambda***) is used to test if the model as a whole is significant. Second, if the *F* test is significant, the individual independent variables are evaluated in terms of their relative contribution in classifying the levels of the dependent variable. A discriminant function prediction equation is a linear combination of the independent variables meant to discriminate between the outcome groups. A discriminant function is of the form:

$$D_i = d_{i1}Z_1 + d_{i2}Z_2 + ... + d_{ip}Z_p \qquad \text{Equation 17.12}$$

where:

      D_i = the score on the discriminant function
      d = weighting coefficients, and
      Z = the standardized values of the p discriminating variables used in the analysis

The weights in a discriminant function are selected based on how well they classify participants into the two groups (i.e., similar to logistic regression). The weighting coefficients in a DA, however, can be interpreted similarly to the coefficients in a multiple regression. They serve to identify the variables which contribute most to differentiation.

The maximum number of functions that can be derived is either one less than the number of groups or equal to the number of discriminating variables, if there are more groups than variables. For a dichotomous dependent variable, this implies that the maximum number of functions is one. The functions are formed in such a way as to maximize the separation of the groups.

Discriminant analysis is based on a series of simplifying assumptions: (a) there is a linear relationship between all pairs of predictors, (b) multivariate normality must exist within groups, and (c) the population covariance matrices for predictor variables must be equal across groups (Leech, Barrett, & Morgan, 2005). Even when these assumptions are violated, however, discriminant analysis is fairly robust. Violations of multivariate normality, however, may affect the accuracy of estimates of the probability of correct classification. Collinearity and multicollinearity (chapter 16) concerns should also be addressed.

Discriminant Analysis in SPSS

Data from the chronic wasting disease study (Vaske, Timmons, Beaman, & Petchenik, 2004) will be used to illustrate discriminant analysis in SPSS. To obtain a Discriminant analysis, the four basic steps in conducting statistical analysis in SPSS discussed in chapter 9 apply:

1. Open the data file: WI – Chronic Wasting Disease.sav
   (see chapter 9 – Introduction to SPSS – for assistance in opening a data file).

2. Select the statistic: Analyze > Classify > Discriminant...   See Figure 17.7

3. Select the variables to be included in the analysis   See Figure 17.8

4. Select additional options
   Statistics button   See Figure 17.9
   Classify button   See Figure 17.10
   Save button   See Figure 17.11

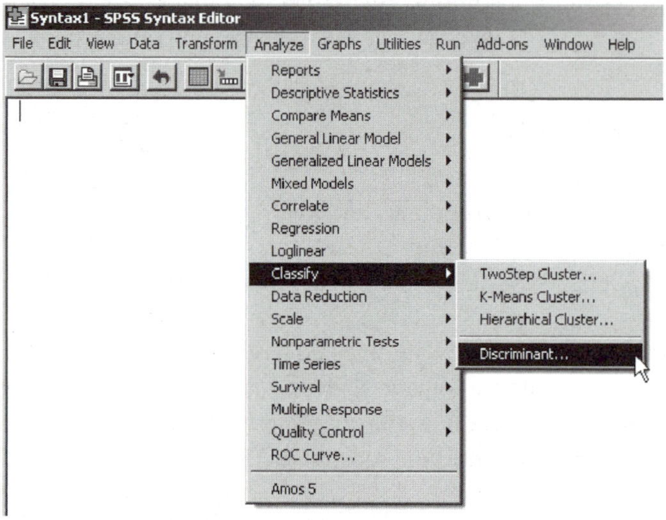

Figure 17.7   Selecting a Discriminant Analysis

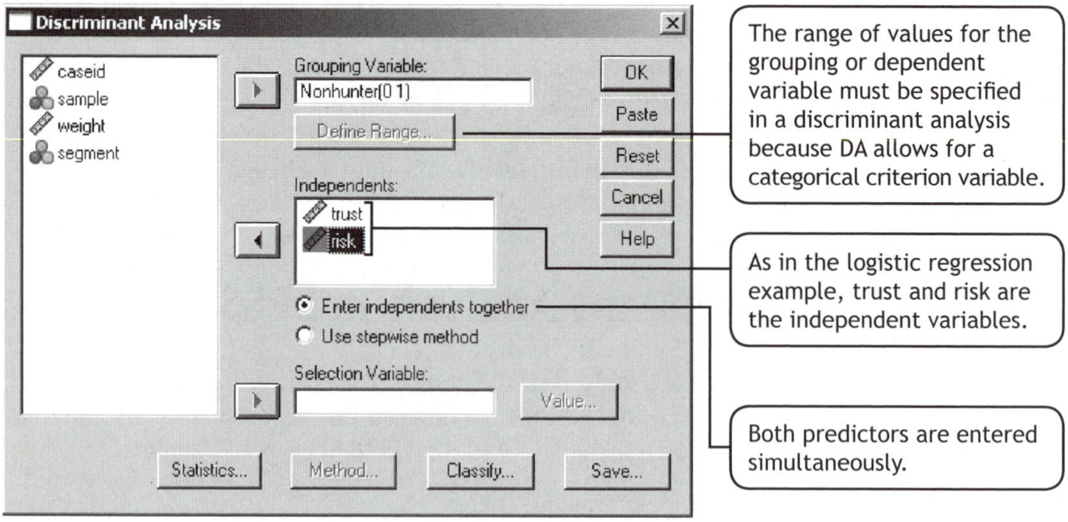

Figure 17.8   Selecting Variables in a Discriminant Analysis

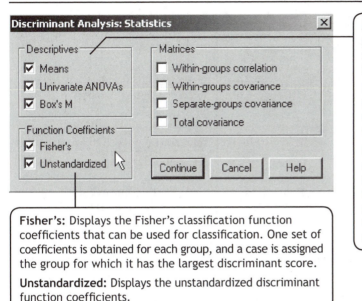

Means: Displays the total and group means, as well as the standard deviations for the independent variables.

Univariate ANOVAs: Performs a one-way ANOVA test for equality of group means for each independent variable.

Box's M: A test for the equality of group covariances. A nonsignificant *p*-value suggests that the covariance matrices do not differ. This test is sensitive to departures from multivariate normality — a DA assumption.

Fisher's: Displays the Fisher's classification function coefficients that can be used for classification. One set of coefficients is obtained for each group, and a case is assigned the group for which it has the largest discriminant score.

Unstandardized: Displays the unstandardized discriminant function coefficients.

Figure 17.9   Selecting the Statistics Button in a Discriminant Analysis

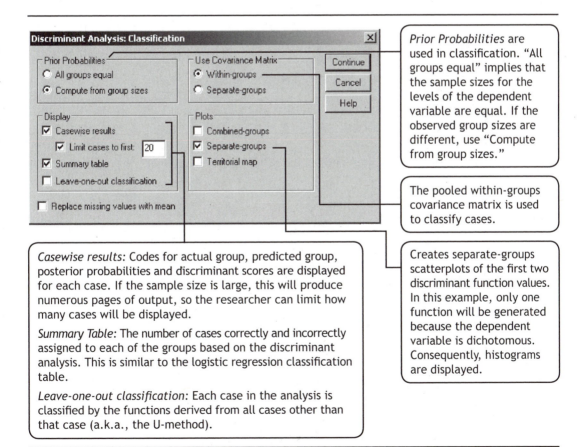

Prior Probabilities are used in classification. "All groups equal" implies that the sample sizes for the levels of the dependent variable are equal. If the observed group sizes are different, use "Compute from group sizes."

The pooled within-groups covariance matrix is used to classify cases.

Casewise results: Codes for actual group, predicted group, posterior probabilities and discriminant scores are displayed for each case. If the sample size is large, this will produce numerous pages of output, so the researcher can limit how many cases will be displayed.

Summary Table: The number of cases correctly and incorrectly assigned to each of the groups based on the discriminant analysis. This is similar to the logistic regression classification table.

Leave-one-out classification: Each case in the analysis is classified by the functions derived from all cases other than that case (a.k.a., the U-method).

Creates separate-groups scatterplots of the first two discriminant function values. In this example, only one function will be generated because the dependent variable is dichotomous. Consequently, histograms are displayed.

Figure 17.10   Selecting Classify Button Settings in a Discriminant Analysis

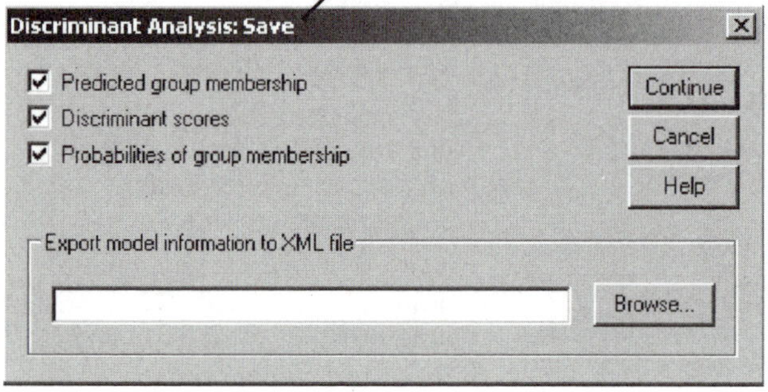

Discriminant Analysis: Save

☑ Predicted group membership
☑ Discriminant scores
☑ Probabilities of group membership

Continue
Cancel
Help

Export model information to XML file

Browse...

The Save button adds new variables to the data file:

Predicted group membership: The group that an individual is predicted to belong to by the model.

Discriminant Scores: One variable for each discriminant function in the solution (i.e., one in this example).

Probabilities of group membership: The probability of group membership, given the discriminant scores (i.e., one variable for each group).

Figure 17.11   Saving Variables Generated from a Discriminant Analysis

The SPSS syntax for the variables and options that have been selected in this example is:

```
DISCRIMINANT
  /GROUPS=Nonhunter(0 1)
  /VARIABLES=trust risk
  /ANALYSIS ALL
  /SAVE=CLASS SCORES PROBS
  /PRIORS  SIZE
  /STATISTICS=MEAN STDDEV UNIVF BOXM COEFF RAW TABLE
  /PLOT=SEPARATE
  /PLOT=CASES(20)
  /CLASSIFY=NONMISSING POOLED .
```

Table 17.2 explains each of the commands in the SPSS discriminant analysis syntax for this example.

Table 17.2   Interpreting the Commands in the Syntax

Line	Command	Description
1	DISCRIMINANT	Runs the Discriminant analysis.
2	/GROUPS=Nonhunter (0 1)	Identifies the grouping or dependent variable and its range of values.
3	/VARIABLES=trust risk	Identifies the independent variables.
4	/ANALYSIS ALL	Includes both predictors listed on /Variables line.
5	/SAVE=CLASS SCORES PROBS	Saves variables generated by the discriminant analysis. In this example, the predicted group membership, discriminant scores, and the probabilities of group membership.
6	/PRIORS SIZE	Computes prior probabilities from group sizes for use in classification.
7	/STATISTICS=MEAN STDDEV UNIVF BOXM COEFF RAW TABLE	Produces descriptive statistics (i.e., means, univariate ANOVAs, and Box's M), and function coefficients (i.e., Fisher's classification function coefficient, and the unstandardized discriminant function coefficient).
8	/PLOT=SEPARATE	Produces scatterplots of separate groups for the first two discriminant function values.
9	/PLOT=CASES (20)	Produces a display of casewise results limited to 20 cases.
10	/CLASSIFY=NONMISSING POOLED .	The pooled within-groups covariance matrix is used to classify cases.

Output 17.12   Case Processing Summary and Group Statistics

Discriminant

Analysis Case Processing Summary

Unweighted Cases		N	Percent
Valid		137	10.0
Excluded	Missing or out-of-range group codes	1191	86.7
	At least one missing discriminating variable	6	.4
	Both missing or out-of-range group codes and at least one missing discriminating variable	39	2.8
	Total	1236	90.0
Total		1373	100.0

A total of 137 (10%) of the 2001 hunters did not hunt deer in Wisconsin in 2002. These individuals were the focus of the study.

90% of 2001 hunters participated in the 2002 deer hunting season.

Group Statistics

Nonhunter		Mean	Std. Deviation	Valid N (listwise) Unweighted	Weighted
0 No CWD influence	trust	3.4684	.96192	66	45.225
	risk	1.2124	.65238	66	45.225
1 Yes CWD influence	trust	3.1354	1.10949	71	43.061
	risk	2.3543	.54839	71	43.061
Total	trust	3.3060	1.04404	137	88.285
	risk	1.7693	.83070	137	88.285

The weighted sample adjusts for oversampling in the CWD counties.

The ANOVA table from the discriminant analysis (Output 17.13) mirrors the ANOVA table from a one-way ANOVA (Box 17.2).

Output 17.13   Test of Equality of Group Means in a Discriminant Analysis

Group Statistics

	Wilks' Lambda	F	df1	df2	Sig.
trust	.974	2.277	1	86	.135
risk	.522	78.854	1	86	.000

Similar to the logistic regression, the discriminant analysis shows that trust in the WDNR did not influence the hunters' decision to participate in the 2002 season ($p = .135$), whereas the perceived risks associated with the disease was significant ($p < .001$).

Box 17.2   ANOVA table from a One-Way ANOVA where:
   Independent variable = NONHUNTER (CWD influenced No vs. Yes)
   Dependent variables = Trust in the WDNR
                Perceived Risk associated with CWD

ANOVA

		Sum of Squares	df	Mean Square	F	Sig.
trust	Between Groups	2.446	1	2.446	2.270	.136
	Within Groups	92.696	86	1.078		
	Total	95.142	87			
risk	Between Groups	28.761	1	28.761	78.593	.000
	Within Groups	31.471	86	.366		
	Total	60.232	87			

The *F*-values in Output 17.13 differ slightly from those in Box 17.2 due to the way the two procedures (discriminant vs. one-way ANOVA) handle missing data.

The **Wilks' lambda** (Output 17.13), also referred to as the *U* statistic, is a multivariate analysis of variance statistic. Lambda tests the equality of the group means or **centroids** (i.e., the separation of the means of the groups). The test statistic ranges from 0 to 1. The smaller the lambda, the more important the independent variable is to the discriminant function. In the CWD data, trust in the WDNR index was not significant ($p = .135$) and Wilks' lambda was .974. Large values of lambda (close to 1) indicate no difference. The perceived risk of CWD was statistically significant ($p < .001$) and Wilks' lambda was .522.

As described in chapter 15, the F-value is based on:

$$F = \frac{SS_{Between} / df}{SS_{Within} / df}$$

Equation 17.13

Wilks' lambda (Output 17.13) for the trust index is calculated as:

$$Wilks'\ Lambda = \frac{SS_{Within}}{SS_{Total}} = \frac{92.696}{95.142} = .974$$

Equation 17.14

The larger the log determinant (Output 17.14), the more that group's covariance matrix differs. In these data, there was more variability in the individuals who were influenced by CWD than those whose decision to not participate in the 2002 season for non-CWD reasons. The "Rank" column indicates the number of independent variables in the model (i.e., 2).

Output 17.14   Box's M Test of Equality of Covariance Matrices

Log Determinants

Nonhunter	Rank	Log Determinant
0 No CWD influence	2	−.976
1 Yes CWD influence	2	−1.050
Pooled within-groups	2	−.937

The ranks and natural logarithms of determinants printed are those of the group covariance matrices.

Box's M tests the assumptions of: (a) the homogeneity of covariance matrices and (b) multivariate normality (Output 17.15). Discriminant analysis is robust even when the homogeneity of variances assumption is not met, provided the data do not contain important outliers. For the CWD data, the test was not significant ($p = .096$); providing evidence that the two groups *do not* differ in their covariance matrices (i.e., the assumption of multivariate normality was not violated). When the sample size is large, small deviations from homogeneity will be significant. Box's M should be interpreted cautiously in these situations.

Output 17.15   Box's M Test

Test Results

Box's M		6.511
F	Approx.	2.116
	df1	3
	df2	1454939
	Sig.	.096

Tests null hypothesis of equal population covariance matrices.

Summary of Discriminant Functions

Output 17.16 shows the *eigenvalues* based on this discriminant analysis. The larger the eigenvalue, the more of the variance in the dependent variable is explained by that function. Because the dependent variable in this example is dichotomous, there is only one discriminant function. If there were more categories to the dependent variable, there would be multiple discriminant functions and the table in Output 17.16 would list them in descending order of importance. The number of functions generated by a discriminant analysis is either:

- 1 less than the number of groups in the dependent variable (i.e., $2 - 1 = 1$), or

- Equal to the number of discriminating variables (i.e., 2 in this example), whichever is smaller.

Output 17.16   Eigenvalues from a Discriminant Analysis

Eigenvalues

Function	Eigenvalue	% of Variance	Cumulative %	Canonical Correlation
1	.939[a]	100.0	100.0	.696

[a.] First 1 canonical discriminant functions were used in the analysis.

An eigenvalue is calculated as in Equation 17.15.

$$\text{Eigenvalue} = \frac{SS_{\text{Between}}}{SS_{\text{Within}}} = \frac{81.029}{86.285} = .939$$

Equation 17.15

The SS_{Between} and SS_{Within} were obtained from a one-way ANOVA where the independent variable was NONHUNTER and dependent variable was the discriminant scores that were saved in the data with the command: / SAVE = SCORES in discriminant syntax. SPSS named this variable DIS1_1 (see Box 17.3).

Box 17.3   ANOVA table from a One-Way ANOVA where:
Independent variable = NONHUNTER (CWD influenced No vs. Yes)
Dependent variable   = Discriminant scores (variable name: DIS1_1)
This variable was saved in a data file with the SPSS command " /SAVE = SCORES."

ANOVA

Dis1_1   Discriminant Scores from Function 1 for Analysis 1

	Sum of Squares	df	Mean Square	F	Sig.
Between Groups	81.029	1	81.029	80.761	.000
Within Groups	86.285	86	1.003		
Total	167.315	87			

The second column (Output 17.16) lists the percent of variance explained by each function. The third column is the cumulative percent of variance explained. When the dependent variable is dichotomous, there will only be one function and the percent of variance explained will always be 100%.

The last column in Output 17.16 is the canonical correlation. A ***canonical correlation*** is a measure of the degree of association between the discriminant scores and the dependent variable. When the dependent variable is dichotomous, the canonical correlation is equal to the Pearson correlation between the discriminant scores (Dɪs1_1) and the dependent measure (Nᴏɴʜᴜɴᴛᴇʀ). This can be verified by running a simple bivariate correlation in SPSS (Box 17.4).

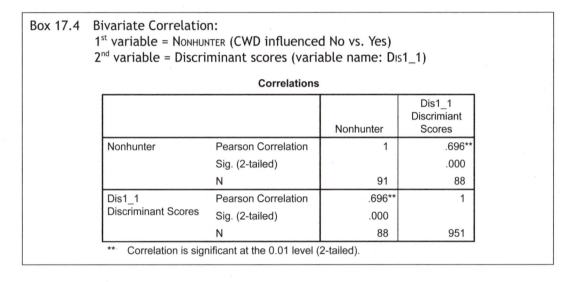

Box 17.4   Bivariate Correlation:
1ˢᵗ variable = Nᴏɴʜᴜɴᴛᴇʀ (CWD influenced No vs. Yes)
2ⁿᵈ variable = Discriminant scores (variable name: Dɪs1_1)

Correlations

		Nonhunter	Dis1_1 Discrimiant Scores
Nonhunter	Pearson Correlation	1	.696**
	Sig. (2-tailed)		.000
	N	91	88
Dis1_1 Discriminant Scores	Pearson Correlation	.696**	1
	Sig. (2-tailed)	.000	
	N	88	951

** Correlation is significant at the 0.01 level (2-tailed).

Output 17.17 shows a second Wilks' lambda and a chi-square. Unlike the lambdas in Output 17.13 that examined each independent variable, this second lambda tests the significance of the eigenvalue for each discriminant function (one in this case), which is significant ($p < .001$).

Output 17.17   Wilks Lambda and Chi-Square

Wilks' Lambda

Test of Function(s)	Wilks' Lambda	Chi-square	df	Sig.
1	.516	56.477	2	.000

The standardized discriminant function coefficients (Output 17.18) serve the same purpose as beta weights in multiple regression. These coefficients indicate the relative importance of the independent variables in predicting the dependent variable. As would be expected from the previous analysis, the standardized coefficient for the perceived risk of CWD was substantially larger than the coefficient for trust in the Wisconsin Department of Natural Resources.

Output 17.18   Standardized Discriminant Function Coefficients

	Function
	1
trust	−.164
risk	.986

The structure matrix (Output 17.19) shows the correlations of each variable with each discriminant function. In this case, there is only one discriminant function. When the dependent variable has more categories, however, there will be more discriminant functions and there will be one column in the table for each function. The correlations are similar to a factor loading in factor analysis. By identifying the largest absolute correlations associated with each discriminant function the researcher gains insight into how to name each function. This function would be labeled a risk function.

Output 17.19   Structure Matrix in a Discriminant Analysis

	Function
	1
risk	.986
trust	−.168

Pooled within-groups correlations between discriminating
variables and standardized canonical discriminant functions
Variables ordered by absolute size of correlation within function.

Output 17.20 shows the unstandardized discriminant function coefficients. These coefficients serve the same purpose as unstandardized B (regression) coefficients in multiple regression or the logit coefficients in a logistic regression. For example, they can be used to construct a prediction equation for classifying new cases.

Output 17.20   Discriminant Function Coefficients

	Function
	1
trust	−.158
risk	1.632
(Constant)	−2.366

Unstandardized coefficients

Output 17.21 is used to establish the ***cutting point*** for classifying cases. If the two groups are of equal size, the best cutting point is halfway between the values of the functions at group centroids (i.e., the average). If the groups are unequal, the optimal cutting point is the weighted average of the two values. Because the computer does the classification automatically, these values are for informational purposes.

Output 17.21   Cutting Points for Functions at Group Centroids

Functions at Group Centroids

	Function
Nonhunter	1
0 No CWD influence	−.935
1 Yes CWD influence	.982

Unstandardized canonical discriminant
functions evaluated at group mens

Prior probabilities (Output 17.22) were used in this classification analysis. The SPSS default is the observed group sizes in the sample for determining prior probabilities of group membership in the dependent variable and should be used if the group sizes differ. When the number of respondents in each group is the same, equal prior probabilities can be specified.

Output 17.22   Prior Probabilities for Groups

Prior Probabilities for Groups

		Cases Used in Analysis	
Nonhunter	Prior	Unweighted	Weighted
0 No CWD influence	.512	66	45.225
1—Yes CWD influence	.488	71	43.061
Total	1.000	137	88.285

The prior probabilities equal the percentages for the weighted data (see Appendix 17.1).

The weights reflect the adjustments made for oversampling in the CWD counties.

Checking "Casewise results" in the "Classify" options of a discriminant analysis produces Output 17.23 (p. 488). The output lists the: (a) actual group, (b) predicted group, (c) probability of the observed group score given membership in the predicted group, (d) probability that the case belongs to the predicted group, based on the independents, (e) squared Mahalanobis distance to the group centroid (i.e., large scores indicate outliers), and (f) discriminant score for the case. In Output 17.23, only the first 20 cases are displayed. Misclassified cases are marked with asterisks. The "Second Highest Group" columns show the probabilities and Mahalanobis distances for the respondent if the individual had been classed based in the other group.

A ***Mahalanobis distance*** is the distance between a respondent and the centroid for each group of the dependent variable. A respondent will have one Mahalanobis distance for each group, and the individual will be classified as belonging to the group for which its Mahalanobis distance is smallest. The smaller the Mahalanobis distance, the closer the person is to the group centroid and the more likely the individual belongs to that group. Because Mahalanobis distance is measured in terms of standard deviations from the centroid, an individual that is more than 1.96 Mahalanobis distance units from the centroid has less than a .05 chance of belonging to the group represented by the centroid.

Output 17.23   Casewise Statistics

Casewise Statistics

		Highest Group					Second Highest Group			Discriminant Scores
Case Number	Actual Group	Predicted Group	P(D>d | G=g) p	df	P(G=g | D=d)	Squared Mahalanobis Distance to Centroid	Group	P(G=g | D=d)	Squared Mahalanobis Distance to Centroid	Function 1
Original 1	0	0	.328	1	.997	.955	1	.023	8.374	-1.912
2	0	1**	.851	1	.806	.035	0	.194	2.987	.793
3	0	0	.077	1	.995	3.121	1	.005	13.567	-2.702
4	0	0	.756	1	.784	.097	1	.216	2.578	-.624
5	0	0	.424	1	.968	.639	1	.032	7.376	-1.734
6	0	1**	.355	1	.503	.857	0	.497	.982	.056
7	0	0	.971	1	.860	.001	1	.140	3.534	-.898
8	0	0	.872	1	.900	.026	1	.100	4.316	-1.096
9	0	1**	.725	1	.921	.123	0	.079	5.143	1.333
10	0	0	.413	1	.969	.671	1	.031	7.484	-1.754
11	0	0	.846	1	.819	.038	1	.181	2.965	-.740
12	0	0	.106	1	.993	2.610	1	.007	12.476	-2.550
13	0	0	.888	1	.896	.020	1	.104	4.235	-1.076
14	0	0	.924	1	.846	.009	1	.154	3.315	-.839
15	0	0	.681	1	.935	.169	1	.065	5.418	-1.346
16	0	0	.800	1	.915	.064	1	.085	4.707	-1.188
17	0	0	.405	1	.572	.694	1	.428	1.174	-.102
18	0	1**	.551	1	.656	.356	0	.344	1.743	.385
19	0	0	.998	1	.869	.000	1	.131	3.685	-.938
20	0	0	.521	1	.958	.411	1	.042	6.543	-1.576

**. Misclassified case

Figure 17.24 is the output resulting from checking "Separate-groups" under Plots in the Classify options of discriminant analysis. If there was more than one discriminant function, the graphs below would be scatterplots showing the relation of the first two discriminant functions. With one discriminant function, bar charts are displayed. If the predictors discriminate between the two groups, the bar graph will have most cases near the mean, with small tails.

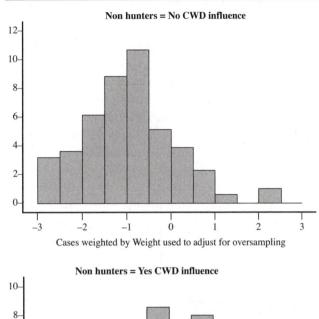

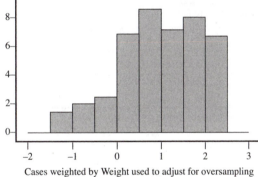

Figure 17.24   Separate Group Bar Graphs from the Discriminant Analysis

Classification Results

Similar to logistic regression, discriminant analysis summarizes the relationship between the observed and predicted group memberships (Output 17.25). This discriminant analysis correctly predicted 83% of the hunters who did not participate in the 2002 season due to reasons other than CWD, and 86% of the respondents who dropped out because of concerns about CWD. Overall, 85% of the hunters were correctly classified. These percentages are identical to those from the logistic regression classification table (Output 17.8, p. 473), although this exact similarity will not always occur for the two procedures. As noted for logistic regression, it is important to examine all three percents. A discriminant model that predicts only one of the two groups is not likely to have much practical utility.

Output 17.25   Classification Results from a Discriminant Analysis

Classification Results[a]

Nonhunter			Predicted Group Membership		Total
			0 No CWD influence	1 Yes CWD influence	
Original	Count	0 No CWD influence	38	8	45
		1 Yes CWD influence	6	37	43
		Ungrouped cases	692	171	863
	%	0 No CWD influence	83.0	17.0	100.0
		1 Yes CWD influence	13.6	86.4	100.0
		Ungrouped cases	80.2	19.8	100.0

a.   84.7% of original grouped cases correctly classified

Chapter Summary

This chapter examined two techniques — logistic regression and discriminant analysis — for estimating the probability that an event occurs. *Discriminant analysis* allows direct prediction of group membership, but the method requires several assumptions (e.g., multivariate normality of the independent variables, equal variance-covariance matrices in the two groups) for the predictions to be optimal. *Logistic regression* (LR) requires fewer assumptions than discriminant analysis; and even when the assumptions required for discriminant analysis are satisfied, LR still performs well.

In contrast to linear regression where the coefficients represent the smallest sum of squared differences between the observed and the predicted values of the dependent variable (i.e., *least squares method*), logistic regression coefficients are selected that make the observed results most likely (i.e., *maximum-likelihood method*). Because logistic regression is nonlinear, an iterative algorithm is necessary for coefficient estimation.

Logistic regression predicts the probability that an event will or will not occur (e.g., vote for or vote against a management action) based on the independent variables in the model. These estimated probabilities for each respondent will always be between 0 and 1. If the estimated probability of the event is < 0.5, the event is predicted to *not* occur for that person. If the probability is > 0.5, the event is predicted to occur.

The *Wald statistic* is used to test the significance of each independent variable in the model. Similar to multiple linear regression, the contribution of individual variables in logistic regression depends on the other variables in the model. The *R* statistic is used in logistic regression to examine the partial correlation between the dependent variable and each of the independent variables. The *R* can range in value from –1 to +1. A positive value of *R* indicates that as the variable increases in value, the likelihood of the event occurring increases. A negative *R* indicates that as the variable decreases in value, the likelihood of the event occurring decreases. Small values for *R* indicate that the variable has a small partial contribution to the model.

In multiple linear regression, the unstandardized coefficient indicates the amount of change in the dependent variable for one-unit change in the independent variable. Logistic regression coefficients are expressed as either the *log odds* (i.e., unstandardized logistic coefficient) or the *odds* (*Exp[B]*) of an event occurring. The *odds* of an event is the ratio of the probability that the outcome occurs to the probability that it does not. Odds ratios (OR) are central to logistic regression, just as the correlation coefficient is central to linear regression. An *odds ratio* is simply the ratio of two odds. The null hypothesis in a logistic regression is that the population odds ratio is equal to 1. If the null hypothesis were true (OR = 1), membership in the two categories of the dependent variable would be unrelated to the independent variable.

In SPSS, *Exp(B)* represents odds rather than log odds. If *Exp(B)* for an independent variable is greater than 1 (e.g., 1.5), when the independent variable increases by one-unit, the dependent variable increases by a factor of 1.5. If *Exp(B)* is less than 1, a unit increase in the independent variable decreases the odds of the event occurring.

There are several ways to assess whether the model fits the data in logistic regression. A *classification table*, for example, compares the predicted group membership to the observed outcomes. If the independent variables correctly predict all individuals in both categories of the dependent variable, the classification table would indicate 100% correct classification. In linear regression terms this is equivalent to an R^2 of 1.00. *Goodness-of-fit tests* provide a second strategy for assessing a logistic regression model. For example, the probability of the observed results, given the coefficient estimates, is known as the likelihood. Since the likelihood is a small number less than 1, it is customary to use *–2 times the log of the likelihood (–2LL)* as a measure of how well the estimated model fits the data. A good model has a high likelihood of the observed results, which translates into small value of *–2LL*. If the model fits perfectly, the likelihood is 1, and –2 times the log likelihood is 0. The *–2LL* can also be used to evaluate the consequences of additional independent variables in a model, where each model builds on the previous equation by adding one new predictor.

Similar to binary logistic regression, discriminant analysis (DA) can be used to classify and predict group membership using one or more continuous or dichotomous predictor variables. Unlike binary logistic, however, the dependent variable in a discriminant can also be categorical. The goals of discriminant analysis are to: (a) classify cases (e.g., respondents) into groups using a discriminant prediction equation, (b) assess the relative importance of the independent variables in classifying the dependent variable, and (c) determine the percent of variance in the dependent variable explained by the independents. The weights in discriminant function are selected based on how well they classify participants into the two groups (i.e., similar to logistic regression). The weighting coefficients in a DA, however, can be interpreted similarly to the coefficients in a multiple regression.

Both logistic regression and discriminant analysis were illustrated using data from a study of hunters' reactions to chronic wasting disease (CWD) in Wisconsin (Vaske, Timmons, Beaman, & Petchenik, 2004). Indices measuring perceived CWD risk and overall social trust in the Wisconsin Department of Natural Resources were used to predict the 2001 Wisconsin deer hunters who did not participate in the 2002 season due to CWD concerns versus non-CWD reasons.

Review Questions

1. In logistic regression, what is the level of measurement for the: (a) dependent variable, and (b) independent variables?

2. What method is used to estimate the probability of an event occurring or not occurring?

3. The probability estimates in a logistic regression for a given individual will always range between what two values?

4. Assume the dependent variable in logistic regression is coded 0 (did not participate in an activity) and 1 (participated in the activity). If the estimated probability for a given individual is .72, would the predicted group membership be 0 or 1? Why?

5. In logistic regression, what does the Wald statistic examine?

6. Why can the Wald statistic sometimes lead to the wrong conclusion?

7. Define the concept of *odds* in a logistic regression.

8. What is an *odds ratio* in logistic regression?

9. If the odds ratio was 1.0, would you reject or fail-to-reject the null hypothesis?

10. What does *Exp(B)* refer to in a logistic regression?

11. If the independent variable in a logistic regression, has an *Exp(B)* of 3.00, what happens to the dependent variable?

12. What does a classification table in logistic regression show you?

13. If a logistic regression correctly classifies 100% of the respondents, what would be the equivalent R^2 in a multiple linear regression?

14. If the model fits perfectly, the likelihood is 1. What is the –2 times the log likelihood in this situation?

15. Give two reasons why stepwise methods are not recommended for entering variables into a logistic regression equation.

16. What is the default cutoff value for the predicted probability in logistic regression in SPSS?

17. In a constant only logistic regression model, what percent of the cases are correctly classified for the group coded as 0 on the dependent variable?

18. In logistic regression, if the *–2LL* for the constant only model equals 150 and the *–2LL* for the model with predictors in the equation is 75, what is the value of the omnibus chi-square test of model coefficients?

19. The omnibus chi-square test in logistic regression is equivalent to what statistic in ordinary least squares regression?

20. Why is the Nagelkerke R^2 preferred over the Cox & Snell R^2 in logistic regression?

21. What does a nonsignificant Hosmer and Lemeshow goodness-of-fit test tell the researcher?

22. If a classification table in logistic regression correctly classified 75% of the group coded as 0, and 43% of the group coded as 1, is the model very good? Why or why not?

23. If an unstandardized logistic regression coefficient equals 4 and the standard error equals 1, what is the value of the Wald statistic?

24. In logistic regression, if the odds [i.e., *Exp(B)*] of an event occurring is 9 to 1, what is the probability of the event occurring?

25. In a discriminant analysis, what levels of measurement are appropriate for the dependent variable?

26. In a discriminant analysis, what levels of measurement are appropriate for the independent variables?

27. The coefficients in a discriminant analysis are interpreted in a similar manner to the coefficients in what statistical technique?

28. What does a Wilks' lambda in a discriminant analysis examine?

29. If independent variable X in a discriminant model has a value of .2 and a second independent variable Z has a value .8, is X or Z a better predictor of the dependent variable? Why?

30. In a discriminant analysis, what does the Box's M statistic test?

31. In a discriminant analysis with a dichotomous dependent variable and four predictor variables, how many functions will be produced?

32. How is an eigenvalue in a discriminant function interpreted?

33. What does a canonical correlation in a discriminant analysis measure?

34. If the dependent variable in a discriminant analysis is dichotomous and the canonical correlation is .75, what is the value of the Pearson correlation between the discriminant scores and the dependent variable?

35. If the standardized discriminant function coefficient for variable X equals .80 and the standardized coefficient for variable Y equals .35, is X or Y a better predictor in the model? Why?

36. If the classification table from a discriminant analysis correctly classified 80% of one group and 38% of the second group, is the model very good? Why or why not?

Appendix 17.1
Alternative Weighting Strategies in SPSS

Data for the Vaske, Timmons, Beaman, and Petchenik (2004) study were obtained from a random sample of 2001 Wisconsin gun deer license holders. Questionnaires were mailed to 1,500 resident gun deer hunters statewide and an additional 600 resident gun deer hunters that lived in the counties where CWD had been detected. Of the 2,100 surveys initially mailed, 43 were undeliverable. A total of 1,373 usable questionnaires were returned, yielding a response rate of 67% (1,373 / 2,057).

Among those who completed the survey ($n = 1,373$), 1,151 (84%) participated in the 2002 gun deer hunting season in Wisconsin and 222 (16%) did not hunt during this season. This 16% dropout rate (unweighted data including the oversample of CWD affected counties) was consistent with the Wisconsin Department of Natural Resources' estimate that 19% of the individuals living in CWD counties did not participate in the 2002 season (Petchenik, 2003).

Of the 222 respondents that did not hunt in 2002, there were 143 nonhunters for whom there were no missing data. A cluster analysis (see Romesburg, 1990) of 14 reasons for not hunting suggested that the perceived risks associated with CWD either strongly (37% – cluster 1) or moderately (15% – cluster 2) influenced individuals in the first two clusters to not hunt deer in 2002. Given the small sample size for cluster 2 ($n = 21$), clusters 1 and 2 were combined into one cluster ($n = 74$, Output A17.1). A final cluster ($n = 69$, 48%) included nonhunters for whom CWD was not a concern. These individuals did not participate in the 2002 deer hunting season due to a lack of hunting partners, lack of a license, or conflicting responsibilities. This implies that about half (estimate = 52% $\pm$ 5%) of the 2001 Wisconsin hunters that did not participate in the 2002 season did not hunt because of CWD.

Output A17.1   Unweighted Distribution

Nonhunter   Non hunters (CWD vs No CWD influence)

		Frequency	Percent	Valid Percent	Cumulative Percent
Valid	0 No CWD influence	69	48.3	48.3	48.3
	1 Yes CWD influence	74	51.7	51.7	100.0
	Total	143	100.0	100.0	

Weighting Strategy 1

The frequency distribution in Output A17.1 is based on unweighted data. To adjust for the oversampling of hunters who lived in the CWD affected counties, the data were weighted. Of the initial statewide random sample ($n = 1,500$ mailout), 154 respondents lived in CWD counties. In the oversampled CWD counties ($n = 600$), completed surveys were received from 389 individuals. The weight factor correcting for oversampling in CWD counties was computed as:

$$Raw\ Weight = \frac{154}{154+389} = .28$$

The SPSS syntax for computing this raw weight is:

```
Value labels sample
      1 'Respondents outside CWD counties'
      2 'Original sample - in CWD counties'
      3 'CWD over sample'.

compute weight = 1.

If (sample NE 1) weight = 154 /(154 + 389).

Frequencies variables = weight / statistics = mean.
```

To adjust for the oversampling, the responses from each individual living in one of the counties where CWD had been detected were multiplied by .28 (Output A17.2). The weighting factor for all other individuals was 1.00. The mean for the WEIGHT variable was .6343. This mean was used to create an adjusted weight variable (ADJWEIGHT) in the second weighting strategy.

Output A17.2   Frequency Distribution of Raw Weight Variable (WEIGHT)

Statistics

weight   Weight used to adjust for oversampling

N	Valid	143
	Missing	0
Mean		.6343

> This mean will be used to create the adjusted weight variable (ADJWEIGHT) in Weighting Strategy 2.

weight   Weight used to adjust for over sampling

		Frequency	Percent	Valid Percent	Cumulative Percent
Valid	.28	73	51.0	51.0	51.0
	1.00	70	49.0	49.0	100.0
	Total	143	100.0	100.0	

> Nonhunters in the oversampled CWD counties were assigned a weight of .28. All other nonhunters had a weight of 1.00.

The SPSS syntax for weighting a variable is simply

```
weight by (name of the weighting variable):
WEIGHT BY weight.

FREQUENCIES VARIABLES=Nonhunter.
```

After weighting by the variable WEIGHT, 49.2% ($n = 45$) did not participate because of CWD concerns and 50.8% ($n = 46$) were *not* influenced by CWD (Output A17.3). Thus, using the WEIGHT variable, the sample was reduced from 143 to 91 respondents.

Output A17.3   Weighted Distribution (Weight Variable = WEIGHT)

Nonhunter   Non hunters (CWD vs No CWD influence)

		Frequency	Percent	Valid Percent	Cumulative Percent
Valid	0 No CWD influence	46	50.8	50.8	50.8
	1 Yes CWD influence	45	49.2	49.2	100.0
	Total	91	100.0	100.0	

Weighting Strategy 2

For analysis, the weighted number of cases should equal the unweighted number of cases and the mean of the weights should be 1 (Glynn, 2004). If the weighted number of cases differs dramatically from the unweighted number of cases, significance tests may not be valid. To address this issue, the weight can be adjusted by dividing the weight by the mean of the weight:

$$\text{Adjusted Weight} = \frac{\text{Weight}}{\text{Mean of the Weight}}$$

Using this weighting strategy, the percentages of respondents in the two groups equal the percentages when the data are weighted by the raw weight (i.e., weighting strategy 1), but the sum of the weighted cases equals the sample size for the unweighted data (Output A17.4). The SPSS syntax for this adjusted weight is:

```
Compute adjweight = weight / .6343.
```
The mean of the raw weight.

```
Frequencies variables = adjweight / statistics = mean.
```

Output A17.4   Frequency Distribution of Adjusted Weight Variable (ADJWEIGHT)

Statistics

adjweight   Adjusted weight

N	Valid	143
	Missing	0
Mean		1.0000

adjweight   Adjusted weight

		Frequency	Percent	Valid Percent	Cumulative Percent
Valid	.45	73	51.0	51.0	51.0
	1.58	70	49.0	49.0	100.0
	Total	143	100.0	100.0	

Using the adjusted weight variable, nonhunters in the oversampled CWD counties were assigned a weight of .45. All other nonhunters had a weight of 1.58.

```
WEIGHT BY adjweight.

FREQUENCIES VARIABLES=Nonhunter.
```

Output A17.5 shows the distribution of responses for the nonhunter variable after weighting by the variable ADJWEIGHT. The percentages for "No CWD influence" (50.8%) and "Yes CWD influence" (49.2%) are identical to the results when the data were weighted data with the raw weight variable (Output A17.3). The overall sample size for the weighted data in Output A17.5, however, equals the *n* for the unweighted data (Output A17.1).

Output A17.5   Weighted Distribution (Weight Variable = ADJWEIGHT)

Nonhunter   Non hunters (CWD vs No CWD influence)

		Frequency	Percent	Valid Percent	Cumulative Percent
Valid	0 No CWD influence	73	50.8	50.8	50.8
	1 Yes CWD influence	70	49.2	49.2	100.0
	Total	143	100.0	100.0	

After weighting by the ADJWEIGHT variable, the overall *n* = the *n* for the unweighted data (i.e., *n* = 143).

After weighting by the ADJWEIGHT variable, the percents are the same as those for the data weighted by the WEIGHT variable (Output A17.3).

Appendix 17.1 Summary

Table A17.1 compares the sample sizes and percentages for the unweighted data against the two weighting strategies. Either weighting strategy results in the same percentages for the No versus Yes CWD influence on decisions to hunt deer in Wisconsin during 2002. The normalized weights, however, retain the same overall sample size as the unweighted data. The raw weight reduced the sample from 143 to 91.

Table A17.1 Comparisons Between Unweighted and Two Weighted Data Strategies

		Weighted Data	
	Unweighted Data	Raw Weight	Normalized Weight
Sample sizes			
No CWD influence	69	46	73
Yes CWD influence	74	45	70
Total	143	91	143
Percentages			
No CWD influence	48.3	50.8	50.8
Yes CWD influence	51.7	49.2	49.2
Total	100.0	100.0	100.0

In the Vaske, Timmons, et al. (2004) article, the findings were analyzed with both the raw and normalized weights. The two weighting strategies produced identical results. In general, however, if the weighted number of cases differs dramatically from the unweighted number of cases, the normalized weight is the recommended approach because it retains the original overall sample.

18

psychological scales and reliability analysis

Many of the concepts of interest to parks, recreation, and human dimensions researchers are not directly observable (e.g., attitudes, beliefs, norms, value orientations). Their existence must be inferred from survey responses that serve as indicators of the concepts. A variety of measurement methodologies and scaling procedures have been proposed for examining these psychological concepts. This chapter describes three common types of scaling procedures: (a) summated rating scales, (b) multiplicative scales, and (c) combined multiplicative and summated scales. Techniques for assessing the reliability of summated rating scales are also discussed in this chapter.

Summated Rating Scales

One method for constructing a summated rating scale was introduced by Likert (1932). This scaling approach begins with a pool of items that are believed to be relevant to the attitude object of interest. Respondents indicate their agreement or disagreement with each statement. For example, recent severe wildfires in the western United States have heightened awareness of the potential risks associated with wildfires (Vaske, Absher, & Bright, 2007; Winter, Vogt, & Fried, 2002). To minimize the negative consequences of wildfires, the USDA Forest Service has shifted from a traditional emphasis on total fire suppression to policies designed to reduce the probability and severity of wildfires. One major technique used is prescribed burning that involves the controlled use of fire to burn off excess vegetation in the forest. A potential set of Likert items for prescribed burning (i.e., the attitude object) is shown in Box 18.1 (p. 502). For each statement, response categories range from –3 (strongly disagree) to +3 (strongly agree). The Likert technique is referred to as a summated rating scale because the responses received from each item are summed (or averaged) to obtain the respondents' total score on the attitude scale.

Another type of summated rating scale is the *semantic differential* (Osgood, Suci, & Tannenbaum, 1957). This scale measures attitudes using a series of bipolar adjectives (e.g., bad-good), each of which is typically separated into seven response categories. Semantic differential statements associated with prescribed burning in National Forests are shown in Box 18.2 (p. 502). Combining the answers from each respondent to this sequence of four items provides an indication of the person's attitude toward prescribed burns.

Box 18.1   Likert Statements Measuring Attitudes toward Prescribed Burning

People have different feelings about using prescribed burning to manage National Forests. Indicate below how strongly you AGREE or DISAGREE with *each* of the following statements. *Circle the number of your response for each statement.*

Prescribed burns in National Forests...	Strongly Disagree	Moderately Disagree	Slightly Disagree	Neutral	Slightly Agree	Moderately Agree	Strongly Agree
...are an effective way to decrease the chances of a large scale fire.	−3	−2	−1	0	1	2	3
...are beneficial in restoring the natural characteristics of the forest.	−3	−2	−1	0	1	2	3
...are too uncontrollable to be an appropriate forest management tool.	−3	−2	−1	0	1	2	3
...minimize the negative consequences of wildfires.	−3	−2	−1	0	1	2	3

Box 18.2   Semantic Differential Statements Measuring Attitudes toward Prescribed Burning

Prescribed Burns in National Forests are:

	Extremely	Moderately	Slightly	Neither	Slightly	Moderately	Extremely	
Ineffective	1	2	3	4	5	6	7	Effective
Harmful	1	2	3	4	5	6	7	Beneficial
Uncontrollable	1	2	3	4	5	6	7	Controllable
Negative	1	2	3	4	5	6	7	Positive

Likert scaling techniques and semantic differential scales are commonly used by parks, recreation, and human dimensions researchers to measure attitudes, beliefs, norms, and behaviors (Vaske, Shelby, & Manfredo, 2006). Scale construction techniques for both types of scales follow a similar logic. The next section focuses on the steps involved in constructing a summated rating scale. Analytical procedures commonly used to test the reliability of summated rating scales are discussed in the last section of this chapter.

Defining Characteristics of a Summated Rating Scale

There are four defining characteristics of a summated rating scale. First, as the name (i.e., summated) implies, the scale must contain multiple items (i.e., survey questions) that will be combined by summing or averaging. Second, each item in the scale must reflect the concept being measured. Third, unlike a multiple choice exam, there are no "right" or "wrong" answers to the items in a summated rating scale (e.g., items concerning attitudes, beliefs, or norms). Fourth, each item in a scale is a statement and respondents rate each statement. Many human dimensions surveys contain 3 to 5 statements per scale, with each statement including 4 to 7 response choices. For example, using norm theory (chapter 2) as the conceptual foundation, Vaske and Donnelly (2007) developed a three-item awareness of consequences (AC) scale in a study of the public's knowledge of and beliefs about the desert tortoise. The three AC statements were:

(a) I am aware of the impacts that humans can have on the desert tortoise, (b) My personal actions can impact the ability of the desert tortoise to recover, and (c) If I touch a desert tortoise, it could hurt the animal's ability to survive. These statements do not have right or wrong answers. Respondents simply stated their beliefs about the impact people can have on the desert tortoise. Each of these items were measured using seven response choices (i.e., a 7-point scale including strongly disagree, moderately disagree, slightly disagree, neutral, slightly agree, moderately agree, strongly agree). Reliability analysis (see discussion in last section of chapter) suggested that the responses to these items were internally consistent (Cronbach's $\alpha = .88$). The scale was constructed by averaging each respondent's answers to the three statements.

Qualities of a Good Summated Rating Scale

Summated rating scales have good *psychometric properties* (Nunnally & Bernstein, 1994; see also chapter 4). In other words, a good scale is reliable, valid, and often precisely measured. *Measurement reliability* means that the multiple items measure the same construct (i.e., the items intercorrelate with each other). *Measurement validity* means that the scale measures what it was intended to measure. When 5 or 7 response options for each statement are used to measure the variable, measurement precision increases. *Precision* reflects the number of response options associated with survey questions. For example, a seven-point strongly agree to strongly disagree scale is more precise than a two-point agree or disagree scale. With multiple response choices (e.g., strongly agree, agree, neutral, disagree, strongly disagree), those who feel strongly can be distinguished from those with moderate feelings.

Steps in Constructing a Summated Rating Scale

The development of a summated rating scale is a multistep process. A thorough effort involves conducting several separate studies to develop the scale. Figure 18.1 (p. 504) illustrates five major steps in the process.

Step 1: Define Construct

A vital step in scale development is the conceptual task of defining the construct (see chapter 2). A scale cannot be developed to measure a concept unless the nature of that construct is clearly delineated. When scales go wrong, more often than not it is because the developer overlooked the importance of carefully and specifically defining the construct. Without a well-defined construct, it is not possible to write good items and to derive hypotheses about constructs for validation purposes.

As an illustration, chapter 2 introduced the concepts of basic beliefs and value orientations. *Basic beliefs* reflect our thoughts about general objects such as nature or wildlife. *Value orientations* are the patterns of direction and intensity among these basic beliefs (Fulton, Manfredo, & Libscomb, 1996; Whittaker & Manfredo, 1997). Vaske and Donnelly (1999) discussed a biocentric-anthropocentric value orientation. Anthropocentric basic beliefs represent a human-centered view of the nonhuman world (Eckersley, 1992; Pinchot, 1910). The approach assumes that providing for human uses and benefits is the primary aim of natural resource allocation and management. The environment is seen as "material to be used by humans as they see fit" (Scherer & Attig, 1983). There is no notion that the nonhuman parts of nature are valuable in their own right or for their own sake. An anthropocentric view of the world emphasizes the

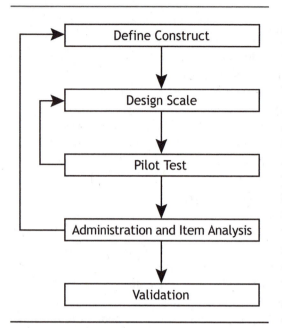

Figure 18.1 Major Steps in Developing a Summated Rating Scale

instrumental value of natural resources for human society, rather than their inherent worth (Shindler, List, & Steel, 1993; Steel, List, & Shindler, 1994). In contrast, biocentric basic beliefs are a nature-centered or ecocentered approach. The value of all ecosystems, species, and natural organisms is elevated to center stage. Human desires and human values are still important, but are viewed from a larger perspective. This approach assumes that environmental objects have inherent as well as instrumental worth and that human economic uses and benefits are not necessarily the most important uses of natural resources. In matters of natural resource management, these inherent values are to be equally respected and preserved, even if they conflict with human-centered values (Thompson & Barton, 1994).

Biocentric and anthropocentric basic beliefs are not mutually exclusive. Rather, these beliefs can be arranged along a continuum with biocentric viewpoints on one end and anthropocentric on the other. When the two sets of basic beliefs are combined, the result is a biocentric-anthropocentric value orientation. This value orientation was thus conceptually defined based on: (a) prior theory (e.g., Eckersley, 1992; Pinchot, 1910; Scherer & Attig, 1983; Thompson & Barton, 1994), (b) the methodology of combining sets of basic beliefs into a single concept (Fulton et al., 1996; Whittaker & Manfredo, 1997), and (c) empirical research (Shindler et al., 1993; Steel et al., 1994).

Overall, a summated rating scale combines multiple items associated with a concept in a single index, rather than analyzing the items separately. Part of construct definition (Step 1, Figure 18.1) is deciding how finely the concept should be divided. For example, the biocentric and anthropocentric basic beliefs might be analyzed separately for some research questions. In other situations, combining the two scales into a single biocentric-anthropocentric continuum may facilitate understanding the construct. The ultimate answer about how finely to divide a construct must be based on both theoretical and empirical utility. If subdividing a construct adds to the explanatory power of a theory, and if it can be supported empirically, then subdividing is indicated.

Step 2: Design Scale

Step 2 involves deciding on the exact format of the scale, including instructions, selection of response choices, and item wording. Box 18.3 contains the statements used to measure the biocentric and anthropocentric basic beliefs reported by Vaske and Donnelly (1999). The instructions for this set of items attempted to clarify what was being asked of the respondents and explicitly noted that there were no right or wrong answers. The first four statements represented items for the biocentric basic beliefs scale; the last five statements were used to measure the anthropocentric beliefs scale. The specific wording for these items reflected minor wording changes from previous work by Fulton and colleagues (1996) in Colorado and Whittaker and

Manfredo (1997) in Alaska that focused on a similar wildlife rights-use value orientation. For some questions, the word *nature* was simply substituted for the word *wildlife*.

In the initial development of the rights-use scale, Fulton and colleagues (1996) identified major issues concerning wildlife in Colorado. These basic belief dimensions were developed in cooperation with wildlife managers and planners from the Colorado Division of Wildlife. After the dimensions of interest were identified, the domain sampling model was used to develop specific measurement items. The ***domain sampling model*** assumes that there is a large pool of items that could be used to reflect the concept of interest (Nunnally & Bernstein, 1994). A scale consisting of several items was developed for each basic belief dimension. Items reflected a sampling of both behaviors and thoughts that indicated the basic beliefs.

The variables in the biocentric-anthropocentric scales (Vaske & Donnelly, 1999), as well as those in the rights-use scales (Fulton et al., 1996; Whittaker & Manfredo, 1997), were measured on seven-point scales ranging from "strongly agree" (1) to "strongly disagree" (7) that included a "neutral" point (see Box 18.3, p. 506). A considerable body of research has examined survey design issues related to the number of response categories and whether a "neutral" response option should be included (see Dillman, 1978, 2007; Salant & Dillman, 1994). Including more response options (e.g., 7 vs. 5) is often desirable for studies conducted in North America and Europe because of the increased precision. For research in developing countries, cultural barriers may limit the use of these types of scales and necessitate a more qualitative approach (Dayer, Stinchfield, & Manfredo, 2007).

Researchers have also debated how to treat respondents who claim to be "neutral," have "no opinion," or are "unsure" of their behavior in a given context (de Leeuw, Hox, & Huisman, 2003; Hall, 2001). These response categories (e.g., neutral, unsure, don't know, no opinion) are generally referred to as *nonsubstantive responses* (NSR; Browne-Nuñez & Vaske, 2006). Some researchers have discouraged NSRs by not offering this response category or by probing until a substantive response is obtained (Gilljam & Granberg, 1993; Schuman & Presser, 1996). If a NSR option is not offered, a respondent without knowledge of an issue, or not having an attitude toward the topic in question, may feel forced to choose a substantive response. Bishop, Oldendick, and Tuchfarber (1980), for example, found that in a question without a NSR option, approximately one third of respondents offered substantive responses. When the question was asked with a NSR option, only 7% volunteered an opinion. To mitigate such issues, researchers have recommended that NSR options be offered on a regular basis (Dillman, 2007). When NSR options are available, the percentage of such responses has ranged up to 90% with rates commonly above 10% (Poe, Seeman, McLaughlin, Mehl, & Dieth, 1988; Schuman & Presser, 1996; van Es, Lorence, Morgan, & Church, 1996).

It is equally important to recognize that not all NSR responses have the same meaning to all individuals (Dillman, 2007). A response option of neutral, for example, could be interpreted as "I have thought about the issue and am unable to make a decision one way or the other." Conversely, Schuman and Presser (1996, p. 113) point out that in telephone surveys, an answer of "I have no opinion" can mean merely "wait a minute, I'm thinking." Their advice, as well as that of others (de Leeuw et al., 2003; Gilljam & Granberg, 1993), is to probe all "do not know" and "neutral" responses that occur in the first few pages of a survey to better understand the basis for the answer (e.g., truly do not know, not willing to volunteer an opinion).

Box 18.3   Statements Measuring Biocentric and Anthropocentric Basic Beliefs

People have different reasons for thinking the National Forests might be important in our society. For *each* of the following statements, think about how you personally feel about the statement, and then please indicate how strongly you agree or disagree. Some of the statements have only slight differences and might sound the same. Please read all the statements first. Then tell us how you feel about each statement by putting a circle around the response that comes closest to the way you feel. There are no right or wrong answers to these statements.

	Strongly Agree	Moderately Agree	Slightly Agree	Neutral	Slightly Disagree	Moderately Disagree	Strongly Disagree
Nature has as much right to exist as people.	1	2	3	4	5	6	7
Forests have as much right to exist as people.	1	2	3	4	5	6	7
Forests have value, whether people are present or not.	1	2	3	4	5	6	7
Wildlife, plants and people have equal rights to live and develop.	1	2	3	4	5	6	7
The value of forests exists only in the human mind. Without people forests have no value.	1	2	3	4	5	6	7
Nature's primary value is to provide products useful to people.	1	2	3	4	5	6	7
The primary value of forests is to provide timber, grazing land and minerals for people who depend on them for their way of life.	1	2	3	4	5	6	7
The primary value of forests is to generate money and economic self-reliance for communities.	1	2	3	4	5	6	7
Forests are valuable only if they produce jobs and income for people.	1	2	3	4	5	6	7

Source: Vaske & Donnelly, 1999

Although the logic of this approach has merit for telephone surveys where a communication dialog is established between the interviewer and the respondent, mail surveys pose a different concern. The goal of writing self-administered surveys is to "develop a query that every potential respondent will interpret in the same way, be able to respond to accurately, and be willing to answer" (Dillman, 2007, p. 32). For mail surveys, research suggests that placement of an undecided or unsure category in the list of possible responses influences use of that option. Willits and Janota (1996), for example, demonstrated that when "undecided" was placed in the middle of the scale, twice as many respondents selected the option compared to when it was at the end of the scale (13% vs. 5%, respectively). To further clarify the meaning of responses, Dillman (2007) recommends a response option of "neither agree nor disagree" as the middle point as well as having a "no opinion" category as the final response option.

Step 3: Pilot Test

All survey questions should be pilot-tested with a small number of respondents who are asked to critique the items. Subjects in these preliminary studies should indicate which items are ambiguous or confusing, and which items cannot be rated along the dimension chosen. The scale should be revised on the basis of the respondents' feedback.

In the initial scale development of the wildlife rights-use wildlife value orientation, Fulton and colleagues (1996) pretested ($n = 27$) the items associated with each scale. Items were refined on the scales that did not provide Cronbach's alpha coefficients of $\geq .60$ (Cronbach's alpha is discussed later in this chapter). A second pretest ($n = 70$) was conducted to test the internal consistency of the refined items and the results demonstrated improvements in scale reliabilities. Given the similarities in concepts (i.e., rights-use vs. biocentric-anthropocentric) the scales developed by Fulton and colleagues (1996; $n = 1,202$), and Whittaker and Manfredo (1997; $n = 971$) can be viewed as a large pretest for the Vaske and Donnelly (1999) study. However, because the biocentric-anthropocentric items did not exactly parallel the rights-use items, the survey questions were pretested on a sample of 100 university students. Based on the pretest data, the reliability coefficients were .82 for the biocentric scale and .81 for the anthropocentric scale.

Step 4: Administration and Item Analysis

Data for the Vaske and Donnelly (1999) study were obtained from a random sample of Colorado residents ($n = 960$). To determine the number of dimensions underlying the basic belief statements, a principal components analysis (PCA) was conducted. PCA is one type of exploratory factor analysis (EFA) commonly used in the social sciences to uncover a cluster of related variables (i.e., a factor) in a larger set of variables. Using this analysis strategy, a large number of variables can be reduced to a smaller number of factors (see Russell, 2002 for more information on factor analysis).

The EFA extracted two factors from the nine basic belief statements. Table 18.1 (p. 508) displays the factor loadings associated with each factor. The factor loadings, also called component loadings in PCA, are the correlation coefficients between the variables (rows) and underlying factors (columns) and are analogous to Pearson's r. The variables strongly correlated with Factor 1 (factor loadings = .60 to .86) were the five anthropocentric basic beliefs. Factor 2 contained the four biocentric basic belief variables (factor loadings = .60 to .93). The internal consistency of the biocentric and anthropocentric basic belief scales was examined using Cronbach's alpha reliability coefficients (discussed at the end of this chapter). The reliability coefficients for the items in each factor were .85 (anthropocentric basic beliefs scale) and .87 (biocentric basic beliefs scale). Two composite basic belief scales (biocentric and anthropocentric) were then computed to create the biocentric/anthropocentric value orientation continuum. One end of this continuum reflected individuals who were mostly biocentric in their orientation; the other end included people who were primarily anthropocentric in their orientation.

Step 5: Validation

Measurement validity deals with the accuracy of generalizations and is concerned with whether the variables in the survey measure the concepts they were intended to measure. Demonstrating validity can take a variety of forms. ***Construct validity***, for example, refers to the way indicators and concepts relate to one another within a system of theoretical relationships (Babbie, 2003).

Table 18.1   Factor Analysis of Biocentric-Anthropocentric Basic Beliefs

Variable	Factor Loadings	
	Factor 1 Anthropocentric Basic Beliefs [b]	Factor 2 Biocentric Basic Beliefs [c]
The primary value of forests is to generate money and economic self-reliance for communities.	.86[a]	−.14
The primary value of forests is to provide timber, grazing land, and minerals for people who depend on them for their way of life.	.82[a]	−.07
Forests are valuable only if they produce jobs and income for people.	.76[a]	−.18
Nature's primary value is to provide products useful to people.	.76[a]	−.29
The value of forests exists only in the human mind. Without people forests have no value.	.60[a]	−.26
Forests have as much right to exist as people.	−.20	.93[a]
Nature has as much right to exist as people.	−.20	.92[a]
Wildlife, plants, and people have equal rights to live and develop.	−.12	.85[a]
Forests have value, whether people are present or not.	−.24	.60[a]

[a.] Designates factor assignment
[b.] Anthropocentric basic beliefs: Cronbach's alpha = .85
[c.] Biocentric basic beliefs: Cronbach's alpha = .87

The Vaske and Donnelly (1999) article examined the value → attitude → behavior cognitive hierarchy (chapter 2) as it pertains to wildland preservation. As predicted by theory, the biocentric/anthropocentric value orientation continuum predicted respondents' attitude toward the preservation of wildlands, and the attitude predicted the behavioral intention to vote for wildland preservation.

Validation of a concept also considers whether the findings are repeatable across different settings and contexts. The biocentric-anthropocentric scales have been used in at least five different studies (Table 18.2). These studies have included: (a) visitors to National Forests (i.e., Arapaho-Roosevelt, Mt. Baker–Snowqualmie, San Bernardino), (b) residents living in the wildland urban interface in Minnesota and Colorado, and (c) residents of southern California who live in or near the Mojave Desert. As discussed later in this chapter, Cronbach's alpha can be used to gauge the internal consistency of survey responses associated with a concept. The alpha coefficients for the biocentric scale ranged from .75 to .87 for the eight studies. The coefficients for the anthropocentric scale revealed a similar pattern of findings. The consistency of these findings for both scales provides partial validation of the scales.

Overall, the five steps shown in Figure 18.1 (p. 504) are essential for the development of a scale. Unfortunately, many scale developers do an inadequate job on the first (i.e., define construct) and/or last steps (i.e., validation). This probably occurs because these steps are the most difficult. Both rely on solid conceptual and theoretical thinking based on relevant research literature. The validation step further involves conducting research studies designed to test hypotheses about the scale.

Table 18.2   Reliability Coefficients for the Biocentric-Anthropocentric Basic Beliefs across Studies

Study	Basic Beliefs [1]	
	Biocentric	Anthropocentric
Colorado residents [2]	.87	.85
Arapaho-Roosevelt National Forest visitors [3]	.86	.77
Mt. Baker-Snoqualmie National Forest visitors [3]	.87	.77
San Bernardino National Forest visitors [3]	.85	.77
Minnesota full-time residents [4]	.86	.78
Minnesota seasonal residents [4]	.86	.76
Northern Colorado residents [5]	.85	.77
Southern California residents [6]	.75	.77

[1.] Cell entries are reliability coefficients (Cronbach's alpha)
[2.] Vaske and Donnelly (1999)
[3.] Bright, Vaske, Kneeshaw, and Absher (2005)
[4.] Bright and Burtz (2006)
[5.] Absher, Vaske, and Bright (2007)
[6.] Vaske and Donnelly (2007)

Before discussing analytical procedures for assessing the reliability of summated rating scales, two additional scale construction strategies — "multiplicative" and "multiplicative and summated" — are introduced. Both types of scales are common in the parks, recreation, and human dimensions literature.

Multiplicative Scales

As the name implies, multiplicative scales involve multiplying two variables. For example, Bright and Manfredo (1996) asked respondents two questions to measure respondents' behavioral intentions. The first question asked: "If you were given the opportunity to vote for or against reintroducing the gray wolf into Colorado, how would you vote?" Responses were coded as +1 for "vote for" and –1 "vote against." After indicating their choice, respondents were asked how certain they were of their decision using a four-point scale from "not at all" (coded as a 0) to "extremely" (coded as a +3). The product of these two responses resulted in a seven-point variable that ranged from –3 (voted against – extremely certain) to +3 (voted for – extremely certain).

Empirical Example (CO – Trapping model.sav)

Wildlife trapping is deeply woven into the exploration, pioneering, and development of the West. Despite this strong tradition, trapping has become controversial and opposition to the activity has grown significantly. In an attempt to develop trapping regulations with broad public acceptance, the Colorado Division of Wildlife (CDOW) initiated a stakeholder review process in November 1994. Part of this review process involved a survey ($n = 900$) of registered voters in the state (Manfredo, Pierce, Fulton, Pate, & Gill, 1999). One of the study's objectives was to determine how residents would vote on a trapping ban. Using a similar method as Bright and Manfredo

(1996), Manfredo et al. (1999) measured behavioral intention with two questions. The first question asked about how the respondent would vote on a wildlife trapping initiative if given the opportunity. Responses were coded: –1 for "allow trapping of wildlife to continue in the state," +1 for "ban trapping in the state", and 0 for "do not know." A follow-up question asked respondents how certain they were of their voting decision: not at all certain (0), extremely certain (6).

A FREQUENCIES analysis of these two variables (VOTEDIR, VOTCERTN) is shown below.

```
Frequencies variables = votedir votcertn.
```

Output 18.1   Variables inthe Multiplicative Voting Intention Scale

Statistics

		votedir Wildlife Trapping Vote	votcertn Certainty of Trapping Vote
N	Valid	900	830
	Missing	0	70

All 900 respondents answered the VOTEDIR question; 70 individuals did not have a valid response on the VOTCERTN variable.

votedir   Wildlife Trapping Vote

			Frequency	Percent	Valid Percent	Cumulative Percent
Valid	–1	Allow trapping	326	36.2	36.2	36.2
	0	Do not know	81	9.0	9.0	45.2
	1	Ban trapping	493	54.8	54.8	100.0
	Total		900	100.0	100.0	

Over half (54.8%) indicated that they would vote to ban trapping. About a third (36.2%) said they would vote to allow trapping and 9% did not know.

votcertn   Certainty of Trapping Vote

			Frequency	Percent	Valid Percent	Cumulative Percent
Valid	0	Not at all certain	16	1.8	1.9	1.9
	1		7	.8	.8	2.8
	2		20	2.2	2.4	5.2
	3		58	6.4	7.0	12.2
	4		139	15.4	16.7	28.9
	5		80	8.9	9.6	38.6
	6	Extremely certain	510	56.7	61.4	100.0
Missing	System		70	7.8		
Total			900	100.0		

Of the respondents who answered the certainty of the trapping vote question, 61.4% were extremely certain of their decision.

In SPSS, there are at least two ways to compute a multiplicative variable. One approach involves the simple multiplication of the two variables of interest. The syntax for this approach is:

```
Compute voteint1 = votedir * votcertn.
Variable labels voteint1 '1st Voting Intentions Scale'.
Value labels voteint1
      -6 'Allow trapping - Extremely certain'
       0 'Do not know'
       6 'Ban trapping - Extremely certain'.
Frequencies variables = voteint1.
```

The output for this analysis follows.

Output 18.2   Multiplicative Voting Intention Scale: Method 1

Statistics

voteint1   1st Voting Intentions Scale

N	Valid	898
	Missing	2
Mean		1.1147
Std. Deviation		4.93742

> Multiplying the two variables resulted in 898 valid responses and 2 missing values. The mean for the computed scale was 1.11 and the standard deviation was 4.94.

voteint1   1st Voting Intentions Scale

		Frequency	Percent	Valid Percent	Cumulative Percent
Valid	−6.00 Allow trapping - Extremely certain	175	19.4	19.5	19.5
	−5.00	31	3.4	3.5	22.9
	−4.00	70	7.8	7.8	30.7
	−3.00	30	3.3	3.3	34.1
	−2.00	10	1.1	1.1	35.2
	−1.00	3	.3	.3	35.5
	.00 Do not know	93	10.3	10.4	45.9
	1.00	3	.3	.3	46.2
	2.00	9	1.0	1.0	47.2
	3.00	27	3.0	3.0	50.2
	4.00	68	7.6	7.6	57.8
	5.00	49	5.4	5.5	63.3
	6.00 Ban trapping - Extremely certain	330	36.7	36.7	100.0
	Total	898	99.8	100.0	
Missing	System	2	.2		
Total		900	100.0		

> Approximately one-fifth of the respondents (19.5%) would vote to allow trapping and were extremely certain of their decision. Thirty-seven percent of the individuals in this computed scale would vote to ban trapping and were extremely certain. The "do not know" category included 93 individuals (10.4% of the sample) using the multiplicative method for creating the scale.

A second strategy for computing a multiplicative variable involves a series of `If` statements in SPSS. The syntax for this example might be:

```
Compute voteint2 = 9.
If (votedir = -1 and votcertn = 0) voteint2 =  0.
If (votedir = -1 and votcertn = 1) voteint2 = -1.
If (votedir = -1 and votcertn = 2) voteint2 = -2.
If (votedir = -1 and votcertn = 3) voteint2 = -3.
If (votedir = -1 and votcertn = 4) voteint2 = -4.
If (votedir = -1 and votcertn = 5) voteint2 = -5.
If (votedir = -1 and votcertn = 6) voteint2 = -6.
If (votedir =  0 and votcertn = 0) voteint2 =  0.
If (votedir =  0 and votcertn = 1) voteint2 =  0.
If (votedir =  0 and votcertn = 2) voteint2 =  0.
If (votedir =  0 and votcertn = 3) voteint2 =  0.
If (votedir =  0 and votcertn = 4) voteint2 =  0.
If (votedir =  0 and votcertn = 5) voteint2 =  0.
If (votedir =  0 and votcertn = 6) voteint2 =  0.
If (votedir =  1 and votcertn = 0) voteint2 =  0.
If (votedir =  1 and votcertn = 1) voteint2 =  1.
If (votedir =  1 and votcertn = 2) voteint2 =  2.
If (votedir =  1 and votcertn = 3) voteint2 =  3.
If (votedir =  1 and votcertn = 4) voteint2 =  4.
If (votedir =  1 and votcertn = 5) voteint2 =  5.
If (votedir =  1 and votcertn = 6) voteint2 =  6.
Missing values voteint2 (9).
Variable labels voteint2 '2nd Voting Intentions Scale'.
Value labels voteint2
        -6 'Allow trapping - Extremely certain'
         0 'Do not know'
        +6 'Ban trapping - Extremely certain'.

Frequencies variables = voteint2 / Statistics = mean stddev.
```

> The `compute` statement initializes the VOTEINT2 variable with a value of 9. The `If` statements selectively change the 9s to valid responses based the individual's answers to VOTEDIR and VOTCERTN.

Output 18.3 Multipicative Voting Intentions Scale: Method 2

Statistics

voteint2   2nd Voting Intentions Scale

N	Valid	830
	Missing	70
Mean		1.2060
Std. Deviation		5.12518

> Using the `If` statements, 70 individuals have missing values on the computed voting intentions scale. Only two individuals were assigned a missing value when the two variables were multiplied together (VOTEINT1). The mean and standard deviation for VOTEINT2 were slightly larger than for VOTEINT1.

Output 18.3   Multipicative Voting Intentions Scale: Method 2 (continued)

voteint2   2nd Voting Intentions Scale

		Frequency	Percent	Valid Percent	Cumulative Percent
Valid	−6.00 Allow trapping - Extremely certain	175	19.4	21.1	21.1
	−5.00	31	3.4	3.7	24.8
	−4.00	70	7.8	8.4	33.3
	−3.00	30	3.3	3.6	36.9
	−2.00	10	1.1	1.2	38.1
	−1.00	3	.3	.4	38.4
	.00 Do not know	25	2.8	3.0	41.4
	1.00	3	.3	.4	41.8
	2.00	9	1.0	1.1	42.9
	3.00	27	3.0	3.3	46.1
	4.00	68	7.6	8.2	54.3
	5.00	49	5.4	5.9	60.2
	6.00 Ban trapping - Extremely certain	330	36.7	39.8	100.0
	Total	830	92.2	100.0	
Missing	9.00	70	7.8		
Total		900	100.0		

> Although the two distributions for VOTEINT1 and VOTEINT2 were similar, there was a difference for the number of individuals in the "do not know" category. With VOTEINT1, 10.4% of the sample (n = 93) was in this category. For VOTEINT2, only 3% (n = 25) were assigned to the "do not know" response.

The difference between the two distributions occurs because of the way SPSS handles missing data when variables are multiplied. *When a valid value of 0 is multiplied by a missing value, SPSS returns a value of 0 for the computed variable* (i.e., 0 * missing = 0; SPSS 15.0, Command Syntax Reference, 2006, p. 90). This outcome can be verified by running the List variables command for respondents in the "do not know" category for VOTEINT1.

```
Temporary.
Select if voteint1 = 0.

List variables votedir votcertn voteint1.
```

The first 15 cases from this output are shown below. The period (.) is a system missing value.

votedir	votcertn	voteint1
0	.	0
1	0	0
0	1	0
0	.	0
0	.	0
0	.	0
0	.	0
0	6	0
0	4	0
0	.	0
0	.	0
0	.	0
0	0	0
0	.	0
0	.	0

SPSS calculated the VOTEINT1 variable as specified in the *Command Syntax Reference Guide*, but this may or may not be the result that the researcher wants. It could be argued that the missing values on VOTCERTN occurred because the respondent truly did not know how they would vote and thus were uncertain about their decision. This uncertainty led to a missing value response for the VOTCERTN variable. From a statistical analysis perspective, however, the researcher's choice of computation methods (i.e., multiplication vs. if statements) influences the resulting distribution. *As the number of missing responses increases, the difference between the two methods will also increase. The decision as to which approach to use, should be made conscientiously and not be determined by SPSS syntax rules.*

Combined Multiplicative and Summated Scales

According to the theory of reasoned action (Fishbein & Ajzen, 1975), attitudes toward a behavior are based on beliefs regarding the likelihood of specific outcomes of a behavior and an evaluation of those outcomes. This relationship between beliefs and evaluation is described by the formula:

$$Att_{act} = \sum_{i=1}^{n} b_i e_i$$

Equation 18.1

where:

Att_{act} = the attitude toward the behavior
b_i = a belief regarding outcome i of a behavior
e_i = an evaluation of that outcome
n = the number of salient beliefs about the behavior
$\sum$ = the sum of the belief * evaluation products across all respondents (n)

The Fishbein and Ajzen (1975) formula for computing an attitude represents a ***combination of multiplicative and additive scales***. An elicitation study is typically conducted where respondents in the population of interest are asked to list the advantages and disadvantages of a given outcome (e.g., a trapping ban) in an open-ended response format. The most frequently mentioned responses are then used to create the final survey questions. Each of these salient beliefs (b_i) about a given outcome is multiplied by the corresponding evaluation (e_i) of that outcome. The resulting products (i.e., $b_i * e_i$) are then summed to create the attitude scale.

Empirical Example

In November 1996, Coloradoans voted on a ballot initiative to amend the state's constitution by restricting wildlife trapping on public and private lands in the state (Amendment 14). The initiative passed by a margin of 4%; 53% voted for and 48% voted against the trapping ban. A phone survey ($n = 408$) of registered voters was conducted immediately after the election (Vaske & Rodriguez, 1996). Using the theory of reasoned action as the theoretical foundation, the study's objective was to explain the voting behavior using measures of the respondents' attitude toward Amendment 14. Descriptive results from the survey mirrored the actual vote: 53% ($n = 218$) voted for and 47% ($n = 190$) voted against the amendment.

An elicitation study ($n = 50$) conducted prior to finalizing the phone survey identified four salient beliefs associated with the trapping ban. The respondents to the elicitation survey believed that a trapping ban would: (a) increase the number beavers and coyotes, (b) reduce the number of problem wildlife, (c) reduce ranchers' ability to protect livestock, and (d) lead to restrictions on hunting. In the final phone survey, these four issues were asked twice. In the first set of questions, respondents were asked whether each outcome was likely or unlikely. Responses to each statement were coded on a seven-point scale ranging from –3 (extremely unlikely) to +3 (extremely likely). For each of the four statements, the second set of questions asked respondents to indicate whether such an outcome was bad or good with possible answers of –3 (extremely

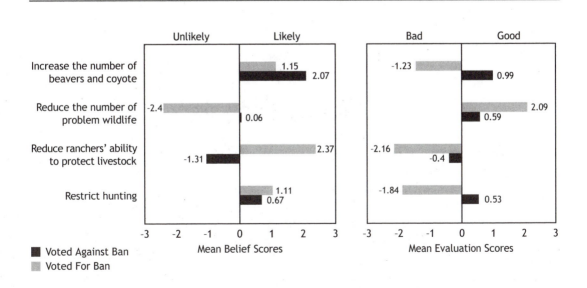

Figure 18.2 Mean Belief (B) and Evaluative (E) Scores for Trapping Ban Outcomes

bad) to +3 (extremely good). The mean scores for those who voted for and those who voted against the trapping ban for both the belief (i.e., unlikely to likely) and the evaluation (i.e., bad to good) components of the attitude are shown in Figure 18.2.

Each respondent's belief was multiplied by his or her evaluation of that outcome. For example, the belief that a trapping ban would lead to an "increase in the number of beavers and coyotes" was multiplied by the person's evaluation that this outcome would be bad or good. This process resulted in four belief * evaluation (BE) product scores. Summing across the four BE products yielded the individual's attitude toward the trapping ban amendment (Figure 18.3). Respondents who were against the ban consistently held a strong negative attitude toward Amendment 14. The averages of these BE products ranged from –2.5 to –5.65. Those who voted for the ban consistently held a positive attitude, but the BE scores were held with less conviction. These BE scores ranged from 0.16 to 1.06. This visual display facilitates understanding how the attitudes of the two groups differed.

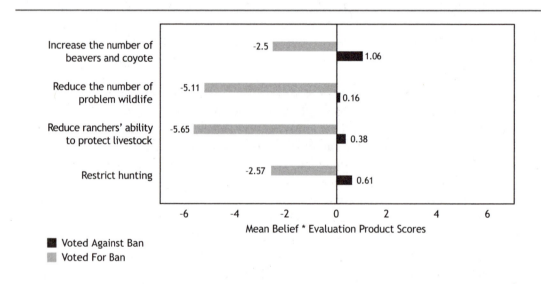

Figure 18.3   Mean BE Product Scores

Reliability Analysis

For summated rating scales (but not multiplicative or combined multiplicative and summated scales), a reliability analysis is commonly performed to estimate the internal consistency of the items. ***Measurement reliability*** refers to the consistency of responses to a set of questions (i.e., variables) designed to measure a given concept. Chapter 4 discussed four basic methods for estimating the reliability of empirical measurement (i.e., test-retest, alternative-form, split-halves, internal consistency). This section elaborates on the internal consistency and split-halves methods. ***Internal consistency*** statistics estimate how consistently individuals respond to the items within a scale. The word *scale* is used here to reflect a collection of survey items that are intended to measure the unobserved concept (i.e., a summated rating scale). There are several internal consistency reliability estimates, for example: (a) Cronbach's alpha (Cronbach,

1951, 2004), (b) Spearman-Brown stepped up reliability coefficient (i.e., Standardized Item Alpha in SPSS terminology), and (c) Kuder-Richardson formula 20 (a.k.a. KR20; Kuder & Richardson, 1937). The Spearman-Brown prophecy formula, a split-halves reliability measure, is discussed at the end of the chapter.

Cronbach's alpha (often symbolized by the lower case Greek letter α) is perhaps the most common estimate of internal consistency of items in a scale (Cronbach, 1951, 2004). Cronbach's alpha measures the extent to which item responses (i.e., answers to survey questions) correlate with each other. In other words, α estimates the proportion of variance that is systematic or consistent in a set of survey responses. The general formula for computing α is:

$$\alpha = \frac{N}{N-1}\left(\frac{\sigma^2_X - \sum_{i=1}^{N}\sigma^2_{Y_i}}{\sigma^2_X}\right)$$

Equation 18.2

where:

   N = the number of components (i.e., survey items in the scale)
   σ^2_X = the variance of the observed total test scores
   $\sigma^2_{Y_i}$ = the variance of component i for person Y

Alternatively, the ***standardized item alpha*** (or the Spearman-Brown stepped up reliability coefficient) can be defined as:

$$r_{SB2} = \frac{N \cdot \bar{r}}{1+(N-1)\cdot \bar{r}}$$

Equation 18.3

where:

   N = the number of survey items in the scale
   $\bar{r}$ = the average of all Pearson correlation coefficients between the survey items

As evident from Equation 18.3, the value of alpha depends on the average inter-item correlation and the number of items in the scale. The statistic can range from 0.00 to 1.00. A Cronbach's α of .90 implies that scale is 90% reliable, and by extension that it is 10% unreliable (100% – 90% = 10%).

When interpreting Cronbach's alpha, there are several issues to consider:

1. Alpha provides an estimate of the internal consistency of the variables in the scale. Alpha *does not* indicate: (a) the stability or consistency of the test over time, which would be estimated using the test-retest reliability strategy, and (b) the stability or consistency of the variables across different survey forms, which would be estimated using the alternative-forms reliability strategy (chapter 4).

2. Alpha is *not a measure of unidimensionality*. A set of items can have a high alpha and still be multidimensional. This happens when there are separate clusters of items (separate dimensions such as biocentric and anthropocentric) that intercorrelate highly. In addition,

a set of items can have a low alpha even when the scale is unidimensional if there is high random error.

3. The items in the scale are assumed to be positively correlated with each other because they are measuring the same theoretical concept. A negative α value can occur when the items are not positively correlated among themselves. In this situation, one or more variables may need to be recoded (see chapter 12) to assure that all items are coded in the same conceptual direction.

4. Alpha will generally increase as the correlations between the items increases.

5. Alpha will be higher for scales containing more variables than for scales containing fewer items. As demonstrated below and explained in Brown (2001), this occurs even when the estimated average correlations are low.

6. Variables with approximately normally distributed scores are more likely to have high Cronbach's alpha reliability estimates than variables with positively or negatively skewed distributions (chapter 11).

Statisticians have debated about what constitutes an acceptable size for Cronbach's alpha (Nunnally & Bernstein, 1994). By convention, an alpha of .65 to .70 is often considered an "adequate" scale in parks, recreation, and human dimensions research. Some researchers require a cut-off of .80 for a "good scale," while others are as lenient as .60.

Cronbach's alpha is a generalization of a reliability coefficient introduced by Kuder and Richardson (1937). The Kuder-Richardson formula 20 (a.k.a. *KR20*) is appropriate for dichotomous variables coded as 0 and 1. The KR20 is defined as:

$$KR20 = \frac{N}{N-1}\left(1 - \frac{\sum p_i q_i}{\sigma_x^2}\right)$$

Equation 18.4

where:

N = the number of dichotomous items
p_i = the proportion of respondents coded as 1 to the ith item
q_i = $1 - p$
σ_x^2 = the variance of the total composite

Since KR20 is simply a special case of Cronbach's alpha, KR20 has the same interpretation. Cronbach's alpha has the advantage over KR20 because it applies to variables with a wider range of response options, not just dichotomous variables (Carmines & Zeller, 1979).

Overall, Cronbach's alpha is a useful and flexible tool for examining the reliability of a set of variables associated with a concept. It is important to remember that reliability, regardless of the strategy used to obtain it, is not a characteristic inherent in the survey itself, but rather is an estimate of the consistency of a set of items when they are administered to a particular group of respondents at a specific time under particular conditions for a specific purpose.

Cronbach's Alpha and Other Measures of Internal Consistency

Jacob and Schreyer (1980) proposed four major classes of determinants of recreation conflict (i.e., resource specificity, activity style, mode of experience, lifestyle tolerance). In this section, Cronbach's alpha is used to examine the internal consistency of a set of items designed to measure resource specificity. Resource specificity relates to the significance recreationists attach to a specific resource. This concept is based on multiple indicators. The survey questions and variable names associated with the resource specificity scale are shown in Table 18.3. The data for this exercise were obtained from a study of recreational conflict between skiers and snowboarders (Vaske, Carothers, Donnelly, & Baird, 2000; CO – Skier-Snowboarder.sav).

Table 18.3   Indicators of "Resource Specificity" Concept

Survey question	Variable name
This area means a lot to me.	PLACE1
A lot of my life is organized around this area.	PLACE2
This area is best for what I like to do.	PLACE3
I identify strongly with this area.	PLACE4

All variables coded on five-point scales ranging from "Strongly Disagree" (1) to "Strongly Agree" (5).

Reliability Analysis in SPSS

As with all analyses, running a RELIABILITY ANALYSIS in SPSS involves four steps:

1. Open the data file   see chapter 9

2. Select the statistical test: **Analyze > Scale > Reliability Analysis...**   See Figure 18.4

3. Select variables for analysis   See Figure 18.5

4. Select additional statistics and options   See Figure 18.6

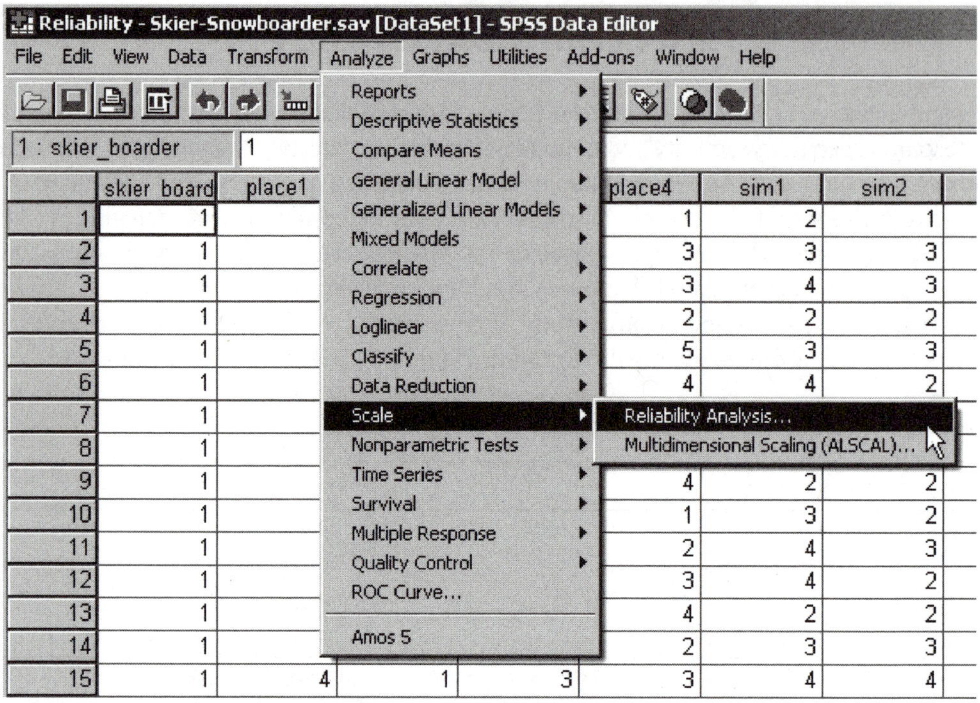

Reliability - Skier-Snowboarder.sav [DataSet1] - SPSS Data Editor

File   Edit   View   Data   Transform   Analyze   Graphs   Utilities   Add-ons   Window   Help

1 : skier_boarder   1

	skier board	place1			place4	sim1	sim2
1	1				1	2	1
2	1				3	3	3
3	1				3	4	3
4	1				2	2	2
5	1				5	3	3
6	1				4	4	2
7	1						
8	1						
9	1				4	2	2
10	1				1	3	2
11	1				2	4	3
12	1				3	4	2
13	1				4	2	2
14	1				2	3	3
15	1	4	1	3	3	4	4

Analyze menu:
- Reports ▶
- Descriptive Statistics ▶
- Compare Means ▶
- General Linear Model ▶
- Generalized Linear Models ▶
- Mixed Models ▶
- Correlate ▶
- Regression ▶
- Loglinear ▶
- Classify ▶
- Data Reduction ▶
- Scale ▶ — Reliability Analysis...
          Multidimensional Scaling (ALSCAL)...
- Nonparametric Tests ▶
- Time Series ▶
- Survival ▶
- Multiple Response ▶
- Quality Control ▶
- ROC Curve...
- Amos 5

Figure 18.4   Select the SPSS Reliability Analysis Procedure

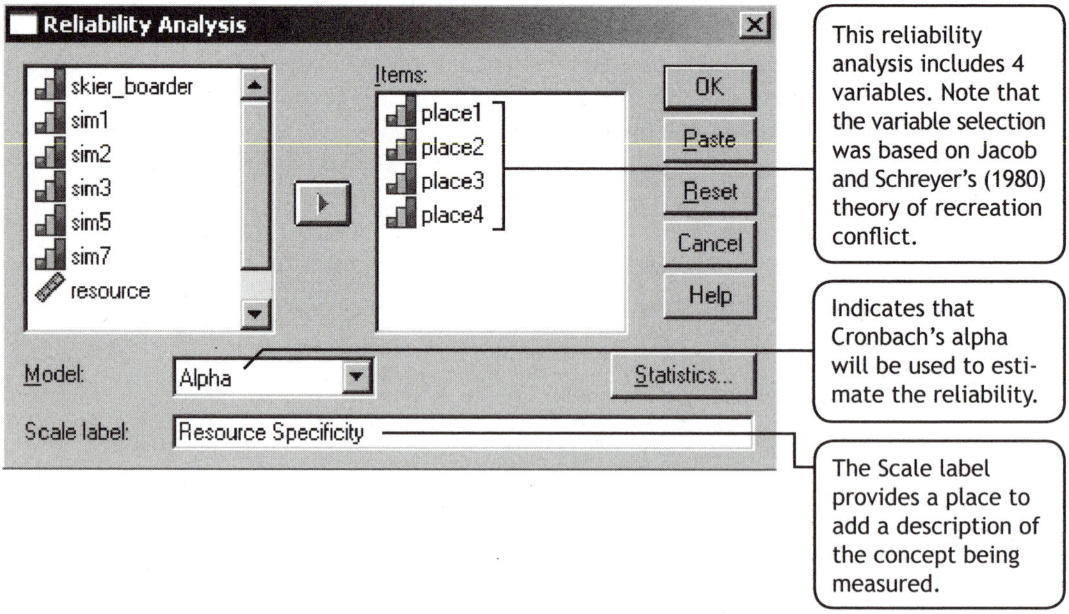

Reliability Analysis

Items: place1, place2, place3, place4

skier_boarder
sim1
sim2
sim3
sim5
sim7
resource

OK   Paste   Reset   Cancel   Help

Model: Alpha

Scale label: Resource Specificity

Statistics...

This reliability analysis includes 4 variables. Note that the variable selection was based on Jacob and Schreyer's (1980) theory of recreation conflict.

Indicates that Cronbach's alpha will be used to estimate the reliability.

The Scale label provides a place to add a description of the concept being measured.

Figure 18.5   Select Variables for the Reliability Analysis

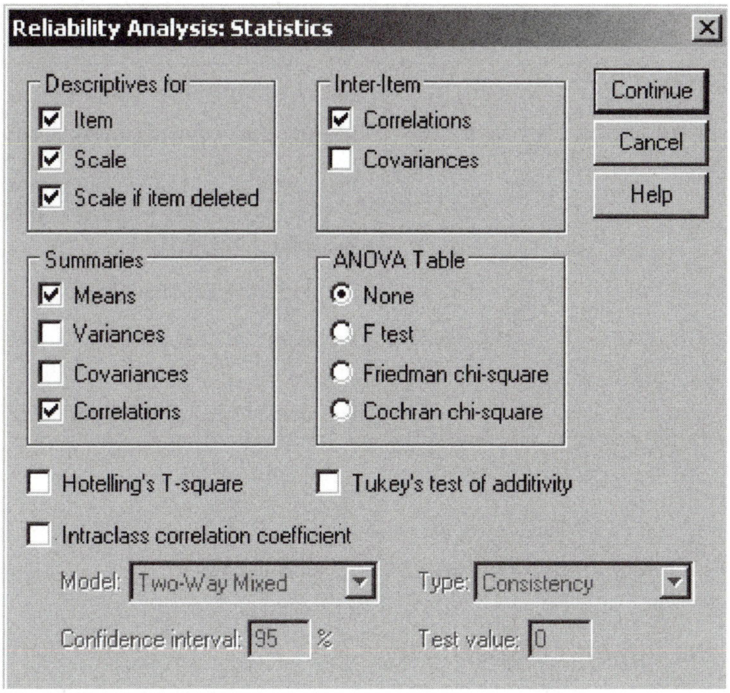

Figure 18.6   Select Statistics Options for the Reliability Analysis

This analysis will produce descriptive statistics for each item, the scale, and scale if item deleted. Summary means and correlations, as well as inter-item correlations will also be produced. After selecting the desired statistics, press the Continue button and the main dialog box for Reliability Analysis will reappear. Use the Paste button to insert the commands into the designated syntax file (Figure 18.7).

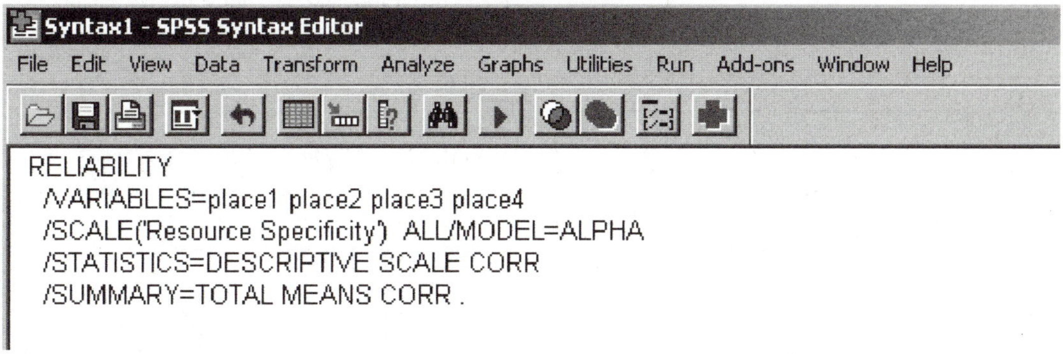

```
RELIABILITY
  /VARIABLES=place1 place2 place3 place4
  /SCALE('Resource Specificity')  ALL/MODEL=ALPHA
  /STATISTICS=DESCRIPTIVE SCALE CORR
  /SUMMARY=TOTAL MEANS CORR .
```

Figure 18.7   Reliability Analysis Syntax

Table 18.4   Interpreting the Commands in the Syntax

Line	Command	
1	`RELIABILITY`	Runs the Reliability Analysis
2	`/ VARIABLES=place1 place2 …`	Identifies the variables to be included in the analysis
4	`/ SCALE('Resource Specificity') ALL`	Includes `ALL` of the variables listed on the `/ VARIABLES` list & labels computed scale as Resource Specificity
	`/ MODEL=ALPHA`	Requests the Cronbach's alpha
5	`/ STATISTICS=DESCRIPTIVE SCALE CORR`	Produces statistics for each variable in the analysis
6	`/ SUMMARY=TOTAL MEANS CORR`	Produces statistics for all variables taken together

Output 18.4   Reliability Analysis of Resource Specificity Scale

Reliability Scale: Resource Specificity

Case Processing Summary

		N	%
Cases	Valid	591	99.3
	Excluded[a]	4	.7
	Total	595	100.0

a. Listwise deletion based on all variables in the procedure.

> Reliability analyses are always based on a listwise deletion of missing values.

Reliability Statistics

Cronbach's Alpha	Cronbach's Alpha Based on Standardized Items	N of Items
.775	.778	4.

> SPSS produces two Cronbach's alpha coefficients (standardized and unstandardized). The ***standardized item alpha*** is the α value that would be obtained if all of the items were standardized to have a variance of 1. When the items in a scale have fairly comparable variances, there is little difference between the standardized and unstandardized alphas. If the items in the scale have widely different variances, the two alphas may differ substantially.

> Means, standard deviations and *N*s (cases) for each variable.

Item Statistics

		Mean	Std. Deviation	N
place1	This area means a lot to me	3.72	.973	591
place2	A lot of my life is organized around this area	2.47	1.177	591
place3	This area is best for what I liked to do	3.08	.996	591
place4	I strongly identify with this area	2.92	1.052	591

Output 18.4   Reliability Analysis of Resource Specificity Scale (continued)

Inter-Item Correlation Matrix

	place1 This area means a lot to me	place2 A lot of my life is organized around this area	place3 This area is best for what I liked to do	place4 I strongly identify with this area
place1 This area means a lot to me	1.000	.452	.511	.519
place2 A lot of my life is organized around this area	.452	1.000	.328	.534
place3 This area is best for what I liked to do	.511	.328	1.000	.461
place4 I strongly identify with this area	.519	.534	.461	1.000

> *Inter-item correlations:* All of the correlations are positive; one of the assumptions in a reliability analysis.

Summary Item Statistics

	Mean	Minimum	Maximum	Range	Maximum/ Minimum	Variance	N ot Items
Item Means	3.047	2.469	3.724	1.255	1.509	.270	4
Item Variances	1.107	.946	1.385	.439	1.464	.039	4
Inter-Item Correlations	.468	.328	.534	.206	1.627	.005	4

> The average correlation among the four variables

> The *Squared Multiple Correlation (R²)* is obtained from a regression analysis (chapter 16) where the item of interest is the dependent variable and all of the other items are independent variables.

> The *Corrected Item-Total Correlation* is the Pearson correlation coefficient between the score on the individual item and the sum of the scores on the remaining items. *In general, these correlations should be ≥ .40. If one of these correlations is < .40, consider dropping the variable from the scale.*

Item-Total Statistics

	Scale Mean if Item Deleted	Scale Variance if Item Deleted	Corrected Item-Total Correlation	Squared Multiple Correlation	Cronbach's Alpha if Item Deleted
place1 This area means a lot to me	8.47	6.541	.621	.394	.701
place2 A lot of my life is organized around this area	9.72	6.063	.539	.327	.747
place3 This area is best for what I liked to do	9.11	6.857	.522	.314	.748
place4 I strongly identify with this area	9.27	6.117	.644	.417	.685

> The *Alpha if Item Deleted* is the unstandardized alpha that would result if a given item was removed from the scale. In this example, the Cronbach's alpha with all four items included in the scale was .775 (p. 522). If "PLACE1" was not in the scale, the Cronbach's alpha would be .701. If "PLACE2" was not included, the α would be .747. In this analysis then, dropping any of the variables lowers the alpha, suggesting that all 4 variables should be retained in the resource specificity scale.

In general, if the overall alpha would increase "substantially" when an item is removed, delete the item from the SPSS reliability syntax, and re-run the procedure. The removal of items should be done sequentially, one variable at a time. In SPSS, a RELIABILITY ANALYSIS is always based on "listwise deletion" (see chapter 19). Removing a single item from a scale may dramatically change the number of individuals included in the analysis and consequently, impact the reliability coefficient. It is equally important to consider validity issues in such analyses. Removing an item from a scale may increase reliability, but decrease the scale's validity. The decision to include or exclude a given variable from a scale should be based on theoretical reasoning, not simply the size of the resulting reliability coefficient.

Scale Statistics

Mean	Variance	Std. Deviation	N of Items
12.19	10.574	3.252	4

The average of the four-item summated scale. Since each variable is coded on a five-point scale with values ranging from 1 to 5, this statistic is not intuitively meaningful.

Overall, the reliability analysis indicated that the four items in the scale had an acceptable level of internal consistency ($\alpha = .775$). Deleting any of the variables did not improve the Cronbach's alpha. This suggests that these indicators of the resource specificity concept could be combined into a summated rating scale. A Compute command would be used to create the scale (see chapter 12 for more information):

```
Compute resource = mean.2(place1, place2, place3, place4).
```

The "mean.2" in this syntax requires two respondent-provided answers for the person to be included in the scale. A more stringent solution would require responses on three of the survey questions (i.e., mean.3).

Table 18.5 illustrates results from three reliability analyses for concepts (i.e., resource specificity, lifestyle tolerance, activity style) that influence recreational conflict as suggested by Jacob and Schreyer (1980).

Correlation Size and Number of Variables in a Scale

The inter-item Pearson correlation matrix for the variables in the resource specificity scale is shown in Table 18.6.

Table 18.6   Pearson Correlation Matrix for Variables in the Resource Specificity Scale

	PLACE 1	PLACE 2	PLACE 3	PLACE 4
PLACE 1	1.000			
PLACE 2	.452	1.000		
PLACE 3	.511	.328	1.000	
PLACE 4	.519	.534	.461	1.000

Table 18.5 Reliability Analyses of Conflict Concepts

	Item Total Correlation	Alpha If Item Deleted	Cronbach Alpha
Resource Specificity			.78
This area means a lot to me	.62	.70	
Lot of my life is organized around this area	.54	.75	
This area is best for what I like to do	.52	.75	
I identify strongly with this area	.64	.69	
Lifestyle Tolerance			.79
Skiers/Snowboarders have similar:			
Lifestyles	.58	.75	
Education	.65	.73	
Income	.53	.77	
Attitudes toward the environment	.59	.75	
Feelings about the value of the area	.52	.77	
Activity Style			.76
Number of skies/snowboards owned	.63	.65	
Money invested in activity	.57	.72	
Skiing/snowboarding ability	.60	.68	

The average of these 6 correlations in Table 18.6 is:

$$\overline{r_{ij}} = (.452 + .511 + .519 + .328 + .534 + .461) / 6$$

$$\overline{r_{ij}} = .4675$$

and the Standardized Item Alpha (from Equation 18.4) is:

$$r_{SB2} = \frac{4 \cdot (.4675)}{1 + (4 - 1) \cdot (.4675)} = .778$$

As suggest earlier, reliability increases as the number of items in the scale increases. Table 18.7 (p. 526) shows the reliability for the four-item resource specificity scale (.778). If the average correlation among the items remains constant (i.e., .4675), but the number of items increases, the scale's reliability increases to .814 with 5 items, and .898 with 10 items. For 20 items, the reliability increases to .946. Conversely, if the scale has only two items and the same average correlation, the reliability declines to .637. Figure 18.8 (p. 526) graphs this relationship between the number of items in a scale and the reliability coefficient.

Table 18.7   Effects of Increasing the Number of Items on Scale Reliability

Number of Items in Scale	Scale Reliability
2	.637
3	.725
4	.778
5	.814
6	.840
7	.860
8	.875
9	.888
10	.898
11	.906
12	.913
13	.919
14	.925
15	.929
16	.934
17	.937
18	.940
19	.943
20	.946

Table 18.8 illustrates the relationship between the number of items in a scale (2 to 20) and the corresponding standardized item alpha for average Pearson correlations of .2, .4 and .8. Even when the average correlation among the items is only .2, the reliability can be substantial ($\alpha = .833$) if there are 20 items in the scale. When the average correlation is .8, a two-item scale has an α of .889. Figure 18.9 graphs these relationships.

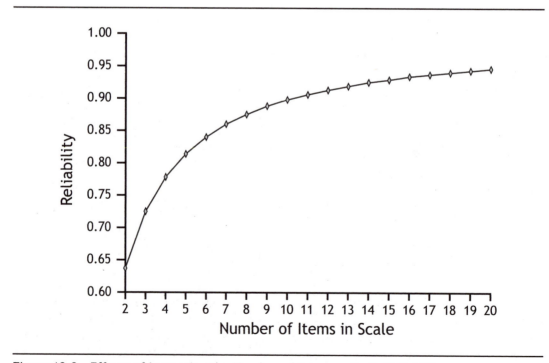

Figure 18.8   Effects of Increasing the Number of Items on Scale Reliability

Table 18.8   Effects of Different Average
Correlations and Number of Items on Scale
Reliability

# of items	Average Correlations [1]		
	.2	.4	.8
2	.333	.571	.889
3	.429	.667	.923
4	.500	.727	.941
5	.556	.769	.952
6	.600	.800	.960
7	.636	.823	.966
8	.667	.842	.969
9	.693	.857	.973
10	.714	.870	.976
11	.733	.880	.978
12	.750	.889	.979
13	.765	.896	.981
14	.778	.903	.983
15	.789	.909	.984
16	.800	.914	.985
17	.809	.919	.986
18	.818	.923	.986
19	.826	.927	.987
20	.833	.930	.988

[1] Cell entries are standardized item alphas

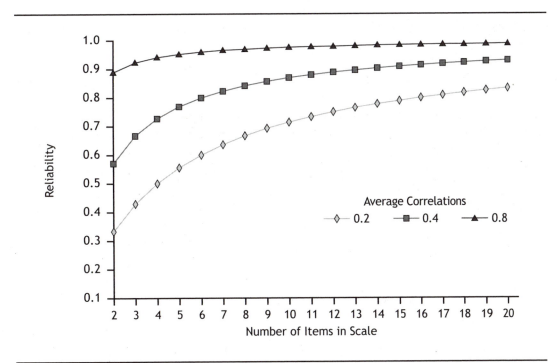

Figure 18.9   Effects of Different Average Correlations and Number of Items on Scale Reliability

Split Halves Reliability

Although internal consistency statistics are commonly used in parks, recreation, and human dimensions research for assessing a summated rating scale's reliability, there are other methods. The *split-halves method*, for example, divides the total set of items into halves and the scores on the halves are correlated to obtain an estimate of reliability. The halves can be considered approximations to alternative forms. Unlike the test-retest and the alternative-form methods for assessing reliability that require two separate administrations with the same group of people, the split-half method can be conducted on one occasion.

The *Spearman-Brown prophecy formula* is a form of the split-halves reliability measure. This measure is briefly reviewed in this section to illustrate the difference between the "prophecy formula" and the Spearman-Brown stepped up reliability coefficient (i.e., the Standardized Item Alpha in SPSS) discussed earlier. The basic Spearman-Brown prophecy formula is:

$$r_{SB1} = \frac{k \cdot r_{ij}}{1 + (k-1) \cdot r_{ij}}$$

Equation 18.5

where:
- r_{SB1} = the Spearman-Brown split-half reliability coefficient
- r_{ij} = the Pearson correlation between form i (1st half) and form j (2nd half)
- k = total sample size divided by sample size per form (k is usually 2)

Alternatively, the Spearman-Brown split-half formula can be expressed as:

$$r_{SB1} = \frac{2 \cdot r_{12}}{1 + r_{12}}$$

Equation 18.6

In SPSS, two Spearman-Brown split-half reliability coefficients will appear in the "Reliability Statistics" portion of the output when split-half is selected under the Model drop down menu: (a) "Equal length" gives the estimate of the reliability if both halves had equal numbers of items, and (b) "Unequal length" gives the reliability estimate assuming unequal numbers.

The SPSS syntax is:

```
RELIABILITY
  /VARIABLES=place1 place2 place3 place4
  /SCALE('Resource Specificity')  ALL/MODEL=SPLIT
  /STATISTICS=DESCRIPTIVE SCALE CORR
  /SUMMARY=TOTAL MEANS VARIANCE CORR .
```

Output 18.5   Split Halves Reliability

Reliability Statistics

Cronbach's Alpha	Part 1	Value	.615
		N of Items	2[a]
	Part 2	Value	.630
		N of Items	2[b]
	Total N of Items		4
Correlation Between Forms			
			.645
Spearman-Brown Coefficient	Equal Length		.784
	Unequal Length		.784
Guttman Split-Half Coefficient			
			.784

a.   The items are PLACE1   This area means a lot to me, PLACE2   A lot of
      my life is organized around this area.

b.   The items are: PLACE3   This area is best for what I liked to do,
      PLACE4   I strongly identify with this area.

Part 1 (the first half) in the output above included the PLACE1 and PLACE2 variables; Part 2 included PLACE3 and PLACE4 (see Table 18.3, p. 519). Although the Spearman-Brown split half coefficient (.784) approximates the Standardized Item Alpha from the earlier analysis (i.e., .778), there is certain indeterminacy in using the split-halves technique to estimate reliability (Charter, 2001). This occurs due to the different ways that the survey items can be grouped into halves. In the example here, the first two items were in the first half (i.e., PLACE1, PLACE2) and the second two items were in the second half (i.e., PLACE3, PLACE4). The variables, however, might also have been grouped by placing the odd-numbered items in one half (PLACE1, PLACE3) and the even-numbered items in the other group (PLACE2, PLACE4). Other ways of partitioning the total number of items include randomly assigning the items into two groups. For ten items, there are 125 different possible splits. Each split will probably result in a slightly different Pearson correlation between the two halves which, in turn, will lead to a different reliability estimate. Since the number of different splits is a function of the number of total items, obtaining a consistent estimate of the reliability changes as the number of items increases. Thus, using the split-halves method, it is quite possible that different reliability estimates will be obtained; even though the same items are administered to the same individuals at the same time.

Chapter Summary

Because parks, recreation, and human dimensions concepts are often not directly observable (e.g., attitudes, beliefs, norms, value orientations), their existence must be inferred from survey responses that serve as indicators of the concepts. This chapter introduced three methods for measuring psychological concepts: (a) summated rating scales (Likert and semantic differential), (b) multiplicative scales, and (c) combined multiplicative and summated scales (e.g., Fishbein & Ajzen's attitude measure).

There are four defining characteristics of a summated rating scale: (a) the scale must contain multiple items (survey questions), (b) each item in the scale must reflect a concept's underlying measurement continuum, (c) there are no "right" answers to the items in a summated scale, and (d) each item in a scale is a statement and respondents rate each statement. A good summated rating scale has good psychometric properties (i.e., reliability, validity, precision).

This chapter highlighted a five-step process for constructing a summated rating scale: (a) define construct, (b) define scale, (c) pilot test the scale, (d) administer the survey and conduct an item analysis, and (e) validate the scale. These steps were illustrated using biocentric and anthropo-centric basic beliefs, and an associated biocentric-anthropocentric value orientation. The five steps are essential for the development of any psychological scale. Unfortunately, many scale developers fall short on the first and last step. These steps are often the most difficult because they require solid conceptual and theoretical thinking.

The second half of the chapter discussed analytical procedures commonly used to test the reliability of summated rating scales. Three internal consistency reliability estimates were presented: (a) Cronbach's alpha, (b) the Spearman-Brown stepped up reliability coefficient, and (c) Kuder-Richardson formula 20 (a.k.a. KR20). The Spearman-Brown prophecy formula was introduced as an example of a split-halves reliability measure. Internal consistency methods can be thought of as "all possible split-halves" and therefore, are the recommended approach for estimating reliability.

An empirical example was presented to demonstrate the calculation and interpretation of Cronbach's alpha using SPSS. The illustration used four indicators of a resource specificity concept from the recreation conflict literature.

The relationship between the number of items in a summated rating scale (2 to 20) and the cor-responding standardized item alpha was examined. As the number of items in a scale increases, alpha increases.

Review Questions

1. Identify three measuring procedures for examining psychological concepts.

2. Describe an example of a semantic differential scale.

3. List four defining characteristics of a summated rating scale.

4. Describe three qualities of a good summated rating scale.

5. Describe the five steps in constructing a summated rating scale.

6. What does the Cronbach's alpha reliability coefficient measure?

7. What is the range of possible values for Cronbach's alpha? What does a Cronbach's alpha of .70 imply?

8. What is the range of possible values for Cronbach's alpha?

9. Discuss the statement "Cronbach's alpha is not a measure of unidimensionality."

10. Describe three situations where a researcher might expect Cronbach's alpha to increase.

11. What is an acceptable size for Cronbach's alpha in parks, recreation, and human dimensions research?

12. What is the relationship between Cronbach's alpha and the Kuder-Richardson formula 20 (KR20)?

13. Briefly describe each of the following statistics:
    - Standardized versus unstandardized item alpha's
    - Corrected item-total correlation
    - Squared multiple correlation
    - Alpha if item deleted

14. If you keep the average correlation between items constant but increase the number of items in the scale, what happens to the reliability coefficient?

19

missing data, response patterns, and outliers[1]

More than a half-century ago, Cochran and Cox (1950) recognized the need for procedures that would reduce bias in statistical estimates (e.g., means, standard deviations) or at least allow the researcher to determine the magnitude of bias in estimates. Reducing bias is an important goal in survey research (i.e., reducing anything that results in systematic error in research findings). That advice is still relevant today. This chapter is concerned with three sources of bias in survey research: (a) missing data, (b) response patterns, and (c) outliers.

Missing Data in Survey Responses

Coping with missing data is a universal data analysis problem. The problem occurs because: (a) some respondents are reluctant to answer some questions (e.g., income), (b) others misread instructions and therefore, do not answer questions that were intended for them, (c) they simply fail to answer some questions, or (d) respondent fatigue (i.e., respondents not answering questions or answering them falsely because completing the survey is overly tiring). Missing data can also arise from data entry errors.

The seriousness of the problem depends on how much data are missing and why the data are missing. If only a few data points are missing from a large data set, the problems are usually not serious and almost any procedure for handling them will yield similar results. Alternatively, if there is considerable missing data in a small- to medium-sized data set, the problem can be serious. Unfortunately, there are no firm guidelines for determining how much is too much missing data for a sample of a given size.

The amount of missing data is less important than the ***pattern of missing data***. When the missing responses are scattered in a ***random pattern*** throughout the data, the problem is typically not serious. When the missing data are nonrandom, the issue is serious no matter how small the number of missing. For example, consider a survey that contains both attitudinal and socio-demographic variables. Refusal to answer an income question (i.e., a demographic variable) may be related to the respondent's attitude. If respondents with missing data on income are

---

[1] This chapter was coauthored with Dr. Lori B. Shelby, George Mason University.

deleted, the sample is potentially biased. To overcome this type of problem, some method of estimating missing data is often desirable.

This section outlines seven techniques or solutions for dealing with missing data in survey research: (a) delete respondent (i.e., listwise deletion in SPSS), (b) delete items, (c) sample means, (d) group means, (e) random assignment within groups, (f) pair-wise *r*, and (g) regression analysis. The amount of missing data in a random pattern is illustrated with a data set from the Lake Mead National Recreation Area (A. Graefe, personal communication, 1998). The pattern of missing data is illustrated using a hypothetical data set examining the relationship between respondents' sex and their beliefs about sexual harassment.

Random Patterns of Missing Data

Delete Respondent Solution

The ***delete respondent solution*** involves deleting any individual for whom values are missing on any of the variables of interest to a given analysis. In SPSS terminology, this solution is referred to as ***listwise deletion*** or ***delete cases***. When the sample size is large, listwise deletion is often the recommended approach (Little & Rubin, 2002; Schafer & Graham, 2002). When the sample is small, deleting respondents (i.e., cases) may be too strict. Consider the hypothetical data matrix in Table 19.1 containing five respondents and four belief statements. A value of 9 has been defined in SPSS by the researcher as missing (chapter 10). If listwise deletion is used in a reliability analysis or a summated index of these four items, all of the respondents would be deleted. In SPSS, a period is automatically used to signify a missing value when the researcher did not declare a specific value. Respondent #1 would not be included because the individual did not answer the BELIEF4 variable. Individual #2 would not be included with listwise deletion because the person did not give a valid response to BELIEF3. Similar scenarios are displayed for respondents 3, 4, and 5. With these hypothetical data then, all of the respondents would be eliminated from the analysis because each individual had failed to answer at least one question of interest. As the number of deleted cases increases, the less tenable the assumption that the available data constitute a random sample of the full sample (i.e., that the missing data are random).

Table 19.1   Data Matrix Containing Missing Data (Listwise Deletion)

ID #	BELIEF1	BELIEF2	BELIEF3	BELIEF4	Summated Index[1]	Reason case was deleted:
1	7	3	1	9	.	BELIEF4 is missing
2	5	4	9	1	.	BELIEF3 is missing
3	9	6	2	3	.	BELIEF1 is missing
4	9	1	1	1	.	BELIEF1 is missing
5	3	9	9	4	.	BELIEF2 & BELIEF3 are missing

[1] A period is used in SPSS to signify a system missing value.

Alternatively, the SPSS `compute` command (chapter 12) allows the researcher to specify how many valid responses a given individual must provide to be included in a summated rating index (chapter 18). In this example, if the analyst believed that three valid respondent provided answers were sufficient for computing a belief index, the SPSS command would be:[2]

```
compute belief_index = mean.3(belief1, belief2, belief3, belief4).
```

Four of the five respondents in Table 19.1 meet this requirement and would be included in the summated rating index. Not all SPSS procedures, however, allow the researcher to specify the criteria for including (or excluding) respondents. Reliability analysis, for example, always performs a listwise deletion. For the data in Table 19.1, a reliability analysis could not be performed on these four belief statements because all of the respondents would be deleted.

What constitutes a "small" versus a "large" number of cases to be deleted is open to debate. In estimating parameters for samples with varying degrees of completeness, some researchers suggest that the parameter estimates do not differ significantly once the completion level reaches 85% (Hertel, 1976; Sharp & Feldt, 1959). Use of the listwise deletion approach is appropriate for samples that have complete data on 85% or more of the cases, although the solution is not as reliable as other alternatives.

Delete Items Solution

Rather than deleting all of the responses from a given individual, sometimes random pattern missing data problems can be solved by removing specific items (i.e., variables) from the analysis. Data from Lake Mead National Recreation Area (NRA) illustrate this solution (A. Graefe, personal communication, 1998). The Lake Mead project included an on-site interview ($n = 3,347$) that asked boaters to indicate the extent to which they felt crowded at different locations during their visit to the NRA. The five specific areas were: (a) at the launch ramp/marina at the start of your trip, (b) out on the lake while boating, (c) along the shoreline areas that you used, (d) at the launch ramp/marina when you stopped boating, and (e) at the boat pumpout facilities. The actual question wording is shown in Box 19.1 with the variable names in parentheses.

Box 19.1 Survey Wording and Variable Names for Crowding Questions in the Lake Mead National Recreation Area Boating Study (A. Graefe, personal communication)

1. Using the following scale, how would you describe the boating conditions at each of the following areas during your visit to Lake Mead National Recreation Area?

1	2	3	4	5	6	7	8	9
Not at all Crowded		Slightly Crowded			Moderately Crowded		Extremely Crowded	

_____ At the launch ramp/marina at the start of your trip	(Crwdstrt)
_____ Out on the lake while boating	(Crwdlake)
_____ Along the shoreline areas that you used	(Crwdshor)
_____ At the launch ramp/marina when you stopped boating	(Crwdstop)
_____ At the boat pumpout facilities	(Crwdpump)

---

[2]   The name given to the computed variable in this example is "BELIEF_INDEX" is 12 characters long. Variable names of this length can be used with versions 12 through 16 of SPSS. Variable names in earlier versions of SPSS are constrained to 8 characters.

The amount of missing data associated with these five variables is shown in Table 19.2. For the first three variables (i.e., start of trip, on the lake, along the shorelines), between 17% and 24% of the respondents did not answer the questions. Approximately half (49%) of the respondents did not answer the crowding question related to the end of the trip, and 84% did not respond to the variable about crowding at the boat pumpout facilities. Pumpout facilities are locations where boaters can empty human waste holding tanks. The large amount of missing data for such facilities might be expected in this situation. Some, not all, of the houseboats on Lake Mead have holding tanks for human waste. If the boat does not have a holding tank, there is no reason for the visitor to use one of these facilities and thus, the question does not apply to the respondent. For houseboats with holding tanks, if the visitor's trip duration was short (e.g., a weekend), the respondent may not have needed to empty the tank. Although such explanations are logical, a strategy for dealing with the missing data must be addressed.

Table 19.2   Missing Data in the Lake Mead NRA Crowding Variables

	Perceived Crowding				
	at launch ramp at start of trip	on the lake while boating	along shoreline areas	at launch ramp at end of trip	at boat pumpout facilities
Sample *ns*					
Valid	2,792	2,672	2,556	1,706	539
Missing	595	675	791	1,641	2,808
Sample %					
Valid	83	80	76	51	16
Missing	17	20	24	49	84

Given the five location-specific crowding variables, a general measure of overall crowding could be computed by creating a summated rating index (chapter 18). Prior to computing such an index, the reliability of the variables comprising the scale should be examined. Table 19.3 contains three reliability analyses that illustrate the consequences of missing data. In general, all three analyses resulted in an acceptable Cronbach's alpha (i.e., .90, .86, .82). Deleting any of the items from a given analysis did not improve the Cronbach alpha. As noted in chapter 18, reducing the number of items in a computed index, reduces the Cronbach's alpha. The primary difference between the three analyses is the amount of missing data. Analysis 1 included only 15% of the sample. Most of this loss of sample can be attributed to missing data on the "pumpout facilities" question. Dropping the "pumpout facilities" variable (Analysis 2) increased the sample size to 1,548 (46% of the sample). Analysis 3 eliminated the crowding at the "end of the trip" where 49% of the data were missing.

The three reliability analyses raise conceptual questions concerning which variables should be used in a summated crowding index. The fact that a majority of boaters may not have used the pumpout facilities, and that Analysis 1 included only 15% (*n* = 486) of the sample, suggests that this variable could be dropped from analysis. Although Analysis 3 retained 70% of the data, a recreation experience includes beginning, middle, and ending aspects (Clawson & Knetsch, 1966; Crompton, 1979). Dropping crowding at "end of the trip" eliminates this conceptual component, and thus the variable might be kept in the index for validity reasons.

Table 19.3   Reliability Analyses for an Overall Crowding Index

	Items in Scale Crowding at:	Number of Items	Alpha if Item Deleted	Cronbach's Alpha	Sample Size	% of Sample
Analysis 1		5		.90	486	15
	Start of trip		.89			
	On the lake		.88			
	Along shoreline		.89			
	End of trip		.87			
	Pumpout facilities		.89			
Analysis 2		4		.86	1,548	46
	Start of trip		.84			
	On the lake		.80			
	Along shoreline		.83			
	End of trip		.84			
Analysis 3		3		.82	2,355	70
	Start of trip		.82			
	On the lake		.67			
	Along shoreline		.77			

When a summated index is computed, the researcher can specify the number of questions a respondent must answer:

```
compute crowding_index1 = mean.3(Crwdstrt, Crwdlake, Crwdshor, Crwdstop).
     versus
compute crowding_index2 = mean.4(Crwdstrt, Crwdlake, Crwdshor, Crwdstop).
```

Table 19.4 illustrates the consequences of conceptualizing the crowding index using different `compute` commands. Both `crowding_index1` and `crowding_index2` include the responses from four variables (i.e., start of trip, on the lake, along the shorelines, end of trip). The two indices differ in the number of valid answers the respondent must provide (i.e., 3 vs. 4). The means, medians, modes, and standard deviations for these two indices are similar, but CROWDING_INDEX1 has 842 missing cases, whereas CROWDING_INDEX2 has 1,799 missing cases (i.e., twice as much missing). Similar to CROWDING_INDEX2, CROWDING_INDEX3 requires four valid responses,

Table 19.4   Comparison of Three Indices Measuring Perceived Crowding

	Crowding Index [1]		
Summary Statistics	CROWDING_INDEX1	CROWDING_INDEX2	CROWDING_INDEX3
Valid *n*	2,504	1,548	1,595
Missing *n*	842	1,799	1,752
Mean	2.73	2.65	2.62
Median	2.00	2.00	2.00
Mode	1.00	1.00	1.00
Standard Deviation	1.87	1.85	1.82

[1].
```
    crowding_index1 = mean.3(Crwdstrt, Crwdlake, Crwdshor, Crwdstop).
    crowding_index2 = mean.4(Crwdstrt, Crwdlake, Crwdshor, Crwdstop).
    crowding_index3 = mean.4(Crwdstrt, Crwdlake, Crwdshor, Crwdstop, Crwdpump).
```

but uses all five measures of crowding. The amount of missing on CROWDING_INDEX2 and CROWDING_INDEX3 are 1,799 and 1,752, respectively. Given the findings in Tables 19.2 through 19.4, CROWDING_INDEX1 is probably the most defensible from a reliability, validity, and missing data perspective.

Sample Means Solution

The sample means solution involves substituting the mean for available data as an estimate of the missing values (Raaijmakers, 1999). The approach assumes that the missing data are random, and therefore, the mean of the available data is an unbiased estimate of the mean for the total sample. Although this solution does not alter the mean for the sample, it does reduce the variance of the sample.

Sample Means Solution: Hypothetical Empirical Example

To illustrate the sample means approach, a hypothetical dataset was constructed to examine beliefs about sexual harassment in the workplace among women and men. The data set included 300 men and 300 women (total $n = 600$). Six belief variables were simulated (Box 19.2). Each of the belief statements was coded on a five-point scale: strongly disagree (-2), disagree (-1), neutral (0), agree (1), and strongly agree (2). A value of 9 was assigned as the missing value for the belief statements.

Box 19.2   Hypothetical Study Examining Relationship between Respondents' Sex and Beliefs about Sexual Harassment

Variable Name	Question
SEX	Sex of respondent
REMARKS	Sexist remarks are heard in my workplace
INNOCENT	Some people mistake innocent remarks for sexual harassment
CAREER1	A *woman* reporting sexual harassment may experience negative effects on her career
CAREER2	A *man* reporting sexual harassment may experience negative effects on his career
INTENTIONAL	An act is sexist if the behavior is intentional
REPORTED	Sexual harassment is reported more often than it actually occurs in my workplace

---

The number of missing values on the six belief statements ranged from 17 (REMARKS) to 22 (CAREER2 and REPORTED) or was less than 4% for any variable.

Output 19.1   Valid and Missing Cases for Six Belief Statements

Statistics

		remarks	innocent	career1	career2	intentional	reported
N	Valid	583	582	580	578	581	578
	Missing	17	18	20	22	19	22

In SPSS, the Sample Means Solution can be computed from the menu system (Figure 19.1). On the main menu, click **Transform > Replace Missing Values**. Among the available choices in the Method drop down is "Series mean."

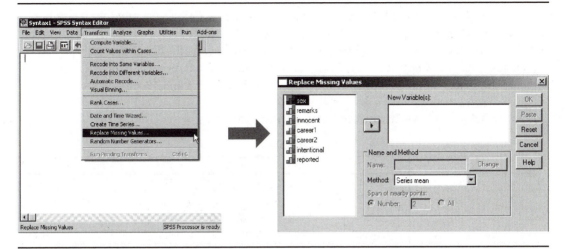

Figure 19.1   Sample Means Solution in SPSS

The syntax for this example is:

```
RMV
  /remarks_1      = SMEAN(remarks)
  /innocent_1     = SMEAN(innocent)
  /career1_1      = SMEAN(career1)
  /career2_1      = SMEAN(career2)
  /intentional_1  = SMEAN(intentional)
  /reported_1     = SMEAN(reported).
```

where:

    RMV = Replace Missing Values
    SMEAN = Series mean

The syntax generates six new variables. SPSS uses the original variable names followed by "_1" (e.g., REMARKS_1). The output shows the number of replaced missing values and 600 valid cases for the six computed variables (Output 19.2).

Output 19.2   Replace Missing Values with Series Mean for Six Belief Statements

Result Variables

	Result Variable	N of Replaced Missing Values	Case Number of Nonmissing Values First	Case Number of Nonmissing Values Last	N of Valid Cases	Creating Function
1	remarks_1	17	1	600	600	SMEAN(remarks)
2	innocent_1	18	1	600	600	SMEAN(innocent)
3	career1_1	20	1	600	600	SMEAN(career1)
4	career2_1	22	1	600	600	SMEAN(career2)
5	intentional_1	19	1	600	600	SMEAN(intentional)
6	reported_1	22	1	600	600	SMEAN(reported)

FREQUENCIES analyses of the six original variables and the six SPSS generated variables high-light: (a) the number of missing values on the computed variables is zero for each of the belief statements, (b) the means for original variables equal the means for the new variables, and (c) replacing the missing values in the original variables with the respective means reduced the standard deviations in the computed variables (see Outputs 19.3 and 19.4).

Output 19.3   Descriptive Statistics for the Original Variables

Statistics

		remarks	innocent	career1	career2	intentional	reported
N	Valid	583	582	580	578	581	578
	Missing	17	18	20	22	19	22
Mean		.1544	.2199	.3862	−.6142	.8709	.9810
Std. Deviation		1.14582	.93493	1.01924	1.02564	.85230	.79075

Output 19.4   Descriptive Statistics for the Computed Variables

Statistics

		remarks_1	innocent_1	career1_1	career2_1	intentional_1	reported_1
N	Valid	600	600	600	600	600	600
	Missing	0	0	0	0	0	0
Mean		.1544	.2199	.3862	−.6142	.8709	.9810
Std. Deviation		1.12944	.92078	1.00208	1.00663	.83867	.77609

The correlations among the original six items were somewhat larger than the correlations among the computed variables. For this data set of 600 respondents, however, the number of missing values was less than 4% on any of the belief statements. As demonstrated later in this chapter, the problem with these hypothetical data is not the amount of missing, but rather the pattern of missing.

Group Means Solution

The group means solution is obtained by the following steps: (a) sort the sample into one or more strata (i.e., groups), and (b) use the means for available data within those strata as estimates of the missing scores. The variables that are used to define the strata should be conceptually related to the variables containing missing data. In the hypothetical example introduced above, SEX (males vs. females) was used to define the strata because SEX is likely to be related to a respondent's beliefs about sexual harassment. By using SEX to identify the strata, relatively homogeneous groups can be identified with respect to the data containing missing values. This homogeneity minimizes errors in using group means to estimate missing values within each group (i.e., males and females).

In SPSS, there is a variety of ways to accomplish this task. One approach is to "split" the file into the desired strata. In this example, the stratum was based on the variable SEX (Figure 19.2).

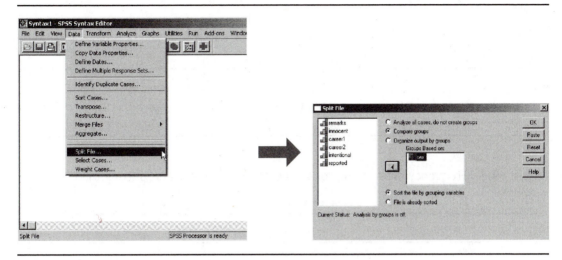

Figure 19.2   Splitting an SPSS Data File into Two or More Strata

Running this procedure, yields the following syntax:

```
SORT CASES BY sex .
SPLIT FILE
  LAYERED BY sex .
```

A FREQUENCIES analysis of the six belief statements displays one set of summary statistics and distributions for males and one set for females (Output 19.5, p. 540). Output 19.6 (p. 540) illustrates one of the frequency distributions for the split sample. The logic of splitting the sample by SEX (males vs. females) is conceptually similar to a ***control*** variable discussed in chapter 13 (Crosstabulations).

Of the 17 individuals who did not answer the REMARKS variable (Output 19.1), 11 respondents were male and six were female. Similar missing data differences were found for the remaining five belief statements. Independent samples *t*-tests (not shown) indicated that the mean scores reported by men were statistically different from those given by women on 5 of the 6 belief statements. The exception occurred for the variable INNOCENT, where both samples were slightly above the neutral response (Output 19.5). The *t*-tests generally supported the assumption noted earlier that the variables used to define the strata should be related to the variables containing missing data.

Output 19.5 Descriptive Statistics for the Original Variables Segmented by Strata

Statistics

sex Sex			remarks	innocent	career1	career2	intentional	reported
0 Males	N	Valid	289	289	288	286	289	288
		Missing	11	11	12	14	11	12
	Mean		.0450	.2249	.0000	−.4231	.9896	1.0556
	Std. Deviation		.97968	.85061	.90296	.98374	.73354	.72080
1 Females	N	Valid	294	293	292	292	292	290
		Missing	6	7	8	8	8	10
	Mean		.2619	.2150	.7671	−.8014	.7534	.9069
	Std. Deviation		1.28104	1.01268	.98470	1.03293	.94204	.84936

Output 19.6 Frequency Distribution for the Remarks Variable after Splitting the File

remarks Sexist remarks are heard at my workplace

sex Sex				Frequency	Percent	Valid Percent	Cumulative Percent
0 Males	Valid	−2.00	Strongly disagree	8	2.7	2.8	2.8
		−1.00	Disagree	96	32.0	33.2	36.0
		.00	Neutral	72	24.0	24.9	60.9
		1.00	Agree	101	33.7	34.9	95.8
		2.00	Strongly agree	12	4.0	4.2	100.0
		Total		289	96.3	100.0	
	Missing	9.00	Missing	11	3.7		
	Total			300	100.0		
1 Females	Valid	−2.00	Strongly disagree	35	11.7	11.9	11.9
		−1.00	Disagree	58	19.3	19.7	31.6
		.00	Neutral	45	15.0	15.3	46.9
		1.00	Agree	107	35.7	36.4	83.3
		2.00	Strongly agree	49	16.3	16.7	100.0
		Total		294	98.0	100.0	
	Missing	9.00	Missing	6	2.0		
	Total			300	100.0		

With the Split File in effect, running the REPLACE MISSING VALUES commands (Figure 19.1) produces Output 19.7. The first 300 cases in the sorted data file were men, the next 300 respondents were female. For both sexes, SPSS generated the same variable names (e.g., REMARK_1, INNOCENT_1). In this example, however, the means for the six variables were based on the average scores for men and the average scores for women. Comparing the FREQUENCIES analysis Output 19.5 against the comparable analysis for the new SPSS generated variables (Output 19.8) shows that: (a) all of the missing values have been replaced with the group means for males or females, and (b) the averages (see mean results) remain the same for the beliefs in the two outputs, but the variances (see standard deviation results) now differ. Across all six belief statements, the females showed more variability in their responses when compared to the males.

Output 19.7   Replace Missing Values with Series Mean for Six Belief Statements Controlling for Sex

Result Variables

sex Sex		Result Variable	N of Replaced Missing Values	Case Number of Nonmissing Values		N of Valid Cases	Creating Function
				First	Last		
0 Males	1	remarks_1	11	1	300	300	SMEAN(remarks)
	2	innocent_1	11	1	300	300	SMEAN(innocent)
	3	career1_1	12	1	300	300	SMEAN(career1)
	4	career2_1	14	1	300	300	SMEAN(career2)
	5	intentional_1	11	1	300	300	SMEAN(intentional)
	6	reported_1	12	1	300	300	SMEAN(reported)
1 Females	1	remarks_1	6	301	600	300	SMEAN(remarks)
	2	innocent_1	7	301	600	300	SMEAN(innocent)
	3	career1_1	8	301	600	300	SMEAN(career1)
	4	career2_1	8	301	600	300	SMEAN(career2)
	5	intentional_1	8	301	600	300	SMEAN(intentional)
	6	reported_1	10	301	600	300	SMEAN(reported)

Output 19.8   Descriptive Statistics for the Computed Variables Controlling for Sex

Statistics

sex Sex			remarks_1	innocent_1	career1_1	career2_1	intentional_1	reported_1
0 Males	N	Valid	300	300	300	300	300	300
		Missing	0	0	0	0	0	0
	Mean		.0450	.2249	.0000	−.4231	.9896	1.0556
	Std. Deviation		.96149	.83482	.88465	.96043	.71992	.70619
1 Females	N	Valid	300	300	300	300	300	300
		Missing	0	0	0	0	0	0
	Mean		.2619	.2150	.7671	−.8014	.7534	.9069
	Std. Deviation		1.26812	1.00076	.97144	1.01902	.92936	.83503

Overall, the group means solution recognizes that there is variance in the sample (e.g., between males and females in this example), and therefore is superior to the sample means solution. Unfortunately, the group means solution may be less appropriate because it exaggerates homogeneity within groups that can overestimate measures of association such as the Pearson r. The solution also requires that researchers have a thorough understanding of which variables should be used to create the group means.

Random Assignment within Groups Solution

If the missing values within the data set are randomly distributed, the researcher can randomly assign values to the variables with missing data such that a complete data set is constructed. The variance that results is an unbiased estimate of the Pearson r (Chen & Shao, 2000). This procedure is called the ***random assignment within groups*** solution. The mechanics for this approach basically parallel those for the group means solution. The difference is that the researcher systematically moves through the data set and replaces any missing value with the mean or median of a selected number of cases above or below the missing value. In SPSS, this can be accomplished by selecting "Mean of nearby points" or "Median of nearby points" from the Method dropdown menu (Figure 19.1). The software allows for specification of a range of points to be included in this selection process (Figure 19.3). For example, if 3 points are chosen, then the mean of the 3 points above in addition to 3 points below the missing value will be computed to replace the missing value.

When the random assignment within groups solution is used, the expected values of the variance are unbiased (Hertel, 1976; Chen & Shao, 2000). Consequently, the expected value of the correlation coefficients is the same as for the full sample.

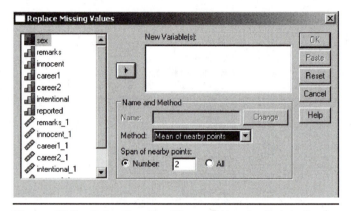

Figure 19.3   Selecting the Mean of Nearby Points from the Replace Missing Values Dialog Box

The Pairwise Correlation Coefficient Solution

With the ***pairwise solution for missing data***, the original dataset is replaced by a correlation matrix for all of the variables being analyzed. The correlation matrix can then be used as input for analyes such as regression analysis, factor analysis, path analysis, or other multivariate techniques. The pairwise solution for missing data deletes only those cases where one or both of the data points for a respondent are missing for a pair of variables. Table 19.5 shows a hypothetical dataset. If pairwise deletion was used to analyze variable X and variable Y respondents 2, 6, and 8 would be deleted from analysis since both data points are missing for these respondents. On the other hand, listwise deletion would result in respondents 2, 3, 4, 6, 8, 9, and 10 being excluded from analysis since all responses for a respondent are deleted if any data point is missing.

The pairwise approach assumes that the data are missing randomly (i.e., the available pairs are a random subset of the pairs of scores for the entire sample). If this assumption is valid, the pairwise *r* solution yields unbiased estimates of sample

Table 19.5   Data Matrix Containing Missing Data

Respondent	VARIABLE X	VARIABLE Y
1	1	8
2	.	9
3	3	.
4	4	9
5	7	2
6	9	.
7	6	7
8	.	.
9	2	.
10	5	9

[1.] A period is used in SPSS to signify a system missing value. A value of 9 is a user-defined missing value.

means and variances and of correlation coefficients for which some scores are missing (Hertel, 1976).

The pairwise solution in SPSS can be accomplished by running bivariate correlations and selecting "Exclude cases pairwise" from the Options dialog box (Figure 19.4).

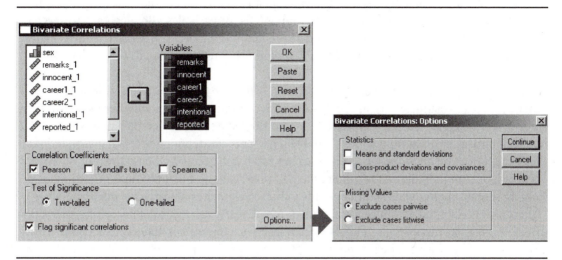

Figure 19.4   The Pairwise Solution to Missing Data in SPSS

There are some problems, however, with this approach. First, the researcher must discard some available data for those records for which a survey response is available for one of the two variables, but not the other. Discarding data may increase existing biases, and reduce efficiency and reliability since the standard error is inversely related to sample size. Second, the lack of a uniform number of cases across the correlation coefficients poses difficulties when assessing the statistical significance of multiple correlation and regression coefficients. If significance tests for multiple correlation coefficients are run using N for the full sample, the level of significance may be exaggerated. Alternatively, the average number of cases available for the correlations can be used as N. If a conservative solution is preferred, the smallest number of cases present in any of the relevant correlations can be used as N, although such caution is ordinarily not necessary.

As long as the missing values were random prior to implementing the pairwise solution, the solution yields an unbiased estimate of variance and of Pearson's r. The variance of the Pearson r is based on a reduced number of cases (i.e., the number of respondents for which data are available for both X and Y). That number, however, is the number of cases on which all components of s_x^2 and s_y^2, and r are based. Consequently, the weaknesses the sample and the group mean solutions have involving biasing the variance and Pearson's r are avoided by the pairwise solution. Overall, although the pairwise solution is preferable to some of the other solutions (e.g., sample means, group means), it does discard available data and therefore is less reliable than the random assignment within groups solution or the regression analysis procedure. In addition, it has limited applications, (e.g., a correlation matrix cannot be used to conduct ANOVA analyses or *t*-tests).

Regression Analysis Solution

This procedure uses regression analysis (chapter 16) for all available scores to estimate missing values. This approach is the most sophisticated of the missing value solutions discussed in this chapter. The following steps are used in the ***regression analysis solution*** to missing data. First, the pairwise r solution is used to obtain a correlation coefficient matrix for all possible pairs of variables. Second, the correlation matrix is then used to produce regression coefficients with all but one variable being regressed on the variable for which missing scores are to be assigned. The researcher systematically proceeds through the list of variables allowing each to serve as the dependent variable with all others used as predictor variables. The approach mirrors the process of computing the squared multiple correlations in reliability analysis (chapter 18).

An advantage of the regression analysis approach is that the procedure uses information on all other variables to estimate missing scores for each missing data variable. There are, however, some disadvantages. First, the regression analysis procedure is based on pairwise rs that were obtained only after discarding some available data. This shortcoming is less consequential in this context because all of the remaining data are taken into account when estimating scores for each variable through regression, unlike the pairwise r solution that provides no estimates of missing scores. Second, this solution yields unbiased estimates of variance and association (Pearson's r) only if all variables are assumed to be linearly related. In other words, interaction effects among the variables used to estimate missing scores are not taken into account. The assumption of linearity can be avoided, however, if all predictor variables are dichotomous and dummy variable regression (chapter 16) is used to estimate missing scores.

*   *   *

Overall, this section has examined seven approaches to handling missing data. Each of these approaches assumes that the *missing values are randomly distributed throughout the data*, and each has advantages and disadvantages. The effects on N for calculating the Pearson r and the effect on r are summarized in Table 19.6. The delete cases and delete items solutions involve straightforward computations in SPSS, but do reduce the available sample size. This is often an acceptable and recommended solution for large data sets. As illustrated by the Lake Mead National Recreation Area example, however, the researcher must consider missing data, reliability, and validity issues when computing summated rating scales. The sample means solution can result in correlation coefficients that are conservative (i.e., smaller), whereas the group means solution tends to inflate estimates of r. The pairwise r can produce unbiased estimates of sample means and variances and of correlation coefficients. The expected r in the regression analysis solution is unbiased, but the approach assumes linearity among the variables. The random assignment within-groups method produces a correlation that equals the r for the full sample, and more reliable estimates can only be obtained by determining the actual values for the missing responses.

Table 19.6   Missing Data Routines and Their Effects on Sample Size and Pearson *r*

Solution	Effect on *N* for calculating *r*	Effect on *r* *
1. Delete cases	Reduces *N* for missing data variables and for other variables.	Estimates of *r* are based on less data than for any other solution and are thus less reliable.
2. Delete items	Reduces *N* to 0 for selected missing data items; use when missing scores are concentrated in a few items.	No *r* can be calculated.
3. Sample means	All available data are included in analysis.	Estimates of *r* are conservative.
4. Group means	All available data are included in analysis.	Estimates of *r* are inflated.
5. Random assignment within groups	All available data are included in analysis.	Expected value of *r* is the *r* for the full sample; more reliable estimates can be obtained only by determining the actual values for missing scores.
6. Pairwise *r*	Slight reduction of available data within each pair of variables.	Expected value of *r* is the *r* for the full sample but such estimates are slightly less reliable than for solutions 5 and 7.
7. Regression analysis	All available data are included in analysis.	Expected *r* is unbiased but requires the assumption of linearity.

* Summary of consequences assumes missing values are randomly distributed. Adapted from Hertel (1976)

Nonrandom Patterns of Missing Data

As noted in the introduction to this chapter, the amount of missing data is less important than the ***pattern of missing data***. If the missing data are nonrandom, the issue is serious no matter how small the number of missing values. To illustrate, consider the hypothetical sexual harassment data set. A researcher might be interested in computing a summated rating scale (chapter 18) representing respondents' general views on sexual harassment (i.e., a latent construct) using the six belief statements. Computing such an index would involve a series of preliminary steps. First, a FREQUENCIES would be run to insure that all missing values had been accounted for and that the values on each of the variables were within the anticipated range (i.e., –2 to +2). Second, a reliability analysis would be performed to verify that: (a) all of the items were positively correlated with each other (i.e., an assumption of reliability analysis), (b) the combination of items produced an acceptable Cronbach's alpha (e.g., $\alpha > .65$), and (c) deleting any of the items from the index did not improve the overall reliability estimate.

Sometimes in a rush to get an answer, researchers mistakenly skip some data manipulation steps. Assume for the moment, that the analyst failed to check that the missing values (i.e., 9) on the six belief statements were declared as missing (step 1) and ran the reliability analysis.

The syntax and output (Output 19.9) for this analysis are:

```
RELIABILITY
  /VARIABLES=remarks innocent career1 career2 intentional reported
  /SCALE('Sexual harassment')  ALL
  /MODEL=ALPHA
  /STATISTICS=DESCRIPTIVE SCALE CORR
  /SUMMARY=TOTAL .
```

Output 19.9 Reliability Analysis of the Six Sexual Harassment Belief Statements (9s not declared as missing)

Case Processing Summary

		N	%
Cases	Valid	600	100.0
	Excluded[a]	0	0
	Total	600	100.0

The analysis is based on all 600 individuals in the sample (i.e., the values of 9 have not been declared as missing).

a. Listwise deletion based on all variables in the procedure.

All of the inter-item correlations are positive and of "substantial" magnitude (chapter 6).

Inter-Item Correlation Matrix

	remarks	innocent	career1	career2	intentional	reported
remarks	1.000					
innocent	.633	1.000				
career1	.709	.643	1.000			
career2	.573	.686	.525	1.000		
intentional	.561	.661	.582	.565	1.000	
reported	.545	.636	.527	.539	.793	1.000

Reliability Statistics

Cronbach's Alpha	Cronbach's Alpha Based on Standardized Items	N of items
.902	.904	6

The overall Cronbach's alpha (.90) is acceptable (i.e., ≥ .65).

Item-Total Statistics

	Scale Mean if Item Deleted	Scale variance if Item Deleted	Corrected Item-Total Correlation	Squared Multiple Correlation	Cronbach's Alpha if Item Deleted
remarks	3.2983	56.143	.728	.581	.885
innocent	3.2200	55.768	.797	.643	.875
career1	3.0300	56.537	.716	.580	.887
career2	3.9650	54.468	.689	.516	.893
intentional	2.5750	57.928	.760	.685	.881
reported	2.4283	58.172	.725	.656	.886

All of the "Corrected Item-Total Correlations" exceed .40 and thus, are acceptable (chapter 18). Deleting any of items does not improve the overall reliability.

Although such results are encouraging and suggest that a summated rating scale can be constructed, none of the missing value responses have been deleted. Rerunning the syntax after declaring the 9s as missing produces Output 19.10.

Output 19.10   Reliability Analysis of the Six Sexual Harassment Belief Statements (9s declared as missing)

Case Processing Summary

		N	%
Cases	Valid	567	94.5
	Excluded[a]	33	5.5
	Total	600	100.0

a.   Listwise deletion based on all variables in the procedure.

> With the 9s declared as missing, 33 respondents were not included in the analysis (valid *n* = 567). A respectable sample size for many survey research projects.

> Unfortunately, many of the inter-item correlations are not positively related to each other, suggesting the need to recode one or more of the belief statements.[3]

Inter-Item Correlation Matrix

	remarks	innocent	career1	career2	intentional	reported
remarks	1.000					
innocent	.045	1.000				
career1	.388	.000	1.000			
career2	−.114	.256	−.199	1.000		
intentional	−.142	.073	−.164	−.066	1.000	
reported	−.119	.099	−.129	−.052	.788	1.000

Reliability Statistics

Cronbach's Alpha	Cronbach's Alpha Based on Standardized Items	N of items
.173	.217	6

> Given the negative correlations, the resulting Cronbach α = .17 (an undesireable result).

Item-Total Statistics

	Scale Mean if Item Deleted	Scale variance if Item Deleted	Corrected Item-Total Correlation	Squared Multiple Correlation	Cronbach's Alpha if Item Deleted
remarks	1.8571	5.048	.047	.163	.175
innocent	1.7848	4.858	.206	.088	.024
career1	1.6120	5.563	−.002	.191	.215
career2	2.6138	5.927	−.078	.123	.283
intentional	1.1323	5.369	.128	.628	.104
reported	1.0265	5.263	.192	.623	.059

> None of the Corrected Item-Total Correlations are acceptable (i.e., > .40, chapter 18). Deleting any of the items does not improve the overall Cronbach's alpha to an acceptable level.

---

[3] Subsequent analysis recoded the variables, but unfortunately, the end result was still negative correlations.

The results from the first reliability analysis (Output 19.9) show an overall Cronbach α of .90 and suggest that the analyst is justified in computing a summated rating scale for the sexual harassment index. Output 19.10 yields an exact opposite conclusion (Cronbach α = .17). The only procedural difference between these two set of results was the listwise deletion of 33 individuals who did not respond to the belief statements. The substantive difference can be attributed to nonrandom patterns in the missing data.

Testing for Patterns in Missing Data

The missing data solutions presented in Table 19.6 (p. 547) assume the missing values are distributed randomly (i.e., there is no pattern). Rather than making this assumption, the safest procedure is to test for patterns in missing data. This can be accomplished in SPSS by constructing a variable with two groups, missing and nonmissing values, for the variables REMARKS through REPORTED.

The syntax for creating the dichotomous variable and running a `Frequencies` is:

```
Missing values remarks innocent career1 career2 intentional reported
().

* Creates new dummy variable (missing vs no missing)

compute missing_nomissing = 0.
formats missing_nomissing (F1.0)

if (remarks      = 9 or
    innocent     = 9 or
    career1      = 9 or
    career2      = 9 or
    intentional  = 9 or
    reported     = 9) missing_nomissing = 1.

value labels missing_nomissing
    0 'No Missing'
    1 'Yes missing'.

Frequencies variables = missing_nomissing.
```

The result (Output 19.11) confirms the reliability analysis showing a total of 33 missing values.

Output 19.11   Frequencies Analysis for the Missing_Nomissing Variable

missing_nonmissing

		Frequency	Percent	Valid Percent	Cumulative Percent
Valid	0 No missing	567	94.5	94.5	94.5
	1 Yes missing	33	5.5	5.5	100.0
	Total	600	100.0	100.0	

Selecting for "Yes missing" (coded 1) on the MISSING_NOMISSING variable and using the List variables command, highlights the pattern of missing values among the 33 individuals who had any missing on the six belief statements.

The syntax for these commands is:

```
Temporary.
Select if (missing_nomissing = 1).
List variables = sex remarks innocent career1 career2 intentional
reported.
```

In this hypothetical data set, 16 of the 33 cases have missing data (males = 10, females = 6; Table 19.7, p. 552) on *all* of the variables. The responses from these 16 individuals constitute a nonrandom pattern (i.e., all 9s). Although an *n* of 16 seems small compared to the overall sample (*n* = 600), the consequences of this nonrandom pattern were dramatic in the two reliability analyses (Output 19.9 vs. 19.10). It could be argued that the researcher simply made a mistake when failing to properly specify the values of 9 as missing, but the error is common among novice analysts who do not check the distributional properties of variables before launching into more complex analyses (i.e., running FREQUENCIES, etc.). *More importantly, the example highlights the consequences of even a small number (n = 16) of nonrandom missing data values in a relatively large data set (n = 600).*

Table 19.7   Patterns of Missing Data on the Six Sexual Harassment Belief Statements

| Pattern of Missing | SEX | Variables | | | | | |
		REMARKS	INNOCENT	CAREER1	CAREER2	INTENTIONAL	REPORTED
Total missing	Male	9	9	9	9	9	9
n = 10	Male	9	9	9	9	9	9
	Male	9	9	9	9	9	9
	Male	9	9	9	9	9	9
	Male	9	9	9	9	9	9
	Male	9	9	9	9	9	9
	Male	9	9	9	9	9	9
	Male	9	9	9	9	9	9
	Male	9	9	9	9	9	9
	Male	9	9	9	9	9	9
Partial missing	Male	−1	9	9	9	1	1
n = 7	Male	−1	0	−1	−1	9	9
	Male	0	−1	−1	9	1	1
	Male	1	0	0	9	1	1
	Male	1	0	9	0	1	1
	Male	2	−1	1	−1	−2	9
	Male	9	1	−1	9	1	1
Total missing	Female	9	9	9	9	9	9
n = 6	Female	9	9	9	9	9	9
	Female	9	9	9	9	9	9
	Female	9	9	9	9	9	9
	Female	9	9	9	9	9	9
	Female	9	9	9	9	9	9
Partial missing	Female	−2	1	−1	−1	1	9
n = 10	Female	−1	−1	0	9	1	0
	Female	−1	0	0	0	0	9
	Female	0	0	0	−1	9	1
	Female	1	1	9	−1	9	1
	Female	1	1	1	−1	1	9
	Female	1	1	0	0	0	9
	Female	1	9	1	−2	2	2
	Female	2	1	2	9	1	1
	Female	2	0	9	−2	2	2

Response Patterns in Survey Answers

When asked to recall a frequency (e.g., days of participation, number of trips) or a quantity (e.g., trip expenditures, number of pheasants bagged), some respondents round their answers to numbers ending in 0 or 5 or multiply days of participation by an integer to approximate expenditures or game harvested (Beaman, Vaske, & Miller, 2005a; Vaske, Beaman, Manfredo, Covey, & Knox, 1996; Vaske, Huan, & Beaman, 2003). These cognitive processes potentially yield responses that differ from what actually happened (Vaske & Beaman, 2006). Approximate or prototype responses are suggested by response heaps (i.e., spikes in response frequency; a.k.a. digit preference or number preference). Heaps appear because some responses occur more often than would be expected by chance (Chase & Harada, 1984; Hultsman, Hultsman, & Black, 1989; Tarrant & Manfredo, 1993). Giving approximate responses such as numbers ending in 0 or 5 potentially distorts findings (Connelly & Brown, 1992; Hiett & Worrall, 1977). If survey responses are systematically in error (i.e., biased), the utility of estimates for planning and management is compromised.

This section provides an overview of recent advances in detecting and correcting for response heaps in parks, recreation, and human dimensions survey data involving responses on frequency (e.g., times participating) and quantity (e.g., game harvest). Six lessons learned from previous research are summarized (see Vaske & Beaman, 2006 for additional lessons). These collective findings and observations are organized in three broad areas: (a) conceptual, (b) methodological, and (c) analytical lessons.

Conceptual Lessons

Lesson 1:
0 - 5 Heaping (Digit Preference) is One Manifestation of Number Preference

Early parks, recreation, and human dimensions research (Chase & Harda, 1984; Hultsman et al, 1989; Tarrant & Manfredo, 1993), as well as studies in other disciplines (Baker, 1992; Bailey & Makannah, 1993) defined digit preference in terms of an individual's preference for numbers ending in 0 or 5. In fact, several studies have found limited 0–5 heaping (Beaman, 2002; Beaman, Vaske, Donnelly, & Manfredo, 1997; Beaman, Vaske, & Grenier, 1998; Beaman, Vaske, & Miller, 2005a, 2005b; Miller & Anderson, 2002; Vaske, Beaman et al., 1996; Vaske et al., 2003). To illustrate, Figure 19.5 (p. 554) shows a frequency distribution of reported angling participation in Colorado (Vaske, Beaman et al., 1996). The study was designed to address the influence of response strategy (e.g., record keeping, guessing) and recall frame (short vs. long time period that respondents must think back to) on exhibiting digit preference. The six subfigures (Figures 19.5a –19.5f) correspond to all possible combinations of levels of response strategy and recall frame. The dark bars show frequencies for numbers ending in 0 or 5. Going down the subfigures, heaping is more evident for longer recall frames (19.5b, 19.5d, 19.5f). Going across the subfigures, heaping is more prominent for those who "guessed" (19.5e, 19.5f) as opposed to "kept records" (19.5a, 19.5b) of their angling participation. Overall, the six subfigures graphically depict frequency distributions for which there is little preference for 0 or 5 to histograms for which most responses end in 0 or 5. Such differences are a function of recall frame (short or long) and response strategy (e.g., record keeping, guessing). Basically,

Figure 19.5a. Number of Anglers – Short Recall/Kept Records

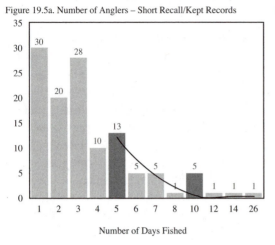

Number of Days Fished

Figure 19.5b. Number of Anglers – Long Recall/Kept Records

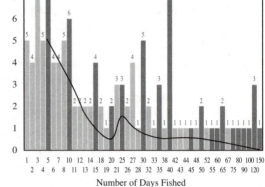

Number of Days Fished

Figure 19.5c. Number of Anglers – Short Recall/Remembered Each Trip

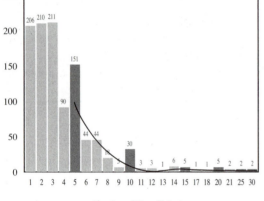

Number of Days Fished

Figure 19.5d. Number of Anglers – Long Recall/Remembered Each Trip

Number of Days Fished

Figure 19.5e. Number of Anglers – Short Recall/Guessed

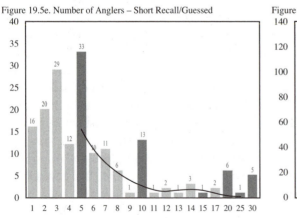

Number of Days Fished

Figure 19.5f. Number of Anglers – Long Recall/Guessed

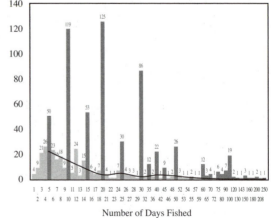

Number of Days Fished

The dark bars show numbers ending in 0 or 5.
The smooth curves define response frequencies for persons not exhibiting digit preference.

Figure 19.5   Response Strategy, Recall Frame, and Digit Preference

respondents are more likely to choose a number ending in 0 or 5 if they are guessing or need to remember back a long time.

Other research, however, shows response heaps at 4 and 8 when the variable "hours of participation during a day" is examined (Rodgers, Brown, & Duncan, 1993). If "duration of a trip" is the variable of interest, respondents tend to overuse 7, 14, 30, and 60 (Huttenlocher, Hedges, & Bradburn, 1990); numbers corresponding to weeks or months as time periods. For "respondents age," individuals tend to overuse numbers ending in 9 (e.g., 29, 39, 49) and under-report numbers ending in 0 (e.g., 30, 40, 50; Bailey & Makannah, 1993). In a similar vein, the number 13 is typically avoided in surveys. *Thus, the "digit preference" phenomenon should be referred to as "number preference," as it does not generally relate to numbers ending in certain digits, but rather to numbers that a person has a disposition to use or avoid* (Beaman et al., 1998; Vaske, Beaman et al., 1996).

Lesson 2:
Response Heaps Occur Because of the Cognitive Processes that Respondents Use

For some respondents, the cognitive process of answering questions about their behavior involves the simple retrieval of information from memory (Burton & Blair, 1991; Nadeau & Niemi, 1995). When the number of events (e.g., trips, annual game harvest) to be recalled is low (e.g., 1, 2), traditional memory models assume that people answer the questions using *episode enumeration* (Sudman & Bradburn, 1974; Sudman, Bradburn, & Schwarz, 1996). Specific episodes are recalled from long-term memory for the relevant time frame, counted, and a response is given. Response errors in these situations occur when individuals fail to recall specific events (*episode omission*) and/or misplace the episode in time (*telescoping*).

As the frequency of participation in a behavior and/or quantity to be estimated increases, episodic enumeration can give way to other cognitive processes (Burton & Blair, 1991; Schwarz, 1990). For example, respondents may use *estimation heuristics* where frequency is estimated by recalling sample episodes (Tversky & Kahneman, 1974). More salient episodes are more likely to be recalled, resulting in overestimation (Vaske et al., 2003). An individual may also use *automatic estimation* when answering behavioral questions (Hasher & Zacks, 1984; Nadeau & Niemi, 1995). Using this cognitive process, responses are based on an innate sense of relative or absolute frequency (e.g., I go fishing every Saturday morning).

When events are numerous, similar, and occur regularly, respondents may use *formula-based multiplier* cognitive processes (Burton & Blair, 1991). For this type of response, individuals recall a frequency rule and apply it to the requested time frame. For example, a person may recall going fishing once a week. When asked how many times did you fish in the last three months, the response might equal 12 (i.e., once a week * 4 weeks per month * 3 months = 12). At least three sources of error arise from formula-based processes. First, the individual may fail to recall exceptions to the rule. For example, the person may typically fish once a week, but thunderstorms prohibited participation two weeks ago and work constraints limited fishing time four weeks ago. Second, response errors can arise when the individual does not account for rule shifts that occur during the time frame for which information is requested. If asked for angling participation during an entire year, the respondent may not adjust for seasonal differences (e.g., spring vs. summer) in frequency. Third, the individual may misestimate the rule when different but similar behaviors are encompassed. An individual, for example, might be an avid trout angler, but fish for walleye only occasionally. If asked about fishing, the multiplier determined for trout fishing might be used for all types of fishing (e.g., walleye, bass).

The recall process may involve use of ***prototypes***. A prototype is defined as a single number that is taken to characterize a set or range of values (Reed, 1996, p. 241). For example, a person may recall fishing somewhere between 8 and 12 times per month. If asked about his or her frequency of fishing, the prototype used in a survey response might be 10. A respondent may see this as the best response because it is central to the interval of 8 to 12. Answers based on 0–5 prototypes are probably the main cause of response heaping and are the most obvious in survey data (Beaman et al., 1997, 2005a; Hultsman et al., 1989; Huttenlocher et al., 1990; Miller & Anderson, 2002; Vaske, Beaman et al., 1996; Vaske et al, 2003). Although prototype responses reflect how the human mind works (Burton & Blair, 1991), grouping responses by assigning them one value influences the value of statistics computed with those responses, and in general, results in biased estimates (Beaman et al, 1997, 2005a, 2005b; Vaske, Beaman et al., 1996; Vaske et al, 2003). Researchers should not treat prototype responses as accurate and precise (Beaman et al, 1998).

Lesson 3:
Prototype Responses Are Not Necessarily Inaccurate

A response on a heaping value (e.g., 0 or 5) does not necessarily imply that the response is inaccurate or approximate. Since 20% of all numbers end in 0 or 5, about one fifth of responses (e.g., days of participation, game harvested) will end in 0 or 5 if preference is not given to certain numbers. A respondent's answer of 5 days hunting or 5 fish caught could be perfectly accurate.

The conceptual problem links to the traditional definition of digit preference (Lesson 1): Individuals giving responses ending in either 0 or 5. Using the individual-based definition, the proportion of respondents exhibiting digit preference is the sum of the frequencies in dark bars (Figure 19.5), divided by the total frequency. The problem at the individual level is determining whether an individual should be classed as exhibiting digit preference. If 25% of the respondents provide answers ending in 0 or 5, all 25% would implicitly be classified as exhibiting digit preference. Since 20% of all positive integers end in 0 or 5, one can argue that only 5% (25% – 20% = 5%) of respondents actually displayed digit preference. Given this logic and example, the obvious question becomes: is 25% or 5% closer to the actual percent of the population exhibiting digit preference?

Beaman and colleagues (1997) developed an unbiased aggregate measure of digit preference. Computation of this aggregate measure involved: (a) defining estimates of those respondents not exhibiting digit preference for numbers ending in 0 or 5, (b) subtracting these estimates from the observed frequencies for numbers ending in 0 or 5 to determine a residual number exhibiting digit preference, (c) summing the number exhibiting 0–5 digit preference to obtain an estimated total number exhibiting digit preference, and (d) dividing this estimated total by the total number of respondents that could have displayed digit preference. In subsequent work (Beaman et al, 2005a), a formula was derived for estimating the proportion of responses in a heap.

Methodological Lessons

Lesson 4:
Survey Methodology Influences Response Heaping and Heaping Related Bias

Research has highlighted the value of shortening the recall period (e.g., a few months vs. an entire year) for which respondents are asked to report estimates of behavior (Beaman et al., 1997; Chu, Eisenhower, Hay, Morganstein, Neter, & Waksbeerg, 1992; Tarrant & Manfredo, 1993; Vaske, Beaman et al., 1996). As discussed earlier, bias increases when respondents are asked to recall events for long time frames. The merits of a reduced recall frame, however, must be taken in the context of the activity under investigation. For hunting and fishing seasons that are less than four months, recall accuracy may only depend on how long after the season harvest information is requested. Big game hunters who are asked to recall the harvest of an animal last year are likely to report an accurate value regardless of recall frame and time since the season. Few animals, if any, are typically harvested and therefore, harvest is easily and accurately remembered. For other activities (e.g., waterfowl, quail, dove, rabbit), with seasons that allow for many days of participation and for which total harvest in a season can be relatively large, collecting data immediately after the end of the season (as opposed to an annual general survey) could be an effective but costly way to increase accuracy. Species-specific surveys, however, might be employed periodically (e.g., every 3 or 4 years) to calibrate annual survey results by correcting for bias. This could be a cost-effective way to obtain accurate and reliable estimates for a variety of species.

Sending hunting activity record-cards prior to a hunting season has also been recommended as a methodology for reducing response heaps and improving the accuracy of participation and harvest estimates derived from survey responses. Miller and Anderson (2002), for example, sent half of the hunters in their sample a record-card for logging their hunting activities (e.g., days spent hunting, harvest on those days). The other half of hunters in the sample did not receive the record-card. Results indicated that hunters who received the record-card were less likely to provide answers that ended in 0 or 5. Additional analyses of the same data (Beaman et al., 2005b), however, demonstrated that although record-card recipients reported less 0–5 heaping, excessive 0–5 heaping explained only 20% or less of the change in means and totals. Changes in these estimates were primarily the result of a higher response rate for record-card recipients reporting low days of participation and/or low harvest. Sending out record-cards prompted more individuals in the sample with low days of participation and low harvest to become respondents. Given that record-cards are relatively inexpensive, state fish and wildlife agencies are encouraged to adopt this methodology.

Methodological changes to reduce bias and increase accuracy, however, can disrupt analysis of trends in data (Beaman, Beaman, O'Leary, & Smith, 2000). If a change between old and new estimates is observed, how much of the difference is a function of: (a) a change in methodology, (b) a change in bias, or (c) a true change in behavior between surveys? To reap the benefits of changing data collection procedures, new methodologies must be phased in. The relationships between estimates based on old and new methodologies can then be determined to allow old trend information to be converted to the base established by the new methodologies.

Lesson 5:
The Pattern of Response Heaps Can Depend on Survey Design / Layout

Some survey designs encourage responses that result in frequency function heaps (Vaske et al., 2003). If frequency of participation and game harvest or trip expenditure questions are asked in sequence, a disposition is created to use multipliers to arrive at a response (e.g., 8 days of participation * 6 birds harvested per day). If the multiplier used is larger than the correct multiplier, the reported response is too large and estimates of means or total harvest (or trip expenditures) are biased. The problem involves knowing the magnitude of bias.

One simple solution for minimizing the use of multipliers and/or 0–5 prototypes is to ask days afield questions separate from and after harvest questions. By physically separating participation (days afield) and harvest questions and asking harvest first, the survey's structure is less likely to motivate harvest responses that are multiples of days. If computer assisted interviewing (CAI) is used for data collection, the program can record harvest responses that are multiples. At the end of the survey, the software can prompt the interviewer to ask respondents how their harvest responses that are multiples of days were determined. Respondents' recall processes for prototype answers could be ascertained in a similar manner. Inquiries about an individual's response strategy should occur at the end of the interview to avoid interrupting the flow of data collection.

Analytical Lesson

Lesson 6:
Bias in Estimates Resulting from Response Heaping Can Be Corrected

Efforts at modeling response heaping in order to make corrections have evolved over the past decade. A preliminary version of a model was outlined in Vaske, Beaman, Manfredo, Covey, and Knox (1996) and important ideas were clarified in Beaman and colleagues (1997). Refinements to this general approach are discussed in detail in Beaman et al (1998).

Overall, the bias correction model involves redistributing responses in heaps back to precise values. Unfortunately, redistribution is complex and estimation of an accurate distribution curve without peaks and valleys requires a number of simplifying assumptions (e.g., nature of prototypes used) and evaluations (e.g., how prototypes of different widths contribute to heaping). The research to date is only an initial step. If a version of the 0–5 redistribution model could be devised for use of multiples, response bias due to multiples could be reduced by modeling. Correcting for bias by modeling can improve estimates obtained from surveys.

State and federal agencies have used hunter / angler surveys for decades to assist in estimating game populations to set seasonal and daily harvest limits, and to communicate season harvests to publics. Unless the goal of data collection is to merely maintain a historical database of hunting participation and harvest from surveys that may be yielding biased estimates, the lessons identified in this review imply the need for changes in the way that harvest survey estimates are produced.

Similar to other data collection methodologies, surveys are subject to bias that does not decrease with sample size. If respondents use prototypes when answering participation and harvest or expenditure questions, bias is present regardless of whether the sample size is small or large. Identifying and developing methods to correct for bias and to obtain reliable and affordable information will enable natural resource managers to have greater confidence in estimates based on survey data.

Outliers in Survey Responses

An *outlier* is an observation that lies outside the overall pattern of a distribution (Moore & McCabe, 1999). For example, assume that a statistics professor wants to demonstrate the calculation of a mean. The variable selected for illustration purposes is the annual income of the students in her class. She conducts a single question survey that asks the students what their income was last year to the nearest whole number. On the day that the survey was conducted, Bill Gates, the chairman of Microsoft Corporation, was sitting in on the class (hey, it is a hypothetical example). With Mr. Gates's annual income included in the sample (approximately 175 million), the average income is likely to be substantially larger than what would have occurred if his income was not used in the calculation of the mean. From this perspective, Mr. Gates's survey response is an outlier. Outliers cause problems when the estimates (e.g., mean income) are much larger than usual and may not be plausible. Problems associated with outliers have been reported for wildlife surveys estimating game harvested (e.g., Moyer & Geissler, 1984, 1991) and tourism surveys estimating trip expenditures (e.g., Beaman, 2006; Huan, Beaman, Chang, & Hsu, in press; Pol, Pascual, & Vázquez, 2006).

Detecting Outliers

A variety of procedures have been suggested for detecting outliers. The first and simplest approach involves a *visual inspection of a variable's distribution*. Run a Frequencies on the variable, note any valid values that seem extreme, and check to ensure that the data were coded accurately. If coding errors are not evident, the extreme values *might* be outliers. Outliers occur because: (a) a data entry error was made, or (b) the respondents are simply different than the rest of the sample.

Second, for an approximately normally distributed variable, outlier values can be defined as *any value beyond 3 standard deviations of the mean* (Stevens, 1992). In a normal distribution, 99% of all responses fall within three standard deviations. Survey responses beyond three standard deviations could be treated as extreme values.

A third method for identifying outliers is the *interquartile range* (IQR). With this approach, the median of the variable of interest is computed. The median of a normal distribution divides the data into two halves. The medians of each of these two halves are then calculated. The result is three points: (a) the first middle point (the median), (b) the median of the lower half of the distribution, and (c) the median of the upper half of the distribution. Each of these points is named Q_1, Q_2, and Q_3, respectively (Figure 19.6, p. 560).

By convention, one definition of a ***mild outlier*** is a value that falls more than 1.5 times the interquartile range below the first quartile or above the third quartile:

$$< Q_1 - 1.5 * IQR$$

or

$$> Q_3 + 1.5 * IQR$$

An ***extreme outlier*** is commonly defined as a value that falls more than 3 times the interquartile range below the first quartile or above the third quartile:

$$< Q_1 - 3 * IQR$$

or

$$> Q_3 + 3 * IQR$$

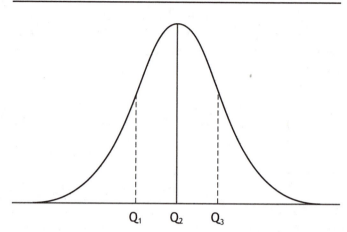

Figure 19.6   Interquartiles in a Normal Distribution

Using these definitions with a normally distributed variable, about 1 in 150 observations will be a mild outlier and about 1 in 425,000 responses will be an extreme outlier.

Finally, Rosner (1975, 1983) describes a generalized ***extreme student deviate*** (ESD) procedure for detecting from 1 to k outliers in a data set. This procedure is based on the statistics, $R_1, ..., R_k$ that are extreme values computed from successively reduced samples of size $n, n-1, ..., n-k+1$ respectively. R_1, for example, is the largest deviation from the mean that is standardized by dividing by the standard deviation. A given survey response is an outlier if the R for that value is greater than λ. Values for λ for normal distributions are presented in Rosner (1983) for various sample sizes. An example illustrating this approach is presented by Moyer and Geissler (1991) for accommodating outliers in wildlife harvest surveys.

Dealing with Outliers

Regardless of how the outliers are detected and defined, it is important to explicitly deal with outliers. Failure to consider the impact of outliers in a data set can lead to meaningless conclusions. In the example above, including Mr. Gates's annual income in the mean of the students' income is likely to increase the average by millions of dollars. His response is valid because he was a student in the class on the day the survey was completed. Given the annual personal incomes of most students, however, the resulting mean would not be very plausible or defensible.

There are at least four ways to deal with outliers. First, the data can be ***transformed*** (e.g., by taking the logarithm of the variable, see chapter 17). Such transformations shrink larger values to a greater extent than smaller values. Although taking the log of a variable reduces the skewness in the distribution, the interpretation may not be straightforward. In addition, the relationship between the logged variable and other variables in an analysis can be different than the relationship between the original variable and the other variables.

A second strategy for dealing with outliers involves the use of ***robust estimators***. For example, ***M-estimators*** are robust alternatives to the sample mean and median for estimating the central tendency of a variable's distribution (Hampel, 1968; Huber, 1964). *M*-estimators calculate the mean by weighting the data. The weights decrease as the observed survey responses move further away from the center of a distribution.

In SPSS, robust estimators are found under Analyze > Descriptive Statistics > Explore...

The resulting dialog box is shown in Figure 19.7. Click on the Statistics button to display the available statistics.

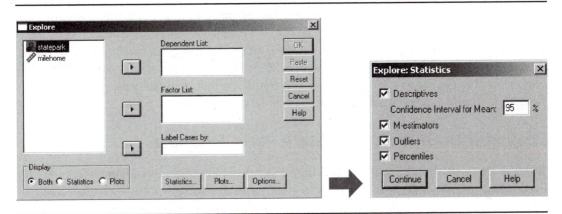

Figure 19.7   Explore Dialog Boxes in SPSS

The four *M*-estimators available in SPSS differ in the weights they apply to the cases: (a) Huber's *M*-estimator uses the weight of $c = 1.339$; (b) Andrews' wave has weight $c = 1.34\pi$; (c) Hampel's *M*-estimator has three weights, $a = 1.7$, $b = 3.4$, and $c = 8.5$; and (d) Tukey's biweight with $c = 4.685$. See Hoaglin, Mosteller, and Tukey (1983) and Huber (1964) for more information on *M*-estimators. See Huan and associates (in press) and Pol et al. (2006) for tourism-related applications and procedures for statistically comparing robust estimators.

A robust estimator not included in SPSS is the ***trimmed mean***. A trimmed mean is the mean of the observations that remain after a certain percentage (α) of the largest and smallest values have been eliminated from the data. For skewed distributions just removing large or small values will produce biased estimates that underestimate the observed values, unless other adjustments are made (e.g., replacing the extreme value with some other value). As noted by Cochran (1977, pp. 12–15), however, biased estimates can be desirable, if high variability is reduced. The total error is reduced if the bias contribution is small relative to the variance decrease. In the hypothetical income example above, removing the annual income of Mr. Gates before calculating the average student income will lower both the mean and variance. Thus, a biased estimate may tend to be more accurate than an unbiased one.

Another robust estimator is the ***Winsorized mean***. Instead of eliminating the α percentage of outliers, the extreme values are replaced with the value of the most extreme response remaining after the highest values have been trimmed from the data. More formally, the Winsorized mean is computed after the k smallest observations are replaced by the $(k + 1)$ smallest observation, and the k largest observations are replaced by the $(k + 1)$ largest observation. In other words, the observations are Winsorized at each end. In parks, recreation, and human dimensions studies, the researcher may not want to Winsorize both ends of the distribution. A value of 0 birds bagged in a study estimating the number of pheasants harvested is a valid and plausible response. The zeroes in this case should not be trimmed from the data. Similarly, in tourism research, 0 expenditures for a given type of expense could logically occur and these valid zero responses should not be eliminated. In the hypothetical income example, a student reporting no personal annual income is also a valid response. For these types of variables, a *semi-Winsorized* approach is commonly used (Guttman & Smith, 1969). With semi-Winsorsized means, only the values on one extreme of the distribution (e.g., the high end) are replaced.

Overall, trimmed and Winsorized means are robust estimators of the population mean that are relatively insensitive to the outlying values. The percentage of values to be deleted (i.e., α), however, is debatable. Moyer and Geissler (1991), for example, suggest that "< 1% of the data should be replaced to avoid excessive bias" (p. 269). The default trimmed value in SPSS EXPLORE is 5%. The safest empirical solution is to run multiple analyses and examine what happens to the estimates. This strategy is used in the example below.

Dealing with Outliers—CO State Parks Example

The data for this example were obtained from a survey of Colorado State Park visitors. Respondents from two state parks—Lory ($n = 600$) and Mueller ($n = 600$)—were selected for illustration purposes. Both of these state parks are relatively small and tend to attract mostly local residents. Lory State Park is located near Colorado State University and therefore, might be used by visiting university scholars who usually live a substantial distance from Colorado.

One of the questions on this on-site survey asked respondents "How far is this park from your home?" Responses were coded as the actual number miles the person traveled to get to the park. Results from the initial FREQUENCIES analysis are presented in Output 19.12.

Output 19.12a   Descriptive Statistics for the Variable MILEHOME

Statistics

milehome   How Many Miles is the Park from Home?

N	Valid	1200
	Missing	0
Mean		155.94
Std. Error of Mean		17.152
Median		56.00
Mode		30
Std. Deviation		594.157
Minimum		2
Maximum		9500

The average number of miles traveled to get to the park was 155.94, but the standard deviation (594.16) is nearly 4 times the mean. As indicated by the maximum (9,500 miles), at least some values were quite extreme.

Output 19.12b   Frequencies Distribution and Bar Graph for the Variable MILEHOME

How many miles is the park from home?

Valid	Frequency	Valid Percent	Cumulative Percent
2	7	.6	.6
5	45	3.8	4.3
7	1	.1	4.4
8	2	.2	4.6
9	5	.4	5.0
10	61	5.1	10.1
12	8	.7	10.8
15	16	1.3	12.1
16	2	.2	12.3
18	2	.2	12.4
19	2	.2	12.6
20	27	2.3	14.8
25	30	2.5	17.3
27	2	.2	17.5
28	4	.3	17.8
29	2	.2	18.0
30	103	8.6	26.6
32	6	.5	27.1
35	31	2.6	29.7
36	1	.1	29.8
37	1	.1	29.8
38	3	.3	30.1
39	1	.1	30.2
40	61	5.1	35.3
42	2	.2	35.4
700	1	.1	95.1
740	1	.1	95.1
750	2	.2	95.3
760	1	.1	95.3
780	1	.1	95.4
800	2	.2	95.6
820	4	.3	95.9
900	5	.4	96.3
950	4	.3	96.7
980	1	.1	96.8
1000	12	1.0	97.8
1050	3	.3	98.0
1100	2	.2	98.2
1140	1	.1	98.3
1200	4	.3	98.6
1250	2	.2	98.8
1290	1	.1	98.8
1300	1	.1	98.9
1400	1	.1	99.0
1500	1	.1	99.1
1600	3	.3	99.3
1900	1	.1	99.4
2000	2	.2	99.6
2500	1	.1	99.7
9500	4	.3	
Total	1200	100.0	

> Due to space considerations, only the first 25 and last 25 values in the distribution are shown.

> In the sample of 1,200 individuals, 21 respondents reported traveling 1,200 or more miles to get to the state park. Of these, 4 people indicated traveling 9,500 miles.

Output 19.12c   Bar Graph for the Variable MILEHOME

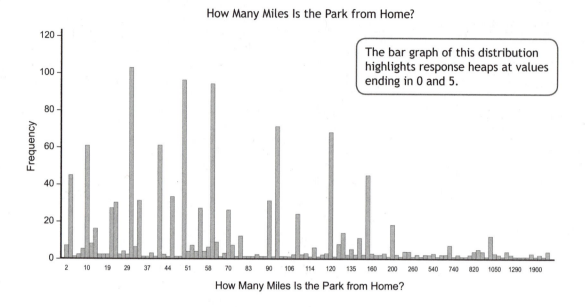

To examine the impact of potential outliers on the mean and standard deviations of the MILEHOME variable, the EXPLORE command in Figure 19.7 was run. For these analyses, the dependent variable was the number of miles traveled to get to the state park (MILEHOME) and the independent variable was the state park visited (variable name = STATEPARK).[4]

The syntax for this analysis is:

```
EXAMINE
    VARIABLES=milehome BY statepark
    /PLOT BOXPLOT STEMLEAF
    /COMPARE GROUP
    /MESTIMATORS HUBER(1.339) ANDREW(1.34) HAMPEL(1.7,3.4,8.5)
TUKEY(4.685)
    /PERCENTILES(5,10,25,50,75,90,95) HAVERAGE
    /STATISTICS DESCRIPTIVES EXTREME
    /CINTERVAL 95
    /MISSING LISTWISE
    /NOTOTAL.
```

The results are shown in Output 19.13.

---

[4] The SPSS menu choice for this analysis is EXPLORE, but the SPSS generated syntax fo this analysis is Examine.

Output 19.13a   SPSS Explore Descriptive Statistics for the Variable Mɪʟᴇʜᴏᴍᴇ

Descriptives

statepark	State Park				Statistics	Std. Error
milehome How Many Miles is the Park from Home?	0 Lory		Mean		206.85	33.256
		95% Confidence Interval for Mean	Lower Bound		141.54	
			Upper Bound		272.16	
		5% Trimmed Mean			93.41	
		Median			60.00	
		Variance			663587.7	
		Std. Deviation			814.609	
		Minimum			2	
		Maximum			9500	
		Range			9498	
		Interquartile Range			75	
		Skewness			10.116	.100
		Kurtosis			111.566	.199
	1 Mueller	Mean			105.03	7.943
		95% Confidence Interval for Mean	Lower Bound		89.43	
			Upper Bound		120.63	
		5% Trimmed Mean			67.56	
		Median			50.00	
		Variance			37855.737	
		Std. Deviation			194.566	
		Minimum			2	
		Maximum			1000	
		Range			998	
		Interquartile Range			70	
		Skewness			3.560	.100
		Kurtosis			11.861	.199

The mean distance traveled for Lory State Park (206.85) is nearly 2 times larger than the mean for Mueller State Park (105.03).

In addition, the standard error for Lory State Park (33.256) is over 4 times the standard error Mueller State Park (7.943).

Much of this difference can be attributed to the 4 extreme values (9,500) in the Lory State Park sample.

As noted earlier, a distance of 9,500 miles traveled for Lory State Park could be valid if the respondent happened to be a visiting scholar on sabbatical at Colorado State University.

Output 19.13b *M*-Estimators for the MILEHOME Variable

M-Estimators

			Huber's M-Estimator[a]	Tukey's Biweight[b]	Hampel's M-Estimator[c]	Andrews' Wave[d]
milehome How Many Miles is the Park from Home?	0	Lory	75.23	67.14	70.16	67.11
	1	Mueller	52.41	46.21	50.65	46.19

a. The weighting constant is 1.339.
b. The weighting constant is 4.685.
c. The weighting constants are 1.700, 3.400, and 8.500.
d. The weighting constant is 1.340 * pi.

> The four robust *M*-Estimators highlight the substantial decrease in the means that occurs when outliers are removed from the analysis.

Output 19.13c SPSS Determined Extreme Values for the MILEHOME Variable

Extreme Values

	statepark State Park				Case Number	Value
milehome How Many Miles is the Park from Home?	0	Lory	Highest	1	597	9500
				2	598	9500
				3	599	9500
				4	600	9500
				5	596	2500
			Lowest	1	3	2
				2	2	2
				3	1	2
				4	19	5
				5	18	5[a]
	1	Mueller	Highest	1	1192	1000
				2	1193	1000
				3	1194	1000
				4	1195	1000
				5	1196	1000[b]
			Lowest	1	604	2
				2	603	2
				3	602	2
				4	601	2
				5	633	5[a]

a. Only partial list of cases with the value 5 are shown in the table of lower extremes.
b. Only a parial list of cases with the value 1000 are shown in the table of upper extremes.

> For both state parks, SPSS lists the 5 highest and 5 lowest extreme values. For each extreme value, the case number (respondent ID) is also displayed.
>
> Given that the case numbers for the 4 values of 9,500 are sequential, these respondents could reflect a family of 4 individuals who had traveled a great distance to the park and happened to be included in the sample. They probably are not, however, representative of the "typical" Lory State Park visitor.

Boxplots are another way to examine a variable's distribution. Output 19.13d shows the boxplots for Lory and Mueller State Parks. Boxplots are based on medians and use the logic of inter-quartile ranges (Figure 19.6, p. 558). With large samples sizes (e.g., $n = 600$ for each state park) and the presence of extreme outliers (e.g., responses of 9,500), boxplots are not very intuitive to understand.

Output 19.13d   Box Plots for Stem-and-Leaf Plot for the MILEHOME Variable

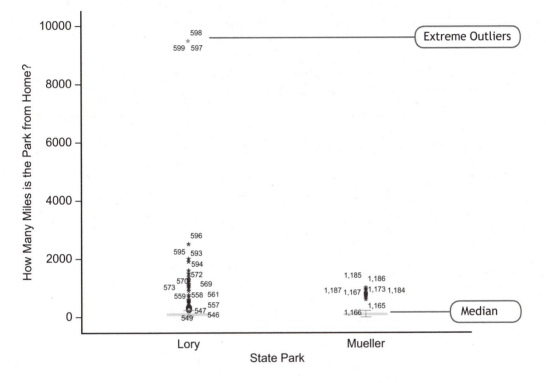

Overall, the FREQUENCIES and EXPLORE analyses identified a number of potential outliers. Respondents who reported traveling 9,500 miles to visit a Colorado State Park, for example, are not likely to be representative of "typical" population of visitors. Such extreme values could be valid, but not probable. To address the impact of outliers in the MILEHOME distribution, four new variables were computed. The variable names and a description of each variable are shown in Box 19.3 (p. 568). Two of the variables – TRIM9500 and TRIM1PCT simply eliminated extreme values from the analysis, with out replacement. The two semi-Winsorized variables — WINSORIZED9500 and WINSORIZED1PCT — eliminated extreme values on the high end of the distribution and replaced the values with the next valid response.

Box 19.3   Computed Variables to Address Outliers in the MILEHOME Variable

Variable name	Variable description [1]
TRIM9500	This variable "trimmed" the 4 values of 9,500 miles from analysis.
TRIM1PCT	Based on the recommendation of Moyer and Geissler (1991), this variable trimmed the upper 1% of the distribution from the analysis.
WINSORIZED9500	This semi-Winsorized variable trimmed the 4 values of 9,500, and replaced those values with 2,500, the next valid value in the distribution.
WINSORIZED1PCT	This semi-Winsorized variable trimmed the upper 1% of the distribution and replaced those values with 1,140, the next valid value in the distribution.

1.   The trimmed variables eliminated extreme values from the analysis
     The two semi-Winsorized variables eliminated extreme values from the analysis and replaced the values with the next valid response.

The syntax for computing these four computed variables is:

```
* * * * * * * * * * * * * * * * * * * * * * * * * * * * *
* Trim 4 values of 9500
* * * * * * * * * * * * * * * * * * * * * * * * * * * * *

Compute trim9500 = milehome.
Formats trim9500 (F4.0).
Recode trim9500 (9500 = 9999).
Missing values trim9500 (9999).


* * * * * * * * * * * * * * * * * * * * * * * * * * * * *
* Trim 1%
* * * * * * * * * * * * * * * * * * * * * * * * * * * * *

Compute trim1pct = milehome.
Formats trim1pct (F4.0).
Recode trim1pct (1200 thru 9500 = 9999).
Missing values trim1pct (9999).


* * * * * * * * * * * * * * * * * * * * * * * * * * * * *
* Winsorized 9500
* * * * * * * * * * * * * * * * * * * * * * * * * * * * *

Compute winsorized9500 = milehome.
Formats winsorized9500 (F4.0).
Recode winsorized9500 (9500 = 2500).


* * * * * * * * * * * * * * * * * * * * * * * * * * * * *
* Winsorized 1%
* * * * * * * * * * * * * * * * * * * * * * * * * * * * *

Compute winsorized1pct = milehome.
Formats winsorized1pct (F4.0).
Recode winsorized1pct (1200 thru 9500 = 1140).
```

A FREQUENCIES analysis was then performed on the original and four computed variables. The FREQUENCIES commands are shown below and the results are displayed in Output 19.14.

```
FREQUENCIES
  VARIABLES=milehome trim9500 trim1pct winsorized9500 winsorized1pct
  /NTILES=  4
  /STATISTICS=STDDEV RANGE SEMEAN MEAN MEDIAN
  /ORDER=  ANALYSIS .
```

Given that at most 1% of the values ($n = 21$) were trimmed from a fairly large data set ($n = 1,200$), the medians and quartiles (i.e., percentiles 25, 50, 75) changed only slightly, if at all, across all five variables in Output 19.14. Compared to the original MILEHOME distribution ($M = 155.95$, $SE = 17.15$), however, all four computed variables show dramatic declines in the means (mean range = 104.44 to 132.61) and standard errors (SE range = 5.13 to 8.14). More severe trimming and winsorizing will increase these differences in the resulting means. The earlier SPSS output (Output 19.13a), for example, trimmed 5% of the sample and the mean for Lory State Park was 93.41 miles; for Mueller State Park, the 5% trimmed mean was 67.56. If the robust M-estimators are used, the mean distance traveled is even lower (Output 19.13b). At Lory State Park, the means for the four robust M-estimators ranged from 67.11 to 75.23 miles. For Mueller, the M-estimators ranged from 46.19 to 52.41.

Output 19.14 Descriptive Statistics for the Original Variable (MILEHOME) and Four Computed Variables Addressing Outliers

Statistics

		milehome Original Distribution	trim9500	trim1pct	winsorized9500	winsorized1pct
N	Valid	1200	1196	1179	1200	1200
	Missing	0	4	21	0	0
Mean		155.94	124.69	104.44	132.61	122.57
Std. Error of Mean		17.152	7.140	5.134	8.141	6.389
Median		56.00	55.00	55.00	56.00	56.00
Std. Deviation		594.157	246.924	176.279	282.007	221.323
Range		9498	2498	1138	2498	1138
Percentiles	25	30.00	30.00	30.00	30.00	30.00
	50	56.00	55.00	55.00	56.00	56.00
	75	110.00	110.00	110.00	110.00	110.00

The choice of one solution over another (i.e., trimmed vs. trimmed and winsorized) partially depends on how the researcher defines an outlier. Response above 1,000 miles traveled might be considered outliers given the two state parks in this example. *What is evident, however, is that failure to address the impact of potential outliers has substantial consequences on the univariate means, standard deviations, and standard errors.*

The influence of outliers transfers to bivariate analyses as well. Output 19.15 displays the results of five independent samples *t*-tests (chapter 14). For these analyses, the independent variable was the state park visited (i.e., Lory vs. Mueller), and the dependent variables were the five different measures of distance traveled to the state park. Across all five analyses, the variances differed statistically (as indicated by the Levene's Test for Equality of Variance). In addition, the mean distances traveled to each state park were statistically different in 4 of the 5 analyses. Only the mean differences for the TRIM1PCT variable did not show a significant difference.

Output 19.15   T-tests Comparing Two State Parks on Five Variables

T-Test

Group Statistics

	statepark State Park	N	Mean	Std. Deviation	Std. Error Mean
milehome	0 Lory	600	206.85	814.609	33.256
	1 Mueller	600	105.03	194.566	7.943
trim9500	0 Lory	596	114.48	289.073	11.841
	1 Mueller	600	105.03	194.566	7.943
trim1pct	0 Lory	579	103.83	155.240	6.452
	1 Mueller	600	105.03	194.566	7.943
winsorized9500	0 Lory	600	160.18	346.135	14.131
	1 Mueller	600	105.03	194.566	7.943
winsorized1pct	0 Lory	600	140.10	244.085	9.965
	1 Mueller	600	105.03	194.566	7.943

Independent Samples Test

		Levene's Test for Equality of Variances		t-test for Equality of Means						95% Confidence Interval of the Difference	
		F	Sig.	t	df	Sig. (2-tailed)	Mean Difference	Std. Error Difference	Lower	Upper
milehome	Equal variances assumed	20.054	.000	2.978	1198	.003	101.818	34.192	34.736	168.901
	Equal variances not assumed			2.978	667.121	.003	101.818	34.192	34.682	168.955
trim9500	Equal variances assumed	8.189	.004	2.770	1194	.006	39.448	14.240	11.509	67.387
	Equal variances not assumed			2.767	1041.493	.006	39.448	14.258	11.470	67.426
trim1pct	Equal variances assumed	7.860	.005	−.117	1177	.907	−1.197	10.274	−21.354	18.959
	Equal variances not assumed			−.117	1137.142	.907	−1.197	10.233	−21.275	18.880
winsorized9500	Equal variances assumed	18.937	.000	3.402	1198	.001	55.152	16.210	23.348	86.956
	Equal variances not assumed			3.402	943.167	.001	55.152	16.210	23.339	86.964
winsorized1pct	Equal variances assumed	6.323	.012	2.752	1198	.006	35.068	12.743	10.067	60.070
	Equal variances not assumed			2.752	1141.276	.006	35.068	12.743	10.066	60.071

Chapter Summary

This chapter described three sources of potential bias in survey research: (a) missing data, (b) response patterns, and (c) outliers.

Missing data problems arise when individuals do not respond to questions that should have been answered. If the amount of missing data is small in a large data set, and the missing data are randomly distributed throughout the data set, the problem is usually not serious. Almost any procedure for handling the missing data will yield similar conclusions. When there is a pattern to the missing data, the problem is serious regardless of the amount of missing data or the size of the data base.

Seven techniques for dealing with random patterns of missing data in survey research:

1. delete respondent (i.e., listwise deletion in SPSS),

2. delete items,

3. sample means,

4. group means,

5. random assignment within groups,

6. pairwise *r*, and

7. regression analysis.

Each of these approaches assumes that the *missing values are randomly distributed throughout the data*, and each has advantages and disadvantages. The effects on *N* for calculating the Pearson *r* and the effect on *r* were summarized. Data from the Lake Mead National Recreation Area were used to illustrate the effects of missing data on computed indices..

The effect of nonrandom patterns in missing data were addressed using hypothetical data (*n* = 600) examining the relationship between respondents' sex and six belief statements about sexual harassment. Two reliability analyses were presented to highlight the seriousness of nonrandom missing data. In the first analysis, the researcher failed to account for missing data correctly and the resulting Cronbach's alpha was .90. The second analysis adjusted for the missing data properly and the Cronbach's α = .17. The difference between these two findings can be attributed to just *16* respondents with nonrandom patterns of missing data.

The section on response patterns in survey data overviewed recent advances in detecting and correcting for response heaps in respondents' answers. Response heaps occur in frequency (e.g., days of participation, number of trips) or a quantity (e.g., trip expenditures, number of pheasants bagged) questions because some respondents round their answers to numbers ending in 0 or 5 (0–5 prototypes) or multiply days of participation by an integer to approximate expenditures or game harvested. Six lessons learned from previous research were summarized. These collective findings and observations were organized in three broad areas: (a) conceptual, (b) methodological, and (c) analytical lessons:

Conceptual lessons

Lesson 1: 0–5 heaping (digit preference) is one manifestation of number preference.

Lesson 2: Response heaps occur because of the cognitive processes that respondents use.

Lesson 3: Prototype responses are not necessarily inaccurate.

Methodological Lessons

Lesson 4: Survey methodology influences response heaping and heaping related bias.

Lesson 5: The pattern of response heaps can depend on survey design/layout.

Analytical Lesson

Lesson 6: Bias in estimates resulting from response heaping can be corrected.

An ***outlier*** is an observation that lies outside the overall pattern of a distribution. Outliers cause problems when the estimates (e.g., mean income) are much larger than usual and may not be plausible. Four procedures for detecting outliers were introduced:

1. Visual inspection of a variable's distribution,

2. Any value beyond 3 standard deviations of the mean,

3. The interquartile range (IQR), and

4. Extreme student deviate (ESD).

Four solutions for dealing with outliers were discussed:

1. Data transformations (e.g., logarithms),

2. Robust estimators (e.g., *M*-estimators in SPSS),

3. The trimmed mean (i.e., eliminating extreme values without replacement of the values), and

4. The Winsorized and semi-Winsorized mean (i.e., eliminating extreme values and replacing those values with some other value).

Data from a Colorado State Parks visitor survey were used to examine the application of four different methods for dealing with outliers. Four new variables were computed for this illustration. Two of the variables — TRIM9500 and TRIM1PCT simply trimmed extreme values from the analysis, with out replacement. The two semi-Winsorized variables — WINSORIZED9500 and WINSORIZED1PCT — eliminated extreme values on high end of the distribution and replaced the values with the next valid response. The results indicated that failure to address the potential impact of outliers has substantial consequences on univariate and bivariate means, standard deviations, and standard errors.

Review Questions

1. List three sources of potential bias in survey data.

2. Why do missing data problems occur in survey responses?

3. Why are patterns in missing data such a serious problem in survey research? Give an example.

4. List four techniques for dealing with random patterns of missing data in survey research.

5. Discuss the advantages and disadvantages of two techniques for dealing with random patterns of missing data. Include in your explanation the effect of each missing data routine on:
   - Sample size
   - Variance estimation
   - Pearson *r*

6. Explain two cognitive processes respondents might use when answering survey questions related to frequency of participation in an activity.

7. Why do "response heaps" in survey responses occur?

8. Explain the statement "0–5 heaping (digit preference) is one manifestation of number preference."

9. What is a *prototype response*?

10. Why are prototype responses not necessarily biased?

11. Why are prototype responses not necessarily inaccurate?

12. How does a survey's design and layout influence the pattern of response heaps?

13. What is an *outlier response* in survey data?

14. Why are outliers a problem in survey data?

15. List four procedures for detecting outliers in survey data.

16. Why might a survey response that is more than three standard deviations from the mean be considered an outlier?

17. List four solutions for dealing with outliers in survey data.

18. What is a *robust estimator*? In general, how is the mean calculated for a robust estimator?

19. What is the difference between a *trimmed mean* and a *Winsorized mean*?

20. What is the difference between a *Winsorized mean* and a *semi-Winsorized mean*?

20

mediator and moderator variables in path analysis

Parks, recreation, and human dimensions researchers are frequently interested in the causal relationships between variables. Fishbein and Ajzen's (1975) theory of reasoned action, for example, assumes that behavior is determined by one's underlying attitudes (i.e., attitudes are predicted to cause behavior, or $X \rightarrow Y$). To gain a deeper understanding of the complexities of human behavior, however, researchers are often interested in exploring the cognitive processes that influenced the evaluation (X) or the outcome (Y). Questions about process rather than simply whether or not an effect exists introduce additional variables that may either directly or indirectly influence the effects between the original X and Y variables. The cognitive hierarchy (chapter 2), for example, predicts that individuals' general value orientations toward nature influence their specific attitudes toward creating more open space, which in turn influences their decision to vote for or against an open space ballot initiative. In this presumed causal sequence, attitude (M) mediates the relationship between value orientations (X) and the behavior (Y). Some studies (e.g., Vaske & Donnelly, 1999) have empirically found attitudes mediate the relationship between value orientations and behavior (i.e., $X \rightarrow M \rightarrow Y$). Even if this causal sequence can be demonstrated, however, the relationships may function differently for males and females. In this situation, the variable SEX is said to moderate the relationship.

This chapter provides a brief introduction to *path analysis*, an analytical technique for estimating the magnitude of the linkages between variables and using these estimates to provide information about the underlying causal process. A distinction is made between mediator and moderator variables. A variable is called a *mediator* "to the extent that it accounts for the relationship between the predictor and criterion" (Baron & Kenny, 1986, p. 1176). A *moderator* is a third variable that affects the direction and / or strength of the relationship between a predictor and a criterion variable.

Mediation Models in Path Analysis

Path analysis was introduced by Sewell Wright (1921, 1923, 1960) and popularized by Duncan (1966, 1975) in the social sciences. The technique can be viewed as a type of multiple regression analysis (chapter 16). In multiple regression, there is a single continuous dependent variable and two or more independent variables. For mediation models in path analysis, there is more than one dependent variable. This chapter focuses on path analysis models that are based on regression analyses. Recent advances in structural equation modeling (SEM) have expanded researchers' opportunities for conducting path analysis, but SEM is beyond the scope of this book (see Byrne, 1994; Hayduk, 1987; Kline, 1998, for a discussion of SEM).

Consider the traditional crowding/satisfaction model discussed in chapter 3 (Figure 20.1). The model predicts that as the actual number of people in an area (actual density) increases: (a) the number of encounters between recreationists (reported encounters) will increase, (b) perceived crowding will increase, and (c) overall satisfaction with the experience will decrease. In addition, as reported encounters increases: (a) perceived crowding will increase, and (b) overall satisfaction with the experience will decrease. Finally, as perceived crowding increases, overall satisfaction with the experience will decrease.

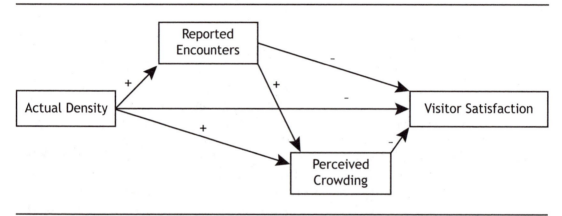

Figure 20.1   Traditional Crowding / Satisfaction Path Model

Such predictions are based on an intuitively logical causal ordering. As the number of people (i.e., actual counts) in a recreation area increases, reported encounters (i.e., a subjective evaluation) between these individuals are likely to increase. Since crowding is the negative evaluation of a certain density, when density or reported encounters increases, crowding should increase. Finally, because most of the early research was conducted in backcountry/wilderness areas where solitude is often a desirable attribute of the experience, as actual density, reported encounters, and perceived crowding increase, satisfaction should decrease (see chapter 3 for more information on the crowding model).

Path analysis is an analytical technique for estimating the magnitude of the linkages between variables and using these estimates to provide information about the underlying causal process. Each arrow and associated sign (+ or –) is a theoretical hypothesis. In this cause-and-effect model, the goal is to examine the strength of each relationship to assess the relative effects of each independent variable and mediating variables on the dependent variable(s) (e.g., perceived crowding, overall satisfaction). Thinking causally about a problem and constructing an arrow diagram that reflects causal processes can facilitate a clearer statement of the hypotheses and the generation of additional insights into the research topic.

A Note on Causation

Most explanatory social research uses a *probabilistic* (as opposed to deterministic) model of *causation*. An independent variable (X) is said to cause a dependent variable (Y), if X influences Y. As noted by Babbie (2003), there are at least three criteria for determining causation: (a) the predictor or independent variable (i.e., cause) and criterion or dependent (i.e., effect) variables must be empirically related to one another, (b) the predictor variable must occur earlier in time than the criterion variable, and (c) the observed relationship cannot be explained away as an artificial product of the effect of another earlier variable. Evidence of the first criterion can be demonstrated with correlation data (i.e., X → Y or Y → X). Support for the second, temporal, criterion is more problematic. Because most applied research employs survey as opposed experimental data, the researcher typically does not know whether X occurred earlier in time than Y. For the traditional crowding/satisfaction model, however, a temporal and logical causal sequence is readily apparent. The causal flow of the variables in Figure 20.1 (e.g., actual density → reported encounters → perceived crowding) is defensible from a deductive reasoning perspective (chapter 3). Before a visitor can recall seeing other visitors (the dependent measure), people have to be present in the area (the independent variable, actual density). Before visitors can evaluate a situation as crowded (the dependent variable), they must remember seeing others (the independent variable).

Testing Mediation Models

This section provides an introduction to testing mediation models.[1] Consider a simple regression model with one independent variable (X) that is assumed to have a causal influence on a dependent variable (Y). The total effect (path c) is the effect of the independent on the dependent (Figure 20.2). If path c is standardized, the regression coefficient equals the Pearson correlation. Although it is common in parks, recreation, and human dimensions research to use standardized regression coefficients, most methods for assessing mediation rely on unstandardized regression coefficients (Sobel, 1982).

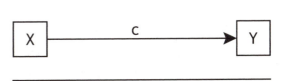

Figure 20.2   Simple Causal Regression Model

If a variable M is causally situated between X and Y and at least partially accounts for the association between X and Y, M mediates the relationship (Baron & Kenny, 1986). A partial mediation model is diagrammed in Figure 20.3 (p. 578). Path a is the causal effect of the independent variable on the mediator. Path b is the causal effect of the mediator on the dependent variable, controlling for the independent variable. Path c' is the causal effect of the independent variable on the dependent variable controlling for the mediator. Path c' is called the ***direct effect*** of X on Y, whereas path c (Figure 20.2) is the ***total effect***. The direct effect partials out from the total effect the causal influence that is shared with M. In other words, path c' is the partial standardized regression coefficient and represents the portion of the effect of X on Y that is unique to X. Path b is also a direct effect (i.e., the direct effect of the mediator on the dependent

---

[1]   For a more complete discussion of mediation models, the reader is referred to the following sources (e.g., Baron & Kenny, 1986; Frazier, Tix, & Barron, 2004; Judd & Kenny, 1981; MacKinnon, Fairchild, & Fritz, 2007; MacKinnon et al., 2002; Mallinckrodt, Abraham, Wei, & Russell, 2006; Preacher & Hayes, 2007; Shrout & Bolger, 2002).

variable). The ***indirect effect*** of X on Y is represented as the two paths linking X to Y through M (i.e., paths a and b in Figure 20.3). The indirect effect of X on Y through M is often quantified as the product of the a and b paths (i.e., a * b, or ab). In simple mediation models such as Figure 20.3, the total effect of X on Y is equal to the sum of the direct and indirect effects (i.e., c = c' + ab). The indirect effect is the difference between the total and the direct effects of X on Y (i.e., ab = c – c').

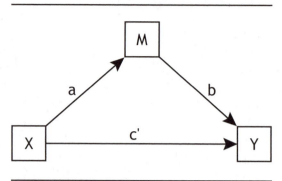

Figure 20.3   A Partial Mediation Regression Model

Mediation hypotheses are typically tested through a causal step approach (Hoyle & Robinson, 2004), where a series of criteria must be satisfied before mediation can be determined. This causal step strategy is attributable to several statisticians (Baron & Kenny, 1986; Hyman, 1955; Judd & Kenny, 1981). Baron and Kenny (1986), for example, outlined a series of four steps for establishing mediation using ordinary least squares regression (Table 20.1).

Table 20.1   Steps in Establishing Mediation Using Ordinary Least Squares Regression[1]

Step	Description	Regression model[2]	Equation
	Demonstrates that the:		
1	Independent variable effects the dependent variable (i.e., X→Y). This step estimates path c in Figure 20.2.	$Y = \beta_1(X)$	1
2	Independent variable effects the mediator (i.e., X→M). This step estimates path a in Figure 20.3.	$M = \beta_1(X)$	2
3	Independent variable and mediator effect the dependent. This step estimates paths c' and b in Figure 20.3.	$Y = \beta_1(X) + \beta_2(M)$	3
4	If M *fully* mediates the X→Y relationship (i.e., X→M→Y), path c' = 0.		
	If M *partially* mediates the X→Y relationship path c' (Figure 20.3) < path c (Figure 20.2).		
	Steps 3 and 4 are estimated in the same regression equation.		

[1.]   Adapted from Baron and Kenny (1986)
[2.]   Y = dependent variable, X = independent variable, M = Mediator

To establish mediation, the following conditions must hold: (a) the independent variable must effect the dependent variable (1st equation in Table 20.1), (b) the independent variable must effect the mediator (2nd equation), and (c) the mediator must effect the dependent variable in the 3rd equation. ***Full mediation*** occurs when the independent variable has no effect on the dependent variable when the mediator is in the model (3rd equation, see also Figure 20.4). ***Partial mediation*** occurs when the

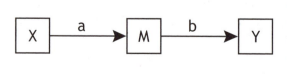

Figure 20.4   A Full Mediation Regression Model

effect of the predictor on the criterion (path c') is less in equation 3 than in equation 1 (Figure 20.3).

The steps outlined by Baron and Kenny (1986) are stated in terms of zero and nonzero coefficients, not in terms of statistical significance for two reasons. First, if the sample size is large, small coefficients can be statistically significant (conversely, with small sample sizes, large coefficients can be nonsignificant). Second, decisions regarding mediation effects should be driven by more than statistical significance. For example, if path a (i.e., X→M) is large and path b (M→Y) is 0, path c = c' (X→Y). However, if X and M are highly correlated, c' could be not significant due to collinearity (i.e., the extent to which the predictor variables are correlated). An analyst in this situation might incorrectly assume complete mediation when in fact there was no mediation given the collinearity. When the independent variables are correlated, it becomes difficult to examine the separate effects in a path analysis.

Chapter 16, for example, examined a regression model predicting the Colorado residents' voting intentions on a wolf reintroduction ballot initiative (Bright & Manfredo, 1996). Two of the independent variables were respondents' "specific attitude toward wolf reintroduction" and their "general attitude toward wolves." Although both of these predictors represent a positive or negative evaluation on an object, the two concepts differ in the specificity of the object. When the object is "wolves," the evaluation reflects general cognitions such as "like or dislike" or "beneficial or harmful" that form a general attitude. When the object is "wolf reintroduction in Colorado during 1996," the evaluation represents a narrower context and time frame, and thus a specific attitude. Using the logic of the cognitive hierarchy (chapter 2), the specific attitude should be a better predictor of voting behavior than the general attitude. The two predictor variables are likely to be correlated, but they could have different and independent influences on voting behaviors. For example, a person may feel that wolves symbolize the natural beauty of the world and should be protected (i.e., the general attitude), but not want them reintroduced into Colorado where they might kill cattle and sheep (i.e., the specific attitude). This logic suggests the partial mediation model in Figure 20.5.

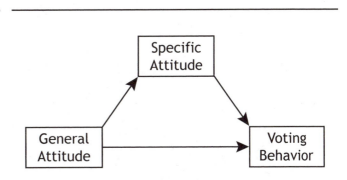

Figure 20.5   Partial Mediation Model Predicting Voting Intentions Based on General and Specific Attitudes

Using the three equations in Table 20.1, produces the SPSS results and path diagrams in Figure 20.6 (p. 580). Examples of the SPSS syntax for running the regressions are found in chapter 16. Equation 1 satisfies the first condition for establishing mediation. The independent variable (general attitude) influenced the dependent variable (voting behavior), $\beta = .75, p < .001$. The second condition for establishing mediation implies that the general attitude should influence the mediator (specific attitude). Support for this criterion is evident in Figure 20.6. The standardized regression coefficient between the two attitudinal measures was $\beta = .82, p < .001$. Equation 3 regressed the dependent variable on both the independent variable and the mediator simultaneously. For full mediation to occur the mediator must affect the dependent variable in

Coefficients[a]

Equation 1

Model		Unstandardized Coefficients		Standardized Coefficients	t	Sig.
		B	Std. Error	Beta		
1	(Constant)	–4.668	.149		–31.246	.000
	General attitude toward wolves	1.136	.027	.751	42.386	.000

a. Dependent Variable: Voting behavior

1st condition for mediation
(Predictor related to Criterion)

Coefficients[a]

Equation 2

Model		Unstandardized Coefficients		Standardized Coefficients	t	Sig.
		B	Std. Error	Beta		
2	(Constant)	–.398	.106		–3.742	.000
	General attitude toward wolves	1.023	.019	.819	53.532	.000

a. Dependent Variable: Specific attitude toward wolf reintroduction

2nd condition for mediation
(Predictor related to Mediator)

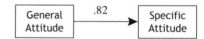

Coefficients[a]

Equation 3

Model		Unstandardized Coefficients		Standardized Coefficients	t	Sig.
		B	Std. Error	Beta		
1	(Constant)	–4.225	.091		–46.637	.000
	Specific attitude toward wolf reintroduction	1.106	.023	.915	49.040	.000
	General attitude toward wolves	.004	.028	.003	.144	.885

a. Dependent Variable: Voting behavior

3rd condition for full mediation
(Mediator related to criterion. Predictor no longer related to criterion)

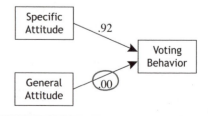

Figure 20.6   Applying the Baron and Kenny (1986) Steps to the Wolf Reintroduction Data

Equation 3 and the influence of the independent variable on the criterion should be reduced to 0. Given that the coefficient for general attitude was reduced from .75 (Equation 1) to .00 (Equation 3), the wolf reintroduction data *could* be interpreted as an illustration of full mediation. The word *could* was highlighted to emphasize that there was a substantial correlation between the general and specific attitude measures ($r = .819$, $p < .001$, see chapter 16). With two predictor variables in a regression model, collinearity exists when the correlation between the independent variables is $> .90$ (Belsley, Huh, & Welsch, 1980). Although the correlation between general attitude and specific attitude does not quite reach .90, it is close and probably contributed to the dramatic decline in the magnitude of regression coefficients (Equation 1 vs. Equation 3).

Measuring Indirect Effects in Mediation Models

The amount of mediation (i.e., *indirect effect*) is defined as the reduction of the effect of the initial independent variable on the dependent variable (i.e., path c – path c'). The difference in these coefficients is approximately equal to the product of the effect of X on M times the effect of M on Y (path a * path b, or ab). This relationship can be expressed as $ab \approx c - c'$ and is illustrated by the wolf reintroduction data (Figure 20.7). The coefficients are standardized regression coefficients from Figure 20.6.

The difference between ab and c – c' will be exactly equal when: (a) multiple regression is used, (b) there are no missing data, and (c) the same independent variables are in the equation. The equality between ab and c – c', however, will only be approximate for logistic regression models (chapter 17) and structural equation models with latent variables (see Byrne,

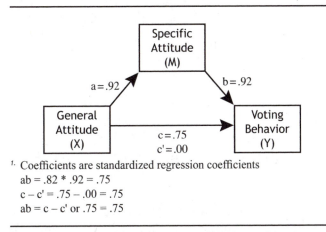

1. Coefficients are standardized regression coefficients
ab = .82 * .92 = .75
c – c' = .75 – .00 = .75
ab = c – c' or .75 = .75

Figure 20.7   Measuring the Indirect Effect of Mediation[1]

1994; Hayduk, 1987; Kline, 1998, for a discussion of SEM and latent variables). For these models, c should *not* be directly computed from step 1 in Table 20.1 (Baron & Kenny, 1986). Rather, c should be inferred from c' + ab. For example, using the wolf reintroduction data this equation is:

c = c' + ab = .00 + .75

When step 2 (the estimate of a) and step 3 (the estimate of b) are met, the effect of X on Y is reduced. The null hypothesis that ab = 0 could be examined by testing that both a and b are zero separately (Steps 2 and 3). Alternatively, Sobel (1982) proposed a single test for examining this null hypothesis. The test is based on the unstandardized regression coefficients and the standard errors associated with the path a and path b coefficients. Using the data from Figure 20.6, the wolf reintroduction path model can be displayed as Figure 20.8 (p. 582).

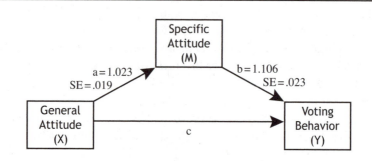

where:

    a & b = the unstandardized regression coefficients for paths a and b in Figure 20.6. The model used
           to obtain coefficient for path b also included the general attitude variable.
    SE = the standard error associated with each coefficient

Figure 20.8   Data for the Sobel Test for Indirect Mediation Effects

A detailed discussion of the Sobel test can be found in (Baron & Kenny, 1986; MacKinnon, Warsi, & Dwyer, 1995; Sobel, 1982), but in general, the formula for this test is:

$$z = \frac{a * b}{\sqrt{b^2 * SE_a^2 + a^2 * SE_b^2}}$$

Equation 20.1

Inserting the data from Figure 20.8 into Equation 20.1 yields:

$$z = \frac{1.023 * 1.106}{\sqrt{(1.106)^2 * (.019)_a^2 + (1.023)^2 * (.023)_b^2}} = 35.865$$

The z-value is a test of whether the indirect effect of the independent variable on the dependent variable via the mediator is statistically different from 0. Because the ratio in Equation 20.1 can be treated as a z-test, absolute values larger than 1.96 are significant at $p < .05$. For the wolf reintroduction data, the z of 35.865 ($p < .001$) indicates that the influence of general attitude toward wolves on voting behavior is mediated by the specific attitude toward wolf reintroduction. As demonstrated here, the calculation of the Sobel test is straightforward. Kristopher Preacher and Geoffrey Leonardelli (2006), however, have developed an interactive webpage that calculates the Sobel test by simply inserting the appropriate unstandardized regression coefficients and standard errors (numbers that can be obtained from the SPSS output, e.g., Figure 20.6). The URL for their web site is: http://www.people.ku.edu/~preacher/sobel/sobel.htm

The Preacher and Leonardelli webpage also includes two variants of the Sobel test: (a) the Aroian test (Aroian, 1944/1947), and (b) the Goodman test (Goodman, 1960). Of these alternatives, Preacher and Leonardelli as well as others (MacKinnon, Lockwood, Hoffman, West, & Sheets, 2002), recommend the Sobel test. For the wolf reintroduction data, the Aroian test ($z = 35.812$) and the Goodman test ($z = 35.869$) were nearly identical to the Sobel test ($z = 35.865$). The Sobel test is one of the most commonly reported tests for mediation in the literature.

Because the Sobel test is conservative (MacKinnon et al., 1995), other researchers (e.g., MacKinnon et al., 2002; Shrout & Bolger, 2002) have explored alternative testing methods such as bootstrapping. Bootstrapping is a statistical method for estimating the sampling distribution of an estimator by sampling with replacement from the original sample (Efron, 1979; Efron & Tibshirani, 1993). The technique is commonly used to derive robust estimates (see chapter 19) of standard errors and confidence intervals of a population parameter like a mean, correlation, or regression coefficient. Preacher and Hayes (2004), for example, have developed a bootstrap method for estimating indirect effects in simple mediation models. Electronic copies of their SPSS macros can be downloaded from the Psychonomic Society's Web archive at www.psychonomic.org/archive/

More Complex Mediation Models

The path analysis models examined thus far have only included one mediator. To understand the logic of more complex mediated path models, it is important to introduce some basic definitions and notations. Consider a generalized version of the traditional crowding/satisfaction path model shown in Figure 20.9.

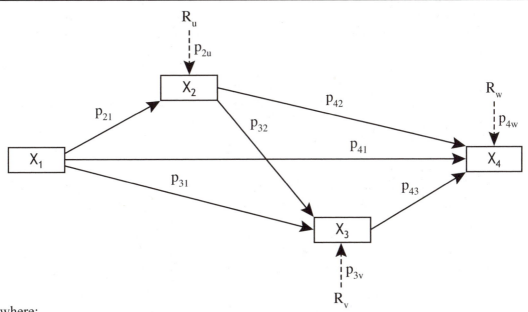

where:

X$_1$ is called an ***exogenous variable*** (independent) since it is not influenced by other variables in the model.

X$_2$, X$_3$, and X$_4$ are ***endogenous variables*** (dependent) that are affected by other variables in the model.

p$_{ij}$s (e.g., p$_{21}$, p$_{31}$) are path coefficients (standardized regression coefficients).

R$_i$s (R$_u$, R$_v$, and R$_w$) are ***residual*** or error terms representing factors that were not measured in the model and/or measurement error.

The X$_i$s are measured variables (variables for which data have been collected), whereas the R$_i$s are unmeasured variables for which observations have not been gathered.

Figure 20.9 Hypothetical Four Variable Path Model

A *path coefficient* is a standardized regression (beta) coefficient showing the direct effect of an exogenous variable on an endogenous dependent variable in the model. In a simple bivariate regression, the beta weight is the same as the Pearson correlation coefficient (chapter 16). When there are two or more causal variables, path coefficients are *partial regression coefficients* that measure the extent one exogenous variable influences an endogenous variable, controlling for the other exogenous variables in a given equation.

An arrow diagram can be converted into a system of equations that reflect the linkages drawn in Figure 20.9. One equation is written for each endogenous variable; thus there will be one equation for X_2, X_3, and X_4. Included in each equation are those variables that directly affect the endogenous variable in question weighted by the appropriate path coefficients. The system of equations for the model in Figure 20.9 is:

$$X_2 = p_{21}X_1 + p_{2u}R_u \qquad\qquad \text{Equation 20.2}$$

$$X_3 = p_{31}X_1 + p_{32}X_2 + p_{3v}R_v \qquad\qquad \text{Equation 20.3}$$

$$X_4 = p_{41}X_1 + p_{42}X_2 + p_{43}X_3 + p_{4w}R_w \qquad\qquad \text{Equation 20.4}$$

This set of equations represents a *recursive system*, meaning that there are no feedback loops or reciprocal linkages. Although more complex nonrecursive models can be analyzed (see Duncan, 1975), most path analyses in the parks, recreation, and human dimensions literature assume that causation is recursive (i.e., one-way). In addition, path analysis assumes that: (a) the variables are measured at the continuous level and are approximately normally distributed in the population, (b) the data are linearly related and the relationships are additive (i.e., no significant interaction between the variables), and (c) the error terms are pairwise uncorrelated with each other. The above equations do not have a constant term because the variables are standardized to a mean of zero and a standard deviation of one.

Estimating Path Coefficients

To obtain estimates of the main path coefficients, regress each endogenous variable on those variables that have arrows pointing to it:

1. p_{21} would be estimated by regressing X_2 on X_1. The relationship between X_1 and X_2 is also the bivariate Pearson correlation between these two variables.

2. p_{31} and p_{32} would be obtained by regressing X_3 on X_1 and X_2. The beta weights are the partial path coefficients for these relationships.

3. p_{41}, p_{42} and p_{43} would be obtained by regressing X_4 on X_1, X_2 and X_3. Again, the beta weights express the magnitude of these paths.

The residual path coefficients can also be ascertained by ordinary regression analysis since they have a direct regression interpretation. The general form of a residual path coefficient is $\sqrt{1-R^2}$ where R^2 is the square of the appropriate multiple correlation coefficient. In the hypothetical model of Figure 20.9:

$$p_{2u} = \sqrt{1 - R_{12}^2}$$
Equation 20.5

$$p_{3v} = \sqrt{1 - R_{3\bullet12}^2}$$
Equation 20.6

$$p_{4w} = \sqrt{1 - R_{4\bullet123}^2}$$
Equation 20.7

R^2 is the proportion of explained variance. Because standardized variables have a variance of 1, the general expression $1 - R^2$ is the proportion of unexplained variance. The residual path coefficient is the square root of the unexplained variation in the dependent variable in question. The dot notation (•) simply means that there was more than one exogenous variable in the equation.

The path model in Figure 20.9 assumes a causal sequence between the variables. If the hypothesized model is not correct, the model is of little value. Path models may be incorrect for a variety of reasons, including: (a) causal misspecification, (b) confounding variables, and (c) omitted variables (Baron & Kenny, 1986; Judd & Kenny, 1981). Because *all* modeling efforts omit some potential predictor and/or criterion variables, no model can ever precisely mirror the cognitive processes underlying the data (MacCallum, 2003). Models such as Fishbein and Ajzen's (1975) theory of planned behavior, Schwartz's (1977) norm activation model, or the cognitive hierarchy (chapter 2), serve as parsimonious approximations of reality. Given the constrained focus of these these theories (e.g., attitudes, norms), no path model is ever totally correct. This does not imply, however, that investigating path models is a pointless undertaking. Rather, the researcher should keep in mind that models are merely tools to clarify our understanding of phenomena, and that some models are better predictive tools than others in explaining certain situations (Preacher & Hayes, 2007).

Moderator Models

A moderator is a variable that affects the direction and/or strength of the relationship between an independent and dependent variable (Baron & Kenny, 1986). More specifically, a moderator is a third variable that affects the zero-order correlation between the other two variables. The appropriate statistical test for moderation depends on the variables' level of measurement (Table 20.2, p. 586). For example, if: (a) the predictor variable is dichotomous (e.g., SEX), (b) the criterion or dependent variable is continuous (e.g., days of participation in an activity), and (c) the moderator is dichotomous (e.g., rural vs. urban place of residence), the test for moderation is a 2×2 analysis of variance (chapter 15). A moderation effect is evident if there is a significant interaction between sex (the independent variable) and place of residence (the moderator). This example treated sex as the predictor variable. Depending on the analysts' theory and the research question of interest, however, place of residence could have been the independent variable and sex could be the moderator. In this case, the research question becomes: does sex moderate the relationship between place of residence and participation rates? Stated otherwise, are males who live in rural areas more likely to participate in the activity than females living in an urban environment?

Table 20.2   Levels of Measurement and Tests for Moderation

Case	Predictor	Criterion	Moderator	Test
1	Dichotomous	Continuous	Dichotomous	2 x 2 ANOVA
2	Continuous	Continuous	Dichotomous	Correlation or Regression
3	Dichotomous	Continuous	Continuous	Dummy Variable Regression
4	Continuous	Continuous	Continuous	Regression

Source: Adapted from Baron and Kenny (1986)

Case 2 in Table 20.2 illustrates a situation where both the predictor and criterion are continuous variables and the moderator is dichotomous. For example, assume the researcher is interested in the relationship between a person's intentions to engage in an activity (i.e., the predictor) and their actual participation (i.e., criterion), where both variables are continuous measures. A moderator in this example might be sex. If correlation analysis is used to test for moderation, the researcher would: (a) correlate intentions with behavior for males, and (b) correlate intentions with behavior for females. A moderation test for differences in two correlations is the Fisher *z* (Fisher, 1925).

Problems can arise, however, when correlations are used to test for moderation. First, the technique assumes that the predictor variable has equal variances at each level of the moderator. In the current example, this implies that the variance of intentions must be equal for both sexes. When the variances differ across levels of the moderator, the correlation between the predictor (i.e., intentions) and the criterion (i.e., behavior) will be smaller for the moderator level (e.g., males) with less variance (as compared to the correlation for the moderator category with more variance). Second, if the amount of measurement error in the criterion (see chapter 18) varies as a function of the moderator, the correlation between predictor and criterion will be spurious. A ***spurious correlation*** occurs when two variables are statistically related, but are not in fact causally linked; usually because the statistical relationship is caused by a third variable. For example, "if researchers found a correlation between individuals' college grades and their income later in life, they might wonder whether doing well in school increased income. It might, but good grades and high income could both be caused by a third variable such as tendency to work hard" (Huff, 1993, p. 132).

Moderation tests for case 2 in Table 20.2 can also be examined using regression analysis. Using this approach, the analyst would regress the criterion (i.e., behavior) on the predictor (i.e., intentions) *separately* for each level of the moderator (e.g., males and females). The test for differences between the regression coefficients can be found in Cohen and Cohen (1983, p. 56). The unstandardized regression coefficients should be used in this situation. However, if there is differential measurement error in the predictor across levels of the moderator, bias will result (Baron & Kenny, 1986). One way to address this problem is to use a structural equation program (e.g., EQS, AMOS, LISREL) to test for differences in measurement error between the categories of the moderator. This approach is sometimes referred to as a multi-group model where the criterion is regressed on the predictor *simultaneously* for each level of moderator (Kline, 1998). The test for a moderation effect is the difference between the models using the $\Delta\chi^2$. The approach is analogous to testing between two models using $-2LL$ in a logistic regression (chapter 17).

Cases 3 and 4 in Table 20.2 involve the use of regression techniques discussed in chapter 16. Case 3 is a dummy variable regression because the predictor variable is dichotomous. Case 4 is ordinary least squares regression because all of variables are measured at the continuous level. The test for moderation in these situations is a significant interaction term between the predictor and the moderator. Unlike case 1, however, where SPSS tests for interactions in the analysis of variance by checking the appropriate boxes (see chapter 15), the interaction term in the regression model must be computed before the model is run. For example, if Y is the criterion, X is the predictor and Z is the moderator, the SPSS syntax for computing the interaction term is:

```
Compute XZ = X * Z.
```

The regression equation that is being evaluated is:

$$Y = B_0 + B_1(X) + B_2(Z) + B_3(XZ) + \varepsilon \hspace{4cm} \text{Equation 20.8}$$

If B_3 is statistically significant, there is evidence of a moderation effect. The moderated multiple regression model with continuous level independent, dependent and moderator variables provides the most power in detecting moderation (Baron & Kenny, 1986). Figure 20.10 diagrams the regression model above.

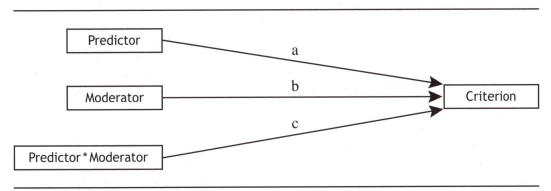

Figure 20.10   A Moderated Regression Model (Baron and Kenny, 1986)

The moderator hypothesis is supported if the interaction (path c) is significant. There may also be significant main effects for the predictor and moderator paths (paths a and b), but these are not directly relevant conceptually to testing the moderator hypothesis. Another property of the moderator variable apparent from Figure 20.10 is that, unlike the mediator-predictor relationship (where the predictor is causally antecedent to the mediator), moderators and predictors are at the same level in regard to their role as causal variables. In other words, the moderator variables always function as independent variables, whereas mediating events shift roles from independent to dependent, depending on where they are in the causal chain.

Moderation Empirical Example

Public support for wildland management policies is often influenced by societal attitudes and behaviors. Understanding attitudes toward and support for wildland fire management is important given the heavy losses to life, private property and natural resources that can occur with wildfires. Of particular managerial interest are questions such as: (a) What is the relationship between peoples' attitudes and their support of agency policies? (b) How strongly are these attitudes held? and (c) Can the views of the public be influenced by education and persuasion campaigns?

An article by Absher, Vaske, Bright, and Donnelly (2006) explored the utility of incorporating a within-individual measure of consensus (i.e., ipsative crystallization, IC) into the traditional attitude-behavior model (chapter 2) to better predict public support for wildland fire management policies. Both the direct and moderating influences of within-individual crystallization were examined.

Study Background

Psychologists have focused on an individual's own state of mind and measured variability within a person's own responses. This property has been referred to as ***ipsativity*** from the Latin *ipse* or "he/she, himself/herself" (Cattell, 1944). Early work by Cattell (1949), for example, recognized the importance of ipsativity when examining response patterns on attitudinal questions. Other researchers (Baron, 1996; Beaman & Vaske, 1995; Cattell & Brennan, 1994; Clemans, 1966; Hicks, 1970) have emphasized that individual variability (or the lack thereof) can be a source of response bias and confound the search for variance that should be measured (see Chan, 2003 for a review). Within-individual (ipsative) research has concentrated on detecting and correcting potential bias in response sets that can lead to erroneous conclusions. Greenleaf (1992a, 1992b), for example, proposed measures and corrections for bias in common response scales. He defined bias due to response variation as one component of attitude data that needs to be separated from actual variation in attitude information. The correction factor in Greenleaf's work was based on an ipsative standard deviation.

Absher et al. (2006) proposed a within-individual crystallization measure that relied on ipsative properties. ***Ipsative crystallization*** (IC) was based on each respondent's standard deviation across a set of items designed to measure an individual's support (or opposition) to wildland fire management alternatives. Individuals who responded to the multiple items with minimal variation were considered to have high crystallization (i.e., consistency). Respondents with greater levels of variation were labeled as low or not crystallized.

Similar to the psychological ipsativity work (e.g., Chan, 2003), within-individual IC measures the respondent's own distribution of scores across a set of survey items to construct an indicator of serial agreement or consensus. In contrast to Chan (2003), however, the Absher et al. (2006) approach considered personal variation in these scores to be substantively important. In other words, the personal variation was not considered as a source of bias, but rather a reflection of an individual's flexibility (or lack thereof) in beliefs. Crystallized attitudes tend to be stronger, resistant to persuasion attempts, influence the processing of information, are stable over time, and guide behavior (Krosnick & Petty, 1995). For example, those who do not vary in their responses regardless of situational considerations were considered highly crystallized and not likely to change their attitudes over time or in response to persuasive communications. Although a practical methodology for differentiating ipsative variation into bias and substantive components has not been identified in the literature, IC effects can be measured and assessed relative to their role in the overall attitude-behavior relationship.

The hypothesized direct and moderating influence of IC, a within-individual ipsative standard deviation measure, on the relationship between respondents' attitude toward wildland fires and their support alternative wildfire policies are illustrated in Figure 20.11. Path a in the figure hypothesizes the traditional attitude-behavior link (Eagly & Chaiken, 1993; Fishbein & Ajzen, 1975). Path b predicts a main effect of IC on support for wildfire policies. Path c tests the moderating effect of IC on the attitude-behavior relationship. Following the conventions of Baron and Kenny (1986), this moderating effect is represented by the interaction of IC and attitude.

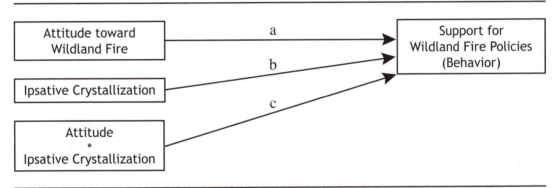

Figure 20.11   Attitude-Behavior Model with Ipsative Crystallization and Moderator Effects

Data for this study were obtained from a mail survey sent to individuals who had visited the Arapaho–Roosevelt National Forest (CO), the Mt. Baker–Snoqualmie National Forest (WA), and the San Bernardino National Forest (CA). A total of 1,288 mail surveys were returned with an overall response rate of 51% (1,288 returned / [2,706 sent – 176 nondeliverables]). Response rates for the individual forests were: Arapaho–Roosevelt 56% (469 returned / [890 sent – 53 nondeliverables]), Mt. Baker–Snoqualmie 54% (498 returned / [987 sent – 70 nondeliverables]), and San Bernardino 41% (321 returned / [829 sent – 53 nondeliverables]).

Respondents' overall attitude toward fire was measured by asking respondents to evaluate the extent to which wildfires are: (1) good or bad, (2) beneficial or harmful, and (3) positive or negative. Each of these variables was coded on a seven-point semantic differential scale (extremely good, beneficial or positive [3]; extremely bad, harmful or negative [–3]). An additive index was calculated from these three items (chapter 18). The index had a Cronbach's alpha reliability of .91.

To measure support, respondents were presented with eight scenarios that described potential effects of a new wildland fire in the Arapaho–Roosevelt, Mt. Baker-Snoqualmie or San Bernardino National Forests. The scenarios manipulated five situational factors (see Kneeshaw, Vaske, Bright, & Absher, 2004, for specifics) related to wildland fires: (a) source of fire ignition (lightning vs. unintentionally caused by humans), (b) impact on air quality in nearby communities (not affected vs. poor air quality), (c) risk of private property damage (low vs. high), (d) forest recovery (few vs. many years), and (e) impact on outdoor recreation within the forest (remain open vs. closed for the rest of the season). Following each scenario, three possible policy actions the U.S. Forest Service might take were presented: (a) immediately put the fire out (full suppression), (b) let the fire burn but contain it so it does not get out of control, and (c) let the fire burn out on its own without trying to contain it. Respondents rated each of the 24 management options (8 scenarios x 3 management options) on seven-point scales ranging from "highly unacceptable" (−3) through "no opinion" (0) to "highly acceptable" (3).

Each individual's set of eight scenario ratings was transformed into a within-individual ipsative crystallization measure for each of three management policies:

$$IC_b = SD_b (S_{1b}, S_{2b}, S_{3b}, S_{4b}, S_{5b}, S_{6b}, S_{7b}, S_{8b}) \qquad \text{Equation 20.9}$$

$$IC_c = SD_c (S_{1c}, S_{2c}, S_{3c}, S_{4c}, S_{5c}, S_{6c}, S_{7c}, S_{8c}) \qquad \text{Equation 20.10}$$

$$IC_p = SD_p (S_{1p}, S_{2p}, S_{3p}, S_{4p}, S_{5p}, S_{6p}, S_{7p}, S_{8p}) \qquad \text{Equation 20.11}$$

where:
- b = "let fire burn,"
- c = "contain fire"
- p = "put fire out"
- IC = the within-individual ipsative crystallization measures for each of three management policies (b, c or p)
- SD = each individual's standard deviation across the eight scenarios for that management policy (b, c or p)
- S_1 to S_8 = each individual's acceptability ratings for a management policy (b, c or p)

Each respondent had three policy-specific, within-individual IC scores, one for each management policy. The direct and moderating influences of within-individual ipsative crystallization on the attitude-behavior relationship were examined through a series of regression analyses for each of the three wildland fire policies (Table 20.3). When considered by itself, attitude explained 12% of variance in "let the fire burn," 14% of the variance in "contain the fire," and 26% in the "put the fire out."

The addition of the ipsative crystallization measure to each of the regression models as a direct effect on behavior increased the explanatory power to between 25% and 32% (R^2 = .255, .249 and .315, respectively). In essence, within-individual IC doubled the explained variance for the "let the fire burn" and "contain the fire" policies and added 6% to the "put the fire out" model. In these equations, both attitude and IC were statistically significant at $p < .001$.

The third regression for each policy included three predictor variables: attitude toward wildland fires, within-individual IC, and the interaction of attitude and IC (i.e., the moderator). Each of the equations supported a moderation effect. For the "let the fire burn" policy, all three predictors were significant. The main effect of crystallization strengthened from $\beta = -.38$ ($p < .001$, equation 2) to $\beta = -.60$ (equation 3), and the influence of attitude increased from $\beta = .25$ (equation 2) to $\beta = .34$ ($p < .001$, equation 3). In the "contain the fire" policy model, the moderator was significant ($\beta = .38, p < .001$), the main effect of IC was reduced from $\beta = .34$ ($p < .001$, equation

2) to $\beta = .03$ (n.s., equation 3), and the main effect of attitude increased from $\beta = .38$ ($p < .001$, equation 2) to $\beta = .54$ ($p < .001$, equation 3). All three predictors were statistically significant in the "put the fire out" policy equation and the main effects of both crystallization and attitude increased.

Table 20.3 Direct and Moderation Effects of Within-Individual Crystallization on the Attitude-Wildland Policy Support Relationship (Absher et al., 2006)

| | Beta Coefficients[a] | | | | |
Dependent variable = Policy	Attitude	Within Individual Crystallization	Moderator[b]	R^2	F-value
Let fire burn					
Attitude	.35	--	--	.121	167.07
Attitude, Crystallization	.25	−.38	--	.255	207.04
Attitude, Crystallization, Moderation	.34	−.60	.28	.262	143.95
Contain the fire					
Attitude	.37	--	--	.136	191.52
Attitude, Crystallization	.38	.34	--	.249	202.87
Attitude, Crystallization, Moderation	.54	.03[*]	.38	.265	147.29
Put fire out					
Attitude	−.51	--	--	.261	431.36
Attitude, Crystallization	−.43	.25	--	.315	282.88
Attitude, Crystallization, Moderation	−.56	.58	−.41	.329	200.82

[a.] Betas and F values are all significant at $p < .001$, except * which was n.s., $p = .688$.
[b.] The moderator was operationalized as the interaction of attitude and within-individual crystallization.

Overall, the Absher et al. (2006) study constituted a first step in improving our understanding of the relationship between attitudes and behavior. One explanation for the moderating effects of crystallization on the attitude-behavior relationship lies in the attitude strength literature. Although there is not a specific operational definition of attitude strength, social psychological theorists have suggested that strong attitudes possess four key characteristics: they (a) are stable over time, (b) resistant to attempts at persuasion, (c) influence information processing, and (d) guide behavior (Krosnick & Petty, 1995). Crystallization is one of a number of attitude strength dimensions that have been suggested to reflect one or more of the four characteristics of strong attitudes (Raden, 1985).

The Absher et al. (2006) article also highlighted a number of unresolved methodological issues that should be addressed in future work. Ipsativity, as operationalized in their work constituted a simple measure of within-individual crystallization. Although the measures proved useful in clarifying the attitude-behavior relationship, there are alternative ways to compute ipsativity. For example, their measure concentrated on each individual's standard deviation across a range of items. As noted by others (Beaman & Vaske, 1995; Romesburg, 1990), ipsative transformations may also compensate for an individual's high or low scoring tendencies by subtracting out the respondent's mean across a set of attitudinal questions. Although this was not directly tested in Absher et al. (2006), an individual's mean and standard deviation should not be treated as irrelevant in examining response patterns (Cattell, 1944; Hicks, 1970; Hui & Triandis, 1985). Individual differences in the mean and/or standard deviation across a response set convey information important to understanding a person's attitudes and behaviors. The extent to which this information represents response bias (Greenleaf, 1992a) or substantive findings remains a topic for future research. Within-individual IC was statistically related to the correspondence between attitudes and behaviors, supporting its role as an important measure of attitude strength and a factor that improves the quality of attitudinal information in natural resource issues.

Chapter Summary

This chapter introduced a statistical technique called path analysis. ***Path analysis*** can viewed as a type of multiple regression analysis (chapter 16). In multiple regression, there is a single continuous dependent variable and two or more independent variables, whereas in path analysis there is always more than one dependent variable, plus two or more independent variables.

A distinction was made between mediator and moderator variables. A variable functions as a ***mediator*** to the extent that it accounts for the relationship between the predictor and criterion. A ***moderator*** is a third variable that affects the direction and/or strength of the relationship between a predictor and a criterion variable. In a path diagram, a mediator can be either an independent or a dependent variable. A moderator is always the independent variable.

If a variable M is causally situated between X and Y and at least partially accounts for the association between X and Y, M *mediates* the relationship. Mediation hypotheses are typically tested through a causal step approach, where a series of criteria must be satisfied before mediation can be determined. Following Baron and Kenny (1986), the steps in establishing mediation using ordinary least squares regression were discussed:

Step 1: Demonstrate that the independent variable effects the dependent variable $[Y = \beta_1(X)]$.

Step 2: Demonstrate the independent variable effects the mediator $[M = \beta_1(X)]$.

Step 3: Demonstrate that the independent variable and mediator effect the dependent variable $[Y = \beta_1(X) + \beta_2(M)]$.

To establish mediation, the following conditions must hold: (a) the independent variable must effect the dependent variable (step 1), (b) the independent variable must effect the mediator (step 2), and (c) the mediator must effect the dependent variable in step 3. ***Full mediation*** occurs when the independent variable has no effect on the dependent variable when the mediator is in the model in step 3. ***Partial mediation*** occurs when the effect of the predictor on the criterion is less in step 3 than in step 1.

The amount of mediation was defined as the reduction of the effect of the initial independent variable on the dependent variable. When step 2 and step 3 are met, the effect of X on Y is reduced. A test developed by Sobel (1982) was discussed for testing whether the indirect effect of the independent variable on the dependent variable via the mediator is statistically different from 0. This simple mediation model was illustrated using data from a study of wolf reintroduction in Colorado (Bright & Manfredo, 1996). Some basic definitions and notations for understanding more complex mediation path analyses were introduced.

All path models assume a causal sequence between the variables. If the hypothesized model is not correct, the model is of little value. Path models may be incorrect for a variety of reasons, including: causal misspecification, confounding variables, and omitted variables. Because *all* modeling efforts omit some potential predictor and/or criterion variables, no model can ever precisely mirror the cognitive processes underlying the data. This does not imply, however, that investigating path models is a pointless undertaking. Rather, the researcher should keep in mind that models are merely tools to clarify our understanding of phenomena, and that some models are better predictive tools than others in explaining certain situations.

A *moderator* is a variable that affects the direction and/or strength of the relationship between an independent and dependent variable. More specifically, a moderator is a third variable that affects the zero-order correlation between the other two variables. Four cases were discussed that illustrated the appropriate statistical test for moderation when the variables have different measurement properties (e.g., dichotomous vs. continuous). These cases involved the use of analysis of variance, correlation, and regression. A moderated multiple regression model was illustrated using data from a wildland fire study (Absher et al., 2006).

Review Questions

1. Explain the distinction between a *mediator* and a *moderator* in path analysis.

2. How does path analysis differ from multiple regression analysis?

3. All path models assume a causal ordering. Explain why the traditional crowding/satisfaction model has a logical ordering of variables.

4. What do the arrows and associated signs (+ or –) in a path model signify?

5. Describe three criteria for determining causation.

6. Describe the basic steps involved in conducting a mediation analysis.

7. Explain the difference between *full mediation* and *partial mediation*.

8. Explain the difference between a *direct effect*, *indirect effect*, and *total effect* in a mediation model.

9. What does the Sobel test examine?

10. Explain the distinction between an *exogenous* and an *endogenous* variable in a path analysis.

11. What do residual or error terms in a path analysis represent?

12. What does a *path coefficient* refer to in a path analysis?

13. What is meant by the term *recursive system*?

14. Explain the phrase: "No path model is ever totally correct."

15. In a moderation analysis, if the predictor is dichotomous, the criterion is continuous and the moderator is dichotomous, what is an appropriate test for examining the relationships among the variables?

16. Explain two problems associated with using correlations to test for moderation.

17. What is a spurious correlation?

18. If the predictor is continuous, the criterion is continous and moderator is dichotomous, what is an appropriate analysis strategy for testing for moderation?

references

Abdi, H. (2007). The Bonferroni and Sidák corrections for multiple comparisons. In Neil Salkind (Ed.), *Encyclopedia of measurement and statistics*. Thousand Oaks, CA: Sage Publications.

Absher, J. (1979). *A sociological approach to crowding in outdoor recreation: A study of the Yosemite National Park backcountry*. Unpublished doctoral dissertation, University of California, Berkeley.

Absher, J. D., & Lee, R. G. (1981). Density as an incomplete cause of crowding in backcountry settings. *Leisure Sciences, 4,* 231–247.

Absher, J. D., Vaske, J. J., & Bright, A. D. (2008). *Basic beliefs, attitudes and social norms toward wildland fire management in southern California* (GTR-PSW-209, 45–56). Albany, CA: USDA Forest Service Pacific Southwest Research Station.

Absher, J. D., Vaske, J. J., Bright, A. D., & Donnelly, M. P. (2006). Ipsative crystallization effects on wildland fire attitude—Policy support models. *Society and Natural Resources, 19,* 381–392.

Achen, C. H. (1982). *Interpreting and using regression*. Beverly Hills, CA: Sage Publications.

Agresti, A. (1996). *An introduction to categorical data analysis*. New York, NY: John Wiley and Sons.

Agresti, A. (2002). *Categorical data analysis* (2nd ed). New York, NY: John Wiley and Sons.

Ajzen, I., & Fishbein, M. (1980). *Understanding attitudes and predicting social behavior*. Englewood Cliffs, NJ: Prentice-Hall.

Alldredge, R. B. (1972). *Some capacity theory for parks and recreation areas* [Reprint]. Washington, DC: USDI National Park Service.

Anderson, D. R., Burnham, K. P., & Thompson, W. L. (2000). Null hypothesis testing: Problems, prevalence, and an alternative. *Journal of Wildlife Management, 64*(4), 912–923.

Argyrous, G. (2005). *Statistics for research: With a guide to SPSS*. Newbury Park, CA: Sage Publications.

Armstrong, J. S., & Lusk, E. J. (1987). Return postage in mail surveys: A meta-analysis. *Public Opinion Quarterly, 51,* 233–248.

Aroian, L. A. (1944/1947). The probability function of the product of two normally distributed variables. *Annals of Mathematical Statistics, 18,* 265–271.

Ashcroft, M. H. (1994). *Human memory and cognition* (2nd ed.). New York, NY: HarperCollins College.

Asher, H. B. (1983). *Causal modeling* (2nd ed.). Beverly Hills, CA: Sage Publications.

Babbie, E. (2003). *The practice of social research with InfoTrac* (10th ed.). Belmont, CA: Wadsworth Publishing Co.

Bailar, B. A. (1987). Nonsampling errors. *Journal of Official Statistics, 3*(4), 323–325.

Baker, B. O., Hardyck, C. D., & Petrinovich, L. F. (1966). Weak measurements vs. strong statistics: An empirical critique of S. S. Stevens's proscriptions on statistics. *Educational and Psychological Measurement, 26,* 291–309.

Baker, M. (1992). Digit preference in CPS unemployment data. *Economics Letters, 39,* 117–121.

Bailey, M., & Makannah, T. J. (1993). Patterns of digit preference and avoidance in the age statistics of some recent African censuses: 1970–1986. *Journal of Official Statistics, 9*(3), 705–715.

Baron, H. (1996). Strengths and limitations of ipsative measurement. *Journal of Occupational and Organizational Psychology, 69,* 49–56.

Baron, R. M., & Kenny, D. A. (1986). The moderator-mediator variable distinction in social psychological research: Conceptual, strategic, and statistical considerations. *Journal of Personality and Social Psychology, 51,* 1173–1182.

Barro, S. C., & Manfredo, M. J. (1996). Constraints, psychological investment, and hunting participation: Development and testing of a model. *Human Dimensions of Wildlife, 1*(3), 42–61.

Baruch, Y. (1999). Response rates in academic studies: A comparative analysis. *Human Relations, 52,* 421–434.

Beaman, J. (2002). Comment on "Digit preference in reported harvest among Illinois waterfowl hunters" by Craig A. Miller and William L. Anderson. *Human Dimensions of Wildlife, 7*(1), 67–72.

Beaman, J. (2006). Obtaining less variable unbiased means and totals for expenditures: Being more cost effective. *e-Review of Tourism Research, 4*(6), 145–152.

Beaman, J. G., Beaman, J. P., O'Leary, J. T., & Smith, S. (2000). The impact of seemingly minor methodological changes on estimates of travel and correcting bias. *Tourism Analysis, 5,* 91–96.

Beaman, J., & Redekop, D. (1990). *Some special considerations in weighting survey data.* Aix-en-Provence, France: Centre des Hautes Etudes Touristiques.

Beaman, J., & Vaske. J. J. (1995). An ipsative clustering model for analyzing attitudinal data. *Journal of Leisure Research, 27*(2), 168–192.

Beaman, J., Vaske, J. J., Donnelly, M. P., & Manfredo, M. J. (1997). Individual versus aggregate measures of digit preference. *Human Dimensions of Wildlife, 2*(1), 71–80.

Beaman, J., Vaske, J. J., & Grenier, M. (1998). A prototype model for estimating and correcting bias in digit preference/number preference. *Tourism Analysis, 2*(2), 77–90.

Beaman, J., Vaske, J. J., & Miller, C. A. (2005a). Cognitive processes in hunters' recall of participation and harvest estimates. *Journal of Wildlife Management, 69*(3), 967–975.

Beaman, J., Vaske, J. J., & Miller, C. A. (2005b). Hunting activity record-cards and the accuracy of survey estimates. *Human Dimensions of Wildlife, 10*(4), 285–292.

Becker, R. H. (1981). Displacement of recreational users between the Lower St Croix and Upper Mississippi Rivers. *Journal of Environmental Management, 13,* 259–267.

Becker, R. H., & Iliff, T. J. (1983). Nonrespondents in homogenous groups: Implications for mailed surveys. *Leisure Sciences, 5*(3), 257–266.

Beimer, P. (1991). *Measurement errors in surveys.* New York, NY: Wiley.

Belay, E. D., Maddox, R. A., Williams, E. S., Miller, M. W., Gambetti, P., & Schonberger, L. B. (2004). Chronic wasting disease and potential transmission to humans. *Emerging Infectious Diseases, 10*(6), 1–14.

Belsley, D. A., Kuh, E., & Welsch, R. E. (1980). *Regression diagnostics: Identifying influential data and sources of collinearity.* New York, NY: John Wiley and Sons

Bem, D. J. (1970). *Beliefs, attitudes, and human affairs.* Belmont, CA: Brooks-Cole.

Binder, A. (1984). Restrictions on statistics imposed by method of measurement: Some reality, some myth. *Journal of Criminal Justice, 12,* 467–481.

Binson, D., Canchola, J. A., & Catania, J. A. (2000). Random selection in a national telephone survey: A comparison of the Kish, next-birthday, and last-birthday methods. *Journal of Official Statistics, 16*(1), 53–59.

Bishop, G. F., Oldendick, R. W., & Tuchfarber, A. J. (1980). Experiments in filtering political opinions. *Political Behavior, 2,* 339–369.

Bishop, G., & Smith, A. (2001). Response-order effects and the early Gallup split-ballots. *Public Opinion Quarterly, 65,* 479–505.

Black, J. S. (1978). *Attitudinal, normative, and economic factors in early response to an energy-use field experiment.* Unpublished doctoral dissertation. University of Wisconsin, Madison.

Blackwood, T. (1977). *Selected characteristics, perceptions and management preferences of day-use rafters on the Upper Wolf River.* Unpublished Master's thesis, University of Wisconsin, Madison.

Blahna, J. B., Smith, K. S., & Anderson, J. A. (1995). Backcountry llama packing: Visitor perceptions of acceptability and conflict. *Leisure Sciences, 17,* 185–204.

Blalock, H. M., Jr. (1979). *Social statistics.* New York, NY: McGraw Hill.

Blasius, J., & Thiessen, V. (2001). The use of neutral responses in survey questions: An application of multiple correspondence analysis. *Journal of Official Statistics, 17*(3), 351–367.

Borenstein, M. (1994). The case for confidence intervals in controlled clinical trials. *Controlled Clinical Trials, 15,* 411–428.

Borgatta, E. F., & Bohrnstedt, G. W. (1980). Level of measurement: Once over again. *Sociological Methods & Research, 9*(2), 147–160.

Bosque, P. J. (2002). Bovine spongiform encephalopathy, chronic wasting disease, scrapie, and the threat to humans from prion disease epizootics. *Current Neurological Neuroscience Report, 2*(6), 488–495.

Box, G. E., Hunter, J. S., & Hunter, W. G. (2005). *Statistics for experimenters: Design, innovation, and discovery* (2nd ed.). New York, NY: John Wiley and Sons.

Bratt, C. (1999). The impact of norms and assumed consequences on recycling behavior. *Environment and Behavior, 31,* 630–656.

Brick, J. M., Waksberg, J., Kulp, D., & Starer, A. (1995). Bias in list-assisted telephone samples. *Public Opinion Quarterly, 59,* 218–235.

Bright, A. D., & Burtz, R. T. (2006). Creating defensible space in the wildland urban interface: The influence of values on perceptions and behavior. *Environmental Management, 37*(2), 170–185.

Bright, A. D., & Manfredo, M. J. (1996). A conceptual model of attitudes toward natural resource issues: A case study of wolf reintroduction. *Human Dimensions of Wildlife, 1*(1), 1–21.

Bright, A. D., Manfredo, M. J., & Fulton, D. C. (2000). Segmenting the public: An application of value orientations to wildlife planning in Colorado. *Wildlife Society Bulletin, 28,* 218–226.

Bright, A. D., Vaske, J. J., Kneeshaw, K., & Absher, J. D. (2005). Scale development of wildfire management basic beliefs. *Australasian Parks and Leisure, 8*(2), 44–48.

Bring, J. (1994). How to standardize regression coefficients. *The American Statistician, 48*(3), 209–213.

Brody, B. A. (1972). Glossary of logical terms. *The encyclopedia of philosophy* (Vol. 5, pp. 57–77). New York, NY: Macmillian.

Brown, J. D. (2001). Statistics Corner. Questions and answers about language testing statistics: Can we use the Spearman-Brown prophecy formula to defend low reliability? *JALT Testing & Evaluation SIG Newsletter, 4*(3), 7–9.

Brown, T. C. (1984). The concept of value in resource allocation. *Land Economics, 60*(3), 231–246.

Brown, T. L., & Wilkens, B. T. (1978). Clues for reasons for non-response, and its effect upon variable estimates. *Journal of Leisure Research, 10,* 226–231.

Browne-Nuñez, C., & Vaske, J. J. (2006). Predicting unsure responses to a proposed moose hunt in Anchorage, Alaska. *Human Dimensions of Wildlife, 11*(5), 371–382.

Bryan, H. (1977). Leisure value systems and recreational specialization: The case of trout fishermen. *Journal of Leisure Research, 9,* 174–187.

Bryan, H. (1979). Conflict in the great outdoors: Toward understanding and managing for diverse user preferences. Bureau of Public Administration. Sociological Studies No. 4. Tuscaloosa, AL: University of Alabama, Tuscaloosa.

Bultena, G., Field, D., Womble, P., & Albrecht, D. (1981). Closing the gates: A study of backcountry use–limitation at Mount McKinley National Park. *Leisure Sciences, 4,* 249–267.

Burton, S., & Blair, E. (1991). Task conditions, response formulation processes and response accuracy for behavioral frequency questions in surveys. *Public Opinion Quarterly, 55,* 50–79.

Byrne, B. M. (1994). *Structural equation modeling with EQS and EQS/Windows.* London: Sage Publications.

Campbell, D. T., & Stanley, J. C. (1966). *Experimental and quasi-experimental designs for research.* Chicago, IL: Rand McNally.

Carmines, E. G., & Zeller, R. A. (1979). *Reliability and validity assessment.* London: Sage Publications.

Carothers, P., Vaske, J. J., & Donnelly, M. P. (2001). Social values versus interpersonal conflict among hikers and mountain bikers. *Leisure Sciences, 23,* 47–61.

Carver, R. P. (1978). The case against statistical significance testing. *Harvard Educational Review, 48,* 378–399.

Cattell, R. B. (1944). Psychological measurement: Normative, ipsative, interactive. *Psychological Review, 51,* 292–303.

Cattell, R. B. (1949). r_p and other coefficients of pattern similarity. *Psychometrika, 14,* 279–298.

Cattell, R. B., & Brennan, J. (1994). Finding personality structure when ipsative measurements are the unavoidable basis of the variables. *American Journal of Psychology, 107,* 261–274

Chan, W. (2003). Analyzing ipsative data in psychological research. *Behaviormetrika, 30*(1), 99–121.

Charter, R. A. (2001). It is time to bury the Spearman-Brown "prophecy" formula for some common applications. *Education and Psychological Measurement, 61*(4), 690–696.

Chase, D. R., & Godbey, G. C. (1983). Research note: The accuracy of self-reported participation rates. *Leisure Studies, 2,* 231–235.

Chase, D. R., & Harada, M. (1984). Response error in self-reported recreation participation. *Journal of Leisure Research, 16,* 322–329.

Chen, P. Y., & Popovich, P. M. (2002). *Correlation: Parametric and nonparametric measures.* Thousand Oaks, CA: Sage Publications.

Chen, J., & Shao, J. (2000). Nearest neighbor imputation for survey data. *Journal of Official Statistics, 16*(2), 113–131.

Chu, A., Eisenhower, D., Hay, M., Morganstein, D., Neter, J., & Waksberg, J. (1992). Measuring the recall error in self-reported fishing and hunting activities. *Journal of Official Statistics, 8*(1), 19–39.

Church, A. H. (1993). Estimating the effect of incentives on mail survey response rates: A meta-analysis. *Public Opinion Quarterly, 57,* 62–79.

Cialdini, R. B., Kallgren, C. A., & Reno, R. R. (1991). A focus theory of normative conduct: A theoretical refinement and reevaluation of the role of norms in human behavior. *Advances in Experimental Social Psychology, 24,* 201–234.

Cialdini, R. B., Reno, R. R., & Kallgren, C. A. (1990). A focus theory of normative conduct: Recycling the concept of norms to reduce littering in public places. *Journal of Personality and Social Psychology, 58,* 1015–1026.

Clawson, M., & Knetsch, J. (1966). *Economics of outdoor recreation.* Baltimore, MD: John Hopkins Press.

Clemans, W. V. (1966). An analytical and empirical examination of some properties of ipsative measures. *Psychometric Monographs 14.*

Cochran, W. G. (1977). *Sampling techniques* (3rd ed.). New York, NY: John Wiley and Sons.

Cochran, W. G., & Cox, G. M. (1950). *Experimental designs.* New York, NY: Wiley.

Cohen, J. (1983). The cost of dichotomization. *Applied Psychological Measurement, 7*(3), 249–253.

Cohen, J. (1988). *Statistical power analysis for the behavioral sciences* (2nd ed.). Hillsdale, NJ: Lawrence Erlbaum Associates.

Cohen, J. (1994). The earth is round ($p < .05$). *American Psychologist, 49,* 997–1003.

Cohen, J., & Cohen, P. (1983). *Applied multiple regression/correlation analysis for the behavioral sciences* (2nd ed.). Hillsdale, NJ: Lawrence Erlbaum.

Cole, S. T. (2005). Comparing mail and web-based survey distribution methods: Results of surveys to leisure travel retailers. *Journal of Travel Research, 43,* 422–430.

Connelly, N. A., & Brown, T. L. (1992). Item response bias in angler expenditures. *Journal of Leisure Research, 24,* 288–294.

Connelly, N. A., Brown, T. L., & Decker, D. J. (2003). Factors affecting response rates to natural resource–focused surveys: Empirical evidence of declining rates over time. *Society and Natural Resources, 16,* 541–547.

Conrad, F. G., & Schober, M. F. (2005). Promoting uniform question understanding in today's and tomorrow's surveys. *Journal of Official Statistics, 21*(2), 215–231.

Cook, C., Heath, F., & Thompson, R. L. (2000). A meta-analysis of response rates in web- or internet-based surveys. *Educational and Psychological Measurement, 60*(6), 821–836.

Cook, T. D., & Campbell, D. T. (1979). *Quasi-experimentation: Design and analysis of issues for field settings.* Boston, MA: Houghton Mifflin.

Couper, M. P. (2000). Web surveys: A review of issues and approaches. *Public Opinion Quarterly, 64,* 464–494.

Coolidge, F. L. (2006). *Statistics: A gentle introduction.* Newbury Park, CA: Sage Publications.

Couper, M. P., Traugott, M. W., & Lamias, M. J. (2001). Web survey design and administration. *Public Opinion Quarterly, 65,* 230–253.

Cottrell, S. P., & Graefe, A. R. (1997). Testing a conceptual framework of responsible environmental behavior. *Journal of Environmental Education, 29*(1), 17–27.

Cottrell, S. P., Vaske, J. J., Shen, F., & Ritter, P. (2007). Resident perceptions of sustainable tourism in Chongdugou, China. *Society & Natural Resources, 20,* 511–525.

Crabb, P. B. (1999). The use of answering machines and caller ID to regulate home privacy. *Environment & Behavior, 31*(5), 657–670.

Crawley, M. J. (2005). *Statistics: An introduction using R.* New York, NY: John Wiley and Sons.

Crompton, J. L. (1979). Motivation for pleasure travel. *Annals of Tourism Research, 4,* 408–424.

Crompton, J. L., & Tian-Cole, S. (2001). An analysis of 13 tourism surveys: Are three waves of data collection necessary? *Journal of Travel Research, 39,* 356–368.

Cronbach, L. J. (1951). Coefficient alpha and the internal structure of tests. *Psychometrika, 16*(3), 297–324.

Cronbach, L. J. (2004). My current thoughts on coefficient alpha and successor procedures. *Educational and Psychological Measurement, 64*(3), 391–418.

Cronk, B. C. (2006). *How to use SPSS: A step-by-step guide to analysis and interpretation* (4th ed.). Glendale, CA: Pyrczak Publishing.

Cumming, G., & Finch, S. (2001). A primer on the understanding, use, and calculation of confidence intervals that are based on central and noncentral distributions. *Educational and Psychological Measurement, 61,* 532–574.

Darlington, R. (1990). *Regression and linear models.* New York, NY: McGraw-Hill.

Dayer, A. A., Stinchfield, H. M., & Manfredo, M. J. (2007). Stories about wildlife: Developing an instrument for identifying wildlife value orientations cross-culturally. *Human Dimensions of Wildlife, 12*(5), 307–315.

de Leeuw, E. D., Hox, J., & Huisman, M. (2003). Prevention and treatment of item nonresponse. *Journal of Official Statistics, 19,* 153–176.

de Leeuw, E. D., Mellenbergh, G. J., & Hox, J. J. (1996). The influence of data collection method on structural models: A comparison of a mail, a telephone, and a face-to-face survey. *Sociological Methods & Research, 24,* 443–472.

DeMaio, T. J. (1984). Social desirability and survey measurement: A review. In C. F. Turner, & E. Martin (Eds.), *Surveying subjective phenomena* (Vol. 2; pp. 257–282). New York, NY: Russell Sage.

DeMaris, A. (2002). Explained variance in logistic regression: A Monte Carlo study of proposed measures. *Sociological Methods & Research, 31*(1), 27–74.

Dickson, J. P., Casey, M., Wyckoff, D., Wynd, W., Erdos, P. L., Barber, B., Leonard, F. B., Abelson, H. I., Skelly, F., & Nejelski, P. (1977). Invisible coding of survey questionnaires. *Public Opinion Quarterly, 41*(1), 100–112.

Dillman, D. A. (1978). *Mail and telephone surveys: The total design method.* New York. NY: Wiley-Interscience.

Dillman, D. A. (2000). *Mail and internet surveys: The tailored design method* (2nd ed.). New York, NY: John Wiley and Sons.

Dillman, D. A. (2007). *Mail and internet surveys: The tailored design method (2nd ed.): 2007 update with new internet, visual, and mixed-mode guide.* Hoboken, NJ: John Wiley and Sons.

Dillman, D. A., Sinclair, M. D., & Clark, J. R. (1993). Effects of questionnaire length, respondent-friendly design, and a difficult question on response rates for occupant-addressed census mail surveys. *Public Opinion Quarterly, 57*(3), 289–304.

Ditton, R. B., Fedler, A. J., & Graefe, A. R. (1983). Factors contributing to perceptions of recreational crowding. *Leisure Sciences, 5*(4), 273–288.

Dolson, D. E., & Machlis, G. E. (1991). Response rates and mail recreation survey results: How much is enough? *Journal of Leisure Research, 23*(3), 272–277.

Donnelly, M. P. (1980). An investigation of hikers' perceptions of the Great Gulf Wilderness Area in New Hampshire. Unpublished Master's thesis. University of Maryland, College Park.

Donnelly, M. P., & Vaske, J. J. (1981). *Turkey hunters in Maryland: A comparison with hunters and fishermen in the Midwest* (MP 955, contribution no. 5774). College Park, MD: Maryland Agricultural Experiment Station.

Donnelly, M. P., & Vaske, J .J. (1995). Predicting attitudes toward a proposed moose hunt. *Society and Natural Resources, 8,* 307–319.

Donnelly, M. P., Vaske, J .J., & DeRuiter, D. (1994). *Economic impact and perceptions of Colorado State Parks* (HDNRU Report No. 13). Fort Collins, CO: Colorado State University, Human Dimensions in Natural Resources Unit.

Donnelly, M. P., Vaske, J. J., & Graefe, A. R. (1986). Degree and range of recreation specialization: Toward a typology of boating related activities. *Journal of Leisure Research, 18,* 81–95.

Donnelly, M. P., Vaske, J. J., Whittaker, D., & Shelby, B. (2000). Toward an understanding of norm prevalence: A comparative analysis of 20 years of research. *Environmental Management, 25*(4), 403–414.

Driver, B. L., & Tocher, S. R. (1970). Toward a behavioral interpretation of recreation engagement with implications for planning. In B. L. Driver (Ed.), *Elements of outdoor recreation planning.* Ann Arbor, MI: University Microfilms Michigan.

Driver, B. L., Brown, P. J., & Peterson, G. L. (Eds.). (1991). *Benefits of leisure.* State College, PA: Venture Publishing, Inc.

Duncan, O. D. (1966). Path analysis: Sociological examples. *American Journal of Sociology, 72,* 1–16.

Duncan, O. D. (1975). *Introduction to structural equation models.* New York, NY: Academic Press.

Dunlap, R., & Van Liere, K. (1978). The new environmental paradigm. *Journal of Environmental Education, 9,* 10–19.

Eagly, A. H., & Chaiken, S. (1993). *The psychology of attitudes.* Belmont, CA: Wadsworth.

Eckersley, R. (1992). *Environmentalism and political theory: Toward an ecocentric approach.* Albany, NY: State University of New York Press.

Efron, B. (1979). Bootstrap methods: Another look at at the jackknife. *Annals of Statistics, 7,* 1–26.

Efron, B., & Tibshirani, R. J. (1993). *An introduction to the bootstrap.* London, UK: Chapman & Hall.

Epstein, D. H. (2003). Problems with odds ratios. *American Journal of Geriatric Psychiatry, 160,* 190–191.

Everitt, B. (1992). *The analysis of contingency tables* (2nd ed.). London, UK: Chapman and Hall.

Feinstein, A. R. (1998). P-values and confidence intervals: Two sides of the same unsatisfactory coin. *Journal of Clinical Epidemiology, 61,* 355–360.

Fidler, F. (2002). The fifth edition of the APA publication manual: Why its statistics recommendations are so controversial. *Educational and Psychological Measurement, 62*(5), 749–770.

Field, A. (2005). *Discovering statistics using SPSS* (2nd ed.). Newbury Park, CA: Sage Publications.

Finch, S., Cumming, G., & Thompson, N. (2001). Reporting on statistical inference in the *Journal of Applied Psychology:* Little evidence of reform. *Educational and Psychological Measurement, 61,* 181–210.

Fishbein, M., & Ajzen, I. (1975). *Belief, attitude, intention and behavior: An introduction to theory and research.* Reading, MA: Addison-Wesley.

Fishbein, M., & Manfredo, M. J., (2002). A theory of behavior change. In M. J. Manfredo, (Ed.), *Influencing human behavior* (pp. 29–50). Champaign, IL: Sagamore Publishing.

Fisher, R. A. (1921). On the "probable error" of a coefficient deduced from a small sample. *Metron, 1,* Part 4, 3–32.

Fisher, R. A. (1925). Applications of "Student's" distribution. *Metron, 5,* 90–104.

Fiske, S. T., & Taylor, S. E. (1991). *Social cognition.* New York, NY: McGraw-Hill.

Fleiss, J. L. (1981). *Statistical methods for rates and proportions.* New York, NY: John Wiley and Sons.

Fowler, F. J., Jr. (1992). How unclear terms affect survey data. *Public Opinion Quarterly, 56,* 218–231.

Fowler, F. J., Jr. (1993). *Survey research methods* (2nd ed.). Newbury Park, CA: Sage Publications.

Fox, J. (1991). *Regression diagnostics.* Thousand Oaks, CA: Sage Publications.

Fox, R. J., Crask, M. R., & Kim, J. (1988). Mail survey response rate: A meta-analysis of selected techniques for inducing response. *Public Opinion Quarterly, 52,* 467–491.

Frankel, J. (1982). *On the definition of response rates: A special report of the CASRO Task Force on Completion Rates.* Port Jefferson, NY: Council of American Survey Research Organizations.

Frankel, M. R., & Frankel, L. R. (1987). Fifty years of survey sampling in the United States. *Public Opinion Quarterly, 51,* 127–138.

Frazier, P. A., Tix, A. P., & Barron, K. E. (2004). Testing moderator and mediator effects in counseling psychology research. *Journal of Counseling Psychology, 51,* 115–134.

Frey, J. H. (1989). *Survey research by telephone* (2nd ed.). Newbury Park, CA: Sage Publications.

Fulton, D. C., Manfredo, M. J., & Lipscomb, J. (1996). Wildlife value orientations: A conceptual and measurement approach. *Human Dimensions of Wildlife, 1*(2), 24–47.

Gad, N. (2000). Telesurvey methodologies for household surveys: A review and some thoughts for the future. *Survey Methodology, 27,* 7–31.

Gaede, D. B., & Vaske, J. J. (1999). Using the Internet as survey research tool: Potential and pitfalls. *International Journal of Wilderness, 5*(2), 26–30.

Gaito, J. (1980). Measurement scales and statistics: Resurgence of an old misconception. *Psychological Bulletin, 84,* 564–567.

Geer, J. G. (1991). Do open-ended questions measure "salient" issues? *Public Opinion Quarterly, 55,* 360–370.

Gilljam, M., & Granberg, D. (1993). Should we take "don't know" for an answer? *Public Opinion Quarterly, 57,* 348–357.

Gitelson, R. J., & Drogin, E. B. (1992). An experiment on the efficacy of a certified final mailing. *Journal of Leisure Research, 24*(1), 72–78.

Glass, G. V., & Hopkins, K. D. (1996). *Statistical methods in education and psychology* (3rd ed.). Boston, MA: Allyn & Bacon.

Gliner, J. A., & Morgan, G. A. (2000). *Research methods in applied settings: An integrated approach to design and analysis.* Mahwah, NJ: Lawrence Erlbaum Associates, Publishers.

Gliner, J. A., Morgan, G. A., Leech, N. L., & Harmon, R. J. (2001). Problems with null hypothesis significance tests. *Journal of the American Academy of Child and Adolescent Psychiatry, 40,* 250–252.

Gliner, J. A., Vaske, J. J., & Morgan, G. A. (2001). Null hypothesis significance testing: Effect size matters. *Human Dimensions of Wildlife, 6*(4), 291–301.

Glynn, P. (2004). *Adjusting or normalizing weights "on the fly" in SPSS* [unpublished document]. Seattle, WA: University of Washington.

Goodman, L. A. (1960). On the exact variance of products. *Journal of the American Statistical Association, 55,* 708–713.

Goodman, L., & Kruskal, W. (1954), Measures of association for cross-classifications. *Journal of the American Statistical Association, 49,* 732–764.

Graefe, A. R. (1980). *The relationship between level of participation and selected aspects of specialization in recreational fishing.* Unpublished Doctoral dissertation. College Station, TX: Texas A&M University.

Graefe, A. R., Donnelly, M. P., & Vaske, J. J. (1986). Crowding and specialization: A reexamination of the crowding model. In *Proceedings: National Wilderness Research Conference* (pp. 333–338). Fort Collins, CO.

Graefe, A. R., & Thapa, B. (2004). Conflict in natural resource-based recreation. In M. J. Manfredo, J. J. Vaske, B. L. Bruyere, D. R. Field, & P. Brown (Eds.), *Society and natural resources: A summary of knowledge* (pp. 209–224). Jefferson, MO: Modern Litho.

Gramann, J. H., & Burdge, R. (1981). The effect of recreation goals on conflict perception: The case of water skiers and fishermen. *Journal of Leisure Research, 13,* 15–27.

Grasmick, H. G., Blackwell, B. S., Bursik, R. J., Jr., & Mitchell, S. (1993). Changes in perceived threats of shame, embarrassment, and legal sanctions for interpersonal violence, 1982–1992. *Violence and Victims, 8,* 313–325.

Greenleaf, E. A. (1992a). Improving rating scale measures by detecting and correcting bias components in some response styles. *Journal of Marketing Research, XXIX,* 176–188.

Greenleaf, E. A. (1992b). Measuring extreme response style. *The Public Opinion Quarterly, 56*(3), 328–351.

Gripp, S. I., Luloff, A. E., & Yonkers, R. D. (1994). Reporting response rates for telephone surveys used in agricultural economics research. *Agricultural and Resource Economics Review, 23,* 200–206.

Grissom, R. J., & Kim, J. J. (2005). *Effect sizes for research: A broad practical approach.* Mahwah, NJ: Lawrence Erlbaum.

Groves, R. M., & Magilavy, L. J. (1986). Measuring and explaining interviewer effects in centralized telephone surveys. *Public Opinion Quarterly, 50,* 251–266.

Gross, J. E., & Miller, M. W. (2001). Chronic wasting disease in mule deer: Disease dynamics and control. *Journal of Wildlife Management, 65,* 205–215.

Groves, R. M., & Mathiowetz, N. A. (1984). Computer assisted telephone interviewing: Effects on interviewers and respondents. *Public Opinion Quarterly, 48,* 356–369.

Groves, R. M., & McGonagle, K. A. (2001). A theory-guided interviewer training protocol regarding survey participation. *Journal of Official Statistics, 17*(2), 249–265.

Groves, R. M., & Lepkowski, J. M. (1985). Dual frame, mixed mode survey designs. *Journal of Official Statistics, 1*(3), 263–286.

Guttman, I., & Smith, D. E. (1969). Investigation of rules for dealing with outliers in small samples from the normal distribution. I: Estimator of the mean. *Technometrics, 11,* 527–550.

Hall, T. E. (2001). Opinion filters in recreation research: The effect of including "no opinion" and "not notice" response categories in questionnaires. *Tourism Analysis, 6,* 1–15.

Hammitt, W. E., & McDonald, C. D. (1982). Response bias and the need for extensive mail questionnaire follow-ups among selected recreation samples. *Journal of Leisure Research, 14*(3), 207–216.

Hammitt, W. E., McDonald, C. D., & Noe, F. P. (1984). Use level and encounters: Important variables of perceived crowding among nonspecialized recreationists. *Journal of Leisure Research, 16*(1), 1–8.

Hampel, F. R. (1968). *Contributions to the theory of robust estimation.* Unpublished Ph.D. dissertation. University of California, Berkeley.

Hasher, L., & Zacks, R. T. (1979). Automatic and effortful processes in memory. *Journal of Experimental Psychology: General, 108,* 356–388.

Hargens, L. L. (1976). A note on standardized coefficients as structural parameters. *Sociological Methods & Research, 5*(2), 247–256.

Harlow, L. L., Mulaik, S. A., & Steiger, J. H., (Eds.). (1997). *What if there were no significance tests?* Mahwah, NJ: Erlbaum.

Hauck, W. W., & Donner, A. (1977). Wald's test as applied to hypotheses in logit analysis. *Journal of the American Statistical Association, 72,* 851–853.

Havlicek, J. E., & Peterson, N. L. (1977). Effect of the violation of assumptions upon significance levels of the Pearson r. *Psychological Bulletin, 84,* 373–377.

Hayduk, L. A. (1987). *Structural equation modeling with LISREL.* Baltimore, MD: Johns Hopkins University Press.

Hays, W. L. (1994). *Statistics* (5th ed.). New York, NY: Harcourt Brace.

Heberlein, T. A. (1971). Moral norms, threatened sanctions, and littering behavior. *Dissertation Abstracts International, 32,* 5906A (University Microfilms No. 72-2639).

Heberlein, T. A. (2004). "Fire in the Sistine Chapel:" How Wisconsin responded to chronic wasting disease. *Human Dimensions of Wildlife, 9*(3), 165–179.

Heberlein, T. A., & Baumgartner, R. (1978). Factors affecting response rates to mailed questionnaires: A quantitative analysis of the published literature. *American Sociological Review, 43,* 447–462.

Heberlein, T., A., & Baumgartner, R. (1981). Is a questionnaire necessary in a second mailing? *Public Opinion Quarterly, 45*(1), 102–108.

Heberlein, T. A., & Laybourne, B. (1978). *The Wisconsin deer hunter: Social characteristics, attitudes and preferences for proposed hunting season changes* (Working paper no. 10). Madison, WI: University of Wisconsin Center for Resources Policy Studies and Programs.

Heberlein, T. A., & Kuentzel, W. F. (2002). Too many hunters or not enough deer? Human and biological determinants of hunter satisfaction and quality. *Human Dimensions of Wildlife, 7*(4), 229–250.

Heberlein, T. A., & Thomson, E. (1996). Changes in U.S. hunting participation, 1980–90. *Human Dimensions of Wildlife, 1*(1), 85–86.

Heberlein, T. A., Trent, J. N., & Baumgartner, R. M. (1982). The influence of hunter density on firearm deer hunters' satisfaction: A field experiment. *Transactions of the 47th North American Natural Resource and Wildlife Conference, 47,* 665–676.

Heberlein, T. A., & Vaske, J .J. (1977). *Crowding and visitor conflict on the Bois Brule River* (Report WISC WRC 77-04). Madison, WI: University of Wisconsin Water Resources Center.

Heitjan, D. F., & Rubin, D. B. (1990). Inference from coarse data via multiple imputation with application to age heaping. *Journal of the American Statistical Association, 85,* 304–314.

Hendee, J. C. (1974). A multiple satisfaction approach to game management. *Wildlife Society Bulletin, 1*(2), 24–47.

Henkel, R. E. (1976). *Tests of significance.* London, UK: Sage Publications.

Hertel, B. R. (1976). Minimizing error variance introduced by missing data routines in survey analysis. *Sociological Methods & Research, 4*(4), 459–474.

Heywood, J. L. (1996a). Social regularities in outdoor recreation. *Leisure Sciences, 18,* 23–38.

Heywood, J. L. (1996b). Conventions, emerging norms, and norms in outdoor recreation. *Leisure Sciences, 18,* 355–364.

Heywood, J. L. (2002). The cognitive and emotional components of behavior norms in outdoor recreation. *Leisure Sciences, 24,* 271–281.

Heywood, J. L., & Murdock, W. E. (2002). Social norms in outdoor recreation: Searching for the behavior-condition link. *Leisure Sciences, 24,* 283–295.

Hicks, L. E. (1970). Some properties of ipsative, normative, and forced-choice normative measures. *Psychological Bulletin, 74,* 167–184.

Hiett, R. L., & Worrall, J. W. (1977). *Marine recreational fishermen's ability to estimate catch and to recall catch and effort over time* (Research Report HSR-RR-77/13-cd). McLean VA: Human Sciences Research.

Hoaglin, J. E., Mosteller, F., & Tukey, J. W. (1983). *Understanding robust and exploratory data analysis.* New York, NY: John Wiley and Sons.

Hofmann, S. G. (2002). Promoting good statistical practices: Some suggestions. *Educational and Psychological Measurement, 61,* 213–218.

Holcomb, Z. C. (2006). *SPSS basics: Techniques for a first course in statistics.* Glendale, CA: Pyrczak Publishing.

Homer, P. M., & Kahle, L. R. (1988). A structural equation test of the value-attitude-behavior hierarchy. *Journal of Personality and Social Psychology, 54*(4), 638–646.

Hopper, J. R., & Nielsen, J. (1991). Recycling as altruistic behavior: Normative and behavioral strategies to expand participation in a community recycling program. *Environment and Behavior, 23,* 195–220.

Hosmer, D. W., & Lemeshow, S. (1989). Best subsets logistic regression. *Biometrics, 45,* 1265–1270.

Hosmer, D. W., & Lemeshow, S. (2000). *Applied logistic regression* (2nd ed). New York, NY: John Wiley and Sons.

Houtkoop-Steenstra, H., & van den Bergh, H. (2000). Effects of introductions in large-scale telephone survey interviews. *Sociological Methods & Research, 28*(3), 281–300.

Hoyle, R. H., & Robinson, J. C. (2004). Mediated and moderated effects in social psychological research: Measurement, design, and analysis issues. In C. Sansone, C. C. Morf, & A. T. Panter (Eds.), *The Sage handbook of methods in social psychology* (pp. 213–233). Thousand Oaks, CA: Sage Publications.

Huan, T. C., Beaman, J., Chang, L. H., & Hsu, S. Y. (in press). Robust and alternative estimators for "better" estimates for expenditures and other "long tail" distributions. *Tourism Management.*

Huber, P. J. (1964). Robust estimation of a location parameter. *Annals of Mathematical Statistics, 35,* 73–101.

Huberty, C. J. (1989). Problems with stepwise methods: Better alternatives. *Advances in Social Science Methodology, 1,* 43–70.

Huberty, C. J. (1994). *Applied discriminant analysis.* New York, NY: John Wiley and Sons.

Huck, S. W., & Cormier, W. H. (1996). *Reading statistics and research* (2nd ed.). New York, NY: HarperCollins.

Huff, D. (1993). *How to lie with statistics.* New York, NY: W. W. Norton & Company.

Hui, C. H., & Triandis, H. C. (1985). The instability of response sets. *Public Opinion Quarterly 49,* 253–260.

Hultsman, W. Z., Hultsman, J. T., & Black, D. R. (1989). "Response peaks" as a component of measurement error: Assessment implications for self-reported data in leisure research. *Journal of Leisure Research, 21*(4), 310–315.

Huttenlocher, J., Hedges, L. V., & Bradburn, N. M. (1990). Reports of elapsed time: Bounding and rounding processes in estimation. *Journal of Experimental Psychology: Learning, Memory and Cognition, 16,* 196–213.

Hunt, L., Haider, W., & Armstrong, K. (2002). Understanding fish harvesting decisions by anglers. *Human Dimensions of Wildlife, 7*(2), 75–89.

Hyman, H. (1955). *Survey design and analysis: Principles, cases and procedures.* Glencoe, IL: The Free Press.

Jacob, G., & Schreyer, R. (1980). Conflict in outdoor Recreation: A theoretical perspective. *Journal of Leisure Research, 12,* 368–380.

Jaeger, R. M. (1990). *Statistics: A spectator sport.* Newbury Park, CA: Sage Publications.

Johnson, D. H. (1999). The insignificance of statistical significance testing. *Journal of Wildlife Management, 63*(3), 763–772.

Joly, D. O., Ribic, C. A., Langenberg, J. A., Beheler, K., Batha, C. A., Dhuey, B. J., Rolley, R. E., Bartelt, G., Van Deelen, T. R., & Samuel, M. D. (2003). Chronic wasting disease in free-ranging Wisconsin white-tailed deer. *Emerging Infectious Diseases, 9*(5), 599–601.

Judd, C. M., & Kenny, D. A. (1981). Process analysis: Estimating mediation in treatment evaluations. *Evaluation Review, 5,* 602–619.

Kalsbeek, W. D., Botman, S. L., Massey, J. T., & Liu, P. W. (1994). Cost-efficiency and the number of allowable call attempts in the National Health Interview Survey. *Journal of Official Statistics, 10*(2), 133–152.

Kalton, G., & Flores-Cervantes, I. (2003). Weighting methods. *Journal of Official Statistics, 19*(2), 81–97.

Kauffman, R. B., & Graefe, A. R. (1984). Canoeing specialization, expected rewards and resource related attitudes. In J. S. Popadic, D. I. Butterfield, D. H. Anderson, M. R. Popadic (Eds.), *Proceedings of the National River Recreation Symposium.* Baton Rouge, LA: Louisiana State University.

Keeter, S. (1995). Estimating telephone noncoverage bias with a telephone survey. *Public Opinion Quarterly, 59,* 196–217.

Keller, D. K. (2006). *The tao of statistics: A path to understanding (with no math).* Newbury Park, CA: Sage Publications.

Kellert, S. R. (1980). Contemporary values of wildlife in American society. In W. W. Shaw, & E. H. Zube (Eds.), *Wildlife values* (pp. 31–60). Tucson, AZ: Center for Assessment of Noncommodity Natural Resource Values, University of Arizona.

Kellert, S. R. (1985). Social and perceptual factors in endangered species management. *Journal of Wildlife Management, 49*(2), 528–536.

Kellert, S. R. (1987). The contributions of wildlife to human quality of life. In D. J. Decker, & G. R. Goff (Eds.), *Valuing wildlife: Economic and social perspectives* (pp. 143–53). Boulder, CO: Westview Boulder.

Kelly, E. J., & Cumberland, W. G. (1990). Prediction theory approach to multistage sampling when cluster sizes are unknown. *Journal of Official Statistics, 6*(4), 437–449.

Kempthrone, O. (1955). The randomization theory of experimental inference. *Journal of the American Statistical Association, 50,* 946–967.

Khurshid, A., & Sahai, H. (1995). A bibliography on telephone survey methodology. *Journal of Official Statistics, 11*(3), 325–367.

Kim, J. O., & Ferree, G. (1981). Standardization in causal analysis. *Sociological Methods & Research, 10,* 187–210.

King, G. (1985). How to lie with statistics: Avoiding common mistakes in quantitative political science. *American Journal of Political Science, 29,* 666–687.

King, J. E. (2003). Running a best-subsets logistic regression: An alternative to stepwise methods. *Educational and Psychological Measurement, 63*(3), 392–403.

Kish, L. (1965). *Survey sampling.* New York, NY: Wiley.

Kirk, R. E. (1968). *Experimental design: Procedures for the behavioral sciences.* Belmont, CA: Brooks/Cole Publishing Company.

Kirk, R. E. (1996). Practical significance: A concept whose time has come. *Educational and Psychological Measurement, 56*(5), 746–759.

Kirk, R. E. (2001). Promoting good statistical practices: Some suggestions. *Educational and Psychological Measurement, 61*(2), 213–218.

Kline, R. B. (1998). *Principles and practice of structural equation modeling.* New York, NY: The Guilford Press.

Knap, N. E., & Propst, D. B. (2001). Focus group interviews as an alternative to traditional survey methods for recreation needs. *Journal of Park & Recreation Administration, 19*(2), 62–82.

Kneeshaw, K., Vaske, J. J., Bright, A. D., & Absher, J. D. (2004). Situational influences of acceptable wildland fire management actions. *Society and Natural Resources, 17,* 477–489.

Kraemer, H. C. (1992). *Evaluating medical tests.* Newbury Park, CA: Sage Publications.

Krippendorff, K. (2004). *Content analysis: An introduction to its methodology.* Newbury Park, CA: Sage Publications.

Krosnick, J. A. (1999). Survey research. *Annual Review of Psychology, 50,* 537–567.

Krosnick, J. A., & Petty, R. E. (1995). Attitude strength: An overview. In R. E. Petty and J. S. Krosnick (Eds.), *Attitude-Strength: Antecedents and consequences* (pp. 1–24). Mahwah, NJ: Erlbaum.

Krueger, J. (2001). Null hypothesis significance testing: On the survival of a flawed method. *American Psychologist, 56,* 16–26.

Krueger, R. A. (1988). *Focus groups: A practical guide for applied research.* Newbury Park, CA: Sage Publications.

Kuder, G. F., & Richardson, M. W. (1937). The theory of estimation of test reliability. *Psychometrika, 2,* 151–160.

Kuentzel, W. F., & Heberlein, T. A. (1998). Why do hunters skybust? Personal disposition or social influence. *Human Dimensions of Wildlife, 3,* 1–15.

Kuss, F. R., Graefe, A. R., & Vaske, J. J. (1990). *Visitor impact management: A review of research.* Washington, DC: National Parks and Conservation Association.

Kvitz, F. J. (1978). Random digit dialing and sample bias. *Public Opinion Quarterly, 42*(4), 544–546.

Kwak, N., & Radler, B. (2002). A comparison between mail and web surveys: Response pattern, respondent profile, and data quality. *Journal of Official Statistics, 18*(2), 257–273.

Labovitz, S. (1967). Some observations on measurement and statistics. *Social Forces, 46,* 151–160.

Labovitz, S. (1970). The assignment of numbers to rank order categories. *American Sociological Review, 35,* 515–524.

LaPage, W. F., & Bevins, M. I. (1981). Satisfaction monitoring for quality control in campground management (USDA Forest Service Research Paper NE-484). Broomall, PA: Northeastern Forest Experiment Station.

Lavrakas, P. (1987). *Telephone survey methods: Samples, selection, and supervision.* Newbury Park, CA: Sage Publications.

Lawson, S. R., Roggenbuck, J. W., Hall, T. E., & Moldovanyi, A. (2006). A conjoint analysis of preference heterogeneity among day and overnight visitors to the Okefenokee Wilderness. *Journal of Leisure Research, 38*(4), 575–600.

Lee, R. (1975). *The management of human components in the Yosemite National Park ecosystem: Final research report.* San Francisco, CA: USDI National Park Service.

Leech, N. L., Barrett, K. C., & Morgan, G. A. (2005). *SPSS for intermediate statistics: Use and interpretation* (2nd ed.). Mahwah, NJ: Lawrence Erlbaum Associates.

Likert, R. (1932). A technique for the measurement of attitudes. *Archives of Psychology, 140,* 44–53.

Little, R. J. A., & Rubin, D. B. (2002). *Statistical analysis with missing data* (2nd ed.). Hoboken, NJ: John Wiley & Sons.

Lohr, S. L. (1999). *Sampling: Design and analysis.* Pacific Grove, CA: Duxbury Press.

Long, J. S. (1997). *Regression models for categorical and limited dependent variables.* Thousand Oaks, CA: Sage Publications.

Loomis, J. (2004). The role of economics in managing natural resources for society. In M. J. Manfredo, J. J. Vaske, B. L. Bruyere, D. R. Field, & P. Brown (Eds.), *Society and natural resources: A summary of knowledge* (pp. 295–304). Jefferson, MO: Modern Litho.

Lord, F. (1953). On the statistical treatment of football numbers. *American Psychologist, 8,* 750–751.

Lynn, P. (1998). Data collection mode effects on responses to attitudinal questions. *Journal of Official Statistics, 14*(1), 1–14.

MacCallum, R. C. (2003). Working with imperfect models. *Multivariate Behavioral Research, 38,* 113–139.

MacKinnon, D. P., Fairchild, A. J., & Fritz, M. S. (2007). Mediation analysis. *Annual Review of Psychology, 58,* 593–614.

MacKinnon, D. P., Lockwood, C. M., Hoffman, J. M., West, S. G., & Sheets, V. (2002). A comparison of methods to test mediation and other intervening variable effects. *Psychological Methods, 7,* 83–104.

MacKinnon, D. P., Warsi, G., & Dwyer, J. H. (1995). A simulation study of mediated effect measures. *Multivariate Behavioral Research, 30*(1), 41–62.

Mallinckrodt, B., Abraham, W. T., Wei, M., & Russell, D. W. (2006). Advances in testing the statistical significance of mediation effects. *Journal of Counseling Psychology, 53,* 372–378.

Manfredo, M. J. (1989). Human dimensions of wildlife management. *Wildlife Society Bulletin, 17*(4), 447–449.

Manfredo, M. J. (1992). *Influencing human behavior: Theory and applications in recreation, tourism, and natural resource applications.* Champaign, IL: Sagamore.

Manfredo, M. J., & Anderson, D. (1987). The influence of activity importance and similarity on perceptions of recreation substitutes. *Leisure Sciences, 9,* 77–86.

Manfredo, M. J., Driver, B. L., & Tarrant, M. A. (1996). Measuring leisure motivation: A meta-analysis of the recreation experience preference scales. *Journal of Leisure Research, 28*(3), 188–213.

Manfredo, M. J., Fix, P. J., Teel, T. L., Smeltzer, J., & Kahn, R. (2004). Assessing demand for big-game hunting opportunities: Applying the multiple satisfaction concept. *Wildlife Society Bulletin, 32*(4), 1147–1155.

Manfredo, M. J., Fulton, D. C., & Pierce, C. L. (1997). Understanding voter behavior on wildlife ballot initiatives: Colorado's trapping amendment. *Human Dimensions of Wildlife, 2*(4), 22–39.

Manfredo, M. J., Pierce, C. L., Fulton, D., Pate, J., & Gill, B. R. (1999). Public acceptance of wildlife trapping in Colorado. *Wildlife Society Bulletin, 27*(2), 499–508.

Manfredo, M. J., & Shelby, B. (1988). The effect of using self-report measures in tests of attitude-behavior relationships. *Journal of Social Psychology, 128*(6), 731–744.

Manfredo, M. J., Teel, T. L., & Bright, A. D. (2003). Why are public values toward wildlife changing? *Human Dimensions of Wildlife, 8*(4), 287–306.

Manfredo, M. J., Teel, T. L., & Bright, A. D. (2004). Applications of the concepts of values and attitudes in human dimensions of natural resource research. In M. J. Manfredo, J. J. Vaske, B. L. Bruyere, D. R. Field, & P. Brown (Eds.), *Society and natural resources: A summary of knowledge* (pp. 271–282). Jefferson, MO: Modern Litho.

Manfredo, M. J., Vaske, J. J., & Decker, D. J. (1995). Human dimensions of wildlife management: Basic concepts. In R. L. Knight, & K. J. Gutzwiller (Eds.). *Wildlife and recreationists: Coexistence through management and research* (pp. 17–31). Washington DC: Island Press.

Manfredo, M. J., Vaske, J. J., & Teel, T. L. (2003). The potential for conflict index: A graphic approach to practical significance of human dimensions research. *Human Dimensions of Wildlife, 8,* 219–228.

Manfredo, M. J., Vaske, J. J., & Sikorowski, L. (1996). Human dimensions of wildlife management. In A. Ewert (Ed.), *Natural resource management: The human dimension* (pp. 53–72). Boulder, CO: Westview Press.

Mangoine, T. W., Fowler, F. J., & Louis, T. A. (1992). Question characteristics and interviewer effects. *Journal of Official Statistics, 8*(3), 293–307.

Manning, R. E. (1999). *Studies in outdoor recreation: Search and research for satisfaction* (2ⁿᵈ ed.). Corvallis, OR: Oregon State University Press.

Manning, R. E., & Ciali, C. P. (1980). Recreation density and user satisfaction: A further exploration of the satisfaction mode. *Journal of Leisure Research, 12,* 329–245.

Maruyama, G. M. (1998). *Basics of structural equation modeling.* London, UK: Sage Publications.

McCarty, C. (2003). Differences in response rates using most recent versus final dispositions in telephone surveys. *Public Opinion Quarterly, 67,* 396–406.

McConnell, K. E. (1977). Congestion and willingness to pay: A study of beach use. *Land Economics, 53,* 185–195.

McDonald, C. D., & Hammitt, W. E. (1981). *Use patterns, preferences, and social impacts of floaters on river resources in the Southern Appalachian Region* (Final project report on file). Southeastern Forest Experiment Station: USDA Forest Service, Asheville, NC

McFarlane, B. L. (1996). Socialization influences of specialization among birdwatchers. *Human Dimensions of Wildlife, 1,* 35–50.

McNutt, L. A., Holcomb, J. P., & Carlson, B. E. (2000). Logistic regression analysis—When the odds ratio does not work: An example using intimate partner data. *Journal of Interpersonal Violence, 15,* 1050–1059.

Menard, S. (2002). *Applied logistic regression analysis* (2ⁿᵈ ed.). Thousand Oaks, CA: Sage Publications.

Mertler, C. A., & Vannatta, R. A. (2005). *Advanced and multivariate statistical methods* (3ʳᵈ ed.). Glendale, CA: Pyrczak Publishing.

Merton, R. K. (1987). The focused interview and focus groups: Continuities and discontinuities. *Public Opinion Quarterly, 51*(4), 550–566.

Miller, C. A., & Anderson, W. L. (2002). Digit preference in reported harvest among Illinois waterfowl hunters. *Human Dimensions of Wildlife, 7*(1), 55–65.

Miller, C. A., & Graefe, A. R. (2000). Degree and range of specialization across related hunting activities. *Leisure Sciences, 22,* 195–204.

Miller, C. A., & Graefe, A. R. (2001). Effect of harvest success on hunter attitudes toward white-tailed deer management in Pennsylvania. *Human Dimensions of Wildlife, 6*(3), 189–203.

Miller, C. A., & Vaske, J. J. (2003). Individual and situational influences on declining hunter effort in Illinois. *Human Dimensions of Wildlife, 8*(4), 263–276.

Mitra, A., & Lankford, S. (1999). *Research methods in park, recreation, and leisure services.* Champaign, IL: Sagamore.

Moore, D. S., & McCabe, G. P. (1999). *Introduction to the practice of statistics* (3ʳᵈ ed.). New York, NY: W. H. Freeman and Company.

Moore, K. A., Halle, T. G., Vandivere, S., & Mariner, C. L. (2002). Scaling back survey scales: How short is too short? *Sociological Methods & Research, 30*(4), 530–567.

Morgan, G. A., & Harmon, R. J. (1999). Sampling and external validity. *Journal of the American Academy of Child Adolescent Psychiatry, 38*(8), 1051–1053.

Morgan, G. A., & Harmon, R. J. (2000). Research questions and hypotheses. *Journal of the American Academy of Child Adolescence Psychiatry, 39*(2), 261–263.

Morgan, G. A., Gliner, J. A., & Harmon, R. J. (1999). Measurement and descriptive statistics. *Journal of the American Academy of Child Adolescence Psychiatry, 38*(10), 1313–1315.

Morgan, G. A., Gliner, J. A., & Harmon, R. J. (2000). Internal validity. *Journal of the American Academy of Child Adolescence Psychiatry, 39*(4), 529–531.

Morgan, G. A., Gliner, J. A., & Harmon, R. J. with Kraemer, H. C., Leech, N. L., & Vaske, J. J. (2006). *Understanding and evaluating research in applied and clinical settings.* Mahwah, NJ: Lawrence Erlbaum Associates.

Morgan, G. A., & Griego, O. V. (1998). *Easy use and interpretation of SPSS for Windows: Answering research questions with statistics.* Mahwah, NJ: Lawrence Erlbaum Associates.

Morgan, G. A., Griego, O. V., & Gloeckner, G. W. (2001). *SPSS for Windows: An introduction to use and interpretation in research.* Mahwah, NJ: Lawrence Erlbaum Associates.

Morgan, G. A., Vaske, J. J., Gliner, J. A., & Harmon, R. J. (2003). Logistic regression and discriminant analysis: Use and interpretation. *Journal of the American Academy of Child Adolescence Psychiatry, 42*(8), 994–997.

Morgan, N. K, Newman, P., & Wallace, G. W. (2007). Conflicts associated with recreational shooting at the Pawnee National Grassland. *Human Dimensions of Wildlife, 12*(3), 145–156.

Morgan, P. L. (2003). Null hypothesis significance testing: Philosophical and practical considerations of a statistical controversy. *Exceptionality, 11*(4), 209–211.

Moyer, L. M., & Geissler, P. H. (1984). Improving stability of annual state waterfowl harvest estimates in highly-skewed data. American Statistical Association, Proceedings of the Section on Survey Research Methods, 467–471.

Moyer L. M., & Geissler, P. H. (1991). Accomodating outliers in wildlife surveys. *Wildlife Society Bulletin, 19*(3), 267–270.

Nadeau, R., & Niemi, R. G. (1995). Educated guesses: The process of answering factual knowledge questions in surveys. *Public Opinion Quarterly, 59,* 323–346.

Nagelkerke, N. J. D. (1991). A note on the general definition of the coefficient of determination. *Biometrika, 78*(3), 691–692.

Needham, M. D., & Vaske, J. J. (2006). Beliefs about chronic wasting disease risks across multiple states, years and interest groups. *Human Dimensions of Wildlife, 11*(3), 215–220.

Needham, M. D., & Vaske, J. J. (2008). Hunters' perceptions of similarity and trust in wildlife agencies and personal risk associated with chronic wasting disease. *Society and Natural Resources, 21,* 197–214.

Needham, M. D., Vaske, J. J., Donnelly, M. P., & Manfredo, M. J. (2007). Hunting specialization and its relationship to participation in response to chronic wasting disease. *Journal of Leisure Research, 39*(3), 413–437.

Needham, M. D., Vaske, J. J., & Manfredo, M. J. (2004). Hunters' behavior and acceptance of management actions related to chronic wasting disease in eight states. *Human Dimensions of Wildlife, 9*(3), 211–231.

Needham, M. D., Vaske, J. J., & Manfredo, M. J. (2005). *Hunters' responses to chronic wasting disease: Regional and state-specific results* (Project Report No. 56). Fort Collins, CO: Human Dimensions in Natural Resources Unit, Colorado State University.

Needham, M. D., Vaske, J. J., & Manfredo, M. J. (2006). State and residency differences in hunters' responses to chronic wasting disease. *Human Dimensions of Wildlife, 11*(3), 159–176.

Norusis, M. J. (2003). *SPSS 12.0 statistical procedures companion.* Upper Saddle River, NJ: Prentice Hall.

Nunnally, J. C., & Bernstein, I. H. (1994). *Psychometric theory* (3rd ed.). New York, NY: McGraw-Hill.

Oksenberg, L., Coleman, L., & Cannell, C. F. (1986). Interviewers' voices and refusal rates in telephone surveys. *Public Opinion Quarterly, 50*(1), 97–111.

Osgood, C. E., Suci, G. H., & Tannenbaum, P. H. (1957). *The measurement of meaning.* Urbana, IL: University of Illinois Press.

Pearl, D. K., & Fairley, D. (1985). Testing for the potential for nonresponse bias in sample surveys. *Public Opinion Quarterly, 49*(4), 553–560.

Pedhazur, E. J., & Schmelkin, L. P. (1991). *Measurement, design, and analysis: An integrated approach.* Hillsdale, NJ: Lawrence Erlbaum.

Petchenik, J. (2003). *Chronic wasting disease in Wisconsin and the 2002 hunting season: Gun deer hunters' first response* (Report No. PUB-SS-582 2003). Madison, WI: Bureau of Integrated Science Services, Wisconsin Department of Natural Resources.

Pinchot, G. (1910). *The fight of conservation.* New York, NY: Doubleday.

Poe, G. A., Seeman, I., McLaughlin, J., Mehl, E., & Dieth, M. (1988). "Don't know" boxes in factual questions in a mail questionnaire: Effects on level and quality of response. *Public Opinion Quarterly, 52,* 212–222.

Pol, A. P., Pascual, M. B., & Vázquez, P. D. (2006). Robust estimators and bootstrap confidence intervals applied to tourism spending. *Tourism Management, 27*(1), 42–50.

Porter, S. R., & Whitcomb, M. E. (2003). The impact of contact type on web survey response rates. *Public Opinion Quarterly, 67,* 579–588.

Potaka, L., & Cochrane, S. (2004). Developing bilingual questionnaires: Experiences from New Zealand in the development of the 2001 Mäori language survey. *Journal of Official Statistics, 20*(2), 289–300.

Preacher, K. J., & Hayes, A. F. (2004). SPSS and SAS procedures for estimating indirect effects in mediation models. *Behavior Research Methods, Instruments & Computers, 36*(4), 717–731.

Preacher, K. J., & Hayes, A. F. (2007). Contemporary approaches to assessing mediation in communication research. In A. F. Hayes, M. D. Slater, & L. B. Snyder (Eds.), *The Sage sourcebook of advanced data analysis methods for communication research.* Thousand Oaks, CA: Sage Publications.

Preacher, K. J., & Leonardelli, G. J. (2006). *Calculation of the Sobel test: An interactive calculation tool for mediation tests.* Available at http://www.psych.ku.edu/preacher/sobel/sobel.htm#refs

Press, S. J., & Wilson, S. (1978). Choosing between logistic regression and discriminant analysis. *Journal of the American Statistical Association, 73,* 699–705.

Puttkammer, A. (1994). *A managerial and theoretical approach to the management of the Mt. Shasta Wilderness.* Unpublished Masters Thesis, Colorado State University, Fort Collins, Colorado.

Raden, D. (1985). Strength-related attitude dimensions. *Social Psychology Quarterly, 48,* 312–330.

Randall, J. (1977). *The windshield experience: Visitor density, perceived crowding and satisfaction in a drive-through dunes park.* Unpublished Master's Thesis, University of Wisconsin, Madison, Wisconsin.

Rao, C. R. (1973). *Linear statistical inference and its application* (2nd ed). New York, NY: John Wiley and Sons.

Rasinski, K. A., Mingay, D., & Bradburn, N. M. (1994). Do respondents really "mark all that apply" on self-administered questions? *Public Opinion Quarterly, 58,* 400–408.

Raymond, G. J., Bossers, L. D., Raymond, K. I., McHolland, L. E., Bryant, M. W., Miller, M. W., Williams, E. S., Smits, M., & Caughey, B. (2000). Evidence of a molecular barrier limiting susceptibility of humans, cattle, and sheep to chronic wasting disease. *European Molecular Biology Organization (EMBO) Journal, 19*(17), 4425–4430.

Robinson, D. H., & Levin J. R. (1997). Reflections on statistical and substantive significance, with a slice of replication. *Educational Researcher, 26,* 21–26.

Rocco, E. (2003). Constrained inverse adaptive cluster sampling. *Journal of Official Statistics, 19*(1), 45–57.

Raaijmakers, Q. A. W. (1999). Effectiveness of different missing data treatments in surveys with Likert-type data: Introducing the relative mean substitution approach. *Educational Psychological Measurement, 59*(5), 725–748.

Reed, S. K. (1996). *Cognition.* Pacific Grove, CA: Brooks/Cole.

Rokeach, M. (1973). *The nature of human values.* New York, NY: The Free Press.

Rodgers, W. L., Brown, C., & Duncan, G. J. (1993). Errors in survey reports of earnings, hours worked, and hourly wages. *Journal of the American Statistical Association, 88,* 1208–1218.

Romesburg, H. C. (1990). *Cluster analysis for researchers.* Alabar, FL: Robert E. Krieger Publishing Co.

Rosenthal, R. (1994). Parametric measures of effect size. In H. Cooper, & L. Hedges (Eds.), *The handbook of research synthesis* (pp. 231–244). New York, NY: Russell Sage Foundation.

Rosenthal, R. (2000). Effect sizes in behavioral and biomedical research: Estimation and interpretation. In L. Bickman (Ed.), *Validity and social experimentation* (pp. 121–139). London, UK: Sage.

Rosenthal, R., Rosnow, R. L., & Rubin, D. B. (2000). *Contrasts and effect sizes in behavioral research: A correlational approach.* Cambridge, UK: Cambridge University Press,

Rosner, B. (1975). On the detection of many outliers. *Technometrics, 17*(2), 221–227.

Rosner, B. (1983). Percentage points for a generalized ESD many-outlier procedure. *Technometrics, 25*(2), 165–172.

Rosnow, R. L., & Rosenthal, R. (1996). *Beginning behavioral research* (2nd ed.). Englewood Cliffs, NJ: Prentice Hall.

Ruddell, E. J., & Gramann, J. H. (1994). Goal orientations, norms, and noise-induced conflict among recreation area users. *Leisure Sciences, 16,* 93–104.

Russell, D. W. (2002). In search of underlying dimensions: The use (and abuse) of factor analysis in *Personality and Social Psychology Bulletin. Personality and Social Psychology Bulletin, 28*(12), 1629–1646.

Salant, P., & Dillman, D. A. (1994). *How to conduct your own survey.* New York, NY: John Wiley and Sons.

Salkind, N. J. (2007). *Statistics for people who (think they) hate statistics* (3rd ed.). Newbury Park, CA: Sage Publications.

Saremba, J., & Gill, A. (1991). Value conflicts in mountain parks. *Annals of Tourism Research, 18,* 155–172.

Savage, I. R. (1957). Nonparametric statistics. *Journal of the American Statistical Association, 52,* 331–334.

Schaeffer, N. C. (1991). Hardly ever or constantly: Group comparisons using vague quantifiers. *Public Opinion Quarterly, 55,* 395–423.

Schaeffer, N. C., & Presser, S. (2003). The science of asking questions. *Annual Review of Sociology, 29,* 65–88.

Scheaffer, R. L., Mendenhall, W., & Ott, R. L. (1996). *Elementary survey sampling* (5th ed.). Belmont, CA: Duxbury Press.

Schafer, J. L., & Graham, J. W. (2002). Missing data: Our view of the state of the art. *Psychological Methods, 7*(2), 147–177.

Schauber, E. M., & Woolf, A. (2003). Chronic wasting disease in deer and elk: A critique of current models and their application. *Wildlife Society Bulletin, 31*(3), 610–616.

Scherer, D., & Attig, T. (Eds.) (1983). *Ethics and the environment.* Englewood Cliffs, NJ: Prentice Hall.

Schmidt, F. L., & Hunter, J. E. (2002). Are there benefits from NHST? *American Psychologist, 57,* 65–56.

Schmitt, N. (1996). Statistical significance testing and cumulative knowledge in psychology: Implications for training of researchers. *Psychological Methods, 1,* 115-129.

Schonlau, M., Asch, B. J., & Du, C. (2003). Web surveys as part of a mixed-mode strategy for populations that cannot be contacted by e-mail. *Social Science Computer Review, 21*(2), 218–222.

Schreyer, R. (1976). Sociological and political factors on carrying capacity decision making. In *Proceedings of the 3rd Resource Management Conference* (pp. 228–258). Santa Fe, NM: National Park Service.

Schreyer, R., & Neilson, M. (1978). *Westwater and Desolation Canyons—Whitewater River recreational study.* Logan, UT: Institute of Outdoor Recreation and Tourism Utah State University.

Schuman, H., & Presser, S. (1996). *Questions and answers in attitude surveys: Experiments on question form, wording and context.* Thousand Oaks, CA: Sage Publications.

Schwartz, S. H. (1977). Normative influences on altruism. In L. Berkowitz (Ed.), *Advances in experimental social psychology* (Vol. 10, pp. 221–279). New York, NY: Academic Press.

Schwartz, S. H. (1992). Universals in the content and structure of values: Theoretical advances and empirical tests in 20 countries. In M. P. Zanna (Ed.), *Advances in experimental social psychology* (Vol. 25, pp. 1–66). San Diego, CA: Academic Press.

Schwarz, N. (1990). Assessing frequency reports of mundane behavior: Contributions of cognitive psychology to questionnaire construction. In C. Hendrick, & M. Clark (Eds.), *Research methods in personality and social psychology* (pp. 98–119). Newbury Park, CA: Sage Publications.

Schwarz, N., Hippler, H., Deutsch, B., & Strack, F. (1985). Response scale: Effects of category range on reported behavior and comparative judgments. *Public Opinion Quarterly, 49*(3), 388–395.

Senders, V. L. (1958). *Measurement and statistics* (Chapter 2). New York, NY: Oxford University Press.

Sharp, H., & Feldt, A. (1959). Some factors in a probability sample survey of metropolitan community. *American Sociological Review, 24,* 650–661.

Shelby, B. (1976). *Social psychological effects of crowding in wilderness: The case of river trips in the Grand Canyon.* Unpublished Ph.D. Dissertation. Boulder, CO: University of Colorado.

Shelby, B. (1980). Crowding models for backcountry recreation. *Land Economics, 56*(1), 43–55.

Shelby, B., & Colvin, R. B. (1979). *Determining use levels for the Rogue River* (Report WRRI-63). Corvallis, OR: Water Resources Research Institute, Oregon State University.

Shelby, B., & Colvin, R. B. (1981). *Carrying capacity for the Illinois River* (Report WRRI-72). Corvallis, OR: Water Resources Research Institute, Oregon State University.

Shelby, B., Vaske, J. J., & Donnelly, M. P. (1996). Norms, standards, and natural resources. *Leisure Sciences, 18,* 103–123.

Shelby, B., Vaske, J. J., & Heberlein, T. A. (1989). Comparative analysis of crowding in multiple locations: Results from fifteen years of research. *Leisure Sciences, 11,* 269–291.

Shelby, L. B., & Vaske, J. J. (2007). Perceived crowding among hunters and anglers: A meta-analysis. *Human Dimensions of Wildlife, 12*(4), 241–261.

Shelby, L. B., & Vaske, J. J. (2008). Understanding meta-analyses: A review of the methodological literature. *Leisure Sciences, 30,* 111–126

Shindler, B., List, P., & Steel, B. S. (1993). Managing federal forests: Public attitudes in Oregon and nationwide. *Journal of Forestry, July,* 36–42.

Shrout, P. E., & Bolger, N. (2002). Mediation in experimental and nonexperimental studies: New procedures and recommendations. *Psychological Methods, 7,* 422–445.

Siegel, S. (1956). *Nonparametric statistics for the behavioral sciences.* New York, NY: McGraw-Hill.

Siegrist, M., Cvetkovich, G., & Roth, C. (2000). Salient value similarity, social trust, and risk/benefit perception. *Risk Analysis, 20*(3), 353–362.

Sills, S. J., & Song, C. (2002). Innovations in survey research: An application of web-based surveys. *Social Science Computer Review, 20*(1), 22–30.

Silva, A. P. D., & Stam, A. (1995). Discriminant analysis. In Grimm L. B., & Yarnold P. R. (Eds.), *Reading and understanding multivariate statistics.* Washington DC: American Psychological Association.

Simon, H. A. (1954). Spurious correlations: A causal interpretation. *Journal of the American Statistical Association, 49,* 467–479.

Singer, E., Frankel, M. R., & Glassman, M. B. (1983). The effect of interviewer characteristics and expectations on response. *Public Opinion Quarterly, 47,* 68–83.

Sirkin, R. M. (2005). *Statistics for the social sciences* (3rd ed.) Newbury Park, CA: Sage Publications.

Sjöberg, L. (2000). Factors in risk perception. *Risk Analysis, 20*(1), 1–11.

Skipper, J. K., Guenther, A. L., & Nass, G. (1967). The sacredness of .05: A note concerning the usefulness of statistical levels of significance in social science. *The Amercian Sociologist, 2,* 16–18.

Slovic, P. (1993). Perceived risk, trust, and democracy. *Risk Analysis, 13,* 675–682.

Snijkers, G., Hox, J., & de Leeuw, E. D. (1999). Interviewers' tactics for fighting survey nonresponse. *Journal of Official Statistics, 15*(2), 185–198.

Snyder, P., & Lawson, S. (1993). Evaluating results using corrected and uncorrected effect size estimates. *Journal of Experimental Education, 61*(4), 334–349.

Sobal, J. (1984). The content of survey introductions and the provision of informed consent. *Public Opinion Quarterly, 48*(4), 788–793.

Sobel, M. E. (1982). Asymptotic intervals for indirect effects in structural equations models. In S. Leinhart (Ed.), *Sociological methodology 1982* (pp. 290–312). San Francisco, CA: Jossey-Bass.

SPSS 15.0 (2006). *Command syntax reference.* Chicago, IL: SPSS Inc.

Stafford, N. T., Needham, M. D., Vaske, J. J., & Petchenik, J. (2006). Hunter and nonhunter beliefs about chronic wasting disease in Wisconsin. *Journal of Wildlife Management, 75*(5), 1739–1744.

Steeh, C. G. (1981). Trends in nonresponse rates, 1952–1979. *Public Opinion Quarterly, 45,* 40–57.

Steeh, C. G., Kirgis, N., Cannon, B., & DeWitt, J. (2001). Are they really as bad as they seem? Nonresponse rates at the end of the twentieth century. *Journal of Official Statistics, 17*(2), 227–247.

Steel, B. S., List, P., & Shindler, B. (1994). Conflicting values about federal forests: A comparison of national and Oregon publics. *Society and Natural Resources, 7*(2), 137–153.

Steinhoff, H. W. (1980). Analysis of conceptual systems for understanding and measuring wildlife values. In W. W. Shaw, & E. H. Zube (Eds.), *Wildlife values* (pp. 11–21). Tucson, AZ: Center for Assessment of Noncommodity Natural Resource Values, University of Arizona.

Stern, P. C. (2000). Toward a coherent theory of environmentally significant behavior. *Journal of Social Issues, 56*(3), 407–424.

Stern, P. C., Dietz, T., & Black, J. S. (1986). Support for environmental protection: The role of moral norms. *Population and Environment, 8,* 204–222.

Stevens, J. (1992). *Applied multivariate statistics for the social sciences* (2nd ed.). Hillsdale, NJ: Lawrence Erlbaum Associates.

Stevens, S. S. (1946). On the theory of scales of measurement. *Science, 103,* 667–680.

Stevens, S. S. (1951). Mathematics, measurement and psychophysics. In S. S. Stevens (Ed.), *Handbook of experimental psychology* (pp. 1-49). New York, NY: John Wiley.

Stevens, S. S. (Ed.). (1966). *Handbook of experimental psychology.* New York, NY: John Wiley.

Student [William Sealy Gosset] (1908). The problem of error of a mean. *Biometrika, 6*(1), 1–25.

Sudman, S., & Bradburn, N. M. (1974). *Response effects in surveys: A review and synthesis.* Chicago, IL: Aldine.

Sudman, S., & Bradburn, N. M. (1983). *Asking questions: A practical guide to questionnaire design.* London, UK: Jossey-Bass.

Sudman, S., Bradburn, N. M., & Schwarz, N. (1996). *Thinking about answers: The application of cognitive processes to survey methodology.* San Francisco, CA: Jossey-Bass.

Sutton, S., & Ditton, R. B. (2005). The substitutability of one type of fishing for another. *North American Journal of Fisheries Management, 25,* 536–546.

Tarrant, M. A., & Manfredo, M. J. (1993). Digit preference, recall bias, and nonresponse bias in self reports of angling participation. *Leisure Sciences, 15,* 231–238.

Teel, T. L., Dayer, A. A., Manfredo, M. J., & Bright, A. D. (2005). *Regional results from the research project entitled "Wildlife Values in the West"* (Project Report No. 58) for the Western Association of Fish and Wildlife Agencies. Fort Collins, CO: Colorado State University, Human Dimensions in Natural Resources Unit.

Thapa, B., & Graefe, A. R. (2003). Level of skill and its relationship to recreation conflict among adult skiers and snowboarders. *World Leisure Journal, 45*(1), 15–27.

Thompson, B. (1989). Editorial: Why won't stepwise methods die? *Measurement and Evaluation in Counseling and Development, 21,* 146–148.

Thompson, B. (1995). Stepwise regression and stepwise discriminant analysis need not apply here: A guidelines editorial. *Educational and Psychological Measurement, 55,* 525–534.

Thompson, B. (1996). AERA editorial policies regarding statistical significance testing: Three suggested frameworks. *Educational Researcher, 25*(2), 26–30.

Thompson, B. (1997). Editorial policies regarding statistical significance tests: Further comments. *Educational Researcher, 26*(5), 29–32.

Thompson, B. (2002). "Statistical," "practical," and "clinical:" How many kinds of significance do counselors need to consider? *Journal of Counseling & Development, 80,* 64–71.

Thompson, S. C. G., & Barton, M. A. (1994). Ecocentric and anthropocentric attitudes toward the environment. *Journal of Environmental Psychology, 14,* 149–158.

Thompson, S. K. (1992). *Sampling.* New York, NY: John Wiley.

Thurstone, L. L. (1927). A law of comparative judgment. *Psychological Review, 34,* 273–386.

Tourangeau. R. (2004). Survey research and societal change. *American Reivew of Psychology, 55,* 775–801.

Tourangeau, R., Rips, L. J., & Rasinski, K. (2000). *The psychology of survey response.* Cambridge, UK: Cambridge University Press.

Tourangeau, R., & Yan, T. (2007). Sensitive questions in surveys. *Psychological Bulletin, 133*(5), 859–883.

Tuckel, P.S., & Feinberg, B. M. (1991). The answering machine poses many questions for telephone survey researchers. *Public Opinion Quarterly, 55*(2), 200–217.

Tucker, C. (1983). Interviewer effects in telephone surveys. *Public Opinion Quarterly, 47*(1), 84–95.

Tversky, A., & Kahneman, D. (1974). Judgment under uncertainty: Heuristics and biases. *Science, 185,* 1124–1131.

Vacha-Haase, T. (2001). *Addressing the clinical significance as against statistical or practical significance: Science and practice working together to benefit the practitioner.* Paper presented at the annual meeting of the American Educational Research Association, Seattle, Washington.

Valliant, R. (2004). The effect of multiple weighting steps on variance estimation. *Journal of Official Statistics, 20*(1), 1–18.

van der Vaart, W. (2004). The time-line as a device to enhance recall in standardized research interviews: A split ballot study. *Journal of Official Statistics, 20*(2), 301–317.

van Es. J. C., Lorence, D. P., Morgan, G. W., & Church. J. A. (1996). Don't know responses in environmental surveys. *Journal of Environmental Education, 27,* 13–18.

Van Liere, K. D., & Dunlap, R. E. (1978). Moral norms and environmental behavior: An application of Schwartz's norm-activation model to yard burning. *Journal of Applied Psychology, 8,* 174–188.

Vaske, J. J., Absher, J. D., & Bright, A. D. (2007). Salient value similarity, social trust and attitudes toward wildland fire management strategies. *Human Ecology Review, 14*(2), 223–232.

Vaske, J. J., & Beaman, J. (2006). Lessons learned in detecting and correcting response heaping: Conceptual, methodological and empirical observations. *Human Dimensions of Wildlife, 11*(4), 285–296.

Vaske, J. J., Beaman, J., Manfredo, M. J., Covey, D., & Knox, R. (1996). Response strategy, recall frame, and digit preference in self-reports of angling participation. *Human Dimensions of Wildlife, 1,* 54–68.

Vaske, J. J., Carothers, P., Donnelly, M. P., & Baird, B. (2000). Recreation conflict among skiers and snowboarders. *Leisure Services, 22*(4), 297–313.

Vaske, J. J., & Donnelly, M. P. (1999). A value-attitude-behavior model predicting wildland voting intentions. *Society and Natural Resources, 12,* 523–537.

Vaske, J. J., & Donnelly, M. P. (2002). Generalizing the encounter-norm-crowding relationship. *Leisure Sciences, 24,* 255–269.

Vaske, J. J., & Donnelly, M. P. (2007). *Public knowledge and perceptions of the desert tortoise* (HDNRU Report No. 81) for the National Park Service. Colorado State University, Human Dimensions in Natural Resources Unit, Fort Collins. CO.

Vaske, J. J., Donnelly, M. P., Doctor, R. M., & Petruzzi, J. P. (1994). *Social carrying capacity at the Columbia Icefield: Applying the Visitor Impact Management framework* (HDNRU Rep. No. 11). Colorado State University, Human Dimensions in Natural Resources Unit, Fort Collins, CO.

Vaske, J. J., Donnelly, M. P., Heberlein, T. A., & Shelby, B. B. (1982). Differences in reported satisfaction ratings by consumptive and nonconsumptive recreationists. *Journal of Leisure Research, 14*(3), 195–206.

Vaske, J. J., Donnelly, M. P., & Petruzzi, J. P. (1996). Country of origin, encounter norms and crowding in a frontcountry setting. *Leisure Sciences, 18*(2), 161–176.

Vaske, J. J., Donnelly, M. P., & Shelby, B. B. (1990). Comparing two approaches for identifying recreation activity substitutes. *Leisure Sciences, 12*(3), 289–302.

Vaske, J. J., Donnelly, M. P., & Tweed, D. L. (1983). Recreationist-defined versus researcher-defined similarity judgments in substitutability research. *Journal of Leisure Research, 15*(3), 251–262.

Vaske, J. J., Donnelly, M. P., & Williamson, B. N. (1991). Monitoring for quality control in state park management. *Journal of Park and Recreation Administration, 9,* 59–72.

Vaske, J. J., Donnelly, M. P., Williams, D. R., & Jonker, S. (2001). Demographic influences on environmental value orientations and normative beliefs about national forest management. *Society and Natural Resources, 14,* 761–776.

Vaske, J. J., Donnelly, M. P., Wittmann, K., & Laidlaw, S. (1995). Interpersonal versus social-values conflict. *Leisure Sciences, 17*(3), 205–222.

Vaske, J. J., Dyar, R., & Timmons, N. (2004). Skill level and recreation conflict among skiers and snowboarders. *Leisure Sciences, 26*(2), 1–11.

Vaske, J. J., Fedler, A. J., & Graefe, A. R. (1986). Multiple determinants of satisfaction from a specific waterfowl hunting trip. *Leisure Sciences, 8*(2), 149–166.

Vaske, J. J., Gliner, J. A., & Morgan, G. A. (2002). Communicating judgments about practical significance: Effect size, confidence intervals and odds ratios. *Human Dimensions of Wildlife, 7*(4), 287–300.

Vaske, J. J., Graefe, A. R., & Dempster, A. B. (1982). Social and environmental influences on perceived crowding. In *Proceedings: Wilderness Psychology Group Conference* (pp. 211–227), Morgantown, WV.

Vaske, J. J., Huan, T. C., & Beaman, J. G. (2003). The use of multiples in anglers' recall of participation and harvest estimates: Some results and implications. *Leisure Sciences, 25,* 399–410.

Vaske, J. J., & Needham, M. D. (2007). Segmenting public beliefs about conflict with coyotes in an urban recreation setting. *Journal of Park and Recreation Administration, 25*(4), 79–98.

Vaske, J. J., Needham, M. D., Newman, P., Manfredo, M. J., & Petchenik, J. (2006). Potential for conflict index: Hunters' responses to chronic wasting disease. *Wildlife Society Bulletin, 34*(1), 44–50.

Vaske, J. J., Needham, M. D., Shelby, L. B., & Hummer, C. (2007). Sensitivity of the potential for conflict index to response scale width for human-wildlife interactions. In *Proceedings of the XXVIII Inter-national Union of Game Biologists (IUGB) Congress* (p. 104), Uppsala, Sweden.

Vaske, J. J., & Rodriguez, D. (1996). *Attitudinal and normative influences on voting decisions to ban trapping in Colorado.* Unpublished manuscript. Colorado State University, Human Dimensions of Natural Resources, Fort Collins, CO.

Vaske, J. J., & Shelby, L. B. (2008). Crowding as a descriptive indicator and an evaluative standard: Results from 30 years of research. *Leisure Sciences, 30,* 111–126.

Vaske, J. J., Shelby, L. B., & Manfredo, M. J. (2006). Bibliometric reflections on the first decade of *Human Dimensions of Wildlife. Human Dimensions of Wildlife, 11*(2), 79–87.

Vaske, J. J., Shelby, B. B., Graefe, A. R., & Heberlein, T. A. (1986). Backcountry encounter norms: Theory, method and empirical evidence. *Journal of Leisure Research, 18,* 137–153.

Vaske, J. J., & Taylor, J. G. (2006). *Visitor and resident acceptability norms toward wolf management actions.* Paper presented at the 3rd International Conference on Monitoring and Management of Visitor Flows in Recreation and Protected Areas. Rapperswil, Switzerland. September 13–17.

Vaske, J. J., Timmons, N. R., Beaman, J., & Petchenik, J. (2004). Chronic wasting disease in Wisconsin: Hunter behavior, perceived risk, and agency trust. *Human Dimensions of Wildlife, 9*(3), 193–209.

Vaske, J. J., & Whittaker, D. (2004). Normative approaches to natural resources. In M. J. Manfredo, J. J. Vaske, B. L. Bruyere, D. R. Field, and P. Brown (Eds.), *Society and natural resources: A summary of knowledge* (pp. 283–294). Jefferson, MO: Modern Litho.

Velleman, P. F., & Wilkinson, L. (1993). Nominal, ordinal, interval, and ratio typologies are misleading. *The American Statistician, 47*(1), 65–72.

Vogt, W. P. (1999). *Dictionary of statistics and methodology: A nontechnical guide for the social sciences* (2nd ed.). Thousand Oaks, CA: Sage Publications.

Wagar, J. A. (1964). The carrying capacity of wildlands for recreation. *Society of American Foresters. Forest Service Monograph, 7,* 23.

Waksberg, J. (1978). Sampling methods for random digit dialing. *Journal of the American Statistical Association, 73,* 40–46.

Wallace, W. (1971). *The logic of science in sociology.* Chicago, IL: Aldine-Atherton.

Watson, A. E., Niccolucci, M. J., & Williams, D. R. (1994). The nature of conflict between hikers and recreational stock users in the John Muir Wilderness. *Journal of Leisure Research, 26,* 372–385.

Watson, A. E., Williams, D. R., & Daigle, J. J. (1991). Sources of conflict between hikers and mountain bike riders in the Rattlesnake NRA. *Journal of Park and Recreation Administration, 9,* 59–71.

Weeks, M. F., Jones, B. L., Folsom, R. E., & Benrud, C. H. (1980). Optimal times to contact sample households. *Public Opinion Quarterly, 44*(1), 101–114.

Weeks, M. F., Kulka, R. A., & Pierson, S. A. (1987). Optimal call scheduling for a telephone survey. *Public Opinion Quarterly, 51,* 540–549.

Weigel, R. H., & Weigel, J. (1978). Environmental concern: The development of a measure. *Environment and Behavior, 10,* 3–16.

Whittaker, D., & Manfredo, M. J. (1997). *Living with wildlife in Anchorage—A survey of public attitudes* (Summary Report 35). Project Report for the Alaska Department of Fish and Game. Colorado State University, Human Dimensions of Natural Resources, Fort Collins, CO.

Whittaker, D., Manfredo, M. J., Fix, P. J., Sinnott, R., Miller, S., & Vaske, J. J. (2001). Understanding beliefs and attitudes about an urban wildlife hunt near Anchorage, Alaska. *Wildlife Society Bulletin, 29*(4), 1114–1124.

Whittaker, D., Vaske, J. J., Donnelly, M. P., & DeRuiter, D. S. (1998). Mail versus telephone surveys: Potential biases in expenditure and willingness to pay data. *Journal of Park and Recreation Administration, 16*(3), 15–30.

Whittaker, D., Vaske, J. J., & Manfredo, M. J. (2006). Specificity and the cognitive hierarchy: Value orientations and the acceptability of urban wildlife management actions. *Society and Natural Resources, 19,* 515–530.

Wildman, R. C. (1977). Effects of anonymity and social setting on survey responses. *Public Opinion Quarterly, 41*(1), 74–79.

Wilkinson, L. and The Task Force on Statistical Inference. (1999). Statistical methods in psychology journals: Guidelines and explanations. *American Psychologist, 54,* 594–604.

Williams, E. S., Miller, M. W., Kreeger, T. J., Kahn, R. H., & Thorne, E. T. (2002). Chronic wasting disease of deer and elk: A review with recommendations for management. *Journal of Wildlife Management, 66*(3), 551–563.

Willits, F. K., & Janota. J. (1996). *A matter of order: Effects of response order on answers to surveys.* Paper presented at the meeting of the Rural Sociological Society, Des Moines, IA.

Wilson, P. D., & Langenberg, P. (1999). Usual and shortest confidence intervals on odds ratios from logistic regression. *The American Statistician, 53*(4), 332–335.

Winter, G., Vogt, C. A., & Fried, J. S. (2002). Fuel treatments at wildland-urban interface: Common concerns in diverse regions. *Journal of Forestry, 100,* 15–21.

Wittmann, K., Vaske, J. J., Manfredo, M. J., & Zinn, H. C. (1998). Standards for lethal response to problem urban wildlife. *Human Dimensions of Wildlife, 3,* 29–48.

Woodside, A. G., & Ronkainen, I. E. (1984). How serious is non-response bias in advertising conversion research? *Journal of Travel Research, 22*(4), 34–37.

Wright, S. (1921). Correlation and causation. *Journal of Agricultural Research, 20,* 557–585.

Wright, S. (1923). Theory of path coefficients: A reply to Niles' criticism. *Genetics, 8,* 239–255.

Wright, S. (1960). Path coefficients and regression coefficients: Alternative or complementary concepts. *Biometrics, 16,* 189–202

Zinn, H. C., Manfredo, M. J., Vaske, J. J., & Wittmann, K. (1998). Using normative beliefs to determine the acceptability of wildlife management actions. *Society and Natural Resources, 11*(7), 649–662.

Zumbo, B. D., & Zimmerman, D. W. (1993). Is the selection of statistical methods governed by level of measurement? *Canadian Psychology, 34,* 390–399.

index

21st Century Leisure: Current Issues, Second Edition
by Valeria J. Freysinger and John R. Kelly

The A•B•Cs of Behavior Change: Skills for Working With Behavior Problems in Nursing Homes
by Margaret D. Cohn, Michael A. Smyer, and Ann L. Horgas

Activity Experiences and Programming within Long-Term Care
by Ted Tedrick and Elaine R. Green

The Activity Gourmet
by Peggy Powers

Advanced Concepts for Geriatric Nursing Assistants
by Carolyn A. McDonald

Adventure Programming
edited by John C. Miles and Simon Priest

Assessment: The Cornerstone of Activity Programs
by Ruth Perschbacher

Behavior Modification in Therapeutic Recreation: An Introductory Manual
by John Datillo and William D. Murphy

Benefits of Leisure
edited by B.L. Driver, Perry J. Brown, and George L. Peterson

Benefits of Recreation Research Update
by Judy M. Sefton and W. Kerry Mummery

Beyond Baskets and Beads: Activities for Older Adults with Functional Impairments
by Mary Hart, Karen Primm, and Kathy Cranisky

Beyond Bingo: Innovative Programs for the New Senior
by Sal Arrigo, Jr., Ann Lewis, and Hank Mattimore

Beyond Bingo 2: More Innovative Programs for the New Senior
by Sal Arrigo, Jr.

Boredom Busters: Themed Special Events to Dazzle and Delight Your Group
by Annette C. Moore

Both Gains and Gaps: Feminist Perspectives on Women's Leisure
by Karla Henderson, M. Deborah Bialeschki, Susan M. Shaw, and Valeria J. Freysinger

Brain Fitness
by Suzanne Fitzsimmons

Client Assessment in Therapeutic Recreation Services
by Norma J. Stumbo

Client Outcomes in Therapeutic Recreation Services
by Norma J. Stumbo

Conceptual Foundations for Therapeutic Recreation
edited by David R. Austin, John Dattilo, and Bryan P. McCormick

Constraints to Leisure
edited by Edgar L. Jackson

Dementia Care Programming: An Identity-Focused Approach
by Rosemary Dunne

Dimensions of Choice: Qualitative Approaches to Parks, Recreation, Tourism, Sport, and Leisure Research, Second Edition
by Karla A. Henderson

Diversity and the Recreation Profession: Organizational Perspectives (Revised Edition)
edited by Maria T. Allison and Ingrid E. Schneider

Effective Management in Therapeutic Recreation Service, Second Edition
by Marcia Jean Carter and Gerald S. O'Morrow

Evaluating Leisure Services: Making Enlightened Decisions, Second Edition
by Karla A. Henderson and M. Deborah Bialeschki

Everything from A to Y: The Zest Is up to You! Older Adult Activities for Every Day of the Year
by Nancy R. Cheshire and Martha L. Kenney

The Evolution of Leisure: Historical and Philosophical Perspectives
by Thomas Goodale and Geoffrey Godbey

Experience Marketing: Strategies for the New Millennium
by Ellen L. O'Sullivan and Kathy J. Spangler

Facilitation Techniques in Therapeutic Recreation
by John Dattilo

File o' Fun: A Recreation Planner for Games & Activities, Third Edition
by Jane Harris Ericson and Diane Ruth Albright

Leisure Education IV: Activities for Individuals with Substance Addictions
by Norma J. Stumbo

Leisure Education Program Planning: A Systematic Approach, Third Edition
by John Dattilo

Leisure for Canadians
edited by Ron McCarville and Kelly MacKay

Leisure Education Specific Programs
by John Dattilo

Leisure Studies: Prospects for the Twenty-First Century
edited by Edgar L. Jackson and Thomas L. Burton

Leisure in Your Life: New Perspectives
by Geoffrey Godbey

The Lifestory Re-Play Circle: A Manual of Activities and Techniques
by Rosilyn Wilder

Making a Difference in Academic Life: A Handbook for Park, Recreation, and Tourism Educators and Graduate Students
edited by Dan Dustin and Tom Goodale

Managing to Optimize the Beneficial Outcomes of Recreation
edited by B. L. Driver

Marketing in Leisure and Tourism: Reaching New Heights
by Patricia Click Janes

The Melody Lingers On: A Complete Music Activities Program for Older Adults
by Bill Messenger

Models of Change in Municipal Parks and Recreation: A Book of Innovative Case Studies
edited by Mark E. Havitz

More Than a Game: A New Focus on Senior Activity Services
by Brenda Corbett

The Multiple Values of Wilderness
by H. Ken Cordell, John C. Bergstrom, and J.M. Bowker

Nature and the Human Spirit: Toward an Expanded Land Management Ethic
edited by B.L. Driver, Daniel Dustin, Tony Baltic, Gary Elsner, and George Peterson

The Organizational Basis of Leisure Participation: A Motivational Exploration
by Robert A. Stebbins

Outdoor Recreation for 21st Century America
by H. Ken Cordell

Outdoor Recreation Management: Theory and Application, Third Edition
by Alan Jubenville and Ben Twight

Parks for Life: Moving the Goal Posts, Changing the Rules, and Expanding the Field
by Will LaPage

The Pivotal Role of Leisure Education: Finding Personal Fulfillment in This Century
edited by Elie Cohen-Gewerc and Robert A. Stebbins

Planning and Organizing Group Activities in Social Recreation
by John V. Valentine

Planning Parks for People, Second Edition
by John Hultsman, Richard L. Cottrell, and Wendy Z. Hultsman

The Process of Recreation Programming Theory and Technique, Third Edition
by Patricia Farrell and Herberta M. Lundegren

Programming for Parks, Recreation, and Leisure Services: A Servant Leadership Approach, Second Edition
by Debra J. Jordan, Donald G. DeGraaf, and Kathy H. DeGraaf

Protocols for Recreation Therapy Programs
edited by Jill Kelland, along with the Recreation Therapy Staff at Alberta Hospital Edmonton

Puttin' on the Skits: Plays for Adults in Managed Care
by Jean Vetter

Quality Management: Applications for Therapeutic Recreation
edited by Bob Riley

A Recovery Workbook: The Road Back from Substance Abuse
by April K. Neal and Michael J. Taleff

Recreation and Leisure: Issues in an Era of Change, Third Edition
edited by Thomas Goodale and Peter A. Witt

Recreation and Youth Development
by Peter A. Witt and Linda L. Caldwell

Recreation Economic Decisions: Comparing Benefits and Costs, Second Edition
by John B. Loomis and Richard G. Walsh

Recreation for Older Adults: Individual and Group Activities
by Judith A. Elliott and Jerold E. Elliott

Recreation Program Planning Manual for Older Adults
by Karen Kindrachuk

Recreation Programming and Activities for Older Adults
by Jerold E. Elliott and Judith A. Sorg-Elliott

Reference Manual for Writing Rehabilitation Therapy Treatment Plans
by Penny Hogberg and Mary Johnson

Research in Therapeutic Recreation: Concepts and Methods
edited by Marjorie J. Malkin and Christine Z. Howe

Service Living: Building Community through Public Parks and Recreation
by Doug Wellman, Dan Dustin, Karla Henderson, and Roger Moore

Simple Expressions: Creative and Therapeutic Arts for the Elderly in Long-Term Care Facilities
by Vicki Parsons

A Social History of Leisure Since 1600
by Gary Cross

A Social Psychology of Leisure
by Roger C. Mannell and Douglas A. Kleiber

Special Events and Festivals: How to Organize, Plan, and Implement
by Angie Prosser and Ashli Rutledge

Stretch Your Mind and Body: Tai Chi as an Adaptive Activity
by Duane A. Crider and William R. Klinger

Taking the Initiative: Activities to Enhance Effectiveness and Promote Fun
by J. P. Witman

Therapeutic Activity Intervention with the Elderly: Foundations and Practices
by Barbara A. Hawkins, Marti E. May, and Nancy Brattain Rogers

Therapeutic Recreation and the Nature of Disabilities
by Kenneth E. Mobily and Richard D. MacNeil

Therapeutic Recreation: Cases and Exercises, Second Edition
by Barbara C. Wilhite and M. Jean Keller

Therapeutic Recreation in Health Promotion and Rehabilitation
by John Shank and Catherine Coyle

Therapeutic Recreation in the Nursing Home
by Linda Buettner and Shelley L. Martin

Therapeutic Recreation Programming: Theory and Practice
by Charles Sylvester, Judith E. Voelkl, and Gary D. Ellis

Therapeutic Recreation Protocol for Treatment of Substance Addictions
by Rozanne W. Faulkner

The Therapeutic Recreation Stress Management Primer
by Cynthia Mascott

The Therapeutic Value of Creative Writing
by Paul M. Spicer

Tourism and Society: A Guide to Problems and Issues
by Robert W. Wyllie

Traditions: Improving Quality of Life in Caregiving
by Janelle Sellick

Trivia by the Dozen: Encouraging Interaction and Reminiscence in Managed Care
by Jean Vetter

 Venture Publishing, Inc.
1999 Cato Avenue
State College, PA 16801
Phone: 814-234-4561
Fax: 814-234-1651